THE YALE EDITIONS OF
The Private Papers of James Boswell

Boswell:

THE OMINOUS YEARS

1774–1776

EDITED BY CHARLES RYSKAMP

ASSISTANT PROFESSOR OF ENGLISH

PRINCETON UNIVERSITY

AND FREDERICK A. POTTLE

STERLING PROFESSOR OF ENGLISH

YALE UNIVERSITY

McGRAW-HILL BOOK COMPANY, INC.

NEW YORK   TORONTO   LONDON

The Yale Editions of the Private Papers of James Boswell will consist of two independent but parallel series. One, the "research" edition, will give a complete text of Boswell's journals, diaries, and memoranda; of his correspondence; and of the *Life of Johnson,* from the original manuscript: the whole running to at least thirty volumes. It will preserve the spelling and capitalization of the original documents, and will be provided with extensive scholarly annotation. A large group of editors and a permanent office staff are engaged in this comprehensive undertaking, the first volume of which may appear by 1963. The other, the reading or "trade" edition, will select from the total mass of papers those portions that appear likely to be of general interest, and will present them in modern spelling and with appropriate annotation. The publishers may also issue limited de luxe printings of the trade volumes, with extra illustrations and special editorial matter, but in no case will the trade volumes or the de luxe printing include matter from Boswell's archives that will not also appear in the research edition.

The present volume is the ninth of the trade edition.

CONTENTS

ILLUSTRATIONS

following page 134

William Miller (1755–1846), son of Thomas Miller, Lord Justice-Clerk; later baronet and Lord Glenlee. From a contemporary oil-painting by David Allan, in the collection of Mario Cellini. Reproduced by permission.

A view of Wilton, the seat of the Earls of Pembroke. From an oil-painting (c. 1775–1779) at Wilton by Richard Wilson. Reproduced by permission of the Earl of Pembroke.

A view of Lichfield, showing on the right the house where Samuel Johnson was born, and beside it the Three Crowns Inn. From an engraving in Stebbing Shaw, *The History and Antiquities of Staffordshire;* the engraving (by Thomas Cook, 12 February 1785), from a drawing by E. Stringer, was first printed in *The Gentleman's Magazine* for February 1785.

A page of the manuscript of the *Life*, describing part of the dinner at Dilly's, 15 May 1776, which introduced Johnson and Wilkes. From the original in the possession of Arthur A. Houghton, Jr. Reproduced by permission.

INTRODUCTION

§I

This part of Boswell's journal begins with nights of gnawing anxiety. There is a threat of a duel, then feverish testing of honour. The story ends in May 1776 with the great dinner at Dilly's—with the laughter of Wilkes and Johnson—and, on the following day, two farewells. One is the climax to a play of extravagant flattery and intrigue with a sorceress, the notorious Mrs. Rudd. Boswell's record is a cryptic huddle of delirium, eyes, ankles, and kisses. Afterwards, "twice 'Adieu'; at last, 'God bless you.'" The other farewell is muted and solemn: Johnson "was not very fluent. I said, 'Thank you for all your kindness.' JOHNSON. 'You are very welcome. Nobody repays it with more.'"

Neither the affability of the dinner, however, nor the poignancy and intimacy of the last moment of each farewell suggests the customary state of Boswell's mind during the years 1774–1776. He had the power of being agreeable and he is on many occasions a most pleasant companion; he realizes the value of a friendship and is a strong friend. But this journal, unlike his *Life of Johnson,* is not significantly the record of friendship. And it is not distinguished as a revelation of harmony and happiness. This is the account of one who hungered to know himself, the whole story of a man of feeling: his passions and pleasures; his hard work, meditation, sympathy, despair—and his confusions and dulness. It is a study of the temptations and the hazards and, only rarely, the achievements of such a man. "I am a being very much consisting of feelings," he writes. "I have some fixed principles. But my existence is chiefly conducted by the powers of fancy and sensation. It is my business to navigate my soul amidst the gales as steadily and smoothly as I can." Nevertheless his ship is battered, and the principles and metaphors whirl away. His portrait, elegant and sure, like one painted by Sir Joshua Reynolds, becomes part of a progress by Hogarth; at last, a dark sketch of despair by Goya: a man torn by violence and saturated with vice.

For Boswell, who had, as he said, "a curious inclination to have an era for almost everything," this is an era of trial, but not an era in which trials are won, nor are they likely to be in the future. These years are not ones of fulfilment, of hopes realized or of ideals reached. The last words of the last day of 1775, "this I could yield or modify"—referring to his "feudal enthusiasm" but implying more—form the most accurate sign of his position during his thirty-fourth and thirty-fifth years. It is the watershed. Standing here we discover where the slope leads. The time is ominous and the recognition of it usually sharp. Boswell admits his limitations with trenchant candour:

It is a certain fact that I have a mind incapable, or at least ill-disposed, for science of any kind. I always remember Sir John Pringle's saying to me some years ago in London, "You know nothing." And now the remark is as just as then. There is an imperfection, a superficialness, in all my notions. I understand nothing clearly, nothing to the bottom. I pick up fragments, but never have in my memory a mass of any size. I wonder really if it be possible for me to acquire any one part of knowledge fully.

From portents like these we can begin to find the shape of the years to come. We can see already in this journal that if no man ever entered upon life with a more overweening ambition, none ever left it with a more complete realization of failure.[1]

These pages reveal how fancy and sensation can be vitiated by the coarse lines of sensuality. At Lichfield Cathedral Boswell is moved by the solemn music and the holy service. Then thoughts of "Asiatic satisfactions" alternate with reflections on the text of the sermon, "Be steadfast and immovable." Finally some "soothing sophistry" leaves his mind at ease. But frequently there is little relief, and when he surveys the long periods of wretchedness, he must write of his life, "What a monstrous account of a man!" For a time, he says, "my moral principle as to chastity was absolutely eclipsed . . . I thought of my valuable spouse with the highest regard and warmest affection, but had a confused notion that my corporeal connexion with whores did not interfere with my love for her." Because his wife is "averse to much dalliance," Boswell feels that he should have a concubine. She says (surely impatiently and without meaning it) that he may go to whoever pleases him; and he can therefore justify his wanderings. Literature perhaps affords no fuller record of that slow process of self-deceit by which men of strong passions and weak wills prepare justification for indulging their appetites. With Boswell words were everything. Promiscuity, if called by its right name, had an ugly sound in his ear, but concubinage was biblical and "Asiatic." Might it provide "Asiatic tranquillity"? "If it was morally wrong, why was it permitted to the most pious men under the Old Testament, nay, specially blessed with fruitfulness? Why did our SAVIOUR say nothing against it?" The word and the idea rise again and again, to be repulsed, to be re-examined, to be toyed with, to be embellished more and more by ingenious sophistry, until the moral fences go down in a murky tide of passion, and Boswell

[1] Here and throughout this Introduction, considerable portions are taken from the Introductions to the tenth and eleventh volumes of the *Private Papers of James Boswell*.

awakes from his dream "cold and disturbed and dreary and vexed, with remorse rising like a black cloud without any distinct form."

Day after day he tells how the love of gaming becomes the rage of gaming; the love of a dram, the mad drinking of a bottle of claret by himself, none of the company drinking with him. His wife waits at home, ill and almost frantic with apprehension, while he spends entire nights at cards and drink. And when he returns to his house, furious and miserably sick, he threatens to hurl furniture at his wife, smashes chairs, throws things in the fire. Even when he is not drunk a dispute over a trifle may arouse his passion so that he cannot command it, and then his inclination is to destroy everything.

The "contagion of fancy" which has always been characteristic of Boswell's ideas remains, but now frenzy predominates. There is sudden rage, and afterwards there is inanimate sullenness. As a result we find that these years contain the most severe hypochondria since his winter in Holland. The depression is extracted from his mind and deposited in the journal in the hope that he can thereby find some alleviation of his burden of tedium, fretfulness, or despair. Similarly the "bad nerves" are laid bare, and the misery of indecisiveness, the timorousness (as well as the boldness), and the terror of duels, of bandits, or of spectres. Romantic oaths are followed by lonely frights, then gloom and indulging in hypochondria. The causes and reactions are childish; the changes come so quickly that one wonders whether some of them are not phantoms of the imagination. But the moods assume an inescapable reality. The macabre scenes are from daily life, not nightmare.

We have come to expect from Boswell—perhaps above all others—contradiction, extreme varieties of experience, the mingling of discordant emotions. Tragicomedy and pathos jostle with puns, light anecdotes, and rollicking humour. We can be thankful that he is a man of contrariety, for after the dulness and the childish fears there is childlike freshness and joy. After his drunken venturousness we shall discover him absorbed in the happiness of his daughters' songs and games, or a London dinner, or travel in a post-chaise, or Oxford college luxury. This volume contains twenty months, only four of which are spent away from Edinburgh. Yet the four months (most of the time with Johnson) fill two-fifths of the book. Here are long stretches of one of the richest London journals we have. The conversation of these journals, whether comic or serious, is delightful. The episodes as well as the talk in London or on the way to and from London are frequently amusing or moving. Boswell describes falling in love (from a seat in a theatre) with a charming singer, and kissing a sweet chamber-maid in the garret of Dr. Johnson's house in Lichfield. Tiresome deliberations about feudal rights are redeemed by spurts of sudden ad-

venture, as when he prances through the streets of London in a one-horse
chair which, by a tip of "only three halfpence," he has charmed a strange
servant into letting him drive. The mists of Scottish anxieties and depres-
sions are blown away by jubilant choruses. In March 1776 in the coach
for London, Boswell is riddled with fears: the prospect of a duel, of falling
from the coach-box, of the highwaymen in the hills. Then fear is banished
as he and the other passengers roar through the Welwyn of Young's *Night
Thoughts* singing—with "prodigious jovial noise"—*Heart of Oak, Gee
Ho, Dobbin,* and *The Roast Beef of Old England.*

On the night before the celebrated dinner at Dilly's when Wilkes and
Johnson meet, Boswell and Wilkes watch a lamplighter borne in procession to his grave by "hundreds of his fraternity with torches." On a day
after a drunken party Boswell saunters up and down Westminster in
search of an accommodating Devonshire wench. He does not find her;
instead he buys laces for his wife. "This," says the lacewoman, having
caught him "in her Mechlin toils," "is *innocent.* This is *grand.*" "O," says
Boswell, "we're past innocence. I'll have the grand." And so the contrasts
and surprises go on. He desires aristocratic dignity and courage, middle-
class security and comfortable morality, but is defeated by weakness and
folly. He wins temporary joy and victory, however, through companion-
ship, conversation, and comedy. Nonsense wells up in him, even if it is at
times merely a rather puerile jocularity. His vivacity and curiosity triumph again and again over depression or fear or feudal pride. The obses-
sions can never erase the spontaneity of the changing feelings of his heart
or the imaginations of his fancy.

There are other qualities in the extraordinary complications of his
character. "Many of my acquaintance would not think that I am devout,"
he writes naïvely; but of course he sometimes is. As the lamplighter's
procession passes, he defends immortality against Wilkes's sneers; he is
"pious and elegantly happy" at the chapel of the Neapolitan ambassador.
And what is perhaps more important for our understanding of Boswell,
he is compassionate. This is particularly true of the scenes with his
brother John, who is mad. Boswell treats him with tender affection when
he waves a poker and cries out wildly, and sheds tears when he sees John
feeble and dejected. Boswell's concern for his own melancholy gives to
these scenes a deeper shading and a feeling of more delicate pathos, but the
central emotion is unselfish love for his lunatic brother. In the visits with
John and in interviews with his impoverished clients there are a nobility
and gentleness which, though they do not purify his debauchery, make us
have a new sympathy for his honest writing and his passionate, proud
heart.

"I have a kind of strange feeling as if I wished nothing to be secret that concerns myself," Boswell writes in his journal for 4 January 1776. "This is a weakness to be corrected." It is not corrected, however, and the secrets develop into the major themes of the volume as stated in this overture. What is written down is done as exactly as if he were a Flemish portraitist or an engraver. He must delineate every winsome feature and blemish in the countenance. But, more important, he also demands that selectivity which finds the spirit to give the whole vitality; he chooses the gesture or movement, and above all, the bits of conversation which build a momentary impression into the drama of a night, a week, or a life.

One may catch a glimpse in his journals of Boswell acknowledging the difficulties of holding both conceptions of portraiture. He turns to metaphor, and one must do the same in talking about him. Boswell—to take an image from his journal—simultaneously collects the gold dust and fashions the ingot. In a single entry of the memorialist one may witness the total action of the artist. His "metaphorical vivacity"—it is really metaphorical pursuit and then savouring—becomes an elaborate game and grows tiresome. His prose is more skilful and lively when he points the sentences directly and a simile or metaphor remains unembellished: "and then I indulged my love of gaming, and insensibly resolved to make a night of it. About seven in the morning my clerk, Mr. Lawrie, came and found us sitting like wizards." He is a master of the complementary parenthetical remark which enables us to hold disparate aspects of himself (serious and comic or wildly romantic and simply matter-of-fact) simultaneously: "with a piece of the Old Castle in my hand, I knelt upon the ruins and swore that if any man had the estate in exclusion of the rightful heir this stone should swim in his heart's blood (I keep the stone)."

We shall never get rid of the old conception of Boswell as a man with a notebook pursuing Johnson for materials to use in the *Life of Johnson*, for it is now one of those established legends of great men which, like the camomile, grow the more vigorously for being trodden upon. But the legend can no longer have any hold on the minds of those who have read the records from which the conversations in the *Life* were quarried. As we come upon familiar scenes in the journal, we realize with a shock that these passages were not, in the first instance, materials deliberately collected for the writing of a biography of Johnson. Each is a fragment of Boswell's autobiography torn loose from its context. His preoccupation during all those years was not with the writing of a book, though he had that in mind; it was with living his own life. He put in a great deal of Johnson as he put in an extraordinary array of other things, but it was seldom from a sense of duty. It was rather from that same insatiable appetite for pleasure which drove him, after fifteen years of familiarity, to walk up and down the streets of London—"a high entertainment of itself. I see a vast museum of all objects, and I think with a kind of wonder that I see it for nothing."

Some of the best-known passages in Boswell's letters and the *Life of Johnson* are more fully recorded here in the journals of 1775 and 1776. The entirely new episodes may not at first reading seem so exciting as the familiar ones, when the familiar ones are given with details that sharpen the outline or complete the picture. Matty, "the handsome chambermaid" at Grantham, for example, at whom Boswell looked twice and then wrote "to Temple, as a priest" a letter full of "speculations on concubinage"— we should be glad to know more of this Matty. Well, we do; she "proved to be a scold, and swore like an oyster wench, and so I was fully cured." It would seem to be impossible to add to the vividness of Johnson's ponderous colloquy with the apprentice boy in Strahan's back yard, yet surely the following irreverent sentence of the journal is more vivid than the one Boswell substituted for it: "The little, short, thick-legged, sniveling urchin, as one may say, was shaking himself and rubbing his pockets, while Johnson rolled superb." And we read not only about Johnson's well-known love of driving briskly in a post-chaise; when he must ride in a jouncing carriage, not with a pretty woman but with an inquisitive Boswell, we find that he may become sharp and irritable: "The rattling of the chaise today prevented me from hearing Dr. Johnson talk. I told him so. 'Then,' said he, 'you may go hang yourself.' " There is a peculiar kind of shock of recognition when Boswell's bent of mind, which one comes to expect in the journal, is added to Johnson's familiar pronouncements from the *Life*. When Johnson bids him "divert melancholy by every means but drinking," Boswell adds, "I thought then of women, but no doubt he no more thought of my indulging in licentious copulation than of my stealing."

§II

After the shock of his grief and indignation following John Reid's execution had passed off, Boswell might well have supposed that all his anxieties arising from that unfortunate man were finished. As it happened, he had at the last moment written a letter to a newspaper; it had failed utterly to be of any service to John Reid, but it was now preparing to recoil upon its author. Throughout this affair he had felt as though he were struggling against a single opponent, Thomas Miller, the Lord Justice-Clerk or president of the High Court of Justiciary. It had seemed very hard to Boswell that the life of his client should be in the hands of a man who had publicly announced a strong prejudice against him. All other avenues being closed, Boswell turned at last to the newspapers, in which he had always had a childlike faith. A strong letter to *The London Chronicle* casting doubts on Miller's impartiality might, he hoped, "have influence in some manner that we cannot exactly foresee." The King himself (the letter was signed "A Royalist") might read it, send off an express with a pardon which would arrive just as John was ascending the ladder, and the Justice-Clerk would be foiled after all. Vain hope: the letter was sent so late that it missed the issue of the paper in which Boswell hoped it would be printed and did not appear until the evening of the day before the execution, when not even the King himself could have got a pardon to Edinburgh in time. All that it accomplished was to bring Boswell a challenge from William Miller, the Lord Justice-Clerk's son.

"I am timid by temperament," wrote Boswell to Rousseau, "and my education did everything to make me the slave of fear. But I have a soul capable of breaking these vile chains and forcing myself to feel the noble courage that belongs to a man." Boswell's remarks about his soul, here as elsewhere, refer to qualities which he hoped he possessed rather than to those about which he was quite certain. If he had not been troubled with doubts, he would not thus have been writing to Rousseau to tell him that he had narrowly escaped a duel some months before. At Berlin, while unwillingly acting as host to a French officer, he had made certain ill-tempered remarks concerning the French nation. The officer had promptly called him a scoundrel. After considering the situation a few minutes, Boswell had apologized and the officer had followed suit. Conflict was avoided, but should it have been avoided? Had he shown sufficient resolution? Ought he to have been less candid and more uncompromising? Had he made the apology because he knew that his words had been childish and petulant, or because he was a coward?

Given such a temperament, it was not to be expected that the affair at Berlin (which took place in Boswell's twenty-fourth year) should have remained unique in his experience. He continued all his life to say indiscreet and insulting things—worse yet, to publish them—and it was an age when a man of honour could hardly reply to an insult save with a challenge. Yet it must cause some surprise to learn that on at least seven occasions Boswell had to consider seriously the prospect of fighting a duel. There was the quarrel at Berlin in 1764. Ten years later came the affair with William Miller, fully narrated in this volume, as well as that of March 1776, when he planned to call out the Lord Advocate (Henry Dundas) for reflections which Dundas had made on Lord Auchinleck. In 1780 an unguarded jest at a card-party brought him a challenge from his brother advocate, Alexander Murray, then Solicitor-General and later Lord Henderland. On 28 May 1785 he made his last will and testament "in perfect soundness of mind but under the apprehension of some danger to my life, which, however, may prove a false alarm." The apprehension was that Henry Dundas would call him to account for the remarks that he had made in the *Letter to the People of Scotland*, just published; it did prove a false alarm. In December 1785 he gave his second, John Courtenay, a formal challenge for Lord Macdonald, who had written, and threatened to publish, an abusive letter concerning the *Journal of a Tour to the Hebrides*. It remained undelivered only because Courtenay was able to persuade Lord Macdonald to yield. And finally in June 1790 he was so grossly insulted by Lord Lonsdale that (to use his own words) "I should have, according to the irrational laws of honour sanctioned by the world, been under the necessity of risking my life, had not an explanation taken place."

Yet in spite of all these alarms, Boswell never faced an opponent on the field of honour. Boswell's son Alexander, whose birth is recorded in this journal, fell in a duel; a duel which he had brought upon himself by precisely the same indiscretion as that which had got his father into trouble with William Miller. That is, he had printed attacks in a newspaper on a man whom he had never openly treated with disrespect. Alexander did not apologize, and sacrificed his life to his intrepidity. His father's duels all somehow got explained away, either by himself or his adversary. With Lord Macdonald and Lord Lonsdale Boswell would have gone to extremities, but Lord Macdonald conceded the point, and Lord Lonsdale apologized. He dropped his quarrel with Dundas in 1776 because Johnson and Sir John Pringle convinced him that what was said about Lord Auchinleck's conduct on the bench was no affair of his. In the other instances he felt as he had at Berlin: "I was fully determined for the worst. Yet I wished that the affair could be made up, as I was really in the wrong."

To us who live in the twentieth century such behaviour seems merely candid and sensible. But to Boswell, who lived in the eighteenth, it left unsettled the rankling doubt which had prompted his letter to Rousseau. He was convinced from the standpoint of reason that duels were silly and wicked. But they did test a man, and he craved to know whether he would not be a more complete man if he had fought. Would not his "spirits be raised by a sense of honour and a sort of gallant vanity which a duel justly fought inspires"? Most important of all, would not a duel tell him once for all whether his shrinking from physical violence was a fundamental trait of his character, deserving the name of cowardice? Hence the many pages in his journal devoted to reflections on duelling; hence the conversations on duelling in the *Journal of a Tour to the Hebrides* and the *Life of Johnson*.

Ten years before this volume, in 1766, Samuel Johnson had written to

Boswell concerning the *Account of Corsica:* "You have, somehow or other, warmed your imagination. I wish there were some cure, like the lover's leap, for all heads of which some single idea has obtained an unreasonable and irregular possession." A single idea, as we have seen, which obtained such possession in Boswell's mind for many months was that of concubinage. Another was his "feudal enthusiasm" for the heirs male of the founder of the family, Thomas Boswell, who had died at Flodden Field in 1513. The unreasonable and tedious hold on Boswell of a belief that only a male could represent his ancestors and transmit the blood of his forefathers created dissension between him and his father and then his own wife and his friends. Boswell's father, Lord Auchinleck, had proposed an entail because he feared profligacy might make it necessary for Boswell to sell the estate or involve it in debts. Lord Auchinleck's plan was to entail the estate upon heirs whatsoever—male and female heirs of his own body—because this would keep the descendants of the dancing-master, David Boswell, from inheritance.

Boswell defended his position on feudal principles of family honour. For a time he thought he saw a precedent for these principles in the action of an ancestor, David Boswell of Auchinleck, who settled the estate upon his nephew, Boswell's great-grandfather, rather than his daughters. In the pages which follow, however, we see Mrs. Boswell answer his violent enthusiasm in the language which he can never resist, that of metaphor. He realizes then that it was possible that David Boswell passed over his daughters because, as Mrs. Boswell said, "The estate was so much burthened, it was more proper for a man than a woman. It was an old coat which he gave to his nephew, because it would not fit his daughter." Shortly after this volume ends, on 7 August 1776, Boswell agreed to a compromise whereby the estate would be entailed upon males descended from Lord Auchinleck's grandfather, but by that time his "old Gothic, Salic male enthusiasm" had abated and he would have willingly supported his father's original principle of settlement.

The spirit of a "feudal Goth," as Boswell calls himself, is seen also in his barbaric raging. It may be traced in quite a different way in his mediaeval and romantic admiration of Highland officers and soldiers. On occasion the eighteenth-century man of sensibility will appear to slip back into the ideas and actions of the Middle Ages. And there are times when he will seem to be looking into the nineteenth or the twentieth century. Intensely, absurdly caught between the past and the future: it is another reason why this volume of Boswell's journal marks the great divide. In one day he visits the founders of one of the most influential modern banks, and then he views Watt's steam-engine at Matthew Boulton's manufactory. "I regretted that I did not know mechanics well enough to comprehend the description of a machine lately invented by him, which he took great pains to show me. 'I sell, Sir,' said he, 'what all the world desires to have— Power.' " And there are days when his association of ideas reminds one, not of Sterne, but of Proust; when the recollection of Auchinleck brings to mind the recollection of Combray. "There was something in the west-country tone of the men that were to be tried that touched me with particular compassion, I believe from some association of it in my youth with distress, while I lived at Auchinleck, as that of a poor tenant unable to pay his rent, or of someone who had lost a father or brother."

But there are many days when he has no opportunity for his enjoyment of the contemplation of greatness, nor the exploration of his mind or times past. He feels then the contraction of his world in Edinburgh; yet he goes on steadily working at his law practice. He endeavours to prepare himself better for his causes—he recognizes his deficiencies as a lawyer—and because of these labours the range of his practice becomes increasingly extensive. In the pages of this volume he notes many successful, if unspectacular, hours at the law. He also has considerable pleasure in his career, not only in making a good speech in court, but also in writing up his causes at home. When he thinks of London and Johnson and the rest of The Club, however, his conclusion must be that "law business consumes my time, and indolence wastes it."

If the beginning of the book is charged with fear and questioning, and there are later periods of feudal obsession and rather unmemorable legal business or indolence, we can be grateful to know that the conclusion is the game of love. It is high comedy, and it is important to this volume because the scene completes the story of Boswell the lover. There has been in it a great deal of sincere, comfortable, husbandly love for his wife, a spirited Griselda; there have been warm flirtations, some meanly furtive, some elaborately open; there have been mad sallies after wenches and wild raging with whores. In the end there is poetic justice in the way in which a siren brings him to heel.

The common statement that greatness of any kind was enough to attract Boswell needs one important qualification: he was attracted by greatness in men but not in women. His male celebrities range from Wilkes to George III, from Sterne to Johnson; but deliberate attempts to record the conversation of a woman for its own sake are extremely rare in his pages. The fact is that in spite of the advantages of his birth and education there was always something gross and undiscerning in Boswell's attitude towards women. Johnson, for all his external roughness, was capable of great delicacy and charm when speaking with young ladies. He loved female society; he could discern talent in women and was always encouraging it. But Boswell really did not care for superior intelligence in women;

it intimidated him and made him uneasy. The one quality in a woman which roused his genuine interest was the power to enchant and allure.

It is therefore not remarkable that the interview with Margaret Caroline Rudd, adventuress, courtesan, and criminal, is one of the few pieces of its kind in the Boswellian treasury. Mrs. Rudd was credited with "irresistible power of fascination"; she was said to have cast her spell over a whole courtroom. Though she was obviously guilty, she had cheated the gallows in an age when the administration of justice was singularly free from sentimentalism. How, Boswell wondered, had she managed it? Could she fascinate him too? He could not rest until he had given her an opportunity.

No specimen of Boswell's art shows greater *finesse* and adroitness than his interview with Mrs. Rudd. In one respect only does he show unusual obtuseness. Intent upon his own "exquisite flattery," he does not realize (at least he does not admit) how successfully she has been playing *her* game from the moment of her carefully arranged entry into the dimly lighted room. Though he believed that he had been "as cautious as if I had been opposite to that snake which fascinates with its eyes," he was in fact an easy victim. True, she did not ask his name "or anything at all" about him, but it was not, we suspect, because of "perfect good breeding." It was because she knew he would come back and tell her of his own accord.

DOCUMENTATION

A. Manuscripts used in their entirety to make the text of this book are the following:

1. Journal in Edinburgh, [2 September] to 26 December 1774: bound octavo notebook with leather spine and marbled paper covers, 188 numbered pages, $4\frac{9}{16}$ by $7\frac{5}{16}$ inches; the text of the present volume begins on p. 72 of this notebook.

2. Journal in Edinburgh, 27 December 1774 to 10 March 1775: bound octavo notebook with leather spine and marbled paper covers, 65 numbered pages, $4\frac{1}{2}$ by $7\frac{3}{8}$ inches. (After 5 blank pages, No. 6, below, follows in the same notebook.)

3. Journal in London, 15 March to 3 April 1775: bound octavo notebook with leather spine and marbled paper covers, 87 leaves, $4\frac{1}{2}$ by $7\frac{3}{8}$ inches, originally numbered by Boswell 1–43, 48–125 (though the journal is continuous between his pp. 43 and 48), but pp. 94–98 (3 leaves), and 121 are missing. Up to p. 59 Boswell wrote on both sides of the leaves; thereafter (with a few exceptions) the right-hand page only is used, the other being left blank for additions and corrections.

4. Journal in London, [3] to 14 April 1775: octavo notebook, full-

bound in leather, with flexible covers and interleavings of blotting-paper, 66 pages, 4⅝ by 7⁵⁄₁₆ inches, originally numbered by Boswell 1–38, 37–64, though pp. 15–30 are loose in the binding, having been torn out by Boswell when he was writing the *Life*. Pages 15–26 (6 April 1775), which he sent to the printer as copy, were recovered at Malahide Castle in 1940, and are now printed for the first time as he originally wrote them.

5. Journal in London and jaunt to Wilton and Mamhead, 16 to 23 April 1775: 8 octavo leaves torn from a notebook, 15 sides written on, loose, 4¾ by 7½ inches. The series seems originally to have been numbered by Boswell 1–12, 19–27 (though it does not appear that anything is missing between p. 12 and p. 19), but pp. 1–6 (which must have contained the record for 15 April) are now missing.

6. "Review of my Life during the Summer Session [13 June to 11 August], 1775," with a review of the period 22–30 August 1775, and an incomplete journal entry for 1 October 1775: 8 octavo pages, numbered by Boswell 71–77, 81 (with three blank pages between 77 and 81), following No. 2, above, in the same notebook with 5 blank pages between. After p. 81 the rest of the book is blank.

7. Journal in Edinburgh, 9 October 1775 to 17 February 1776: bound quarto notebook with leather spine and blue paper board covers, 171 pages, 6¼ by 7⁵⁄₁₆ inches, originally numbered by Boswell 1–180, but p. 118 is blank, and pp. 55–58, 107–110 are missing.

8. Journal in Scotland and England, 18 February to 3 April 1776: bound quarto notebook with leather spine and blue paper board covers, 186 pages, 6⁵⁄₁₆ by 8 inches, numbered by Boswell 1–13, 16–188, but continuous and complete. Pages 187–188 (3 April 1776) are loose in the binding, having been removed by Boswell to serve as printer's copy for the *Life*. They were recovered at Malahide Castle and are now printed for the first time as Boswell originally wrote them.

9. Journal in London, 3–19 April 1776: bound quarto notebook with leather spine and blue paper board covers, 72 pages, 6⅜ by 7¹³⁄₁₆ inches, originally numbered by Boswell (if no mistakes in the missing portions) 1–84, 83, 86 (83 being a mistake for 85); but pp. 19–20, 25–34, 37–38 are now missing. Pages 1–8 (3–4 April 1776) and 63–72 (13 April 1776) are loose in the binding, having been removed by Boswell to use as printer's copy for the *Life*. They were recovered at Malahide in 1940 and are now first printed as Boswell originally wrote them.

10. Letter to his wife, "but not sent," 23 April 1776 (the interview with Mrs. Rudd): 6 leaves, 12 sides written on, 7⅜ by 9 inches; not signed.

B. Other Boswellian documents of the period, as follows, have been drawn upon at will for annotation and for patching the gaps in the journal:

1. Manuscript of the *Life of Johnson,* 16 September 1774 to 17 May 1776: main draft on 190 quarto leaves (7 now missing) rectos numbered by Boswell (if no error in the missing folios) 427 to 616, some with additions on the versos, roughly 8⅛ by 9⅞ inches, loose; plus 61 leaves of supplementary documents or "papers apart" which the printer was directed to insert at specified places in the draft, of various sizes, loose. Folios 497 to 616 are for the greater part (98 leaves out of 120) in the collection of Mr. Arthur A. Houghton, Jr., New York City. Our most extensive quotations are from Boswell's folios 478–489, 566–568, 595–607, the narratives for 18 April 1775, 7 April 1776, and 15 May 1776.

2. Three sets of notes for journal, greatly condensed and frequently obscure: jaunt to Twickenham to visit Richard Owen Cambridge, 18 April 1775, 4 small octavo leaves, 8 sides written on, loose, roughly 4⅛ by 6½ inches; notes on a visit to Auchinleck, 24 August to 3 September 1775, 2 octavo leaves, 3 sides written on, loose, roughly 4⅝ by 7½ inches; notes for journal in London, Bath, Bristol, and Scotland, 12 April to 5 June 1776, 25 octavo leaves, 48 sides written on, including a "paper apart," dated 16 May 1776, written on the blank side of a leaf torn from an almanac, loose, various sizes.

3. Upwards of 160 letters sent and received by Boswell, 24 September 1774–14 May 1776. Boswell's letters to William Johnson Temple for this period (18 in all) are in the Pierpont Morgan Library. Few of the manuscripts of his correspondence with Johnson have ever been recovered, but the *Life of Johnson* provides texts of 35 letters for the period, Boswell's being excerpted and abridged. Nine other letters by Boswell for the period repose in collections other than Yale's. With the exception, however, of letters to Temple and letters to and from Johnson, all letters quoted or mentioned in our apparatus are at Yale. One of the manuscripts of Boswell's letters at Yale is an original; the others are his drafts, or file copies made by himself or others. Boswell's Register of Letters, also at Yale, is useful for fixing the dates on which letters were sent or received, and for listing of unrecovered letters.

4. Upwards of 35 miscellaneous documents, 24 September 1774–May 1776. These include (the enumeration is not exhaustive) notes by Boswell on legal cases or books he was reading; original verses and songs; copies of epitaphs and inscriptions; bills; manuscripts by or about Johnson collected as materials for the *Life;* letters preserved by Boswell but not written by him or addressed to him.

C. Boswell's minor published works, when cited, will be identified at the places where they are quoted or referred to. The most authoritative edition of the *Life of Johnson* is that by G. B. Hill, 6 vols., Clarendon

Press, 1887, revised by L. F. Powell, 1934–1950. The fifth volume of this edition is the *Journal of a Tour to the Hebrides with Samuel Johnson,* as published by Boswell himself (1st edition 1785). The text of the Hebridean journal as actually written by Boswell on the tour was published in 1936 by the Viking Press and William Heinemann, Ltd., under the editorship of F. A. Pottle and C. H. Bennett; a new printing, with additional notes by F. A. Pottle, appeared earlier in the present year with the imprint of the McGraw-Hill Book Company and William Heinemann, Ltd. (Throughout this volume we refer to the *Life of Johnson* as *Life* and *The Journal of a Tour to the Hebrides*—edition by Pottle and Bennett—as *Hebrides.*) Boswell published his correspondence with Johnson in the *Life of Johnson,* and, as explained above, the *Life* still furnishes the only text for the letters of 1774, 1775, and 1776. Boswell's letters to Temple were published, with some omissions, more than a century ago (1857) by Sir Philip Francis; this volume was reprinted in 1908 by Thomas Seccombe. Professor Chauncey Brewster Tinker printed the letters of Temple from the manuscripts, with nearly 300 additional letters, in his *Letters of James Boswell,* Clarendon Press, 1924. The greater part of the text of the present volume was published by F. A. Pottle in 1931 in the tenth and eleventh volumes of the *Private Papers of James Boswell from Malahide Castle in the Collection of Lt.-Colonel Ralph H. Isham,* an expensive privately printed edition limited to 570 copies. The present printing is the first to make this matter available to the general reader.

We have printed the fully written journals without any omissions or editorial interruptions, linking them together with editorial summaries, selections from Boswell's journal notes, and passages from the manuscript of the *Life.* Appendices contain a previously unpublished letter of Boswell's which reinforces what we have said about his kindness of heart; also genealogical tables, information on the Scottish courts and legal system, and a glossary of legal terms.

The spelling, capitalization, and punctuation of text and notes (including quotations from printed works cited) have been brought close to modern norms, Boswell being allowed to retain certain idiosyncrasies. Abbreviations and contractions have been expanded. The standard of spelling for all but proper names is *The Concise Oxford Dictionary* (1956). For place names, F. H. Groome's *Ordnance Gazetteer of Scotland,* J. G. Bartholomew's *Survey Gazetteer of the British Isles,* and *London Past and Present* by Peter Cunningham and H. B. Wheatley have been followed. Family names have been brought into conformity with the usage of *The Dictionary of National Biography,* Mrs. Margaret Stuart's *Scottish Family History,* G. E. Cokayne's *Complete Baronetage* and *Complete Peerage,*

Sir James Balfour Paul's *Scots Peerage,* and various other special books of reference. Names of speakers in conversations cast dramatically, whether supplied by Boswell or by the editors, are set in small capitals without distinction. A few clear inadvertencies have been put right without notice. Square brackets indicate words added where the manuscript shows no defect, but where for one reason or another the editors have made an insertion; angular brackets indicate reconstruction of words lost through defects in the manuscript, where the reconstruction is not entirely certain.

We have tried to give the reader the knowledge he needs for placing Boswell accurately in relation to the people he meets and the events he lives through, but exhaustive annotation—such as full and systematic explication of his legal cases—has been reserved for the research edition. The index of the volume is intended to serve not only as a finding tool but as a supplement to the annotation; thus, we have frequently reserved for the index the function of supplying the Christian names, professions, and titles of persons mentioned.

Both the textual editing and the annotation of this volume owe much to earlier works of scholarship already mentioned: the edition of the *Private Papers of James Boswell* by Geoffrey Scott and F. A. Pottle, that of Boswell's *Letters* by C. B. Tinker, the great edition of the *Life of Johnson* by G. B. Hill as revised by L. F. Powell, and the edition of the *Letters of Samuel Johnson* by R. W. Chapman. To these titles should be added F. A. Pottle's *Literary Career of James Boswell, Esq.,* 1929, the catalogue of the *Private Papers of James Boswell* by F. A. Pottle and Marion S. Pottle, 1931, and *A Catalogue of Papers relating to Boswell . . . found at Fettercairn House,* by Claude Colleer Abbott, 1936. A considerable amount of unpublished preliminary work has also been available. We have occasionally drawn upon Dr. John Murray's unpublished Yale dissertation, "James Boswell in Edinburgh" (4 vols., 1939), an editing of Boswell's journal notes in Edinburgh for the years 1771–1774, with elaborate attention to the institutions and customs of the city and to Boswell's literary and legal career. The research of the late Dr. Charles H. Bennett has been invaluable. He reviewed the text and prepared systematic annotation for the journal and notes of the period covered in this volume. Using such of the foregoing materials as were available and others resulting from his own researches, F. A. Pottle more than twenty years ago compiled a text and notes for a trade or reading edition of these journals. The subsequent recovery of papers from Malahide Castle and of other documents, and the release of those that had been found at Fettercairn House, necessitated the planning of a quite different volume, with extensive revision of the earlier editing.

ACKNOWLEDGEMENTS

As formerly, the Editorial Committee has helped the editors to settle the general plan of the book. Professor Pottle directed the revision of the maps, and Mrs. Iola S. Haverstick, Secretary to the Committee, collected the illustrations. Mr. John X. Evans, graduate student in English at Yale, did research on various problems, and Mr. Douglas R. Jenner, Yale '63, Bursary aide in the Boswell Office, 1961–1962, and Mr. Leonard W. Riches, Princeton '61, helped extensively in various ways. Miss Harriet Chidester, editorial assistant, typed parts of the manuscript, and she and Mrs. Haverstick prepared the whole for the printer. The index was compiled by Miss Delight Ansley.

The proofs for this volume were read by the Editorial Committee, Sir James Fergusson and Dr. Powell of the Advisory Committee, Mr. N. S. Curnow, Miss Marion Park, and the office staff. In addition, Sir James Fergusson has replied to many queries on particular points.

We gratefully acknowledge various kinds of expert assistance from the following: Keith Andrews, Richard Brown Baker, John K. Bates, William Beattie, James Biddle, the British Museum, Lord Bruce, Mrs. Genevieve Butterfield, Signora Vera Cacciatore, J. V. Langmead Casserley, James L. Clifford, the Earl of Crawford and Balcarres, N. S. Curnow, the Master and Fellows of Davenport College, the Countess of Elgin, Allen T. Hazen, Arthur A. Houghton, Jr., R. E. Hutchison, Mr. and Mrs. Donald F. Hyde, Ronald Ireland, Helge Kökeritz, W. S. Lewis, Lawrence C. McHenry, Jr., Robert F. Metzdorf, Charles S. Minto, the Earl of Pembroke, A. E. Popham, Mrs. Marion S. Pottle, Graham Reynolds, Peter Ward-Jackson, C. P. Willard, William K. Wimsatt, Jr.

Princeton and   C. A. R.
New Haven   F. A. P.
15 June 1962

BOSWELL:

THE OMINOUS YEARS

1774-1776

I paid my house-rent to John Buchan, Writer to the Signet, at whose house I saw some old boxes full of manuscript books and papers and printed pieces belonging to the family of Napier, which he allowed me to tumble and examine. There were several little pieces in manuscript, mostly in figures, which had been the operations of the celebrated Napier of Merchieston. There were also some journals by different persons; in particular, notes by this Lord Napier's grandfather, of what his Lordship saw when travelling. It was melancholy to see what had been written with care, and preserved as valuable, treated as lumber; and I could not but moralize on what might become of my own journals. However, they serve to entertain and instruct myself; and though the importance of a man to himself has been the subject of ridicule, it is clear to me that nothing is equally important to a man with himself. A man is called selfish in a bad sense who prefers a small good to himself to the happiness of others; or whose enjoyments are without reference to others. But surely happiness of every kind must ultimately center in a man's own breast.

[26 OCTOBER *1775*]

What misery does a man of sensibility suffer!

[*11* MARCH *1776*]

Boswell: The Ominous Years

1774—1776

SKETCH OF BOSWELL'S LIFE TO 24 SEPTEMBER 1774. "I am a Scots gentleman of ancient family"—it was thus that Boswell began his celebrated letter of introduction to Rousseau. A month earlier, when he was appealing to the Margrave of Baden-Durlach for the Order of Fidelity, he had said, "It may sound strange, but, Sir, I can count kindred with my sovereign from my being related to the family of Lennox and the royal family of Stuart. Sir, I am one of your old proud Scots." About his pride there could be no question, but he was giving an accurate description of his lineage and connexions: his mother was in direct descent from the grandfather of Lord Darnley and he could boast that through both her and his father the blood of the Bruce flowed in his veins. His father was Alexander Boswell, eighth Laird of Auchinleck in Ayrshire. Though the Lairds of Auchinleck (in the eighteenth century generally pronounced Ahfléck) had not attained to a title of nobility, they were connected by marriage to many of the noble families of the land, and through one of them, the Hamiltons, Earls of Arran, to the House of Stuart. Alexander Boswell, like his father and like his eldest son, was a member of the Faculty of Advocates in Edinburgh. When this book opens, he has been for twenty years one of the fifteen judges of the Court of Session, the highest court for civil processes in Scotland, and one of the six judges of the High Court of Justiciary, the court for criminal causes. His style as judge was Lord Auchinleck, but this title conveyed no honours to his son.

James Boswell was born at Edinburgh on 29 October 1740; he had two brothers, John and David, born in 1743 and 1748. Until he was nine, Boswell lived mainly in that city, at his father's house in Blair's Land, Parliament Close; but after 1749 he must have spent half the year at Auchinleck, where he could ride for ten miles in a straight line on ancestral land. He went to James Mundell's private school in Edinburgh, and afterwards, at the age of thirteen—it was not unusual at that time—he entered Edinburgh University, where he proceeded through the arts course. He then studied law at Edinburgh and at Glasgow, but was really by this time interested in scribbling poems or essays or reading *belles-lettres* or attending

1

the theatre. He was at first timid and nervous and subject to depression. After what seems to have been a nervous collapse in his seventeenth year, he grew suddenly vigorous, gregarious—and amorous. In 1760 he ran away to London, where he joined the Roman Catholic Church for a brief time, became a libertine, lived with the witty and the wicked and the great, and longed for a commission in the Foot Guards.

He returned to Edinburgh after three months to a tense and exasperating life with his father. Lord Auchinleck was strict and sarcastic, and they were always in opposition. Boswell boisterously pursued nonsense and an assortment of pleasures and vices, and languidly studied law, according to his father's command and under his personal instruction, until he passed his Civil Law examination on 30 June 1762. In the autumn of that year he toured the southern counties of Scotland with Lord Kames, one of his father's colleagues in the Court of Session and the High Court of Justiciary. On 15 November he set off for London in the hope of obtaining a commission, of finding adventure, and of discovering himself—that is, "by attending to the feelings of his heart and to his external actions." He determined for this purpose to keep a daily journal in which, he said, "I shall set down my various sentiments and my various conduct, which will be not only useful but very agreeable. It will give me a habit of application and improve me in expression." The record of that trip, containing his meeting and the development of his friendship with Samuel Johnson, was discovered in 1930 by Professor C. Colleer Abbott at Fettercairn House and in 1950 was published as the first volume in this series.[1]

His attempts to gain a commission were fruitless and his adventures increasingly gross, though not altogether unamusing. There were also sober moments of moral reflection, and after he met Johnson he strove to reform. In August 1763 he went to Utrecht to study law; he remained until June, studying hard, frequently dull and depressed but always chaste. He then began his Grand Tour: through a number of the German courts, to Switzerland—where he conversed intimately with Rousseau and Voltaire—and to Italy. In Naples he hob-nobbed with the notorious rake and political exile John Wilkes; in Rome and afterwards he travelled with the young, rich, and handsome Lord Mountstuart, eldest son of Wilkes's adversary, Lord Bute; in Siena he had a grand amour with the wife of the mayor (the "Capitano del Popolo"). But much more important than any of these encounters or affairs was his visit to Corsica in October and November 1765. He was deeply stirred by the heroic Corsican general, Pasquale de Paoli, whose intense convictions and incorruptible leadership were re-

---

[1] *Boswell's London Journal, 1762–1763,* published by the McGraw-Hill Book Company, Inc. (New York) and William Heinemann, Ltd. (London). For the titles of subsequent volumes, see above, p. i.

flected in the lives of his countrymen and in their fight for political and social liberty. From Corsica Boswell went to Genoa and from there into France. At Paris he read of his mother's death; he therefore hurried home, stopping briefly in London, and arrived in Edinburgh in March 1766.

The next years were complicated by half-serious endeavours to find a wife and by amorous entanglements, especially with that "Circe," Mrs. Dodds, who bore him a daughter, Sally, in December 1767. Nevertheless he managed to settle down to a legal practice, in which he enjoyed professional success, and in 1768 he also realized literary acclaim, for his *Account of Corsica* was widely praised. The year 1769 was marked by three celebrations: the night early in March when the news reached Edinburgh that the House of Lords had reversed the decision of the Court of Session in the famous Douglas Cause, and Boswell led the mob which broke the windows of the judges (including his father) who refused to acknowledge the event by "illumination"; the sortie in September to Garrick's Shakespeare Jubilee at Stratford, where Boswell appeared at the masked ball as an armed Corsican chief; and the day of 25 November when James Boswell and his cousin, loyal and forbearing Margaret Montgomerie, both dressed in white, were married at the seat of her family, Lainshaw, in Ayrshire.

The marriage began in domestic felicity; Boswell was the very model of an earnest advocate and a faithful husband. And he became (legitimately) a father. The son born at the end of August 1770 died within two hours, but in March 1773, and fourteen months later, were born his beloved daughters Veronica and Euphemia. He took an exhilarating jaunt to London in the spring of 1772, and another the following spring, when he became a member of The Club—the great club of Dr. Johnson and other distinguished literary men and politicians. The following summer and autumn he and Johnson made their celebrated tour to the Hebrides.

Yet after the first two years of marriage Boswell became restless and unhappy. This was chiefly because of his father (who had remarried) and because of the "narrow" society of Edinburgh. The routine of his professional life could give little solace: the humdrum civil causes which he argued were undoubtedly burdensome. As a result his heavy drinking grew habitual, and gaming began to last through the night. His spirits were otherwise not often intensely aroused, nor his sympathy engaged except when he was concerned in some unfortunate and desperate criminal cause. For these hopeless clients he risked his career and wore himself out in the court-room and in the prison-cell—exhorting them personally and pleading before the juries. The most extraordinary of these causes was that of John Reid the sheep-stealer, who had been, in the autumn of 1766, Boswell's first criminal client. The verdict of guilty was this time almost inevitable, but by every means he could think of Boswell frantically worked for a pardon or a commutation of sentence, and when all those efforts failed, entertained a mad scheme of resuscitating Reid after he was cut down. The macabre, poignant, yet slightly comic scenes involving the two tormented men—client and counsel—and the dramatic oratory of the court-room form the story of the summer of 1774. The poor wretch was hanged and, on the day before this journal opens, his widow buried him in Muiravonside churchyard.

The journal as printed in this volume begins half-way through the entry for Saturday 24 September 1774. Boswell and his wife are departing for a family party at Valleyfield, a mile or two from Culross, both scenes of his mother's youth where he himself was "very healthy and very happy" as a boy. Valleyfield was the seat of Sir George and Lady Preston, who have been like parents to Boswell ever since his marriage. Lady Preston, daughter of William Cochrane of Ochiltree and Lady Mary Bruce, eldest daughter of the second Earl of Kincardine, was his mother's aunt. Sir George's eldest son, Patrick ("Mr. Preston"), had attained the rank of major in the British army stationed in Minorca, and afterwards that of brigadier-general in the service of Portugal. He was now retired to Valleyfield and no longer addressed by his military title. In the past Boswell had found him "a jolly, agreeable, pretty man." His younger brothers were Major Charles and Captain Robert, the latter of whom was in command of the *Hillsborough* in the East India Company's service. Dr. Alexander Webster, who is accompanying Boswell, was also a family connexion: his wife, now dead, had been a sister of Boswell's mother. A well-known figure in Edinburgh and very fond of his claret ("Dr. *Bonum Magnum*"), he was minister of the Tolbooth Church and a leader of the strict ("high-flying") party in the Church of Scotland. George Webster, his son, was a cloth-merchant in Edinburgh. Lt.-Col. James Webster, Dr. Webster's second son and an older brother to George, later served in the American War and died of wounds received at the battle of Guilford Court House.[2]

SATURDAY 24 SEPTEMBER. . . . . At ten we set out in a post-chaise for Valleyfield, my wife having been with difficulty persuaded to leave her children for a night or two. Dr. Webster was in another chaise. We got a fine passage at the ferry in a yawl, but the burgh elections had taken up all the chaises on the north side. We had therefore to send an express to Valleyfield for Mr. Preston's chaise, and had to sit several hours in the inn

[2] For a table of Boswell's Cochrane, Preston, and Webster connexions see below, Appendix C, Chart V.

at the North Ferry. I found that Dr. Webster and I by ourselves could not make good company. I suppose he is never lively but when he has a considerable circle. We tired somewhat. Mr. Preston's chaise came and carried us to Valleyfield, where we found a warm reception; but there was a violent noise about the election, Colonel and George Webster and their father being for Sir Lawrence Dundas; Sir George, my Lady, and Captain Preston for Colonel Campbell.[1] * * * [2]

SUNDAY 25 SEPTEMBER. It was agreeable to be at Valleyfield, where I had been in my earliest years, and to find myself amidst so many friends, all so well in life. I went in the chaise with my wife and Lady Preston to Culross. They went into church. I called on Lord Cochrane for a minute, and told him we were to visit him after the church came out. We did so. I felt an enthusiasm at Culross. I made my wife observe the burial-place where Lady Mary Cochrane cried, "Valuable dust," and the grand Abbey, of which my mother thought that it was like "This Babylon which I have built." [3] Lord Cochrane gave us a collation of fruit, bread, and wine. I

[1] Dundas was M.P. for Edinburgh from 1768 until his death in 1781. He had been Commissary General and Contractor to the Army, by which he acquired a large fortune, and was now a powerful politician. His descendants became Earls and later Marquesses of Zetland. Boswell did not meet him until 19 September 1780: "It was adding a new distinguished character to my collection. He appeared to me not a cunning, shrewd man of the world as I had imagined, but a comely, jovial Scotch gentleman of good address but not bright parts." Colonel Campbell was later General Sir Archibald Campbell of Inverneil, Governor of Jamaica and then of Madras. He had been wounded at Wolfe's attack on Quebec in 1758. In 1775 he was taken prisoner in Boston harbour by the insurgents, who later exchanged him for Ethan Allen. A year later he led the campaign in Georgia, which was entirely successful and ended in the capture of Savannah. Boswell found him "a man of admirable parts, a good deal like General Paoli" (see below, 12 October 1774).—After the dissolution of Parliament on 30 September, Boswell himself will become involved in burgh politics. Fifteen of the forty-five members whom Scotland sent to Parliament were chosen by the burghs: the city of Edinburgh returned one member, and the remaining burghs, divided into fourteen districts, returned one member from each district. The right of election was vested in the magistrates and town councils. Each of the councils chose a delegate, who on election day went to the presiding burgh (a privilege which all the burghs enjoyed in rotation) to cast his vote. In the Michaelmas election of magistrates Campbell was opposing Dundas's interest in the Stirling district. Dundas was not himself seeking office from this district; he was to stand for re-election as member for Edinburgh. But at this time he held control of the town councils and therefore of the parliamentary representation of the district. The election was completed on 26 September, Colonel Campbell's forces having prevailed.

[2] These symbols probably indicate conjugal relations between Boswell and his wife. See *Boswell for the Defence,* 19 August 1774, where the symbol appears in the journal for the first time.

[3] Daniel 4. 30. The burial-place was the Bruce Chapel, attached to the north wall of the Culross Abbey Church, where Sir George Bruce (d. 1625) and his descendants are

made my wife walk in the garden and admire the fine situation. She and I and Lady Preston drove back to Valleyfield immediately; Colonel Webster rode. The Captain and George walked. Dr. Webster, Miss Preston, and Miss Susie Wellwood stayed the afternoon's sermon, and came in another chaise.⁴ (Why need I be thus particular? especially, too, as I am now writing on the 6 of October, having neglected my journal for many days, and John Reid having required so much writing in it.) We had good hospitable entertainment from Patrick Preston. We drank claret, not quite to excess, but freely; and this night our political disputes were very noisy. *

MONDAY 26 SEPTEMBER. It was a very wet day. However, Mr. Preston and I got upon horse-back and he showed me a good part of his farm, where he was improving substantially. I thought if he, who had been bred in the Guards and seen so much of the world, could bring himself to apply to farming, I might do so, too. He showed me that he followed it as a branch of trade, kept regular books of all his transactions and all his expenses and profits, and found his estate rising excellently. I saw that the keeping of books was a great help to make a man like farming; at least it would be so to me, who will go through almost anything with a degree of satisfaction if I am to put an account of it in writing. We drank more than usual after dinner today. I had a joy in it. At night Lady Preston prevailed with me to break up the company early. *

TUESDAY 27 SEPTEMBER. My wife and I and Dr. Webster left Valley-field after breakfast, in Mr. Preston's chaise, and drove pleasantly to the North Ferry. It was a fine day. Mrs. Cuninghame, the landlady, said to me, "We did not know it was you, Sir, the other day, till you was gone—you that has done so much for the poor man, who gives you a blessing in his last speech." ⁵ We had a fine passage again and dined at the Hawes.⁶ We

---

buried. The dust of Culross (pronounced "Coórus") was especially valuable to Lady Mary Cochrane, Sir George's grand-daughter, who was the great-grandmother of Boswell and the mother of Lady Preston. She occupied the seventeenth-century Culross Abbey House after the death in 1705 of her brother, Alexander, third Earl of Kincardine, and transmitted the house and estate to her descendants, but failed, in repeated litigation, to establish her own right to the title. Her son, Thomas Cochrane, eighth Earl of Dundonald, inherited them after the deaths of his elder brothers, Charles and James. The hanging gardens of Culross Abbey House were a wonder of the countryside and would have been well known to Boswell's mother, who grew up in the interesting old house (still standing) in Culross called "the Colonels' Close."
⁴ Susan, daughter of Robert Wellwood of Garvock, was grand-daughter of Sir George and Lady Preston.
⁵ In *The Last Speech, Confession, and Dying Words of John Reid,* Reid had concluded with a wish for Boswell, that "when he comes to leave the earthly bar . . . he will be fully rewarded for the services done to fellow men in their afflictions." *The Last Speech* was drawn up by Alexander Ritchie, an Independent lay preacher who attended people under sentence of death, from what Reid had said to him.
⁶ Hawes is the Scots pronunciation of Halls, which is the spelling Boswell actually

then had two chaises; and for the first half of the way I went with Dr. Webster, and then with my wife. When we got to Edinburgh, I felt that my nerves were yet weak at times, for I had a sensation of being wild and timorous, as if I had been for years in the country, and all the objects in the town—the houses, the coaches, the people—hurt me in an unaccountable manner. Our children were at Dr. Webster's. We went and drank tea there. ✳

WEDNESDAY 28 SEPTEMBER. I dined at Bailie Macqueen's with the two reverend doctors to meet whom he had asked me, and with his brother-in-law, Mr. Stirling, the town treasurer.⁷ Mrs. Macqueen was a genteel, obliging body. We had a good comfortable dinner, strong ale and shortbread after it, a dram of Ferintosh whisky, port, and punch.⁸ I was well recovered and in good spirits. This was quite a new scene to me: a good burgher's dinner. The Bailie bolted the door after dinner that we might not be disturbed after his wife and Mr. Stirling left us. We talked a great deal about John Reid. I had written to him and each of the two doctors to give me an attestation concerning John. Dr. Macqueen wrote one; Dr. Dick chose rather that I should mention his account, and he would revise it. Bailie Macqueen intended, when he was less agitated with the melancholy scene, to put down what occurred to him.⁹ I thought myself a kind of Burke today. We contrived to sit together till past eight, but did not drink more than did us cordial good. Dr. Macqueen went away. Dr. Dick and I drank tea. I engaged the Bailie and the two doctors to dine with me on Monday next. Dr. Macqueen asked me to be an elder in his parish, the Old Kirk, but I told him that I did not think myself fit for the office.¹

---

used. Lovel and Jonathan Oldbuck dined here in Scott's *Antiquary,* and it was at the Hawes Inn, in Stevenson's *Kidnapped,* that Ebenezer Balfour and Captain Hoseason planned the abduction of David Balfour.

⁷ George Macqueen was Bailie of Edinburgh (that is, one of the magistrates who, at common law, had the same power within a burgh as the sheriff in his county). The Reverend Daniel Macqueen and the Reverend Robert Dick, like the Bailie, were convinced of Reid's innocence. James Stirling was afterwards Lord Provost of Edinburgh and a baronet.

⁸ The whisky was made at Ferintosh in Ross-shire by Duncan Forbes of Culloden under a privilege granted by the Scottish Parliament (withdrawn in 1785, Burns lamenting the fact in *Scotch Drink:* "Thee, Ferintosh, O sadly lost!").

⁹ The Reverend Daniel Macqueen's attestation ("a full impression of his sincerity") and the Bailie's letter reporting that he felt himself "as yet uncapable of that degree of composure of mind with which I could wish to write on a subject so interesting" are in the collection at Yale. Dick's account may have been given orally; no written report is among the Yale papers.

¹ At the Reformation the church of St. Giles was divided into four parts: the New Church (the choir), the Old Church (the central part), the Tolbooth Church, and Haddow's Hole Church.

THURSDAY 29 SEPTEMBER. The Laird of MacLeod was returned to town from a jaunt to the south.[2] I called on him, and begged he would come and take a family dinner with me. I then played at bowls. At three I came home and found MacLeod, and Balbarton, whom my wife had invited.[3] Grange had called for me in the forenoon and promised to dine, but some business called him out of town.[4] MacLeod and I and Balbarton were very social, and drank each his bottle of claret. But MacLeod did not appear so well to me as when I saw him in the Hebrides. He threw out some modern ideas, as if feudal principles could not now be kept up, which made me angry with him. We all drank tea. He went away. I made Balbarton agree to pass the evening with us. I went for Mr. Donaldson to come and play at whist, but he was busy preparing to set out for London next day.[5] So we had nothing for it but to play at catch-honours.[6] We were very comfortable, and at night took a little warm punch. This was an idle day, but a plain social one.

FRIDAY 30 SEPTEMBER. Lord Gardenstone had applied to me in behalf of a Mr. Smith who had been deprived of the office of Surveyor of the Customs at Aberdeen.[7] I went to Commissioner Cochrane, who seemed to be very unfavourable to him.[8] I wrote to Lord Gardenstone that the Boards of Customs and Excise were secret and severe as the Inquisition, and obstinate as the Medes and Persians. The Commissioner told me he heard that I drank hard pretty often. That I should take care, or it would put me wrong in the head. I should have mentioned that Gordon the bookseller, the chancellor of John Reid's last jury, called them together on Thursday, and, being a hot-headed man, proposed that I should be prose-

---

[2] Norman MacLeod, Chief of the clan and only twenty years old, was visited by Boswell and Johnson at Dunvegan in 1773. Johnson had said of him (when at Raasay): "He's a fine fellow, MacLeod. I have not met with a young man who had more desire to learn, or who has learnt more. I've seen nobody that I wish more to do a kindness to than MacLeod" (11 September 1773).

[3] James Boswell of Balbarton was a distant cousin, seventy-four years old.

[4] John Johnston of Grange, a writer (solicitor) in Edinburgh, was Boswell's most intimate friend in Scotland. They had both been in Robert Hunter's Greek class in 1755. He was loyal, affectionate, sentimental in his Scottish interests, but—like Boswell—often depressed.

[5] Alexander Donaldson, the Edinburgh publisher and friend of Boswell, was sometimes called by him "the Great Donaldson" because of his manner and his ambitions in publishing.

[6] The same as catch-the-ten or Scotch whist, a card game that can be played by any number of people from two to eight. The main object is to take a trick containing the ten of trumps, which counts ten points.

[7] Francis Garden, Lord Gardenstone, was one of the Lords of Session.

[8] Basil Cochrane, Commissioner of Customs, was Boswell's mother's uncle and brother of the Earl of Dundonald.

cuted for the paragraph in the newspapers about Reid's declaring that his sentence was unjust.⁹ But it seems the rest of them, or at least a majority, were wise enough to see the folly of the proposal. I played at bowls today.

SATURDAY 1 OCTOBER. Sir Alexander and Lady Dick and Miss Dick sent in a friendly manner that they would come and take pot luck with us today.¹ I got Grange to be of the party. After playing at bowls, I was in excellent humour, and we had a very agreeable day of it. I had not seen Sir Alexander for a long time. After tea Grange and I walked awhile on the Castle Hill.

SUNDAY 2 OCTOBER. I was too late for the New Church, and sauntered down the street in a disagreeable state of irresolution whether to go to any place of worship or not. I envied Sir Adolphus Oughton for his uniform decency as I saw him driving with his lady to the English Chapel.² I felt a kind of bashfulness and unwillingness to be looked at. I slunk quietly to Grange's, lounged, drank some tea, read reviews, and talked a little. In the afternoon my wife and I went to the New Church and heard Mr. Walker. Lady Betty Cochrane came home with us and drank tea.³ We supped at Dr. Webster's. Mr. Mingay, an officer of the 66, was there.⁴

MONDAY 3 OCTOBER. The 66 Regiment was out at exercise in the King's Park for the last time this season. I went about eight and saw them awhile, and then breakfasted at Lord Dundonald's. By the time I got to the Cross, Gamelshiels told me the news that the Parliament was dissolved.⁵ It vexed me, as I imagined the election of Ayrshire would be lost by the great families.⁶ I played at bowls. Bailie Macqueen and Bailie John Grieve,

⁹ "When upon the ladder, with the rope about his neck, just as he was turning over and dropping into eternity, his last words were, '*Mine is an* UNJUST SENTENCE'" (*Caledonian Mercury,* 21 September).

¹ Sir Alexander was a retired physician whom Boswell called "a *Corycius senex*" after the contented and hospitable bee-keeper of Virgil's *Georgics* (iv. 127), adding that he was "quite a classical man and much of an Italian in pleasantness of disposition" (to Temple, 22 June 1767). Sir Alexander inhabited a fine house at Prestonfield, near Edinburgh, and was a close friend of Boswell, though nearly forty years his senior.

² Lieut.-Gen. Sir James Adolphus Oughton had for some years been acting Commander of the forces in Scotland (North Britain); he was appointed Commander-in-Chief in 1778.

³ She was the daughter of the eighth Earl of Dundonald, and cousin of Boswell's mother.

⁴ Lieutenant Eyre Robert Mingay married Dr. Webster's daughter Ann in June 1777.

⁵ James Home Rigg of Gamelshiels, very rich, lived in an elegant mansion in the old and fashionable Gosford's Close. The Parliament of Great Britain was dissolved unexpectedly by royal proclamation on 30 September. Such a dissolution had not occurred since 1747.

⁶ In the last general election (1768), the Earls of Loudoun and Cassillis had pooled their "interest" and had secured the election as M.P. of Cassillis's younger brother, David Kennedy. The Earl of Eglinton had since joined their coalition. But they were

who had been the principal means of acquitting John Reid on his former trial, and Drs. Macqueen and Dick dined with us. Lady Betty Cochrane was so obliging as to come and grace this curious dinner. Matters went on very well. But we drank too much; and I was too open in my disapprobation of the Justice-Clerk.[7] John Grieve told us that when he was with Cochrane and Hamilton, their shop was broke, and, the goods having been advertised, a man was found at Linlithgow offering them to sale. He was apprehended, and application was made to the King's Counsel to have him prosecuted. But Mr. Grant, then King's Advocate, and the present President, then Solicitor, would not bring him to trial, saying, "It is true he had your goods; but can you prove that he broke your shop?" "This shows," said Mr. Grieve, "that great men of the law differ as to the import of being possessed of stolen goods, and I have always considered it as insufficient to infer theft."[8] We drank claret till nine at night. Bailie Macqueen left us rather earlier. The two ministers stayed and drank tea.

TUESDAY 4 OCTOBER. Grange dined with us. He and I were calm and quite sober. The Valleyfield family were now returned. We supped at Sir George's. I visited the Lodge of St. Patrick's at the earnest request of the Master, Mr. Daniel Miller.[9]

---

now opposed by a group of "independent" landed gentlemen who proposed to elect Sir Adam Fergusson of Kilkerran. Boswell's emotions were deeply involved because he had rashly assumed that his father would allow him to deliver the Auchinleck "interest" to the "noble association" and had suffered humiliation when Lord Auchinleck declared for Fergusson.

[7] Thomas Miller, Lord Justice-Clerk, the actual head of the High Court of Justiciary, the supreme court of Scotland for criminal causes. Boswell had written in his journal for 19 September that he "felt an indignation at the Justice-Clerk, whose violent report had prevented my obtaining for John Reid the royal mercy" (*Boswell for the Defence*).

[8] Grieve's memory (or Boswell's) has erred. William Grant, Lord Prestongrange, became Lord Advocate in 1746 at the same time as "the present President," Robert Dundas (the younger), Lord Arniston, resigned as Solicitor-General. In declining to consider unexplained or implausibly explained possession of stolen property as proof of theft, they differed radically from the Lord Justice-Clerk, who had twice been keen to convict Reid on the combined grounds of possession of stolen sheep and a bad reputation. On the occasion of Reid's trial in 1766, Boswell (then defending his first criminal cause) had secured a jury verdict of "not proven." Some months later, in giving judgement in the Douglas Cause, Miller had indulged in an *obiter dictum* directed at Reid and his counsel: Reid, he said, had been acquitted though there was a moral impossibility of his innocence. And again, at the trial of 1774, Miller and the five other judges of the Justiciary Court had considered the verdict of guilty appropriate, though the prosecution had advanced no direct proof of theft.

[9] In 1759 Boswell had been admitted a mason and member of the Canongate Kilwinning Lodge, No. 2. He became Junior Warden in 1761, was Depute Master, 1767–1768, and Master, 1773–1775.

WEDNESDAY 5 OCTOBER. I played at bowls. My wife and I dined at Sir George Preston's. Colonel Campbell, who carried the burghs of Culross, etc., against Sir Lawrence Dundas, was there. We were now engaged in a series of dinners and suppers along with Captain Preston. After tea I went home and wrote to Treesbank, etc.[1] I received a letter from Mr. Samuel Johnson on his return from Wales. It was a cordial to me. I sauntered awhile in the streets; returned to Sir George's to supper. Had heated myself and catched cold. Drank to intoxication. ✻ conat.[2]

THURSDAY 6 OCTOBER. We dined at Lord Dundonald's[3] with the Valleyfield family. Commissioner Cochrane was there. I drank moderately. We supped at Mr. Wellwood's, along with Captain Preston and his friends.[4] I drank little.

When I came home, I found my wife in great distress. She had been home about an hour before me; and a letter had come for me, without any postmark. She imagined that it contained some merchant's account, and opened it. But it proved to be a letter from the Justice-Clerk's son,[5] demanding to know if I wrote a paper signed "A Royalist" in *The London Chronicle,* which he set forth as an injurious charge against his father; and, if I did write it, to know if I would avow in the public papers that the insinuations contained in that attack against his father were false and scandalous, and ask forgiveness of the injury offered him; and that I knew the consequences of answering in the negative.[6] My wife was gone to bed

[1] James Campbell of Treesbank was Lord Auchinleck's cousin; his second wife was Mary Montgomerie, sister of Mrs. Boswell. See below, Appendix C, Chart VI. The letter was almost certainly political: Boswell wanted to fix Treesbank for the "old interest."

[2] Probably an abbreviation of the past participle of *conor;* that is, "attempted."

[3] His house at Belleville was in the environs of Edinburgh, between Holyrood Palace and the Abbey Hill. His principal residence was La Mancha in Peeblesshire.

[4] Robert Wellwood of Garvock (d. 1791) was an advocate. He was son-in-law of Sir George Preston and father of Susie Wellwood (above, 25 September).

[5] William Miller, at this time nineteen years old, became an advocate and was raised to the bench in 1795 (four days after Boswell's death) as Lord Glenlee. He was the only son of the Justice-Clerk. See the portrait following p. 134. William Miller's letter and other documents in this affair seem not to have survived.

[6] "John Reid . . . is remarkable because he was formerly tried and acquitted by a very worthy jury, notwithstanding which some persons in high office publicly represented him as guilty. In particular one great man of the law exclaimed against him in his speech in the great Douglas Cause. This is a striking specimen of what goes on in this narrow country. . . . A respite for fourteen days was sent to Reid from the office of Lord Rochford. . . . But, according to my information, an opinion from Scotland was desired upon the case, an opinion from that very man who exclaimed in the civil court against a man acquitted by a jury in the criminal court when his life was staked upon the issue" (*London Chronicle,* 17–20 September; the whole paper is quoted in *Boswell for the Defence,* 13 September 1774).

in a miserable alarm. She said she hoped I had not written a paper signed "A Royalist." I said I had. "Then," said she, "you will be called to account by the Justice-Clerk's son." "Nonsense," said I. "Oh," said she, "it is done already. There is his letter lying." I was confounded at reading such a peremptory address from a boy. My wife said he was nineteen or twenty. I said I would either give him no answer, or write to him that he had no title to question me; and I would give him no satisfaction. My wife cried bitterly, and said that would not do. The lad would insist to fight. "Well," said I, "let him do so." "What!" said she. "And make me and your poor children quite miserable?" She was really like a person almost frantic, and earnestly begged I would give her my word of honour that I would deny having written the letter. I did so, being quite shaken by her distress. And, indeed, it is a kind of principle or resolution which I have long held, though with some dubiety, that a man is as well entitled to deny an anonymous publication as to say that he is engaged when asked to a house where he does not choose to be, or to make his servant say that he is not at home when he does not choose to be seen. The difference, however, is that a man who thinks himself hurt by an anonymous publication has perhaps a right to ask a man suspected of it if the suspicion be true; and, though one may make his servant say he is not at home to an ordinary visitor, it would not be well to do so to a gentleman who calls upon him for satisfaction. Yet, if a man is obliged to confess or deny to a person hurt by an anonymous publication, it would be a great check on a due censure of men in public office; as a man must be zealous indeed for propriety and the general good who would expose himself to a duel for it. It occurred that perhaps the Justice-Clerk's friends had obtained from the printer my original manuscript, and, if I should deny it, then they would have a hold of me. My wife was for my setting out for London immediately, quite privately, to get the manuscript, if the printer still had it, and to determine whether to deny or not according as I found that matter to stand. I liked the proposal at first, as in a matter of such deep consequence I would have the advice of Mr. Samuel Johnson, with whom I would hold secret and solemn interviews. But then I considered that my going out of the way would have a strange appearance, that it would be an idle expense, and that my wife and I would suffer terrible anxiety during our separation. She was for doing anything for safety, even flying to a foreign country. I was very ill of a cold, which added to my uneasiness. We lay awake in a sort of burning fever all night, suggesting various schemes.

FRIDAY 7 OCTOBER. After five we got a little broken sleep. At seven I rose, and went to worthy Grange, whom we considered as a real comfortable friend. He rose, and we walked on the Castle Hill. He was much perplexed with the affair, and knew not well what to advise. Sometimes he thought I should write to the lad that he had no title to question me. Sometimes that I should write to him that I would answer the Justice-Clerk himself if he called upon me. Sometimes that I should go west to my father, let him know the affair, and his prudence would settle it properly. He considered it as most disagreeable to be thus engaged with a boy, so that I could gain nothing in any way. But then he was anxious that the world should not have it in their power to represent me as without the proper resolution of a man. He came home with me. My wife was up, and appeared pale as a spectre. She was quite wretched, and looked most melancholy when poor little Veronica came into the room. For myself, as I had heard Mr. Johnson demonstrate that it is lawful for a Christian to fight a duel, as it is lawful for him to engage in war,[7] I had no scruple; and notwithstanding the vivacity of my imagination, which figured dreary pictures, while my wife's misery softened and tormented my mind, I felt that if it really should be necessary to fight, I could do it. I considered how many duels had been fought without any hurt, or without much hurt; and that, if I should even be killed, it was not a worse kind of death than what might happen to me in the ordinary course of things; and that my father and friends would certainly take care of my wife and children. But it vexed me to think that I had a boy for my antagonist.

My wife grew rather better and said she was anxious that my honour should be preserved. I resolved that we should take a chaise and go out to Commissioner Cochrane, who, being my uncle and an old soldier, could give a most proper advice. Charles Hay had been told by me of the "Royalist"; and therefore it was absolutely necessary to talk with him in case I should deny it.[8] I sent for him, and he was very uneasy at the incident. Grange thought it best that Hay should not know that he was told of it. Hay said it would be very unlucky if a man so well known in the world, and so well esteemed as I was, should be thought deficient in courage. At the same [time], he thought that as my wife knew of this affair, and as it was a boy who had written to me, there was great difficulty in determining what to do. He consulted with a most friendly attention. He was once for denying it; but, then, as I had been so long of receiving the boy's letter, it occurred to him that it was probable evidence was already procured that I had written the "Royalist." I myself hit upon this plan: to write to the boy, telling him that the letter was written by me; but assuring him, as I truly could, that he was in a mistake in supposing that I attacked either his father's honour or honesty. That I meant no injury, and, if I had used any expressions which had been misunderstood, I was sorry for it. That if

[7] On 10 April 1772 and 19 April 1773. See the *Life.*
[8] Hay was an advocate, later Lord Newton; he had been almost as eager as Boswell to save John Reid.

after this candid explanation any disagreeable consequences should ensue, I should have the comfort to think I was not to blame. Hay was quite pleased with this. I sat down directly and wrote a scroll, and put it in my pocket to show to Commissioner Cochrane.[9]

My wife and I drove out in an anxious state. She said she envied every passenger we met, as unconscious of future evil. I left her at the gate of the avenue, and found the Commissioner walking. I told him the story, and read to him the passages in the "Royalist" relative to the Justice-Clerk. He thought there was little in them, but they might have been spared. I then read him the boy's letter, and my answer. He approved entirely of it. Said that I had not said too much. That I had said I meant no injury, and was sorry that one was supposed. That was enough; and there would be no more of it. He said it would have been quite wrong to have denied it; and he was of opinion that a son might call upon a man for satisfaction if he thought his father's character attacked. He said I should never write in newspapers. It was below me. He talked with such coolness, indifference and ease, like a man who knew the world, and looked on the boy's letter as a youthful flash, that I was much relieved. We went for my wife, and he told her there would be no more of it. We walked a little, then went in and took a glass of wine and a biscuit, and then re-turned to Edinburgh.

Worthy Grange was waiting for us. My wife relapsed and had almost fainted. Never did I see so affecting a scene. She viewed herself as on the brink of the deepest affliction. I wavered in my resolution while I beheld her, but she bid me arm myself with fortitude. Hay called again too, and thought that the letter which I was to write could not fail to settle the affair. We had been engaged to dine at Mr. Webster's with Sir George Preston's family. My wife was so ill that she insisted to be excused. I went by myself. I found the company so comfortable and friendly-like that I thought she would be soothed if there, and kept from brooding over her woe by herself. They were all for her coming still, saying that her complaint was only low spirits. George and I went for her; and with much entreaty I got her to take a chair and come. She had a faintness in her countenance that was very interesting, and her anxiety about me endeared her to me. The kind attention which everybody showed her, particularly Lady Preston's motherly kindness, did her good, and she grew easier. I was for a while like a man with some mortification or gnawing distemper at his heart, and envied worthy Sir George and every man whose heart was at ease. It was so vexatious to be entangled with a boy, and to run the risks of a serious duel with one that would make it really ludicrous, being not only young, but a little, effeminate-looking creature. I however re-

[9] A scroll is a draft.—Cochrane lived at Pinkie, in Inveresk parish.

solved to take the comforts of life heartily in the mean time. I eat a good dinner, and drank freely of excellent claret, and by degrees I felt myself firm.

My wife called me into another room, and begged I would allow her to mention the affair to Lady Preston. I thought it would relieve her much to have a female friend to whom she could unbosom herself; and therefore, since she had unhappily come to the knowledge of it, I allowed her to mention it in the utmost confidence. When the company went to tea, I spoke of the affair to Dr. Webster, as to a sagacious man. He said, if my letter did not give satisfaction, the boy's father should confine him as a Bedlamite. My wife had desired that I would speak of it to Captain Preston, who was a younger man than Commissioner Cochrane, for she was anxious that there should not be the least imputation on my spirit. I did so; and he was of opinion with the Commissioner. I engaged him to be my second in case matters should come to an extremity; and I begged of him that, as I was so much concerned on my wife's account, and might therefore lean to a too gentle conduct, he would as a true friend take care that I should do nothing but what was perfectly becoming a gentleman. He said he would. He made me read both the letter and the answer twice over, and was satisfied that I was doing quite properly. After tea I went home and wrote out my answer, with a very little variation. My wife and Grange sat by me. Then Grange went with me, and saw me put it into the posthouse.

My wife and I supped at Sir George's, and were pretty easy. At night she told me that Captain Preston said to her she might make herself quite easy. Let the boy give what answer he pleased, he would not leave Scotland till he saw the affair ended without any harm being done. Wearied both in body and mind, we slept tolerably.

SATURDAY 8 OCTOBER. This was our day of entertaining Captain Preston and his friends. My wife would fain have had an apology made that she was ill. But I prevailed with her to have the resolution to do her best. As Captain Preston was so very good a friend, it would have been wrong to have disappointed him of a social party. Besides, I thought that keeping in a constant scene of company would do both her and me good.

Mr. Hay and I took a walk in the King's Park and piazza of the Abbey of Holyroodhouse. He was clear that my letter was enough; and that if the boy should return an impertinent answer, I should treat him as a boy, and despise it. Mr. William Wilson had sent me some papers to consider.[1] It was an irksome task in my present state. I however did it, and called on

---

[1] Wilson was a Writer to the Signet. On the day Boswell put on the gown, 29 July 1766, he had given him his first fee, which, Boswell said, "has made me ever since look upon him with particular regard" (14 March 1772).

him for a little this forenoon. I had a serious conversation with Grange, walking backwards and forwards in the court of the Royal Bank. He said he was really puzzled. He did not imagine the boy would be satisfied by my letter, otherwise he would make a foolish figure after writing to me with so much keenness. He was for acquainting his father or uncle of the affair, before fighting, lest they might have reflections against me as going to extremities with a minor without their knowledge. Yet he had some suspicion that they already knew of it.

We had at dinner Lord and Lady Dundonald and Lady Betty Cochrane, Sir George and Lady Preston, Miss Preston, Colonel Preston,[2] Captain Preston, and Mr. Patrick Preston, who just arrived from Valleyfield, in his boots, about three; Dr. Webster, Miss Webster, George Webster and Sandy Webster, Mr. and Mrs. Wellwood, and Miss Susie Wellwood. We were in all eighteen. I had some excellent pint bottles of claret, which I called Captain Preston's marines. We drank jovially. Dr. Webster left us. I said this was *the first time of his appearing in that character*.[3] I was much intoxicated.

Captain Preston had agreed at my request to take Andrew Boswell, a younger son of the old family of Balmuto, as one of his midshipmen.[4] I presented the boy to him this evening; and he promised to take care of him. The smallpox being frequent, and little Effie unfit for inoculation, her nurse and she went this day to Prestonfield, where they were kindly received.

SUNDAY 9 OCTOBER. The riot of yesterday had been great among the servants, as well as in the dining-room. Twenty-four bottles of small beer were drank. This was a specimen of what goes on in disorderly families. I got up tolerably well, and called on Grange, who now thought there would be no more of the quarrel. I was at the New Church and heard Mr. Walker and Mr. Stuart of Cramond, who preached on a gloomy subject: death being without any order.[5] The text, I think, was in Job.[6] Sir George, Colonel, Captain, and Mr. Patrick Preston and I went in a coach

---

[2] Lieutenant-Colonel Robert Preston was Sir George's brother.

[3] In the language of the playbills.

[4] The Boswells of Auchinleck were originally cadets of the Boswells of Balmuto. The "old family" declined, and in 1722 Balmuto was purchased from the laird by John Boswell of the Auchinleck branch, younger brother of Boswell's grandfather. Boswell considered Godfrey Bosville, the Yorkshire squire, his chief because he believed the Boswells of Auchinleck were ultimately cadets of the Bosvilles of Gunthwaite, Yorkshire.

[5] The Reverend Charles Stuart resigned his parish in 1776; he later studied medicine and practised as a physician. In 1822 his eldest son, James, killed Boswell's eldest son, Sir Alexander, in a duel.

[6] "A land . . . of the shadow of death, without any order" (Job 10. 22).

and dined with Commissioner Cochrane at Pinkie. At night we all supped at Dr. Webster's, and were wonderfully quiet. Colonel Webster was to set out for London next morning. I kept up my spirits as well as I could wish.

MONDAY 10 OCTOBER. Sir George and my Lady and Miss Preston and my wife and I went in a coach to the Hawes to take a fish dinner from Captain Preston. The Colonel, Mr. and Mrs. and Miss Wellwood and George Webster were there. Colonel Campbell should have been with us, but was obliged to be at Edinburgh. We dined well, and drank not to excess, but till we were mellow; and then took tea. It was really a comfortable jaunt—though I was at intervals haunted with the disagreeable idea of the quarrel. We supped at Sir George's.

TUESDAY 11 OCTOBER. In the morning Mr. Moir, agent for Colonel Campbell, came, and desired that I would be at Dunfermline as counsel for the Colonel when a delegate was to be chosen for that burgh, which was to be on Thursday next, and asked also if I would accept of being delegate for Culross. I agreed to both proposals, and was pleased to be thus selected. It was a diversion to the disagreeable thoughts which clouded me. No answer had come to my letter; so I concluded that it was satisfactory. At breakfast my wife suggested very well that I was not bound to answer the young man. That if an injury had been done to his sister or any female relation, or to an old superannuated father, he might step forth. But that in this case the father was my proper antagonist. This view of the case seemed quite just. Hay called, and was of that opinion; Grange also agreed. My wife had written to my cousin Claud, begging that he would come to town, as she had something that made her very uneasy to communicate.[7] He came with a most friendly readiness, and she told him the story. He agreed with her; and then he came and called on me. I showed him all that had passed. He thought there was nothing in the "Royalist" that could be made the subject of a serious question, and that I had written a proper and spirited answer to the young man. He said to fight with a boy would be like fighting with a footman, as no honour could be had by it, in any event; and he was clear that I should hold the Justice-Clerk as the only person to whom I was bound to answer. It gave me much satisfaction to find Claud, who is both very sensible and abundantly resolute, agreeing with me. He and Charles Hay dined with us. Then my wife and I accompanied him in a coach to Leith, and saw him sail for Kinghorn. Grange drank tea with us when we came home. Sir George's family were all abroad this day. We supped by ourselves.

[7] Claud Boswell, later Lord Balmuto, was son of the John Boswell who purchased Balmuto (above, p. 16 *n.* 4). See below, Appendix C, Chart III.

WEDNESDAY 12 OCTOBER. Sir George and Captain Preston called on me, and we went and waited on Colonel Campbell, who was to set out for Dunfermline this forenoon. It was settled I should go with him. We set off in a post-chaise with four horses, and I enjoyed the quick driving as Mr. Johnson does. It kept my spirits brisk. I found the Colonel to be a man of admirable parts, a good deal like General Paoli. We had a fine sail across the ferry, and got to Dunfermline in good time. The lively cry of "Campbell for ever" was animating. The people seemed to be in the greatest joy on his arrival. He just stopped at my acquaintance John Adie's inn to dress. We then drove to Sir John Halkett's, at Pitfirrane, to dinner. There was a large company there. We were well entertained. At five we took our chaise and drove to Culross, as there was some little difficulty about the choice of a delegate, one of the bailies being anxious to be it. We stopped at the Red Lion, where we were visited by the councillors. My being delegate was very proper, from my natural connexion with Culross; and the Colonel got it settled that I should be chosen on Saturday. We drove back to Dunfermline, and had some of the Colonel's friends to sup with us at John Adie's. I had a kind invitation to lodge at Mr. William Adie's, being one of his trustees.[8] I was very well there.

THURSDAY 13 OCTOBER. After a good breakfast I went and visited the Colonel, who had all his friends of the Council about him. It was curious to see with what address he spoke to them. Mr. Wellwood came this morning. He and I and the Colonel walked about while the Council was sitting, till there was like to be some confusion. I was then called in by the magistrates to give my advice whether the council chosen by the minority, who had already protested that they were the legal council and declared how they would have voted, could be allowed to have a second protest minuted that their votes were now refused. I was somewhat uneasy when called in, as I had very little knowledge of burgh politics. However, I saw the matter here was plain, and very gravely gave my opinion that it was idle, and that the Council should take no notice of it. I then said I supposed they would not wish to be disturbed with people who had no right to be with them. I left them; and the man who came to protest again withdrew, upon which they locked the door. I was sent for again to hear a protest taken by the minority of the real council read. I was of opinion it required no answer. The Colonel and a few of us dined at John Adie's. I was then invited to the Town House, and received a burgess-ticket.[1]

---

[8] William Adie, a merchant in Dunfermline, was a brother of John, and probably a son of Peter, a surgeon, who died in 1769. In the same year Boswell was appointed a trustee of Peter Adie's estate.

[1] A certificate of citizenship in the burgh.

The Colonel and I and Mr. Wellwood drank tea at Mr. William Adie's, after which we drove to Inverkeithing to prepare for the election of a delegate there, which was to be next day. Mr. Moir had been with us today, and went also to Inverkeithing. We put up at the house of Kellock, one of the present bailies. We went to the house of Henderson, a councillor, where they were all met in a small room with a fire, and a deal of punch on the table; so that it was a very disagreeable scene. We left them, and supped at Kellock's, where I had a tolerable room, and slept wonderfully well.

FRIDAY 14 OCTOBER. A better method was followed at Inverkeithing than at Dunfermline, for the council chosen by the minority were not allowed to go into the court-house, but were told that they might send in any protest they had to make. They sat long, and I wearied somewhat; but considered that I was in the way of my business, so was contented. Mr. Wellwood talked of the system of fatality, which revived that sort of uneasy doubts about free will which have sometimes disturbed me, but which have not for this long time arisen in my mind. I was a little gloomy from a near view of the uncertainty of life, as a quarrel might suddenly deprive one of it. A life of Mr. Johnson in *The Westminster Magazine* copied into *The Weekly Magazine* did not interest me as it would have done on some occasions.[2] A man must have his powers in a good degree of vigour to relish anything properly, either corporeal or mental. We dined at Henderson's, and I was made a burgess. Mr. Wellwood went for Edinburgh; the Colonel and I and Mr. Moir to Culross, where we had the three bailies (Johnston, Halkerston, and Bald), Ireland the town clerk, and Mr. Christie, who had written several songs on the Colonel's side, with us at supper.[3] The Colonel, ever since the writ was issued, made a point that every man who had a vote should pay his club.[4] All these days there was no hard drinking. I kept myself warm with liquor, but was never intoxicated. I wish to keep myself from being too particular in my journal, but it is not easy for me to refrain. Bailie Bald came and told me, "I have provided a *sappy*[5] bed for you—at Miss Erskine's of Balgonie." Accordingly he conducted me to her house; and there I found a very plump hospitable landlady, well advanced in years, and quite in the style of a

---

[2] "An Impartial Account of the Life, Character, Genius, and Writings of Dr. Samuel Johnson" (*Westminster Magazine*, September 1774, reprinted in *The Weekly Magazine* for 13 October).

[3] Probably James Christie, schoolmaster of Kennoway, who in 1776 was elected master of the Song School, Dunfermline.

[4] After the issuance of the writ for choosing a representative to serve in Parliament, thirty days before the election, any treating of a delegate might be construed as a bribe. Campbell, as well as Dundas, was suspected of bribery, not without cause.

[5] Plump, soft.

Scots good gentlewoman of the last age, or early in this. I had an excellent room with a Bible, a prayer-book, and *The New Whole Duty of Man*⁶ lying in it. I read some before I went to bed; and, though to a certain degree disturbed with the idea that a hot-headed young man might force me into a situation which might prove fatal, I became upon the whole calm with devout resignation.

SATURDAY 15 OCTOBER. Miss Erskine and I breakfasted very cordially. I then visited Bailie Johnston, in whose house the Colonel lodged. Captain James Erskine of Alloa had been with us at Inverkeithing.⁷ He came this day to Culross from the Queensferry. I was chosen delegate unanimously and without any protest. The Captain insisted that we should go for a night or two to Alloa. He and I talked a little of duelling. He said the best way was to fire immediately, and that he who fired first had a great advantage, having many chances to kill his man. He talked quite coolly of this, as of a matter of science. We dined at a place called the Sands, a little way from Culross, with Captain ———— Roberton, brother to Earnock, who was tenant there.⁸ At night we went to Alloa. It was pleasing to me to come at last to this ancient seat of which I had so often heard. I was glad to see my old class-fellow Johnny Erskine in his own house, and his lady, formerly Miss Floyer, whom I had seen in London in the year 1763, when my friend Temple admired her much.⁹ We found

⁶ *The New Whole Duty of Man* was an anonymous devotional work like the old *Whole Duty of Man* (1658) and equally popular. First published in 1744, it was now in its twenty-second edition.

⁷ James Francis Erskine had unsuccessfully opposed Sir Lawrence Dundas in the election for Edinburgh city on 13 October. His mother was the daughter and successor of the attainted Earl of Mar, whose estates were forfeited because of his involvement in the uprising of 1715; her husband, James Erskine ("Old Mar"), son of Lord Grange, an advocate and Knight-Marshal of Scotland, was her first cousin. Boswell's grandfather, Colonel John Erskine, was grandson of John, Earl of Mar, the close friend of James VI (James I of England), and was stepfather, by his second marriage, of the attainted earl. See below, Appendix C, Chart IV. The earldom was later (1824) restored to James Francis's elder brother John Francis. After the forfeiture, their estate in Clackmannanshire, Alloa (in the possession of the Erskine family since 1365), had been purchased for them from the Government by Lord Grange and another relation, David Erskine, Lord Dun.

⁸ Earnock was Captain James Roberton of Earnock; this brother was probably William, a captain of Marines.

⁹ In 1756–1757 Boswell and John Francis Erskine had been enrolled in John Stevenson's class in logic and metaphysics in Edinburgh University. In 1770 Erskine had married Frances Floyer, only daughter of Charles Floyer, formerly Governor of Fort St. David, Madras. The Reverend William Johnson Temple, Rector of Mamhead in Devonshire, also a member of Stevenson's class in 1756–1757, was Boswell's most intimate friend. On 1 February 1775 he wrote to Boswell: "Miss Floyer . . . was when we knew her, if not a beauty, at least desirable. What I admired in her was that truly

nobody else but Mrs. Rachel Erskine and a Mr. Grant, a little one-eyed clergyman who spoke English and, I suppose, had a living somewhere in England.[1] Mr. Campbell of the Bank's son had come with Captain Erskine.[2] We had tea, then whist, then supper; plain living—no claret. Accounts came that Sir Adam Fergusson had carried the election of Ayrshire. I was vexed, but bore it properly; though indeed the reflection that the noble families of the county to which I belong had been defeated, even accidentally, by a kind of democratical coalition, kept me awhile awake after I went to bed.[3]

SUNDAY 16 OCTOBER. I was to have stayed here with the Colonel till Monday; but Captain Erskine having had information that Captain Robert Preston was to set out on Monday morning, and I being very anxious to see the Captain before he went, as he was the man on whom I depended in my disagreeable affair, I resolved to leave Alloa after breakfast. I got a short walk taken, and reserved my seeing the place to another occasion. The Colonel ordered his chaise to be ready to carry me to the North Ferry. I told him I was sorry that we should part. He said he should wish too to see Captain Preston before he went, and after a little consideration he determined to go to town with me. This was a happy change for me, as I should have been dull alone. The old house, the large rooms, and the pictures at Alloa gave me sober and grand ideas of family. The Colonel and I drove charmingly to the North Ferry; and he gave me on the road a detail of his spirited progress as an engineer—as one invited to be chief engineer to the Venetians—as chief engineer in Bengal. His activity, his application, his command of accurate expression pleased me, though I myself was somewhat low-spirited. We dined at five at Cuninghame's, having made the landlord's Sunday's supper our dinner. We got to Edinburgh about eight. I felt no such sensations as affected me when I last returned

---

feminine diffidence and softness so highly engaging when united with pleasing features and sweetness of voice." Boswell's and Temple's private name for Erskine was "the Horse."

[1] Mrs. Rachel Erskine, a spinster, was the sister of "Old Mar."

[2] The banker was John Campbell, cashier of the Royal Bank since 1745.

[3] Only freeholders with large property qualifications could vote in parliamentary elections, but some of the landholders had sold redeemable life rents for nominal sums in order to split their qualifications, and thus, through friends and dependants, they could cast more than one vote. Such votes had always been considered fictitious by Lord Auchinleck: he had maintained this stand in his *Observations on the Election Law*, dictated to Boswell in 1771. In the present election, both sides were well supplied with fictitious votes. Boswell held that the noble families had been defeated "accidentally" because he believed that, had not Sir Adam Fergusson's brother George proposed putting the oath of *bona fide* possession, their coalition, which supported Kennedy, would have won. As it turned out, more of Fergusson's friends than of Kennedy's were willing to perjure themselves in taking the oath.

to town.⁴ We supped at Sir George's, where my wife was. We sat too late, and I drank too much.

MONDAY 17 OCTOBER. William Fergusson, a schoolmaster, called on me after breakfast and consulted me, with a confused appearance of secrecy, what he should do with a bond granted by one of the candidates for the burghs of Inverkeithing, etc., to a deacon, which he said was in his possession, and that he was offered £500 by Sir Lawrence Dundas's party to *give it back*. This made me believe it was a bond by Colonel Masterton.⁵ I told the wretch that as he had communicated this to me unwarily, I should not betray him, but would give him no advice, desiring him to go again to Lord Pitfour, whom he said he had consulted. I was uneasy at this visit, for I wished to inform Colonel Campbell of so strong a circumstance against his antagonist; yet was restrained by the fidelity of my office, as the creature, though he gave me no fee, appeared to advise with me as a lawyer. I suspected too that he was a rogue, and wanted to discover the bond to Colonel Campbell to get money for it, and might say that I had told what he mentioned in confidence.

We dined at Sir George's with Colonel Campbell. Captain Preston gave out that he was not to leave Edinburgh till next morning, that he might shun a farewell parting with his parents, whom he had little chance of finding alive on his return from India; but he let me and his brother, etc., know that he was to go this afternoon. We rose soon after dinner, and went out before tea, as it were to return. We met at Mrs. Brown's in the Exchange, where was Dr. Webster; and there we drank a couple of magnum bonums of claret to the Captain's health and success. Webster sat still, and the rest of us saw the Captain to his chaise. He assured me that there would be no more of the disagreeable affair as to which he had engaged to stand by me. But I understood that he had mentioned it to his brother, Mr. Preston, who would willingly take his place. I spoke to Mr. Preston, and he assured me that he would conduct the affair with prudence and honour, if anything more was necessary. Webster had whispered to him that he and I should return to Mrs. Brown's. We did so, and we three drank two more pints very cordially.

We supped at Sir George's. I was called into another room after supper, and found my wife in a most miserable state, as she had notice that the Justice-Clerk's son was come to Paxton's, and wanted to see me there.⁶

⁴ 27 September.

⁵ The deacon was Thomas Gibson of Inverkeithing. Lieutenant-Colonel James Masterton, Colonel Campbell's opponent and a creature of Sir Lawrence Dundas, was M.P. for Stirling, 1768–1774. Fergusson wanted Campbell to offer him more for the bond (forged: see below, 21 October), as evidence of bribery, than had allegedly been offered to him by Dundas.

⁶ James Paxton's inn in the Grassmarket.

This appeared to be a determined purpose of a duel, and she was quite overcome with fear. Mr. Preston was called out and bid her be easy; advised that no notice should be taken of the thing tonight; and that, when the young man's letter came in the morning, we should send for Mr. Preston, and he would settle matters properly. We went home and gave orders not to open the door, though there should be a knock. After we were in bed, somebody knocked several times, but no answer was made. I felt myself somewhat uneasy, but sufficiently determined. No doubt the claret which I had taken was of use to me.

TUESDAY 18 OCTOBER. I slept pretty well till near six. As I was now a delegate, I was bound in honour to Colonel Campbell to run no risk till the election was over; so at any rate there was time to prepare.

My wife never shut her eye the whole night. At six she rose and called for Grange, that he might come down to me immediately; and also for Mr. Preston, that he might be in the house when the message came. Grange was with me before I got up, and spoke calmly to me as a true friend, but was very anxious. Mr. Preston came between seven and eight. Grange went away and was to return between nine and ten. A note from the young man came before eight, insisting to see me before nine, either at Paxton's or my own house; and mentioning that it would be proper I should have a friend with me. My wife was like one in a kind of delirium. Mr. Preston made her give us some tea, and told her that he would go and talk with the young man. I sent a card by him with my compliments, and that my friend Mr. Preston would communicate my sentiments. As he went away I took him by the hand, and told him I trusted that he would say nothing inconsistent with my honour. He promised he would not. That he would say he thought my letter was a sufficient satisfaction; but, if anything farther was necessary, I was ready to answer my Lord Justice-Clerk. That, if he could not convince the young man himself, he would endeavour to get him to agree that the advice of his uncle, Mr. Peter Miller, Mr. Preston's very good friend, should be taken. After Mr. Preston was gone, Grange came; and he and I walked backwards and forwards in my dining-room. I was at ease enough to tell him all the history of Colonel Campbell.

A long time passed without any appearance. At last between ten and eleven a servant of the Justice-Clerk's came running into the court, and went to the house of Mr. Peter Miller, who lived in the same stair with me; and in a little he went back, followed by Mr. Peter Miller. This made me think all was well. Grange followed, and saw them go to the Grassmarket. He was obliged to go as far as Linlithgow this day, but from kind anxiety kept his chaise waiting till he should know what was done. By and by Mr. Preston and Mr. Peter Miller came down the court arm in arm.

Mr. Preston told me when he came in that he had gone to the bottom of the matter, and it was now as we could wish. I informed Grange, who waited in the next room; and he went to his chaise in peace. My wife was, as she herself said, like one who had been upon the rack, so that she felt a most pleasing relief. Mr. Preston told me that he was much pleased with the young man, and with his friend whom he had with him, Principal Robertson's son.[7] That he had some difficulty to convince young Miller, or to get him to agree to send for his uncle; but when his uncle came and was of the same opinion with Mr. Preston, things went smoothly. That the young man expressed great concern on being told that his letter had fallen into my wife's hands. Mr. Preston then went down and brought up Mr. Peter Miller, and we three talked over the matter. Mr. Peter Miller acquitted himself with great good sense, proper spirit, and an uncommon ease and propriety of expression. He said that I was in a disagreeable situation; for in whatever way this matter might end, his nephew would have the world on his side. That had his advice been taken by either party, he would have been against the writing of his nephew's letter, and my answer. But as matters stood it was of consequence to me to avoid an affair with this young man. That he thought I had said what was sufficient; and that at any rate to be sure the Justice-Clerk was the only person whom I was bound to answer. "At the same time," said he, "my nephew, though not yet known in the world, is, I assure you, an uncommon young man. He is a thinking, metaphysical fellow, and he will argue himself into a persuasion that he is in the right; and though upon this occasion he has nothing to say, he may keep a resentment in his mind, and some years after this easily contrive to make a quarrel with you, in which he shall be a principal. It were therefore to be wished that this affair were effectually settled, that no bad blood may remain." He told me that so far from there being any reason for blaming the Justice-Clerk for being severe against John Reid, the fact was that Lord Rochford sent the respite to him with a power to deliver it or put it in the fire as he should judge proper. That the Justice-Clerk would not take upon him such an exercise of the royal prerogative, but delivered the respite; and though he sent up his own opinion, sent also up a full copy of the trial that it might be judged of by the King in Council. Mr. Peter Miller said he imagined that when I knew this, I would wish to tell Lord Justice-Clerk that I was sorry any paper of mine had been understood to be injurious to his character. I said I would tell him so.

It was then agreed that Mr. Peter Miller with his nephew should meet Mr. Preston and me in half an hour at Mrs. Brown's in the Exchange. Mr.

[7] Probably William, eldest son of William Robertson, the historian, Principal of Edinburgh University; he was later, like William Miller, a Lord of Session.

Preston and I called at the Custom House and told Commissioner Cochrane what had passed, and he was quite satisfied. We then went to Mrs. Brown's; and in a little appeared the two Millers. The young man and I met and took each other by the hand as easily as at any meeting. He seemed to be quite calm and mild and genteel, with spirited ideas of honour and the regard he owed to his father's character, but not clearly knowing how he should proceed. I told him that I had given him more satisfaction than I should have done in a common case, because I was pleased with the feelings which he showed; that he could not expect, and I was sure would not wish, that I should make any improper concessions. I had assured him he was mistaken. He declared that he was satisfied. I said I hoped this was not merely a ceremonious adjusting of the affair, but that he was quite satisfied and that nothing would lurk behind. He said nothing should. I told him that his father was certainly the person whom I was bound to answer. That I would wait on him and assure him of my regret that anything I had written had been misunderstood to mean an attack upon him, and I was sure he would be satisfied. I asked the young man as a favour that this affair might not be mentioned; for, though I had owned to him as a gentleman that I had written the "Royalist," I did not choose it should be known. He said he would not speak of it. We parted in perfect good terms. Thus did my friend Preston relieve me from a very disagreeable dilemma. He dined with my wife and me comfortably; and he and I just drank a pint bottle of claret. We all drank tea and supped at Sir George's.

WEDNESDAY 19 OCTOBER. Mr. Preston went home to Valleyfield. I dined at home with my wife. After so many days of warm living and agitation I felt a sort of depression. We had M. Dupont and Grange at tea.[8] Dupont was become very deaf and seemed failing visibly. Poor Mr. George Frazer had died while I was with Colonel Campbell at the burghs.[9] This was a striking circumstance to me, as I had known him long, and liked him much; but in the busy frame I was in, I did not feel it much at the time. This forenoon I called on Charles Hay, and told him how the disagreeable affair was happily settled. We supped at Sir George's.

I had now another uneasiness. I had not adverted that every one who votes in the election of a Member of Parliament may be obliged to take the Formula.[1] I had scruples as to this, and was in very great anxiety

---

[8] The Reverend Pierre Loumeau Dupont was pastor of the French Protestant congregation in Edinburgh.
[9] Frazer, an excise officer, had died on 12 October.
[1] The Formula, prescribed by a parliamentary act of 1700, required the taker to prove that he was not a Roman Catholic by declaring that he "denied, disowned, and abhorred" certain tenets assumed to be peculiar to the papal obedience.

lest it should occur to Sir Lawrence Dundas's party to put it, and by my delicate conscientiousness one of Colonel Campbell's delegates should be cut off; and as my refusing the Formula would prevent me from ever being in Parliament or even voting at an election, and would also make my father do all that he could to my disadvantage, I should be in such a situation as to make it advisable for me to leave Scotland. This was a secret of such importance to me that I resolved to mention it to nobody whatever. Sometimes I thought of falling sick, or of pretending to have important business in London, and to get another delegate chosen in my place. At last I thought that as putting the Formula was very unusual I would take my chance. My difficulty in taking the Formula was that I could not well swear I *abhor* all the tenets there mentioned, such as *purgatory,* the *invocation of angels and saints,* and believe them *contrary to* and *inconsistent with* the written word of GOD; for, indeed, I do not see that they are. At least I do not recollect the passages against them. I hoped that, even if the Formula should be put, I might get Mr. Wight, my brother lawyer, a delegate for Sir Lawrence, to waive it by entrusting him in confidence as a gentleman, and assuring him that he would lay me under the utmost obligation for life.[2] Much did I wish that I had not been delegate, and impatiently did I long to have the election over. Lady Betty Cochrane supped with us at Sir George's.

THURSDAY 20 OCTOBER. Mr. James Erskine of Grange breakfasted with us, and was as lively as ever.[3] Commissioner Cochrane carried me out in his chaise, and I dined with him. There was nobody with us but his housekeeper, Mrs. Webster. He was sensible and prudent and kind. I came to town in the fly. Mr. Forbes, the non-jurant bishop at Leith, was

---

[2] Wight was delegate for Queensferry; he was later Solicitor-General.

[3] James Erskine was a rather remote blood relation (third cousin once removed) of Boswell, and more interestingly connected with him by marriage—Boswell's grandfather, Colonel John Erskine, as was indicated above, having been stepfather to Erskine's father, Lord Grange, and his uncle, the Earl of Mar. Erskine's family history is an epitome of Scots violence, which by no means ended with the seventeenth century. His mother's father, John Chiesly of Dalry, murdered the Lord President of the Court of Session in the streets of Edinburgh, and in consequence was tortured, executed, and his body hung in chains. His uncle, John Erskine, Earl of Mar, led the rebellion of 1715 in favour of the Pretender, and was attainted and exiled. His mother, Rachel Chiesly, a violent and intemperate woman, was abducted at the instance of his father, Lord Grange, judge in both the supreme courts of Scotland, spirited away to the Hebrides, and kept incommunicado in various places there (seven years on the remote rock of St. Kilda) till her death eleven years later. Erskine, who was an advocate, was married to his first cousin, Frances Erskine, daughter of the attainted Earl of Mar, and was the father of John Francis Erskine and James Francis Erskine (above, 15 October).

in it.⁴ He revived ideas of High Church and Jacobitism, etc. I drank tea with Lady Betty Cochrane at Belleville, where she was by herself, her father and mother having gone to La Mancha; and supped with my wife at Sir George's.

FRIDAY 21 OCTOBER. I called on worthy Grange in the morning. We pleased ourselves with thinking in what a comfortable state we were now, in comparison of what we were when I called last in a morning. I took him home with me to breakfast. Mr. Moir came in and breakfasted and informed me that the rascal Fergusson was in prison, having been detected in attempting to sell to Sir Lawrence's party a bond forged as if granted to a deacon by Colonel Campbell; and it seems the wretch had been trying to get money on the like pretence from both sides. The Colonel wanted to see me immediately. I dressed and went to him. We went with John Stewart, who acted as sheriff-substitute of Midlothian, to the house of Alexander Fergusson, writer in Edinburgh, who was sick; and he was examined on a precognition, the wretch having employed him to negotiate a bargain as to the delivery of the bond. I and Mr. James Hardie and Mr. Moir attended from between twelve and one till between seven and eight. The Colonel came and went, but was with us a good part of the time. We then went to Sommers's tavern to precognosce Major Bruce, who had treated for having the bond given up, believing it to be a real one. We eat some dinner and drank a few glasses. Maclaurin was there on our part, Sandy Murray on the part of Major Bruce.⁵ It was a novelty to allow counsel to attend for a witness. I objected to it. But Maclaurin would not make a point of the objection. We took the Major's declaration for about an hour, and adjourned till next morning at nine. I felt myself in a sort of wild state of mind, metaphysical and fanciful, looking on the various operations of human life as machinery, or I could not well describe what; and not in the plain steady view which I have had in the midst of a busy session. I was introduced to Sir James Campbell of Ardkinglass. We took

⁴ Robert Forbes resided at Leith, where he had a church for non-jurors. Since 1769 he had been Bishop of Ross and Caithness in the Episcopal Church in Scotland, which was descended from the church established by the Stuarts, and still loyal to that line. (Forbes was an ardent Jacobite.) Although the statutes were no longer enforced, the congregations of the Scottish Episcopal Church were compelled to meet quietly because their priests were forbidden under severe penalties to minister to more than four persons at a time besides their own families. The majority of Scots Anglicans attended "qualified" chapels (or "English" chapels), which were legal and public. Their priests were in English or Irish orders and read the liturgy of the Church of England.

⁵ John Maclaurin (later Lord Dreghorn) was one of Boswell's most intimate friends in the Faculty of Advocates. (The others were Andrew Crosbie and William Nairne.) Alexander Murray became Solicitor-General in 1775 and was raised to the bench as Lord Henderland in 1783.

well to each other. He and I and the Colonel and Captain Erskine and Mr. Moir and Mr. Duncan Campbell, the Colonel's brother, supped at Sommers's. We did not drink much, but were just properly social.

SATURDAY 22 OCTOBER. By nine in the morning I was at the sheriff's chamber, to be present at the farther examination of Major Bruce. I breakfasted with Colonel Campbell. I said to Sandy Murray I wished Mr. Lockhart might die Dean of Faculty.[6] Were he to get to the bench, it would be *sitting in state* before his funeral. Sir James Campbell, Captain Erskine, the Colonel's brother, Maclaurin, Moir, and I dined at Sommers's. They all but Maclaurin supped with me. We had also Hardie and Sir George, my Lady and Miss Preston. Thomas[7] the gown-keeper, my old servant, came and officiated. Fergusson had escaped. A lad who was catched carrying a letter to Miss Charlotte Fergusson, in whose clothes he went off, was put in the Guard. The Colonel and I went and examined him, but could learn nothing. The soldiers showed me a vault in the Guard in which five riotous earls were confined at one time. The Colonel and I returned to the company. We were very sober.

SUNDAY 23 OCTOBER. Lay too long. Stayed at home with Veronica. After dinner missed Mr. Charles Hay, who was to take me to New English Chapel.[8] Walked out to Lady Colville's.[9] Found her and Lady Anne and the three brothers and Arbuthnot at dinner. I drank a bottle of claret. Many jokes passed about elections, particularly that of Ayrshire. Lord Kellie, after giving Sir A. Fergusson, said to me, "I'm going to give a toast you'll like still worse—'Good afternoon.'" I called on Colonel Campbell a little. Supped home. ✳

MONDAY 24 OCTOBER. Attended an examination of Miss Charlotte Fergusson in the Council Chamber, on the part of Colonel Campbell. Dined with him at his lodgings. Went and saw Breslaw perform. Was much entertained with his legerdemain. My wife and I supped at Sir George's.

[6] Because of his Tory and indeed Jacobite politics, Alexander Lockhart, Dean of the Faculty of Advocates, was seventy-five years old before he was raised to the bench as Lord Covington in 1775. He died in 1782.

[7] Thomas Edmondson.

[8] A "qualified" chapel, which had been opened for public worship only two Sundays earlier. It had been built somewhat in the form of St. Martin's in the Fields, London, by the united congregations of the three small Anglican chapels in Edinburgh. The building (now a Roman Catholic church) still stands in the Cowgate.

[9] To Drumsheugh (site of Drumsheugh Gardens today), where he was "always soothed, comforted, and cheered." Elizabeth, Lady Colville was now twice widowed. She lived with her brother, Captain Andrew Erskine, Boswell's friend since 1761. He was unmarried, as were his sister, Lady Anne Erskine, and his two older brothers, Thomas Alexander, sixth Earl of Kellie, and Archibald, afterwards seventh Earl of Kellie.

TUESDAY 25 OCTOBER. Mr. Alison, clerk to Mr. Alexander Orr, breakfasted with me, and consulted me on a bill of advocation from the proceedings of the commissioners of supply of the Stewartry of Kirkcudbright.[1] I was on Laird Heron's side. My wife and I drank tea at Mr. Robert Boswell's. It was agreeable to see his family in a real cheerful state. Fergusson was catched tonight. We supped Sir George's. Dr. Webster was there.

WEDNESDAY 26 OCTOBER. It was necessary to go out to Lord Hailes's to have the Kirkcudbright advocation judged.[2] Alison had a post-chaise at the head of James's Court by eight. We breakfasted and drove out. The Galloway names of the parishes *Urr* and *Lochrutton* revived Scottish southern ideas. Lord Hailes gave us a speedy judgement, and we came back in good spirits. Mr. Robert Boswell and his wife, Balbarton, and young Donaldson dined and drank tea with us. I went again to Breslaw's. My wife went. I was again well entertained. Miss Webster supped with us.

THURSDAY 27 OCTOBER. We dined at Sir George's. Mrs. Wellwood was there. George Webster came to tea and brought a letter from Digges, giving an account of his expedition in Ireland.[3] It revived my old theatrical ideas. I went home and wrote my journal, being always behind with it, and went back to Sir George's to supper.

FRIDAY 28 OCTOBER. My wife and I dined at Prestonfield and saw Effie, who was a fine thriving child. I valued Sir Alexander the more from reflecting on the death of Mr. Keith and Mr. Frazer, two of his friends and cotemporaries. Dr. Young was there.[4]

I had called in the forenoon on David Hume to pay him half an year's rent of his house.[5] He told me he thought I should write the history of

[1] The commissioners of supply would be chiefly concerned with collection of the land-tax.

[2] Sir David Dalrymple, Lord Hailes, a Lord of Session who corresponded with Boswell on antiquarian and historical matters, lived at Newhailes, in Inveresk parish about five miles east of Edinburgh.

[3] West Digges, actor and the manager of the Theatre Royal, had been engaged to play twelve times in Ireland. Boswell had come under his spell as early as 1757. In the period of the London journal 1762–1763, Digges was his chief model of a man of fashion.

[4] He was Professor of Midwifery at Edinburgh University and Mrs. Boswell's obstetrician.

[5] In May 1771 Boswell and his wife had moved to a house which belonged to David Hume the philosopher, in James's Court, in the Lawnmarket. Though they were still paying rent to Hume, they had not been living there since May 1773, when they sublet the apartment and moved downstairs into two floors of "very handsome and spacious rooms" in the same building. Boswell admired Hume for his kindness and good humour; respected him for his learning and literary achievement; but he had deep uneasiness, growing into rancour, at his scepticism.

the Union, which might be a neat popular piece of history. That when Wedderburn was a young man, and wished to be known, he asked Mr. Hume to suggest a subject of history for him to write; and he suggested the Union. That Wedderburn made himself known in another line and so did not pursue the plan.[6] He said I would find materials in the Advocates' Library. That I might with great justice to my countrymen please the English by my account of our advantages by the Union. That we had made many attempts. But when the English inclined to it, then our Jacobites opposed it. That we never gained one battle but at Bannockburn;[7] and as we did so ill even in rude feudal times, we could not have made any defence long in the present state of the art of war. That our great improvements are much owing to the Union. That for these several years there must have been a famine in Scotland if we had not had the liberty of importing corn, which the English could have prevented. I felt strongly my own ignorance, but said I should think of it. Sir Alexander Dick has more than once recommended to me this very plan. Mr. Hume said he had heard the Balcarres family had some papers which would throw light on the Union.

I drank rather too much today, wishing still to keep off the ghost of the Formula. I wandered in the streets at night, out as far as the Meadow by the Chapel of Ease; an unlucky practice *bs*.[8] My brother John had been a week in town without letting me know.[9] I heard of it by chance, and sent him a note asking him to sup with us tonight. I found him when I came home. He was in the same formal silent state as usual. It was vexing to see my *heir male*. But I hoped for a son, and considered that at any rate he was but an individual.[1]

SATURDAY 29 OCTOBER.[2] Counsellor Archibald Macdonald breakfasted with us. At ten Mr. Moir, Mr. Flockhart, Colonel Campbell's brother, and I set out in a coach. Thomas attended me as my servant for the occasion. We took a dram at Queensferry, and another at the North Ferry, from whence they went for Dunfermline and I went by Pitliver in a post-chaise, and took up Mr. Wellwood, and he and I met Colonel Camp-

---

[6] Alexander Wedderburn, now a great man in the British government, was a self-made Scot. He was a member of the Faculty of Advocates. In 1793 he became Lord Chancellor and on his resignation in 1801 was created Earl of Rosslyn.

[7] In 1314, when Robert Bruce routed the English under Edward II and assured the independence of Scotland.

[8] A private symbol which occurs nowhere else in the journal.

[9] Lieutenant John, three years younger than James. He suffered from periodic attacks of insanity and had been under the care of Dr. John Hall and Dr. Andrew Wilson at St. Luke's House (a "private house for lunatics") in Newcastle.

[1] That is, John was unmarried and the *line* would not pass to him.

[2] Boswell's thirty-fourth birthday.

bell at Valleyfield; nobody there but Mr. Preston and the Colonel, his uncle. We drank moderately, took tea, supped, and drank moderately again.

SUNDAY 30 OCTOBER. The Colonel carried Mr. Wellwood in his chaise, and I and my servant got Mr. Preston's chaise, and after breakfast we proceeded to Dunfermline, that we might appear decently at church. We had a most curious sermon from old Mr. Thomson, of which a very genuine account was given in *The Caledonian Mercury*.[3] We dined and drank heartily between sermons, and went to church again in the afternoon. The sight of the old church made the Formula more disagreeable to me.[4] The Colonel took me to drink tea at old Provost Wilson's, who, to distinguish him from others of the same name, is called Water-Wynd from his residence, and who has been of great service to the Colonel. Maclaurin was now come, and we had also Mr. Erskine of Mar and several more gentlemen.[5] Mr. Wellwood and I kept ourselves quiet all the evening in a room at John Adie's, and Bailie Buncle, who claimed to be delegate from Queensferry, supped with us.[6] John Adie went with me to my quarters at his brother's, where we had two bottles of excellent claret. I kept myself warm during all this time that the fear of the Formula might not sink me.

MONDAY 31 OCTOBER. I considered that this was the important day of trial for me, or rather the important day of risk. There were some paltry images upon my chimney-piece, which revived ideas of *saints*. In a bookcase I found Tillotson's *Sermons*. I turned to where he endeavours to confute some doctrines of the Church of Rome contained in the Formula. But he did not satisfy me. I recollected that Mr. Johnson said "we had no authority in Scripture for the invocation of saints. It was therefore *safer* not to practise it."[7] But surely he could not say he *abhorred* it and thought it *contrary to* and *inconsistent with* Scripture. Sometimes I thought that I might swear the Formula against the doctrines there mentioned, meaning as they are practised in the Church of Rome, they being greatly abused. But alas! the Formula seems to hold an abhorrence of the doctrines themselves as the test of not being a papist. I thought I would plead that no man is by law obliged to take the Formula unless he is *suspected* of being a papist, which I am not. But then I considered

[3] See below, 4 February 1775.
[4] The Norman church, founded by Queen Margaret late in the eleventh century, superseded Iona as a royal burial-place. In 1818 the grave of Robert Bruce was discovered there.
[5] Maclaurin had been chosen delegate from Dunfermline.
[6] James Buncle, the delegate chosen by Campbell's party, who were in a minority at Queensferry.
[7] *Life*, 7 May 1773.

what an appearance my refusal of it would have in the House of Commons; and besides, that the fact of my having once embraced the Romish faith might be brought out.[8] I dressed myself in my crimson and silver suit; resolved to be as thoughtless as a young officer going into a battle; breakfasted well; took a dram of brandy after it. Went down to John Adie's and met Colonel Campbell and the other delegates for him and several more friends. There I took another dram of brandy; and at least *felt bold.* At twelve we met the delegates in the opposite interest and their friends upon the street, and walked in procession to the Town House, where we delegates, commissioned and noncommissioned, sat round a large table, and proceeded to the business of the day. I sat in great anxiety till all the protests and government oaths were over. When it was agreed that we should then give our votes, I was like a man relieved from hanging over a precipice by a slight rope. Mr. Wight behaved with great propriety, and quite like a gentleman.

After the election, and being jostled by the joyous mob, I waited on Colonel Campbell in a large room, with a numerous company at dinner, and wished him joy.[1] Then we three delegates and Captain Erskine and some others dined together and drank heartily, after which we went to Colonel Campbell's room, and there I drank much more. Sir James Campbell, Captain Erskine, and some more of us went to the Cross and drank the Colonel's health. The mob became so fond of me that the cry changed from "Campbell for ever" to "Paoli for ever." It was a sad rainy night. Most of the windows were illuminated. The mob broke several which were not. I threw my glass at one and made it crash one pane of it. Sir James Campbell had proposed our going to the Cross, and my popular mobbish spirit still broke forth in a smaller degree.[2] We returned to the large room. Many songs were sung. I gave *The Jolly Beggar* and made them drink to the memory of James V.[3] I went to my lodgings about nine, fully intoxicated.

[8] Boswell embraced Roman Catholicism in London in 1760. His adherence was brief; but he occasionally attended mass throughout his life, and in a codicil to his will he requested the prayers of friends for his departed soul, "considering how reasonable it is to suppose that it may be detained some time in a middle state."

[1] Campbell secured control of three of the five burghs (Culross, Dunfermline, and Inverkeithing).

[2] In March 1769 Boswell had led the mob in Edinburgh that broke the judges' windows (including his father's) after the Lords reversed the decision of the Court of Session in the Douglas Cause.

[3] *The Jolly Beggar,* a song later imitated by Byron, was attributed to James V. Its chorus:

> And we'll gang nae mair a roving
>   Sae late into the night
> And we'll gang nae mair a roving, boys,
>   Let the moon shine ne'er so bright.

TUESDAY 1 NOVEMBER. I was pretty well, and got up before nine. Captain Erskine insisted that I should go to Alloa to give him my assistance as counsel on Thursday, the day of election for Clackmannanshire, where he was a candidate. He and Colonel Campbell and young Paterson of Bannockburn went with Mr. Erskine of Mar in his coach. I chose the chaise as being the most airy and pleasant conveyance. Mr. Hardie and I went together. We found at Alloa two Miss Rollos, sisters to young Bannockburn. Two Miss Grants of Grant and Mr. Paterson Rollo came.[4] I told Colonel Campbell in confidence what a dilemma I had been in. He said he was glad I had not told him, as he would have been very uneasy, both on my account and his own. He promised as a man of honour not to mention it. It was an ease to my mind, or rather now a pleasure, to communicate my anxiety to the gentleman next concerned to myself.[5] Old Erskine was here in his usual good spirits. We had also Mr. Paterson Rollo of Bannockburn, who had been out in 1745, and diversified our conversation a little with his ideas. He told us of a curious kind of historical play on the events of 1745. I must inquire about it. Real characters are introduced. Time passed very well. I lived full and jolly.

WEDNESDAY 2 NOVEMBER. In my room were lying a folio history of Scotland by _____, also Ker of Kersland's *Memoirs*. I glanced over part of them and found some materials for a history of the Union. In the forenoon I revised a number of protests which Captain Erskine was to take next day. Time passed as yesterday.

THURSDAY 3 NOVEMBER. After breakfast Lord Alva, Mr. Barclay Maitland, and the rest of the freeholders for Captain Erskine came, and we went to Clackmannan in goodly form with I forget how many carriages.[6] I was introduced to Colonel Masterton, whom I had never seen before. General Scott was made praeses, and appeared as a sensible, respectable man of good family and great property. But it was an odd reflection that his great distinction was owing to his having been a professed gamester.[7] We returned to Alloa and had a grand dinner. Fortune's cook

---

[4] Young Paterson of Bannockburn was Hugh James Paterson Rollo; his sisters Mary and Davida were married in 1777. The father (called by Boswell "Mr. Paterson Rollo"), son of James Rollo of Powhouse, had assumed the name of Paterson when he married Mary, daughter of Sir Hugh Paterson of Bannockburn and his wife, who was a sister of the attainted Earl of Mar and of Lord Grange.

[5] A change of quill here suggests that Boswell continued the entry after an interruption, which would account for the repetitious references to Erskine ("Old Mar") and "Paterson Rollo."

[6] James Erskine, Lord Alva, Judge in the Court of Session, was second cousin to Boswell, both of them being great-grandsons (by different wives) of Sir Charles Erskine of Alva, younger son of John Erskine, Earl of Mar (c. 1562–1634). See below, Appendix C, Chart IV.

[7] Major-General John Scott of Balcomie, M.P. for Fife, had indeed acquired his great

and Steele the confectioner and his man were brought from Edinburgh.[8] The family of Mar, though by accident defeated in the county (supposing a petition to the House of Commons not to succeed), appeared with becoming magnificence.[9] So many of us drank from dinner till ten at night, when we were told supper was on the table. We had no ladies with us today. I was in high spirits, supped voraciously, drank more after it, but had reason enough to go to bed while I could walk.

FRIDAY 4 NOVEMBER. Colonel Campbell and I set out in his chaise about eight. I was not much indisposed. We breakfasted at the North Ferry, stopped at Queensferry, and drank a glass at Bailie Buncle's; drove to town, and came out of our chaise at the Exchange, that all who were at the Cross might see us after our victory. I went home and saw my wife and Veronica, then dined with the Colonel at his lodgings, and, as he was to be busy, just drank half a bottle of port; then sallied forth between four and five with an avidity for drinking from the habit of some days before. I went to Fortune's; found nobody in the house but Captain James Gordon of Ellon. He and I drank five bottles of claret and were most profound politicians. He pressed me to take another; but my stomach was against it. I walked off very gravely though much intoxicated. Ranged through the streets till, having run hard down the Advocates' Close, which is very steep, I found myself on a sudden bouncing down an almost perpendicular stone stair. I could not stop, but when I came to the bottom of it, fell with a good deal of violence, which sobered me much. It was amazing that I was not killed or very much hurt; I only bruised my right heel severely. I supped at Sir George's. My wife was there, and George Webster.

SATURDAY 5 NOVEMBER. Fortune's wine was excellent, for I was neither sick nor uneasy. The sacrament was to be administered next day in this city. I had some doubt whether I should go to it, as I had been so riotous of late. But, considering that it was truly no more than a public declaration of my faith in the Christian religion, and that there was no

fortune at the gaming table. Writing of him in 1755, at the beginning of his notoriety, Walpole said he had "nothing but a few debts and his [captain's] commission." At the time of his death he was reputed to be the richest commoner in Scotland (his "fortune has never been estimated at less than half a million"). His three daughters became respectively Duchess of Portland, Lady Doune (had she lived, she would have been Countess of Moray), and Viscountess Canning.

[8] Fortune's was the most fashionable tavern in Edinburgh, and Robert Steele was one of the two earliest confectioners there.

[9] On 7 April 1775 a committee of the House of Commons made a report favourable to Ralph Abercromby, who had defeated Colonel James Francis Erskine. The problem again was chiefly the property qualifications for being on the roll of voters. See above, 15 October and below, p. 130.

opportunity for solemn devotion in a Presbyterian kirk, I resolved to go. Charles Hay called, and I kept him to an early dinner. At three my wife and I went to the New Church. I drank tea at Sir George's.

SUNDAY 6 NOVEMBER. Was at New Church forenoon and afternoon. Was much displeased with the Presbyterian method. My attendance was just a piece of decent attention to Christianity in the form established in my native country. I however thought that perhaps I was to blame in not regularly attending public worship in a form of which I approved, especially as there was now a fine Episcopal chapel in Edinburgh. But then I reflected that my doing so would offend my father. Mr. Wellwood drank tea with us.   ✳

MONDAY 7 NOVEMBER. Not thinking it necessary to attend sermon today,[1] I stayed at home and wrote an opinion on a case before the Synod of Lothian and Tweeddale on which James Gilkie[2] consulted me. It was Helen Amos against Robert Hope; and the question was in what circumstances the oath of purgation could be put.

TUESDAY 8 NOVEMBER. Mr. Lawrie was now with me, having come to town above a week before.[3] I this day studied with great attention Sir John Hall's cause. I dined with my wife at Dr. Grant's. In the evening I attended the Synod and heard Gilkie plead the cause of Hope, as I would not appear in an inferior kirk court. I was asked to sup at Walker's with the Synod, which I did. There were ten ministers and George Webster and I. Dr. Webster took the lead. I was disgusted with their coarse merriment, which frequently seemed to me to be profane, as it turned on absurd passages in sermons. Webster kept so many sitting till towards two in the morning. I was against sitting, but could not refuse Webster.

WEDNESDAY 9 NOVEMBER. I was very ill after my Synod riot, and could not get up till about two. I really suffered severely. I was easier in the afternoon. My wife very justly said that it was inexcusable to be riotous in such low company. I have often determined to be strictly sober, and have often fixed an era for the commencement of my proper conduct. I have a curious inclination to have an era for almost everything. The period of my being strictly sober has been advanced from one time to another. I this day thought I should have it to say that I had not been drunk since I supped with the Synod of Lothian and Tweeddale in November 1774.

[1] The service of thanksgiving held on the Monday following Holy Communion.
[2] A "writer" of doubtful repute and an author of eccentric treatises: *Speak Evil of No Man*, 1774, and *Every Man His Own Procurator*, 1778. Boswell had been his counsel in 1767 when there was an alleged attempt on Gilkie's life (see William Roughead, *Rascals Revived*, London, 1940, pp. 129–183).
[3] John Lawrie was Boswell's clerk; "a sober, diligent, attentive lad" who "goes errands, copies letters, and is very serviceable." Lawrie had been at his father's house during the vacation.

THURSDAY 10 NOVEMBER. Sir George, my Lady, and Miss Preston dined with us. Lady Betty Cochrane obligingly came with them, though not invited. They stayed tea and supper, except Lady Preston, who had a little cold and went home. I was very indolent, and my heel was painful; so I sent Mr. Lawrie to make my apology at St. John's Lodge,[4] and completed my study of Sir John Hall's cause, to whom I had written making an apology for delay and telling him that when he pleased I should be ready to deliver him my opinion.

FRIDAY 11 NOVEMBER. I breakfasted at Lady Colville's. My father arrived in the afternoon. My wife and I called in the evening. He was cold as usual, but I liked to contemplate his uniform steady character in general, though in politics he had been misled by the President.[5] He talked much of his politics. I thought it was to divert a consciousness that he was wrong.

SATURDAY 12 NOVEMBER. I called at my father's before he went to the Parliament House, and took Veronica to see him. There was no quorum of the Lords today. The session did not promise well. The crop appeared thin. I called on my brother John yesterday, and engaged him to dine with me today. He had never called of his own accord. I had Dr. Boswell with him.[6] The contrast between them was striking, yet both had the same constitution differently modified. M. Dupont came to tea and brought with him M. le docteur Dunant, a young Geneva physician, nephew of the Reverend Monsieur Chais at The Hague.[7] He revived my travelling ideas, but I felt myself much rusted. The Doctor and the Lieutenant went away before tea, after having seen the two foreigners. Sir John Hall supped with us, and I gave him my opinion in writing on his cause. This was a good comfortable day, all spent with *family connexions,* as I may call every one of them. The Doctor and Lieutenant at dinner; M. Dupont and a nephew of M. Chais at tea; Sir John Hall at supper.[8]

SUNDAY 13 NOVEMBER. Having taken a dose of lenitive electuary to cool me after my riotous engagements, I was at home all day. I finished Carstares's *Letters,* and read a part of the second volume of Burnet's *His-*

---

[4] Canongate Kilwinning Lodge.
[5] The Lord President of the Court of Session, Robert Dundas, had misled him into making fictitious votes.
[6] John Boswell, M.D., younger brother of Lord Auchinleck, was in temperament somewhat like Boswell.
[7] Boswell had known Chais at The Hague, where he was pastor of the French church and an intimate friend of Boswell's relatives, the Sommelsdycks.
[8] Sir John Hall was a "family connexion" in that he was the nephew of Sir John Pringle, the physician, close friend of Lord Auchinleck. Dupont's connexion was through very old acquaintance. The successive terms which he and his father served as pastors in Edinburgh amounted to more than a hundred years, 1685–1786.

tory of His Own Times.[9] But I cannot say that I enjoyed much pleasing meditation, as I hope to do when I stay at home on a Sunday.

MONDAY 14 NOVEMBER. I dined at Lord Dundonald's by invitation. He made me drink about a bottle of port, which heated me. My Lady and I had a conference on her cause.

TUESDAY 15 NOVEMBER. After being in the Parliament House, Maclaurin and I went and attended awhile at the election of the peers of Scotland.[1] I drank tea at Balmuto's.

WEDNESDAY 16 NOVEMBER. The Earl of Loudoun, John Hunter, Writer to the Signet (his agent), Lady Dundonald and Lady Betty Cochrane, the Hon. A. Gordon and Lady Dumfries, Colonel Stopford and Captain Skeffington of the 66th supped with us.[2] This was the first time that Lord Loudoun was in my house. I liked to be well with one of the nobles of the county of Ayr. But I must own that I was somewhat cooled towards the peers when, upon talking to Lord Loudoun of the sheriffship of our county yesterday, he told me that he was not at liberty to speak on the subject, as he believed measures were already taken about it, and from his conversation I guessed that he was engaged for one of whom I thought meanly.[3] I also perceived that his Lordship had not that dignity of spirit which I should have wished, but was ready to join with Sir Adam Fergusson if he saw it for his interest, though Sir Adam had been the avowed opposer of the great families of the county. My scheme of taking the sheriffship and letting Mr. Duff retain the salary for life, was by no means fixed in my mind. It would secure me an office somewhat respectable, and be a step to the bench. But then it would be very laborious, and engage me too intimately in my own county, which I would not like; and besides Mr. Duff might live many years, during which my having all the trouble for nothing would be irksome.[4] And after all, my warm wish was to be employed in London. And I pleased myself with keeping loose from all en-

---

[9] *State-Papers and Letters Addressed to William Carstares,* 1774, and *Bishop Burnet's History of His Own Time,* 1724–1734. Both men were Scots and their works would help Boswell in his proposed history of the Union (see above, 28 October): Carstares had been greatly influential in overcoming the opposition of the Presbyterian clergy to the Union; Burnet had despaired of any success in the negotiations between Scotland and England.

[1] The election at the Palace of Holyroodhouse of the sixteen representatives of the Scottish peerage to the House of Lords.

[2] John Campbell, Lord Loudoun, had been the ineffective Commander-in-Chief of the British forces in America, 1756–1757. Lady Dumfries (widow of the fourth Earl) was Alexander Gordon's wife.

[3] Probably William Wallace, Professor of Scots Law in Edinburgh University, who shortly afterwards succeeded William Duff as sheriff of Ayrshire. Boswell at one time thought well of Wallace, but later changed his opinion. See below, 17 January 1775.

[4] Duff did not die until 1781.

gagements in Scotland, that I might more easily take the great English road. I drank rather too much tonight.

THURSDAY 17 NOVEMBER. On Tuesday last I sent a card to Lord Justice-Clerk begging to know when I might have the honour of waiting on him. He fixed between six and seven. I went accordingly. He was very polite; that is to say, civil and obliging and even kind. I told him all the matter of my paper in *The London Chronicle* which had occasioned the correspondence between me and his son; that I considered his Lordship as my proper party and hoped he was satisfied with my explanation. He declared he was; that he was glad I was come to put an end to a very disagreeable affair; that he read the paper at Aberdeen, considered it as calculated for the meridian of London and thrown in *valeat quantum valere potest;*[5] that he should have taken no notice of it, and would have prevented his son had he known. But his son never mentioned it to him, supped with him on Sunday evening, when there was a good deal of company, and was quite cheerful. But in the middle of the night carried off horses and a servant, and in the morning my Lord had a letter from him from which it appeared he was gone about some affair of honour, but to what place or against whom no information was given; and my Lord remained above two days in the greatest anxiety. His Lordship, after declaring that he was satisfied that I did not mean what his son had imagined, said that he was conscious he did his duty to the best of his abilities, which satisfied his own mind; but he should be sorry that a prejudice was entertained against him, especially by me; that it [was] unnatural to be attacked by me, as our families had lived in the greatest friendship, he might say, for ages; at least for generations. (Here I had some difficulty to refrain from being at him, knowing that his grandfather, a surgeon in Kilmarnock, was the first of *his* family. However, I let him go on, as he spoke very well in the main.)[5a] He said that, after making out his report on the case of John Reid, he could not assemble all the judges, being in the country, but he knew all their opinions. He however rode over to one for whom he had a great respect, Lord Auchinleck, and showed it to him, and he entirely approved of it. He then said he would give me an advice as a father, not to go beyond the line of my profession for any client; that he imputed his success in life much to his adhering to that rule. That he had often won-

---

[5] "For whatever good it might do."

[5a] In view of Boswell's contempt for the Miller family, it is a little ironic that his eldest son, Alexander, was to marry a grand-daughter of Thomas Miller's sister. Thus within fifty years of this journal entry, the owner of Auchinleck and of the journals—Boswell's grandson, Sir James Boswell—had both Boswell and Miller blood in his veins.

dered that I did not think more of myself. That a young fellow of no solid foundation in learning or connexions might make a splash in life to distinguish himself and perhaps by a kind of chance to get forward. But a man of my rank and fortune and standing as a lawyer had a higher character to support. He said the less I wrote in newspapers the better, as my being known to do it gave people an opportunity of ascribing to me every abusive thing that appeared.

Upon the whole this was a good interview, and I was really pleased with the Justice-Clerk's warmth of heart and the justice of his reasoning. I am sensible that my keenness of temper, and a vanity to be distinguished *for the day,* make me too often *splash* in life, as he well expressed it. I am resolved to restrain myself and attend more to decorum. I thought that I would not court the Justice-Clerk, with whom I had somehow never been well since the decision of the Douglas Cause; but, if it could easily happen, I should be glad to be on a good footing with him.[6]

This day, though I had not drank to intoxication last night, I had a severe headache. I went with George Webster and dined at Lord Dundonald's, where we just drank one bottle of claret, and rose cheerful. At five I came home. Lieutenant Graham of the Scots Dutch, and Mackenzie of Dolphinton and his brother—with the two latter I was to consult on a cause of poor Monkland's[7]—drank tea, and then we sat a long time on business. I felt a kind of wonder in observing them pay much deference to my opinion. Young Robert Syme came and gave me my first guinea this session. I called at Paxton's for my friend Captain Hoggan's father, who

[6] Besides attacking John Reid and Boswell (see above, 3 October, *n.* 8), he had voted against Douglas. The Douglas Cause, which has been called the greatest civil trial affecting status in the whole of Scottish history, was initiated at the instance of the Duke of Hamilton and his brother, both small boys, with the intent of proving that another youngster, Archibald Stewart, who had assumed the name and inherited the estates of the Duke of Douglas, was an impostor. According to the account of his ostensible parents, Lady Jane Douglas and her Jacobite husband Colonel John Stewart, he was the survivor of twin sons born to Lady Jane in her fifty-first year at Paris in 1748 under circumstances of remarkable obscurity; according to the Hamilton party, he was the child of a poor French glass-grinder whom Colonal Stewart had bought or stolen. After considering the cause for five years (1762–1767) the Lords of Session divided evenly, seven and seven, whereupon the Lord President, by his casting vote, gave the verdict against Douglas. Lord Auchinleck, like his son, had been a Douglasian; the Lord Justice-Clerk was a Hamiltonian. Douglas appealed, and in February 1769 the House of Lords reversed the decision of the Court of Session.

[7] "Poor David Hamilton of Monkland, on account of his vote in Lanarkshire, was made one of the macers of the Court of Session. He had a constant hoarseness, so that he could scarcely be heard when he called the causes and the lawyers, and was indeed as unfit for a crier of court as a man could be. I said he had no voice but *at an election.*" (*Boswelliana,* ed. Charles Rogers, London, 1874, p. 296).

wanted to see me on some business, and then supped at Sir George's; my wife, Dr. Webster, and Peter Colvill there.

FRIDAY 18 NOVEMBER. Matthew Dickie and I drank tea at John Tait's and talked over a submission between Lord Dumfries and Hugh Mitchell in Craigman.⁸ I mark each day anything that is not just the common course.

SATURDAY 19 NOVEMBER. I dined at Sir Alexander Dick's. Captain Gunning, brother to the Duchess of Hamilton, and his lady, one of the Miss Minifies the authoresses,⁹ were there, as also Dr. Young and old John Forrest. Effie was in vigorous health.

SUNDAY 20 NOVEMBER. Was at the New Church in the forenoon; Mr. Walker preached. My wife stayed at home. I dined at my father's between sermons. Colonel Webster, lately returned from London, and George were there. Went to Tolbooth Church and heard Dr. Webster, afternoon. George and I called on my brother John, and brought him to my house to tea. After George went away, Annie Cuninghame and David arrived.¹ I was very happy to see them again. John would not stay supper.

MONDAY 21 NOVEMBER. I went with George Webster and David Cuninghame and saw Astley ride in Comely Garden.² They and Annie dined with us. Colonel Campbell was come again to town. I supped along with him at Mr. Moir's.

⁸ Mitchell, Boswell's client, was a tenant of Lord Dumfries.

⁹ John Gunning, later Lieutenant-General, brother of Elizabeth Gunning, Duchess of Hamilton, had married Susannah Minifie, who in her first novel had collaborated with her sister Margaret.

¹ Annie Cuninghame and her brother David were younger children of Mrs. Boswell's eldest sister, Elizabeth, who became heiress of Lainshaw on the death of her brother, James Montgomerie, late in 1766. She had married in 1754 Captain Alexander Montgomerie-Cuninghame, heir to Sir David Cuninghame of Corsehill, Bt., but he had predeceased his father in 1770, and her eldest son, Walter, had succeeded to the baronetcy in that same year. See below, Appendix C, Chart VI. The ages of the Lainshaw children have not yet been run down, but it is the guess of the editors that in 1774 Walter was about nineteen, Alexander eighteen, Annie sixteen, David fifteen, James thirteen, and Henry Drumlanrig eleven. Mrs. Montgomerie-Cuninghame was a warm-hearted, brilliant, improvident woman, of whom Boswell had been very fond, but when she contracted with John Beaumont a second marriage which he considered "low," he disowned her and forbade Mrs. Boswell to have any intercourse with her. She had borne Beaumont a daughter, and had now gone to London, taking James and Henry with her, probably already afflicted with the illness from which she died a little more than a year later. The Lainshaw children, impoverished, high-spirited, well-born but under-bred, were orphaned and dispersed while most of them were in their teens. Boswell, who constituted himself a sort of unofficial guardian, was to be much plagued by the importunities and lawlessness of Sir Walter and David. David succeeded Sir Walter, and held the Corsehill baronetcy for a few months in 1814.

² Philip Astley was at the beginning of a career which made him the best equestrian performer of his time. Comely Gardens was a lower-class pleasure park, a "paltry imitation of Vauxhall."

TUESDAY 22 NOVEMBER. My father and Lady Auchinleck, Colonel Campbell, Sir George Preston, Charles Hay, Annie and David Cuninghames dined. My wife and I and Annie supped at Sir George's.

WEDNESDAY 23 NOVEMBER. Miss Cuninghame had slept in our house these two last nights. She was grown quite a woman, as amiable as ever, and the better of a little of the English accent which she had acquired in Ireland. She and David were going to London to their mother. Mr. Spottiswoode the solicitor, who was to accompany them, and his sister breakfasted with us today. They set out after breakfast. In the evening Grange came to town, and kindly supped and drank some brandy punch with us.

THURSDAY 24 NOVEMBER. Grange dined with us. We supped at Sir George's. Lady Betty Cochrane and Dr. Webster there.

FRIDAY 25 NOVEMBER. We dined at Lady Colville's with Sir George and nobody else; a comfortable party. I supped at Moncrieffe's. Ten there. Drank cheerfully and no more.

SATURDAY 26 NOVEMBER. Claud came to me to read over long papers in a cause in which we were engaged together. He dined with us. At six I went to Charles Hay's, where Maclaurin and I had an appointment to play at whist. William Aytoun was the fourth man. I felt all the former symptoms of gaming which have at times fevered me: anxiety, keenness, etc., etc. I lost about two guineas. We supped and drank but a little. When I came home, I of my own accord gave my word of honour to my wife that I would never play at whist for more than a shilling the game and two shillings the rubber.

SUNDAY 27 NOVEMBER. Was at New Church all day. Dr. Blair forenoon; Mr. Walker afternoon. At my father's between sermons; Dr. Webster there. Evening spent at home, not very profitably; a little of the Bible read. The weather, frost and snow. ✳

MONDAY 28 NOVEMBER. In the morning was the burial of a son of Mr. Hill's, writer in Glasgow. Supped at Mr. David Dalrymple's, advocate, Grand Master elect, with several Master Masons.[3] We were jovial and no more.

TUESDAY 29 NOVEMBER. Was at the burial of Mr. Alexander Orr, Writer to the Signet. Dined at Lady Colville's, a party of her brother Lord Kellie's inviting: General Colville, Captain Edgar,[4] Matthew Hender-

[3] Dalrymple was elevated to the bench as Lord Westhall in 1777.
[4] Probably James Edgar, collector of customs at Leith, a middle-aged bachelor and a well-known Edinburgh eccentric. Matthew Henderson, antiquary and member of various convivial clubs, was later closely associated with Robert Burns, who wrote a moving elegy on his death. Although not actually a blood relation of Boswell, Henderson was nearly connected, being a first cousin of the second Lady Auchinleck, Claud Boswell, Hugh and Bruce Campbell, whose mothers had been sisters of Matthew's father. See below, Appendix C, Charts III and VI.

son, young Pitfour. We drank profusely. Even Captain Archibald went deep. I came home very drunk. A strange riot! I was not able to see Mr. and Mrs. Campbell of Treesbank, who came this night to our house.

WEDNESDAY 30 NOVEMBER. Waked in sad disorder. Struggled up between nine and ten. Saw Mr. and Mrs. Campbell. Dr. Monro and Mr. Wood[5] agreed that Mr. Campbell's lip should be cut a second time to remove a hard swelling which might prove cancerous. The idea of that distemper was gloomy. In the afternoon, having done all that I had to do in the Court of Session in the forenoon very tolerably, I officiated as Master of St. John's Lodge at the procession and feast on St. Andrew's day.[6] I was calmly cheerful; quite well.

THURSDAY 1 DECEMBER. Mr. Hugh Campbell of Mayfield and Matthew Dickie dined with us.[7]

FRIDAY 2 DECEMBER. [No entry for this day.]

SATURDAY 3 DECEMBER. Dined at Fortune's with the *Stoic Club,* a society begun by Foote.[8] I had promised at Lady Colville's to Matthew Henderson to be there; and though I had not much inclination to go, I did not choose to break an appointment, and I thought it not amiss to see this club for once. It was just a dinner with Lord Kellie and the other frequenters of Fortune's. Nothing particular. I drank one bottle and came home to tea. In the evening Mr. Moir was with me about Colonel Campbell's politics. He supped.

SUNDAY 4 DECEMBER. Was at the New Church in the forenoon; ———— preached. Between sermons Dr. Boswell and Mr. Wood came to have Treesbank's lip cut. Poor man, he looked like one under sentence of death. I was much affected with the idea of the painful operation, which made me think drearily of the various terrible distempers to which man is liable. I could not be present at the operation. It was soon over. Dr. Boswell dined, and we sat at home in the afternoon.

[5] Alexander Monro, M.D. (1733–1817), the "secundus" of three famous physicians of the name, was Professor of Anatomy and Surgery at Edinburgh University. Alexander ("lang Sandy") Wood, surgeon, had recently been called in to give his advice concerning the lameness of the infant son of Walter Scott, W.S., and against his better judgement had joined in Boswell's scheme to resuscitate John Reid. He was much beloved for philanthropy and conviviality, made pets of a raven and a sheep named Willy, and is said to have been the first man in Edinburgh to carry an umbrella.

[6] This was a Grand Lodge festival. The members of the various lodges in Edinburgh met in the Parliament House for the election of officers of the Grand Lodge, and then marched in procession to the Assembly Hall in New Assembly Close for a feast and entertainment.

[7] Hugh Campbell was Boswell's second cousin, his grandmother, Margaret Boswell, being a sister of Boswell's grandfather, old James. See below, Appendix C, Chart VI.

[8] Samuel Foote, actor and dramatist, played in Edinburgh in 1759 and again in 1770–1771. Irresistibly comic—a wit and a buffoon—and a gourmand, he was anything but a stoic.

MONDAY 5 DECEMBER. Was at home on business all day. Andrew Boswell dined.

TUESDAY 6 DECEMBER. Balbarton and Mr. MacDougall, a son of Lorn's and apprentice to Mr. Wood, dined.

WEDNESDAY 7 DECEMBER. Grange dined.

THURSDAY 8 DECEMBER. Lady Dundonald having lost her cause before both Lord Hailes and Lord Alva on the bills, I wished to dissuade her from carrying it farther. With that view, I went and dined at Belleville and had Mr. George Cooper, her agent, to meet me there. But I found her resolved to go on. The Earl set two bottles of port at once upon the table after dinner, and insisted that Cooper and I should drink them. I was mellow with my bottle. I drank tea. At seven I attended a consultation at Macqueen's on Colonel Campbell's politics. There was now a pretty deep snow lying.

FRIDAY 9 DECEMBER. My poor brother John was now seized with a return of delirium so as to be confined in his room at Mr. Weir the painter's. I called this day, but did not go into his room.

SATURDAY 10 DECEMBER. Mr. James Hunter, with whom I deal as a banker, with whom I was at the College, and who is an Ayrshire laird, had complained some days ago that we never met at each other's houses; and indeed I have been to blame on that account.[9] I engaged that my wife and I should dine with him this day, along with Sir Adolphus and Lady Oughton, which we did. Colonel Skene and some more company were there. Sir Adolphus always inspirits me. We drank tea.

SUNDAY 11 DECEMBER. Was at New Church forenoon. Dr. Blair preached. Dr. Boswell and Mr. Macredie dined with us, and we sat at home in the afternoon. It was proposed to send my brother John to the house of one Campbell at Inveresk, who takes in disordered people. Mr. Wood was against this, as he heard that Campbell was harsh; but he told me that I need not try to oppose it, for my father was resolved, his wife being clear for it. Wood seemed to think the plan by no means consistent with a proper concern for a relation.

Between five and six I went to Mr. Weir's. John was somewhat calmer. The maid told him his brother was there and wanted to see him. He said he would be glad to see me. Upon which I went up to his room, accompanied by Mr. Weir, an apprentice of Mr. Weir's, and Alexander Macduff, a Guard soldier who was there as a keeper.[1] John had on his night-

---

[9] About this time Hunter took the name of Blair after that of Hunter, in consequence of his wife's having succeeded to the property of Dunskey; he later was created a baronet. He was the banking partner of Sir William Forbes, Bt. (Boswell's trustworthy adviser and confidant), in Forbes, Hunter, and Co.

[1] He was a member of the Town Guard, which was composed, for the most part, of old Highlanders. Their dress was a soldier's red uniform.

gown and nightcap with a hat above it, and he waved a poker in his hand, singing some strange articulate sounds like Portuguese or some foreign language to the tune of *Nancy Dawson,* and ending always with "Damn my heart!" He cried, "Come on," and uttered wild sounds. I was at first seized with a kind of tremor. But Macduff and the apprentice having taken the poker from him, and removed the shovel and tongs, I ventured to go near him. He had then taken up his cane, but Macduff and I got it from him with little difficulty. He had taken a liking for Mr. Lawrie, who had been with him several times. I got him set down by the fireside, and, when I asked him if Mr. Lawrie had been with him, he answered very distinctly that he had been with him yesterday. He had sent for him. Poor man! he was much extenuated, and being now calm, and holding my hand cordially, I felt a tender affection for him. Indeed he was more agreeable than when better in his judgement but sour in his temper. We carried him downstairs to a room more convenient for him. I then took all his keys and locked up everything that belonged to him. It was remarkable to see the great exactness in which he had all his things. I continued with him awhile in his new apartment, but he would not or could not speak to me. It was a curious sensation when I saw my brother, with whom I had been brought up, in such a state. Madness of every degree is inexplicable. I could not conceive *how* he did not talk as usual. I reflected with deep seriousness on the melancholy in our family, and how I myself had been afflicted with it.

I came to my father's, and being much affected spoke against sending John to Musselburgh.[2] My father seemed to have no other concern than to be free of trouble by him, and of a kind of *reproach,* as he called it, from having a relation in such a state. It was resolved that Commissioner Cochrane's opinion should be taken next morning.

MONDAY 12 DECEMBER. The Commissioner agreed with me that it was better to keep John at Mr. Weir's till we should see how he was, and if he did not grow soon well, the best thing to be done was to send him to Newcastle, where he was formerly well taken care of in a regular house kept by Dr. Hall. And so it was fixed. I had a load of papers to write, yet was listless. I however was obliged to move on, though uneasily. In the evening I went to the Justiciary Court and heard Lord Advocate and Mr. Wight charge the jury in the trial of Downie for murder. I could not help feeling a great superiority when I reflected on my own appearances in that court; and it was painful to one who wishes to think highly of human nature to see Lord Advocate on this occasion making every allowance, nay every supposition, in favour of the panel, because he had been impressed with a notion that what he had done was not murder—when in the case

[2] That is, to Campbell's madhouse. Musselburgh was then in Inveresk parish.

of a poor thief, I have seen him so desirous to urge every circumstance against him.[3]

TUESDAY 13 DECEMBER. Grange dined with us.

WEDNESDAY 14 DECEMBER. Amidst my throng of business, I could not resist an invitation to dine with Colonel Stopford at the mess kept by him, Captain Skeffington, and Lieutenant Vowel. The other guests were Sir William Erskine of Torrie, Captain Schaw, and Captain Gunning, brother to the Duchess of Argyll. We were very jolly. But I observed they talked mostly of military matters and I of law cases. The mess was at Mrs. Brown's in the Exchange. At seven I came home to tea and found Claud, and then went to a ball for young ladies at Madame Marcoucci's given by Miss Schaw, the Captain's daughter.[4] There was a great deal of company at it. I felt myself quite easy, and was very pleasingly amused.

THURSDAY 15 DECEMBER. This day Crosbie told me that he and Maclaurin, etc., had dined the day before at Lord Monboddo's along with Mr. Bruce, the great traveller.[5] I was somewhat hurt that Monboddo had not asked me, too; and I was also somewhat hurt at being told that Bruce was displeased with my mentioning in *The London Magazine* that it had been said he was "Nec visu facilis nec dictu affabilis ulli." [6] I had made an apology for his appearing in that style, so he had no reason to be displeased with me.[7] But I could see plainly that he did not like me; probably because I

---

[3] John Downie, engaged in a scuffle with John Darling, struck at him with a scythe through a gate and wounded him fatally. He was sentenced to be hanged; but was pardoned, on the recommendation of the Lord Justice-Clerk. The Lord Advocate was James Montgomery, who had given a summation of unusual warmth in the John Reid case.

[4] Madame Marcoucci was mistress of a dancing-school. Boswell later saw his own daughter Veronica dance a minuet there.

[5] Monboddo was the "notorious theorist about human kinship with the orang-outang." James Bruce of Kinnaird had just returned from his travels. He announced and no doubt believed himself to be the discoverer of the source of the Nile, but the source he had reached was really that of the Nile's largest tributary, the Blue Nile; and even there he had been preceded by the Portuguese priests Paez and Lobo in the first quarter of the seventeenth century. Boswell had met him on 9 August when "Monboddo set him dead, and Maclaurin snuffed him keen." In the face of determined resistance, Boswell had extracted from him a considerable amount of information, and had published an account of his travels in *The London Magazine,* August and September.

[6] "Forbidding in appearance, in speech to be accosted by no one" (*Aeneid,* III. 621, describing Polyphemus, the Cyclops).

[7] Boswell had written: ". . . it should be considered that a gentleman of fortune, and who has the *blood of Bruce* in his veins, is entitled to maintain a dignity of character. He has travelled for his own instruction and amusement, and he is not bound to communicate his knowledge, but when and how he himself pleases. . . . When he meets with men of knowledge and of classical enquiry, he is very ready to take the trouble

had given the public a good dish of his travels, better dressed than he could give himself. I took myself,[8] and considered it was below me to mind whether I was agreeable to him or not. No man can be agreeable to all kinds of people. And surely I am agreeable to as many as I could well expect. Bruce is a rough-minded man, and has not such principles as that one would court him. I had seen him as a curiosity and extracted from him a good essay for *The London Magazine;* and there was enough.

Sir William and Lady Forbes, Mr. Nairne, and Colonel Webster dined with us.[9] After the ladies went away, we got into a conversation on human liberty and GOD's prescience. Sir William and Mr. Nairne would not give up the latter, yet maintained the former; which I cannot help thinking an absolute contradiction; for if it is *certainly foreknown* that I am to be at the play tomorrow, then it is certain I am to be there; and if it is *certain* I am to be there, then I cannot have a liberty either to be there or not. This is the subject which most of all has perplexed and distressed me at different periods of my life. Montesquieu in one of his *Lettres Persanes* made it clear to me in 1769, when I was with my friend Temple at Mamhead.[1] But to meditate on it makes me melancholy. Lady Colville and Lady Anne Erskine drank tea with us. I was quite sober today. But the abstruse question saddened me.

FRIDAY 16 DECEMBER. Continued dull, but was obliged to write a representation, which did me good, as it kept me from thinking on myself. I have long admired this expressive passage in one of Dr. Young's tragedies, I think *Busiris:*

> Auletes, seize me, force me to my chamber,
> There chain me down and *guard me from myself.*[2]

No words can convey a more striking idea of a disturbed mind.

SATURDAY 17 DECEMBER. Laboured all day after the Court rose at answers for Colonel Campbell's friends at Inverkeithing.[3] Got into better spirits, but they were only temporary.

---

of giving them the satisfaction of which they are worthy" (*London Magazine,* September 1774, p. 431).

[8] A Scotticism: "I controlled myself."

[9] William Nairne was later Lord Dunsinnan and a baronet. He had accompanied Boswell and Johnson in the beginning of their tour to the Hebrides.

[1] It was the sixty-ninth letter. Montesquieu's argument, in brief, is that, although God's foreknowledge is boundless if He chooses to exercise it, He usually does not choose to do so as far as man's actions are concerned; therefore God's foreknowledge is not inconsistent with human liberty.

[2] *Busiris,* Act III.

[3] Probably, as had happened at Dunfermline, a petition of complaint concerning the election had been presented to the Court of Session.

SUNDAY 18 DECEMBER. Was at New Church in the forenoon. I forget whether I was out in the afternoon or not.

MONDAY 19 DECEMBER. Busy with the Inverkeithing paper. Was roused at night by seeing Mr. Johnson's *Journey to the Hebrides* advertised.[4]

TUESDAY 20 DECEMBER. I drank tea with Crosbie and talked over the case of McGraugh, for whom he had undertaken to write answers to a reclaiming petition for the Procurator-Fiscal, and had now almost finished it.[5] I have always the same ideas when I drink tea with Crosbie: learning, antiquities of our courts, etc. While I sat with him, I could not believe that he was a mere *fatal* or *foreknown* machine. Yet I was uneasy because it *might* be so.

WEDNESDAY 21 DECEMBER. The ordinary course of business went on. I made a resolution that I would not dine abroad, except on some particular occasion, while Treesbank was with me. He was recovering pretty well; and I entertained him with accounts of the causes determined in the Court of Session. This forenoon I met with D. Boswell at Leith in P. Williamson's Coffee-house, lent him three guineas, and drank a dram.[6]

THURSDAY 22 DECEMBER. Grange dined with us. After tea I met, along with Robert Boswell, with Mr. Robert Balfour, etc., on a submission between him and the representative of the old family of Balmuto.[7] Then came home and was consulted to draw replies for *Hope*[8] against Goodlet about a bill of suspension and liberation as to which dispatch was asked. I did them directly, which pleased Mr. Robert Syme, the agent.

FRIDAY 23 DECEMBER. I was late in the Court of Session hearing the Lords give judgement in a cause, Shaw against Bean, interesting in some degree, as character was concerned, and as it respected a charge of defama-

[4] *The London Chronicle* for 15–17 December announced it for publication on 18 January.

[5] Henry McGraugh, an Irishman, had been sentenced to public whipping and banishment because he had ordered food and drink in taverns and then said he could not pay for them. Boswell had sought the man out in the Tolbooth and had written a bill of suspension which had saved him from the execution of the sentence. But on 24 November Robert Gray, the Procurator-Fiscal (the public prosecutor of a district), had reclaimed. McGraugh remained in prison until 4 February 1775, when he was set at liberty because of the length of his confinement.

[6] David Boswell, whom Boswell sometimes calls "Craigston," though his grandfather had sold that property, was the impoverished dancing-master at Leith whom Lord Auchinleck was determined to exclude from his entail. Boswell was forced to meet him at a public house because Mrs. Boswell refused to have him in her home. See below, Appendix A, for a letter which Boswell later wrote for David to send to Lord Auchinleck in the hope of softening the old man's heart.

[7] David Boswell.

[8] Boswell sometimes indicates his own client by underlining.

tion for expressions thrown out in a paper before the sheriff; so that it respected the *liberty of the bar,* as some of the Lords said, practitioners in inferior courts being entitled to the same liberty with practitioners in the Court of Session.[9] While the Lords were giving their opinions, and a crowd attended with much curiosity, I was wondering if all the particulars of this cause and its determination were predetermined. My brother lawyer, Mr. Grant of Corrimony, sat by me, and I observed to him that it was in vain to argue to the Lords when they were met to decide a cause, for then their opinions were fixed. The bench then was set sail and would pursue its course. While the pleading lasts, the bench is like a ship in the harbour. You may direct it or have a chance to direct it. But when the Lords are met to decide, you may as well call to a ship fairly sailed to return. I drank tea at Captain Schaw's and supped at Moncrieffe's.

SATURDAY 24 DECEMBER. Was, after the House rose for the Christmas recess, at the burial of old Drummond the bookseller. Being specially invited to eat venison at Colonel Stopford's mess, I found him, Captain Skeffington, and Mr. Vowel and nobody else. I don't know how it was, but the Colonel got into the humour of drinking, which was very extraordinary for him; and we drank a great quantity of port. Captain Skeffington was to set out for London in a day or two, and, as I intended to be up in the spring, he promised to introduce me to Gerard Hamilton and Dean Marlay, two friends of his, both of whom admired Mr. Johnson. I was pleased this day to find myself so intimate with the brother of the Earl of Courtown and the brother of Lord Massereene, officers of the army and Irishmen, both which circumstances please me. We sat till near ten. I was very drunk, roved in the street, and went and stayed above an hour with two whores at their lodging in a narrow dirty stair in the Bow. Luckily I had seen enough to prevent me from running any risk with them. But I might certainly by a little degree more of intoxication have done what might have got me a distemper which might have been very fatal. I found my way home about twelve. I had fallen and rubbed some of the skin and flesh off the knuckle of the middle finger of my left hand.

SUNDAY 25 DECEMBER. Lay in bed all forenoon, very ill and very much vexed at reflecting on my depraved wandering last night. I most firmly resolved for the future to be sober and never to come home at night but in a chair. Grange dined with us according to annual custom on Christmas-

[9] George Bean, legal agent for some English merchants, had alleged before the sheriff of Inverness that Angus Shaw, a merchant in Inverness, was a "fraudulent bankrupt." For this and similar allegations, Shaw brought a process of defamation before the Court of Session. After reading hundreds of pages of proof and hearing a defence which lasted ten days, the Lords found Shaw's process "groundless, vexatious, and **oppressive**" (*Edinburgh Advertiser,* 23–27 December 1774).

day, and in the afternoon he and I went to the New English Chapel. It was striking to see so grand a place of worship in Edinburgh. But I cannot say that I was in so good a frame as I could have wished to be in on Christmas-day.

MONDAY 26 DECEMBER. Sir George, ————,[1] Mr. Charles Hay drank tea. It was now fixed that my brother John should set out next morning for Newcastle under the care of Macduff, the Guard soldier, and Thomas Edmondson, my old servant. I had called for him since I last mentioned it in my journal. This evening I went down and had Mr. Lawrie with me, and put up and inventoried what things were to go with him and put the rest in his trunks, which were to be brought up to stand in my house. Poor man! he was quite calm tonight and in a sort of gentle stupor, for he could not speak to me.

TUESDAY 27 DECEMBER. John set out in the morning early. Mr. Lawrie saw him into the chaise. I this day bought *Lettres Persanes,* and the letter on prescience made me as clear as ever. But indeed I am sensible that this difficult subject affects me rather according to a kind of sentiment at the time than by reasoning; for the very same arguments have quite different effects on different occasions. My father and Lady Auchinleck, Colonel Webster, Balbarton, and Lieutenant Graham dined with us, and drank tea. Treesbank for the first time came to the table. In the evening, it being St. John the [Evangelist's] day, I was at St. John's Lodge.

WEDNESDAY 28 DECEMBER. Was at home all day.

THURSDAY 29 DECEMBER. Dr. Webster drank tea with us. He returned and supped. Treesbank was much entertained with him. He and I drank each a bottle of claret slowly. This was too much, though it did not hurt me. But Webster is so social it is not easy to resist the inclination of taking a good glass with him.

FRIDAY 30 DECEMBER. Dined at Lady Colville's, where were Lord Kellie, Sir William and Lady Forbes, and Mr. Nairne. I took but a moderate glass. Captain Erskine had been reading Carte's life of the Duke of Ormonde. He talked of it and revived ideas of Tory men of fashion.

SATURDAY 31 DECEMBER. Having resolved to pay off every account that I owed, and begin with the year 1775 to deal in ready money, I had been busy in that way for some days.[2] George Webster accompanied me

---

[1] Boswell left the greater part of a line blank, intending to record other names.

[2] Paying off every account included writing some long-promised letters. Boswell's letter to Bennet Langton on this day begins: "Epistolary debtors are like other debtors. As time advances, what they owe becomes heavier and heavier; and they sink into a kind of despondency, when by a vigorous exertion they might soon clear themselves. In the unhappy state which I have been describing do I now feel myself, for indeed, my much esteemed friend, I am seriously distressed with my debt to you."

this forenoon to Peter Ramsay's, where I paid Peter's account, and George and I got a dram of cherry brandy. I really love drams like a savage. I then called on Mr. Isaac Grant to talk of a paper that I was to draw for a client of his and mine, and he gave me a dram of most excellent gin. I said that of all human arts I valued distilling the most. I dined at my father's. My wife, Treesbank and Mrs. Campbell, and Sir George and Miss Preston, and Robert Boswell and his wife were there.

1775

SUNDAY 1 JANUARY. Was at New Church in the forenoon; Mr. Walker preached. Afternoon, heard Dr. Webster preach on the awful cry of the angel in the Revelation that *Time shall be no more.* Went up to his house awhile with Annie, the Colonel, and George. They were very lively in a particular way. Imagined their brother John fighting with the Americans—come home with a wooden leg—all that he would say himself—his father would say—Sir George would say—most naturally. I drank tea by special appointment with worthy Sir William Forbes, to let him read my Hebrides journal to prepare him for Mr. Johnson's book. He was much entertained, and I left him my three volumes, after reading him a great deal.[1]

MONDAY 2 JANUARY. I was with Sir William Forbes at his counting-house in the forenoon, as he had obligingly agreed to show me his account-book, and put me on an accurate plan of management. I gave him a state of my affairs, and reckoning £300 a year from my father, and as much by the practice of the law, my income was £600. For the interest of my debts and other burthens we allowed £100. And the remaining £500 was regulated thus:

My wife to have £20 a month for the expense of the family, exclusive of wine but including servants' wages and children's clothes	240
My wife's clothes	60
House-rent £50 and wine £30	80
My own clothes and pocket-money	50
	£430

So that I should have £70 for contingencies, such as a London jaunt, and smaller expenses and charities. It was admirable to see what a proportion of Sir William's money went in charity, the last year upwards of £70. He said that he had been so much more prosperous than he had reason to expect that he thought giving about a tenth of his income in charity was a proper acknowledgement of gratitude to Providence. It gave me great satis-

[1] On 6 January Sir William returned the three volumes of the journal, which, he said, "has both instructed and delighted me to a very high degree. I am perfectly of opinion with your learned companion that it will be a treasure to you in all time to come."

faction to see myself in prospect an accurate man, and my dear wife cheerfully resolved to help me. She and I dined today at Lord Dundonald's. My
father and Lady Auchinleck, Dr. Webster, and the Colonel were there. I
was firm and would not drink more than enough. Mr. Lawrie went home
to his father's for a day or two this morning.

TUESDAY 3 JANUARY. Grange and Mr. Wood dined with us. Mr.
Wood raved ignorantly about the uncertainty of the soul's being immortal
or immaterial. But I had not arguments ready to silence him. I must get a
summary from Mr. Johnson.[2] Treesbank and Mrs. Campbell were to go
next day. So Grange and Mr. Wood stayed to tea to take a kind of cordial
farewell of them. Miss Cuninghame, niece to Mr. Trotter the confectioner,
supped with us. She entertained me with that kind of intelligence and wit
which goes on in an Edinburgh *sweetie-shop*. It was a variety to me. Life
and light and cheerfulness are found in all places in different modes.

WEDNESDAY 4 JANUARY. Treesbank and Mrs. Campbell left us. Mr.
Lawrie had gone home on Monday to his father's for a few days. I had
therefore this day to write with my own hand answers for Mr. Anderson
of Inverness to be boxed next day. The agent's memorial served for the
greatest part of the paper. But I wrote eleven pages. I was asked very particularly to dine today at Lord Dundonald's, to meet the Countess Dowager of Galloway. The chaise was sent, and carried down Colonel Webster
and me. There was fine sobriety this day. My wife and I supped at Sir
George's.

THURSDAY 5 JANUARY. Mr. Lawrie returned before dinner.

FRIDAY 6 JANUARY. Miss Mary Foulis of Colinton and Balbarton
dined and drank tea with us.

SATURDAY 7 JANUARY. We dined at my father's, where were Lord
and Lady Dundonald and Lady Betty, Mr. Nairne, Mr. George Fergusson,
and Mr. Henderson, Sir Robert's son. We drank tea there, and supped at
Sir William Forbes's, with him and Lady Forbes alone.

SUNDAY 8 JANUARY. At New Church forenoon; Dr. Blair. My father's between sermons. New Church afternoon. Mr. Grove, an English
kind of Independent minister, who officiated in Lady Glenorchy's chapel,
preached.[3] My wife and I drank tea at Sir George's, then came home, and I
read to her part of an account which the late Mr. Cumine of Pitullie in
Aberdeenshire had written of his first wife, and which was lent to me by

---

[2] There is no record of his having done so.

[3] Thomas Grove was one of the students expelled from Oxford in 1768 for methodis-
tical practices. He preached in Lady Glenorchy's chapel for several months during
1774–1775, but was not appointed minister because he disapproved of the Establishment and would not sign the Formula.

Sir W. Forbes.[4] My wife thought *her* a *simple woman,* and the husband a *double fellow.* I thought so too; for *she,* though pious, seemed to be persuaded with little or no argument; and *he,* notwithstanding great professions of grief and constancy, took another wife.[5] Perhaps it is too hard a censure to call him *double.* But he certainly was not the man which his manuscript would make one think him. We also supped at Sir George's.

MONDAY 9 JANUARY. Commissioner Cochrane carried me out with him in his chaise. He had called on me a few days before, and talked strongly about the differences between my father and me as to settling the estate.[6] He said my father had entailed the old estate on heirs male as far as Claud, but there he stopped; and that he had vested his own purchases in trustees, to be entailed upon the same series of heirs; but that if any of his heirs should call in question his entail, it should be a forfeiture of his own purchases, which should go past the heir challenging the entail, and his descendants. I was vexed to think that the family acquisitions should be separated, but I remained firm for the support of the male succession, as I considered that to be the only true representation of an ancient barony. I was under great temptations to quit my feudal resolution, for my father would make no immediate settlement on my wife and children, and my wife, who could not understand my feudal principles, upbraided me with want of affection. I was conscious that I had as warm an affection as any husband or father whatever, but I had the resolution of a Roman for the support of my family; and indeed I considered myself bound in honour and fidelity to our ancestor,[7] who, though he had four daughters, gave the estate to his nephew and made it a male fief, that Thomas Boswell, who fell at Flodden Field, might be represented by one of his sons to the latest posterity. At the same time, I suffered great anxiety of mind from the thought that *perhaps* I might die before my father, and leave my wife and children in a very poor situation. Mr. Johnson had said [8] that I should not be uneasy, for my wife and children had for them the probabilities of human life, and that was enough. I hoped that my father would not settle his own acquisitions past the family. But suppose he should, it was better to reject a considerable bribe to cut off so many of the sons of the family from a succession which might open to them. That, if they were excluded, the real family might come to an end, while many

[4] In his letter of 6 January, Forbes had called the manuscript "a great curiosity."
[5] George Cumine's first wife was Jean Urquhart; his second, Christian, daughter of Sir John Guthrie of Ludquharn, by whom he had seventeen children.
[6] See Introduction.
[7] David Boswell, the fifth Laird of Auchinleck. The nephew (sixth Laird) was also named David. See below, Appendix C, Charts II and III.
[8] Probably on 21 March 1772.

of its sons existed; and that, as the acquisitions of one man might be equalled by the acquisitions of another at some future period, it would be wrong to sacrifice so many men for a present addition of land. That the family had increased and diminished its possessions during the lives of different lairds, according as they were prudent or lavish; and that, while the old barony remained, the family was still preserved. All these considerations and the recollection of solemn oaths, one in spring 1767, when I swore to my father that if the estate was fixed on heirs whatsoever I would cut my throat, and one in winter 1769, when, with a piece of the Old Castle in my hand, I knelt upon the ruins and swore that if any man had the estate in exclusion of the rightful heir this stone should swim in his heart's blood (I keep the stone)—these kept me as firm as the old rock itself. The Commissioner and I did very well when we kept off the question of settlements. He had no company with him. The evening went on well enough. I was dreary in my room at night, being in an old house, and far from the rest of the family. I stupefied myself as much as I could by reading old newspapers, but heard sounds which gave me a kind of fear. At last I fell asleep.

TUESDAY 10 JANUARY. Not having slept quite well, I got up somewhat gloomy. Knowing that I would be immediately relieved when I got to town, I indulged hypochondria, which I had not felt of a long time. I called up into my fancy ideas of being confined all winter to an old house in the north of Scotland, and being burthened with tedium and gnawed with fretfulness. It is humiliating for me to consider that my mind is such that I can at any time be made thus wretched, merely by being placed in such a situation. But let me comfort myself that I can keep out of it. My body would be tormented were it put into a fire, as my mind would be tormented in such a situation. But as the one thought gives me no uneasiness, neither should the other. As I would not wish to have my body of stone, so I would not wish to have my mind insensible.

After breakfast I returned to town with the Commissioner, and at once was well. I called at my father's, willing to talk with him, but as usual felt myself chilled. I was restless today and went and dined at Dr. Webster's because I could not sit at home. He and I and the Colonel, George, and Annie were very social. There is to me a double satisfaction in sociality with near relations. It is like knowing that wine is wholesome while we drink it. I came home to tea, and found Lieutenant Graham of the Scots Dutch. In the evening Mr. Preston of Valleyfield called, and he and I talked fully of my father's settlements. He did not believe that any harm would really be done, but was for my keeping a strict look-out. My wife and I went with him and supped at Sir George's.

WEDNESDAY 11 JANUARY. This was a very wet day. I went in the forenoon to the Advocates' Library, and in returning felt myself seized with a cold. Grange drank tea with us.

THURSDAY 12 JANUARY. My cold was heavy. I kept the house all day. I wrote a long letter to my brother David, told him my difficulties and my heroism for the family, and said that I trusted any heir male who should get the estate through my firmness would behave handsomely to my wife and children.[9]

FRIDAY 13 JANUARY. I was engaged to dine with Mr. George Wallace. My cold was so ill that I sent him an apology. He wrote to me in such terms that I saw he would be much disappointed if I did not come. He is a worthy fellow, and I made a stretch for him. Old Professor Stevenson and Craig of Riccarton and his brother were the men.[1] They revived some particular ideas. There were two Miss Gunnings there.[2] One of them was as fine a seraglio figure as I could wish to see. I passed my time cheerfully and came home early.

SATURDAY 14 JANUARY. Dined at Fortune's with so many of the members of Moncrieffe's tavern giving him an entertainment. There was not much hearty merriment, and I was shocked with profanity. I felt however a desire to sit and indulge in intoxication. But having pleased myself with the idea of being always sober after the last day of the year 1774, when I got drunk with Colonel Stopford, etc.,[3] I came home, and I had a consultation on the Earl of Cassillis's Ayrshire politics.

SUNDAY 15 JANUARY. Lay in bed almost the whole day; read the first volume of *Histoire des Révolutions de Corse, par l'Abbé de Germanes,* a new book.[4] It entertained me to see a subject on which I myself had written well treated by a Frenchman. I read a little in Walton's *Lives,* and felt the same *unction* as formerly.

MONDAY 16 JANUARY. At home all day.

[9] At this time Boswell's brother Thomas David stood third in the line of heirs male to the estate of Auchinleck, preceded by his older brothers, James and John.

[1] John Stevenson, Professor of Logic in Edinburgh University (Boswell had attended his class in logic in 1756–1757); Thomas and Robert Craig, bachelors about ten years older than Boswell, sons of the Professor of Law in Edinburgh University and descendants of Sir Thomas Craig, the great Scottish feudal lawyer.

[2] Margaret and Catherine, daughters of Captain William Gunning, were fairly close cousins of those celebrated beauties, the Gunning sisters. Catherine, the younger, in 1782 became the second wife of William Campbell, the "Young Fairfield" of Boswell's journal entries of 7 and 8 March 1776.

[3] Boswell forgets; this bout took place on Christmas Eve.

[4] The first two volumes of the Abbé's *Histoire* were published in 1771. Since Boswell calls it "a new book," he may have read the second edition of the first volume, published in 1774.

TUESDAY 17 JANUARY. At the anniversary meeting of the Faculty of Advocates I intended to make a motion that if the Collector of Decisions did not publish annually he should forfeit his office. I yesterday sent notice of my intention to Mr. Wallace, the Collector. He was very much offended, and told me he did not expect [it] from *me*. He spoke to some of our brethren, and they, from friendship to him, begged that it might be delayed. At the meeting I rose and said there seemed to be a necessity for some effectual proviso, and wished that some of my senior brethren would suggest one. The Dean said it well deserved consideration; but some of Wallace's friends got the matter slurred over at this time. However, the alarm would, as I thought, probably produce dispatch, and, if it did not, I resolved to have a party prepared for a determined regulation next year.[5] I did not go to Fortune's to the entertainment given by the Dean, as he was not able to attend himself. My wife and I supped at Sir George's.

WEDNESDAY 18 JANUARY. Sandy Murray spoke to me in a very friendly way in the House, and told me that I should check expressing my disapprobation of characters, as people were getting a notion that I was an ill-natured man, which he knew was not my character. That it was of consequence to me to have a general good-will, with the view of representing Ayrshire in Parliament. I took his admonition kind, and considered that I really did express myself against many people in strong terms; that I had made several enemies, and might add to the number till I should be thought by the *world* a malevolent being. That men must be taken as they are, and their faults must be overlooked. At least not keenly detected. Sir George and Lady and Miss and Mr. Preston and Colonel Stopford dined with us, and drank tea. Then Mr. Burnett, younger of Kemnay, called.[6] He who had been in Prussian campaigns was an excellent companion for Mr. Preston. While we were in the drawing-room, Mr. Johnson's *Journey to the Western Islands of Scotland* came to me in thirteen franks.[7] I have still a kind of childish satisfaction in seeing many packets come to me, and thinking that I appear important at the post-office. I opened the franks with impatience, read a short letter from Mr. Johnson and a part of the book; and, as I had received it the very day on which it was published at

[5] Boswell's efforts in this matter seem to have been unavailing. Wallace did not publish the *Decisions* for 1772–1774 until 1784; those for 1775 were not published until after his death in 1786.

[6] Boswell had met Alexander Burnett, "a solid, clear-headed fellow," in 1764 at Berlin, where Burnett was secretary to the British Minister, Andrew Mitchell, and had probably not seen him since.

[7] Johnson sent the book in sheets, two sheets in each packet, because a franked packet could not exceed two ounces in weight if it was to go free. Johnson probably received the franks from his publisher, William Strahan, who enjoyed the privilege of franking as M.P. for Malmesbury.

London, I was pleased at my being so privileged. I was engaged to sup with Mr. Burnett at Mr. Andrew Stewart, Junior's, where we had Messrs. A. Keith and W. Dunbar, Writers to the Signet. I was lively though ill of a cold, being inspirited by Mr. Johnson. I came home as early as I could, sat down by the drawing-room fire, and read on till I had reached the end of the *Journey*. It was then about three in the morning, and the fire was very low and the night very cold. The song of fair Hebe says,

> I found
> The wine in my head, but the love in my heart.[8]

I on this occasion felt cold and pain in my head, but much noble imagery and reflection in my mind; though I must own that the hurry in which I read, and my bodily uneasiness, made me not relish the book so highly as I *knew* I should afterwards do.

THURSDAY 19 JANUARY. I could not but mention that I had a hidden treasure. But as I had written to Mr. Johnson that I would not let a soul see it till Mr. Strahan's cargo was arrived, I kept it close, though I had many solicitations. I felt a secret pride in knowing that Mr. Johnson had spoken so handsomely of me, and that the public would soon read what he had said. Matthew Dickie and Lawrence Hill dined. I wrote to Mr. Johnson at night. But my Register of Letters written and received makes it unnecessary for me to mention the particulars of my correspondence.[9] I this day read passages of the *Journey* with more pleasure than last night.

FRIDAY 20 JANUARY. Dined at Lord Dundonald's; Colonel Stopford, Captain and Mrs. Schaw and Miss there.

SATURDAY 21 JANUARY. Dined at Walker's Tavern—the anniversary meeting of Mundell's Scholars, a good institution.[1] We have always a kind of curious merriment, the same jokes every time, and all are willing to be pleased. Came home quite sober.

---

[8] The words are attributed to John West, Earl de la Warr:

> Fair Hebe I left with a cautious design,
> To escape from her charms, and to drown 'em in wine.
> I tried it, but found when I came to depart,
> The wine in my head, and still love in my heart.
>
> (*Gentleman's Magazine*, August 1752, p. 376.)

[9] The register for 1769–1777 was among the Boswell manuscripts found at Fettercairn House. In his letter Boswell "exulted in contemplating our scheme fulfilled."

[1] The former pupils at James Mundell's private academy in Edinburgh, which Boswell entered some time between October 1745 and October 1746 and left in 1748 or 1749. The anniversary meeting was usually held on the third Saturday in January. The members of the club tried to relive their school-days; each was addressed by the nickname he had had when one of the "schule laddies" and any deviation was punishable by a fine.

SUNDAY 22 JANUARY. Lay in bed, read Mr. Johnson's *Journey* with much relish. Enjoyed the excellence of passages at leisure, as one does fine paintings. Read in the Old and New Testament, and some of the Apocrypha. The oriental style always gives me a kind of Asiatic tranquillity. Read also some of the second volume of Burnet's *History of His Own Times.* ✶ (This is the history of Sunday the 29. On the 22 I was at New Church.)

MONDAY 23 JANUARY. Grange dined with us. M. Dupont came after dinner and drank tea.

TUESDAY 24 JANUARY. Nothing particular to mention.

WEDNESDAY 25 JANUARY. It was a very rigid frost. I sat long in Parliament House hearing Solicitor plead Elliot against Hewit, etc. His forcible manner gave me satisfaction. My cold grew worse. As I walked home, I felt the frost sensibly dart into my head. The French speak of a *coup de soleil;* I felt a *coup de gelée.* Hallglenmuir walked home with me.[2] He and Dr. Dunant, the *genevois,* and M. Dupont and Miss Scott and Grange dined. My head ached violently. I could scarcely sit till dinner was over. I then went to bed, and was in a violent fever all the afternoon. Mr. Wood gave me some mixture to make me sweat. I was ill all night.

THURSDAY 26 JANUARY. Was little better. Mr. Wood would not let me attempt going out. Mr. Lawrie got anything I had to do in the Court done for me by some of my brethren. We are very kind to one another in that respect; and the Court put off Lady Dundonald's cause, which was to have come on. I was comforted by a cordial letter from Mr. Johnson which had come last night. My wife was most tenderly careful of me. In the afternoon I was pretty easy. I never knew before that one could have a fever for a short while. I thought if once it begun it took at least a week to exhaust its force.

FRIDAY 27 JANUARY. Ventured to the Court in a chair at ten, but felt myself weak and feeble. I had gone out to attend the moving of a violent complaint drawn by me against Mr. Gordon, minister at Keith. There was a curious contrast, at the time when it was moved, between *its* force and *my* weakness.[2a] I came home immediately. Hallglenmuir, Mr. Anderson, jeweller at Inverness, a client of mine, and Mr. Isaac Grant, his agent, supped with me. Hallglenmuir diverted me with an account of his brother-in-law, Dernconner,[3] being persuaded that after he was *infeft* as one of my father's fictitious voters, he would be obliged to take the trust oath. The poor man said he would not perjure himself. He would fly to

[2] Alexander Mitchell of Hallglenmuir was a neighbour at Auchinleck. His mother was a sister of John Boswell, "Old Knockroon." See below, Appendix C, Chart II.

[2a] We have not yet been able to discover the nature of this complaint.

[3] James Lennox.

France. Said Hallglenmuir: "They can bring you back from any country and make you take it, and we're to have a stout man to watch you that you may not escape." At last he told him the election was to come on before my father's votes were ready, and he would not have to swear. Hallglenmuir assured me that, besides Dernconner, he and James Johnston and Wallacetown [4] had all resolved not to take the oath. This pleased me. A chat with him revived Auchinleck ideas.

SATURDAY 28 JANUARY. Sitting up somewhat late last night had done me harm. I was not able to get up, but lay in bed all forenoon. Grew better. Lady Colville and Lady Anne Erskine, Miss MacLeod of Raasay, and Mrs. Vernon (with whom she lodged), Colonel Stopford, Mr. Nairne, and Claud dined with us, as did Miss Campbell of Skerrington. My wife and I had called for Miss MacLeod, but missed her. I was pleased at seeing her again, and she appeared as well at Edinburgh as in Raasay.

SUNDAY 29 JANUARY. See page [58].[5] I have only to add that my wife came home from church in the afternoon not at all well.

MONDAY 30 JANUARY. My wife continued ill. I was afraid of a miscarriage, she being about a month gone with child. Made her keep her bed.

TUESDAY 31 JANUARY. My wife much in the same way. Still in bed. I was in a kind of indifferent frame.

WEDNESDAY 1 FEBRUARY. A sameness of life. Grange dined with me while my wife was confined to her bed.

THURSDAY 2 FEBRUARY. My wife better. Evening at St. John's Lodge. The Grand Master with us.[6]

FRIDAY 3 FEBRUARY. After the Court rose, Lord Monboddo desired to have some conversation with me. We walked in the large new room of the Advocates' Library, and he told me that my father had been talking to him of his family settlements, and that he was to disinherit me of his own acquisitions since I would not agree to the limitations of succession which he wished. I repeated to him part of the same arguments mentioned on page [53] and following pages of this volume. He paid no regard to them, and said that my being so mad upon male succession was in his opinion a sufficient cause for not entrusting me with the estate. I was calm and determined, and told him that Mr. Johnson approved of my resolution. "But," said he, "if Mr. Johnson knew that you would submit to be disinherited yourself of a great proportion of your inheritance rather than take the chance of cutting out a ninth cousin, he would not approve; and then you would not persist." "Nay," said I, "even Mr. Johnson could

---

[4] William Wallace.

[5] Here and elsewhere in the text, Boswell's references have been conformed to the pagination of the present edition.

[6] David Dalrymple. See above, 28 November.

not change me *there. Amicus Plato; sed magis amica veritas.*" [7] I changed the subject, and then he and I were very social. I supped with him at night; Messieurs Bannatyne MacLeod and Charles Hay there. He told us that he was of opinion numbers of spirits besides mankind were in the universe; that they might have communications with our minds; and that he had been told such facts concerning the second sight that *he believed it.* He mentioned Duncan Forbes as giving faith to it, which I have often heard. I was in fine cheerful spirits tonight, spoke a good deal, fancied myself like Burke, and drank moderately of claret.

SATURDAY 4 FEBRUARY. This forenoon came on before Lord Gardenstone two actions of defamation, one at the instance of Robert Scotland in Dunfermline against the printer of *The Caledonian Mercury* for inserting a card to him from the pillory.[8] The other at the instance of the same Robert, John his father, and David his brother, against Mr. Thomson, minister at Dunfermline, for having attacked them from the pulpit on the 30 of October, of which I have made mention in my journal of that date.[9] Colonel Campbell's lawyers were consulted on these causes last night at Macqueen's. We all gave our advice, but some of us were to plead the one, some the other. Ilay Campbell and Maclaurin put me in good spirits by their defence of the *Mercury;* and I pleaded Thomson's cause really as well as I could wish to plead. I had full command of myself and a fluency that was pleasant to feel, and at proper intervals I threw out

[7] "Plato is dear to me, but truth is dearer still": a proverb which has appeared in various forms; that given here is found in *Don Quixote,* Part II, Ch. li.

[8] Really three actions, for action was taken against *The Edinburgh Advertiser* as well as *The Caledonian Mercury.* The "card," as reprinted in *The Scots Magazine,* began as follows: "The PILLORY presents its most respectful compliments to *Robert Scotland,* and begs leave to assure him that in due season he shall be honoured with a comfortable armed chair and collar, in consideration of his faithful services to Colonel Masterton. The circumstances of six hundred guineas to himself, [and] a kirk at Edinburgh for his brother, being scarcely a sufficient recompence for his taking in his grey-headed father to break his faith with Colonel Campbell, and for his attempt to seduce different gentlemen at Dunfermline . . ." (February 1775, p. 107).

[9] Scotland, "one of [Campbell's] political agents, who was charged with having been unfaithful to his employer, and having deserted to the opposite party for a pecuniary reward, attacked very rudely in a newspaper the Reverend Mr. James Thomson, one of the ministers of that place, on account of a supposed allusion to him in one of his sermons. Upon this the minister, on a subsequent Sunday, arraigned him by name from the pulpit with some severity; and the agent, after the sermon was over, rose up and asked the minister aloud, 'What bribe he had received for telling so many lies from the chair of verity'" (*Life,* iii. 58). Scotland, in a letter to *The Caledonian Mercury,* had called Thomson "a blustering blunderbuss of an old military chaplain." Thomson took as his text Ephesians 4. 25 ("Wherefore putting away lying, speak every man truth with his neighbour") and applied it directly to Scotland, his brother, and his father.

sallies of vivacity and humour which had an instantaneous effect on Lord
Gardenstone himself and on the most numerous audience that I ever saw
at a Lord Ordinary's hearing.[1] Mr. Rae, who spoke after me, began with
saying, "I have heard Mr. Boswell with great pleasure." "And I dare say,
so has everybody that heard him," said Lord Gardenstone. Macqueen said
to me, "I would give a great deal to make such a speech as you have done
just now." I can believe that he was in earnest. That kind of oratory which
excites lively and gay emotions *nescio qua dulcedine nos allicit.*[2] I went
far against Robert Scotland for having betrayed Colonel Campbell. I
said, "He is an *infamous fellow,* and I will prove it." I knew he was standing at my back. When I retired from the bar, bad as he was, I could not
help relenting a little. I have really a compassionate heart. I could have
given him a little balsam to his bruises. I thought no man is so bad but if
we see him much hurt we will help him. Suppose one of the most worthless
—nay, the most mischievous—of men were shipwrecked and terribly cut
upon the rocks, and exhausted with famine, we should put him into a
warm bed, and be most tenderly careful of him, at least very soft and attentive about him. I comforted myself by thinking that Robert Scotland
was not too severely hurt.[3] I felt some uneasiness from imagining that perhaps my peculiar violence of declamation against him might make him
attempt to take revenge. I have a timidity in my temper which it requires
an exertion to counteract.

SUNDAY 5 FEBRUARY. Was too late for church in the forenoon. My
wife was pretty well again. In the afternoon went and heard Dr. Webster

[1] Each judge took his turn for a week as Lord Ordinary to hear causes in the Outer
House. Either party in the action could appeal from his decision to the full bench of
fifteen judges in the Inner House.

[2] "Allures us with an indefinable charm."

[3] *The Scots Magazine* for this month (pp. 108–109) gives a very full summary of
Boswell's speech. The defence was (1) that as the Scotlands had attended Mr. Thomson's ministry for many Sundays after the offensive sermon was preached, there was
a virtual *remissio injuriae;* (2) that it was the duty of a clergyman to preach against
vice, and that the Scottish clergy (witness John Knox and others) had always exercised
this privilege; (3) that as the Scotlands had first attacked Mr. Thomson and had also
publicly replied to him in very injurious language, they had precluded themselves
from legal redress; (4) finally, that if the Court would allow a proof (as it should), it
would be shown that everything Mr. Thomson had said about Robert Scotland was
strictly true. Memorials were ordered, and on 28 February Lord Gardenstone acquitted
Mr. Thomson and ordered the Scotlands to pay costs of suit. But on 19 December
1775, in an interlocutor signed by Lord Auchinleck (the Lord President being absent)
the Court of Session by a majority reversed Lord Gardenstone's decision. Johnson
wrote an argument for Mr. Thomson, but Boswell was dissuaded by Edward Thurlow
from appealing to the House of Lords. See below, 19 December 1775, and *Life,* iii.
58–64, 91.

in the Tolbooth Church. Drank tea at his house with the Colonel, Annie, and George. Fell a talking of my travels, and was in such a flow of spirits that I sat with them till near eight.

MONDAY 6 FEBRUARY. Busy all day writing answers to Dr. Memis.[4] Grange supped with us.

TUESDAY 7 FEBRUARY. Dined Sandy Gordon's, a company for David Moncrieffe: Lord Gardenstone, Peter Murray, and several more. Quite an Edinburgh dinner. Local talk, and noise, and wine. I drank rather too much, and lost the afternoon. Played awhile at brag.[5] Was cautious and would not venture so as to risk more than a trifle. Won half a guinea.

WEDNESDAY 8 FEBRUARY. Mr. James Macdonald, factor to Sir Alexander, young Cowhill, Mr. John Graeme, Writer to the Signet, and Adam Bell dined with me. In the evening I was kept busy correcting the proof-sheets of my paper against Dr. Memis.

THURSDAY 9 FEBRUARY. Logan drank tea with us. I had such accounts of his behaving unhandsomely in the Ayrshire elections that I had no liking for his company. Clownishness and duplicity make a sad mixture.[6] At six I was at the examination of Mr. _____, younger of _____, upon civil law.[6a] Sandy Murray was our *praeses* and acquitted himself so well that I was humbled tonight, and roused to prepare myself better for another occasion. In many things we may do without censure, though we are very imperfect. But how agreeable is it to do well or to see a thing well done.

FRIDAY 10 FEBRUARY. Mr. James Hardie consulted me to write a memorial for Mr. Thomson against Scotland, and drank tea. I got a letter

[4] John Memis, M.D. from St. Andrews, practised as a physician at Aberdeen. He was the author of the *Midwife's Pocket Companion*. Boswell explained Memis's absurd cause to Johnson in a letter of 19 January 1775: "In a translation of the charter of the Infirmary [at Aberdeen] from Latin into English, made under the authority of the managers, the same phrase in the original is in one place rendered *physician,* but when applied to Dr. Memis is rendered *doctor of medicine.* Dr. Memis complained of this before the translation was printed, but was not indulged with having it altered; and he has brought an action for damages on account of a supposed injury, as if the designation given to him were an inferior one, tending to make it be supposed he is *not* a *physician,* and consequently to hurt his practice." On 6 May Johnson dictated to Boswell a refutation of Memis. Boswell was counsel for the managers of the Infirmary, who finally won the case.

[5] A card-game, essentially the same as poker.

[6] Hugh Logan of that ilk, a frequent guest at Auchinleck, was well known for lavish hospitality and broad humour: his witty sayings gave rise to a nineteenth-century collection of anecdotes entitled *The Laird of Logan.* Boswell did not like to be compared to him.

[6a] The blanks should be filled respectively with "James Paterson" and "Carpow" (Faculty of Advocates Records 59).

from Dr. Wilson at Newcastle, who was just setting out for London, where he was to settle, informing me that my brother John was better, being calm and able to answer questions pretty distinctly. I had also an excellent letter from my friend Temple. I felt highly the value of such a friend, who was not only steadily affectionate but learned and elegant in taste.

SATURDAY 11 FEBRUARY. This was a busy and a gainful week to me. I received twenty-seven guineas in fees, two more than I had ever received in one week before. Charles Hay walked with me to Sir Alexander Dick's. The Knight was amiable and classical as usual. He was very fond of Mr. Johnson's *Journey,* which I had lent to him, and was writing notes on it. When I came home in the evening I found Lady Wallace and Miss Susie Dunlop with my wife.[7] I received a letter from Mr. Johnson contradicting a story told against him by Macpherson's supporters.[8] This was like supplying me with sufficient arms to fight in a cause which I had much at heart. He was angry with me for begging to be allowed to read to more people than to Lord Hailes some verses on Inchkenneth which he had sent me.[9] He said, "Your love of publication is offensive and disgusting, and will end, if it be not reformed, in a general distrust among all your

[7] Susan Dunlop was not only the niece of Lady Wallace (Antonia, daughter of Francis Dunlop, second wife of Sir Thomas Wallace, Bt.), but also her step-granddaughter. Lady Wallace was Boswell's subtenant for Hume's apartment in James's Court. Susan's mother, Mrs. Frances Anna Dunlop of Dunlop, later became the favourite correspondent of Robert Burns, who often mentions Susan in his letters to her.

[8] The story, as reported by Boswell himself in a letter to Johnson, was as follows: "It is confidently told here that before your book came out [Macpherson] sent to you to let you know that he understood you meant to deny the authenticity of Ossian's poems; that the originals were in his possession; that you might have inspection of them, and might take the evidence of people skilled in the Erse language; and that he hoped, after this fair offer, you would not be so uncandid as to assert that he had refused reasonable proof. That you paid no regard to his message, but published your strong attack upon him; that then he wrote a letter to you in such terms as he thought suited to one who had not acted as a man of veracity" (2 February 1775). Johnson, after scolding him for paying any attention to the "disposition of your countrymen to tell lies in favour of each other," denied that Macpherson had ever offered him "the sight of any original or of any evidence of any kind."—James Macpherson's epic poem, *Fingal,* published at the end of 1761, professed to be the work of Ossian, son of Fingal, the king of Morven in the third century A.D. Although its authenticity was readily denounced by many in England, partly because of political prejudice, and was suspected by a number of Scots, it enjoyed enormous popular and critical success, especially on the Continent. Macpherson never seriously attempted to refute the charge of forgery. Eventually nearly everyone came to agree that though he drew on a considerable amount of heroic poetry, the epic work was his own invention. In 1785 Boswell declared that the subject of Ossian had "now become very uninteresting"; the controversy, however, broke out again after Macpherson's death in 1796.

[9] Johnson's Latin verses, *Insula Sancti Kennethi,* were later published in Boswell's *Journal of a Tour to the Hebrides.* See 17 October 1773.

friends."[1] This was too severe, as Lord Hailes had agreed with me that the verses should be freely shown. My wife, who is more touchy than I am, was really angry for a little. I began first to be vexed, and then somewhat angry too. But I soon recollected the authority which Mr. Johnson had over me as a preceptor, and his real kindness for me, and was satisfied. In this very letter he said, "I am just now engaged, but in a little time I hope to do all that you would have." I supped at Mr. John Swinton's, in whose house I had not been for many years.[2] There were just Maclaurin and his wife, David Stuart and his wife, a Miss Rose, and a Miss Mercer. We had a single rubber at shilling whist, and a genteel easy supper. I cannot account for it, but it so happened that it was a better evening than I imagined could have been passed in Edinburgh. No rioting—no private stories—no loud laughing. A company is like a chemical composition. Materials may come together and form a *whole* that is better than perhaps more valuable ones united.

SUNDAY 12 FEBRUARY. Last night before I went to Mr. Swinton's I called on my father, and had a little serious conversation. I had the better of him, for I told him that I was now doing all that could be wished. I was sober.[3] I was diligent in business. I was successful in business; and if he would tell me anything with which he found fault, I would amend it. He owned he had nothing particular to mention. But still he was cold and dry and indifferent. I could not help it. I was at the New Church today, forenoon and afternoon. Called on Crosbie between sermons, and talked with him of Mr. Johnson's *Journey*. He promised me many remarks. Dined at home. My father's dinner between sermons is an unpleasant scene, and I attend only as a piece of duty, and when in finer frame I avoid it. I was at New Church in the afternoon. Went home with young Donaldson and got the *Monthly* and *Critical Reviews* on Mr. Johnson's *Journey*, which were a feast. Drank tea at Sir George's. Found Mr. Nairne when I came home, and read the reviews on Mr. Johnson to him.

MONDAY 13 FEBRUARY. Busy with Mr. Thomson's memorial. Miss Foulis of Colinton, Messrs. James Hardie, Matthew Dickie, and young Donaldson dined, as did Mr. Matthew, clerk in the post-office, who dines with me annually.[4] I went in the evening in a hackney-coach with so many

---

[1] Boswell did not print in the *Life* this portion of Johnson's letter.

[2] John Swinton, advocate, later a Senator of the College of Justice, was first cousin to Sir Walter Scott's mother. Scott was always very proud of his Swinton ancestry, the Swintons having then maintained their connexion with their ancestral lands (in Berwickshire) perhaps for a longer time than any other family in Scotland. The John Swinton here mentioned was reckoned the twenty-seventh of that ilk.

[3] Though on 7 February he says that he "drank rather too much," Boswell seems not to have been drunk since Christmas Eve.

[4] Thomas Matthew had been in the post-office for nearly thirty years. A copy of

of my brethren of Canongate Kilwinning, or St. John's, Lodge and visited Leith Lodge. My spirits were vigorous, and I sung my nonsensical Scotch song, "Twa wheels," etc.[5]

TUESDAY 14 FEBRUARY. This morning in the Court, I joked to John Grant, Junior, on an oath, which was wrong. His client had produced several writings to show that she had debts against the estate of my client. I insisted that she should swear that she believed them to be just debts. Grant objected and said he did not see why she should be obliged to swear. I, laughing, answered, "She need not swear but what she likes; she is not *legally* obliged to swear the truth. You have not explained to her the nature of an oath." I meant to say in a jocular manner that if she was unwilling to swear there must be some fallacy in the writings. But an oath is of so solemn a nature, and people are so apt to think too lightly of it, that it should never be mentioned in merriment.

WEDNESDAY 15 FEBRUARY. Finished Mr. Thomson's memorial before five in the afternoon. Drank tea first at home, then at Captain Schaw's; went with him and Mrs. Schaw to *The Beggar's Opera,* performed by desire of several ladies of quality. There was an elegant audience. Digges looked and sung as well as ever. I was quite in London. A girl from Ireland who played Polly, by the name of Mistress Ramsay, pleased me very well. Only her notes were sometimes not sweet enough, but like the cry of a peacock. I sat between Lady Betty Cochrane and Mrs. Schaw in one of the rows of the pit taken by Lady Dundonald. I was cheerful and happy, having no pretensions, being very well established as an agreeable companion, and being a married man. Life is like a road, the first part of which is a hill. A man must for a while be constantly pulling that he may get forward, and not run back. When he has got beyond the steep, and on smooth ground—that is, when his character is fixed—he goes on smoothly upon level ground. I could not help indulging Asiatic ideas as I viewed such a number of pretty women, some of them young gay creatures with their hair dressed with flowers. But thoughts of mortality and change came upon me, and then I was glad to feel indifference.

After the play and the farce of *The Miller of Mansfield,*[6] I went to Princes Street Coffee-house, joined Sinclair the advocate, Grant the advocate, and three other Highlanders, eat roasted cheese and drank strong rum punch. There was soon to be a trial of Captain Belsches for attacking

---

Douglas's *Peerage of Scotland,* 1764 (owned by Mr. Richard Brown Baker), bears this inscription in Boswell's hand: "James Boswell. Edinburgh 1780. A present from Mr. Thomas Matthew. One of the clerks in the post-office."

[5] Not known to have been preserved; probably indecent. The full title was "Twa wheels and an axletree."

[6] By Robert Dodsley.

Stirling, the fishmonger, with a red-hot poker.[7] This was a common topic of conversation. One of the Highlanders said, "A red-hot poker was a species of *firearms*." I observed, either now or before, that Stirling should have had a good large fish by way of a shield, and, as it would have been broiled by the poker, he might have eat his shield as Æneas and his companions eat their tables.[8] It was said that Stirling was a good gentleman. "Poh," said somebody, "a fishmonger a gentleman!" I ludicrously said, "Was not Jonah as good a gentleman after he came out of the whale's belly as when he went into it?" This produced a loud laugh, though the application was not very just. I was vexed that I had brought in a story from Scripture ludicrously. But I was in tumultuous spirits. David Moncrieffe spoke in character as a *feaster* when he said that, when Stirling pulled his hand from the red-hot poker, which he had catched hold of to defend himself, it broiled like a beefsteak. We did not drink to excess. I was disposed for it, but checked myself, confessing, however, my inclination thus: "Well, drink is a strange thing. It gives me acute pain to rise now." I came home in a chair to shun the cold of the night and the noise of my companions on the street. I was home before twelve, I think. I have been guilty of the *dilatory notation* which Mr. Johnson censures.[9] I have this night, February 20, written my journal from page [59], being February 2, from short notes kept by my clerk. I shall be more regular after this. But I find that I do not enough mark the state of my mind and its changes. I shall try to do better.

THURSDAY 16 FEBRUARY. Good resolutions woefully fail. I have not begun to my journal again till Sunday the 5 of March; but as I consider the study of myself to be very improving, I do not scruple to write it on this day of recollection, and I hope to bring it up. Thursday the 16 February was passed in the usual course of a session day without anything to mark it.

FRIDAY 17 FEBRUARY. My wife and I dined at my father's; Mr. Stobie's family and Balbarton were there. I know not how, Balbarton got

[7] "Mr. Belsches in riding with unusual speed down the Cowgate had very near rode down an old woman, when Mr. Stirling caught hold of her and saved her; and at the same time challenged Mr. Belsches for his rashness, which produced some altercation between them. A short time thereafter Mr. B. sent for Mr. S. to an inn at the foot of the Cowgate; Mr. S., upon entering the room, was not a little astonished at Mr. B.'s locking the door, and taking a pair of red-hot tongs out of the fire, with which he threatened to twist his nose, and would have accomplished his threats, it is thought, had not Mr. S. sacrificed his fingers for the safety of his face, by grasping the tongs, hot as they were, and at the same time alarming the house; upon which the landlord breaking into the room prevented further mischief" (*Gentleman and Lady's Weekly Magazine*, 18 January 1775, p. 92).

[8] *Aeneid*, vii. 107–147.

[9] In the *Journey to the Western Islands*, when he was with Sir Allan Maclean in the cave on the coast of Mull.

into unusual spirits and wished to drink heartily. I could not resist indulging a sensible and learned kinsman of seventy-four years of age, and
so he and I drank too much. I saw him home carefully, and I supped at
Moncrieffe's, and drank a good deal more.

SATURDAY 18 FEBRUARY. Was exceedingly ill after yesterday's excess. I went to the Court of Session, where I had some trifling causes to attend and had a few words to speak. But I was grievously incapacitated. I
went to Leith in a coach with my wife and the children, which made me
better. Balbarton, MacGuarie, Torloisk, young Coll, Dr. and Miss Grant,
and Colquhoun Grant dined with me.[1] I loved to find myself cordial with
Highlanders and Hebrideans. We were not riotous. Mr. Johnson's health
was drank in a bumper, and much praise was bestowed on his *Journey,*
though some of the company stickled for Ossian and insisted that in the
Highlands and Islands Erse was written long ago.[2] No instance however
was given, except that MacGuarie said he had an old paper in his family
at which Maclean's subscription was in Erse. But this paper may not be
very old. I remember the Laird of MacLeod told us that his ancestor Rorie
More signed his name in Erse.

My wife and I supped with Lady Preston and Miss Preston; Sir George,
who had been ill for some time, having gone early to bed. It affected me
with some degree of melancholy to see his seat vacant. It made me think
of his being dead, which must be at no great distance, as he is seventy-two.
Hospitality such as his makes a man be missed more than greater qualities
do. But why be gloomy because a friend dies when he is old, and the course
of the world goes on?

SUNDAY 19 FEBRUARY. Was at New Church forenoon and afternoon,
and at my father's between sermons. I drank tea at Lord Kames's, not
having been to see him this long time.[3] He was in moderate spirits, so that
he was really very good company, as he gave me rational conversation; but
there was nothing important enough or ingenious enough to be put down
except his denial that taxation depended on representation. "For," said
he, "not only are all artificers and a great proportion of those who pay
taxes not represented, but *women,* who have a large share of the property
of the kingdom and pay land-tax, and who in other situations pay other
taxes, are not represented." He thought taxation depended on protection.

[1] Alexander Maclean, younger brother of Boswell's and Johnson's host in the Hebrides,
succeeded his father Hugh as fourteenth Laird of Coll. "A very amiable man, though
not marked with such active qualities as his brother" (Boswell's letter to Johnson written on this day). Torloisk was Lachlan Maclean, seventh Laird of Torloisk.
[2] Johnson had denied that there were any old manuscripts of Erse at all.
[3] Henry Home, Lord Kames, Lord of Session and of Justiciary, a prolific writer on subjects so diverse as agriculture and theory of criticism, has left a well-earned reputation
for judicial severity and a partly legendary reputation for judicial indecorum. He
was thin, able, arrogant, and at this time seventy-eight years old.

An artificer or farmer is guarded by government, so that he can labour in security and gain much more than he could do if interrupted by defending himself, and therefore it is reasonable he should contribute to the support of government. Mrs. Drummond, his lady, always revives youthful ideas in my mind, as in my most dissipated days I was much in their house.[4] I ought to be oftener there now. She was fond of Mr. Johnson's *Journey,* and my Lord spoke of it more favourably than I had any notion his prepossessions against Mr. Johnson would have allowed him. But he was firm to Ossian, was satisfied of its antiquity from *internal evidence,* and wanted to have a splendid edition of it with plates published by subscription. Mr. Nairne and Mr. Stewart Moncrieffe were here. Nairne supped with me. I spoke to Lord Kames to give me notes of his life. He said he would if I would write it before his death. But like Cicero he would ask to have it done in a flattering manner.[5] I told him I would do it fairly. I know not if he has eminence enough to merit that his life should be written. Perhaps I may do it.[6]

MONDAY 20 FEBRUARY. Busy at home. Miss Annie Dick dined with us. At night read an account in the newspapers of Lord Strichen's death, being the first vacancy on our bench after *eight* years, and the opening for Mr. Lockhart, our Dean of Faculty, to be a judge at last, after having been fifty-two years at the bar.[7] What a thought! Had sentence been pronounced on him to do this—to stand fifty-two years at the bar, and to write such a number of long papers—it would have been shocking. It makes one recollect *The Castle of Indolence:*

> O mortal man that livest here in toil,[8]
>
> .   .   .
>
> That like an emmet thou must ever moil,
> Is a sad sentence of an ancient date.

His being made a judge would give him comparative ease and a security of above £600 a year; and he would have the pleasing delusion that he had a new life to live. At the bar he had the notion of ending. As a judge

[4] Lord Kames's wife was styled Mrs. Drummond because she had succeeded her brother in the estate of Blair Drummond in Perthshire.
[5] Probably an allusion to Cicero's highly flattering memoir of his own consulate, which he sent to several of his friends in the hope that they would write on the same subject.
[6] Boswell did later collect a considerable quantity of materials for Lord Kames's biography.
[7] The last death of a judge of the Court of Session was that of Andrew Fletcher, Lord Milton, 13 December 1766.
[8] Boswell left a blank for the second line of Thomson's poem. The first two lines run properly:
> O mortal man, who livest here by toil,
> Do not complain of this thy hard estate.

he would think of beginning. Lord Strichen had been a judge forty-three years.[9] Mr. Lockhart might stretch his imagination very far. I had not of a long time been so much roused as by this event, which was to produce a change which I considered in so many lights. I had resolved to write Mr. Lockhart's life, as he had been the first barrister that ever practised in the Court of Session;[1] and the first man in my own line of life was a proper subject for my biographical exertion.[2]

TUESDAY 21 FEBRUARY. Lord Strichen's death was in everybody's mouth in the Court. I said to Crosbie that I felt today that death was necessary, for that we should be very dull were there no changes. Worthy Lord Strichen could not be regretted, as he had lived to a good old age. In the evening I was at St. David's Lodge, the Grand Master being there;[3] and then I supped at Crosbie's with Charles Hay and Fergusson of Craigdarroch, concerting measures to be taken in case Crosbie should stand candidate to be Dean, I having promised to be for him long ago. Lord Advocate appeared to have a considerable majority on reading the list of advocates. I was against having a King's Counsel for our Dean, but was for a man quite independent.[4] Mr. Johnson, I remember, thought this foolish. I argued today in the Court with some of my brethren on the subject. I said we should have no man's servant at our head. Said Sandy Gordon: "You would have a practising lawyer, who is every man's servant." "Yes," said I; "he is every man's servant, but he is his own master." We did not drink to excess at Crosbie's, which was wonderful.

WEDNESDAY 22 FEBRUARY. M. Dupont drank tea with us. I wrote to Dempster that his living cheerfully in the country all winter was to me more wonderful than the second sight which he treated as a superstitious fable, though it has no more to do with superstition than electricity has. I could not imagine how, after London and Parliament and Burke, he could bear vacant hours and the conversation of Angus lairds. To de-

[9] Actually he had been judge nearly forty-five years.

[1] That is, first in general reputation and practice.

[2] In his journal Boswell often mentions that he took notes for Lockhart's life; but they have apparently not survived. According to one report, Boswell "hovered like a vulture above the dying judge, in quest of anecdotes" (John Ramsay, *Scotland and Scotsmen in the Eighteenth Century*, Edinburgh, 1888, i. 138 *n*. 1). *The London Magazine* for March 1775 contains a "short account" of Lockhart, probably written by Boswell.

[3] Sir Walter Scott was later a member of this lodge, which had branched from the Leith Kilwinning Lodge and always maintained a very close connexion with the Canongate Kilwinning Lodge. It met in Hyndford's Close.

[4] James Montgomery, Lord Advocate, who became Lord Chief Baron of Exchequer in May, was not made Dean; but Boswell was disappointed in his hope for "a man quite independent." The new Dean was the ambitious Henry Dundas, who had made his first speech in the House of Commons on the preceding day, and in May replaced Montgomery as Lord Advocate. See below, "Review" of the Summer Session, 1775.

liver me if he could from a dreary possibility in my imagination of my sufferings on retiring to the country from disappointments, I begged to have a particular account from him how he lived, not in book language about domestic society, etc., but in our own language, so as to be understood and felt. If he can dispel the horrors of my idea of a country gentleman's life, he will relieve me much; for it is a kind of distress to have even a possibility so near to probability of dreariness at a future period. I was busy this evening studying the cause of Colonel Campbell's friends in the town of Stirling to have the election of magistrates and Council there set aside.[5] It was to be heard by the Lords next day.

THURSDAY 23 FEBRUARY. I opened the cause of the reduction of the Council of Stirling in the Inner House, and was quite easy and master of myself. I imagined myself pleading at the English bar. The President said, "Mr. Boswell, you have pleaded your cause very neatly and very well." It is pleasant to receive praise in public from a man with whom one is not on speaking terms in private. Nothing gives me such spirits as making a good speech in public. Craigengillan and Matthew Dickie dined with me.[6] I was clear-headed and cheerful, and talked with Craigengillan of his trade as a drover, and was instructed in it. He insisted that I should sup with him at Matthew Baillie the stabler's in the Grassmarket, where he lodged.[7] After some hours of law labour, I went to him and found him encircled by Matthew Dickie, Robert Aiken, and other Ayrshire inferior men. He and I drank brandy punch, the rest rum punch. Our conversation was hearty, and we did not drink much. I suppose out of all the conversations that one is engaged in during a whole life, or indeed all conversations in general, the proportion of instruction or wit that can be extracted is very small; and I suppose one should be content if he usually has cheerfulness. But Mr. Johnson and our Club in London have made me luxurious.

FRIDAY 24 FEBRUARY. In the evening attended at Walker's the taking of a proof, *Hope* against Tweedie, about a foot-race for a pipe of

[5] Three leading men of Stirling had entered into a bond to unite their interests in all matters relating to the election and government of the burgh, and to divide all profits and emoluments which any of them should procure from Members of Parliament. Campbell's friends presented a cause of reduction, an action to render void the election of magistrates in Stirling. The Court so decided on 1 March and severely censured the signatories; on an appeal in November 1775, the House of Lords affirmed the decree.

[6] Boswell later wrote that John McAdam of Craigengillan had "certainly made the greatest fortune that any inland man ever did. I mean without trading beyond seas." McAdam sent an "obliging" letter to Burns at the beginning of his poetical career, and Burns responded with a poem, "Sir, o'er a gill I gat your card."

[7] Edward Topham remarked that Edinburgh innkeepers "have modesty enough to give themselves no higher denomination" than "stable-keepers" (*Letters from Edinburgh, Written in the Years 1774 and 1775*, London, 1776, p. 18).

port.[8] Hope, who had won it, was carried on horseback through a river in the way. I was not sure but this might, in strict *race-law,* forfeit the bet. I did not intend to go to Moncrieffe's, but this night I went in the way of my *business,* as we have several members skilled in all kinds of gaming who could inform me as to this *point.* But I got no clear light. I came to think it a quibble, as Hope had run wherever he could, and rode only where it was hardly practicable to go on foot. I marked the conversation tonight at this club, and it was local jocularity and bawdy, and nothing else. I came home a little after twelve.

SATURDAY 25 FEBRUARY. Bedlay was keen to have a bill of suspension drawn. He was with me himself and helped to frame it, and dined in a hurry, and then to it again. My wife and I were at the play in the evening—*Hamlet*—with Lady Anne Erskine, etc. After the play I went behind the scenes and saw Mr. Digges, whom I had not seen this winter before. Engaged him to dine with me on Tuesday sennight.

SUNDAY 26 FEBRUARY. Was at New Church forenoon. Dined at my father's; my wife there. Afternoon, walked down to Lord Dundonald's; drank a dram of brandy with him. My Lady was ill. Lady Betty came home and made tea. She and I walked and had some very pleasant conversation. I then called on Mr. Lockhart, and sat above an hour with him alone, and asked him a variety of questions about his life and the history of practice at our bar. I have put down in notes of his life what he told me. He was engaged to dine with me on Tuesday, but was indisposed and hesitated. I insisted on his coming. "Then," said he, "I shall be with you if I am alive. If not, my ghost shall attend you."

MONDAY 27 FEBRUARY. Busy writing law as usual on Mondays, when there is no Court and I stay at home.

TUESDAY 28 FEBRUARY. This day I gave my valedictory dinner to Mr. Lockhart. Colonel Stopford, Captain and Mrs. Schaw, Miss MacLeod of Raasay, Miss Jeanie Henderson, Miss Susie Dunlop, Lord Elphinstone, and Mr. Crosbie were of the party. It went on very well. I drank so as to be heated, but no worse.

WEDNESDAY 1 MARCH. Nothing remarkable.[9]

THURSDAY 2 MARCH. Was somewhat fretted by being hurried to write law-papers. St. John's Lodge in the evening for a little, having first written to Lord Pembroke and Beauclerk, a gleam of fine spirits having come.[1]

---

[8] The cause occupied the Court at least until December 1776. Tweedie's defence was that the wager on the foot-race was not in earnest and was therefore not actionable. Eventually the Court dismissed the cause, finding "expenses due to neither party."

[9] But see above, 22 February, *n.* 5.

[1] This is Topham Beauclerk. "His great veneration for Mr. Johnson and Johnson's

FRIDAY 3 MARCH.[2] John Boswell of Knockroon, Grange, and young Robert Syme supped. I foolishly sat pretty late drinking brandy punch.

SATURDAY 4 MARCH. Dined at Mr. Lockhart's; Macqueen, Wattie Campbell, and four more advocates there. We drank hard for a little and were inflamed, at least I was, and then fell to whist. I had a rage for gaming and had once lost *eight pounds* and the loss did not move me. I won it all back but five-and-twenty shillings. Macqueen and Maclaurin and I supped and played after supper. It was humiliating to see the Dean, the eminent barrister whose life I was writing, peevish because he lost. It lessened him. His conversation indeed is very barren. You can see little more of *him* by being in company with him than you see of an eminent engraver or musician.[3] We were impatient for his commission as a judge. He said he was more indifferent about it than any of us. After I came home I promised or rather vowed to my wife that I would never play higher than shilling whist.

SUNDAY 5 MARCH. Stayed at home in the forenoon. My wife with great justice complained that my conversation with her was never rational, but merely childish nonsense. It is not easy to give a distinct specimen of that puerile jocularity in which alone I exert myself at home. The reason of it may be partly indolence, to avoid thought; partly because my wife, though she has excellent sense and a cheerful temper, has not sentiments congenial with mine. She has no superstition, no enthusiasm, no vanity; so that to be free of a disagreeable contrariety, I may be glad to keep good humour in my mind by foolish sport. Was at New Church afternoon. Drank tea at Lord Alva's very cordially. Mr. Nairne, Lady Wallace, and Miss Dunlop supped with us.

MONDAY 6 MARCH. Sir Alexander and Lady Dick came and breakfasted with us. It was a most cheerful meal. I was in high spirits, and the

---

love for him are enough to make me value him; and from what I have seen of him he appears to be a man of wit, literature, and fashion in a distinguished degree" (*Boswell for the Defence*, 7 April 1773). Boswell's acquaintance with Lord Pembroke had begun the preceding summer, though there had been a "connexion" since 1768, when Pembroke had gone to Corsica and had requested a letter of recommendation from Boswell to Paoli. He was a charming and licentious man, Lord of the Bedchamber and Lieutenant-General in the Army, author of a treatise on the handling of horses which was the basis of the system generally adopted in the British cavalry. He had a genuine affection for Boswell and repeatedly showed a willingness to do favours for him; he also furnished him with a not-altogether-fortunate model of personal behaviour.

[2] The first line of this entry has been cancelled and is illegible.

[3] Lockhart "was by no means a lively or entertaining companion, being always well pleased to let other people take his share of the discourse. . . . However little he might shine in conversation, such was his courtesy and attention to his guests, that his house was all along frequented by people of distinction" (Ramsay's *Scotland and Scotsmen*, i. 137–138).

prospect of being in London elevated me. At eleven I was at Mr. Macqueen's at a consultation for Sir Allan Maclean. I got into a dissipated
state of mind, called on Maclaurin, and talked with him in a desultory
way, walking up and down his room till three. Dined at home.

Drank tea with David Hume, having half a year's rent of his house to
pay him. He spoke of Mr. Johnson's *Journey* in terms so slighting that it
could have no effect but to show his resentment. He however agreed with
him perfectly as to Ossian. But then he disbelieved not so much for want
of testimony, as from the nature of the thing, according to his apprehension. He said if fifty barea—d Highlanders should say that *Fingal* was an
ancient poem, he would not believe them. He said it was not to be believed that a people who were continually concerned to keep themselves
from starving or from being hanged should preserve in their memories a
poem in six books. He said that Homer had once been written, which
made a great difference. He said that the late Mr. Wood had written a
very ingenious dissertation to prove that the use of letters was not known
in Homer's time.[4] But that he was wrong; for we find in Homer a letter
is brought from the King of _____.[5] He said that the extensive fame of
Ossian was owing to the notion that the poems were so ancient; that if
Macpherson had given them as his own, nobody would have read them to
an end. He acknowledged that there were some good passages in them,
and perhaps there might be some small parts ancient. He said the Highlanders, who had been famed as a warlike people, were so much flattered
to have it thought that they had a great poet among them that they all
tried to support the fact, and their wish to have it so made them even
ready to persuade themselves into it. I told him Mr. Johnson's saying that
he could undertake to write an epic poem on the story of Robin Hood
which the half of the people of England should say they had heard in their
youth.[6] Mr. Hume said the people of England would not be so ready to
support such a story. They had not the same temptation with the Highlanders, there being many excellent English poets.

This night the newspapers informed me that Mr. Lockhart's commission as a judge was come. It gave me a fresh agitation. Lockhart having
been so long a fixed planet at the bar, his being metamorphosed to a judge
was an event which my mind did not easily follow. Ordinary men may
change their situations and appearances without surprising us. We never
dwell long enough upon the contemplation of them to mind them much.

[4] Robert Wood, *An Essay on the Original Genius of Homer*, 1769. The subject of the
essay is not so narrow as Boswell, or Hume, implies; the discussion of "the use of
letters" is preliminary to a study of Homer's style.
[5] Bellerophon carried a tablet from Proetus, King of Argos, to the King of Lycia (*Iliad*,
vi. 152–170). Wood himself mentioned this "letter," but said that it was "symbolical,
hieroglyphical, or picture description" (ed. 1775, p. 250).
[6] *Hebrides*, 10 November 1773.

But a great man who has for years been in a particular sphere strikes us with a kind of wonder when he moves.

TUESDAY 7 MARCH. I went between nine and ten to congratulate Mr. Lockhart. He was gone out to the President's, but his daughter, Miss Annie, spoke to me from a window, seemed sensible of my attention, and promised to tell him. This forenoon he sat within the bar and in the Outer House as Lord *Probationer.* A crowd followed with a strange curiosity wherever he went. Mr. Digges and Colonel Stopford and Miss MacLeod of Raasay dined with us. It was quite an easy, genteel dinner. We had two kinds of Greek wine, port, Madeira, mountain, claret. Digges was to play Macheath at night.[7] So went away early. Stopford and I sat awhile cordially by ourselves, and then drank tea with the ladies. I had many papers to write, and the wine which I had drank made me restless and idle, so that I was unhappy. I went early to bed.

WEDNESDAY 8 MARCH. I rose pretty early, and got somewhat forward in my business. I was again pleased with seeing Lockhart followed. My wife and I drank tea at Mr. Samuel Mitchelson, Junior's. I then came home and laboured, and then she and I supped cordially at Sir George's. I was quite in love with her tonight. She was sensible, amiable, and all that I could wish, except being averse to hymeneal rites. I told her I must have a concubine. She said I might go to whom I pleased. She has often said so. I have not insisted on my conjugal privilege since this month began, and were I sure that she was in earnest to allow me to go to other women without risk either of hurting my health or diminishing my affection for her, I would go. Thus I thought; but I was not clear, for though our Saviour did not prohibit concubinage, yet the strain of the New Testament seems to be against it, and the Church has understood it so. My passion, or appetite rather, was so strong that I was inclined to a laxity of interpretation, and as the Christian religion was not express upon the subject, thought that I might be like a patriarch; or rather, I thought that I might enjoy some of my former female acquaintances in London. I was not satisfied while in this loose state of speculation. I thought this was not like Izaak Walton or Dr. Donne. But then the patriarchs, and even the Old Testament men who went to *harlots,* were devout. I considered indulgence with women to be like any other indulgence of nature. I was unsettled.

THURSDAY 9 MARCH. Another day of seeing Mr. Lockhart. Yesterday and today both, he *reported* causes with a distinctness which humbled me. I got my table so well cleared that I was not groaning as I had done some of the former days of this week. At night was at Mr. Alexander

---

[7] The hero of Gay's *Beggar's Opera.* Digges was the best Macheath of his time, perhaps the best who ever played the part.

Murray's, determining a case in which he and I were arbiters between Simpson of the Bank and William Taylor. I perceived that each of us leaned to the side of the party who chose us, he to Simpson, I to Taylor. This I suppose almost always is the case. We struck a kind of medium.

FRIDAY 10 MARCH. It was a fine day. Mr. Lockhart finished his trials.[8] When he took the oaths Harry Erskine said that was the hardest part of his trials.[8a] I said no; for I supposed he did not think any king had a *right*.[9] There was a complacency in his countenance. He was like an old post-horse turned into a clover field. To see him in his gown struck me with a boyish impression of novelty. He made a fine appearance. Crosbie said he only looked too much like a gentleman for a Lord of Session. I said he was like a Lord of Parliament in his robes, and now that he had his gown, he was upon the whole a fortunate man. He had a full crop of fame and money by continuing so long at the bar; and now he was to enjoy, comparatively speaking, *otium,* as he would have vacations, which he had not known for many years, and he would have *otium cum dignitate*.[1] To see him so much pleased with his promotion raised my notion of being a Lord of Session, which had for some time appeared little to me. When he took his seat there was a joyous agitation in the crowd. I began a clap slyly with my foot. The galleries catched it at once. The President was very angry, as he did not like Lockhart's Toryism. They tried a second time to clap. In the afternoon . . .

[EDITORIAL NOTE: The journal breaks off here. That evening Boswell may have attended a "grand ridotto" (masked ball) given by Digges in the Theatre Royal, which was "honoured with the presence of many persons of the first rank and fashion, and was exceedingly crowded, the number amounting to near five hundred" (*Scots Magazine,* March 1775, pp. 165–166). On 15 March Boswell resumes the journal with his jaunt to London.]

[8] Edinburgh, 11 March: "Yesterday Alexander Lockhart, Esq., reported a cause to the Court of Session, which finished his trials; after which the usual oaths [of abjuration and allegiance] were administered, and he took his seat on the bench, under the title of Lord Covington" (*London Chronicle,* 14–16 March 1775).

[8a] Henry Erskine, later Lord Advocate and Dean of Faculty, was already widely known as orator and wit. He was six years younger than Boswell and his distant cousin, being second son of the tenth Earl of Buchan. Thomas Erskine, later Lord Chancellor, was his younger brother. See Appendix C, Chart IV.

[9] Lockhart's father, George Lockhart of Carnwath, was a zealous Jacobite, and his son's sympathies were suspected to be with the exiled family. He won prominence by serving as voluntary counsel for several of the rebels tried at Carlisle in 1746.

[1] "Leisure with honour," a phrase common in Cicero.

Jaunt
to London and Mamhead
Spring 1775

WEDNESDAY 15 MARCH. Got away with more ease than usual. The hurry did not give my wife and me time to be pathetic. I most gratefully felt her attention and activity in having everything in good order for my journey. At six I walked down to the fly, Mr. Lawrie, my clerk, with me. A fine morning. Mr. Innes of the Bank's son and a servant of Captain John Nisbet, Dirleton's son, were with me. Innes was a great-grandson of Lord Fountainhall's.[1] The idea pleased me, and I thought I should get anecdotes of Lord Fountainhall on my return. The servant, ———, a Yorkshireman, was a civil, conversable fellow, and curious sometimes in his phrase. He said Sir Watkin Williams-Wynn's house in Wales was built "in the Roman Catholic form."[2] He meant, no doubt, something antique. At Fala Dam, where we breakfasted, we were joined by Mr. Walter Scott, Writer to the Signet, and his wife, who, with Innes and an ugly girl who had joined us at the same time, went out at Bridgehaugh.[3] I dined at Kelso, and after dinner called in ———, my fellow-traveller, and gave him some port, for which he was very thankful. He gave me useful instruction as to servants in London. He said a servant, tolerably acquainted, could hardly want victuals when out of place, as he was invited by other servants in place, who also invite their companions who are on board wages. But

[1] Sir John Lauder, Lord Fountainhall, was a respected Scottish judge and a celebrated chronicler with a Jacobite bias who opposed the union with England. A granddaughter, Marion Lauder, married George Innes of Stow, Cashier of the Bank of Scotland. This is their son Gilbert, later for many years Deputy Governor of the same bank and a very rich man.

[2] Wynnstay, in Denbighshire, which dated in part from the early seventeenth century, was considered "Gothic" (that is, rude and inelegant) because it had been built over a long period of time and in very different styles of architecture.

[3] Mr. Scott had probably come out on business, and his wife may have accompanied him to visit at Sandyknowe their lame boy, Walter, at this time about three and a half years old.

he said a servant might make money in London on half a guinea a week board wages. He might buy any bit of meat he chose, go into a public house and have it dressed, a cloth laid and pepper and salt and vinegar for nothing, calling only for a halfpenny worth of bread and a pint of beer. At night came to Wooler. Joined company with the fly *from* Newcastle. There was in it only one gentleman. He named me, and turned out to be Mr. Robertson, wine-merchant in Leith. We supped together and drank a bottle of port.

THURSDAY 16 MARCH. Set off about five. Nobody with me but _____. Spoke little. Breakfasted at Glanton.⁴ In the forenoon was in vigorous spirits, and, recollecting my debts, resolved to push this spring for something—for an office by interest—urging to Lord Mountstuart his warm professions, and that I really required his aid.⁵ I thought too of doing anything decent to get money in the mean time. Mr. Johnson might put me on a scheme of writing or translating something that would bring me money. I even meditated on being employed as a reviewer. I looked diligently over the lists of *places* in the *Almanac*.⁶ I thought I would take a good employment abroad, but soon recollected that I could not give up being with Mr. Johnson on any account. I was keen for the English bar, but frightened that my father, from his notions that my being in England would totally estrange me from Auchinleck, might sell it. I thought I would have patience.

At Morpeth called on Mrs. Collingwood.⁷ Had a son of one of the proprietors in the fly to that town. After we left it, the coachman took in his brother (a butcher), a woman and a young girl (her daughter), and a sergeant's wife and a young child.

Got to Newcastle to dinner. Sent to Dr. Hall and got a ticket of admission to his St. Luke's House, where my brother John was. Mr. Robert Sinclair and Mr. Alexander Stevenson, advocates, and Mr. William Dick, writer, who were going to York, called on me. I was pleased with their attention, and we drank a glass or two of port. Then Mr. Wilson, landlord of the Cock, and I walked about two miles to St. Luke's. Was shown into a very neat room. Mr. Jackson, who had the charge of it, was a sensible, good-humoured Northumbrian, and his wife, a decent, well-behaved

---

⁴ Boswell, by mistake, wrote *Granton*.

⁵ John Stuart, Lord Mountstuart, later fourth Earl and first Marquess of Bute, had been Boswell's travelling companion in Italy (see below, 25 March 1775). His father, the third Earl of Bute, Prime Minister 1762–1763, was thought to have secret influence with the King.

⁶ By *places* Boswell means appointive public offices with salaries paid by the Government.

⁷ An aunt of Mrs. Temple. Boswell generally paid her the compliment of a call when he passed through Morpeth.

woman. John was soon brought to me. He was silent at first, and looked eagerly at me. But he knew me, and soon began to answer questions. We walked into the garden with Mr. Jackson. John asked for his father, said he wished to see him, and cried a little. He asked me if I was going to London, and spoke several things quite rationally. We went in again, and he said, "Will you leave me alone with my brother?"—which was done. He seemed to be affectionate, and was so feeble and dejected in his appearance that I shed tears. He asked if I was really alive, for he thought it was my ghost. I shook hands with him strongly to convince him I was not a ghost. He said he thought he sometimes saw ghosts, but that he could not be sure; for GOD, who made us, may make what appearances he pleases. He said he wanted no books. It was strange to talk with him and think of his situation. He said, "I am confined and have lost my senses, and I am surely dying." Poor man, my heart melted for him. It was a great satisfaction to me that he could have so much intercourse with me. I said I hoped he prayed to GOD. He said yes. I asked if he would have any money. He at first said no; but afterwards said, "You may give me two or three shillings," and I gave him three. He seemed to like some oranges which I gave him. I had seen several of the lodgers in a common parlour, all pretty much disordered. He complained of being disturbed by them, and expressed an inclination to be out. I told him he was better there for some time yet, and he was satisfied. Wilson, my landlord, had waited in the kitchen. John knew him as we were going, named him, and asked how he did, or said, "Your servant, Mr. Wilson." Wilson told me John had dined alone a long time at his house, and he never knew who he was till he was brought to it last winter under confinement. I was much softened by this interview.

Drank tea at my inn, wrote to my wife, and put down this journal from the beginning.[8] Dr. Hall, the physician who keeps St. Luke, called on me, and I found him to be a sensible, pretty kind of man, and of a humane appearance. He sat a good while with me; said he could not understand Battie's book on madness.[9] That it was meant as an attack on old Monro of London, and that young Monro and Dr. Schomberg had written an answer to it.[1] I was comforted that John was in such hands, and Dr. Hall said whatever I should suggest should be done. Supped quietly alone, Dr. Hall being engaged. Wished to write to Temple. But

[8] That is, from Wednesday 15 March.
[9] William Battie, *A Treatise on Madness*, 1758.
[1] James Monro ("old Monro") was censured because of his unwillingness to admit students to Bethlehem Hospital, of which he was physician. His son John's reply to Battie, *Remarks on Dr. Battie's Treatise on Madness*, 1758, does not indicate any collaboration with Dr. Isaac Schomberg.

found my time consumed by my journal. I must learn abbreviation or omission. A word or two may suffice to excite ideas.² But then, if I do not write intelligibly at the time, I never can find leisure afterwards. Thought I would write to Temple at Grantham. Had pious thoughts and moderate views of life.

FRIDAY 17 MARCH. Set out at three; quite alone, cold, and somewhat dreary at first. Got a kind of sleep. Reached Durham about six. After breakfast was stout and hearty. Was joined by a plump, swarthy man in mourning. I found he was a mercer in Holborn, but was to remove to another part of London. He told me he was bred with a shopkeeper at Durham, and that his old master had made £30,000 and now kept his coach. He said they made coarse camlets at Durham, and one warehouse-man in London took of them to the value of £10,000 a year.

I should have mentioned that at Durham I sent for Mr. Banks, a chorister, and *negotiated* with him, as Mr. Digges expressed it in a letter to me, about some music for an oratorio in the Edinburgh Theatre. It struck me somewhat to see a man who was probably a good musician heavy and clumsy. But was not Thomson our beautiful poet so?³ Banks told me he had never been sixty miles from Durham. I cannot think that a man who has seen so little can have much *compass* either of feeling or execution, so far as mind is exerted.

The mercer told me that he, his man, and his maid kept house in London for £60 a year, that he drank tea twice a day, and had sometimes a friend to dine with him, or eat cold meat at night. He was like me in one particular. He talked in very high terms of the comforts of London, where he had now lived twenty years, and said, "When I come down to Durham, I say, 'I think you *less* and *less, poorer* and *poorer.*'" He said, to a man accustomed to dine between two and three, it seemed strange to dine at one, as they do in this country. Everything is comparative. He looked big, as one who dined between two and three. How *little* and how *poor* would he seem to a fashionable man in London who dines between four and five! He went with me as far as Northallerton, where I learnt that his name was Picket or Pigott, and that his father had been vicar of that parish and died very lately.⁴

Here I was shown in to dinner with a plumper man than the last, but fair and more reserved. I could not guess whether he was a player or a country gentleman or a trader. We talked little in the time of dinner, and

² A clear indication that Boswell considered his abbreviated or "shorthand" notes to be hints for remembering, not a definitive record.
³ Johnson said that he was "gross, unanimated, uninviting" (*Life of Thomson*).
⁴ Richard, son of Robert Pigott, Vicar of Northallerton; he was mercer at No. 23, Holborn.

when he spoke at all, it was with a kind of indifference such as I have often found in Englishmen. We had some brandy punch. I gave the King's health. He gave "The Lord Mayor of London." I, "Lord North." He, "Sir Watkin Lewes."⁵ This contest of toasting, though not warm, could not bring us together. I therefore tried him with "Mr. Burke." "With all my heart," said he; and then he gave "Great men honest, honest men great." He had been irresolute which road he should take. At length he resolved to take a place to Grantham, and away we set together. In a little, he mentioned a Bob Fergusson at Ayr in Scotland, and said he was married to his sister, but had never yet been down to see him. (I mean to express that *he* was married to Fergusson's sister. I know not how I could have done it at once without any ambiguity.) We came at night to Wetherby, became a little more social, and had no difference.

SATURDAY 18 MARCH. Being waked at three in the morning, when it is dark, occasions a kind of convulsion in the frame of man. It is an untimely and violent birth from insensibility or unconsciousness to life, and shocks our sensibility. There is a coldness in the body and a dreariness in the mind; and the cessation of human existence or activity, which then prevails, affects one with gloom. Formerly, when my nerves were bad, such a scene was terrible to me. Now that they are vigorous and well-braced, I shudder a little, but soon recover.

I slept pretty sound in the fly most part of the way to Ferrybridge. When we got there, I read in a newspaper an extract from Mr. Johnson's new pamphlet, *Taxation no Tyranny*, and was of new struck with admiration of his powers.⁶ I was proud, and even wondered that the writer of this was my friendly correspondent. I thought that he who thinks well of my abilities might recommend me to the Sovereign and get me highly advanced, and how should I delight to add riches and honour to my family in a Tory reign, by the recommendation of Mr. Samuel Johnson. What I read now elevated my mind wonderfully. I know not if I can explain what I have felt, but I think the high test of great writing is when we do not consider the writer, and say, "Here Mr. Johnson has done nobly"; but when what we read does so fill and expand our mind that the writer is admired by us instantaneously as a being directly impressing us, as the soul of that writing, so that for a while we forget his personality, and, by a reflex operation, perceive that it is Mr. Johnson who is speaking to us. I feel quite well what I have now written. I wish I could make it clear in words.

After breakfast my companion grew more chatty, and informed me

⁵ An alderman of London, later (1780–1781) Lord Mayor.
⁶ Extracts from *Taxation no Tyranny* were printed in *The London Chronicle* for 7–9 and 9–11 March.

that he was an attorney in London and had been down at Newcastle under a commission of bankruptcy against one Ramsay there, who was run off to France. At Doncaster we saw some fine fish in the market. He proposed that we should buy a plaice, and carry it on with us for dinner. We did so, and got one of four pounds weight at fourpence a pound. I can when I please be as great an epicure as any man, and upon this occasion I outdid my English companion; for I talked of eating this plaice —a fish which I had never tasted before—with a relish beyond his in proportion to my greater vivacity. At Barnby Moor we had it boiled, and excellent it was. I was diverted to observe the economy of this man of law. He did not grudge eightpence extraordinary for dinner. But though he wanted to write, and had half a sheet of paper brought to him, he checked his inclination; because, having (I don't know how, as I was not in the room) taken it into his head to ask what they would charge for this half sheet, he was told a *halfpenny,* and he said to me that he would not submit to such imposition, for that the paper was but fourpence a quire; and he actually did not use the paper. I do not believe that any Scotsman would have thought of this. The Scots may be greedy, but they have something of a gentlemanly spirit that keeps them from giving attention to the difference between a halfpenny and a farthing. What will Mr. Johnson say to this?

This day I meditated on the subject of concubinage. If it was morally wrong, why was it permitted to the most pious men under the Old Testament, nay, specially blessed with fruitfulness? Why did our SAVIOUR say nothing against it, if an alteration was to take place by a new positive institution? Suppose a man is *too many* for one woman, to use a common phrase, may he not be allowed to have more? The Elector of Hesse had an indulgence from Luther to have two.[7]

We got to Grantham at night. I expatiated on the excellency of coal fires in Scotland, where we have large pieces, "and," said I, "build a fire like—" "Like a church," said the attorney, very slyly. Then he added, "A fire should be like a church. They should both warm us." I had at Grantham an acquaintance, the Reverend Mr. Palmer, who was chaplain to Sir John Cust when Speaker of the House of Commons, and is now one of the Prebends of Canterbury. I sent a card that if it was not inconvenient for him, I would wait on him next day to breakfast. His answer was that in the present situation of his family, breakfasting would be inconvenient, but that he would be glad of the favour of my company to a family din-

---

[7] Philipp I, Elector of Hesse, while married to Elisabeth, daughter of George, Duke of Saxony, fell in love with Margaretha von der Saal, maid of honour to his sister. He applied to Luther and Melanchthon for a dispensation to permit him to marry Margaretha, and received it.

ner. How breakfasting could be inconvenient and dining not, I could not guess. Some men have odd fancies in trifles for which there is no accounting.

SUNDAY 19 MARCH. The attorney and I had slept, as we did the night before, in a two-bedded room. It seems we had both talked in our sleep. He had asked something at me, and waked speaking and hearing me answer him, but he could not tell distinctly what either of us said. Men, we are told, will answer questions when asleep, put to them by people who are awake, and will answer very coherently. But I have never heard that two people, both asleep, could carry on a dialogue at all to the purpose.

I got up this morning between five and six and wrote to Temple as I intended. There was a handsome chambermaid lighted the fire in the parlour for me, and came again to see if it was burning. I was taken with her in a slight degree, and I mentioned to Temple, as a *priest,* my speculations on concubinage: that no man was ever more attached to his wife than I was, but that I had an exuberance of amorous faculties, quite corporeal and unconnected with affection and regard, and that my wife was moderate and averse to much dalliance. Why might I not then be patriarchal? To this purpose I wrote to my old and most intimate friend.[8] I observed Dr. Young says,

A fever argues better than a Clarke.[9]

With as fair reasoning I might say that Matty, the handsome chambermaid, reasons better than whom you please.

At breakfast we were joined by a passenger from London, a Stockton man, a sensible, communicative man. Dr. Palmer called on me and I went to church with him. It is a noble old building and there is an excellent organ.[1] The minister, Mr. Easton, read prayers and preached very well. I was in as good a frame as could be, only disturbed a little by my doubtful speculations on concubinage. Between sermons Dr. Palmer and I walked about the town. In the market-place is a dial with an inscription on each quarter in Latin:

On the north, *Luceo et lateo.*
On the south, *Tempus edax rerum.*

[8] "I am *too many,* as the phrase is, for one woman; and a certain transient connexion, I am persuaded, does not interfere with that attachment which a man has for a *wife,* and which I have as much as any man that ever lived; though *some* of my qualifications are not valued by her, as they have been by other women—ay, and well-educated women too." The letter is throughout much less explicit than this journal entry.
[9] That is, better than Samuel Clarke, the great divine and metaphysician. The line is from Young's *Satires,* iv. 56.
[1] St. Wulfram's Church dates in part from the thirteenth century, and has a celebrated fourteenth-century steeple (272 feet). The organ was installed in 1736.

On the west, *Tarde sed certe.*
On the east, *Truditur dies die.*[2]

Before an ale-house there is a singular sign which Dr. Palmer told me had been there these thirty years. There is a beehive elevated pretty high like a small pigeon-house, and upon a board, which hangs waving, is the following inscription:

> Stop, traveller; this wondrous sign explore,
> And say, when you have viewed it o'er and o'er,
> Now, Grantham, now two rarities are thine:
> A lofty steeple and a living sign.[3]

Dr. Palmer told me the hive is always stocked with bees, and that in summer they are buzzing before the door. This must surely incommode those who sit and soak in the sun, so that the rare wit is dearly bought. There are a number of fine monuments in the church. There is one for Mr. ———, who, being a profligate, irreligious man, left it specially in his will that he should be laid not east and west as a Christian, but north and south, with his head towards his country seat. I think it was wrong to receive him into the burying-ground within the church in that way. It was very near the same as receiving a man with an infidel inscription on his tombstone.

I dined very comfortably with Dr. Palmer, his lady, and younger son, the eldest being at St. John's College, Cambridge, and his daughter confined with a lameness. We went to church again in the afternoon, and returned to coffee and tea. The ease at which I was here pleased me much. Grantham has no trade nor manufactures, but several people of good fortune live in it, and there is a rich neighbourhood. There is a literary society here which has subsisted these thirty years.[4] Dr. Palmer, who is a member of it, told me that at first it consisted of clergymen only, and very respectable clergymen; but now they have apothecaries and others amongst them, and are not so respectable. Any member may propose buying a book, and it is seldom opposed. They buy a good many, and settle their account with their bookseller, Mr. ——— in London, every half year. They used at the end of the year to divide their books by lot. But as a member sometimes got a parcel for which he had no mind, they now sell them all by auction every year; so every man buys just what he likes. He said the expense of their books and pamphlets did not

[2] "Now in light and now in shade"; "Time, devourer of all things" (Ovid, *Metamorphoses,* xv. 234); "Slow but sure"; "Day presses hard on day" (Horace, *Odes,* II. xviii. 15).
[3] The public house, the "Beehive," still stands in the Castlegate.
[4] The literary society, like the profligate, irreligious man, has not been traced.

exceed a guinea a year each member. They meet once a month. He said Mr. Johnson's *Journey* was by all of them thought not equal to his abilities. I bid him consider what materials Mr. Johnson had.

Dr. Warburton was in his younger days a member of the literary society here, and then used to abuse Pope both as a philosopher and a satirist. He afterwards was wiser and defended Pope, and became his intimate friend, and so got his promotion.[5] Dr. Palmer showed me a little volume of *Miscellanies* by Warburton, published I think in 1724, translations from Cicero, Claudian, etc., in prose and verse, with a Latin dedication signed *Willielmus Warburton.*[6] He said it was lately in a catalogue at seven shillings for the curiosity of it; that Warburton would be glad to have it back. He showed me a letter to Warburton against David Hume, which he *knew* was written by Warburton himself.[7] He said that only a few copies went abroad, for Warburton recalled the impression soon after it came out.[8] (He had come in his coach to the publishers and got them. It was a letter addressed to Warburton himself. It says, "You shall never know more of me than you do at present." Dr. Johnson afterwards observed, "Then Warburton had resolved not to know himself better.")[9]

He said that Mr. Gray was fond of *Fingal,* and, without staying to examine its authenticity, let himself be carried along. But that Dr. Hurd did not believe its general authenticity, and said if it were worth while he could point out a variety of imitations from other authors in it; and Dr. Palmer observed that Dr. Hurd's able criticism could show how these were imitations and not coincidences.

He said Dr. Ogden was a very good man, but though he liked his sermons much, he had heard them little mentioned. He said when the

---

[5] William Warburton, Bishop of Gloucester, was a native of Newark, which is about fifteen miles from Grantham. Warburton once wrote of Grantham: "There are half a dozen worthy men there, with whom, for a course of years, I have spent the most pleasurable parts of my life" (*Letters from a Late Eminent Prelate,* London, [1808], p. 40). In the early part of his life Warburton spoke of Pope's "want of genius"; later he defended the *Essay on Man* against the attack by Crousaz and became Pope's friend. This eventually led to a close association with Ralph Allen of Prior Park, the immensely rich patron of genius, to marriage with Allen's niece and through her the inheritance of his estate, and as a consequence, to a bishopric.

[6] *Miscellaneous Translations, in Prose and Verse, from Roman Poets, Orators, and Historians,* 1724. The dedication is actually signed "W. Warburton," but as it is entirely in Latin, "Willielmus" would legitimately be inferred.

[7] It was a collaboration between Warburton and Richard Hurd: *Remarks on Mr. David Hume's Essay on the Natural History of Religion: Addressed to the Rev. Dr. Warburton,* 1757.

[8] It was republished, however, in 1777, and was included in Warburton's *Works.*

[9] The parenthesis is a later addition.

Duke of Newcastle was at Cambridge when Chancellor of the University, Ogden had been well recommended to him.[1] The Duke took out his pocket-book and pencil, and said, "Then I'll put him down for—" While he paused, the levee were conjecturing, "for dean of such a place," or some other preferment. His Grace however finished "for—a very ingenious man."

We had some conversation on religion. Palmer seemed to be a sincere believer. He read from his pocket-book that the suffering of Christ was at once having the effect of repeated executions, to deter from sin, His sufferings alone being equal to many. But that this was but secondary, there being a great sacrifice. I was glad that he agreed with me on this point. But I told him my great difficulty was upon the occasion for the sacrifice; how upon principles of reason and justice we were liable to punishment for the sin of our first parents. "If," said I, "there were a generation of *souls,* I can see how guilt may be transmitted in a series. But I consider that each human soul is a new being, totally distinct from any other. How then can a being, created now, be answerable in any degree for the fault of beings who existed so long ago, and with whom it is not connected?" He said he was of opinion that it might be explained very rationally, but he was not willing, I saw, to enter upon it. So I only said that he should put his explanation in writing. This kind of conversation always produces some degree of melancholy in my mind. I was gloomy for a little and wished to be again in the fly frame, with common thoughts about the roads and the price of provisions. I must really get Mr. Johnson to put me down a short, clear system of religion. Mrs. _____, an ugly, sensible woman, drank tea with us. She was well versed in Mr. Johnson's *Journey,* and talked a great deal of it and seemed to be much entertained. Thus did I pass a very comfortable day at Grantham. I was asked to stay and eat cold meat, but I resolved to go to bed early.

I therefore went to the inn at seven. But I sat down and wrote a long letter to my father, with much anxiety to persuade him to be satisfied with me. Then my two companions, who had been together all day, looked so social towards me that I thought I would sup heartily with them, and sleep in the fly in the morning. We were now joined by Ensign Becher of the 16 Regiment of Foot, who was going to London in the fly. He had been drinking with his friends at Newark, as he was to go to

---

[1] Samuel Ogden, Fellow of St. John's, Cambridge, was a popular preacher at the "round" church. In 1753 he performed his exercise for the D.D. in the presence of the Duke, "who was much gratified at the contest of intellect, and conferred on him, in 1754, the vicarage of Damerham in Wiltshire" (DNB). Boswell "set a very high value" on his sermons and mentioned them frequently in the *Hebrides:* he even "preached" one of them in the ruined cathedral of Iona.

Pensacola, and was in tumultuous spirits, and, being dull of hearing, he roared very loud. He asked a friend to sup—Mr. Holmes, an attorney's clerk. I treated the company with a bottle of port, as I had not dined at the inn, and then we drank good brandy punch in moderation. We got to bed half an hour past eleven.

MONDAY 20 MARCH. We were called before two, which was hard campaigning. My pretty chambermaid proved to be a scold and swore like an oyster wench, and so I was fully cured. The attorney, the Captain,[2] and I came on very well to Barnet. The night was very dark, and there had been several robberies on Finchley Common; so the Ensign and I resolved to put up at Barnet all night, to shun the disagreeable feeling of fear.[3] We were as social as two men quite strangers to each other could be. He told me he had an estate not far from Newark.

TUESDAY 21 MARCH. Rose about six; took some boiled milk and toast to comfort my stomach and make me in a good frame for enjoying the approach to London. The pleasure of a post-chaise driving quick is always vivid to me. But the morning being hazy, I could not have the *coup d'œil*, the striking view of London. Either yesterday or today I had a thought which amused me for a moment. I considered that all my anxiety and all that restrained me from pushing my fortune in England or in India was a terror that my father might sell Auchinleck. I saw upon the road so many pretty places that I thought, "The Boswells came from England. If my Father should do so desperate a deed, may I not transplant the family of Auchinleck into a more benignant soil, and, bringing with me the pride of considerable antiquity, authenticated in the Heralds' Office, settle in one of the best southern counties, and vigorously acquire riches?" But the Old Castle, the romantic rocks and woods of Auchinleck, must never be forsaken; and if the family is destroyed, it shall be by a fatality which no means that I can use can avert. As I came into London this time, I felt less of novelty and agitation than formerly, when I had been absent from it less than a year.[4] I came into the capital of

[2] That is, the Ensign.
[3] The highwayman who had gained notoriety by these robberies had, however, just been captured and carried to Hertford gaol (*London Chronicle*, 21–23 March). Boswell may have been made especially apprehensive because of the attempted robbery of his cousin, Captain Robert Preston and a Captain Richardson during the previous autumn. As these men "were coming in a post-chaise and four from the north to town, they were attacked near Finchley by a highwayman well-mounted, who thrust his pistol into the chaise and demanded their money; but on their presenting a blunderbuss he rode off with the utmost precipitation" (according to a report from London, for the week ended 5 November, in the Edinburgh *Weekly Magazine*, 10 November 1774, p. 221). Boswell had seen Captain Preston off from Edinburgh on 17 October. See above, p. 22.
[4] Boswell was on his first visit since the spring of 1773.

our island as one well acquainted with it. I found Messrs. Dilly as hospitable as usual.[5] I dressed, breakfasted, and then Mr. Edward Dilly and I walked out.

Called on Mr. Johnson. Run upstairs to him and was received as kindly as he can receive anybody. He had with him Mr. Garrick of Lichfield (the elder brother of Roscius, a mild, plain man, but very like David) and Dr. Levett, his old aide-de-camp.[6] He said Beauclerk was very ill, but there was comfort, for all the medical people agreed now that his life was not in danger. The other day he called Heberden, to try the effect of a new understanding.[7] He could not yet tell what the distemper was.

Mr. Garrick observed that, as Scotland was so near Norway, timber could be imported cheaper than it could be raised, which might in some measure account for the neglect of planting. I said Mr. Johnson's account of the want of trees was true in the main, but that he was wrong in saying there was not one tree older than the Union between Edinburgh and England. That the proper punishment for him would be that he should receive a stripe at each tree of a hundred year old to be found in that space. Said Mr. Johnson: "I believe I might agree to this for a *bawbee.*" [8] I mentioned David Hume's observation that he would not believe the authenticity of *Fingal,* though fifty bare-arsed Highlanders should swear it. "No," said Mr. Johnson, "nor though fifty Lowlanders should; for you know that all Scotsmen to a man—nay, not all, but *droves* of 'em—would come and attest anything which they think for the honour of Scotland."

He wanted me to sit longer, but I told him I was in a hurry in quest of lodgings, and I agreed to meet him in the afternoon at Mr. Thrale's.[9] He was very civil to Dilly. There came in as we went out a Mr. Macbean; I take it the same who wrote a book of ancient geography to which Mr. Johnson gave him a preface.[1]

[5] Charles and Edward Dilly, booksellers in the Poultry, had published Boswell's *Account of Corsica* in 1768, and were later publishers of the *Life* and the *Hebrides.*
[6] Boswell refers to David Garrick, as did others, by the name of the most famous Roman comic actor. David's brother Peter was a wine-merchant. In the *Life* Boswell describes "Dr." Robert Levett as "an obscure practiser in physic amongst the lower people, his fees being sometimes very small sums, sometimes whatever provisions his patients could afford him." He lived with Johnson and occasionally prescribed for his household.
[7] William Heberden was "the last of the learned physicians" according to Johnson, whom he attended during his life and in his last illness.
[8] Scots for a halfpenny.
[9] The winter house of Henry Thrale, the rich brewer and M.P., was in Southwark, next to his brewery. Here and at Streatham, he and his wife Hester Lynch (later Mrs. Piozzi) entertained many guests, most notably Johnson. "There are many," Mrs. Thrale said to Boswell, "who admire and respect Mr. Johnson; but you and I *love* him."
[1] Alexander Macbean's *Dictionary of Ancient Geography,* 1773.

Mr. Garrick walked so far with Mr. Dilly and me. Called on Sir John Pringle: "Gone to the country for a day." Found Colonel Campbell at his house in Sackville Street; was glad to be received by him with much attention and cordiality now that I was no longer of much use to him. He asked me to dine with him. We then walked out, and he was clear for my coming to the English bar. I should have mentioned that I had first been with Mr. Dilly at the House of Commons and seen two committees on the Bedfordshire and Sudbury elections.[2] They were pretty courts. Fifteen men of fashion, or a majority such, attending closely to business as judges, was pretty. I heard Counsellor Lucas speak. I thought I could do as well. Colonel Campbell accompanied me while I called at General Paoli's: "Gone out to ride." We then parted, and I called at Lord Mountstuart's: "Gone out of town for a few days." The Hon. James Stuart's: "Not at home"; but found Mrs. Stuart, who was, or seemed to be, very happy to see me.[3] She was now in Hertford Street. She had with her a Miss Hale, and they were eating cold pigeon pie and cold beef and drinking Madeira and water at two o'clock. I joined them in beef and Madeira. Mrs. Stuart asked me to dine today tête-à-tête with her. I said I was afraid to trust myself, but was besides engaged. It was very pleasing to me to see Peggie Cuninghame, my wife's companion, in so great a style, and so pretty, easy, and agreeable. She engaged me to dine next day.

Miss Hale went away. Somehow or other the subject of polygamy was introduced. Mrs. Stuart was clear for it, because she said there were so many men who could not afford to marry that a number of women were useless; that supposing as many men as women in the world, a man who can maintain many wives or women, having them, is not depriving some other men of their share; because you deprive a man of nothing when you take what he at any rate would not have. This she said in answer to an argument which I quoted from Mr. Johnson, and which is marked in my journal while at Dunvegan.[4] I really agreed with her. But I asked how she would like her husband's having several wives. She said, well enough if she was the favourite sultana, and that the difference between men and women was that men could have connexions with women without having their hearts engaged. Women could not with men.

I dined very well at Colonel Campbell's. A Captain Duncan Campbell was there. I then walked by Blackfriars Bridge to Mr. Thrale's; found

---

[2] It was Bedford borough, not Bedfordshire.

[3] Mrs. Stuart was the wife of James Archibald Stuart, younger brother of Boswell's friend Lord Mountstuart. She was Mrs. Boswell's "most intimate friend" and Boswell's confidante; he will shortly find himself very fond of her.

[4] *Hebrides,* 16 September 1773.

Mrs. Thrale, Mr. Johnson, and Baretti [5] and Peter Garrick. Drank some tea. I said we were not sure but there were old Erse manuscripts. Mr. Johnson said, "We have seen none; and we have no reason to believe that there are not men with three heads, but that we have seen none." He again spoke of the Scots being ready to attest anything which they thought did honour to their country. "Well," said I, "that is patriotic. Give them credit for their patriotism." He said, "That is very well." Peter Garrick took a hackney-coach and set me down in Fleet Street, and then I walked home to Dilly's.

WEDNESDAY 22 MARCH. A most obliging letter from Lord Pembroke, which had gone to me in Scotland and been returned, put me in high spirits. Yesterday I had wandered about looking for lodgings at a guinea a week, my fixed price, and was amused by the variety of them which I saw. Mr. Dilly had found one at Mr. Goodwin's, a tailor in Gerrard Street, Soho, a very neat first floor at sixteen shillings; and he cried, by way of humouring my love of nonsense, *"Goodwin Sands."* [6] I own I love nonsense. I deluge my mind with it at times, as Egypt is overflowed by the Nile, and I think I produce better crops. To be perpetually talking sense runs out the mind, as perpetually ploughing and taking crops runs out land. The mind must be manured, and nonsense is very good for the purpose. I dined with Mr. and Mrs. Stuart. Nobody there. I spoke of succeeding Mr. David Ross in the office of one of the commissaries of Edinburgh. Mr. Stuart said he would ask it for me, but bid me speak to his brother too. He and I drank a bottle of claret each. I went to the St. James's Coffee-house and wrote to Lord Pembroke, who, I heard, was at Wilton. [7] Here I met Captain William Bosville of the Guards, who

[5] This was Giuseppe Marc' Antonio Baretti, the Italian critic, whom Boswell had first met in Venice in 1765. He lived at times with the Thrales (as tutor to their children) and accompanied them and Johnson on their trip to France in the autumn of this year. Johnson said of him: "I know no man who carries his head higher in conversation than Baretti. There are strong powers in his mind" (*Boswell in Search of a Wife*, 28 March 1768).

[6] Sandbanks off the east coast of Kent, which are exposed at low water. "To set up shop on Goodwin Sands" is an old proverb. There may be an equivocation in *Goodwin*: to gain wealth.

[7] "Your letter is not a few lines which your Lordship has deigned to write to me as a king deigns to speak a few words at his levee. Your Lordship has written as a particular king, as Charles the Second spoke, when he found a man who was fortunate enough to please him. . . . That you are not in town is a disappointment for the time, as I was very impatient for the pleasure of another interview with one who, though so much my superior, contrives it so that I am quite happy in his company, and happiness cannot be without ease. Ease is the ground on which happiness is embroidered. I am glad that your Lordship likes Mr. Johnson's book in any view. I own that I have a very high admiration of him. His powers are vast, so that your

invited me to dine at his father's on Friday. I was glad that my being on bad terms with Sir A. Macdonald made no difference between me and my Yorkshire cousins.[8] It was late before I reached Mr. Dilly's.

THURSDAY 23 MARCH. Mr. Langton, who had been calling on me, was now in London with his lady and one of his sisters.[9] I sat awhile with him this forenoon at his lodgings in New Bond Street, then went to the House of Lords and heard Lord Advocate and Mr. Wedderburn plead the cause of Annan and Colquhoun against Mrs. Scott.[1] Thought I could do very well. Dined General Paoli's at his house in Hill Street, Berkeley Square. He asked me to take an apartment in his house, but I told him that the newspapers would say that a hungry Scotsman had got him a pension that he might live gratis with him; so that it was better not to lodge with him. We had at dinner Count Gentili, and a Mr. Dossie, who writes on agriculture, etc., a fat, pale-faced Englishman who affected to treat religion lightly, saying, "I forget how many sacraments we have."[2] He however knew Mr. Johnson a good deal, and respected him highly. I eat and drank heartily here as usual.

In the evening I called on Mr. Beauclerk; found him in his easy chair in the drawing-room with a number of books all about him, as in a confused library. Lady Di and her two brothers, Lord Robert and Lord Charles Spencer, were there.[3] I was pleased with seeing people of high fashion, who, though no doubt of the same clay of which we are all made, have had it refined, and are like figures of Indian earth. I had engaged to eat a fowl with Langton. Beauclerk sent for him that we might be all together. The two lords went away, and Langton and I supped with Mr. Beauclerk and Lady Di. After supper Garrick came in and was pleasant as usual. We got however, by talking of Mr. Johnson's *Journey*, into

---

Lordship's criticism on his pomposity is just. I mean his pomposity when he mentions trifling or, if you please, little matters. He should be *Omnia magna loquens*. He should speak only of great subjects."

[8] Sir Alexander Macdonald (after 1776, Lord Macdonald) had married the "Yorkshire beauty," Elizabeth Diana Bosville, sister of Captain William Bosville, Boswell's "namesake," a *bon vivant* with a large fortune, whom he had first met in London in 1763. The quarrel with Macdonald arose during the tour of the Hebrides, at Armadale in September 1773, because of Sir Alexander's mean living, his unpopularity with his people, and his wife's "nothingness and insipidity."

[9] Bennet Langton, one of the original members of The Club, had married the widow of the ninth Earl of Rothes. He had three sisters, one of them unmarried.

[1] The question was whether creditors could claim a woman's estate conveyed to her by her father in the event of her husband's insolvency.

[2] Robert Dossie, author of *Memoirs of Agriculture and other Economical Arts,* 3 vols., London, 1768.

[3] Beauclerk's wife, Lady Diana, was the daughter of the Duke of Marlborough and sister of Lady Pembroke.

a conversation on the second sight and apparitions. They all joined against me. Garrick said he had persuaded Alderman ———— of Rochester, the most sensible man of the place, that he made a man who had been dead some time—old Ewnit—appear to him with his red cloak and crutch. He went with him into a room by themselves, with a candle burning not very bright, and by tones and gestures so operated on his imagination that he believed he saw old *Ewnit* or *Unit.*[4] Garrick owned that the alderman was half drunk, and even with that advantage I did not believe the story quite. But I nonplussed Garrick by an unexpected supposition. "How do you know," said I, "but that, at the very time when you was playing this trick, the ghost of Unit did appear, as you say the alderman was a very sensible man?" Garrick certainly could not disprove my supposition; and it was about as probable as that he should have made a sensible alderman believe that he really saw the figure of a person deceased.

Some of them mentioned a story of ————,[5] the famous wicked parson in Hogarth's *Modern Midnight Conversation,* who after his death was seen by a waiter at the ————,[6] which he frequented, and the waiter went and delivered some message to two women of the town with whom ———— had been intimate, and they became grave ever after and reformed. But then some of them observed that we had no certainty that the waiter told the story; or, if he did tell it, that he was not lying. Beauclerk said that Mr. Johnson was very much acquainted with ————, who admired him highly. Beauclerk said that his mother dreamt that a poor relation, a woman who lived in the house with her, was going to murder her. She awaked with the fright, fell asleep again, dreamt it again. Waked, fell asleep, and dreamt it a third time, and then waked crying out. When she stretched out her hand she felt the arm of her poor relation, who was standing at her bedside, and seemed very confused; and next day when she charged her with an intention to murder, burst into tears and could give no distinct account of herself. He said his mother went to her grave persuaded that this woman really intended to murder her. But he accounted for the story very well, without anything being supernatural. His mother had happened to dream once that the woman was going to murder her, as one will by chance dream anything once. The dream had made a deep impression upon her, and therefore she dreamt the same

[4] Robert Unitt (d. 1738), also an alderman of Rochester.
[5] Cornelius ("Parson") Ford, a first cousin of Johnson. He was, as Boswell himself wrote in the *Life,* "a man in whom both talents and good dispositions were disgraced by licentiousness."
[6] Hummums (Boswell supplies the word in the *Life*). The Hummums (a corruption of an Arabic word for hot bath, *hammam*) was a bagnio in Covent Garden.

thing again, which is not uncommon in such a case. The third time she had called aloud in her sleep. The poor relation, who lay in the next room, had been waked by the noise, and had run in a confused, half-waked state to my lady's bed-side, and so was there when she awaked; and when charged with so horrid an intention as to murder her benefactress, no wonder that she wept and was disconcerted. I said, "You have melted it down." "Ay, Sir," said Garrick, "philosophy is the crucible in which all these stories are melted down." I told General Oglethorpe's story of Prendergast.[7] But they would not allow of it, as not sufficiently vouched.

Garrick went away. We fell a talking of religion, and then was the most perfect contrast between Langton and Beauclerk. The one earnestly and seriously arguing for the truth of Christianity. The other with indifference and vivacity parrying every argument, or springing out of its way. Langton quoted passages from books. Beauclerk threw out immediate sparkles from his own mind. I tried to aid Langton a little. But being fond of my belief, rather kept it snug in my bosom than ventured to hold it out in my hand, and defy Beauclerk to pull it, or rather *whip* it (if that be an English phrase for getting a thing by a jerk) away from me. It made me somewhat melancholy to find that even Langton, who had studied religion so much, was, like myself, unable to convince another; nay, could not make a strong impression upon his antagonist. Arguments for Christianity are not always ready to a man. A Christian may have a good controversial sword which for want of use rusts in the scabbard, so that he cannot draw it. Beauclerk very subtly said, "The belief of Christianity does not influence a man's conduct. I *know*, Langton, it did not keep you from whoring." Worthy Langton with great formality answered, "One could accuse one's self much more than you do. The principles of religion are not always present to the mind of a Christian in their full force, and passions will prevail. But religion keeps us from committing many

[7] General James Edward Oglethorpe, founder of the colony of Georgia in 1732, had been Boswell's loyal and generous friend since the publication of *An Account of Corsica* in 1768. His story (which Boswell tells in the *Life,* but in an unusually confused and uncircumstantial manner) was something as follows: Thomas Prendergast and Sir John Friend were both privy to a plot to assassinate King William in 1696. Prendergast turned informer, and Friend, with several others, was executed for high treason. Prendergast received many marks of royal favour, including a baronetcy, and rose to be a brigadier-general in the Army. Some time before his death, he made a notation in his pocket-book that he had "dreamt or—" (Boswell thought that the blank meant "was told by an apparition") that Sir John Friend would meet him on 11 September 1709. He thereupon told his friends that he would die on that day. On 11 September 1709 occurred the battle of Malplaquet. When the order to cease firing was given, Prendergast was still alive, and his brother-officers joked him on the failure of his prophecy. But a shot came from a French battery which had not yet received the order, and he was killed on the spot.

sins which we would commit were we not restrained by it." To see Langton's concern and Beauclerk's lively carelessness was truly comic; but I was checked from indulging it by a cold shiver of dubious speculation when I saw so acute a man as Beauclerk an infidel, and by a kind of wild regret from the supposition that so pretty a man should cease at death and his qualities be annihilated. By wild I mean that feeling which one has in a sort of delirium of mind. Beauclerk said Johnson did not practise religion. He seldom went to church. He was with him three Sundays at _____,[8] and never once went. One Sunday he went and lay on a tombstone in the churchyard, and was in that posture when the people came out of church. Beauclerk said to him he was like Hogarth's Idle Apprentice.[9]

FRIDAY 24 MARCH. Breakfasted with Mr. Garrick. He was hurried and I saw little of him. His brother Peter very kindly asked me to take a bed at his house when I came to Lichfield in my way to Scotland, which I told him I intended to do to see Mr. Johnson's native town. He said a lady, a very fine woman, said to him that Mr. Johnson was a very seducing man among the women when he chose it; and he added that it was suspected he had seduced her. This was not very probable. In the forenoon found Sir John Pringle, who was cordial as ever and said to me, "Between ourselves, I think it is very rational for you to come up once a year and shake off the dust of Edinburgh." [9a] Dined at my worthy kinsman, Mr. Bosville's. Miss Julia was grown a prodigious fine woman, with all the elegance of dress and scented powder. I was charmed with her, and she was very glad to see me, and frank as ever. Master Tommy was grown to six foot three, had quitted being a merchant in the city, and was a candidate for the Guards. The hospitable, cheerful ease of this family pleased me much. Mr. Grinfield, one of the adjutants of the third regiment of Guards, dined with us; and after dinner came Mr. Phipps, Mr. Bosville's parson, a jolly fellow, to whom the honest squire readily presented me: "Mr. Boswell from Scotland, a gentleman of my family."

I had been with Dilly yesterday morning to visit my old acquaintance Wilkes in the Mansion House as Lord Mayor of London.[1] He received

---

[8] Windsor (Boswell supplies the word in the *Life*).

[9] The third plate of *Industry and Idleness* shows the Idle Apprentice in a churchyard stretched out on a coffin-lid beside a newly-opened grave, gambling with some tattered and filthy companions.

[9a] A Scotsman who had been a professor at Edinburgh University, he now lived in London; physician to the King, President of the Royal Society, an important reformer of military hygiene.

[1] Boswell seems to have met Wilkes only once since returning from the Continent, and then casually, in 1773. Besides achieving the mayoralty, Wilkes had again been elected to Parliament and seated without opposition, and so was now almost respectable.

me very politely, and while I drank chocolade was lively as formerly. I made him a kind of mock formal introductory speech. "My Lord, there being now a happy union between the two kingdoms, and no distinction between Englishmen and Scotsmen, and London being the capital of the island, I come to pay my respects to the chief magistrate of that great city." It entertained me to see Wilkes, whom I had known so much abroad, now Lord Mayor of London. If one could always look at men just as objects of contemplation, studying their characters and variegations, it would be very entertaining. I am sometimes quite in that humour, and think that I could attend the levees of ministers and the toilettes of fine ladies without any schemes either of ambition or love. Wilkes carried us to his daughter's dressing-room and she presented us with tickets to a ball at the Mansion House on Friday, April 7.

This evening there was a ball at Mr. Bosville's. I could not attend it completely, as it was the night on which The Club meets, to which Mr. Johnson introduced me, and which I valued so highly. However, though I was dressed only in a grey second-cloth frock suit with white metal buttons, which I had brought from Edinburgh, Miss Bosville insisted that I should stay awhile. I did so, and was enlivened with seeing a good deal of company, and danced two or three country dances with Miss Bathurst, a niece of the Lord Chancellor's.

At nine I went to The Club. Mr. Charles Fox, Sir Charles Bunbury, Mr. Steevens, one of the annotators of Shakespeare, and Dr. [George] Fordyce, the chemist, four new members since I was in town, were there; as also Messrs. Johnson, Colman, Beauclerk, Langton, Percy, and Vesey.[2] I was disgusted by Fordyce, who was coarse and noisy; and, as he had the Scotch accent strong, he shocked me as a kind of representative of myself. He was to me as the slaves of the Spartans, when shown drunk to make that vice odious. His being a member lessened the value of The Club. He flattered Charles Fox grossly, saying that we had had speeches of late better (I think) than those of Demosthenes. Charles defined eloquence to be the art of saying common things in an elegant manner, or in a striking manner. He meant eloquence that is to have effect; for if an orator speaks of uncommon things, he will not be understood.

Mr. Johnson attacked Swift, as he always does, saying that the *Tale of the Tub* is so superior to his other writings that one can hardly believe

---

[2] Charles James Fox, the statesman; Sir Thomas Charles Bunbury, Bt., M.P. for Suffolk; George Fordyce, Scottish physician, who had settled in London where he was a popular lecturer on medical science; the dramatist George Colman the Elder; Agmondesham Vesey, Accountant-General of Ireland, husband of Elizabeth Vesey, the bluestocking. George Steevens had brought out an edition of Shakespeare in ten volumes in 1773. Boswell calls him an "annotator" because the edition was a revision of Johnson's and bore Johnson's name on the title-page as well as Steevens's.

he was the author of it: "There is in it such a vigour of mind, such a swarm of thought, so much of nature and art and life." *Gulliver* he treated lightly, allowing merit however to the inventory of what was found on the Man Mountain, in particular the conjecture as to his watch. I was keen for Swift, and tried to rally the troops, but in vain. They durst not engage Mr. Johnson. He said, "Swift put his name but to two things after he had a name to put: the *Plan for the Improvement of the English Language,* and the last *Drapier's Letter."*

He told what he had said to Sheridan at Oxford about Home's *Douglas.*[3] "This," said he, "was wanton and insolent; but I meant to be wanton and insolent. A medal has no value but as a stamp of merit. Sheridan had no right to give that stamp. He was counterfeiting Apollo's coin." He took up a long time with a trifling dispute whether he was generous or not in giving a man half a crown in Percy's parish because he drank half a pint of his wine. Percy would maintain that he *was* generous. It is wonderful how he will dwell on a trifle sometimes; like an ox in warm weather running after a fly—if that ever happens, of which I am not quite sure.

I had found Percy in his study at Northumberland House in the forenoon.[4] He told me Mr. Johnson spoke of me with more affection than he had heard him do of almost anybody. Before Mr. Johnson came to The Club this night, I said he was only willing to believe the second sight. I really believed it. The evidence was enough for me. What could not fill a quart bottle might fill a pint bottle. I was filled with belief. Said Coleman: "Cork it up."

This night, as well as some former ones, I had wandered about with women of the town pretty late, but had not proceeded to completion. I was alarmed at finding myself approaching to viciousness, and resolved to shun such temptations; for my arguments in favour of concubinage had, either from their own weakness or by being met by prejudice from long habit, ceased to appear even plausible to me now. Besides, concubinage was something settled. This was approaching to *vaga Venus.* I this night went to my lodgings.

SATURDAY 25 MARCH. Breakfasted with Captain James Erskine, and talked over the merits of his petition in the Clackmannanshire election. There was something comfortable in being with one who, though well acquainted with London, knew Scotland well too. The ideas of both countries were well mixed; and London really seemed in my imagination the

[3] "Mr. Sheridan, how came you to give a gold medal to Home for writing that foolish play?" This was Thomas Sheridan, actor, elocutionist, and lexicographer; his son was Richard Brinsley Sheridan, just emerging as the leading dramatist of the day.
[4] Percy was chaplain to the Duke of Northumberland. See below, 2 April.

capital of both, and not a strange capital. I found Lord Mountstuart at home. He had sent a card to me to dine with him yesterday, and he received me kindly. His brother Jamie was with him. He *threatened,* as he thought, that if I mentioned any of his follies in print, he would publish my letters to him while I was in Italy.[5] I desired to hear some of them; and I declare I was delighted with them, and cried, "Better than Lord Chesterfield, upon honour."

I called on Langton, and he and I drove in his coach to dinner at Dilly's, where we had Mr. Alexander Donaldson, bookseller, Dr. ———, physician, Dr. Mayo, and Mr. Fell, a dissenting clergyman. It was but a poor crop of conversation, though we were manured with a good dinner. Somebody said that Mrs. Sheridan, formerly the famous singer Miss Linley, had fifty pounds for one song. "Then," said I, "we can no longer use the phrase 'for a song' to signify 'for a mere trifle.' " It was said Sheridan, the father, and his son were not on *speaking* terms.[6] Said I: "They should be on *singing* terms." Some nights ago Davies, a clergyman, at Dilly's was finding fault with General Paoli as doing nothing but eat English beef. Said I: "He is a game-cock, ready to fight whenever there is a main. In the mean time he must be fed—George the Third, feeder." David Cuninghame found me here. He had been left by his mother in a manner destitute, and was hanging on to see if he could get a commission. I received him coldly, to make him reflect, but my heart was sore for him.

I went to Mr. Strahan, the printer's, and drank tea, having engaged to meet Sir John Pringle there, where he had dined. The conversation was all of Mr. Johnson and his journey with me. I was lively and communicative, perhaps too much so. I had called yesterday for Mr. Woodfall of *The Public Advertiser,* and felt myself welcomed. Mrs. Woodfall was at Mr. Strahan's. Sir John carried me in his chariot to the Adelphi, where I found Langton with Beauclerk, and also Lord William Gordon, whom I had never seen before. He was very lively, and much of a man of fashion. Lady Pembroke came, and I was presented to her. She was quite enchanting; at least my group of ideas was charming. Langton and I supped. Garrick also came in.

SUNDAY 26 MARCH. Breakfasted with Lord Loudoun. I remember nothing worth marking. Then called on Lord Pembroke; was very well received. Lord William Gordon was with him. Was carried up to Lady

---

[5] Boswell had no doubt mentioned his plan to publish an account of his travels on the Continent. In his letter to Temple of 18–19 March, he had written: "For my own part, I have continual schemes of publication, but cannot fix." The follies of Boswell and Mountstuart in Italy were not published until 1955: *Boswell on the Grand Tour: Italy, Corsica, and France.* The letters to Mountstuart have apparently not survived.

[6] Thomas Sheridan considered his son's marriage to Miss Linley a disgrace.

Pembroke's apartment, and paid respects to her while her hair was dressing, and Lord William showed her a large Italian dog. My Lord and Lord William talked a great deal of mere fashionable conversation about people whom I did not know, so that I could not get in for long intervals. I however contrived to introduce Johnson and the Western Isles, where my Lord had been, and Lord Eglinton; and was lively and easy, at least felt myself so. My Lord said he would be happy to see me at Wilton. The Sunday's forenoon was far spent in this gay lounging, and I in some degree reproached myself for not being at church.

I called on Percy, and luckily found him just going to the Chapel Royal to hear Dr. Hurd, the new Bishop of Lichfield, preach. I went with him, and got a good place very near the pulpit, having a kind of reading desk covered with crimson velvet and gold lace to lean upon. The Bishop of London read prayers remarkably well.[7] The music was admirable; and actually to see the KING at his devotions was a high object for my mind. I was quite a Royalist, and a High Church man—*in worship,* for I went no farther. Dr. Hurd preached from these words: "Never man spake as this man." [8] He displayed the divine influence of our Saviour's discourses in a distinct, elegant, and persuasive manner, and like music calmed my spirit.

I dined with Langton. There were only he and I and his lady and sister. It was rather dull compared with what society I can have in London. There was not enough. It was dining on plain boiled and roast, with some sauce too. But I am used to variety and high relish. In the forenoon I found General Oglethorpe. He had Thuanus's history and Nelson's *Feasts and Fasts* lying on the table before him. He was reading Thuanus. He received me with his usual cordiality, and we drank chocolade. He told me that Basil Kennett was his tutor, and told him that a man who follows a learned profession, as a lawyer, should have a commonplace-book; but a man who is only intended for a general scholar should not, as it hurts the memory.[9] Kennett, I take it, was right. A man who accustoms himself to unload his memory almost as soon as he has received ideas has his faculty of retention weakened.

Langton and his ladies and I went to prayers in the evening at St. George's, Hanover Square. It was very cold, and I wearied. I wished I had not been there. There was something dreary which chilled the warmth of my Chapel Royal fervency. I am a being very much consisting of feelings. I have some fixed principles. But my existence is chiefly conducted

[7] Dr. Richard Terrick.

[8] John 7. 46.

[9] Dr. Basil Kennett, a writer of antiquarian and religious works, was President of Corpus Christi College, Oxford, when Oglethorpe was admitted there in 1714.

by the powers of fancy and sensation. It is my business to navigate my soul amidst the gales as steadily and smoothly as I can. I think Erasmus has a treatise on dying,[1] where he allows much to music and even pictures. I have thought of translating it, but it is long since I looked into it.

I went to Lord Mansfield's levee, if an evening's meeting should be so called.[2] He received me politely. Said, "We have all been reading your travels, Mr. Boswell." I said, "I was a humble attendant on Mr. Johnson." Said my Lord: "He speaks ill of nobody but Ossian." He commended highly *Taxation no Tyranny.* But I forget the words which he used. He mentioned a dispute in Neuchâtel, whether hell was eternal or not, which became so violent between different parties that the King of Prussia forbid their clergy to mention hell, *ou en bien* [*ou*] *en mal.*[3] (I doubt if this was true.)[4] I said I believed that amidst the religious disputes in this country that question had never been a party contest. My Lord, mistaking me as if I spoke of the present time, said, "In this country they don't trouble themselves about hell, whether it is eternal or not" (laughing). Said Lord Despencer, in a very humorous manner: "They take it as they find it." This was upon the whole rather an improper exchange of pleasantry at the Lord Chief Justice's on a Sunday.

I concluded the evening at Sir John Pringle's, who has a learned levee. Dr. Baker, Dr. Watson, and Dr. Hunter, the Queen's Physician, were there. We spoke a good deal of Mr. Johnson's *Journey,* and I gave them some lively anecdotes. I stayed awhile with Sir John after they were gone. He told me that Bruce was thought a brute here, and was not fully believed. I was glad that I was not wrong in my opinion as to the first part of his character. I was calm and comfortable, and got home between twelve and one, being the first night of a good while that I have reached my bed at a reasonable hour.

MONDAY 27 MARCH. Called on Mr. Johnson early. He was gone to Mr. Strahan's; found him there, and we breakfasted. He mentioned his being engaged to go at night to Mrs. Abington's benefit.[5] "She was visit-

[1] *De Praeparatione ad Mortem.*

[2] William Murray, Baron (later first Earl of Mansfield, Lord Chief Justice, was a Scot; a man whom Boswell admired but never felt easy with. He "spoke as well as I could conceive any man to do," but his "cold reserve and sharpness" were sometimes "like being cut with a very, very cold instrument" (*Boswell for the Defence,* 10 April 1772, 11 April 1773).

[3] "Either favourably or unfavourably."

[4] This famous quarrel ravaged the canton of Neuchâtel from 1754 to 1762. Frederick, King of Prussia (Neuchâtel had belonged to Prussia since 1707), tended to side with the civil authorities; but his chief interest was to bring about peace. Whether he actually sent any such order as that described seems unlikely, as Boswell thought.

[5] A theatrical performance the receipts from which would go to Frances Abington, then the queen of comedy at Drury Lane in such roles as Shakespeare's Beatrice, Congreve's Millamant, and Isaac Bickerstaffe's Charlotte (*The Hypocrite*).

ing," said he, "some ladies whom I was visiting, and begged that I would come to her benefit. I told her I could not hear. But she insisted so much on my coming that it would have been brutal to have refused her." I thought that if she had not been a woman much in fashion, he probably would have been less complying. He was vain of a fine actress's solicitations. The play was *The Hypocrite,* altered from Cibber's *Non-juror.* He said he did not think the character just as to the Methodists, but that it was very just as to the non-jurors. He said to Dr. Madden, a clergyman of Ireland, who was a great Whig, that he believed a non-juror would have been less criminal in taking the oaths than by refusing them; because refusing necessarily laid him under almost irresistible temptation to be more criminal.[6] "For," said he, "a man *must* live, and, if he precludes himself from the supports of the Establishment, will probably be reduced to very wicked shifts to get a support." I said that a man who took the oaths contrary to his principles was a determined wicked man, because he was sure that he was committing perjury. Whereas a non-juror might be insensibly led to do what was wrong without being so directly conscious of it. "Why, Sir," said he, "a man who goes to bed to his patron's wife is pretty sure that he is committing wickedness." BOSWELL. "Did the non-jurant clergy do so, Sir?" JOHNSON. "I am afraid many of them did." After all, I am not clear that his proposition is just. Had not his own father taken the oaths, he would probably have been more violent against a swearing Jacobite: "Had he not resembled my father as he *swore*."[7]

Strahan, of his own accord, urged my coming to the English bar. He said Wedderburn was once in such a style as to apply to him to recommend him in the City; and in what a great situation was he now![8] I liked to hear Strahan argue for this, as Mr. Johnson and I had formerly talked in favour of it, and I was so desirous to come. I liked to hear a fast-headed fellow like Strahan, who had made so much money in London, encourage my scheme.[9] I said my difficulty was that I made now £300 at the Scotch bar, and it would be foolish to quit a certainty. Strahan said very well, "Small certainties are the bane of men of genius and abilities. Are they

---

[6] Johnson's conversation with Samuel Madden probably took place about 1745, when Madden submitted a long "panegyrical poem," *Boulter's Monument,* to him for castigation. Johnson later recalled that he had "blotted a great many lines, and might have blotted many more, without making the poem worse." For his work Madden generously gave him ten guineas, which was a great sum to Johnson, who was then living in obscurity and poverty.

[7] Michael Johnson, in order to be elected a magistrate of Lichfield, took the oaths of allegiance, supremacy, and abjuration in 1712 and again in 1726. The quotation is *Macbeth,* II. ii. 12–13, parodied.

[8] He was Solicitor-General.

[9] William Strahan had made his money in the printing business. He was King's Printer and publisher to Johnson, Hume, Gibbon, Adam Smith, etc.

not, Sir?" JOHNSON. "Yes, Sir." Strahan said if he had had £100 a year, he never would have left Scotland. I said I was of opinion that, although I should fail here, there would be no good reason to reproach me with folly; because I should have done well to take my chance of something great. But that my father was so averse to my leaving Edinburgh (having an old contracted notion as if London were a foreign capital, whereas in reality it is now the capital of all the island, and an Aberdeenshire man might as well be confined to Aberdeen as his capital, as a Scotsman to Edinburgh)—he was so averse that he would give me nothing; and I was afraid he might sell his estate in order to disappoint me. "Nay," said Mr. Johnson. "He will no more sell his estate than he will hang himself. He *may*, to be sure, do the one as well as the other; but the one is as improbable as the other." I said that we were unhappily so different in our notions as to be on very bad terms. Said Mr. Johnson: "Not to be at war, they are on as bad terms as can well be supposed"; and he added that he did not see a chance of our being well together unless I got a great deal of money here and went down and saw him. Strahan thought my being at a distance from him would be the best way of getting on better terms; that I should frequently go down and see him, though I said I certainly would, because I would by no means estrange myself from my paternal estate. "Nay," said Mr. Johnson, "I see nothing against his coming here if he can be maintained in the mean time." I objected that I might get nothing. Said Mr. Johnson: "There is no fear of that. In the first place, you are a Scotsman; and all your countrymen would assist you to get on, while the English would not keep you back, for that is the way here." "But," said I, "how many men of abilities and knowledge are at the bar here, and get nothing?" Said Strahan: "There are no such men who get nothing, unless they want application and activity." Mr. Johnson agreed. And Strahan and I resolved to talk with Sir John Pringle on the subject, and try to get him to prevail with my father to consent to my coming here.

Mr. Johnson said my paper against Dr. Memis was very well done. That he wondered how I had found so much to say. He owned he had not read it all regularly through, which he hardly ever does any book or pamphlet. He threw out some of his usual sallies against the Scotch, saying, wildly enough, that "they would say there were trees behind that house" (pointing out of the window), "though they were sure that I would immediately go and detect them. I will undertake that your judges in their robes should do this from the bench." Such extravagance is really ludicrous.

Strahan had taken a poor boy from the country as an apprentice on his recommendation. He asked five guineas from Strahan, I suppose to account of his literary rents and profits, and, speaking of the boy, said, "I'll give him one. Nay, if one recommends a boy, and does nothing for him, it is not well" (or some such phrase). "Call him down to me." I went after him into Strahan's back yard, and there I had an example of what I have heard Mr. Johnson profess, that he talks alike to all. "Some people," said he, "tell you that they let themselves down to the capacity of their hearers. I never do that, Sir. Let a man speak intelligibly and uniformly." (Of the last words I am not quite certain, as the observation was made to me at Harwich in the year 1763, and my journal at that period has been lost.) "Well, my boy," said he, "how do you go on?" "Pretty well, Sir. But they are afraid I an't strong enough for some parts of the work." JOHNSON. "Why, I shall be sorry for it; for when you consider with how little mental power and corporeal labour a printer can get a guinea a week, it is a very desirable business for you." (The words were pretty exactly these; and the little, short, thick-legged, sniveling urchin, as one may say, was shaking himself and rubbing his pockets, while Johnson rolled superb.) "Do you hear—take all the pains you can; and if this does not do, we must think of some other way of life for you. There's a guinea." The creature thanked him, but had not parts enough to do it well.[1]

I walked home with him. Dr. Hunter, the Queen's Physician, sat awhile. Then Mr. Johnson and I drove to Sir Joshua Reynolds's. Mr. Johnson went to Miss Reynolds, who, I believe, was drawing his picture.[2] "You," said he, "go to Sir Joshua." I had a very pleasing reception from Sir Joshua, and read him some passages of my journal on the tour with

---

[1] It is a pity to mar one of the very best anecdotes in the journal, but the fact is that Boswell was misled by the apprentice's appearance (he seems to have been deformed), and made unwarranted conclusions as to his attainments. His name was William Davenport; he was the orphan son of a clergyman, and had been brought up by the Reverend William Langley, Master of Ashbourne School. That he had received an excellent grammar-school education is shown by the fact that he later qualified for an annuity created by William Bowyer for a journeyman compositor who should "be able to read and construe Latin, and at least to read Greek fluently with accents." It should be noted that the journal makes clear (as the *Life* does not) that Johnson's remark about not talking down to people was not made on this occasion. The boy's failure to thank Johnson gracefully was perhaps not entirely due to lack of "parts." In 1783 he wrote to Mr. Langley, "Thus to toil in the drudgery of life, without hope of advantage or of ease; to be deprived of all opportunities of amusing or improving my mind by reading; to struggle occasionally with disease and hunger, and so far to impair my constitution as to be sensible each day of its decline—are the advantages I have acquired from the recommendation and interest of the great Dr. Johnson" (*Gentleman's Magazine*, December 1878, p. 703).

[2] The only extant portrait of Johnson by Miss Frances Reynolds, sister of Sir Joshua, was completed in 1783. The sittings for this portrait were protracted (Johnson sat ten times), and it is possible that Johnson was now sitting for a picture completed in 1783. No separate "drawing" is known.

Mr. Johnson, and he said, "It is more entertaining than his." As Mr. Johnson and I came along in the hackney-coach, he advised me not to show my
journal to anybody, but bid me draw out of it what I thought might be
published, and he would look it over. This he did upon my telling him
that I was asked to publish; but he did not seem desirous that my little
bark should "pursue the triumph and partake the gale."[3] He will assist
a friend, when desired. I doubt if he spontaneously sets one forward. Perhaps he thinks that no man deserves his assistance who does not so far set
forward himself.

I dined at Mr. Bosville's, in dress, it being Sir Thomas Wentworth's
birthday.[4] A Mr. _____ Wentworth and a Yorkshire Mr. Cockson were
there. I drank cheerfully, but I thought not too much. Went to the play,
having taken a ticket from Sir Joshua in the morning. He had forty places
which he was to fill mostly with *wits,* Mrs. Abington being vain of their
attendance. Sir Joshua himself dined with so many sea-officers, Mediterranean friends as he called them; and I suppose they had drank like fishes,
for he did not appear at the play, when he should have been at our head.
However, we had General Johnson, who sat on the seat behind me; but
as he could neither see nor hear at such a distance from the stage as a front
box, he was quite a cloud amidst all the sunshine of glittering and gaiety.
I wondered at his patience in sitting out a play of five acts, and a farce,
Bon Ton, of two.[5] He spoke very little. He said that Dryden had written
prologues superior to any by Garrick. But that Garrick had written more
good ones than Dryden had done. He said it was wonderful how Garrick
wrote such a *variety* of them. In short he said pretty much what I said in
my last letter to Garrick.[6]

There were not many wits in Sir Joshua's places. They were mostly
filled with ladies. Mr. O'Brien, formerly a player, now Lord Ilchester's
son-in-law, sat behind me, and named me, and was chatty and lively
enough. Percy came, but as there was not room, went to another place.
Mrs. Horneck and Miss Reynolds sat on the same seat with me. Mr. Johnson and I saw them to their carriage. I half persuaded him to go with me

[3] This and the preceding line from Pope's *Essay on Man* (iv. 385–386) were printed on
the title-page of Boswell's *Hebrides* (1785).
[4] Mrs. Bosville's brother.
[5] By Garrick. The play, as Boswell has already noted, was Bickerstaffe's *Hypocrite.*
[6] "You write prologues and epilogues with new varieties of fancy. You have
certainly a particular muse to yourself as an inspirer of that species of writing, for
your genius is inexhaustible. I am always struck with an agreeable surprise when another of those pieces issues from your *forge,* for I cannot imagine how you can give
us one of a different form from any of those which we have already had" (4 February
1775).

to Beauclerk's. But he suddenly took a resolution to go home, saying, "But I don't love Beauclerk the less"; or something quite to that effect, for I am so nice in recording him that every trifle must be authentic. I draw him in the style of a Flemish painter. I am not satisfied with hitting the large features. I must be exact as to every hair, or even every spot on his countenance.

At Beauclerk's was a Mr. _____, a clergyman. Beauclerk, without knowing that I had any serious intention, encouraged me in coming to the English bar by observing that a man who succeeds ever so well in Scotland cannot advance his *family*. Whereas here, a man may by the practice of the law get not only riches, but arrive at a British peerage, and have his children married into the greatest families. He roused my ambition. He said that now in England being of an old family was of no consequence. People did not inquire far back. If a man was rich and well educated, he was equally well received as the most ancient gentleman, though if inquiry were made, his extraction might be found to be very mean. He instanced Langton, to whom he said the antiquity of his family was of no service. I said I hoped they were not yet such barbarians, and that all who had birth valued it. That a gentleman of old standing in a county would have more influence than an upstart. That *he* would not for £10,000 be the son of a *linen-draper*. Lady Di told me afterwards that Mr. _____ was a linen-draper's son. These unlucky circumstances will sometimes fall out. I drank port pretty heartily, but not a whole bottle; for _____ had his share. Garrick came in, and said I was as drunk as *muck*.[7] I told him Mr. Johnson's compliments on his prologues. Of Garrick I have omitted that he argued that the Scotch were really national. "Now," said he, "the Adams are as liberal-minded men as I know.[8] But I don't know how, all their workmen are Scotch. You," said he to me, "employ the only Scotch shoeblack in London." He took off Johnson well in these lines:

> Os homini sublime dedit—caelumque tueri
> Jussit—et erectos ad sidera—tollere vultus.[9]

[7] Thoroughly and disgustingly drunk.

[8] Robert Adam and his brother James, the architects. Garrick lived in the Adelphi, built by them.

[9] "He gave man the uplifted face, and bade him look up at the sky, and hold his countenance erect towards the stars" (Ovid, *Metamorphoses*, i. 85–86). The malice in Garrick's choice of a quotation is made clearer in the *Life:* "He imitated the manner of his old master with ludicrous exaggeration; repeating, with pauses and half-whistlings interjected [here occur the lines from Ovid], looking downwards all the time, and, while pronouncing the four last words, absolutely touching the ground with a kind of contorted gesticulation."

TUESDAY 28 MARCH. Breakfasted at Colonel Campbell's.[1] Sat at Dr. Percy's several hours. He read to me anecdotes of Goldsmith, taken from his own mouth and confirmed by his brother, Maurice Goldsmith, a cabinet-maker, who came over from Ireland on his death, thinking to get something, when, alas! poor Goldie was drowned in debt. He also showed me a bunch of papers of Goldsmith's which he had got from him in a present. They seemed to be just a handful of what was lying on his table or in his bureau: letters, notes, scraps of all kinds. Percy had also bits cut out of newspapers about him; in short, many materials for a life of him, which he intended to write.[2] He let me sit in his excellent study and read letters of Voltaire to Rolt, who wrote a dictionary of commerce and I believe a history of the war before last.[3] I read till I was quite composed; nay, in a kind of stupor, as by drinking too much capillaire.[4]

I took boat at Somerset Stairs, I think, and sailed to Mr. Thrale's, from whom Mr. Johnson had delivered me a general invitation to dine when not otherwise engaged, as he was to be much there. This was exceedingly kind, and I valued both the kindness and the advantage of it, as one values an *useful* dish or vase of *fine* metal (a bad simile enough, I fear). Thrale welcomed me with his manly, true English heartiness. We had a plain, plentiful family dinner. Mr. Johnson and Baretti were there. Baretti said Burke, by associating with factious people, had lost his relish for Johnson; as a man by living in a tan-yard loses his relish for a rose. "But," said he, "it is good tan too, for it produces excellent pineapples.[5] His productions are beautiful." Thrale had some delightful French liqueur, which he produced to me, as I declared my fondness for a dram and said that in the Western Isles it acted like a lever, and made me get up in the morn-

---

[1] Opposite this page of the manuscript Boswell has added the following note: "By my *dilatory notation* I have misplaced the breakfasts of Tuesday and Wednesday. On Tuesday I was at Spottiswoode's and also called on Crosbie to have his aid about the petition of appeal; and on Wednesday I was at Colonel Campbell's."

[2] The "Percy Memoir" of Goldsmith, based on these materials, was not published until 1801. The greater part of the actual writing was done by the Reverend Thomas Campbell, who was assisted by contributions from Henry Boyd and Samuel Rose.

[3] Richard Rolt's widow was a connexion of Percy, who allowed her a pension after Rolt's death. This explains the presence of the letters in Percy's study. Rolt was the author of *A New Dictionary of Trade and Commerce*, 1756 (for which Johnson wrote a long preface), and *An Impartial Representation of the Conduct of the Several Powers of Europe Engaged in the Late General War*, 1749–1750.

[4] A syrup of maidenhair fern, flavoured with orange-flower water. Johnson used to pour it into his port. A great many medicinal properties were ascribed to the syrup: it was said to be "serviceable in obstructions of the liver, in the jaundice, in cleansing the lungs, and in helping difficulty of breathing."

[5] The spent bark from tan-pits was used in hotbeds by gardeners.

ing when nothing else would.[6] He said he had a dozen of bottles of this liqueur, and he would keep them for me, bringing them out only when I was there.

Mr. Johnson attacked Mr. Gray, and said he was a dull fellow. I said he was reserved and might appear dull in company. But surely he was not dull in his poetry, though he might be extravagant. "No, Sir," said Mr. Johnson. "He was dull in company, dull in his closet, dull everywhere. He was dull in a new way; and this made many people think him great. He was a mechanical poet." Then he repeated _____,[7] and said, "Is not that great, like his odes?" Mrs. Thrale tried to defend him, and said they were melodious. He repeated, or she did,

> "Weave the warp and weave the woof";

and while he sneered, I solemnly tried,

> "The winding sheet of Edward's race.

There is a good line." "Ay," said he, "and the next is a good line" (pronouncing it contemptuously),

> "Give ample [room and verge enough.]"[8]

I owned it was not good. "No, Sir," said he. "There are but two good stanzas in Gray's poetry, in his *Churchyard*." Then he repeated,

> "For who to dumb forgetfulness a prey," etc.,

mistaking one word: *confines* he said instead of *precincts*. And he said there was another stanza; he forgot which.

Baretti, happily for me, went to bed pretty early, having fallen asleep at the fireside.[9] At tea we talked of Lord Ilchester's family's conduct towards O'Brien. Mrs. Thrale seemed to be for their forgetting Lady Susan's misconduct. Mr. Johnson distinguished well. "Were I a man of rank, I would not let my daughter starve who has made a mean marriage; but,

[6] *Hebrides,* 2 and 9 October 1773.

[7] The *Life* adds: "some ludicrous lines, which have escaped my memory."

[8] The manuscript gives only the first two words of this line. In the *Life* Boswell expanded it, but incorrectly, transposing "room" and "verge." This and the two lines quoted above are from *The Bard,* ll. 49–51.

[9] Boswell's aversion to Baretti was caused partly by Baretti's rough manners, but principally by his scorn for the Corsicans, very frankly expressed in a letter to Boswell on the publication of the *Account of Corsica*. When Baretti accidentally killed a man in a street brawl in the autumn of 1769, Boswell considered him guilty of murder, and said so openly. Matters were made worse by Baretti's demanding and receiving a written apology, which Boswell later regretted as "weak" and "absurd."

as she has voluntarily degraded herself from the state which she was originally entitled to hold, I would support her only in the state which she herself has chosen, and would not put her on a footing with my other daughters."

Sir Joshua had told me that Mr. Johnson was of opinion that the "respectable Hottentot" in Lord Chesterfield's *Letters* was not meant for him, because Lord Chesterfield had never seen him eat or drink; and he said to Sir Joshua he thought it was meant for Lord Lyttelton, who was, to be sure, very awkward.[1] Sir Joshua had ventured to ask Mr. Johnson about this. But both Murphy and Baretti agreed, in my hearing, that it was clearly meant for Mr. Johnson. The caricatura might have been increased by my Lord, as to the eating and drinking, from his fancy. I ventured this afternoon to speak of it. Mr. Johnson seemed persuaded that it was not meant for him. "One thing," said I, "certainly does not apply. You do not throw your meat anywhere but down your throat."[2] He said he did say these letters taught the morals of a whore and the manners of a dancing-master. I endeavour to get as many of his sayings as I can authenticated by himself. I wondered how these letters had so great a sale. Mr. Johnson said there was no wonder, considering that they were the letters of a statesman and a wit; one who had been so much in the mouths of mankind—*volitare per ora virum.*

Time passed on till it was near twelve. Mr. Thrale has no supper, as he dines at five. I set off on foot, there being no coach on the stand in Southwark. I walked over London Bridge. It was a fine, soft night, and the *City* had a grand appearance in the tranquillity. I rung at Dilly's door once. But as nobody answered, I would not disturb the house, and so walked on all the way to my lodgings.[3]

WEDNESDAY 29 MARCH.[4] I received a note from Spottiswoode, the solicitor, that a petition of appeal for Bedlay, which he had employed me to draw, should be lodged with the Clerk of the House of Lords this evening. As I was not quite expert in the form, I went to him, breakfasted, and wrote the petition while he was by and gave me some directions. I called on Crosbie this forenoon and sat a little with him. David Cuninghame found me at Spottiswoode's, who was his mother's man of business

---

[1] Dr. George Birkbeck Hill was convinced that the portrait in Chesterfield's letter of 28 February 1751 was intended for Lord Lyttelton rather than for Johnson, and presented impressive evidence for his belief. See his edition of the *Life*, i. 267 *n.* 2. The *Letters* had appeared about a year before this date, but as Boswell had not seen Johnson during 1774, this was his first opportunity to discuss them.

[2] Chesterfield referred to his drink, not his meat: "He throws anywhere, but down his throat, whatever he means to drink; and only mangles what he means to carve."

[3] From the Poultry to Gerrard Street, Soho—about two miles.

[4] See the first note to 28 March.

in London, and whom I begged to try to prevail with her to advance money for a commission to him. Spottiswoode gave him my fee of two guineas for drawing Bedlay's petition. I dined at Sir John Pringle's. I had in the forenoon found Lord Mountstuart, and gone with him and Captain Baillie, a great connoisseur, to look at some pictures for sale.[5]

I got to Sir John's about a minute after four. He said he was just telling the company that I was like all Scotsmen—irregular in appointments. "But," said I, "Sir John, you had not time to tell them. I have come to prevent you." He had a Mr. Baillie from the north of Scotland and his lady, and I think a Miss Chudleigh, a very decent-like woman with whom they lodged, Colonel Pringle, Mr. Crosbie, Mr. Alexander Murray, and Mr. Strahan. I mentioned my love of a dram; I said people thought of a dram when I appeared as when a goose appears. Sir John gave us very excellent cherry-brandy. Somebody said I talked as if I wished to have a second dram. I said I would not take it unless Sir John prescribed it. He ordered it directly. He is a liberal physician, and I took it comfortably: *Nil nocet praesente medico.*[6] My writing so much about a dram is proof positive of my love for it. I cannot recollect any of our conversation. It was very pleasant for the time, and that is very well. As Mr. Johnson said of Mallet—that he had talents enough to be distinguished while he lived, and that this was a good deal [7]—so a man ought to be very well satisfied if his conversation serves to entertain the present company, though it should not, like Johnson's, be such as to be worthy of preservation. If it is sparkling for the time, one must not regret that it is not strong enough to keep for ages.

I supped with Lord Mountstuart. He had, with some degree of a pressing invitation, asked me to dine with him, and he would send an apology to Sir John Pringle. But this I would not do. Lady Mountstuart was very civil. Sir William Cunynghame came, and rattled and teased us with his fabulous gallantries. The Duchess of Guadignola, whom Lord Mountstuart had adored at Rome in vain, was, it seems, an easy conquest to Sir Willy. He told us at last that she came to his lodgings. My Lord then burst out a laughing in my face. Sir William saw we were tired of him, said he saw we had something to talk of, and left us about one in the morning. My Lord complained that he had lost us the evening. However, we sat on more than an hour. He was noble in his thoughts, and warm in his affections. Assured me that he would use his interest for me, and spoke in the most friendly manner. But he was against my coming to London, as he

[5] William Baillie, an engraver and etcher, was most celebrated for his imitations of Rembrandt.

[6] "Nothing will hurt you if your doctor is by."

[7] *Life,* 29 April 1773.

did not think that I could get forward at the English bar over so many men bred to it from their youth. "But," said I, "your Lordship may as easily make me a judge in Scotland if I fail here, as if I continued in Scotland." "What?" said he. "A good reason to make you a judge—because you failed! No. I could much more easily get a gown for you if I could say, 'It is for Mr. Boswell, a gentleman eminent at the Scotch bar.'" There was shrewd sense in his remarks. But I was very unwilling to quit my beloved ambition and agreeable living in the mean time, both of which are to be found in my plan of practice here. I suggested to him Baron Maule's office of Clerk to the Register of Sasines.[8] He said if the Duke of Queensberry would ask it for me, he would negotiate a resignation. I remonstrated to him against his indolence and inactivity. He said I did not know his present situation. He said he wished to be called up to the House of Lords, as his mode of speaking was better suited to that House than to the House of Commons. He is quite a prince.

THURSDAY 30 MARCH. I breakfasted with Colonel Campbell. Called at several places. Had seen Mr. Thomas Davies before at his house for a little. This day (I think) sat with him a good while. Talking of Percy's industry and activity in collecting curious things, he said he would go to Grand Cairo to fetch a straw. To account for Mr. Johnson's perpetual hostility to Swift, he told me George Faulkner said to him that Johnson had applied to Swift to get him made Master of Arts. That Swift informed him it was not in his power, but that Johnson still thought it was; and, being irritated by the supposed refusal, had been so violent against Swift.[9] I dined at Mr. Alexander Donaldson's, where I found Mr. Murphy, Mr. Crosbie, and Mr. Porter, merchant at St. Petersburg, an acquaintance of mine.[1] We were very hearty, but there was no conversation fit for bottling. I shall only remark as an instance how difficult it is to get at the authenticity of Mr. Johnson's stories, or indeed at truth on almost any occasion. Mr. Murphy told in my presence how he was at Tom Davies's when a Scotch gentleman was introduced to Mr. Johnson; and having said, "I come from Scotland, Sir, but I can't help it," Mr. Johnson answered, "That, Sir, is what a great many of your countrymen can't help." Now it was to me that this was said, and Murphy was *not* present. He went on

[8] Approximately, the registry of land titles. John Maule of Rankeillor, a Baron of the Court of Exchequer, was Keeper, not Clerk, of the Register of Sasines. He lived until 1781.

[9] Johnson denied that this was the cause of his disliking Swift. "I once took the liberty to ask him if Swift had personally offended him, and he told me he had not" (*Hebrides,* 16 August 1773).

[1] Boswell had had correspondence with William Porter about a proposed Russian translation of the *Account of Corsica.*

and said that the same gentleman then got the noted answer of the noble wild prospects. Whereas that was said to Ogilvie, the poet.[2] I could not contradict Murphy after he had said he was *present,* without being rather too hard upon him. So he passed.

FRIDAY 31 MARCH. I breakfasted with the Hon. Mrs. Stuart. When in a former part of this journal [3] I said she was glad, or *seemed* to be glad, to see me, I did her injustice in not being sure of her kindness of heart. She has, I am persuaded, a great deal. She had given Davy Cuninghame some shirts and stocks and stockings; and this morning told me she had got £50 from her husband to give him. She spoke so feelingly of his having the spirit of a *gentleman* that she charmed me, though I was not quite sure that the obstinate dog deserved her good opinion. She was pleasing and elegant this morning. I have found her at home on other occasions omitted in my journal. On one of these, she restricted somewhat her latitude as to plurality of women, for she found fault with Lord Pembroke for going to other women when it made my Lady very uneasy. *"There,"* said she, "is the crime—to do what gives another pain." This morning we talked of gallantry. I explained or illustrated the manners of Italy; said that a gay society of people of gallantry there was like an orrery. The planets were in continual rotation: as one falls, another rises. If I grow indifferent to one lady, I catch a warmth for another, and my former *flame* beams kindly on some man who has grown cold to some other, and thus it goes round. That there is thus more immediate happiness is certain, for people are kept constantly in the delirium of love. But I told her that an Italian lady said to me that our ladies were much happier, who married from attachment and preserved a constancy, for when Italian ladies grow old, they are in a sad situation. "But," said I, "it may be said age is a bad thing at any rate; and we are not to lose exquisite happiness while we can enjoy it, merely because we shall afterwards be worse in age." That one might reason according to the song in *The Beggar's Opera:* "Youth's the season made for joy, etc., Age is nought but sorrow." [4] Mrs. Stuart said she did not think it was. I said the women were great cheats; they were so cold. That the men talk of them in such terms, and imagine them so much occupied with amorous inclinations, but they find very little reality of that kind. She said she had often laughed at the men on that account; and she really believed that very few women ever thought

[2] The two famous conversations are, of course, recorded in the *Life:* 16 May and 6 July 1763 ("the noblest prospect which a Scotchman ever sees is the high road that leads him to England!").

[3] 21 March.

[4] "Joys" in the original: *The Beggar's Opera,* II. iv. Air XXII.

of it when young girls; that she used to have an aversion to the very idea of it; and that she never had any conversation with her . . .⁵

. . . life written. I understood he had done it. For when I said that if it was [not] done soon many particulars would be lost, he said he had taken care to secure it. I passed a few minutes very pleasantly with him. Then called at Mrs. Bosville's, where I was asked to spend the evening, and, she not being at home, left a card of excuse. The only want of a servant which I feel in London is to go messages. I contrive to carry them myself upon most occasions, and now and then sixpence to a porter or chairman is all my other expense on that account. My barber, Mr. Grandmain in Prince's Street, just at the end of Gerrard Street, who shaves and dresses my wig for sixpence, finds me a *messenger* for sixpence. A shilling is generally paid for both. So I am quite a master of economy this time.

Mrs. Stuart sung me several songs; in particular, "My lodging is on the cold ground," a fine plaintive Irish one on the subject of love.⁶ I tried to learn it, but said it was ill to catch, being like a swallow's flying, the notes wavered so and did so dip and rise and skim along. I resolved to get it from her. I was in the most pleasing spirits, and, as she sung, expressed my joy in metaphor borrowed from my favourite *liqueur:* "This is quite a dram. This is the very kernel taste." ⁷ Speaking of Mr. Johnson's roughness to me at times, I told her that he said to me at Edinburgh, before Dr. Blair and some more, that he reckoned the day on which he and I became acquainted one of the happiest days in his life. "Now," said I, "What a number of little attacks will it take to counterbalance this. If he gives me a hundred thousand pounds, and takes from me a shilling, or even a guinea, now and then, what a time will it take before he gets his great gift back again." "Nay," said she, "he never can take it from you." I went home with her, and we eat some cold mutton and drank a little white wine.⁸

I then called at my lodgings; then dined at Lord Mountstuart's. His

⁵ Five pages were removed from the manuscript at this point, not earlier than 1912. A typescript made at that time (also mutilated) enables us to recover the last six words. When the journal begins again, Boswell is in conversation with Allan Ramsay, the painter, on the subject of a life of his father, the poet. This identification was made by Mr. N. S. Curnow from a journal entry of 1778 in which Boswell refers to this conversation.

⁶ A song in the fifth act of D'Avenant's *Rivals.* The air, which is probably English rather than Irish, was that for which Thomas Moore wrote "Believe me, if all those endearing young charms."

⁷ As in "kernel-water," which was a liquor made of the kernels of cherries and apricots, pounded and steeped in brandy.

⁸ The chronology is badly confused because of the hiatus in the manuscript. Apparently Boswell went out with Mrs. Stuart in her carriage, left her to attend to affairs of her own while he made some calls, and then returned with her to her house.

brother James only there. We had a bottle of champagne, and drank about two bottles apiece of admirable claret. My Lord was very cordial, and I could not easily rise and leave him. Lord Denbigh came in with two bottles and a half in his head. At eleven I insisted to go to The Club. My Lord had a kind of joy in disabling me. However, go I would, and having either been told or fancied that Mr. Johnson was not to be there, I was forsooth so full of wisdom and abilities that I would, as I thought, supply his place. But I found him sitting there, and intoxication could not keep off awe. I made a foolish attempt to combat with him. Went and stood leaning over his chair. "Why, Sir, did you go to Mrs. Abington's benefit? Did you see?" JOHNSON. "No." BOSWELL. "Did you hear?" JOHNSON. "No." BOSWELL. "Why, then, did you go?" (roaring boisterously). JOHNSON. "Because she is a favourite of the public; and when the public cares the thousandth" (I think) "part about you that it does about her, I'll go to your benefit too." This was a good lick.° I cried, "Well, I'm satisfied, and shall now go and eat my pigeon in peace," a dressed pigeon having been brought for me to a side table. I eat it heartily and drank small beer. Then returned to the table. I remember there were, besides Mr. Johnson, Charles Fox, Percy, Langton. I was sadly in liquor, and harangued Fox, who sat next me, about his *certainly* being Prime Minister; but that then he would not have the same pleasure from his speaking as now, as he would imagine the applause was given to the *Minister*. Whereas now he was sure it was to Mr. Fox. He did not like my vinous compliments, and went to another part of the table from that where I sat. Worthy Langton very attentively and kindly put the bottle past me, that I might drink no more, though indeed it would have been better that I had taken as much as would have knocked me up quite, so that I might have been carried to bed; for I got into the streets, and wandered among the women of the town, first with one, then with another; but had reason enough left to prevent me from proceeding to the last risk.

SATURDAY 1 APRIL. Awaked very uneasy after my intoxication. David Cuninghame called and breakfasted, and gave me a dish of tea in bed, and then I desired to have my apartment darkened, and that I should be called at three. I slept some; but Gerrard Street being very noisy, was disturbed by twelve, and got up. Went to Old Slaughter's Coffee-house, and drank some brandy and water; was a sad being for a while, but recovered pretty well by walking in the streets of London, which is really to me a high entertainment of itself. I see a vast museum of all objects, and I think with a kind of wonder that I see it for nothing.

Mr. Johnson had proposed that he and I should dine together this day at the Mitre. But Mr. Thrale sent me a card that the meeting should hold

° In the *Life* Boswell suppressed the fact that it was he himself who received this "lick."

at his house. Mr. Johnson, however, was engaged to dine today with Gerard Hamilton to meet Bruce the traveller, and, I take it, his having this invitation was the reason of Mr. Thrale's card, that Mr. Johnson might get off. But perhaps I am wrong in my conjecture. I called on Mr. Johnson. He had this morning received a diploma from the University of Oxford as Doctor of Laws, his doctorate formerly having been from Dublin. He did not vaunt of his new dignity, but I understood he was highly pleased with it. Levett and Macbean were with him. They soon were dismissed, and then he reproved me for coming drunk to The Club, but he did not dwell upon it, for he soon made a transition to some of the manuscript of Lord Hailes's *Annals of Scotland,* which he was to revise.[1] We went to his bedchamber to look for it, and there I won a bet of five shillings from Lady Di Beauclerk about one of his particularities. It seems he has been frequently observed at The Club to put in his pocket the peel of the oranges which he has squeezed into his drink, which he makes for himself. Garrick and Beauclerk told me of it and seemed to think that he did it with a wish not to be discovered. We could not divine what he does with those peels; and Lady Di laid me a crown that I should not ask him. I was resolved to have come out with it slapdash some day. But this morning I saw on his table some fresh peels with all the pulp taken out of them, nicely scraped in the inside, and cut into pieces. "O, Sir," said I, "I see now what you do with the peels which you put into your pocket at The Club." JOHNSON. "I have a great love for them." BOSWELL. "And pray, Sir, what do you do with them? You scrape them, I see, very neatly; and what next?" JOHNSON. "I let them dry, Sir." BOSWELL. "And what next?" JOHNSON. "Nay, Sir, you shall know their fate no farther" (with a jocular but determined air). BOSWELL (laughing pretty heartily). "The world then must be left in the dark. 'He scraped them and let them dry, but what he did with them next, he never could be prevailed with to tell.' " JOHNSON. "Nay, Sir, you should say it more emphatically,—'he could not be prevailed with even by his nearest' " (I think) " 'friends to tell.' "[2] We went up again into the study, and he re-

[1] Opposite this page of the manuscript two notes were added later. The first reads, "Colman told me afterwards that when some of them asked Mr. Johnson, 'Well, Sir, did you see Mr. Boswell next day?' 'Yes, Sir.' 'And what did he say?' Mr. Johnson answered, 'Sir, he said all that man should say. He said he was sorry.' " The second is: "Tom Davies called for a little, and engaged us to dine with him next Thursday."

[2] Dr. Thomas Campbell, who was with Johnson and Boswell at Thrale's, recorded (from Boswell) that Johnson's reply was " 'his dearest friend should not know that.' This has made poor Boswell unhappy, and I verily think he is as anxious to know the secret as a greensick girl" (*Dr. Campbell's Diary*, ed. James L. Clifford, Cambridge, 1947, p. 68). Johnson probably used the dried peels, powdered, as a cure for indigestion (see Johnson's letter to Miss Hill Boothby, 31 December 1755).

vised Lord Hailes's sheets and wrote some notes with red ink, which he bid me tell my Lord did not sink into the paper, and might be wiped off with a wet sponge, so that he did not deface his manuscript. An attention to a small particular of this kind, when its use or convenience appears, is not unsuitable to him. But it is strange that he should maintain such mystery and concealment about a trifle like the orange peel; and he does so in many other such instances. He said, "Does Lord Hailes love *me?* I love *him."* While he revised, I wrote to my wife. I appointed to come to him in the evening.

I then went to St. Paul's Church, with intention to be solemnly penitent. But the doors were locked. I stood a little at the _____ door, which was, though fastened by a chain and lock, open enough to let me see into that holy sanctuary, and I knelt against a pillar and prayed, and my mind was calmed.

I called at Donaldson's a minute, and then walked over London Bridge to Mr. Thrale's. We had there Murphy, a Dr. Campbell, a clergyman from Ireland, and Baretti. Murphy again told his story of a Scotsman's introduction to Mr. Johnson, "come from Scotland," etc., as if he had been present. "Why," said Baretti, "it was Mr. Boswell." Murphy tried to escape by saying that I was not then of such consequence as to make him remember that I was the person. I could not resist any longer correcting his inaccuracy, and told him he was *not present.* "You are confounding what you have *heard* with what you have *seen,"* said I. Dr. Johnson (for I shall *now* give him always his *title*) said to me this forenoon, when I told him how Murphy narrated the story at Donaldson's, "Sir, you never again can quite believe Murphy, even when he tells a thing of some consequence." I said it was hard to get at authenticity. He said Langton meant to be authentic as much as Beauclerk, but he did not know so well when he was telling truth. To Beauclerk he allowed full credit. Said I: "There are few from whom I can put down in writing your sayings." JOHNSON. "Why should you put down my sayings?" BOSWELL. "When they are good." JOHNSON. "Nay, you may as well put down the sayings of any one else that are good."

We had a good dinner at Thrale's, and I had my liqueur. Murphy and Thrale both concurred in having heard Mr. Johnson tell that Dr. James came one day in his chariot (or coach) and took him up. There was a lady in it, whom Mr. Johnson treated with great respect. She proved to be Dr. James's kept mistress. Mr. Johnson was very angry, and told him, "Sir, at my time of life and your time of life, it is indecent to be driving about the streets with a whore." Said James: "I am very sensible it is very indecent for both of us. But such is my infirmity, that if I go six weeks without a woman, my ballocks swell so that I cannot keep them in my breeches." "Was not this a gross fellow?" said Mr. Johnson. The curiosity was that he should pronounce such a saying. Murphy said that Garrick could lead him on to speak the plainest bawdy. As thus: "What is the greatest pleasure, Sir?" "Why, f—king." [3] Thrale and I sat a little by ourselves when the company went to tea. He was rather *for* my coming to the English bar. He said I should be introduced to the King now, as he was fond of Mr. Johnson's *Journey,* and it might do me good to be introduced.

In the evening I called on Mr. Johnson, and he and I drank tea with Mrs. Williams in the old style. I had called and seen her before. BOSWELL. "Is not Bruce a sensible man, Sir?" JOHNSON. "Why, Sir, he is not a distinct relater. I should say that he is neither abounding nor deficient in sense. I did not perceive any superior sense." BOSWELL. "But has he not a nobleness of resolution?" JOHNSON. "That is not to the present purpose. We are talking of his sense. A fighting cock has a nobleness of resolution." He said that Jackson, the Member of Parliament, was a man who knew a great deal; that he was sometimes called "sensible Jackson" and sometimes "all-knowing Jackson," and that he did not believe Bruce. I read Mr. Johnson's ludicrous "Meditation on a Plum-pudding," which I took down at Inveraray.[4] But I observed that it was very easy to write in that manner, that anybody might do it as well as he, as people run equally well downhill. The simile is bad, for I believe it requires as much strength to run downhill well as uphill. At least, difference of strength will appear in the one as well as in the other. This was rather a dull night. The conversation did not flow.

SUNDAY 2 APRIL. I intended to hear high mass in the Bavarian Minister's Chapel, but was too late after having breakfasted on chocolade with General Paoli. The Bavarian Chapel was the first where I heard the Romish service, with a wonderful enthusiasm; and therefore I love to go to it once while I am in London. Count Haslang, the Minister when I was there first, is still there. General Paoli said that Lord Bute now in-

---

[3] Dr. Campbell corroborates Boswell's report in every respect, and even enlarges on the bawdy speeches. According to his *Diary* (pp. 68–69), Johnson was represented by Murphy as having said that the second greatest pleasure was drinking. "And therefore he wondered why there were not more drunkards, for all could drink though all could not f—k." Campbell also records the story of Dr. Robert James—to which, he said, the company all agreed—with this conclusion: "James apologized by saying that he always took a swelling in his stones if he abstained a month, etc. 'Damn the rascal,' says Johnson, 'he is past sixty; the swelling would have gone no farther.'" Two things, however, should be noted: that Boswell himself never at any time heard Johnson talk bawdy; that of the two speeches, one was made by Dr. James and merely repeated by Johnson, who wished to censure James's grossness, and the other rests on the sole authority of Murphy, who has just been proved to be no authority at all.

[4] See *Hebrides,* 24 October 1773.

volved himself in a cloud, *un turbine,* of smoke which he imagined was luminous. He said Mr. Johnson was too apt to take personal qualities of some [of] those whom he met in Scotland for national ones. I called on Adam Smith at his lodgings in Suffolk Street. He had an amanuensis writing to him. He said that he was near finishing his book on commerce.[5] That he intended once to give only his own nostrums, but that he was now convinced that a book should be complete and without references to other books. (I afterwards observed to Beauclerk that this was hard on your readers, as you made them pay for all that others said on the subject. "That will be cheaper," said Beauclerk, "than, by referring, to make them buy all the books.") Smith said that he imputed Johnson's roughness to a certain degree of insanity which he thought he had. I found that Smith himself would not take now with[6] his having been formerly low-spirited, though I talked freely of my having been so; and well do I remember his being so at Glasgow, and talking of "a day in bed—a day in bed." [7]

I called on Dr. Percy, and he and I walked in the Mall, where we were joined by Hoole. The number of beauties today was enchanting. I said that when there were many of them I was kept on gay fancy. There were feathers enough to make me hover and bear me up. But when there was but one, I fell down plump on sensuality. Hoole asked us to dine with him, as he had Dr. Johnson. Percy at first agreed. But afterwards recollected that the Duchess was at home by herself, and might want him.[8] Whether this was a mere court excuse to get a better dinner, as Beauclerk afterwards imagined, I know not. As Hoole and I walked along to his house in Shire Lane, Temple Bar, I observed that Garrick had been so much abused he could not feel an ordinary kind of abuse. He was now so hardened that it would require a very sharp sword to pierce him. Hoole seemed to think otherwise, upon which I very readily changed the metaphor. "He is all raw," said I, "and is easily hurt." Mrs. Hoole was a good-humoured, talkative woman; young Hoole, an obstinate-looking lad, so that he displeased me.[9]

We had a good plain dinner. Mr. Johnson then walked into the garden. We talked of his not being very strict in the practice of going to church. Mrs. Hoole said that he would loiter over tea, and then find that

[5] *The Wealth of Nations,* which was published in March of the following year.
[6] Admit: a Scotticism.
[7] Boswell attended Smith's lectures in philosophy and *belles-lettres* at the University of Glasgow, 1759–1760.
[8] The Duchess of Northumberland. See above, 24 March.
[9] Susannah Hoole, "the handsome Quaker" of Bishop Stortford, was the wife of John, the translator, and mother of Samuel, who was now about seventeen years old. John and Samuel Hoole were intimate friends of Johnson.

it was too late to go. Hoole said he once passed some fast day with him. They did not dine, but drank tea several times, and he looked at some of Hoole's *Tasso,* which Hoole wondered he should do on a day which he kept so religiously.[1] I said he should be put in mind to go to church this afternoon; and that he should be asked if he would have tea in good time. Accordingly either Mr. or Mrs. Hoole went to him. His answer was, "I shall not go to church this afternoon, and I'm in no haste for tea." Whether he had been at church in the forenoon, I know not. But as I had not, I went to St. Clement's to prayers, came away before the sermon, and returned to Hoole's to tea.

He said, "Pope wrote his *Dunciad* for fame. If it had not been so, the dunces might have railed against him enough. He delighted to vex them, no doubt; but he had more delight in seeing how well he could vex them." BOSWELL. "They could not have a malignity against Pope without knowing him." JOHNSON. "Yes, Sir, very well. I hate Gray and Mason, though I do not know them. Colman's *Odes* in ridicule of them are his best things." BOSWELL. "It is said that Lloyd and Colman together made these *Odes.*" JOHNSON. "Nay, man, how can two people make an ode? Perhaps one made one of them, and one the other.[2] The first is the best. They exposed a very bad kind of writing." BOSWELL. "Are there not some good passages in Mason's *Elfrida?*" JOHNSON. "There are now and then some good imitations of Milton's bad manner."

His *Taxation no Tyranny* was mentioned. He said he was not attacked enough for it. Attack was the reaction. He never thought he hit hard unless it rebounded. BOSWELL. "I don't know, Sir, what you would be at. Five or six shots in every newspaper, and cannons of pamphlets, may satisfy you." I repeated to him from Temple's letter the expostulation how "he would not say my *pious,* but my *moral* friend" could "support barbarous measures of administration which they had not the face to ask even their infidel pensioner Hume to defend."[3] This made more impression upon him than almost anything that I ever witnessed. Indeed I can make

---

[1] Johnson had said to Boswell, 17 October 1773: "I do not like to read anything on a Sunday but what is theological" (*Hebrides*).

[2] Boswell adds a note here: "I observed that two people had made a play; and I quoted the anecdote of Beaumont and Fletcher, when one of them cried, 'I'll kill the king.'" The source of Boswell's anecdote is the first volume of the 1750 edition of Beaumont and Fletcher.

[3] "When we have the pleasure of seeing you, American affairs will be better known to you; but I hope you will receive your information from Mr. Burke rather than Dr. Johnson. Is it consistent in your pious friend, I should have added *moral* too, to commence in his old age a writer in support of at least unpopular and violent measures? They dare not require such a return from another of their pensioners, even the infidel D. Hume, the fattest hog of Epicurus's sty" (26 March 1775).

no exception. However firm in his own sentiments, it might affect him a little seriously to find in what a light his conduct could be viewed by others. BOSWELL. "You'll never make out this match with Mrs. Macaulay, Sir, since you are so severe against her principles."[4] JOHNSON. "Nay, Sir, she is like _____,[5] the Amazon; she must be courted by the sword. Though I've not been hard upon her." BOSWELL. "Yes, you've made her ridiculous." JOHNSON. "That was already done. To make Macaulay ridiculous is like blacking the chimney."

I mentioned the landlord at Ellon saying that he was the greatest man in England except Lord Mansfield.[6] "Ay," said he, "the exception defined the idea. A Scotchman could go no farther:

> The force of nature could no farther go"[7]

(laughing). At dinner there was a very good pudding. Mr. Hoole made bring another of them. Mr. Johnson repeated,

> Two puddings smoking on the board.[8]

What struck me was that from first to last there was not the smallest appearance of genius, not an aiming at it, in Hoole's conversation. He was a civil, good man; but nobody could have imagined that he had had tragedies acted and translated Italian poets.

I mentioned Miller[9] of Batheaston's collection of verses by the fine people. Mr. Johnson said that *bouts rimés* was a conceit, and an old conceit *now;* that he wondered how people were persuaded to write so for Miller. I said Captain Phipps wrote.[1] JOHNSON. "He was a blockhead for his pains." BOSWELL. "The Duchess of Northumberland wrote." JOHNSON. "Sir, the Duchess of Northumberland may do what she pleases. Nobody

---

[4] Mrs. Catharine Macaulay, famous as a female historian, was "a great republican." Five of the eight volumes of her best known work, *The History of England,* had appeared by this time. In his *Taxation no Tyranny,* Johnson had described her as "a female patriot, bewailing the miseries of her friends and fellow citizens."

[5] Hippolyta. See *A Midsummer Night's Dream,* I. i. 16.

[6] *Hebrides,* 24 August 1773.

[7] From Dryden's lines on Milton.

[8] "And lo! two puddings smok'd upon the board": Pope, *Moral Essays,* iii. 360.

[9] Changed to "Lady Miller" in the *Life.* These "Parnassus fairs," as Horace Walpole called them, were held on Thursdays at Sir John Miller's Batheaston Villa, near Bath. Rhymes and themes were given out, and the extemporaneous verses which the company composed were placed in a Roman vase adorned with ribbons and myrtles. Later the winning compositions were selected and prizes awarded. A selection from the Batheaston verses (*Poetical Amusements at a Villa near Bath*) had been published in January of this year.

[1] Constantine John Phipps, later Lord Mulgrave. Boswell suppressed his name in the *Life.*

will say anything to a lady of her high rank. But I should be apt to throw Phipps's verses in his face." Indeed *bouts rimés* is a childish thing, a ridiculous thing, and should have no other name than what Edward Dilly gave them to me when talking of Miller, but with no jocular intention—*boots rhymes.*

I passed the evening at Sir John Pringle's. Much was talked of Mr. Johnson's *Journey.* I sat awhile with Sir John after his company were gone, and got home quietly a little after twelve, which was extraordinary for me. My landlord always gets up and lets me in. It vexes me somewhat to disturb him so much; and it has come into my mind that such violent exercise, agitation of spirits, and want of sleep might bring on a fever. But my avidity to put as much as possible into a day makes me fill it till it is like to burst.

MONDAY 3 APRIL. Called on Earl Fife about ten; was very politely received, and had ideas of Scotch interest reproduced in my mind. I found he had breakfasted, so did not sit long with him. He said he was obliged to me for the visit, and would have me to *meet* his brother some day, by which I understood to *dine,* which I liked well, as nobody dines with more elegance. I then found Lord Pembroke, and breakfasted with him on good chocolade. He was in his usual good humour and spirits; talked to me of all the fine people as if I had known them as well as he did, and it seemed to me that hearing them talked of in so easy and rapid a manner made me in some degree acquainted with them, at least with parts of their characters. He told me that last year there was a black bawdy-house in London. That _____ went there one evening, and finding himself sitting in a company all black, he thought he was in hell. He said there were now whites mixed with them; but if I had a mind to go and drink tea there any evening, he would show me blacks enough. He said one night he had drank and whored till he was quite exhausted. _____ Hamilton was with him. That as they were coming home, a great strong whore accosted them. My Lord told her he was incapable. "Never fear," said she, "I'll make it do." And away she took them to . . .[2] In this way he rattled on quite freely. He assured me that he never had the venereal disease in his life. "Then," said I, "my Lord, it is wonderful how people lie; for I have heard that you gave it twice to Lady Pembroke." "It is not true," said he. "Lady Di had it."

He told me that to *air* his house at Wilton, that is to say, to keep fires in it and have it taken care of when he was not there, cost him £100 a month. He must certainly be much cheated. He told me that he would be there from the 16 to the 26, and hoped to see me there. That he had spoke to General Paoli, who said he would come with me. While I was

---

[2] One page of the manuscript has been torn out at this point.

quite free and gay with Lord Pembroke, I could not help recollecting how little pretension I in reality had to be so, having been educated narrowly and awkwardly, and, though I had been from Scotland roving for a small portion of my life, was now an advocate at Edinburgh. However, that "facility of manners" which Adam Smith allowed me, and the incidental excursions of several springs, have, it seems, qualified me to pass muster wonderfully, or rather to be unobserved as an *awkward man.* He carried me about in his chariot while he called for different people, of whom he had a long list. He spoke in favour of the Quakers as an honest people. I did not imagine that he had ever thought of any diversity of sects. But as Astley will pick up a handkerchief while riding full speed, so Lord Pembroke, while he gallops through life, catches ideas which one would not suppose he would.

I had engaged to call on Lord Mountstuart to walk with him to Kensington and see an apartment which he had got in the Palace. I was a little too late. But he excused me at once, and we walked briskly. We got upon our old subject of monarchy. I said, "Surely the *jus divinum* of kings cannot be maintained." He answered, "I am not sure of that," or, "that is not so clear," or something to that purpose; and pointing to a detachment of the Horse Guards which were passing through Hyde Park, where we were, "Those fellows should believe it." This was truly *Stuart;* I loved it. He complained that we had at present no Prime Minister. That each Secretary of State insisted on giving away the offices in his own department without consulting Lord North. That Lord Bute never suffered this. He *was* Minister. I said we were governed at present by an aristocracy of ministers. That the King should either govern himself, or by a minister as his deputy who should solely be supreme. I was in a grand, calm kind of frame in the Palace at Kensington, pleased to be so intimate with Lord Mountstuart, pleased that I had now the same feelings as ever. He complained that Johnson never wrote in support of Lord Bute, who either gave him his pension, or who might have stopped it and did not; and he promised to ask Lord Bute about it.[3] As we were coming out of Hyde Park to London, he pointed to an advertisement placarded on a board, that His Majesty *desired* nobody might walk on the grass. "Were I King," said he, "it should be in a very different style. I would give my *orders,* and send my guards to enforce them."

[3] Alexander Wedderburn suggested the pension to Lord Bute, "solely as the reward" of Johnson's "literary merit." Lord Bute, then Prime Minister, made the announcement of "this instance of his Sovereign's bounty." When Johnson waited on the Prime Minister to thank him, "Lord Bute said to him expressly, 'It is not given you for anything you are to do, but for what you have done.' His Lordship, he said, behaved in the handsomest manner. He repeated the words twice, that he might be sure Johnson heard them, and thus set his mind perfectly at ease" (*Life,* 20 July 1762).

It was near five before we got to Hill Street, and I was engaged to dine with General Paoli. He had waited for me till then. Abate André was there. I was in high regal spirits. After coffee I went to Lord Mountstuart's and sat awhile. Then went home about ten, and found a card from Spottiswoode requesting my attendance at a consultation on the Clackmannan election, at Mr. Madocks's chambers at seven.[4] I was vexed to think that I had missed this, as a little business as a lawyer in London was desirable both as helping to defray my expense and giving me a *solid* apology of *business* for being there. I went directly to Spottiswoode's to know what was to be done. He was not come home; so I went and sat awhile at Beauclerk's, where was Langton. Then found Spottiswoode, who told me they had sat at the consultation till near twelve, and he desired I might be at the House of Commons next day with a wig and gown and band. I called on Crosbie for a little as I went home, and was told that there was a great deal to consult still. I resolved to go in the morning to my friend Claxton and borrow the appurtenances of a counsellor.[5]

TUESDAY 4 APRIL. Got up early. Got from worthy Claxton a gown and wig, which one of the porters of Lincoln's Inn carried home for me; and I bought two ready-made bands at a milliner's, ordered my landlord to make me a suit of black clothes, and he borrowed one for me in the mean time. I saw at Claxton's Mason's *Life of Gray*, in which he introduces a character of him by an anonymous author, which he says is well written, and which he takes from *The London Magazine*. This was originally in a letter from my friend Temple to me, and I communicated it.[6] I wrote to Temple of this with great elation, and in high spirits told him that my mind, formerly a wild, had been for some years well enclosed with moral fences; that a storm of passion had lately come and shaken them, but that I found them now firm. I should have added, as I afterwards thought, that as we plant roses and honeysuckles in hedges, and sometimes adorn them at the roots with borders of flowers, so moral hedges should be made pleasing by agreeable circumstances.

I breakfasted with Captain Erskine. Hardie, the writer from Edinburgh, was with him. I called on Cosmo Gordon, and on Chalmers, the solicitor, and on Crosbie, and engaged to call on him with a hackney-coach, when I was dressed, that we might go together to the House of Commons.[7] I did so. In the Court of Requests I met Edmund Burke, who

---

[4] John Madocks, later K.C. and M.P. for Westbury.
[5] John Claxton ("Clack") was a lawyer and antiquary whom Boswell had first met in London in 1763 with Temple, who had been Claxton's intimate friend at Cambridge.
[6] Temple's letter was written 3 September 1771. It was communicated to *The London Magazine* (March 1772) without Temple's knowledge.
[7] James Chalmers was a Writer to the Signet in Edinburgh, where Boswell had formerly

knew me in my wig and gown.[8] I did not think he could have *extracted* my physiognomy from the heap of disguise. "What," said I, "can you take the snail out of his shell?" I said I wished he would be upon the Clackmannan committee, that I might see if he could enliven it; as it was the dullest matter, the most barren moor. "You should apply to Dr. Johnson," said he. "He has been cultivating the Highlands." I went on, "If you can make flowers grow upon this, *Eris mihi magnus Apollo.*[9] You shall be *Titan* himself." "Ay," said Burke, "a *tight one*" (for he loves a pun, and will make a very poor one). I was introduced to Madocks, whom I thought a sensible but a wondrous dull man. Archie Macdonald in his flippant way said, "Boswell, you can't go in unless Madocks stays away. The Speaker will turn you out. They never allow more than *two* counsel."[1] I made Spottiswoode inquire, and it was so. I was therefore obliged to be a third wheel to the cart, as I said—a counsel out of livery—and did not go in to the balloting.[2]

I had been asked last night to dine this day at Mrs. Montagu's; but was engaged at Sir John Pringle's, where were Mr. and Mrs. Mitchelson, a Mr. Lockhart, an apothecary, and a Captain Campbell of the Navy. Nothing material passed. After coffee Sir John talked to Campbell and me

---

known him. Boswell has mistaken the day. *The Journals of the House of Commons* show that Erskine's petition was appointed to be taken into consideration on this day, but that the order was adjourned to Wednesday 5 April because of lack of a quorum.
[8] This was the court for the recovery of small debts. It was part of the old Westminster Palace.
[9] "You shall be my great Apollo": Virgil, *Eclogues,* iii. 104.
[1] Macdonald and Rae were counsel for Ralph Abercromby, the sitting M.P. for Clackmannanshire; Madocks and Crosbie were counsel for the petitioner, Erskine. Archibald Macdonald was brother to Lord Macdonald; he was afterwards a baronet.
[2] The names of all the members of the House had previously been written on pieces of paper of the same size, and these ballots, rolled, were put in six glass containers and shaken together. The Clerk then drew ballots successively out of the containers, and the Speaker read out the names to the House. The sitting member and the petitioner were each allowed to nominate one member. The names of absent members were put to one side, as were also, for various reasons, the names of sixteen members present. When forty-nine names had been drawn, the Clerk gave one list of these names to the counsel for the petitioner and another to the counsel for the sitting member, whereupon Erskine withdrew, together with the counsel and the agents for both sides, and the clerk appointed to attend the projected Select Committee. On their return to the bar, the Clerk announced that the counsel on each side had alternately struck off one of the forty-nine names from the list till the number was reduced to thirteen; these thirteen, plus the two nominees, constituted the Select Committee which was to try the petition. Each was sworn by the Clerk; the petitioner, counsel, and agents were directed to withdraw; and the Select Committee was ordered to meet forthwith in the Court of Chancery. They met on the sixth, and on the seventh reported to the House that they had found the sitting member duly elected.

about the measures against the Americans: that they had been condemned without being heard, though they asked to be heard. That they had behaved so well during the last war that our Parliament voted them £_____.³ That their assemblies were just the same as the Parliament in Ireland. That they would never refuse sufficient supplies, nor throw off the power of this country, unless forced by severe usage; but that if we persisted in our present measures, the provinces might unite against us. He made a strong impression on my mind.

Before eight I was at the Queen's Arms in St. Paul's Churchyard, it being the first Tuesday of the month, when the partners of *The London Magazine* hold their monthly meeting. Having thus saved my distance ⁴ by showing myself to Mr. Robert Baldwin, our publisher, who gives a crown to each partner who is present when the clock of St. Paul's strikes eight, I run to Mr. Madocks's to a consultation on the Clàckmannan election. The Reverend Mr. Erskine, uncle to Captain Erskine, was there. I received my five guineas, and got back to the Queen's Arms a little before ten, just as supper was begun. I found Henry and Robert Baldwins, John Rivington, Edward Dilly, Thomas Becket, and Mr. Mayo, who was now one of our editors. Captain Thompson was the other, and did the theatrical part.⁵ The partners were in great spirits at seeing me. I drank a glass with each, and my spirits rose prodigiously. In the crowded part of Holborn my pocket had been picked of my handkerchief. I told it. "Well," said Harry Baldwin, "you have been picking somebody else's pocket"— alluding to my having got a fee: "Gamesters and lawyers, etc., your pockets they'll pick," etc.⁶ I pleased the partners much by telling them how our magazine had furnished a character of Gray which Mason had thought worthy of being placed as the top stone of his monument. I talked a vast deal, and we drank a great deal too much. I went home to Dilly's.

WEDNESDAY 5 APRIL. Last night's riot was sore upon me, and upon poor Dilly. I took a little coffee, and then went to the King's Arms Coffee-

³ Boswell neglected to insert the figure mentioned by Pringle. During the period 1758–1763 Parliament had voted nearly a million pounds as "compensation."

⁴ A term of horse-racing, meaning to be near enough the finish in a heat-race so as to avoid elimination.

⁵ Captain (later Commodore) Edward Thompson alternated naval commands with excursions into the fields of verse and drama. He had made fun of Boswell's Stratford posturings in *Trinculo's Trip to the Jubilee.*

⁶ *Beggar's Opera,* II. iv. Air XXIV:

> The gamesters and lawyers are jugglers alike,
>   If they meddle, your all is in danger.
> Like gipsies, if once they can finger a souse,
> Your pockets they pick, and they pilfer your house,
>   And give your estate to a stranger.

house and took a basin of gravy soup, and a basin of pease soup, and was made somewhat better. I walked over London Bridge, met Thrale in his coach, and called on Mrs. Thrale. I told her that I had asked Dr. Campbell, the Irish clergyman, to dine today at Dilly's, as he was so desirous to see Mr. Johnson, was so good-humoured a man, and so thankful for any civilities. That he was quite like a *pet* sheep (Mrs. Thrale gave me the English phrase, a *cade* sheep), went with the cows, walked about the house, and everybody, even the children, gave him clover or a handful of corn or a piece of bread out of their pockets. Everybody gave something to Campbell—"Poor Campbell." She thought my idea a very good one. I went with her in her coach by Westminster. I said that Mr. Johnson, by supporting the Court now, had given room for a plausible charge of acting contrary to his former principles:

> Here let those live whom pensions can incite
> To vote a patriot black, a courtier white.

She said that in *general* a pension was given to a state hireling.[7] That Mr. Johnson's was given as a reward of merit, and without any condition. That he had not changed, but the Court had changed. While the Court was Whig, he opposed it; was then a patriot. Now it has become Tory, he is a friend to it. She said he was more superior to other men in goodness than in abilities. She set me down at my lodgings.

I then went to the House of Commons door, but did not go in to the ballot. Took a boat at Westminster and sailed down the Thames. One of the watermen said that they who fixed the fares on the Thames never rowed them. Mr. Johnson told me afterwards he believed that was not true, and that they were, upon the whole, good enough. The waterman complained of the high price of provisions, and said if a poor man could live now, he might live for ever. This was a curious expression that provisions never would be dearer. I landed at the Temple, took up Campbell at the Grecian Coffee-house, and he and I walked to Dilly's. Here was Dr. Johnson, John Scott the Quaker, Mr. Langton, and Mr. Miller of Batheaston, who appeared to me much better than I expected; for I expected to see a mere fribble, and found him a tall, well-looking man, very elegantly dressed, and, though a coxcomb, not so trifling as I imagined.

We talked of speaking in public. Mr. Johnson said that one of the first wits of this country, Isaac Hawkins Browne, got into Parliament and never opened his mouth. Mr. Johnson said that it was more disgraceful

---

[7] "State hireling" is from Johnson's own definition of the word "pension": "An allowance made to any one without an equivalent. In England it is generally understood to mean pay given to a state hireling for treason to his country." The couplet is also Johnson's: *London,* ll. 51–52 (read "reign" for "live").

not to try to speak than to try and fail, as it was more disgraceful not to fight than to fight and be beat. His argument here I thought fallacious; for if a man does not speak it may be said that he would have done very well had he tried, whereas if he has tried and failed, there is nothing to be said for him. I asked, "Why, then, is it thought universally disgraceful for a man not to fight, and not disgraceful not to speak in public?" "Because," said he, "there may be other reasons for a man's not speaking in public than want of resolution. He may have nothing to say" (laughing). "You know _____ [8] makes courage the greatest of all virtues; because unless a man has that, there is no security for his preserving the others."

Mr. Johnson said that the acts against bribery were intended to prevent upstarts with money from getting into Parliament. That if he were a gentleman of estate [he] would turn out all tenants who did not vote for the candidate whom he supported. Worthy Langton contended that this was checking the freedom of election. Mr. Johnson said the law did not mean that the privilege of voting should be independent of old family interest, of permanent property.

At seven I went to Madocks's chambers to another Clackmannan consultation; came to Dilly's again at night, drank some old hock, and went to bed cool.

THURSDAY 6 APRIL. As my journal is written from imperfect notes a good while after the days have passed (I now write at Mamhead, April 27), several particulars, such as where I breakfasted, sometimes have escaped my record. This day at ten the Clackmannan committee sat. I was much pleased with Mr. Montagu, the chairman, and Sir George Savile. Madocks was heavy, Rae's barbarous Bath-metal English shocking to my ear. [9] Macdonald was pert, and disgusted me, though he was lively and spoke very good language. He was like a boy whipping a top while he pleaded: he licked away and looked up in the faces of the committee. Crosbie was manly and clear, though his pronunciation was pretty much Scotch. I felt a great keenness to speak, but could only sit by in my ordinary dress.

Burke and his brother came and sat awhile in the Court of Chancery, where this committee met. I maintained a strange proposition to Burke:

[8] Boswell neglected to fill this blank, and, in the *Life*, saved labour by generalizing: "courage is reckoned." Johnson probably said "Aristotle." In the *Life of Pope* he says, "Aristotle is praised for naming fortitude first of the cardinal virtues, as that without which no other virtue can steadily be practised." "Fortitude" translates ἀνδρεία of the *Nicomachaean Ethics*, III. vi. Johnson's manuscript of the *Life of Pope*, now in the Pierpont Morgan Library, reads "courage," as here in Boswell.

[9] David Rae, later Lord Eskgrove. On 6 April 1772 Boswell had said, "As people had a vanity in founding new sects, Mr. Rae had a mind to found a new language" (*Boswell for the Defence*). Bath-metal was a kind of brass used in cheap, flashy jewelry —pinchbeck.

that it was better for a Scotsman and an Irishman to preserve so much of their native accent and not to be quite perfect in English, because it was unnatural. I would have all the birds of the air to retain somewhat of their own notes: a blackbird to sing like a blackbird, and a thrush like a thrush, and not a blackbird and other birds to sing all like some other bird. Burke agreed with me. Englishmen would laugh heartily, and say, "Here an Irishman and a Scotsman, each with his own country tone strong, attempt to prove that it is better to have it." I said it was unnatural to hear a Scotsman speaking perfect English. He appeared a machine. I instanced Wedderburn. "A man of wood," said I, "or a man of brass." "Ay, a man of *brass*," cried Burke. Lord Lisburne and I had afterwards a dispute on this subject.[1] My metaphor of the birds he opposed by saying, "A Scotsman may do very well with his own tone in Coll; but if he comes into the House of Commons, it will be better if he speaks English. A bagpipe may do very well in the Highlands, but I would not introduce it into Bach's concert." "This," said I, "shows what it is to argue in metaphors. One is just as good as another." But I maintained to my Lord that it put me in a passion to hear a Scotsman speaking in a perfect English tone. It was a false voice. He speaks as if he had some pipe or speaking instrument in his mouth. And I thought always, "Can't he take this confounded pipe out, and let us hear him speak with his own organs?" I do still think I am right. Lord Lisburne said Sir Gilbert Elliot had just a little of the Scotch accent.[1a] "Well," said I, "he has just what I wish: as much of the native note as to mark his species." I said to Burke, "You would not have a man use Scotch words, as to say a *trance* for a *passage* in a house." "No," said he, "that is a different language." "But," said I, "is it not better, too, to try to pronounce not in the broad Scotch way and to say *passage* and not *pawssage*." "Yes," said Burke, "when once you're *taught* how they pronounce in England; but don't *try* at English pronunciation." Said Richard Burke, "Better say *pawssage* than *pissage*." And indeed some Scotsmen, such as Rae, the advocate, make blunders as bad as this.

I dined at Tom Davies's, where were Mr. Johnson, Mr. Moody, one of the players of Drury Lane Theatre, and a Mr. Hickey, a painter.

Mr. Johnson, as usual, abused Colley Cibber. He said it was wonderful that a man who for forty years had lived with the great and the witty should have acquired so ill the talents of conversation. That he had but half to furnish, for one half of what he spoke was oaths. He, however, allowed considerable merit to his comedies, and said there was no reason

[1] Presumably during Boswell's visit in Devonshire later in the month. See below, 23 April.
[1a] Sir Gilbert Elliot was a very able orator (in the *Life* he was Boswell's model for Scotsmen); M.P. for Roxburgh.

to believe they were not written by himself. Davies said he was the first dramatic writer who introduced genteel ladies upon the stage. "No," said Mr. Johnson, and instanced several characters in comedies before his time. "I mean," said Davies (to try to defend himself from a charge of ignorance), "genteel moral characters." I think," said Hickey, "gentility and morality are inseparable." "By no means," said I. "The genteelest characters are often the most immoral. Does not Lord Chesterfield give precepts for uniting wickedness and graces? A man is not genteel when he gets drunk; but most vices may be committed very genteelly. A man may debauch his friend's wife genteelly. He may cheat at cards genteelly." "I do not think *that* is genteel," said Hickey. "Sir," said I, "it may not be like a gentleman but it is genteel." Said Mr. Johnson, "You are meaning two different things. One means exterior grace; the other honour. It is certain that one may be very immoral with exterior grace. Lovelace, in *Clarissa,* is a very genteel and a very wicked character. Tom Hervey, who died t'other day loaded with all kinds of vice, was one of the genteelest men that ever lived." [2] Tom Davies instanced Charles II. Mr. Johnson got into a generous rage. "Charles II," said he, "was licentious in his practice; but he always had a reverence for what was good. Charles II knew his people and rewarded merit. The Church was at no time better filled than in his reign. He was the best king we have had from his time till the reign of his present Majesty, except James II, who was a good king, but unhappily believed that it was necessary for the salvation of his subjects that they should be Roman Catholics. *He* had the merit of endeavouring to do what he thought was for the salvation of the souls of his subjects, till he lost a great empire. *We,* who thought that we should *not* be saved if we were Roman Catholics, had the merit of maintaining our religion at the expense of submitting ourselves to the government of King William (for it could not be done otherwise), to the government of one of the most worthless scoundrels that ever existed. No; Charles II was not such a man as George II. He did not destroy his father's will. He was not a thief. He took money from France. But he did not betray those over whom he ruled. He did not let the French fleet pass ours. George I knew nothing, and desired to know nothing; did nothing, and desired to do nothing; and the only good thing that is told of him is that he wished to restore the crown to its hereditary successor." He roared with prodigious violence against George II. When he ceased Moody interjected in an Irish tone, "Ah, poor George II." There was a fine print of him on horseback hanging behind Mr. Johnson. Mrs. Davies told him so. "Madam," said Mr. Johnson, laugh-

[2] The Hon. Thomas Hervey, second son of the first Earl of Bristol, had died 20 January 1775.

ing, "be where he will, he was a scoundrel." Moody seemed to be pleased, and I imagined he was one of the Irish Jacobites.

I mentioned that Dr. Campbell had come from Ireland to London, principally to see Mr. Johnson. He growled at this. Said Tom Davies, "Why you know, Sir, there came a man from Spain to see Livy; and Corelli came to England to see Purcell, and when he heard he was dead, went back again to Italy." [3] Said Mr. Johnson, "I should not have wished to be dead to disappoint Campbell, had he been so foolish; but I should have wished to have been a hundred miles off." This was apparently perverse; and I do believe it would not have been Mr. Johnson's real way of thinking. He would have liked a man who came so far to see him. He laughed with some complacency when I told him Campbell's odd expression to me of him, that having seen such a man was a thing to talk of a century hence—as if he could live so long.

Judge Page, of whom Mr. Johnson speaks in his *Life of Savage,* was mentioned. [4] Said Davies, "He will live as long as Mr. Johnson's *page.*" "What a pun," said I. "Nay," said Tom, " 'tis a good one, for it's a *lasting* one."

We got into an argument whether the judges who went to India should trade. [5] Mr. Johnson warmly maintained that they might, for why should not judges get riches, as well as those who deserved them less? I said they should have sufficient salaries, and have nothing to take their attention from the affairs of the public. "Sir," said Mr. Johnson, "no judge can give his whole attention to judging. And it is very proper that he should employ what time he has to himself, for his advantage in the most profitable manner that he can." "Then," said Davies, who enlivened the dispute by making it somewhat dramatic, "he may become an insurer; and when he is going to the bench, he may be stopped, 'Your Lordship cannot go yet. Here is a bunch of invoices; so many ships are going to sail.' " "Then," said Mr. Johnson, "you may say a judge should not have a house. They may come and say, 'Your Lordship's house is on fire'; and so instead of minding the business of his court, he is to be occupied in getting the engine with the greatest speed. There is no end of this. Every judge who has land trades to a certain extent in corn or cattle, and in the land itself, undoubtedly. His steward acts for him, as clerks for a great merchant. A judge may be a farmer; but he's not to geld his own pigs. A judge

[3] Davies was mistaken in this, as Dr. Burney later pointed out (notes to the third edition of the *Life*).

[4] Sir Francis Page, the judge at Savage's trial in 1727.

[5] Robert Chambers, a member of The Club, with the three other judges of the supreme court of judicature in Bengal, had sailed for India just a year before.

may play a little at cards for his amusement; but he's not to play at marbles, or at chuck-farthing in the piazza. No, Sir, there is no profession to which a man gives a very great proportion of his time. It is wonderful, when a calculation is made, how little the mind is actually employed in the discharge of any profession. No man would be a judge upon the condition of being obliged to be totally a judge. The best-employed lawyer has his mind at work but for a small proportion of his time. A great deal of his occupation is merely mechanical. I once wrote for a magazine. I made a calculation that if I should write but a page a day, at the same rate, I should in ten years write nine volumes in folio of an ordinary size and print." BOSWELL. "Such as Carte's *History?*" [6] JOHNSON. "Yes, Sir. When a man writes from his own mind, he writes very rapidly." (*He* certainly does, who has a mind stored with knowledge and teeming with imagery.) "The greatest part of a writer's time is spent in reading in order to write. A man will turn over half a library to make one book."

I argued keenly against the judge's trading, and gave Hale as an instance of a perfect judge. Mr. Johnson said Hale left a great estate. No matter. That was because what he got accumulated without any risk and anxiety in him. [7]

While the dispute went on, Moody once tried to say something upon our side. Tom Davies clapped him on the back to encourage him. (Beauclerk, to whom I told this, said that he could not conceive a more humbling situation than to be clapped on the back by Tom Davies.) Mr. Johnson demolished poor Moody by a word or two, and concluded, "You're an Irishman." In a little Moody was, or affected to be, convinced by Mr. Johnson. "Nay," said I, "if you go over, *we'll* say you're an Irishman." Moody was an old acquaintance of mine. Poor Derrick introduced him to me in the year 1760. [8] He sat by today with a kind of timorous humour that durst not play for fear of Mr. Johnson. He was once in danger of a reproof for bringing in Scripture too lightly. Talking I think of Reed's *Dido: a Tragedy,* he said it was no more like a tragedy than the first chapter of Genesis. Tom gave him a significant hush; and Mr. Johnson either did not hear it, or took no notice.

We spoke of Rolt, to whose dictionary of commerce Mr. Johnson has written the Preface. He said he never saw either the man or the book. But

[6] Thomas Carte announced the plan of his *General History of England* in 1738, and requested subscriptions to carry on his great project. Volumes were published in 1748, 1750, 1752, and 1755.

[7] In the *Life,* Boswell puts the last two sentences in direct discourse, assigning the second to himself.

[8] Samuel Derrick in 1760 had shown Boswell the low life of London "in all its variety of departments, both literary and sportive." At that time John Moody had just created his celebrated character of Sir Callaghan O'Brallaghan in Macklin's *Love à la Mode.*

Rolt used to say, "I have been with Sam Johnson." He was such a fellow that when he went over to Dublin, he published Akenside's *Pleasures of Imagination* (which had come out with no name) with his own name to it, and was received for a while as the author of that poem.[9] He said old Gardner the bookseller employed Rolt and Smart to write a monthly publication called *The Visiter*.[1] "There was a formal written contract, which Allen the printer saw. Gardner thought as you do of the judge. They were bound to write nothing else; they were to have, I think, a third of the profits of this sixpenny pamphlet; and the contract was for ninety-nine years.[2] I wish I had thought of giving this to Thurlow in the cause about literary property.[3] What an excellent instance would it have been of the oppression of booksellers to poor authors." Davies, jealous for *the trade,* said Gardner was not properly a bookseller. "Nay," said Mr. Johnson, "he certainly was. He had served his time regularly, was a member of the Stationers'

[9] No edition with Rolt's name on the title-page is known. The report is a myth, or, as Malone suggested to Boswell, "the poem being then anonymous, Rolt acquiesced in its being attributed to him in conversation" (*Life,* Boswell's note to beginning of 1761).

[1] *The Universal Visiter* appeared in 1756, the same year as Rolt's *New Dictionary of Trade and Commerce.* Johnson contributed six articles in order to assist his friend Christopher Smart, "with whose unhappy vacillation of mind he sincerely sympathized" (*Life,* beginning of 1756).

[2] In the second edition of the *Life,* Boswell added a note expressing doubt whether he or Johnson had not been mistaken in the terms of this extraordinary contract. The actual document has since turned up. It shows that Rolt and Smart were each to have one-fourth part of the clear profits, and that all the parties bound themselves not to engage "in any work or undertaking of a like nature" as long as the contract continued in force. The period *was* ninety-nine years, but there was a saving clause freeing any or all of the parties if the magazine failed to pay its expenses for six months. It was not profitable and expired with the twelfth monthly issue.

[3] Boswell himself had been greatly involved in this victory over the London booksellers, who had generally maintained, in spite of the Copyright Act, that an author's copyright existed in perpetuity and could be transferred to his assignees. In 1769, in the case of Millar v. Taylor, the Court of King's Bench had ruled that there was perpetual copyright at common law. The London booksellers secured an injunction from the Court of Chancery to stop Donaldson, the Edinburgh publisher, from issuing reprints in England, and then raised an action (Hinton v. Donaldson) against him in Scotland, to which the decision in Millar v. Taylor did not extend. In July 1773 Boswell won an almost unanimous verdict for Donaldson in the Court of Session in this cause, and at the end of the year published a pamphlet giving the speeches of the Scots judges. Donaldson had meantime appealed to the House of Lords from the injunction of the Court of Chancery, and Boswell's pamphlet appeared just in time to be read before the appeal (Donaldson v. Becket) came up. Donaldson's counsel, Edward Thurlow, later Lord Chancellor, argued eloquently against perpetual copyright, and on 22 February 1774 the Lords reversed Millar v. Taylor and rendered a decision coinciding with that of the Court of Session. Donaldson v. Becket is still the basis of all English and American copyright acts.

Company, kept a shop in the face of mankind, purchased copyright, was a *bibliopole*,⁴ Sir, in every sense. I wrote for some months in *The Visiter* for poor Smart while he was mad, not knowing the terms on which he wrote, and thinking I was doing him good. I hoped his wits would soon return to him. Mine returned to me, and I wrote in *The Visiter* no longer." We had a good dinner at Davies's, and drank tea too, very comfortably. I supped at Lord Mountstuart's. Mr. David Ross was there.⁵ He talked of the Duke of Buccleuch's imagining that he should be Prime Minister for Scotland, and that Harry Dundas was to act along with him; and such was their scheme. Lord Mountstuart heard this with contempt, and said of Dundas, "I hate the fellow." My Lord showed me tonight how he could adapt himself to a Scotch company. He made bumpers of claret circulate quickly, drank "the beggar's benison"⁶ and a number of such toasts, and we three finished five bottles. I liked very well to hear him and Ross talk of the *interest* of the Bute family; and I hoped that I and some of my friends should be the better for it.

FRIDAY 7 APRIL. At eight o'clock was at Mr. Stuart's and saw the *show,* as I called it, of *his Honour* breakfasting at that early hour, that he might be at the Haslemere committee at ten.⁷ Mrs. Stuart was amiable as ever. He and I went to Westminster Hall. I walked a little in it with Lord John Cavendish, who was on Erskine's committee, and talked with him on a hasty resolution which they had made yesterday, not to *judge* of the *sufficiency* of qualifications. I had known Lord John at The Hague. Erskine in a very handsome manner declined giving the committee any farther trouble, as their resolution of yesterday, which went deeper than an answer to the question which he put, had precluded him.⁸ I said, in

⁴ Johnson is introducing a word into the language, and he and Boswell know it.
⁵ Another actor; the manager of the Edinburgh Theatre Royal.
⁶ "May your prick and purse never fail you." The toast takes its name from its alleged origin, which is recorded as follows in the *Records of the Most Ancient and Puissant Order of the Beggar's Benison and Merryland, Anstruther,* printed (understandably) for private distribution only, 1892: "King James V, the 'Gudeman of Ballangeish,' in the disguise of a bagpiper, was journeying to the East Neuk of Fife. Failing to cross the Dreel Burn, in spate, a buxom gaberlunzie [beggar] lass came to the rescue, tucked up her petticoats, and elevated her Sovereign across her *hurdies* to the opposite bank. Enamoured with the high favour, His Majesty in return gave the damsel her *fairin'* [present], for which 'the gudeman' got her 'benison' [blessing]."
⁷ Concerning a controverted election in the borough of Haslemere, Surrey.
⁸ Erskine's case had rested mainly on his contention that his opponent was not qualified for election from the county of Clackmannan, and the committee had the day before refused even to consider this question. As a consequence he withdrew his petition altogether. But there was a sequel on 20 April when Colonel Abercromby, offended by a publication of Erskine's on the result of the election, met him in a duel which ended without harm to either man. By that date Boswell was at Wilton, and he did not refer to the affair.

blooding him they had cut an artery. Spottiswoode ludicrously said, "The committee make corks for the mouths of our counsel." Erskine said that Lord George Germain was for his going on, and thought he would succeed with the committee, and surely *he* knew them better than we did. I said he knew them better as private gentlemen, but had not seen them on a committee, as we had done. It was like one who had seen horses going [9] in a field, but had never seen them draw. We had seen them draw. I was hurt to see a branch of the family of Mar lose the county of Clackmannan; but the candour of the committee, though I thought them mistaken as to the point which they determined, prevented all reflections of a murmuring nature against *them*.

This day our Club dined together, there being now an institution that there should be a dinner instead of a supper the first Friday of every month. There were present Johnson, Beauclerk, Langton, Reynolds, Chamier, Percy, Steevens, a Mr. Gibbons whom I had not seen before, and myself.[1] The ham was not very good. But Percy said, when somebody cried to take it away, that it was not so bad as to deserve *expulsion*. Said I: "It should only be *rusticated, as it is rusty."* This conceit was allowed to pass as laughable.

Mr. Johnson said he had been reading Twiss's *Travels*, which were just come out. ("There's not a mouthful of sense in them," said Beauclerk, but I do not know if Mr. Johnson heard him.) "They are as good as the first book of travels that you will take up. They are as good as Keysler or Blainville or Addison, if you take out the learning. (Said Beauclerk: "They are nothing without the learning.") They are not so good as Brydone, but they are better than Pococke or _____.[2] I have not, indeed, cut them up yet, but I have read in them where the pages are open, and I do not suppose what is on the pages which are closed is worse than what is on the open pages." He said, what I have heard him say before, that Addison has not introduced the Italian learning into any of his writings, so that it would seem he has not acquired it.[3] That the only passage he quotes is, *"Sta bene; per star miglior star qui."* [4] (Tom Davies told me that there

[9] That is, running wild, not pulling in harness.

[1] Anthony Chamier in this year was appointed Under-Secretary of State. Edward Gibbon was little known at this time but leaped into prominence the following year with the publication of the first volume of his *Decline and Fall of the Roman Empire*. Boswell grew to dislike him intensely.

[2] The *Life* has simply, "better than Pococke's."

[3] Addison was not ignorant of Italian. In his *Remarks on Several Parts of Italy,* 1705, he discusses the opera and comedies and translates St. Anthony of Padua's sermon to the fishes.

[4] Boswell is clearly losing his Italian. The *Life* gives a more nearly correct form of the epitaph: *"Stavo bene; per star meglio, sto qui."* Being a pun on two meanings of

was more, and that he said to Mr. Johnson, "Because you find *some* Italian learning in a writer, that is not an argument that he had not more.") I mentioned Addison's having borrowed from Leandro Alberti. Beauclerk said he was said to have borrowed too from Capaccio.[5] Mr. Johnson said that all the men who went to look for what the classics had said of Italy *must* find the same passages, and that he should think it would be one of the first things the Italians would do on the revival of learning: to collect all that the Roman authors had said of their country.

I should have mentioned that I called on Sheridan this forenoon at his lodgings in [Frith] Street, Soho. He was always very friendly to me, and his conversation is to me improving and entertaining. He said Johnson discovered a black heart when he said it was time for him to give up his pension when Mr. Sheridan got one, for that *he* had been the person chiefly instrumental in procuring Johnson his pension by applying to Wedderburn, who applied to Lord Bute. Lord Mountstuart did tell me last night that he had asked his father about it, and was told by him that it was Wedderburn who insisted with him to have it done, and, when he neglected it, took care to put him in mind. Sheridan said he was the man employed to announce to Johnson that a pension was intended for him; and he painted him very well, rolling in the greatest agitation, and at last saying, "If the chief magistrate of this great nation chooses to honour me with a pension, I should be a fool to refuse it." I told Mr. Sheridan this was very odd, for that Murphy assured me he was the man employed to communicate it. Mr. Johnson had confirmed to me what Murphy told; and he afterwards assured me that Sheridan had never formally communicated the matter to him; and if he had spoken of it at all at any time, it was only in an overly[6] way, as, "It would be right you should have a pension," or, "Would not you accept of a pension?" or something in that style. I was shocked that Sheridan should tell so downright a falsehood. He said Mr. Johnson was the vainest and the proudest man in the world, and would have no other man praised but himself. That it was Swift's great fame which made him always attack him, and no personal quarrel; and that the great test was that Swift's works sold more than any others, which Davies too told me. He said he saw Cumming the Quaker fairly thresh

---

stare, it is really untranslatable. An expanded paraphrase would be something as follows: "My health was good, but I wanted it to be better, consulted a physician, and here I am."

[5] In the *Life* Boswell wrote: "borrowed many of his classical remarks from Leandro Alberti" (his *Descrittione di tutta Italia*), and referred to Capaccio as "another Italian author" whom Addison put under service. Capaccio's most important work was a history of Naples.

[6] Careless, cursory.

Johnson one night with a forcible natural eloquence when fully provoked by him; and that Johnson cried mercy.[7] Now Mr. Johnson told me that he had been rather severe upon Cumming; that Cumming was drunk and attacked him with rudeness; and that he did not answer him because he was in such a situation; and that he walked home with him. Sheridan said Johnson was a bully. That he never feared him; and that Mr. Johnson never said an ill-bred thing to him but once, which was, "Sir, you have said this three times already. I do not see why you should say it again." He said he had found General Fraser and Wedderburn both grow cold to him;[8] but he lamented the fickleness of human nature very candidly. He and I were both in high spirits, and talked keenly. It is impossible to put down an exact transcript of conversation with all its little particulars. It is impossible to clap the mind upon paper as one does an engraved plate, and to leave the full vivid impression. I insisted with Sheridan that I should bring Mr. Johnson and him together again, as it was wrong that two such men should have a coldness. But, indeed, I could not well defend Mr. Johnson's saying about Sheridan's pension. I told him, as Mr. Johnson told me, that it was said *jocularly.* But I do not see the joke. It has been a splenetic explosion. Mr. Johnson said to me today that he would willingly meet with Sheridan and set it to rights.[9] I told at The Club Mr. Sheridan's answer to Mr. Johnson when he defied him to show ten good lines in *Douglas:* "Lines, Sir? I would not talk with a man who looks for lines in a drama."

We talked of Ossian. Mr. Johnson said that supposing the Irish and Erse languages to be the same, which he did not believe, yet as there was no reason to believe that they ever wrote their native language in the Highlands and Isles, we could not believe a long poem was preserved. That if we had no evidence of writing having ever been practised in one of the counties of England, we were not to believe that they had a long poem preserved *there,* though the neighbouring counties, where the same language was spoken, could write. Beauclerk observed that the ballad of *Lilliburlero* had been in the mouths of all the people of this country, and was said to have had a great effect in bringing about the Revolution.[1]

[7] Tom Cumming had died the previous year. The only time that Boswell met him was at Dilly's on 30 March 1768.

[8] See below, 28 March 1776.

[9] But they were never reconciled.

[1] The words seem first to have been sung in 1641, but became famous in 1686–1687 as the refrain of a song satirizing the Earl of Tyrconnell, who was going to Ireland as James II's papist lieutenant. Burnet had written in his *History* that "the whole army, and at last all people both in city and country, were singing it perpetually. And perhaps never had so slight a thing so great an effect." It was also, of course, perpetually

Yet he questioned if anybody could repeat it now, which showed how improbable it was that much poetry should be preserved by tradition.

Percy mentioned an objection to the antiquity of Ossian: that wolves are not mentioned in it.[2] After this had been discussed, and Langton and Sir Joshua were carrying on some dialogue which Mr. Johnson did not hear, he, in the midst of it, broke out, "Pennant talks of bears—" (I forget what.)[3] They went on, while he, being dull of hearing, did not perceive it, or, if he did, was not willing to mind them. So from time to time he roared out remarks, and the word *bear* ("like a word in a catch," as Beauclerk said) was always heard at intervals, and, coming from Mr. Johnson, while we who were sitting round tried to stifle laughter, produced a very ludicrous effect. Mr. Johnson said, "we are told the black bear is innocent, but I should not like to trust myself" (or "engage") "with him." Said Gibbons (aside): "I should not like to trust myself" (or "engage") "with you." [4]

Johnson said, "Patriotism is the last refuge of scoundrels." Sir Joshua and I maintained that all patriots were not scoundrels. Said Steevens: "Name some who are not." "Sir George Savile," said I. "Come, shoot at him if you can. Nobody bids for this lot. Put him by." "Burke," said Sir Joshua. Said Mr. Johnson: "I do not say that Burke is not honest. But we have no reason to conclude from his political conduct that he is so. Were Burke to accept of a place from this ministry, he would lose that character for firmness which he has, and might be turned out of his place in a year. This ministry is neither stable nor grateful to their friends as Sir Robert Walpole was. So that Burke may think it more for his interest to take his chance of the Rockingham Party coming in." I argued against this, and mentioned Burke's resisting offers, as I supposed. "Sir," said Mr. Johnson, "you are arguing because you know it is uncivil to answer you; uncivil to an absent member." "Well," said I, "I do admire Burke's resistance." JOHNSON. "And I do admire your resistance." Any other man would have been repressed by such a rebuke. Mr. Steevens and I stayed a little after the rest. We had taken a pretty hearty glass of port. He said that it was a pity Mr. Johnson was so rough, as it prevented many people from knowing his excellence (or some such expression). This very day, though Mr. Johnson was willing to be reconciled with Sheridan, he, upon

---

whistled by my uncle Toby in *Tristram Shandy,* and was one of the best-known airs in *The Beggar's Opera.*

[2] Percy was writing the history of the wolf. See below, 17 March 1776.

[3] Thomas Pennant, in his *British Zoology,* had given classical and Celtic references to the existence of bears in Britain.

[4] In both instances the manuscript has a third choice, "to meet." In the *Life* Boswell chose "to trust myself."

William Miller (1755-1846), son of Thomas Miller, Lord Justice-Clerk; later baronet and Lord Glenlee. From a contemporary oil-painting by David Allan in the collection of Mario Cellini. Reproduced by permission.

A view of Wilton, the seat of the Earls of Pembroke. From an oil-painting (c.1775-1779) at Wilton by Richard Wilson. Reproduced by permission of the Earl of Pembroke.

A view of Lichfield, showing on the right the house where Samuel Johnson was born, and beside it the Three Crowns Inn. From an engraving in Stebbing Shaw, *The History and Antiquities of Staffordshire*; the engraving (by Thomas Cook, 12 February 1785), from a drawing by E. Stringer, was first printed in *The Gentleman's Magazine* for February 1785.

A page of the manuscript of the *Life,* describing part of the dinner at Dilly's, 15 May 1776, which introduced Johnson and Wilkes. From the original in the possession of Arthur A. Houghton, Jr. Reproduced by permission.

Joseph Brant (Thayendanegea), the Mohawk Chief (c. 1740-1807). From the
engraving originally printed as the frontispiece to *The London Magazine* for
July 1776; the engraving was made from a drawing in the possession of James
Boswell, which has dropped out of sight.

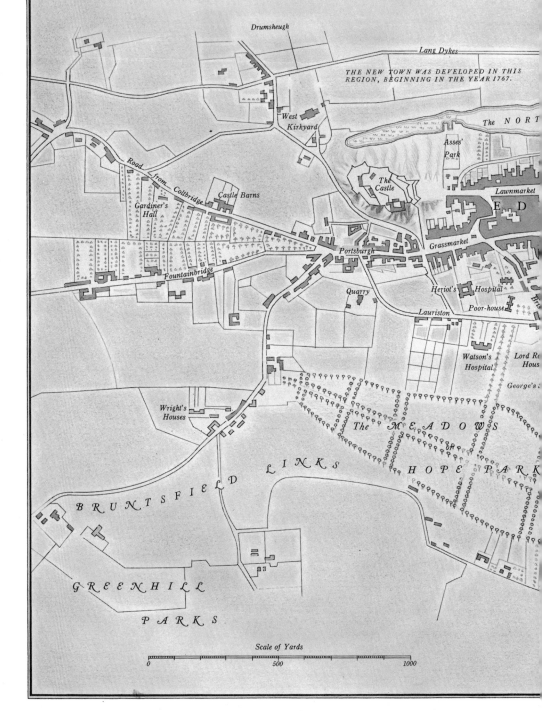

A MAP OF THE ENVIRONS OF EDINBURGH

locating many of the places mentioned in the text

REDRAWN BY HAROLD K. FAYE FROM AN ANONYMOUS MAP, CIRCA 1767

Drumsheugh

Lang Dykes

THE NEW TOWN WAS DEVELOPED IN THIS
REGION, BEGINNING IN THE YEAR 1767.

West
Kirkyard

The NORT

Asses'
Park

The
Castle

ED

Lawnmarket

Road from Coltbridge

Castle Barns

Gardiner's
Hall

Grassmarket

Portsburgh

Fountainbridge

Quarry

Heriot's Hospital

Lauriston

Poor-house

Watson's
Hospital

Lord Re
Hous

George's

Wright's
Houses

The MEADOWS

HOPE PARK

BRUNTSFIELD LINKS

GREENHILL

PARKS

Scale of Yards

0   500   1000

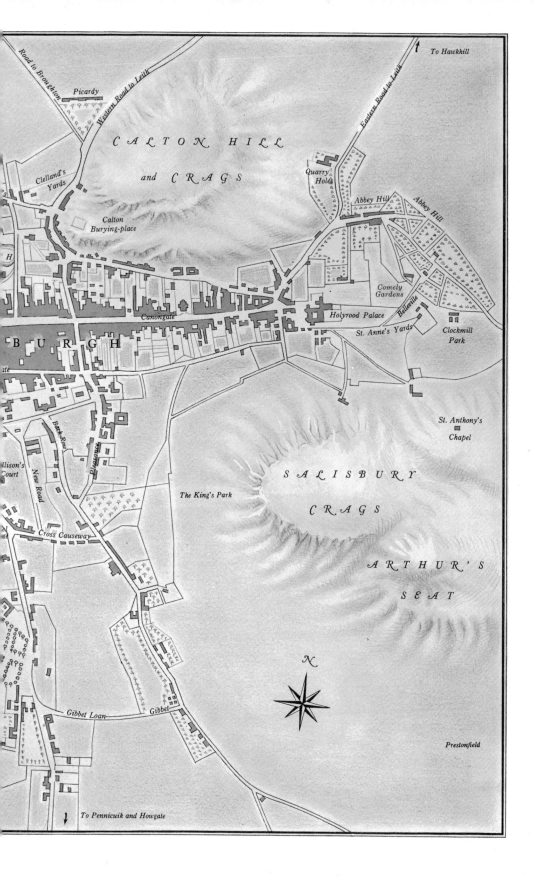

Margaret Caroline Rudd (c. 1745 — apparently living 1794) at the bar of the Old Bailey. From an engraving by Gaetano Bartolozzi, Jr., 15 December 1775. Photograph by courtesy of the Trustees of the British Museum.

some story of him being told, called him a foolish fellow, and a _____ whelp (I forget the adjective).

I went to a ball at the Mansion House. It was very splendid. Mr. Bosville's family was there, all but the Captain. Mr. Orme, the East Indian historian, to whom Dempster once introduced me, knew me again, and accosted me. We talked together a good while of Mr. Johnson's *Journey,* which he admired much. He said he had more fancy than any man in this country; and that there were in his *Journey* great thoughts which had been rolled and rolled in his mind, as in the sea. The image appeared very good at the time. I doubt if I have taken it well down.[5] Edward Dilly was here tonight. I took up my room in the Poultry tonight.

SATURDAY 8 APRIL. Wrote my journal at Dilly's quietly in the forenoon. Tom Davies called. I said, "I am quite full of Mr. Johnson's sayings. I am tapping myself." "Well," said he, "it will be good wine to draw off for the public." I dined at Mr. Thrale's by invitation. Mr. Johnson, Dr. Campbell, Baretti, and a Mr. Gillon, a nephew of Gillon of Wallhouse's, who had never been in Scotland, but had been at Guadaloupe and sent Mr. Thrale the fine liqueurs, were there. Mr. Johnson had been last night with Sir Joshua to sup at Mrs. Abington,'s where were Lady Fitzroy, General Irwin, and other fine people. This was a kind of new scene to him. He seemed to be much pleased with having been there. I suppose vanity was the chief cause of his pleasure. Mrs. Thrale told us that Mr. Johnson had said that Barry was just fit to stand at the door of an auction-room with a long pole: "Pray, gentlemen, walk in." She said Murphy said Garrick was fit for that, and would pick your pocket after you came out. Mr. Johnson said there was no wit there.[6] "You may say of any man that he will pick a pocket. Besides, the man at the door does not pick pockets. That is to be done within, by the auctioneer."

Yesterday at The Club Mr. Johnson said Mrs. Pritchard's playing was quite mechanical. It was wonderful how little mind she had. She had never read the play of *Macbeth.*[7] She no more thought of the play out of which her part was taken than a shoemaker thinks of the skin out of which the piece of leather of which he is making a pair of shoes is cut.

Mrs. Thrale told me yesterday that Tom Davies repeated in a very

[5] In a note to his *Hebrides,* Boswell wrote it down thus: "There are in that book thoughts which, by long revolution in the great mind of Johnson, have been formed and polished—like pebbles rolled in the ocean!"
[6] Boswell later (probably when he was revising for the *Life*) changed this sentence and the preceding to read, "and that Mr. Murphy said another eminent actor . . . no wit there, only abuse." When he printed the passage, he suppressed not only Garrick's name but also Barry's and Murphy's.
[7] Hannah Pritchard was Lady Macbeth in her last appearance on the stage, 24 April 1768, when she spoke an epilogue by Garrick.

bald manner the story of Mr. Johnson's first repartee to me, telling it thus: "I was born in Scotland," instead of, "I come from Scotland"; so that Mr. Johnson's saying, "That is what a great many of your countrymen can't help," had no point or even meaning. Upon this Fitzherbert had observed, "It's not everybody that can carry a *bon mot.*" [8] I reminded Mrs. Thrale of the noted story of the coat being too short—"Long enough before I get another"—being bungled.

Mr. Thrale told me, I am not sure what day, that there is a book of Johnsoniana kept in their family, in which all Mr. Johnson's sayings and all that they can collect about him is put down.[9] He told me they had seen _____,[1] a surgeon at Birmingham, who was a schoolfellow of Mr. Johnson's, had some of his exercises, and could tell a great deal about him, and that he had promised to give them a great deal. I must try to get this *Thralian* miscellany, to assist me in writing Mr. Johnson's life, if Mrs. Thrale does not intend to do it herself. I suppose there will be many written.

> Be there a thousand lives,
> My great curiosity has stomach for 'em all.[2]

There was either little said today, or I remember little.[3] I supped at Lord Mountstuart's. He asked me to come and dine with him next day, when he should have no company.

SUNDAY 9 APRIL. I breakfasted with Mr. Burke, and stayed so long with him that I was too late for mass at the Bavarian Chapel, which I intended to hear after breakfasting with the Irish (reputed *popish*) orator.[4] I went directly after leaving him to the Parliament Street Coffee-house, and put down what passed, which is to be found on a separate paper.[5] I walked awhile in the park with Colonel Campbell. Called a little at Mrs.

[8] This conversation must have occurred some years earlier, for William Fitzherbert died at the beginning of 1772. In her diary Mrs. Thrale wrote that Davies had said, "I could not, you know, help being a *Scotsman*" (*Thraliana,* ed. Katharine C. Balderston, 2nd ed., Oxford, 1951, i. 62–63).

[9] This early collection, of which only a few fragments survive, can probably be identified with the "Table Book" which is mentioned in *Thraliana.*

[1] Edmund Hector, who later supplied Boswell with many details of Johnson's early life and gave him his school exercises.

[2] Parodied from *Othello,* V. ii. 74–75.

[3] Perhaps because "the Doctor was not in as good spirits as he was at Dilly's" (*Dr. Campbell's Diary,* p. 76).

[4] Burke's mother was a Roman Catholic, as was also his wife, though on her marriage she conformed to the Church of England. Because of these associations and his Irish origin, his political opponents had not been slow to carry on a whispering campaign to the effect that he was a papist.

[5] This paper has disappeared.

Stuart's. Stopped a few minutes at the Portuguese Chapel about four, knelt before the altar, and was secretly pious, public prayers being over. Dined happily with Lord Mountstuart. Nobody there but Lady Windsor.[6] He was warmly friendly, and we shook hands with that spontaneous motion of cordiality which comes from the heart. I observed that, though I saw we were as friendly together as ever, there was no intercourse between us for long intervals. He never wrote to me. "What can I write?" said he. "Why," said I, "to tell me that you are well." "That," said he, "is like two girls who live in different streets corresponding." There is great manliness about him, and this thought was that of a man. But surely there is an amiable affection not unworthy of a man which is kept more lively by mutual letters. He gave me a bottle of the best old hock that I ever drank. It was some which Lord Bute got from Sir Lawrence Dundas. I drank only that bottle. General Paoli sent his coach to my lodgings, and I drove in it to Lord Mansfield's. Lord Essex told of some very mischievous boys who took up handfuls of dust in the street and threw them in the wind just in the face of the coaches going along the street, to disturb the horses; and that he saw a coachman cut a boy severely with his whip. "He deserved it," said Lord Mansfield, "and yet after all what are half the age doing but throwing dust in other people's eyes?" "There seems to be a want of coachmen, my Lord," said Lord Dalhousie. Lord Mansfield's joke was quaint and pedantic; Lord Dalhousie's, good wit. I supped at Beauclerk's. Langton was there.

MONDAY 10 APRIL. I breakfasted at Lord Mountstuart's with Sir Alexander Gilmour, on whom I called in the morning. I had engaged to go with my Lord to hear the petition of Shawfield on the Lanark election tried by the committee of which he was one. Gilmour and I sat together and heard the pleadings. Hardinge was petulant, but very clever; that is to say, he spoke with readiness and accuracy, and I doubted if I should ever attain to such perfection, where he did well. I dined at General Oglethorpe's, where were Mr. Johnson, Langton, Mr. ———, a pretty young man just returned from his travels (a relation of Mrs. Oglethorpe's), a lady whom I did not know, and Dr. Campbell, whom the General had allowed me to bring.

Before dinner Mrs. Oglethorpe plagued Mr. Johnson about his giving such a book as Cocker's *Arithmetic* to the young woman at Anoch.[7] He said it was the only book he had. But I said, "How came you to buy it, to take it in a post-chaise?" He said, "Sir, it is inexhaustible."

We had a good dinner and Sicilian wine as usual. But I missed poor

[6] Lord Mountstuart's mother-in-law.
[7] In the tour of the Hebrides, 31 August 1773.

Goldsmith.[8] Mr. Johnson told that Bruce said the Abyssinians were white; whereas we had always been told they were black. The General went into a dissertation on the different gradations of black. "Sir," said Mr. Johnson, "the question is precisely between black and white."

He said the present was never happy, and that every part of life was at some time future. That is Pope's thought:

Man never *is* but always *to be* blest.[9]

I said, "Is a man *never* happy for the present?" JOHNSON. "Never but when he's drunk."

He pressed General Oglethorpe to give his life, saying, "I know no man alive whose life would be _____."[1] The General seemed very unwilling to enter upon it. He[2] said he had given Savage money several times.

Scott's *Elegies* were lying in the room. Mr. Johnson said they were very well, but that they were such as twenty people might write. I argued against Horace's maxim, "mediocribus esse poetis."[3] Mr. Johnson repeated the common remark that, "as there is no necessity for our having poetry, it should be excellent." I was not satisfied. "Horace and you must settle it," said he. He was not in the humour of talking, and I tried several times to set him a going, which displeased him; for Langton told me he said when they were in the coach, "When Boswell gets wine, his conversation consists all of questions."[4]

[8] Goldsmith, who had died just a year before, used to dine with Boswell at Oglethorpe's.
[9] *Essay on Man*, i. 96.
[1] Boswell left a blank for the rest of this sentence. The *Life* reads: "I know no man whose life would be more interesting. If I were furnished with materials, I should be very glad to write it." Campbell wrote in his *Diary:* "Dr. Johnson pressed him to write his life, adding that no life in Europe was so well worth recording, etc. The old man excused himself saying the life of a private man was not worthy public notice. He however desired Boswell to bring him some good almanac that he might recollect dates, and seemed to excuse himself, also, on the article of incapacity, etc., but Boswell desired him only to furnish the skeleton and that Dr. Johnson would supply bones and sinews, etc. 'He would be *a good doctor,*' says the General, 'who would do that.' 'Well,' says I, 'he is *a good doctor,*' at which he, the Doctor, laughed very heartily" (p. 78). Later Boswell himself projected a life of Oglethorpe. His notes are among the papers at Yale.
[2] Johnson.
[3] That is, that mediocrity in poetry is not to be tolerated (*Ars Poetica,* ll. 372–373).
[4] Campbell gave a more vivid account of Johnson's displeasure: "Boswell desirous of eliciting his opinion upon too many subjects, as he thought, he rose up and took his hat. This was not noticed by anybody as it was nine o'clock, but after we got into Mr. Langton's coach, who gave us a set down, he said, 'Boswell's conversation consists entirely in asking questions, and it is extremely offensive,' etc.; we defended it upon Boswell's eagerness to hear the Doctor speak" (*Dr. Campbell's Diary,* p. 79).

I called on Sir John Pringle and walked up and down his parlour with him a good while. I convinced him that if my father would give me what was sufficient to maintain my family decently in London, it would be advisable for me to try the English bar. We got upon religion. He was keen for Socinianism, for Dr. Priestley's kind of Christianity.[5] He talked with vivacity against the Trinity, the satisfaction of Christ, and the eternity of hell's torments, and said that at the Day of Judgement people would be ashamed of having entertained such notions. He said when Condamine was here he was astonished when he (Sir John) told him he was a Christian, Condamine's idea being that a man could not be a Christian without believing such doctrines as those which Sir John had now ridiculed; and he asked him, "Croyez-vous la trinité? que trois sont un?" and the other points.[6] "No," said Sir John, and gave him his rational creed. I drank some small beer with Sir John as a cooling beverage. This kind of conversation relaxed my mind somewhat; and the effect was thus: if churches for ages, if bishops and most learned clergy, if I myself have so grossly erred in *doctrine* as Sir John thinks (and as to which he *may* be right, for I cannot answer him), may not there be as much error as to *morals?* And I saw no great risk of vice in running after fine girls. In this frame I quitted Sir John; and, having met a beautiful Devonshire wench in the Strand, was lasciviously fond of her; and dallied for a while, and was restrained from completion by other considerations than religion. I supped at Beauclerk's, where was Langton.

TUESDAY 11 APRIL. Called on Sir John Pringle between nine and ten. Wished to see him as often as I could, and he took it kind that I called when I passed by his door. I breakfasted with Mr. Douglas of Douglas.[7] Found the Duke of Queensberry there. Took him aside and mentioned to him his having formerly said that if Baron Maule would resign, he would try what could be done for me to get the Clerkship to the Sasines, and told him that Lord Mountstuart would get the resignation managed. He said he would talk with Lord Mountstuart, and Douglas promised to keep him in mind.

It was a warm day and my blood was on fire. I went to Peter Street, Westminster, to the Devonshire girl's lodgings, and toyed with her awhile. She was like a marble statue of antiquity. I heard Thurlow plead in the House of Lords an appeal about the voters of Linlithgow. He was masterly. I did *not* think I could do as well as he did.

I dined at Beauclerk's. Sir Joshua and Langton were there. Sir Joshua

---

[5] As we should say, Unitarianism.
[6] "Do you believe in the Trinity? that three are one?" Charles Marie de La Condamine, French traveller and mathematician, visited England in 1763.
[7] This is Archibald Douglas, the principal in the Douglas Cause.

said that the more artificial wants we could make to be gratified, the greater our happiness. That this was the advantage of civilized society. He said he saw in this nation all the symptoms of a great and flourishing state: magnificence, elegance, plenty; everybody living better than formerly. He took up _____, and read some of _____, where are sage remarks upon the simplest truths, as that it is wonderful "quand on est malade on n'est pas bien."[8] He said if one had time one might introduce this well into a comedy. I gave an account of M. Dupont, our French minister at Edinburgh, who says such things as this: "Il est mieux pour M. Douglas qu'il a gagné son procès."[9] Beauclerk said, "I wish M. Dupont lived near me, for he would teach my children to speak French and to tell truth." At this time in London I was wearing out as my dressed suit an old crimson suit embroidered with silver, made at Dublin in 1769. It was now old-fashioned, though a good handsome dress. I said, "I feel myself quite different in this suit from what I am in my frock" (meaning that I felt myself better). Said Beauclerk: "So should I feel myself quite different, but I should not feel agreeably" (meaning that I was ridiculous). He has a fine malignity about him. He talked of Johnson's supping with Mrs. Abington and Sir Joshua's getting into the club at Almack's, and said, "I hope to see Johnson an old rake" (I think) "and you, Sir Joshua, without a coat."[1] He did not mean any serious ill will; but the oddity of the transitions amused his fancy.

I supped at Mr. Henry Baldwin's, where were Edward and Charles Dilly, Robert Baldwin, and Dr. Mayo; Mrs. Baldwin supped with us. Mr. Waller, the lawyer, came in late. His *smartness* displeased me. We had a pretty good evening. But by having been so much in company and sitting up late so often, I was somewhat sleepy.

WEDNESDAY 12 APRIL. Breakfasted with Langton. Lounged at his lodgings all the forenoon talking of Mr. Johnson and Langton's affairs, and his coming to live in London, which I found he was almost determined to do, and imagined he could live for £800 a year; and of my coming to the English bar, of which he approved. I wished to be introduced to Dr. Lawrence, who had been long Mr. Johnson's physician, and who could tell a great deal about him, for no man knows one better than his physician. Langton said he would introduce me directly. Away we went to [Essex] Street in the Strand, where the Doctor lives; but were too late, as he would dine about three.

Langton went with me to Somerset House, where I called on my client, Dr. Alexander Johnson, who had lodgings taken there. He had been

---

[8] "When one is sick one is not well."
[9] "It is better for Mr. Douglas to have won his cause."
[1] That is, that he would lose it by gambling. Almack's was noted for deep play.

twice to call on me, and I was pained to think that I had neglected to return his visits, especially as I had his cause to talk to him about. I thought that I was quite *idle* in London. I left a note that I would breakfast with him on Saturday. Langton and I walked near an hour in Somerset Gardens, where I never had been before. It was very agreeable to find quietness and old trees in the very heart of London. My dissipation and hurry of spirits were cured here. We talked of religion. It was quite such a scene as *The Spectator* pictures.[2] I valued worthy Langton.

I dined at Sir Alexander Gilmour's. Lord Mountstuart and his brother James, Lord Dalhousie, Captain John Elphinstone, Douglas, and Shawfield were there, so that there was an excellent Scotch company. But Gilmour had absurdly asked Walker, a little paltry *writer* from Edinburgh, who sat like a spy. I was really hurt by this strange leaven. We drank a good deal. I was much intoxicated. So many of us supped at Mr. Stuart's. I was very fond of Mrs. Stuart tonight and made wondrous speeches to her. I had reflection enough to go home soon after supper.

THURSDAY 13 APRIL. David Cuninghame has the odd luck of finding me in the morning after I have been drinking. I was very ill. I carried him to Old Slaughter's to breakfast. He was a burthen to me. I sauntered up and down Westminster. The Devonshire girl was not at home. I called for her, as I thought that by dalliance I might divert the uneasiness of yesterday's debauch.

Walked in the park up by Buckingham House, and went to Mrs. Stuart's. Found Mrs. Chancellor, the great lace-woman in Duke Street, with her.[3] Was glad to find that I had given her no offence last night. Drank a great deal of tea, and was entertained by looking at a variety of beautiful laces, and hearing Chancellor speak in the most flattering terms of all the great ladies. At length my fancy was taken with the laces. I was catched in her Mechlin toils.[4] My valuable spouse never yet would allow me to buy her a suit of laces. I determined to do it now, while her friend should approve of my choice. I mounted up gradually from sixteen guineas to thirty. I wished to have a suit not merely genteel but rich. I was *flattered* by the speeches which the old beldame made to me, who even called me a *handsome* gentleman. I was quite a fine fellow this morning. I was all levity and did not care how much money I spent. It was amazing with what copiousness and variety of expression Mrs. Chancellor set off her laces. "This," said she, "is *innocent*. This is *grand*."

---

[2] *Spectator* No. 77 opens with the writer and Will Honeycomb strolling and reflecting in Somerset Gardens.

[3] Elizabeth Chancellor's greatness soon suffered a decline. Five years later she was listed as a bankrupt.

[4] Lace made at Mechlin in Belgium.

"Oh," said I, "we're past innocence. I'll have the grand." I wanted to have a suit for the lady of a *baron*. I said to Mrs. Stuart, "This is just contracting thirty guineas of more debt. You must become bound to pay it in case I die in ten years, and then I can make myself easy by thinking that, by taking this lace, I do not make my creditors worse." Accordingly she wrote a note declaring that she was bound for thirty guineas if I died within ten years without paying my debts; and Miss Hale, who came in, signed witness.[5] Mrs. Stuart and she and I drove to the Green Park and walked a good while. I was now quite well and in delightful spirits. (When I told Mr. Johnson of the lace, he said, "Well, you've done a wise thing and a good thing." "I've done a good thing," said I, "but I don't know if I've done a wise thing." "Yes, Sir," said he. "No money is better spent than what is laid out for domestic satisfaction. A man is pleased that his wife is dressed as well as other people, and a wife is pleased that she is dressed.")

We came back to Mrs. Stuart's and eat cold mutton and I drank beer. I dined at General Paoli's, having engaged several days ago to him, when he complained of seeing me seldom. After coffee I called on Lord Mountstuart, and promised to sup with him. Went home and wrote letters and returned to him about nine. Mr. Kennedy of Dalquharran, or Dunure rather, who had just come from Geneva, was there. My Lord had purchased a noble collection of prints of great men, put up in volumes. He knew me so well that he would with difficulty show them to me, as he said I did not care for them. I owned that I did not care enough; but that a taste was acquired by looking at pictures or prints. I prevailed with him to show me the volume of Charles the First's reign. My Lord said tonight I was like a jack: wind me up, and I would run down again.[6] In this manner he represented my conversation. "My Lord," said I, "you are never wound up." "Because," said he, "I'm always at the top." We parted in good time tonight. Kennedy pleased me as we walked home, for he told me the fate of the Ayrshire election had kept him a night from sleeping. He got the news in France, I think.

FRIDAY 14 APRIL. This being Good Friday, I resolved as usual that it should be solemnly spent. I breakfasted with Mr. Johnson, drank a good deal of tea, and eat cross-buns. Dr. Levett made tea to us. I observed Mr. Johnson took no milk to his tea. I suppose because it is a kind of animal food. Nor did he eat any bread at all. I was not quite so strict; and I will own that the minute circumstance of the buns being marked with the cross had *some* effect on my mind.

[5] Mrs. Boswell may be wearing the suit of lace in the Auchinleck portrait of her reproduced as frontispiece to *Boswell in Search of a Wife*.

[6] A jack was a machine for turning a spit, which was wound up like a clock.

Mr. Johnson said that the great loss now was that government had too little power; that all that it had to bestow was necessary to be given to support itself; so that government could not reward merit. No man, for instance, could now be made a bishop for his learning and piety, but because he is connected with somebody who has parliamentary interest. That our several ministries in this reign had outbid each other in concessions to the people. That Lord Bute, though a very honourable man, a man who meant well, a man whose blood was full of prerogative, was a bookman, and thought this country could be governed by the influence of the Crown alone. That he had foolishly given up much. In particular, that he had advised the King to agree that the judges should hold their places for life, instead of being removable at the accession of a new king. I wished to hear him on this topic, as his opinion was so different from what I had always heard. Said he: "Lord Bute thought to make the King popular by this concession; but the people never minded it, and it was a most impolitic measure. There is no reason why a judge should be for life more than anyone else. A judge may be partial otherwise than to the Crown. We have seen judges partial to the populace. A judge may become corrupted, and yet there may not be legal evidence against him. A judge may become froward from age. A judge may grow unfit for his office in many ways. It was desirable that a possibility of being delivered from him by a new king should be in contemplation. That is now gone by an Act of Parliament *ex gratia* of the Crown. Lord Bute gave up £5———,[7] for which nobody thanked him. It was of consequence to the King, but nothing to each of those among whom it was divided." (Lord Mountstuart afterwards owned to me that he thought his father wrong as to that money, but maintained that making the judges for life was noble.) "Lord Bute," said Mr. Johnson, "showed an improper partiality to Scotsmen. He turned out Dr. Nicholls, a very capital physician, to make room for Duncan, a very low man who had cured him.[8] Wedderburn and John Home went errands for him. He had occasion for people to go errands; but he should not have had Scotsmen."

I told him that Lord Mountstuart informed me that John Home's going into Lord Bute's room before the first people in England was no more than what happens at every minister's levee, where those who attend are admitted in the order that they have come, which is better than admitting them according to their rank, so that when a man has waited

[7] In a note in the *Life* Boswell sets this figure at £900,000.
[8] According to Lord Eldon, the King was asked to make Duncan a baronet on the ground that he was an eminent Scottish apothecary. The King replied, "What, what, is that all? It shall be done. I was afraid you meant to ask me to make the Scotch apothecary a physician; that's more difficult."

all the morning a peer might come and go in before him and keep him waiting still. Mr. Johnson said, "Yes. But Home should not have come to the levee to be in the way of people of consequence. He saw Lord Bute at all times, and could have said what he had to say at any time as well as at the levee."

He said there was now no Prime Minister. Lord North was only the agent for Government in the House of Commons. He said we were governed by the Privy Council; but that there was no one head there, as in Sir Robert Walpole's time. I said Parliament was just a larger council to the King. "Yes," said he, "and the benefit of a numerous council is having a greater number of men of property engaged in the legislature, who, for their own interest, will not consent to bad laws." He said Lord Bute took down too fast, without building up something new. "Because," said I, "he found a rotten building. The political coach was drawn by a set of bad horses." "But," said Mr. Johnson, "he should have changed them one by one."

When I put down Mr. Johnson's sayings, I do not keep strictly to chronology. I am glad to collect the gold dust, as I get by degrees as much as will be an ingot. I told him that Mr. Orme said many parts of the East Indies were better mapped than the Highlands of Scotland. Said Mr. Johnson: "That a country may be mapped, it must be travelled over." "Nay," said I, "can't you say it is not *worth* mapping?" [9]

He and I went to St. Clement's Church. As we went and saw many shops open, I said one disadvantage of the greatness of London was that, as nobody was attended to, there was no fear of censure for not observing Good Friday. He said this was true. London was too big. But it was nonsense to say the head was too big for the body. It would be as much too big if the body were ever so large, the country ever so extensive. It had no similarity to a head connected with a body. Dr. _____, the _____,[1] preached well enough; but Mr. Johnson thought it wrong that his sermon was not particularly adapted to the day. Mr. Wetherell, Master of University College, Oxford, was at St. Clement's and walked with us to Mr. Johnson's. He told me that he had managed the getting Mr. Johnson's diploma from Oxford, as in so numerous a body some management was required to unite them. I could gather that there were at Oxford some who did not admire and reverence Mr. Johnson as some of us do. After

[9] This anecdote almost surely belongs to the dinner at Thrale's on 8 April. Dr. Campbell recorded in his *Diary* for that date: "Boswell lamented there was no good map of Scotland. 'There never can be a good of Scotland,' says the Doctor sententiously. This excited Boswell to ask wherefore. 'Why, Sir, to measure land a man must go over it; but who could think of going over Scotland?'" (p. 76). Boswell had met Orme at the Mansion House the night before, 7 April.

[1] Presumably "Dr. Burrows, the rector."

Wetherell left us, Batheaston Miller and Edward Dilly called. Miller talked foolishly about the methods practised in France by men to prevent their wives from having children. "You, Sir," said he to Mr. Johnson, "have been a married man and will understand it"; and he spoke gross bawdy and said he had intrigued with men's wives in France. I wondered that Mr. Johnson let him alone. This kind of conversation was to prove that taxes discourage population, as poor people cannot maintain many children when provisions are dear. Mr. Johnson laughed at him while he recited the common remarks that by taxes labour would be dear, other nations would undersell us, and our commerce would be ruined. Mr. Johnson said our commerce was in a very good situation, and suppose we had no commerce at all, we could live very well on the produce of our own country.

Mr. Johnson and [I] went again to St. Clement's in the afternoon. Mr. _____,[2] the curate, preached very well on a suitable text: "It is finished."[3] Mr. Johnson then said, "Come, you shall go home with me and sit just an hour, and no longer." He however was much better than his word, for after we had drank tea with Mrs. Williams, he asked me to go upstairs with him, and we sat a long time in a sort of languid, grave state, like men watching a corpse; or nearly like that.[4] He said, "All knowledge is of itself of some value. I would rather know _____ than not. In the same manner, power. A man would not sit down and learn to hem a ruffle of his wife or his wife's maid. But if a mere wish could do it, he would rather wish to be able to hem a ruffle."

I told him Goldsmith's observation to me that he had come too late. That Pope and other poets had taken up the places of fame; and that a man could hardly get reputation now, as but a few can have it. Mr. Johnson said that was one of the most sensible things he had ever heard of Goldsmith. "It is difficult to get literary fame," said he, "and is every day growing more and more difficult. Ah," said he, "that should make a man think of securing happiness in the other world, which all who try sincerely for it may attain. In comparison of that, how little are all other things!" (Now let me here fairly mark the sentiments of my mind. It damped me to have an idea that the great fame of Johnson was little, compare it as you will; and a comparison which made me have the impression that Johnson's was *little* hurt me, in so much that the prospect of futurity was in this view unpleasant. I could not bear to have my im-

[2] S. Popham.
[3] John 19. 30.
[4] "Boswell and I went to church, but came very late. We then took tea, by Boswell's desire, and I eat one bun, I think, that I might not seem to fast ostentatiously. Boswell sat with me till night; we had some serious talk" (Johnson's *Prayers and Meditations*).

mediate enjoyment of the contemplation of greatness diminished.) He said immortality was impressed upon all men, and that all men acted under an impression of it, however they might talk, or however they might perhaps not be sensible of it. I said several people had not the least notion of immortality, as, for instance, Charles Fox. "Sir," said he, "if it were not for an impression of immortality, Charles Fox would cut a throat to fill his pockets." (When I quoted this to Beauclerk, he said, "Charles Fox would, etc., if it were not for fear of being hanged.")

Mr. Johnson said that there was a great cry about infidelity, but that there were in reality very few infidels. He had heard Dr. Brocklesby, a man once a Quaker and afterwards loose in his notions, say that he did not believe there were in England above two hundred infidels. He repeated tonight Dr. Cheyne's saying upon a proper attention both to this life and the next, in his *English Malady*.[4a]

He was very cordial, and I told him the story of my being in danger of having a duel last autumn. He said I had done as well as I could do in the circumstances; but that I had no business to go to the newspapers with a trial in a court of justice. Talking of Mr. Steevens, he said he was a great writer in the newspapers. I thoughtlessly asked, "What pleasure can he have in that?" "Nay," said Mr. Johnson, "*you* can best tell that." He said, "If you come to settle here, we will have one day in the week on which we will meet by ourselves. That is the happiest conversation when there is no competition, no vanity, but a calm interchange of sentiments." (I know not if I have his very words, but I have the meaning.) I took this as a high compliment. Our conversation having taken a turn to futurity, and to think that all is vanity, I felt myself clouded and depressed, and much in the way that I felt myself at Grantham when Mr. Palmer talked of the fall of man. I suppose my *not having dined*[5] was, according to Pope's doctrine, a considerable addition to the cause of my gloom. I walked home quietly, eat some figs and drank some wine, and was in a state altogether different from that heat of blood, vigour of nerves, and fever of spirits in which I have found myself for many nights.

SUNDAY 16 APRIL.[6] I had engaged to go with General Paoli to Wilton on Tuesday. But there came yesterday a card to me from Sir Joshua Reynolds, that Mr. Owen Cambridge would be happy to see me at

[4a] On 5 September 1773 when at Armadale during the tour of the Hebrides, Johnson had said that Cheyne's rule "should be imprinted on every mind: 'To neglect nothing to secure my eternal peace, more than if I had been certified I should die within the day; nor to mind anything that my secular obligations and duties demanded of me, less than if I had been ensured to live fifty years more.'"

[5] *Moral Essays*, i. 80.

[6] The record for 15 April (six pages) has been removed from the manuscript. The reason will be plain in a moment: because of an "irregularity" in Boswell's behaviour.

dinner that day at his house at Twickenham with Sir Joshua and Dr. Johnson.[7] This was a scene not to be lost if the invitation was properly given. I breakfasted with Sir Joshua and Miss Reynolds in good cheerful humour, and having found that Mr. Cambridge wished to see me, I resolved to try if I could prevail on the General to wait another day. This was Easter day, which is always to me a very noble festival, when I can worship in the grand cathedral, St. Paul's Church. By Sir Joshua's pleasing conversation I was kept somewhat late; but I got in before the sermon was ended, and joined in a few prayers after it. And then was the communion service, which had full effect upon me, and I received the Holy Sacrament with great devotion. Last night's irregularity, or whatever it should be called, did not disturb me. I was all piety. I went and drank coffee and read the newspapers comfortably in the Chapter Coffee-house.

Then went to Dr. Johnson's, where I was engaged to dinner. Dr. Burney was there.[8] I renewed my acquaintance with him. Dr. Johnson, Mrs. Williams, and I dined together. We had soup, beef *à la mode,* boiled pork and pease-pudding and potatoes, roasted lamb and spinach, porter and port. We were hearty and easy.

After dinner I said Horace was wrong in placing happiness in *nil admirari.*[9] I was sorry I had lost much of my disposition to admire, as people generally do as they grow up. Said Mr. Johnson: "One gets a better thing—judgement to estimate things at their true value." I said admiration was more pleasing than judgement, as love is more pleasing than friendship; and I repeated what I said one day to Mrs. Stuart: that friendship was like being comfortably filled with roast beef; love like being enlivened with champagne. "No," said Mr. Johnson, "admiration and love are like being intoxicated with champagne; judgement and friendship like being enlivened with champagne. Waller has hit upon the same thought with you."[1] I said I did not imagine I had borrowed from Waller. I doubted if I had seen the passage. "I don't believe you *have* borrowed," said he. "I believe it is from your own powers." I said, "I don't talk much from books; but there is a very good reason for it. I have not read many books." Said Mr. Johnson: "I wish you had read

---

[7] Richard Owen Cambridge was an author of satiric verse and an essayist, whose villa in the meadows opposite Richmond Hill was the resort of wits, writers, and politicians.
[8] Charles Burney was a musician and author of many books on music, including the *History of Music,* 1776–1789, and, later, a member of The Club. Johnson said of him, "Dr. Burney is a man for all the world to love: it is but natural to love him."
[9] " 'Marvel at nothing'—that is almost the only thing . . . which can make and keep one happy": *Epistles,* I. vi. 1–2.
[1] Boswell left a blank here for a quotation from Waller's *Epistles,* which he gives in the *Life* in a foot-note.

more books. The foundation must be laid by reading. General principles must be had from books. But they must be brought to the test of real life. In conversation you never get a system. What is said upon a subject is to be gathered from a hundred people. The parts of a truth which one gets thus are at such a distance from each other that one never gets a full view." He had said before dinner that Lord Elibank's great excellence was not his having read a great many books, for we can go to the books ourselves; but it was his having improved his knowledge by being much in the world.

I called on Dr. Wilson from Newcastle at his house in Cecil Street in the Strand, and was pleased to find him quite calm in London, with old books about him. I then called at Beauclerk's. He was at dinner, but having been told I had been at the door he sent after me, and begged I would come in. Miss Herbert, Adam Smith, and Mr. Norbury, one of the under masters of Eton, were there. I was in the very finest spirits, and stayed and drank tea, and thought myself agreeable, though I might be mistaken; for as Mr. Johnson observed of Sir Joshua Reynolds, "He has now got a good deal into great company and drinks to raise himself to a level with his company, without considering that when a man is agreeable to himself, he may not be so to others."

I called on General Paoli, and found that he was a little averse to delay the Wilton jaunt. However, I was so desirous to go to Cambridge's that I trespassed on his goodness, and he consented to wait. I then went to Lord Mountstuart's. Supper was over. I had some bread and cheese and a bottle of claret. Lord Northington and John Ross Mackye were there. Lord Northington told us that the Duchess of Hamilton solicited his father to come and vote against Douglas, and that his father answered, "Madam, you're so pretty that I'd do any wickedness *with* you, but not *for* you." He said Douglas did not look like a Frenchman, but neither did he look like a man of high birth. I stayed a little with my Lord by ourselves.

MONDAY 17 APRIL. I got up early, finished my duplies, and was easy; dressed, and in passing to the City, called on Mr. Walter Scott, the agent against Dr. Memis, who was now in London, and read the paper to him, with which he was pleased. I had called yesterday morning in my way to St. Paul's and left an apology for not being ready on Saturday. However, it was soon enough by this night's post. Yesterday Mr. Seton of Touch called while I was writing my apology, and he and I had a little conversation on *the old political faith.*[2] Today I went with Mr. Edward

---

[2] Hugh Seton of Touch (born Smith) had married the heiress of that ancient family, which, like his own family, had strong Jacobite connexions.

Dilly and dined at the Mansion House. Mr. Colman sat by me.[3] I also stayed to the ball, which was very elegant. I lay at Dilly's.

TUESDAY 18 APRIL.[4] . . . [Dr. Johnson] and I were engaged to go with Sir Joshua Reynolds to dine with Mr. Cambridge at his delightful seat on the banks of the Thames near Twickenham. Dr. Johnson's tardiness was such that Sir Joshua, who had an appointment at Richmond early in the forenoon, was obliged to go by himself on horse-back, leaving his coach to Johnson and me.[5] He was in such good temper that everything seemed cheerful to him as we drove along and I was uncommonly easy with him.

[JOHNSON. "Miss Reynolds ought not to paint. Public practice of staring in men's faces is inconsistent with delicacy."] I happened to start a question of propriety, whether, when one knows that some of his intimate friends are invited to the house of another friend, with whom they are all equally intimate, may he go also without an invitation? [JOHNSON. "You're not to go where others are invited." BOSWELL. "Not I to Thrale's when you and Langton are there?" JOHNSON. "No, we may be invited to abuse you."]

As a curious instance how little a man knows, or wishes to know, his own character in the world, or perhaps as a convincing proof that Johnson's roughness was only external, and had no participation with his heart, the following dialogue actually passed between us: JOHNSON. "It is wonderful, Sir, how rare a quality good humour is in life. We meet with very few good-humoured men." I mentioned four of our friends, none of whom he would allow to be good humoured.[6] One was *acrimonious,*

[3] "At the Mansion House dinner on Easter Monday Mr. Boswell, who had taken care to secure good room at the table, seeing Mr. Colman in want of a place called to him and gave him one beside himself, saying, 'You see what it is to have a Scotsman for your friend at Mr. Wilkes's table.' A little time after there came a foreign waiter with something. Mr. Boswell talked to him in German, upon which Mr. Colman observed, 'I have certainly mistaken the place today; I thought I was at the Mansion House, but I must surely be at St. James's; for here are none but Germans and Scots'" (*Public Advertiser*, 1 May 1775, doubtless written by Boswell himself).

[4] Boswell's record for this day survives only in the form of notes. As printed here, the text is taken from the manuscript of the *Life*—the first draft, in so far as this can be determined. In a few instances passages from the notes (somewhat expanded by the editors) are interpolated within brackets.

[5] According to the notes, Boswell, while waiting for Johnson, went to the shop of Dodsley the bookseller. In order to prepare himself for conversation at the villa, he read several essays contributed by Cambridge to *The World:* Nos. 118–119 (on gardening), No. 123 (on turtle-eating), and No. 206 (on a career of gallantry).

[6] The notes show that these were Reynolds, Burke, Beauclerk ("acrimonious" or "acid"), and Langton ("muddy").

another was *muddy,* and to the others he had objections which have
escaped me. Then, shaking his head and stretching himself at his ease
in the coach, and smiling with much complacency, he turned to me and
said, "I look upon *myself* as a good-humoured fellow." The epithet *fellow*
applied to the great lexicographer, the stately moralist, the masterly critic,
as if he had been *Sam* Johnson, a mere pleasant companion, was highly
diverting; and this light notion of himself struck me with wonder. I
answered, also smiling, "No, no, Sir; that will *not* do. You are good-
natured, but not good-humoured. You are irascible. You have not patience
with folly and absurdity. I believe you would pardon them if there were
time to deprecate your vengeance; but punishment follows so quick after
sentence that they cannot escape."

I had with me a great bundle of Scotch magazines and newspapers, in
which his *Journey to the Western Islands* was attacked with all the
weapons which could be got together; and I read them to him almost the
whole of the way to Richmond. I wish the writers of them had been
present. They would have been sufficiently mortified. One ludicrous imitation of his manner, by Mr. Maclaurin, was distinguished by him from
the rude mass.[7] "This," said he, "is the best. But I could caricature my
own style much better myself." He defended his remark upon the general
insufficiency of education in Scotland. He confirmed the authenticity of
his witty saying on the learning of the Scotch—"Their learning is like
bread in a besieged town. Every man gets a little, but no man gets a full
meal." "There is," said he, "in Scotland a certain diffusion of learning
widely and thinly spread. A merchant there has as much learning as one
of their ministers."

He spoke of Izaak Walton's *Lives,* which was one of his most favourite
books. Dr. Donne's life, he said, was the most perfect. He said it was
wonderful that Walton, who was in a very low situation in life, was
familiarly received by so many great men, and that at a time when the
ranks of men were kept more separate than they are now. He supposed
he had then given up his business as a [linen-draper],[8] and was only a
writer; and that Walton was a great panegyrist. BOSWELL. "No quality will
get a man more friends than a disposition to admire the qualities of
others. I do not mean flattery, but a sincere admiration." JOHNSON. "Nay,
Sir, flattery pleases most people.[9] In the first place, the flatterer may think

---

[7] John Maclaurin had written a verse parody, "On Johnson's Dictionary," printed in
The Weekly Magazine for 14 January 1773.
[8] Johnson was wrong. Walton had been a friend of men like Donne and Henry King,
Bishop of Chichester, long before he retired from business.
[9] On two occasions, in the *Hebrides* and in the *Life,* Boswell reports that Johnson was
"somewhat susceptible of flattery."

what he says. But, in the second place, whether he thinks so or not, he certainly thinks us of consequence enough to be flattered."

No sooner had we made our bow to Mr. Cambridge in his library than Johnson ran eagerly to one side of the room, intent on poring over the backs of the books. Said Sir Joshua, "He runs to examine books as I do to the pictures. But I have the advantage. I can see much more of the pictures than he can of the books." Mr. Cambridge, upon this, politely said, "Dr. Johnson, I am going, with your pardon, to accuse myself, for I have the same custom which I perceive you have. But it seems odd that one should have such a desire to look at the backs of books." Johnson, ever ready for contest, instantly started from his abstraction, wheeled about, and answered, "Sir, the reason is very plain. Knowledge is of two kinds. We can know a subject ourselves, or we can know where we can be informed upon it. When we inquire into any subject, the first thing we have to do is to know what books there are upon it. This leads us to look at catalogues, and the backs of books in libraries." Sir Joshua observed to me the extraordinary promptitude with which Johnson flew upon an argument. "Yes," said I, "he has no formal preparation, no flourishing with his sword. He is through your body in an instant. [Cambridge had not his sword drawn."]

Johnson was here solaced with an elegant entertainment, a very accomplished family, and much good company, amongst whom was Mr. Harris of Salisbury, who paid him many compliments on his *Journey to the Western Islands.*

The common remark as to the utility of reading history having been made: JOHNSON. "We must consider how very little history there is. I mean real authentic history. That certain kings reigned, and certain battles were fought we can depend upon as true. But all the colouring, all the philosophy, of history is conjecture." "Then, Sir," said I, "you think all history no better than an almanac, a mere chronological series of remarkable events."[1] . . .

[After dinner: JOHNSON. "People soon return to their original mode: Boswell soon reverts to oatmeal. Early habits are such that though reason —nay, our senses—approve a different course, the other habits return. . . ."]

The Beggar's Opera, and the common question whether it was pernicious in its effects, having been introduced: JOHNSON. "As to this matter, which has been very much contested, I myself am of opinion that more influence has been ascribed to *The Beggar's Opera* than it in reality ever

[1] Gibbon was present at this conversation, but, as Boswell wrote in the final draft of the *Life,* he "did not step forth in defence of that species of writing. He probably did not like to *trust* himself with JOHNSON!"

had; for I do not believe that any man was ever made a rogue by being present at its representation. At the same time, I do not deny that it may have some influence, by making the character of a rogue familiar, and in some degree pleasing." Then collecting himself, as it were, to give a heavy and comprehensive stroke: "There is in it such a *labefactation*² of all principles, as may be injurious to morality."

While he delivered this response, we sat in a comical sort of restraint, smothering a laugh, which we were afraid might burst out. . . . [Cambridge] was told by Quin that during the first night of its appearance it was long in a very dubious state of danger; that there was a disposition to damn it; and that it was saved by the song, "Oh ponder well! be not severe!"³ Quin himself had so poor an opinion of it that he refused the part of Macheath, and gave it to Walker, who acquired such celebrity by his grave yet animated performance of it.

Johnson arraigned the modern politics of this country, as entirely devoid of all principle of whatever kind. "Politics," said he, "are now nothing more than means of success in life. With this sole view do men engage in politics, and their whole conduct proceeds upon it. How different in that respect is the state of the nation now from what it was in the time of Charles the First, during the usurpation, and, after the Restoration, in the time of Charles the Second. *Hudibras* affords a strong proof how much hold political principles had upon the minds of men. There is in *Hudibras* a great deal of bullion which will always last. But, to be sure, the brightest strokes of his wit owed their force to the impression of the characters which was upon men's minds at the time; to their knowing them at table and in the street; in short, being familiar with them; and above all, to his satire being directed against those whom a little while before they had hated and feared. The nation in general has ever been loyal. The murder of Charles the First was undoubtedly not committed with the approbation or consent of the people. Had that been the case, Parliament would not have quietly given up the regicides to their deserved punishment. And we know what exuberance of joy there was when Charles the Second was restored. If Charles the Second had bent all his mind to it, had made it his sole object, he might have been as absolute as Louis the Fourteenth." BOSWELL. "And he would have done no harm if he had." JOHNSON. "Why, Sir, absolute princes seldom do any harm. But they who are governed by them are governed by chance. There is no security for good government." CAMBRIDGE. "There have been many

---

² In the manuscript Boswell began to write "labefaction." The hesitancy may cast some doubt on "labefactation." Neither word (both mean overthrow or downfall) is given in Johnson's *Dictionary*.

³ The twelfth air in Act I.

sad victims to absolute power." JOHNSON. "So have there been to popular factions." BOSWELL. "The question is, shall we have one wild beast or many?" . . .

Johnson praised *The Spectator,* particularly the character of Sir Roger de Coverley. He said, "Sir Roger did not die a violent death, as has been generally said. He was not killed. He died only because others were to die, and because his death afforded an opportunity to Addison for some very fine writing. We have the example of Cervantes killing Don Quixote.[4] I cannot account why Sir Roger is represented as a little cracked. It appears to me that the story of the widow was intended to have something superinduced upon it.[5] But the superstructure did not come."

Somebody found fault with writing verses in a dead language, maintaining that they were merely arrangements of so many words, and laughed at the Universities of Oxford and Cambridge for sending forth collections of them not only in Greek and Latin, but even in Syriac, Arabic, and other more unknown tongues. JOHNSON. "I would have as many of these as possible; I would have verses in every language that there are the means of acquiring. Nobody imagines that an university is to have at once two hundred poets; but it is to show two hundred scholars. Peiresc's death was lamented, I think, in forty languages.[6] And I would have at every coronation and every death of a king, every *gaudium* and every *luctus,*[7] university verses in every language that can be shown. I would have the world to be thus told, 'Here is a place where everything may be learnt.'"

[In drawing-room he clapped me on shoulder kindly. I said, smiling, "Well, you gave me my oatmeal." JOHNSON (imagining I was vexed). "Digest it; digest it. I would not have given it you if I thought it would have stuck in your throat." . . .

Walking with Sir Joshua, I spoke of coming to London. Sir Joshua said, "Every man must judge for himself." I said, "Johnson has more power in his own person than any man. He has not sought money. He has end without means." SIR JOSHUA. "By other means." BOSWELL. "Yes; he has gold, so needs not silver; or rather, he has goods, so needs not money."]

[4] "The reason which induced Cervantes to bring his hero to the grave, *para mi solo nacio Don Quixote, y yo para el* [for me alone was Don Quixote born, and I for him], made Addison declare, with an undue vehemence of expression, that he would kill Sir Roger; being of opinion that they were born for one another, and that any other hand would do him wrong" (Johnson, *Life of Addison*).
[5] *Spectator* No. 113.
[6] Nicolas Claude Fabri de Peiresc (1580–1637), French archaeologist and patron of letters.
[7] Every gaudy (annual dinner of commemoration in a college) or day of mourning.

WEDNESDAY 19 APRIL.[8] About ten o'clock General Paoli and I set
out in a post-chaise attended by Giacomo Pietro, a Corsican, his *valet de
chambre,* and Alessandro, an Italian footman. We had a good journey to
Wilton. The magnificence of the house was striking.[8a] My Lord and my
Lady were very civil. At supper I talked a good deal of Dr. Johnson, and
the company were well entertained. General Paoli and I had each a very
good room near to one another, and each had a small room adjoining
where a servant slept. My Lord went after supper and saw us to our rooms.

THURSDAY 20 APRIL. We went and saw my Lord ride some manège
horses. He generally rides four every morning. Lord Herbert was a fine,
healthy, good-looking young man, not sixteen.[9] There was an excellent
breakfast. The servants made chocolade and tea in what is called the
coffee-room, and brought it to us in the next room; and there were fine
hot rolls baked every morning, and good fresh butter. Colonel Phillipson,
Lieutenant-Colonel of my Lord's regiment, and some more gentlemen
were here. We were all weighed after breakfast. Lord Herbert performed
the ceremony. It seemed to be a great mode of judging here, at least a
great object of curiosity. There was a puppy of which Lord Herbert said,
"It is strange. That puppy is but nine weeks old, and it weighs five-and-
twenty pound and a half." [1] After breakfast the General and I and Captain
Charles Medows and Lord Herbert and Mr. Brompton the painter walked
out. There is here no extensive park. But the river Avon runs beautifully
through fine verdant turf, and it has been contrived to cut it so as to
form _____ islands with tall trees on them. Lord Herbert rowed Mr.
Brompton and me up the river, and we landed on one of them. They
are very near the house. There are here some cedars of extraordinary size.
I admired much a rock bridge across the Avon by Sir William Chambers.
It had quite the appearance of nature. On the other side of the river is
a beautiful mass of green ground and trees, from whence is a prospect of
Salisbury steeple.[2]

[8] On this day the battle of Lexington inaugurated the American War.
[8a] A contemporary view of Wilton is reproduced following p. 134.
[9] Lord Pembroke's eldest son, later eleventh Earl of Pembroke.
[1] Among Boswell's memoranda now at Yale: "Wilton House, 20 April 1775. I was
weighed by Lord Herbert, who liked to weigh man and beast, and I was eleven stone
twelve pounds" (166 pounds).
[2] "The river Nadder [which joins the Avon at Salisbury, three miles away] runs near
the house, and there used to be some small islands, I believe, some three or four
hundred yards from the house, where the boat-house now is. They were done away
with during the latter half of the nineteenth century. The 'rock bridge' spans the
Wylye, which also runs through the gardens. This is now known as the Image Bridge,
as there are two life-size stone figures on it, just below the parapet. The facing of the
stones of the bridge is roughly carved to look like rocks. The bridge carries a road,
still used, which used to be the old carriage drive to the entrance of the house on the

At dinner we had two Mr. Sheldons, Roman Catholic gentlemen—brothers. One of them, a counsellor in Gray's Inn, told me that Lord Dormer's family has had the second sight for several generations, and he promised to get me some proofs about it. Lord Pembroke, who laughs at all mysterious belief, told us as a matter of *chance* that he dreamt at Paris that a lady with whom he was in love had a mole on a particular part of her body which was concealed, and when he attained to his wishes, he found the mole on that very spot. I drank cheerfully today. The afternoon, however, went but tiresomely after London. There is a billiard-table to which all the company go in the evening, to play or look on.

FRIDAY 2 1 APRIL. I had undertaken to write out a clean copy of the notes which I took of the speeches of the Lords of Session on the reduction of the Town Council of Stirling. I tried to do it here; but was so indolent, though I had nothing to do, that I could hardly write any. There was at Wilton no state, no grand order, not a cook—in short, not what one would wish to see at a nobleman's country seat. My spirits flagged. I was even hypochondriac. It is unnecessary to mark all the shades of such a state. In vain did I recollect that I was now at Wilton, that I was with the Earl of Pembroke, that here was the very walk where Sir Philip Sidney composed his *Arcadia*. I was sunk and nonchalant. General Paoli tired exceedingly. My Lord could not take the trouble to be magnificent. My Lady went this day for London. Mr. Brompton and I walked to Salisbury; saw the Cathedral, which is beautiful and curiously light. Then took a post-chaise and drove to Stonehenge. I was struck only with a general sensation of stupendousness. I had seen prints and read of it so much that there was little novelty. Mr. Brompton accounted for the stones being raised by telling me that they raise immense stones in the East Indies by making a bank of earth, rolling them up it, and then taking away the earth. Brompton talked well, which was lucky; for I could hardly articulate, so relaxed was I. When we returned to Wilton, we found the celebrated Mrs. Greville, her daughter the beautiful Mrs. Crewe, and the Hon. Miss Monckton, accompanied by Dean Marlay, to whom I had been introduced one day in the street in London, but did not recollect him.[3] I imagined the parson of the parish and his wife and

---

east side, before Wyatt made the present entrance to the north. There are two of the original cedars still standing in the garden, and another five or six in the park. One big cedar died in 1916 or 1917, and it was about three hundred years old" (Lord Herbert, now Lord Pembroke, to F. A. Pottle, 6 April 1943).

[3] Mrs. Greville, the wife of Fulke Greville and godmother of Fanny Burney, was the author of the ode, *A Prayer for Indifference*. Her daughter, later Lady Crewe, was considered one of the most beautiful women of her time. The Hon. Mary Monckton, daughter of the Earl of Galway and later Countess of Cork and Orrery, was a vivacious bluestocking. Dickens drew on her for his Mrs. Leo Hunter in *Pickwick Papers*.

daughters were come on a visit, and I would needs from much humanity be very civil and encouraging to the good folks. Had not Brompton undeceived me, there might have been fine sport. Mrs. Greville would have played me off. They went away after dinner. We had a long, long evening, though the billiards were tried awhile. I was next day to proceed on a visit to my friend Temple.

SATURDAY 22 APRIL. Mr. Brompton showed me the finest things in the house, as also the library. *That* roused me a little. The General and I set out at twelve, and Mr. Brompton with us. At Salisbury we saw at Mr. _____, a banker's, several pictures, in particular a very excellent one of Butler by Sir _____.⁴ We dined, and I set out in the Exeter coach, leaving the General to return to London. At Salisbury is a curious signpost: "John Holdaway, late Turnkey to the County Gaol. Spirituous liquors sold here." How a man's having been a turnkey should recommend him, unless people wanted to be confined, was not clear. I got to Blandford about seven, had tea and finished the Stirling notes, and was relieved. I waited here for the Exeter chaise, which was to go through about one in the morning.

SUNDAY 23 APRIL. About one the chaise arrived. But unluckily it was full to Axminster. Keenness to get forward made me resolve to follow it on horse-back. A heavy rain came on, so I took a chaise to Dorchester. There it grew fair, and I mounted a hack; but not being used to ride, and having no boots, it was very hard on me. When I had rode eight miles it began to rain again. One of the travellers in the chaise cried, "Come, I'll give you a spell." So he took my horse and put me into the chaise. The other two were fishermen; and I got so much into their favour that they declared I should ride no more. They'd go out of the chaise time about.⁴ᵃ Breakfasted at Bridport. My spirits rose. One of the fishermen agreed to go by water. So I had a snug seat. From Axminster I had only for my companion the first obliging traveller, Mr. Zachary John of Stoke Newington, a Cornish man, going to Penzance. We were very social. We got to Exeter between three and four, ordered fine salmon and soles for dinner, and went to the Cathedral, which is truly grand. Service was going on. I offered up my devotions fervently. Mr. John had been educated at Exeter. He showed me the place. I had a wonderful pleasure in walking among crowds, not one of whom knew me, or I them. Mr. John told me his father had a Cornish dictionary in manuscript. I must inquire about it. We agreed to meet again if we could.

⁴ These blanks may be filled respectively by "Hayter" and "Peter Lely" (James Granger's *Biographical History of England*, London, 1779, iv. 38–39).
⁴ᵃ Scots for alternately.

I took a post-chaise and drove to Mamhead.[5] The evening was fine. I was as well as I could wish to be. The driver could not find the way to the parsonage. So I knocked at the door of Lord Lisburne's house to get a guide. To my surprise, his Lordship opened the door. I had seen him on a committee.[6] I did not imagine he had been in the country. He was polite and lively and obliging, and made a servant show me to Temple's with a lantern, and asked Mr. Temple and me to come and breakfast next day with him. My worthy friend received me with warm affection. Mrs. Temple got me at my desire some warm bread and milk, and [I] had my feet bathed in warm water, and went to bed and slept after my weary journey most calmly and placidly under the roof of my old and most intimate friend. It was the next comfort to being at my own house.

[EDITORIAL NOTE: While Boswell was at Mamhead (probably until 30 April), Temple read his Hebrides journal, which he had brought with him and which was later left at Streatham for Mrs. Thrale to read after he returned to Edinburgh from London. Two events of this Devonshire jaunt we know: he was taken to dine at Ugbrooke with Lord Clifford—a Roman Catholic—in order that he might "feast his imagination" with old trees and priests; and Temple pledged him to sobriety under a venerable yew (Boswell was not to drink more than six glasses at a time). He was back in London on 2 May. His landlord in Gerrard Street having had an advantageous offer for the lodging he was occupying, he at last yielded to Paoli's urging and moved into his friend's house, which thereafter remained his headquarters while he was in London. On 12 May he slept for the first time under Johnson's roof, finding (to his surprise) "everything in excellent order." The next day he dined with John Wilkes and his daughter at the Mansion House; they were "classical and gay . . . as when at Rome and Naples" in 1765. During these weeks, as a non-committal step towards coming to the English bar, Boswell began his terms at the Inner Temple, and ate enough meals at commons to fulfil the requirements of one term's residence.[7]

[5] Mamhead is eight miles south of Exeter. Temple's small and ancient church, very little changed since 1775, stands in the park of Mamhead House, the best part of a mile from the Lodge entrance, in full view of the House (then a residence of Lord Lisburne). The venerable yew under which Boswell pledged sobriety (see below, p. 178) may still be seen in the churchyard. The thatched house that served as a rectory during Temple's incumbency was converted by his successor into a mansion which stands today.

[6] At the Lanarkshire election committee on 10 April.

[7] As was customary, Boswell had to give a commons bond with two sureties (Johnson joined in his bond). The formality of his admission to the Inner Temple had been arranged for him by Thomas Sheridan many years before, on 19 November 1761.

On 16 and 17 May he went with Johnson to the Thrales' villa at Streatham and after that to Beauclerk's villa at Muswell Hill, near Highgate, with its splendid library, its "greenhouses, hothouse, observatory, laboratory for chemical experiments—in short, everything princely." Yet Boswell remained in such a "dissipated state of mind" that he absolutely could not write. His last day, none the less, was delightful: breakfast with Paoli, worship in St. Paul's, a tête-à-tête with Mrs. Stuart, supper with Johnson at Dilly's. He left London on 22 May, at two in the morning, in order to be in Edinburgh for the meeting of the General Assembly. That night at Grantham he was in almost as good spirits as on the way to London, though Mattie, the handsome chambermaid, was not there. Fortunately in the fly with him was an "amiable creature," Miss Silverton, and he could "unite little fondnesses with perfect conjugal love." Near Newcastle he visited his brother John, who did not seem to be unhappy, and when he arrived in Edinburgh, he found his wife and daughters as well as he could wish. But "it required some philosophy to bear the change from England to Scotland. The unpleasing tone, the rude familiarity, the barren conversation of those whom I found here, in comparison with what I had left, really hurt my feelings."]

REVIEW OF MY LIFE
DURING THE SUMMER SESSION 1775

I do not remember any portion of my existence flatter than these two months.[8] I was indolent in body and in mind; and the scenes of most lively enjoyment that I had were two dinners in the Castle with the mess of the 66 Regiment. Dr. Samuel Johnson being on a jaunt in different parts of England, I had not a single letter from him during this Session; so that my mind wanted its great Sun. Some letters from Temple and one from my brother David were comforts. My father's coldness to me, the unsettled state of our family affairs, and the poor opinion which I had of the profession of a lawyer in Scotland, which consumed my life in the mean time, sunk my spirits woefully; and for some of the last weeks of the session I was depressed with black melancholy. Gloomy doubts of a future existence harassed me. I thought myself disordered in mind.[9] Yet I was able to discharge my duty as a lawyer, wrote sixty papers, though none of them were very long indeed, and got one hundred and eighteen guineas and one pound in fees.

Mrs. Grant of Ballindalloch, the handsome gay widow, disturbed me

[8] That is, 12 June to 12 August.
[9] "While afflicted with melancholy, all the doubts which have ever disturbed thinking men come upon me. I awake in the night, dreading annihilation or being thrown into some horrible state of being" (Boswell to Temple, 12 August 1775).

at one period.[1] I supped with her three times at her own house. She was several times at ours; and I was with her at Lord Dundonald's and Comely Garden. I got into a style with her somewhat like the beginning of my former connexions with actresses, particularly one Saturday forenoon. It vexed me to have any degree of such a fever while I was conscious of the most sincere regard for my valuable spouse, who was hurt by it. I resolved to check myself; and luckily one evening that she supped with us near the end of the Session she talked to me in an ill-bred manner, which disgusted me a good deal, and I became indifferent; and when I afterwards dined along with her at Lord Chief Baron Montgomery's, where she tried her allurements, I felt myself quite easy.[2] My notions of intercourse between the two sexes are perhaps too licentious. I am somewhat of a Solomon in that. But, without any argument, it is clearly wrong for me to let my *affection* be at all carried away from my wife and children.

During this session I was visited by M. Le Clerc de Septchênes, a young Parisian recommended to me by Sir John Pringle, and by Mr. Paradise, born in Greece, recommended to me by Mr. Langton.[3] He and his lady and Mr. Gosset, an English clergyman, came a jaunt into Scotland.[4] The Reverend Mr. Donald Macqueen, Captain Maclean from Coll, and Coirechatachan were in town.[5] I entertained them cordially, but could not show them so much kindness as I met with in the Hebrides. The truth is, as somebody observed to me, that *there* they had Dr. Johnson and me only to mind. Whereas in a town a man is taken up by a variety of peo-

[1] Elizabeth Grant, widow of Major William Grant of Ballindalloch (died 1770). They had separated in 1764. She later married James Burnett of Countesswells, Aberdeenshire. Except for one or two extremely guarded references in the journal (like the present one), the Boswell papers contain nothing on Mrs. Grant.

[2] Chief Baron Ord had resigned; the Lord Advocate (Montgomery) had been advanced to his place, and Henry Dundas, the Solicitor-General, had been made Lord Advocate.

[3] Presumably N. Le Clerc de Septchênes, translator of Gibbon's *Decline and Fall of the Roman Empire*. In a letter of 29 May, Pringle had introduced him as "modest, sensible, and well-behaved"; a young man who "is breeding for being one of the private secretaries to the King of France, and that for the department of English affairs." Le Clerc planned also to meet Hume, Kames, Monboddo, and Sir Alexander Dick. John Paradise was recommended by Bennet Langton in a letter of 9 June as the son of a man of "handsome fortune" who had been "our consul at Thessalonica in Greece." He had an extraordinary talent for languages. He became a friend of Johnson, Reynolds, and Sir William Jones. His wife Lucy, a celebrated beauty, was the daughter of Philip Ludwell, a Virginia planter.

[4] Isaac Gosset, the younger, a book collector since a boy and very deformed; he was the son of the artist who modelled portraits in wax.

[5] Lachlan Mackinnon of Coirechatachan was "a jolly big man" whom Boswell and Johnson had visited in Skye, 6–8 and 25–28 September 1773.

ple. Also we had them only to receive us there. In a town they have numbers to receive *them*. Of the 66 Regiment, I had several times with me Major Coates, a Yorkshireman, and Captain Castle of the Grenadiers, and sometimes Captain Vowel, and once Major Macdonald of Keppoch (a captain who sold out),[6] Ensign and Adjutant Duncan, Surgeon Gauld.

There was some stir about a competition for the office of Dean of the Faculty of Advocates. I was clear for Crosbie as a man of learning and independency. But there was so great a majority for Harry Dundas, the young Lord Advocate, that Crosbie declined standing, and he and his friends voted for Dundas that there might be no division.[7] I was hurt to find no spirit in our society.

On Sunday the 18 of June I dined with Lord Kames, having gone to call for him between sermons, and having got from him particulars of his life with design to write it, and so sat on. He was in a good frame. I was sometimes at Moncrieffe's club, at Prestonfield, at Lord Dundonald's. I tried some medicines, thinking my melancholy might be owing to some corporeal disorder. I had really a sad session of it. I could do nothing but what I was obliged to do; so kept no journal. Mr. Lawrie marked briefly each day. I keep his paper.[8]

The engagements in America roused me somewhat; but notwithstanding Dr. Johnson, I was inclined to the side of the provincials.[9] Captain George Preston of the Marines came home from the East Indies. I was often at Sir George's. I attended a course of chemistry by Dr. Black between two and three. We were mostly lawyers who agreed to take a course. I did not feel much curiosity for the science. But the truth is, I have never been properly disposed to acquire any regular stock of knowledge.[9a]

On Tuesday the 22 of August 1775 I went west to pay a visit to my

[6] That is, though a major in the Army, he had been a captain in the regiment but had just sold his commission.

[7] "Only think, Temple, of a law promotion in Scotland. Harry Dundas is going to be made King's Advocate—Lord Advocate at thirty-three. I cannot help being angry and somewhat fretful at this. He has, to be sure, strong parts. But he is a coarse, unlettered, unfanciful dog. Why is he so lucky? . . . Tell me, is it wrong to feel thus at his success?" (Boswell to Temple, 22 May 1775).

[8] It has since disappeared.

[9] "I am growing more and more an American. I see the unreasonableness of taxing them without the consent of their assemblies. I think our ministry are mad in undertaking this desperate war" (Boswell to Temple, 12 August 1775).

[9a] Joseph Black (1728–1799), Professor of Medicine and Chemistry in Edinburgh University, though curiously averse to publication and the defence of his own claims, made more fundamental contributions to the science of chemistry than any other British chemist of his time: he isolated carbon dioxide and defined the principles of combining weights, latent heat, and specific heat. He was also a very capable popularizer.

father. I got to Treesbank on Wednesday to dinner, and as I understood that it was *the preaching week,* as it is called, at Auchinleck, and did not think myself anyhow obliged to undergo the weariness of long tiresome discourses, I remained quietly at Treesbank. He and I visited Fairlie, Mr. Bruce Campbell, and Skerrington.[1] On Sunday afternoon we walked to Riccarton Kirk, where I had fully the ideas of an Ayrshire country kirk, and we drank tea at Caprington with Sir John Cuninghame and Lady Betty. It was comfortable to me to find Treesbank quite well,[2] and to be kindly entertained by his good wife, and see his sons promising children. There are ideas attached to particular places which it is almost impossible to express. I had my old ones of Treesbank quite lively. On Monday August 28 Treesbank and Mrs. Campbell went with me to Auchinleck. It was a fine day. The dry gravel roads and new-whitened pavilions gave a fine air to the place, which really looked grand. Mrs. Campbell went home that night. Treesbank stayed till Wednesday afternoon. He and I sauntered about the old house, the Mains, Tenshillingside, etc., with ideas of my grandfather, etc., quite fresh. James Bruce was just the same man as ever.[3]

SUNDAY 1 OCTOBER.[4] On Saturday, the day before, I had called on Mr. John Donaldson, miniature painter, who after many years' residence in London had come on a visit to Edinburgh.[5] He showed me some drawings, played some tunes both on the German flute and common flute,[6] and let me read an essay which he had written on the connexion between *sound* and *sight* and *morals,* in which there were really some

---

[1] John Campbell of Skerrington.

[2] A premature diagnosis. His operation had come too late. Within a year he was dying of "a monstrous incurable cancer." Though James Campbell was in his sixties, his sons were quite young, the elder six and the younger four. See Appendix C, Chart VI.

[3] Unfortunately for Boswell, his father was also just the same man as ever. Boswell wrote to Temple on 2 September: "It is hardly credible how difficult it is for a man of my sensibility to support existence in the family where I now am. My father . . . has a method of treating me which makes me *feel* myself like *a timid boy,* which to *Boswell* (comprehending all that my character does, in my own imagination and in that of a wonderful number of mankind) is intolerable. His wife, too . . . is so narrow-minded, and, I don't know how, so set upon keeping him totally under her own management, and so suspicious and so sourishly tempered that it requires the utmost exertion of practical philosophy to keep myself quiet. I, however, have done so all this week to admiration, nay, I have appeared good-humoured; but it has cost me drinking a considerable quantity of strong beer to dull my faculties."

[4] The scene shifts to Edinburgh. Only a fragment of the journal for this day remains among the Boswell papers.

[5] Donaldson painted a miniature of Boswell in 1769, and of Mrs. Boswell in December 1775 and again in 1784. None of them has so far been located.

[6] Boswell's "common flute" resembled a recorder; the German or transverse flute has entirely superseded it.

ingenious observations. As an old acquaintance and a man of merit, though somewhat odd, I asked him to dine with me. He lodged at the end of the New Bridge opposite to the Theatre. I called at the Theatre, and found Mr. Digges, and . . .

[EDITORIAL NOTE: At this point the journal breaks off. On 9 October, being inspirited by the birth of his son Alexander, Boswell started again to keep a journal regularly.]

Journal in Edinburgh
Autumn and Winter 1775—1776

MONDAY 9 OCTOBER. My wife having been seized with her pains in the night, I got up about three o'clock, and between four and five Dr. Young came. He and I sat upstairs mostly till between three and four, when, after we had dined, her labour became violent. I was full of expectation, and meditated curiously on the thought that it was already certain of what sex the child was, but that I could not have the least guess on which side the probability was. Miss Preston attended my wife close. Lady Preston came several times to inquire, but did not go into the room. I did not feel so much anxiety about my wife now as on former occasions, being better used to an inlying. Yet the danger was as great now as ever. I was easier from the same deception which affects a soldier who has escaped in several battles. She was very ill. Between seven and eight I went into the room. She was just delivered. I heard her say, "God be thanked for whatever he sends." I supposed then the child was a daughter. But she herself had not then seen it. Miss Preston said, "Is it a daughter?" "No," said Mrs. Forrest, the nurse-keeper,[1] "It's a son." When I had seen the little man I said that I should now be so anxious that probably I should never again have an easy hour. I said to Dr. Young with great seriousness, "Doctor, Doctor, let no man set his heart upon anything in this world but land or heritable bonds; for he has no security that anything else will last as long as himself." My anxiety subdued a flutter of joy which was in my breast. I wrote several letters to announce my son's birth. I indulged some imaginations that he might perhaps be a great man. Worthy Grange came and cordially congratulated me. He and Dr. Young and Lady Preston and Miss Preston supped with me.

I have resolved to keep a journal of my life every day from this important era in my family, and I shall never omit putting down something of each day's history. To record fully and minutely how every hour was employed would be an intolerable labour, or would prevent action in a great measure. If I can look back and see how my life has been passed, by having so many marks of each day preserved, it is enough. I shall

[1] Sick-nurse.

try to register the state of my mind, and although I am now writing this journal from short notes on the 24 of October, I am resolved for the future to put down the marks of each day before I sleep, or at latest the day after. I may at times make a review of a period and try to form something general out of a number of various ideas, and I think it would be agreeable to have my life drawn out in tables: by months or years, by my progress in knowledge, or by any other plans. I was this night most devoutly grateful to GOD.

TUESDAY 10 OCTOBER. This morning my little son's nurse, Nellie Anderson, wife to William Colville, a tailor in the suburbs of Edinburgh at a place called Goosedub, came. She was a pretty little woman about _____, but a mere simpleton, which we thought no disadvantage. I dined at Sir George Preston's, who was warmly happy upon the joyful occasion. I drank tea in my wife's room and then went down to worthy Grange's, and he and I and Mr. James Loch drank a couple of bottles of Malaga, except a few glasses which Mr. Lawrie drank. At night Mrs. Montgomerie, dowager of Lainshaw, came. She and I supped by ourselves.

WEDNESDAY 11 OCTOBER. Dr. Webster was not returned from a jaunt into England. I engaged Dr. Erskine to be with me in the afternoon, when I intended to have my son baptized.[2] Commissioner Cochrane dined at Sir George's with Mrs. Montgomerie and me, in order to be at the baptism. But as we did not keep precisely to the hour of four, and he was afraid of travelling in the night air, he left my house before the ceremony. There were present Sir George and Lady Preston and Miss Preston, Mrs. Montgomerie, Grange, and my cousin Bruce Boswell, who was just returned from an East India voyage.[3] Veronica and Effie, and all the servants too but one, were in the room. It was pretty to see the two little sisters well dressed and quiet. I was serenely happy. Robert Boswell came in after the ceremony, which, as an Independent, he did not like to attend. After drinking some wine and tea, I took Dr. Erskine down to my wife's room, and he said a prayer with much fervency. He then said to me, "Allow me to express a wish for your infant son. May he have all the genius and spirit of one connexion, all the sense, knowledge, and application of another, and all the unaffected piety of a third; and then he will not only be an useful member of society but a happy man.

[2] In naming his children, Boswell followed the custom usual in Scotland with established families: first son named for father's father, second son for mother's father, third son for father's grandfather (Alexander for Lord Auchinleck, David for David Montgomerie of Lainshaw, James for James Boswell of Auchinleck).

[3] Bruce Boswell, Dr. Boswell's son, became a captain in the service of the East India Company. Robert was his older brother. When Boswell calls Robert an Independent, he uses the term loosely. Robert, like his father, was a Glassite or Sandemanian, and opposed the principle of an established church. See below, 6 January 1776.

And may his parents live to see him such." I understood this to mean myself, my father, and my mother. Dr. Erskine, I firmly believe, was sincere. This was a most comfortable afternoon.

THURSDAY 12 OCTOBER. Dr. Boswell breakfasted with me, and expressed much joy. I dined at Sir George Preston's, where I had a general pressing invitation while my wife was confined to bed, that no jack might disturb her.[4] I supped at Mr. Wood's to be made acquainted with his family. He had drank too much at dinner, a very rare thing with him, and he was noisy and incoherent. Poor Veronica was taken ill with a sudden hoarseness. I brought him home with me, but he was not fit for advising very clearly. I was sadly alarmed. She grew better.

FRIDAY 13 OCTOBER. Veronica was pretty well. I wrote a memorial against one Dick, applying for a *cessio bonorum,* and found myself ready enough in dictating. Dined at Maclaurin's, where were Wight, David Erskine, etc. Played at whist. Was seized with the rage of gaming which is in my blood, and played till three in the morning. Lost.

SATURDAY 14 OCTOBER. Having heard that the Royal Highland Regiment was to march in today to the Castle, I was eager to meet them. Grange went with me, and Mr. Lawrie also went. We overtook Dr. Boswell near the West Port, who harangued what fine fellows the Highlanders were in 1745. He was going but a little way. We walked to the other side of the Coltbridge. I had wrought myself into a kind of enthusiasm about *The Highland Watch,* recollected their not having been in Scotland since the year 1744, and never in Edinburgh Castle, and I said to Grange that he and I would talk of their entry into *Auld Reekie* many years hence.[5] I have straw or chips in my mind which a little matter will kindle into a blaze. But I have more solid materials, hard coal and old wood, which require stronger heat to inflame them. I should, however, take care. A chimney has been set on fire and a house burnt by an inconsiderable kindling. We were disappointed, for there were no more of the Regiment came in than fifty-five men, which were all they had for four companies. There were three officers: Captain Macpherson of _____,[6] who commanded them, Lieutenant Graham, son to my cousin the late Colonel Gordon Graham, and Ensign Dalrymple. I spoke with young Graham as a relation, and it seems he had seen me before.[7] There

[4] If Boswell dined out, it would not be necessary to turn the spit with the jack, which was noisy.

[5] The regiment, better known as the Black Watch, was famous for its foreign service ever since its founding in 1739. They embarked not in 1744, as Boswell writes, but in 1743. "Auld Reekie" ("Old Smoky") is a sobriquet of Edinburgh.

[6] Probably Duncan Macpherson of Bleaton.

[7] Lt.-Col. Gordon Graham's eldest son, Charles, was a captain, and his second son, William, a lieutenant in the 42nd. William is probably here referred to. But there were

was a great number of people meeting them. The windows in Portsburgh and Edinburgh were crowded. I liked to see them enter the West Port. We saw them fairly enter the Castle.

I then met with Mr. Spence, Treasurer to the Bank of Scotland, at his lodging in the Bank, consulted on his cause against Lawrence Spens *as a friend,* and was treated with Malaga and biscuits. I dined at Sir George Preston's, and was in such lively spirits and cordial frame that I drank about a bottle of port quickly, which intoxicated me somewhat. And away I went to the Castle, and viewed it in possession of the Highlanders; and as I saw the tartan in the sentry-boxes and the square swarming with filibegs, I felt as if in the days of one of the ancient kings of Scotland. The officers were engaged in different parties. But I got the sergeant upon guard, Monro, a fine black fellow who had been twenty years in the Regiment, and a sergeant of the Invalids,[8] who turned out to be John Taylor, a Kilmarnock man (who when in the Royal Scots was tried for murder at Guildford, and got off), as also Shearer, the head gunner—and with these three I drank strong beer for two hours. I wanted to have had a number of the men with us. But Monro said they got as much this night from their friends as would do them good. But I made him promise to have all the men then upon guard to meet me next day at four o'clock in the afternoon in the place where we were then drinking; to wit, the little room in which Queen Mary was delivered of King James VI.[9] This was a strange satisfaction to me. I was quite military and Highland. Monro was a true specimen of the Scotch Highlanders: robust and intrepid. It is curious how the character is continued through generations. I came home and Mr. Wood supped with me.

SUNDAY 15 OCTOBER. Was a little vexed at last night's adventure, and not a little uneasy to think of my engagement for today, which, as it was with soldiers, I resolved to keep. I went down to Grange and prevailed with him to promise to accompany me. I was at the New Church both forenoon and afternoon, and at home between sermons; so that I had a good counterbalance of decency. At four Grange and I repaired to the *cantine.* But luckily for me, Mr. Monro had either thought that I was joking or in liquor, or would not remember my appointment, and he was not there. I had resolved to drink only a single glass and leave

---

also in the 42nd a Lt. James Graham and a Lt. John Graham who may have been sons of Colonel Gordon. He was a great-great- and Boswell was a great-great-great-grandson of James Boswell, fourth Laird of Auchinleck (d. 1618), Graham being descended, through his mother, a Schaw of Sornbeg, from Isobel, second daughter of David Boswell, the fifth Laird (d. 1661). See below, Appendix C, Chart II.

[8] Disabled soldiers unfit for active service.

[9] The room was long used as a canteen for the soldiers.

them. But it is hard to say what might have happened if the Highlanders had been quite to my mind. I gave Sergeant Taylor money to buy beer for them, and came off. I meditated on the Highland character, which I really believe is truly Scythian and does not know the weaknesses which occasion distress to most men. There is a hardiness of body and a firmness of spirit quite peculiar. Grange and I walked to the Abbey calmly, and then he came home and drank tea with me, and I read to him from the manuscript history of our family, and we were most comfortable.[1]

MONDAY 16 OCTOBER. A supine indolence relaxed me. I began from immediate feeling an essay for *The London Magazine* on impotence of mind, wishing earnestly to have a cure for it, which perhaps some correspondent had.[2] Sir George Preston was ill again.

TUESDAY 17 OCTOBER. My indolence continued, but I finished my essay and sent it off. I was vexed that I was making no progress in any kind of knowledge. I could not read. I however was easier than I have been sometimes, as I had no instant call upon me to labour. I this day received a letter from my brother David, enclosing a genteel settlement on my wife and daughters in the event of his becoming proprietor of Auchinleck. I had asked it of him, to make my mind easy, and was very happy to find that a mercantile life had not made him selfish and evasive. I could have wished that he had not asked of me to make a settlement on him to the extent of from £1,000 to £1,500 in case of his getting no more than he already had from his father. For I should have spontaneously done as much for him. However, I thought that his behaviour to me deserved a good return, and I resolved that he should have it. Though he recommended secrecy, I could not but tell my wife and Grange to comfort them. I was still very indolent notwithstanding this cordial from David. I had some time ago during this autumn been reading Robertson's *Charles V* and *Gil Blas*, but had not looked at either for a week past.[3] I dined today tête-à-tête with my wife in her bedchamber.

WEDNESDAY 18 OCTOBER. Went out with Commissioner Cochrane in his chaise to Pinkie. Captain Campbell, a half-pay captain, dined, drank tea, and played at catch-honours all the evening, and supped with us. His fortune was strange. He was cousin german to three successive Dukes of Argyll: the great John, Archibald, and the present Duke's father, and yet had neither pension nor any good office. He seemed to be a good

[1] The history was drawn up by Boswell's grandfather. See below, 31 December.

[2] "A Cure Requested for Occasional Impotence of Mind," *London Magazine*, November 1775, pp. 570–571. A sequel in the form of a reply, also by Boswell, appeared in the issue for November 1776.

[3] On 6 November Boswell wrote to Temple: "I have read the first volume of Robertson's *Charles V*. When I have finished the book, I shall give you my opinion. In the meantime I am really disappointed."

worthy Highlander, and his bad luck made one regard him with a sort of kind regret. The Commissioner and I played off rough jokes as usual. As a specimen, when I told that the hangman of Edinburgh had two guineas apiece for all that he hanged, he said, "James, you would hang all the folk in Edinburgh at the same rate." I answered, "Indeed would I, Commissioner; and I would begin with the Boards of Custom and Excise." When I went to my room after supper, I read some of Lord Kames's *Sketches;* thought them very inferior compilations.[4]

THURSDAY 19 OCTOBER. Breakfasted early with the Commissioner, and came to town with him in his chaise. The great lines of characters may be put down. But I doubt much if it be possible to preserve in words the peculiar features of mind which distinguish individuals as certainly as the features of different countenances. The art of portrait painting fixes the last, and musical sounds with all their nice gradations can also be fixed. Perhaps language may be improved to such a degree as to picture the varieties of mind as minutely. In the mean time we must be content to enjoy the recollection of characters in our own breasts, or by conversation and gestures with people acquainted with the particular persons as much as we are. I cannot portray Commissioner Cochrane as he exists in my mind. It pleased me today to see a man of seventy-four without any wretched effect of age, neat in his person, pleasant in his temper.

This forenoon I had a letter from my father wishing me joy on the birth of my son. As the weather had been bad, he had not sent for some time to Ayr for letters, so had not received mine. Knockroon had informed him of it, from the newspapers. His writing to me thus, before he got a letter from me, showed plainly that he was very happy, though he said little. My wife dined upstairs today. Colonel Archibald Campbell was in town. I supped with him at his lodgings. Hardie and Moir, his agents, and some more of his people were there. He told me that there are some of the British regiments that have particular fates attending them. For instance the 4th, or King's Own, is never in service but its Grenadiers are severely mauled. He said that regiment is the only one which has a record from their first being raised, and it is kept at headquarters. I think there should be a little chronicle of all the regiments in the service. I should like to write it if I could get materials.

FRIDAY 20 OCTOBER. Dempster had written to me that he was to lodge under my roof on Friday evening in his way to the meeting of Parliament. He came before dinner and sent me a note from Peter Ramsay's Inn. I went to him immediately, and found him as agreeable as ever. But I suppose a little more time and a little more application to business as a lawyer had given a greater degree of solidity and rigidness to

[4] *Sketches of the History of Man, 1774.*

my mind; for he appeared to me not so strong in sense as a man and a politician should be. He had with him a Mr. Heming, his brother-in-law, for whom I secured a room in the same stair with my house.[4a] Their baggage was sent to my house directly. But I was engaged to dine at Robert Boswell's, and Dempster had to see several people. So it was agreed that he should come to me in the evening. I dined and drank tea at Robert Boswell's in a good family way, the Doctor, his two daughters and Bruce, and Captain MacLeod, formerly of the *Mansfield* East Indiaman, being there. He and the Doctor and his two sons and Maclaurin supped with me, along with Dempster and Heming.

SATURDAY 21 OCTOBER. It was rather unlucky that Dempster came at this time, for as my wife could not yet dress to appear before company, it obliged her to be again confined to her room. Maclaurin breakfasted with us today. Then we went to the Advocates' Library, where Sir Adam Fergusson, Dempster's companion to London, came, and got Dempster away with him. George Webster dined with my wife and me. Heming dined at Mr. Samuel Mitchelson's, Junior, along with Maclaurin. I went there in the afternoon to play at whist. We had two parties, and played from six in the evening till three next morning, taking only a bit of supper cold, and drinking a little wine and punch by the by. I lost several pounds, and my rage for game made me sit at it on Sunday morning, which I disapproved of as an offence against the notions of decency in Scotland; and I was vexed at having kept my wife awake so long, especially before she was well recovered. Her anxiety prevents her from sleeping till I come home.

SUNDAY 22 OCTOBER. I lay long and then got up and had Heming to breakfast with me. I was entertained by him with a number of stories of dining at taverns and travelling in stage-coaches and other adventures, which, whether true or borrowed from books, amused me. He dined at Maclaurin's. I dined quietly at home, and then went to the New English Chapel. My fatigue from sitting up late made me more susceptible of good impressions. This I *felt*. Heming, Captain George Preston, and Grange supped with me. Heming gave us several stories. He went early to bed, as he was to set out in the fly for London next day. I was in an excellent frame. I had been awhile with Sir George Preston. Dr. Erskine, that primitive saint, visited him, and prayed. It gave me satisfaction, while I turned my eyes on Sir George without being observed, that he looked up to heaven from his bed of sickness with all the appearance of sincere devotion. There are more pious minds than is believed to be. Many of my acquaintance would not think that I am devout.

[4a] George Heming, son of a Jamaica planter and Member of Assembly, had since 1769 been the tenant of Caldecote Hall in Warwickshire.

MONDAY 23 OCTOBER. Sat awhile with Maclaurin. Dr. Boswell dined with me. Donaldson, the miniature painter, drank tea, as did Mrs. Mitchelson, after which I played at whist with my wife, Mrs. Montgomerie, and Mrs. Mitchelson.

TUESDAY 24 OCTOBER. Began this journal. Drank tea with Grange, who was to set out next day for Annandale. When I do not mention dinner at all, it is understood that I dine at home and no company with me.[5]

WEDNESDAY 25 OCTOBER. Passed a part of the forenoon in the Advocates' Library with Maclaurin and Mr. Andrew Lumisden.[6] Talked of foreign literature, while I had a humbling consciousness that I could at present study none, and could seldom study much. We then walked in the Meadow with Dr. Boswell, and continued the same kind of conversation. In the afternoon I had Maclaurin and young Honyman to play at whist with me and Mrs. Montgomerie. I grew keen, and would go on after supper, and betted sometimes half a guinea, sometimes a guinea extraordinary on the rubber. Lost several pounds, and sat till between two and three. Gave a promise of my own accord to my wife that I would never again play higher than half-crown whist, and never bet on the rubber.

THURSDAY 26 OCTOBER. Walked out with Mr. Lumisden to Dr. Boswell's, and breakfasted. We were most comfortable, and it was most agree-

---

[5] Boswell wrote to Langton on this day: "My wife is recovering remarkably well, and young Alexander (named for my father) is a stout little fellow. You know what an acquisition a son is to an old feudal Goth like your humble servant. My earnest study, however, is to guard myself against being too much attached to what is very uncertain. Indeed it is in vain to think of attaining to such a frame as to enjoy a good, and not suffer by being deprived of it. Horace's *Laudo manentem* [I praise (Fortune) while she remains] and careless *resigno quae dedit* [I resign what she has given] is poetical stoicism, and I am persuaded unpracticable philosophy. Christianity opens to us a pleasing moderation, which I believe has been attained. . . . It is my intention to visit London every spring unless something extraordinary prevents me. I still indulge the scheme of trying my fortune at the English bar. . . . [Dr. Johnson's] journey to Paris [he left on 15 September] is an excellent incident in his life. I am exceedingly curious to have some account of it from him. A little before he set out, he wrote to me very kindly bidding me not be uneasy, though he did not write again for some time, as he was going to set out 'on another journey,' but not a word did he say of a French expedition. This reserve you have remarked to me on lesser occasions. . . . You promised to me, or at least resolved to put down in writing, all the sayings of Dr. Johnson that you remember. Pray favour me with them, that the crown of his own jewels which I am preparing may be more brilliant.—Tory as I am I cannot help being doubtful upon the American controversy, or rather inclined to think that our common monarch's subjects in the colonies are hardly treated."

[6] In 1765, when Boswell was in Rome, Lumisden had been his closest friend among the Jacobites who gathered about the court of the Old Pretender (for them, of course, James VIII and III). Lumisden was then the Pretender's secretary.

able to me to recollect my being at Rome with Mr. Lumisden and talking of the good Doctor when there was no prospect of our all meeting in this world, and then to have the immediate perception of our society this morning. I paid my house-rent to John Buchan, Writer to the Signet, at whose house I saw some old boxes full of manuscript books and papers and printed pieces belonging to the family of Napier, which he allowed me to tumble and examine. There were several little pieces in manuscript, mostly in figures, which had been the operations of the celebrated Napier of Merchiston.[7] There were also some journals by different persons; in particular, notes by this Lord Napier's grandfather, of what his Lordship saw when travelling. It was melancholy to see what had been written with care, and preserved as valuable, treated as lumber; and I could not but moralize on what might become of my own journals. However, they serve to entertain and instruct myself; and though the importance of a man to himself has been the subject of ridicule, it is clear to me that nothing is equally important to a man with himself. A man is called selfish in a bad sense who prefers a small good to himself to the happiness of others; or whose enjoyments are without reference to others. But surely happiness of every kind must ultimately centre in a man's own breast. I dined at Sir George Preston's with my Lady and Miss Preston.

FRIDAY 27 OCTOBER. Wrote to my brother David, and sent him a settlement of £1,500 in case the sum of £4,000 was not made up to him by our father. Though it occurred to me that it might possibly happen that my circumstances might be embarrassed, and David and I disagree, and then I might repent this settlement and appear very foolish, I *trampled on such ideas* (to use a phrase of his after suggesting difficulties which he *might* have had of making a settlement on my wife and daughters), and I felt a nobleness of mind. I dined at Sir George Preston's, Mr. Preston being come to town. I also supped there along with Dr. Webster and his son George. Mr. Preston and I talked almost the whole time of cookery. He is really skilled. I affect it, and am improving.

SATURDAY 28 OCTOBER. Mr. Preston, Dr. Webster, and Mrs. Mitchelson dined with us. I really enjoyed the luxury of a black-cock and claret. We did not drink to excess. The news of Mr. Sayre's being committed to the Tower on a charge of high treason agitated me.[8] I was rather in-

---

[7] John Napier, the inventor of logarithms.

[8] Stephen Sayre, a banker and "patriot" of American birth and education (College of New Jersey, 1757), had enjoyed the unusual distinction of serving in 1773 as Sheriff of London. An outspoken and intemperate partisan of the cause of the colonies, he had been arrested and lodged in the Tower on the charge (preferred by another American, one Richardson, adjutant of the Guards) of plotting to seize the King's person and take possession of the Tower. He was soon released for want of evidence and brought an action against Lord Rochford, Secretary of State, for false imprisonment; won the verdict, but was unable to collect damages.

clined to the American side of the present grand dispute, notwithstanding Dr. Johnson's eloquence; and I spoke warmly pretty often, from the spirit of opposition principally, I believe, as well as from a regard to what appeared to me just and reasonable. I did, however, see that it would be more prudent for me to say nothing, because the reduction of America to an implicit submission to the British legislature was a favourite object of the King himself, who might put a negative on any man against violent measures, and so Lord Mountstuart's friendship might be of no service to me. A kind and charming letter from the Hon. Mrs. Stuart had pleased me much. I supped at Maclaurin's along with Mr. Lumisden, Mr. John Fyfe, etc. We played at whist before supper. I won fifteen shillings, and was moderate in every respect this night, and home in good time.

SUNDAY 29 OCTOBER. This was my birthday, when I completed thirty-five years. I did not keep it, nor was I sensible of any remarkable reflections upon it. I stayed at home in the forenoon. Was at the New Church in the afternoon and heard Mr. Walker preach very well on the duty incumbent on every man professing the Christian religion to act according to its precepts. That some people excused themselves by saying that they made no great professions of holiness, but that professing Christianity included holiness. I walked out to Lady Colville's and drank tea. Her brother Andrew and Mr. Arbuthnot were with her, as was Lady Anne. When I came home I found Sir Walter Montgomerie-Cuninghame arrived from Minorca, and was pleased to find him appear improved and attached to me. Mr. Preston and Captain George and Mr. Wood supped with us.

MONDAY 30 OCTOBER. Sir Walter, whom I lodged at my friend Grange's, set out early for Lainshaw. I took Mr. Lawrie with me in the forenoon to Leith to talk with Captain Spears of the *Champion* about taking out James Boswell, eldest son to David, in his ship to Jamaica. David and his son had been with me some days before, informing me that Charles Boswell had written to his brother John to have the boy sent out, and he would pay his passage and take care of him.[9] We sat a little at David's, and met Captain Spears at Mrs. Ritchie's, and I agreed to advance the money for the boy's passage, being seven guineas in the steerage.[1] It was curious to find David, who had not a shilling but was in debt, making some objections to his son's not going in the cabin. I knew not whether to be angry at his folly or pleased at such a symptom

[9] David Boswell was the dancing-master; Charles and John ("Old Knockroon") were his uncles, younger sons of David's grandfather (also named David), who sold Craigston. Charles Boswell had settled in Jamaica. See below, Appendix C, Chart II.
[1] Mrs. Ritchie was a vintner at Leith, in the district called "on the shore."

of his having the blood of a gentleman. I dined at home and supped at Sir George's, along with Dr. Webster.

TUESDAY 31 OCTOBER. James Boswell came after breakfast, and I gave him an order for his passage and a guinea and six bottles of wine, recommending to him good behaviour and coming home rich. I liked to see a branch of our family going abroad with a probability of doing well and becoming a creditable connexion.

I dined at Dr. Webster's, where were his son George, Colonel Preston, and Mr. Preston. Annie was out of town. We had a truly social meeting. After tea George went with me, along with some others of Canongate Kilwinning Lodge, to visit St. Giles's Lodge. Webster's claret had enlivened me pretty well, and some strong negus which I drank at the lodge put me in such a frame that I could not finish the evening but in merry company. George Webster had received a card to come to Wares', formerly Macduffie's, to young Kincaid and Andrew Balfour to sup and play at whist and bring a fourth hand. As there is an appetite for meat, a *fames canina*[2] which will make a man devour anything, there is an appetite of the same kind for company. Away I sallied with George, and we carried with us young Hay, the surgeon. I was directly in such a fit as often seized me in the days of the Soaping Club, and supped and drank and roared and played with vast keenness.[3] Balfour went away soon. Kincaid sat till about five. Webster and Hay and I sat till between six and seven. We were in a low room known by the name of "Hell." I had sent home to tell that I was upon business; and the rage of play so heated me that I abandoned myself to it, and half-persuaded myself that my wife would be fallen asleep. I had once lost about six pounds, but when we rose my loss was only £2.16. It might have amounted to a great sum, for I was quite in the humour of venturing. When I got home there was really a dismal scene. My wife had been up all night in anxiety and terror what I could be about, and poor Veronica had been again taken ill with a hoarseness worse than last time. To reflect on all this, and at the same time on my having passed a whole night in such company, and so employed, vexed me sadly; and my wife's upbraidings galled me. I was miserably humbled.

WEDNESDAY 1 NOVEMBER. Got up about ten. Was somewhat consoled, as Veronica was better. Called at Sir George Preston's. Mr. Preston said he wished I could be set in a pillory for my conduct last night. That the ordinary pillory in presence of the rabble would not do. But he wished there were some genteel pillory where I might be made ashamed

[2] "Dog's hunger."
[3] The Soaping Club was a convivial Edinburgh society instituted by Boswell in 1760 or 1761. It met on Tuesdays at Thom's.

before creditable people. Lieutenant Graham of the Royal Highlanders, Dr. Cairnie, and Balbarton dined with me. I took a steady moderate cup of good port, and was sagacious and well again. John Boswell and his nephew David called, and I brought them in to drink a glass with us.[4] When the company went to tea, I had a private conference with my two kinsmen about David's family and Charles, and I was quite as a Highland chief with two of his clan. Mr. Preston called for a little, and by his advice I bathed my feet in warm water, went early to bed, and took a potation of sack whey. The recollection that this was All Saints' day calmed my mind.

THURSDAY 2 NOVEMBER. Veronica was hoarse again, and appeared to have a bad cold. It is amazing how little I can do at present in the way of study, and how indolently my time is spent. Dr. Cairnie sat with me a little, and we talked of the family of Stuart. I observed there is now an end of the party for them. In this reign *omnes eodem cogimur.*[5] (This happened on Friday the 3—for I am now writing on Saturday the 4.) In the evening I was at Canongate Kilwinning Lodge, and supped at Sir George Preston's with Dr. Webster and Mr. Wood. Mr. Preston was to go to Valleyfield next day. He said on hearing that I had been again at a Mason lodge,

> "Tho' list'ning senates hung on all he spoke,
> The club must hail him master of the joke."[6]

FRIDAY 3 NOVEMBER. Wrote a little journal and read part of Langhorne's edition of Collins's poems. Dr. Cairnie sat with me a little. So did Mr. Lumisden, who recalled to my mind the ideas of foreign parts and of Scotland forty years ago, when there was more politeness and gentility than now. My little son's nurse had not milk enough, and my wife was very uneasy. I called on Mr. Wood a little after three. He had dined, so I eat a bit with him and drank some glasses of wine, and then he went with me to see another nurse, whom we engaged. Her name was _____, wife to _____ Ross, a sawer in Nicolson Street. I thought that my son would perhaps read this journal and be grateful to me for my attention about him, for I was twice out speaking to his nurse. My wife, who does not like journalizing, said it was leaving myself embowelled to posterity[7]—a good strong figure. But I think it is rather leaving myself em-

---

[4] Perhaps Mrs. Boswell's exclusion of the dancing-master extended only to a ban on invitations. In any case, she could hardly have refused him admission when he came in the company of his uncle, and when she had other guests.

[5] Horace, *Odes,* II. iii. 25: "We are all impelled in the same direction."

[6] Pope, *Moral Essays,* i. 184–185: for "list'ning," read "wond'ring."

[7] The phrase occurs in the prolegomena to *The Dunciad:* "embowel and embalm him

balmed. It is certainly preserving myself. It was a kind of distressful scene
to remove the first nurse, who was anxious to stay. Mrs. Ross came to
him tonight. Veronica's cold was worse. Mr. Wood thought it might be
the measles; I was tortured with apprehension for her. I was ill of a cold.

SATURDAY 4 NOVEMBER. Veronica was easier. I lay long in bed with
my cold, stayed at home all day, finished Collins's poems with Langhorne's
observations, and brought up my journal from 27 October. Was in a
calm, mild frame, and resolved never again to fall behind with my journal.

SUNDAY 5 NOVEMBER. Having taken physic for my cold, lay in bed
till the afternoon, drank tea and took onion soup, and was relaxed and
quiet. My son had a rush [8] which alarmed my wife's anxiety. Veronica
was still indisposed, and Effie had a severe cold. The house was quite an
hospital. I considered that I could do no good, and lay still. Read Lord
Pitsligo's *Thoughts*, a little book which Dr. Johnson commended in a
letter to old Drummond, the bookseller. [9] Was disappointed somewhat.
It was pious indeed, but had not accuracy or force of mind nor the unction of Izaak Walton. Read also *The Monthly Review* for September
last. Found in it an account of a virtuous religious family by Mrs. Cha-
pone, and how they passed their time. [1] It seemed to me a very dull life.
But I believe no life will appear happy from a particular description. I
thought how insipid, and to many how disagreeable, would the greatest
part of my own life appear if exactly put down in writing. I know not
if I now express clearly the impression which I had. Mr. Nairne drank
tea with us. Sir Walter M.-C. [2] came to town with his mother (very ill),
and also drank tea. I could have written my journal at night, but thought
it better to write each day's history the day after, having then the day
complete. This I now do, and it shall be my regular practice. I shall
mention when it is otherwise.

MONDAY 6 NOVEMBER. It was very wet. Time passed away in the
forenoon idly enough. In the afternoon I had a consultation, and relished
a new cause as a little particular history. I finished today the reading of
a very pretty French piece which I had in a present from Mr. Lumisden:
Consultation sur la Discipline des Avocats. [3] It puts the office of a lawyer
in a high point of view, and is beautifully expressed. I really felt myself

---

for posterity." Mrs. Boswell may have read it there, but it is just as likely that she hit
on it by accident.

[8] That is, "rash": a Scotticism.

[9] Alexander Forbes, fourth Lord Forbes of Pitsligo, *Thoughts concerning Man's Condition;* published in 1763.

[1] An extract from her *Miscellanies in Prose and Verse.*

[2] Montgomerie-Cuninghame.

[3] A pamphlet of twenty-one pages, written by one Duvergier, published at Paris in this
year by the *Conseil de l'Ordre des Avocats de Paris.*

elevated by it. If I execute my plan of writing an essay on my profession, it will aid me much.[4]

I went to Dr. Young's about eight; was averse to be in company, but meeting there no formal people, but just Mr. Lumisden, his sister Mrs. Strange, John MacGowan, etc., I played at loo cheerfully, and got into high spirits. After supper I maintained with ingenuity and force that a man who accumulates money has the most probable security for happiness, providing that he really has a taste for being rich and saving, which has this advantage: that it always increases. I said that misers in general were sneaking fellows, because they cringed under the censure of mankind, and tried to conceal their taste. But if a man of good parts would with firmness and spirit avow wealth to be his great object, and steadily pursue it, he would be respected. Let him walk about in a warm plain frieze suit, and in every circumstance avoid expense and tell fairly why, and he might strut with a dignity which the world would acknowledge. I drank too much old hock.

TUESDAY 7 NOVEMBER. Whether from the quantity or quality of the hock, or from having catched more cold, I awaked exceedingly ill and could not get up till about three. Sir Walter dined with us. The children were all pretty well again. My son's second nurse was an excellent one, and he was visibly fuller in flesh and healthier in looks. I really had practical philosophy enough not to set my heart anxiously upon him. Though I was indolent and did nothing this day, I felt no uneasiness. I was only hurt somewhat to perceive that when Sir Walter talked with me about his affairs, I could not give him a decisive sensible opinion. I am sensible that I am deficient in judgement, in good common sense. I ought therefore to be diffident and cautious. For some time past I have indulged coarse raillery and abuse by far too much. There is hardly any character that one may not attack, either with violent accusation or lessening ridicule. I know there is a kind of mischievous gratification in such indulgence; but it is an unworthy gratification, and makes enemies to him "that uses it."[5] If people have faults, one would not wish to be the hangman to them. If reputations may be stained, one would not wish to throw the dirt. Besides, a man often finds that he was mistaken as to characters when it is too late, as he has rankled the persons by his rash expressions. I am resolved to be on my guard for the future against evil speaking of every kind, and to cultivate a benevolent disposition, at least an external mildness. I had today a letter from the Laird of Raasay on the birth of my son, in terms most cordial, which pleased me much. He expressed a great regard for me, and mentioned my wife's educating one of our

---

[4] The essay was never written.
[5] A reference to the conclusion of Hamlet's advice to the players: III. ii. 50.

daughters to be empress of his _____.[6] I actually looked on this as an event that might happen, and I exulted in it. I am a man of old times.

WEDNESDAY 8 NOVEMBER. Lay long. Had the forenoon taken up by a number of visits of Dr. Cairnie, George Webster, Bob Wellwood, Sir Walter, and Lieutenant Graham, who showed me his father's settlement, which he wished to set aside in part. Dr. Cairnie dined and drank tea with us. I had one gold consultation, and one gratis.[7] Went and sat awhile with worthy Sir George. At night was in a sullen frame at supper with my wife and Mrs. Montgomerie. I indulged bad temper in silence, disregarding politeness. Grew better.

THURSDAY 9 NOVEMBER. (I am now writing on Saturday the 11.) Lieutenant Graham and Robert Boswell breakfasted with me. I had engaged Robert to be here, that we might consider if any relief could be obtained at law from the hard terms of Colonel Graham's will. Robert spoke with knowledge and accuracy. I was sensible of a sad want of promptness of memory or attention in business. I am better for being a barrister than a counsellor. This was the fast day before the sacrament. I stayed at home in the forenoon. Mr. Lumisden, who was to set out for Paris next day, came and sat awhile with me. I would have gone with him to dine with Sir Alexander Dick, as I do not think a fast before the sacrament necessary, but my father was to come to town today, and my being absent would have offended him. Sir Walter dined with us. I went to the New Church in the afternoon; drank tea at Dr. Webster's comfortably with him and Annie. My father came in the evening. I sat a good while with him.

FRIDAY 10 NOVEMBER. After breakfast my father and Lady Auchinleck paid us a visit. He was very guarded last night against expressing joy on the birth of my son, and today when he saw him he said very little. I however flattered myself that I detected symptoms of satisfaction in his behaviour. He tasted a little liqueur. It is strange to see such a niggardliness of fondness. Excess of it is no doubt weakness; and to be secure from this, which my uncle the Doctor shows, my father is in the other extreme.

I dined with Mr. Alexander Mackenzie, Writer to the Signet, with Barrock, a Caithness laird, and his lady and two daughters, my client Ardross and his lady, and my cousin Lieutenant Graham.[8] I got into a Highland humour and drank first plentifully of port and then of claret,

[6] "Realm." Blank in the manuscript; recovered from Raasay's letter.

[7] Boswell's Consultation Book shows that it was customary to pay an advocate's fees in guineas.

[8] Barrock's name was Alexander Sinclair; Ardross's family name was Mackenzie and his Christian name Murdoch. Boswell later (31 January and 3 February 1776) makes extended reference to Mackenzie's cause, a family action which went on for generations.

which cost only £16 a hogshead; and, as intoxication rose, I disregarded my solemn engagement of sobriety to my friend Temple, and pushed the bottle about with an improper keenness, as I was not the entertainer. About nine Graham and I drank tea with Mr. and Mrs. Mackenzie. I was able to be decent then. But when I got into the street I grew very drunk and miserably sick, so that I had to stop in many closes in my way home, and when I got home I was shockingly affected, being so furious that I took up the chairs in the dining-room and threw them about and broke some of them, and beat about my walking-stick till I had it in pieces, and then put it into the fire and burnt it. I have scarcely any recollection of this horrid scene, but my wife informed me of it. She was in great danger, for it seems I had aimed at her both with chairs and stick. What a monstrous account of a man! She got me to bed, where I was excessively sick.

SATURDAY 11 NOVEMBER. My intemperance was severely punished, for I suffered violent distress of body and vexation of mind. I lay till near two o'clock, when I grew easier, and comforted myself by resolving vigorously to be attentively sober for the future. There is something agreeably delusive in fresh resolution. Reason tells me that I cannot expect to be better restrained now than by former vows; and yet, like a man who has had several blanks in the lottery and fancies that another ticket will certainly be a prize, I flatter myself that I shall have it to say that from the 11 of November 1775 I maintained an uninterrupted moderation in drinking. Indeed the horrid consequences with which my last night's debauch might have been attended may probably awe my mind.

Sir Walter dined with us. I went to the New Church and heard Mr. John Gibson preach very well on "Glory to God in the highest." I drank coffee comfortably at home, and my wife seemed to have quite forgotten my bad conduct. Her unhappy sister, Sir Walter's mother, was still in Edinburgh, ill of a consumption, and preparing to go to France. I allowed my wife to go and see her, as the feelings of natural affection may be indulged towards an unworthy object when dying. Her debasing herself by a mean marriage ought, from a just regard to preserve the honourable distinctions of civilized society, to prevent her from enjoying the countenance of her relations in cheerful intercourse. But sickness and the approach of death may be indulged with a humane attention. I have been rigidly firm in giving no countenance to my wife's unhappy sister. Dr. Johnson, in a conversation at Mr. Thrale's which I have marked,[9] judiciously settled the manner in which women who make low marriages should be treated by their relations. It is proper to supply them with

[9] See above, 28 March.

necessaries if they are in want, but it is improper to keep them on a footing with those who have not acted unsuitably.

I was disappointed this evening with a book which I borrowed from the Advocates' Library, entitled, *The Great Law of Subordination Considered, or the Insolence and Unsufferable Behaviour of Servants in England duly Inquired Into,* printed London, 1724.[1] On glancing a little on it, my curiosity was excited. But it was a poor low performance.

SUNDAY 12 NOVEMBER. There had been a fall of snow in the night. When I looked out from my bed in the morning and saw everything white, I felt a kind of agreeable wintry sensation which the sight of snow always gives me. I was at the New Church forenoon and afternoon, and took the sacrament as a commemoration of Christ's death and a testimony of my belief in His religion. But the Presbyterian communion has nothing of solemn devotion in it. I felt a kind of reluctance at giving my countenance to it, especially as the clergy of that profession appear to me to have no good authority to celebrate the Holy Sacrament, not having ordination flowing from the Apostles. But then I considered that there could be no harm in joining a number of people of my own country in a Christian duty according to the established mode; and that my doing so was essential to my having my father's good opinion. Mrs. Montgomerie and I dined with him between sermons. I made my wife stay at home all day, as she was not quite recovered yet. The tediousness of the service in the New Church was really tiresome. I drank tea at home, then sat awhile with Sir George. Supped at home with my wife, just by ourselves.

MONDAY 13 NOVEMBER. Was at the New Church in the forenoon, and heard Sir Harry Moncreiff preach on "O death, where is thy sting," [2] etc. He represented death under its various dreary views, and then suggested the consolations of Christianity. A strange thought struck me that I would apply to David Hume, telling him that at present I was happy in having pious faith. But in case of its failing me by some unexpected revolution in my mind, it would be humane in him to furnish me with reflections by which a man of sense and feeling could support his spirit as an infidel. I was really serious in this thought. I wonder what David can suggest. I was struck with thinking that the preacher and all who heard him were certainly to undergo death in one way or other. I sat awhile with old Mrs. Boswell of Balmuto and her two unmarried daughters.[3] I have had for some time past a high relish of thinking: just speculating within myself on the objects around me, and looking backwards and for-

[1] By Defoe.
[2] I Corinthians 15. 55.
[3] Lady Auchinleck's sisters, called in the family Peggie and Menie.

wards on the various effects produced in the progress of time. Thinking itself seemed to be a positive pleasure.

My father and Lady Auchinleck, Messieurs Kincaid, senior and junior, and Sir Walter dined with us.[4] My father was observed to be visibly duller or failed. Mr. Kincaid said, with an air that he thought the contrary, "Is he as *vif* [5] as he used to be?" He indeed had an old look, and a sort of indifference in his manner. He has never been cordial in my house, but today there was something about him like one worn out. I was affected by it tenderly in my own mind, for all his coldness of late to me. My wife very prudently said that I should by no means appear to be sensible of any failure about him. He and Lady Auchinleck went away early, and, as he was going down the stair, he took my wife kindly by the hand, as if by stealth, and said, "God bless you all." This pleased me much. The Kincaids and Sir Walter and I were very cordial as relations, and the old gentleman talked from experience of the advantage of relations keeping up their connexion. I guarded against any excess in drinking, though such a meeting justified a little more than usual. I found that my constitution was quite unfit for the least excess in wine, for although I had but the smallest share of three bottles of claret among four, I was feverish and even sick. Messieurs Kincaids drank tea.

I wrote to Lord Mountstuart and his brother James to ask for me the place of one of the commissaries of Edinburgh, vacant by the death of Mr. Smollett yesterday. I had resolved day after day to write to Lord Mountstuart, that my friendship with him might be kept alive, but amazing indolence had hitherto prevented me. He had promised to assist me in getting something better,[6] but I wrote to him that it would be of great consequence to me to show my father that I had his Lordship's patronage, and therefore a smaller office speedily obtained would serve me much. I was in the frame of an old baron, and hoped that my application would have effect, were it only to make him write a letter to my father expressing his friendship for me, which he had promised to do.[7] I am curious to see how he will act. I went to bed early.

TUESDAY 14 NOVEMBER. The weather was fine and clear, but frosty. The Court of Session met, but there was not a quorum of the Lords. The advocates went through the customary form of dissimulation, or rather unmeaning expression, wishing one another a good session, when in reality

[4] Alexander Kincaid, His Majesty's printer and stationer, was later Lord Provost of Edinburgh. His son, Alexander, was also a printer; his wife, the Hon. Caroline Ker, was, like Boswell, a great-grandchild of the second Earl of Kincardine.
[5] Lively.
[6] See above, 29 March.
[7] "I have told you my situation, and I leave it to your nobleness of mind how to act . . . I remain with the sincerity and warmth of an old baron."

if the meaning of most of them were known, it would be wishing a bad session, or little business, to every rival; for the profits of our bar do not afford many good shares. Nothing particular struck my mind at the opening of this session. I walked out to the Abbey Hill and met the first division of the 31 Regiment, and walked along and was cheered by their drums and fifes and martial air. Got before them into the Castle, and saw them enter the square. They were to relieve the Highlanders, who were to go to the Forts and other parts of Scotland. I had several session papers to write, having let them lie over instead of writing in the vacation. I was very averse to labour. However, I did tolerably.

WEDNESDAY 15 NOVEMBER. (I am now writing on Friday the 17.) I went on better with my business. There is nothing else to mark. For I am never to put down that I rose, breakfasted, etc. I am to mark only what company I have kept, and any occurrences or reflections which at the time I think worth preserving.

THURSDAY 16 NOVEMBER. This forenoon I was glad to find myself able to speak freely and distinctly before the Lords in a cause, Mrs. Rickson against some officers of the 19th Regiment of Foot. But I was sensible at one moment of a sort of confusion of mind which sometimes affects me, either from having too many ideas, or not vigour enough to arrange them and keep back all but those immediately necessary. At such times the mob breaks in upon the regular troops. Mason's *Ode to Memory* begins,

> Mother of Wisdom! thou whose sway
> The throng'd ideal hosts obey.

I know not if the ideas can be said with propriety to obey the memory at any time. But I am sure that mine are at times turbulent. They either secrete themselves, so that they cannot be found when I want them, or are disorderly when they appear. My luxury in thinking, which I remarked some days ago, had ceased. I just jogged on in existence, with little vivacity of any kind. In the general course of life, when a man feels no positive uneasiness, he should be satisfied.

Mr. Peter Colvill from Torryburn drank tea with us. I dictated in business pretty easily this evening. Sir Walter, who had convoyed his mother as far as Greenlaw in her journey to France, returned and supped with us. I was in a more social humour than usual with my wife and him. Mrs. Montgomerie supped abroad. I projected that he might, by uniting with me and Treesbank, form a good interest in Ayrshire. But I did not allow my mind to fix much on this, as I doubted his stability; and what was worse, doubted my own prudence and perseverance.

FRIDAY 17 NOVEMBER. My father was ill of a cold, a most frequent complaint this winter. He had kept the house yesterday, and he continued to do so today. I was with him a little yesterday. But today I sat with him a good while, and he entered on the subject of my debt. I had bought Dalblair in 1767, and borrowed £2,000 upon heritable security on it, as also £500 from Lord Marischal on my personal bond. Full of the idea of being the heir of a great estate, I had been very extravagant; and I was so the more freely that I had laid down a resolution to marry no woman but one with a fortune of £10,000, so that any debt I should contract might be cleared off at once. Dalblair cost me £2,435.[8] The price belonged to a number of creditors, who had various perplexed claims, so their trustees were in no hurry for payment. This was unlucky for me, for it left me the command of the money which I had borrowed. I indeed soon paid up £1,400. But the remainder I dissipated, and was in debt a great deal more when I married. I hoped that my father would then have made me clear. But he let things hang on, and I was unwilling to disturb him. I found now that, after applying in payment of debt and in expense of living my wife's portion of £1,000, I was in debt between twelve and thirteen hundred pounds to Dalblair's trustees, and upon a state of debit and credit in other particulars was owing about £200 more. My father was bound along with me for the price of Dalblair, and he spoke of it today with dissatisfaction. I calmly reasoned that I had formerly been foolish, but was now acting a proper part, and that I hoped he would make me easy. I suggested that the money might be wanted soon. He seemed to acquiesce pretty quietly in his being obliged to pay it.[8a] When I got home I considered that he had given me only £200 this year, though my allowance was £300, and therefore I had a claim for £100, which would reduce what he had to pay to £1,175; and I thought it would be better to take £1,000 neat from him rather than have reflections why I had allowed the interest to run on, and that I might in no long time be able to make myself quite clear, and then begin to pay off part of the value of Dalblair. As the interest of the price at five per cent exceeded the present rent (£26 a year), it was an immediate burthen to me. My father was willing to take it off my hands, and my wife pressed me to part with it. But as I hoped good things of myself, and wished to appear in the family archives as having added Dalblair to our territories, and had pleased myself with thinking that at least that estate in the parish of Auchinleck should be entailed on the heirs male of Thomas Boswell, the founder of our family,

[8] Boswell's bid at the auction was £2,410. He was also burdened with an annuity of £25, which he thought he could compound for £80 or at most £90.

[8a] Lord Auchinleck's visible failure (above, 13 November 1775) and his gentleness on the subject of Boswell's debts on this day and the day following were probably due to his being ill with influenza, an epidemic of which was sweeping Europe, as many contemporary references show. He regained his harshness with his health.

I determined to keep it. It pains me that my wife has not a spark of feudal enthusiasm, but is always opposing me upon the subject of family.

Sir Walter dined with us. I was very busy with a paper in the afternoon. Donaldson, the painter, came and drank tea. I would have dismissed most visitors sooner. But knowing his temper, and wishing not to hurt him, I bestowed a good portion of time upon him. He was, as usual, constantly aiming at extensive thought and general reflections, such as: "We admire extension. One who kills a single man is abhorred; but a man-killer, a hero who has destroyed numbers, is a high character." He made one remark which seemed just: that the common observation that heroes are the most merciful is not true. For we imagine so because mercy is more conspicuous in such a ferocious being. After he went away I said his conversation was a kind of whale fishing. He always launched into the wide ocean and pursued vast objects. But he catched nothing.

After finishing my paper, I went to David Stewart Moncrieffe's, the first evening of his club, or tavern as he calls it, for this session. I played pretty well at whist, and won a little. We were sixteen at supper. The conversation was flashy and vociferous. I was in the humour of laughing at any joke, even such as Captain James Gordon calling Sir Adolphus Oughton "Sir Orang-outang." Sandy Maxwell was a strenuous man for a militia in Scotland. I called him "General" Maxwell. Captain Gordon, alluding to General Putnam's complaisance to Mrs. *Gage* and Maxwell's being a wine-merchant, said, "Ay, he'll bow to Madam *Gauge*." [9] This had an excellent effect at the time. I was in good moderate spirits, and had resolution to check some absurd sallies of profanity which some of the company threw out. I resolved to be at this club every Friday, as a place where I can play whist, see the best company of this country, hear intelligence from various sources, and be exhilarated with sociality once a week. I came away before twelve. My purpose is to do so always, and to speculate without paying the tax of drinking much and sitting up late.

SATURDAY 18 NOVEMBER. (I am now writing on Monday the 20.) After being in the Court of Session, called on my father, who still kept

[9] After the Battle of Bunker Hill, General Gage shut himself up in Boston, which the provincial troops blockaded on the land side. The following, purporting to be a letter dated 15 September 1775, from an officer in Boston to his father in London, had appeared in the newspapers: "Why should I complain of hard fate? General Gage and his family have for this month past lived upon salt provisions. Last Saturday General [Israel] Putnam, in the true style of military complaisance, which abolishes all personal resentment and smooths the horrors of war when discipline will permit, sent a present to the General's lady of a fine fresh quarter of veal, which was very acceptable, and received the return of a very polite card of thanks" (Frank Moore, *Diary of the American Revolution*, New York, 1860, i. 136, from *The Constitutional Gazette*, which quotes an unnamed London paper).

the house, and informed him of my having had a letter from Mr. Miller, writer in Ayr, factor for Dalblair's creditors, giving me notice that the remainder of the price should now be paid. It was lucky that my father had happened to talk of it to me yesterday before the letter came, as I got him prepared for letting me have the money. Mr. Stobie was present when he and I talked together today.[1] I was obliged to hear an unpleasing recapitulation of my extravagance. But after a good deal of dialogue, and Mr. Stobie throwing in a word sometimes in my favour, it was agreed that my father should have £1,000 ready at Candlemas,[2] and with this, and what I had to advance, the bond should be cleared. Stobie said he might take an obligation from me for repayment. "No, no," said I. "Let me once be clear, so that no man can look me in the face as a debtor." I was touched with parental affection when I found my father agree to make me easy.

He found fault with me for being against him in the last Ayrshire election. My apology was that he had told me he was to take no side; otherwise I should not have interfered in the least. He said that he had connected himself with his father's friends, and that they were the surest. I had fallen out with the President, though I knew that there had been an intimacy between his father and himself with my father. I said nothing to this. But allowed Stobie to say it was wrong. I was conscious that I connected myself with Sir John Pringle, who was my father's friend, and also with Lord Monboddo, and that my quarrel with the President was for a very sufficient reason: because after I had taken a warm side in the Ayrshire election, in the faith that my father was to take none, the President, without consulting me, beset my father and persuaded him to take the opposite side with great keenness, by which *I* appeared quite insignificant, and to split the superiorities of his estate and make fictitious votes, by which *he* appeared acting contrary to his professions both in public and private. This was a most ungentlemanly conduct. I think it was rascally. I therefore have not seen the President for about two years. Yet I wished today that I could accidentally fall in again to a kind of decent intercourse with him to please my father; and I could be aware, and keep myself out of his power in any degree.

My father mentioned his having made an entail of the family estate, and that, to insure it, he had made a proviso that if a reduction of it was so much as attempted, all his own purchases should be forfeited by me and the heirs of my body. I asked him on what series of heirs he had settled the estate. He said on the heirs whatsoever of his own body. This confounded me, and I calmly spoke a little for the male line. I knew he

[1] John Stobie was Lord Auchinleck's clerk.
[2] 2 February; in Scotland one of the quarter-days.

had not power without my consent to disappoint the male succession. But to lose his own acquisitions was a great hardship. I said with an easy good humour, "You should let the heir male have Tenshillingside and the lime quarry at Stonebriggs as essential; the first as a part of the policy,[3] the other for the improvement of the estate." In my own mind, I quietly thought that I would give up both, with all that he had bought, rather than let a female and her race by a stranger cut out the *sons of the Family.* My father had the money to borrow with which he was to pay off my debt. Stobie said it should be borrowed in small sums, and he could clear it off at his convenience. I was not certain whether Stobie was much my friend or not. I thought he might really be so. If that is the case, I shall not forget it. My father seemed to be failed today. He was gentler than usual, and I was sincerely grateful to him. He is an excellent man upon the whole, though he has, as I have, appearances of narrowness and harshness.

Sir Walter dined with us. I drank a little strong ale with him, which, though less than half a bottle, confused me somewhat. My drinking vigour is either quite gone or in abeyance. I was busy writing session papers. In the forenoon I had been to see a little creature shown as a curiosity under the name of a *Corsican Fairy.*[4] It was a very well-made woman not above three feet high. It was said she was born in Ireland, but *Corsican* was a good show title. A man who spoke Italian, and said he was her brother, showed her, and the rogue, having been told who I was, pretended that he had seen me in Corsica. General Paoli will tell me about this. I had also called for one Carmichael, a shopkeeper in Morpeth, confined for debt in the Canongate prison, for whom I was to draw a paper.

I told my wife of the conversation between my father and me, and she was violent to a degree that hurt me, complaining that I would not only disinherit my own daughters, but deprive my own son of a part of his inheritance. I told her that it was a principle in honour and justice with me that the heirs male of Auchinleck should not be deprived of their succession; that a settlement depriving them could not be effectual unless I approved of it, and that my father's acquisitions were no doubt a considerable bribe to act contrary to my principle, but that I could resist it, and might make an equivalent for my son. I was made really uneasy by my wife's violence tonight, though it was natural and excusable. She said I would be looked upon as a madman if I acted as I intended to do; and

[3] A Scottish term for the embellishments or plantations of an estate.
[4] ". . . Maria Teresa, a CORSICAN FAIRY, born on the mountain of Stata Ota in 1743; only thirty-four inches in height, and only twenty-six pounds in weight; has a good deal of vivacity, and speaks Italian and French" (*Scots Magazine,* Appendix, 1775, p. 733).

when I insisted on our title to the estate from the worthy old laird who gave it to his nephew though he had four daughters, she answered with a very good metaphor: that the estate was so much burthened, it was more proper for a man than a woman. It was an old coat which he gave to his nephew, because it would not fit his daughter. The fact however was that, although there was a load of debt, my great-grandfather got a sub-stantial fund.

SUNDAY 19 NOVEMBER. In the early part of last night my mind had been so much agitated with thinking of the entail which my father told me he had made, and with momentary apprehensions of my approving of it, from the temptation of my father's purchases, that I was actually for a little in a state of insanity. The idea of the Old Castle of Auchinleck going to a female in exclusion of *Boswells* was horrid. I composed myself by resolving firmly. I was at the New Church all day, but did not profit by it. The cold was intense. Coughs were so frequent that it would have required the voice of an old field-preacher to be heard. I dined at my father's between sermons, with Mrs. Montgomerie and George Webster. I used to drink as much at this weekly meeting as to bring on a degree of comfortable stupefaction. I resolved today not to allow myself this gross kind of indulgence, and I kept my resolution. I drank tea at Belleville. Lady Dundonald had the cold and was in bed. Lady Betty and I drank tea beside her. Lady Betty's marriage with Mr. Heron of Heron was fixed to be very soon.[5] This was a very . . .'[6]

[THURSDAY 23 NOVEMBER]. . . . of the children kept her at home.[7] I liked to be with the Baron as a friend of Lord Mountstuart's. At eight I went to an oratorical society in Mary's Chapel, called the "Pantheon," as a militia for Scotland was to be debated; and, as I thought it of con-sequence to rouse a general spirit for it, I made a vigorous harangue and introduced an eulogium on Lord Mountstuart as the tutelary patron of this country.[8] I believe I did very well. I got applause enough from the

[5] Patrick Heron's first wife was Jean Home, Lord Kames's only daughter. Heron had divorced her in 1772 for adultery with a young officer. In 1762 she had been Boswell's mistress.

[6] Four pages of the manuscript, containing the record for 20, 21, and 22 November, have been removed at this point. Somewhere in the missing portion (probably in the latter half of the entry for this day) was an account of a clandestine visit to the unidentified woman of the entry for the following Sunday, 26 November.

[7] This sentence perhaps read: "My wife was also invited to dine, but the illnesses of the children kept her at home." "The Baron" is almost certainly William Mure, who was a great friend of Mountstuart's.

[8] A bill for establishing a Scots militia was debated in the House of Commons in April 1760, and since that time the controversy concerning it had been kept alive by its Jacobite supporters. Opponents of the militia feared that while Charles Edward

company, about one hundred writers, wrights, etc., etc., and the question carried *for a militia* upon the votes of all present being taken. I suppose the visitors bore a great proportion above the members. There were a number of officers of the 31 Regiment there who all voted *against a militia*. They were not fair judges. I was made an honorary member. I supped with my wife quietly. Found two fees lying for me, but was not clear for business.

FRIDAY 24 NOVEMBER. This forenoon I resumed what I had neglected for above two years: reading the records of the Privy Council of Scotland and copying any curious passage. My father has four volumes of abstracts from them by old Robert Mylne.[9] Some books have been found since his death, and these I examine. Mr. Robertson, one of the keepers of the records, has been always very obliging to me. I was glad today to find that I could read the old hand pretty easily after a long interruption. I have a kind of calm, comfortable satisfaction in being thus employed in the Laigh [1] Parliament House. I think that I may make a good publication of these abstracts. Sir Walter dined with us. The first week of the session produced me but three guineas. This produced six, and I had but little labour. Lord Eglinton was in town, and had called on me. I called on him yesterday, and this night I met him at Moncrieffe's. I had not an opening for a party at cards. We were eleven at supper. There was nothing to remark. I kept quiet and sober, and came home soon after twelve. As I am minutely exact, I must observe that the most part of this day's journal was written after twelve at night, so, on Sunday the 26.

SATURDAY 25 NOVEMBER. (I am now writing on Monday the 27.) My father sent for me this morning into the robing room to engage me and my wife and Mrs. Montgomerie to dine with him today, along with the Countess Dowager of Galloway. He and I had a quiet, comfortable chat together, and were very well. The dinner took place and we also drank tea. I sat awhile with Thomas Boswall, who had been very ill and was not yet recovered. To see so stout a man feeble was humbling. But I felt myself philosophically steady. I supped at Sir George Preston's. He himself was asleep. It was the night before Captain George was to set out for his Marine Corps. George Webster was there. He told that George Fergusson was appointed one of the commissaries of Edinburgh. This was

and Cardinal York were still alive in Italy, such a body would lend its strength to a new rebellion. On 2 November, Mountstuart had moved in the House of Commons for leave to bring in a bill for the militia. It was brought in and read on 7 December; thrown out on 5 March 1776.

[9] Boswell actually wrote "Mill," in accordance with the pronunciation.

[1] That is, low; the basement storey of the Parliament House.

a small disappointment to me. I was remarkably placid tonight. I had not a single paper upon my hands. I had therefore no immediate labour to oppress me.

SUNDAY 26 NOVEMBER. Was at the New Church forenoon and afternoon, and at my father's between sermons, where were George Webster and his sister and Mr. Claud Boswell. My father was not very well, and stayed at home in the afternoon. While at church I was very impatient as = had promised to be at home at V.² I drank tea at my father's, and was solid with him and Lady Auchinleck. Last night there came a present of silk caps from her to my daughters, and of a silk hat and cloak from my father to my son. This was an agreeable attention. My father seemed to be really kinder of late. I had real happiness in being well with him, and I wished him long life, feeling also a sort of discouraging apprehension that the Family of Auchinleck would not be properly supported by me. Without reserve there cannot be dignity, and my warmth and gaiety, which procure immediate small applause, counteract the wish which my pride forms for respect in general. I *may* restrain them as I grow older. If not, why should there not be a diversity of characters in the succession of lairds?

A ³ little after five I stole gently to ='s room, which I found to be neat and cosy. I sat about an hour. She indulged me in amorous dalliances of much familiarity, but though I preached from the Old Testament, could not think of allowing me ingress. I was much pleased with her unaffected goodness, and being for the time calmed, I thought we might do more afterwards. There was nothing of art or feverishness on either side. I was clear that I was doing no ill. Such was my sensation or immediate impression. I sat awhile with Sir George, then came home and began for the first time Macaulay's *History of St. Kilda.* I read about one half of it.

MONDAY 27 NOVEMBER. (I am now writing on Wednesday the 29.) Having no business immediately pressing, I finished *St. Kilda.* It afforded me some curious speculation, though I was really uneasy at the contempla-

² With this sentence Boswell began the practice of spelling with Greek characters some of the words in certain passages of his journal which he did not wish Mrs. Boswell to be able to read. (Here the words are προμισεδ and χομε.) In this edition all such words have been transliterated. The disguise was childish and failed of its main purpose (see the entry for 4 December); and to preserve the Greek characters in a printed text is only to make the passages in question unpleasantly prominent. In this case he has provided work for his editors by later inking over the latter part of the sentence. The lady's name is represented in the manuscript by some initial or symbol which we have been unable to make out. (She may have been Mrs. Ross, Sandy's nurse.) The reading "V" (that is, "five") is not certain, but is confirmed by what follows.

³ Boswell wrote much of what follows in this entry in Greek characters; later he carefully cross-hatched everything from this word to "no ill." Some of the readings are not quite certain.

tion of human beings living in so wretched a state of ignorance, want of cleanness, and dependence. Dr. Johnson and I had discovered from Macaulay's conversation, and from what we were told in Skye, that he had not written the book to which his name is prefixed, but only collected some materials for it. Dr. Macpherson, minister of Sleat, is supposed to have arranged them and put them in language, with illustrations and reflections.[4] The book indeed is not like the genuine narrative of a traveller himself, and is too much loaded with dissertation and allusion. It is deficient in many respects. There is not near so minute an account of the peculiar state of life in St. Kilda as might have been given. I am sure I could give a much better. Dr. Johnson is a great model to travellers. I dictated some today. Sir Walter and Mr. Adam Bell dined. In the evening I was at George Alexander Stevens's "Lecture on Heads."[5] He appeared to me to be duller than when I heard him in 1768 in this town. Supped quietly at home. Fell into a fit of bad humour because my wife did not pay me respect enough.

TUESDAY 28 NOVEMBER. I had kept my bad humour all night with a strange obstinacy, persisting in a principle or passion never to change till my wife solicits me. When I came home from the House this forenoon, she tried to soothe me; but my sullenness had been allowed to continue too long, and I could not get free from it quickly. I verily believe that I could persist in it for years. I sat awhile with worthy Grange, who had hurt his leg and was a little feverish. I laboured pretty well today. Lord Eglinton, Captain Hugh Montgomerie, Sir Robert Laurie, Sir Walter, Mr. John Graeme, Writer to the Signet, and Matthew Dickie supped with us. My Lord made two pretty good observations. He said he liked Cardinal de Retz's *Memoirs,* because he is short. "When a man is short," said he, "I take it he writes truth. If he writes long, there must be some reason for his saying so much, and I doubt his veracity." He also said advice never did good. "If," said he, "a young man has not sense enough to find out from the conversation of proper people what is thought right, the sooner he is ruined the better; for he must be good for nothing. Direct advice will never be of any service." I was calm and placid and easy tonight, though still not reconciled to my wife. I drank weak brandy punch. The Earl, who had dined hard, grew suddenly intoxicated, and was passionate and noisy. However, we broke up before one in the morning.

[4] It is now known that Kenneth Macaulay, great-uncle of Lord Macaulay, not only collected the materials for this book, but also wrote it in its original form. It was thoroughly revised and enlarged, however, by Dr. John Macpherson.
[5] Stevens was the pioneer of the monologue. His "Lecture," a series of characterizations satirizing the follies of the time, is said to have gained him £10,000.

Annie Mill, Effie's nurse, went away yesterday, after having been about eighteen months with her; the separation was a distress to both. We got a fine comely girl to take care of Effie: Jeanie Hardie, a Dunbar girl, who had served at Dumfries House. To divert Effie was a study to me. These little domestic incidents engage me much. After I went to bed, my wife got the better of my bad humour by asking me to be friends before I fell asleep; "For," said she, "the consequence of sleep is uncertain." I was struck with the awful reflection that I might not awake again in life, and that it would be shocking to die in such a frame; and I was softened by her tender anxiety. Much do I value and love her.

WEDNESDAY 29 NOVEMBER. (I have fallen too much behind; for I am now writing on Sunday the 3 of December.) Business went on well. Sir Walter supped with us, after which he and I went down and drank a little mountain comfortably with Grange.

THURSDAY 30 NOVEMBER. This being St. Andrew's day, I walked as Master of the Canongate Kilwinning Lodge in the procession of the Free Masons from the Parliament House to the Theatre Royal. It had an excellent effect upon the New Bridge, while the flambeaux blazed in a luminous train. The Theatre was our place of meeting this year, as the Assembly Hall was newly painted. I was in perfect good spirits, and harangued and sung with ease and vigour. When I observed in a speech that this was *"our first appearance on this stage,"* it had a cheerful influence like one of Burke's sallies.

FRIDAY 1 DECEMBER. I make it a general rule neither to dine abroad nor have company with me on Friday, as Moncrieffe's supper is enough for one day. This day, however, we were asked to dine at my father's, and I did not like to refuse. Mrs. Montgomerie and Sir Walter were there. It was but a dull day somehow. When I came home I found a letter acquainting me that my lottery ticket was drawn a blank; but to balance that I also found a most friendly letter from Lord Mountstuart telling me that the Commissary's place had been engaged, but that he had no doubt that the Duke of Queensberry and he would be able to obtain something for me. This comforted me. I went to Moncrieffe's, played at cards and lost a little, supped well, and was pretty joyous, and as Lord Monboddo was there, sat till one.

SATURDAY 2 DECEMBER. Mrs. Montgomerie left us this morning. Sir Walter went west with her. I sat a little with Crosbie, who was confined with the epidemical cold, and talked with him of the cause, Carmichael against Scott, on which the Lords had ordered a hearing in presence to be on Tuesday.⁹ I had made Mr. Crosbie be taken in to assist

⁹ The cause was determined on Wednesday, 6 December; Boswell was chief counsel for Carmichael, and Maclaurin was counsel for Scott. William Scott, merchant in

me in it. I dined with Nairne. He had Lord Kellie's brothers, young Pitfour, and Captain Turnbull, etc., with him. We had a deal of profane licentious jocularity and Edinburgh ill-bred raillery. I disliked the company much. Captain Erskine said little. Captain Andrew was seized with the humour of the place. The only satisfaction I had was from Captain Turnbull's relating some of the military operations last war. I drank rather more than I should have done. I was now rather loaded with business to be done, and intended to have gone home and laboured; but I received a note from Sandy Gordon to come and play at whist at his house, and I could not resist it. Maclaurin and I played against Lady Dumfries and him, and lost. Maclaurin then went to sup with Lord Monboddo, and Sandy and I and the Countess fell to brag. We grew keen, supped, drank a bottle of claret slowly, having resumed our cards, and so much bewitched were we that we played on till past four in the morning. I was sensible that this was very indecent; I was ill from such rakishness and knew that my dear wife would suffer. Yet I could not quit gaming. I had once won a good deal. When we parted, I had won only seventeen shillings.

SUNDAY 3 DECEMBER. (I am now writing on Wednesday the 6.) Was at New Church forenoon and afternoon, and at my father's with my wife between sermons. In the afternoon paid another visit to _____. Sat awhile with Sir George.

MONDAY 4 DECEMBER. Was busy studying a process against the kirk session of Borrowstounness, and writing a paper in it. At nine went to Crosbie's to talk over the cause of Carmichael on arrestment of an Englishman *judicio sisti,* on which he and I were to plead before the Lords next day. John MacGowan and I supped with him, drank moderately, and talked of the history of painting and engraving in Scotland. I talked of a design which I had to collect all the engraved portraits of Scotsmen. Lord Mountstuart has a great collection of British heads. My plan is confined and such as I can afford. Mr. MacGowan mentioned several Scotch heads that I never knew had been engraved. He said there was a rage in England at present for making collections of that sort. He looked on it as a bad taste. I considered it as amusing to curiosity, and somewhat instructive, besides, in assisting historical memory.

When I came home, I found that my wife had been reading this

Newcastle, claiming that John Carmichael, merchant in Morpeth, had gone to Edinburgh to avoid paying his debts, caused him to be arrested and imprisoned there. Carmichael declared that his imprisonment was illegal, inasmuch as he was not subject to the jurisdiction of Scotland. On this and on other grounds, the Lords decided in favour of Carmichael.

journal, and, though I had used Greek letters, had understood my visits to ———. She spoke to me of it with so much reason and spirit that, as I candidly owned my folly, so I was impressed with proper feelings; and, without more argument than that it was disagreeable to so excellent a spouse, resolved firmly to keep clear. And when I reflected calmly, I thought it lucky that my journal had been read, as it gave an opportunity to check in the beginning what might have produced much mischief. I wondered at my temporary dissipation of thought when I saw the effects of my conduct. I valued and loved my wife with renewed fervour.

TUESDAY 5 DECEMBER. Pleaded Carmichael's cause with composure and ease, and, the Solicitor told me, very well.[7] Heard Ilay Campbell, Crosbie, and Maclaurin plead it, and was interested. I had dictated any notes that I had for it this morning. Was idly inclined after dinner. Called for Mr. Digges at the Theatre, and drank a glass of wine with him. He was as laborious in his profession as I in mine, but he observed that there was more entertainment in his. "Yes," said I, "you are a silversmith. I am a blacksmith. You make fine, glittering, ornamental pieces of work. I make coarse black grates and shovels, and chains sometimes." It was curious to look back fifteen or sixteen years ago, when I viewed him as a being of high dignity and a kind of mysterious refinement, as if he were as superior to most other men as a page of Shakespeare's most exquisite poetry to ordinary prose. However, I must own that he appeared very well in my imagination still. I came home and drank tea, and had two consultations. Young Coll, who was to go for London next day, sat a little with me.[8] Though I had some papers to write, I did nothing at all today in business except Carmichael's cause. I yielded to indolence.

WEDNESDAY 6 DECEMBER. After the Court of Session rose, walked in the Meadow with Ilay Campbell and Charles Hay, the only time that I have walked for above two months. Was quite an idler in the afternoon, and did nothing. Sat awhile with Grange, and was comfortably social.

THURSDAY 7 DECEMBER. (I am now writing on Saturday the 9.) The day was passed in the ordinary way during a winter session, without anything particular, only that I was at Canongate Kilwinning Lodge in the evening.[9]

FRIDAY 8 DECEMBER. After my business in the Court of Session was over, I called on Mr. Donaldson, the painter, for a little. He offered to

[7] Alexander Murray had succeeded Henry Dundas as Solicitor-General in May 1775.
[8] Boswell gave Alexander Maclean, the young Laird of Coll, a letter of introduction to Johnson, who was pleased with him, and took him to dine at the Mitre.
[9] He was notified that he had been unanimously elected an honorary member of the "Pantheon," the literary debating society, and was informed that the question to be debated this night would be: "Does the passion of love proceed most from a regard to ourselves, or to the object beloved?" (letter from William Downie, the clerk of the society, 6 December).

assist me in making my collection of Scottish engraved portraits. He put into my hands some extracts which he had taken from Hawthornden's poems, some of which were very fine. He wished to see a selection of that poet's pieces published. He also showed me some fancy drawings of his own, very well imagined. He said he did not like painters choosing always subjects from books. It made painting a secondary art. Let it supply itself with ideas. I find myself always led into a curious train of thinking by Donaldson, and as he is really a man of genius, and seems sensible of my kindness for him, I wish to befriend him.

I then called on Mr. Robert Syme, Writer to the Signet, who was sitting in his chamber in a green night-gown, confined with the cold, and surrounded with processes; a very different scene from Donaldson's, but a very proper one for me, as Mr. Syme employs me much as a lawyer. George Webster observed one day lately that the world is just a succession of scenes as on the stage. The thought was the same as Shakespeare's, "All the world's a stage." But George rendered it more applicable to immediate observation. "Shakespeare," said he, "wrote plays in five acts. But we see innumerable acts"; and then he rapidly gave a number of different instances of what we see even in this town of Edinburgh.

(I am now writing on Sunday the 10th December.) Business was now going on with me very well, though I did not rise early. But still I read nothing but law cases or authorities. When I compared myself to a blacksmith when talking with Digges, I should have added that studying dull causes before pleading them or writing on them is the worst part of our profession. If the iron is once heated and laid on the anvil, it is not very disagreeable to wield the hammer or instruments for shaping it into various forms. But it is irksome to have a mass of a *process* laid cold on one's table, and to be obliged to blow the bellows of application in the heat of attention till I can mould it.

Mr. Claud Boswell drank tea with us. There is little congenial sympathy between him and me, so that, though I regard him as a worthy cousin, we meet seldom. I however wish to be more with him, and shall be so for the future. Between six and seven I met at John's Coffee-house a detachment of my Lodge of Canongate Kilwinning, and we went and visited St. Andrew's Lodge held in Niddry's Wynd. This evening for the first time I saw a kind of quarrel like to fall out in a Mason lodge. The junior warden, _____, an Irish student, was drunk and spoke a little impertinently. Captain Hamilton of the 31st, one of my attendants, took him up; and if there had not been a prudent interposition, they might have fought. I went to Moncrieffe's. The news of General Scott's having died suddenly that morning had come by express. There is no denying it that this event excited the mind in a manner rather agreeable. Surprise is pleasant, and a purse-proud man of immense opulence is not regretted.

There is to other men a kind of satisfaction when such a man, who has great advantages over them, is at once laid low. Maclaurin said very well, "This is a great death," as they say "a great marriage." Moncrieffe himself appeared to be sorry. But the company was not in the least saddened. I played at whist and won a little. I drank rather freely while I sat; but after some wavering between an inclination to indulge and my good resolution of sobriety, I came off before one.

SATURDAY 9 DECEMBER. General Scott's death was the universal topic in the Parliament House, and in justification of my last night's philosophy, everybody seemed to be rather merry. His riches, his young widow, and witticisms on his gaming applied to death were the remarks produced.[1] I sat awhile with worthy Grange, who observed that this was a strong instance to us that great wealth did not procure real friends. That Scott's death was not regretted, while a man of perhaps £100 a year had the sincere goodwill and affection of his neighbours. I went at one to the burial of James Bannerman, who had been for many years Glasgow William Wilson's clerk, an honest, intelligent, and assidous being. William was chief mourner, and the burial letters bore, "James Bannerman, my *friend,* died," etc. I then sat a little with Sir George, then a little with Dr. Webster, and then took a walk in the Meadow with Nairne.

We talked of my notion of an obligation in moral honesty, at least in honour, to continue the male line of succession of an estate, if a predecessor has devised it so, and a man has received it merely because he is an heir male. Nairne did not agree with me. Said he: "If my predecessor gives me an estate because I am an heir male, I am obliged to him; but I am under no obligation in conscience to follow the same line of succession. If he had been resolved on that, he might have entailed the estate under a prohibitory irritancy. But if he has not done so, but has left me the power of choosing what line of succession I like, I will without scruple choose what I think best at the time. If my predecessor, who leaves me an estate or a large sum of money, signifies an inclination that a house on a certain plan should be built, and I think it a bad plan, I will not build it." My answer was that it is not right to counteract the destination of a predecessor, who, instead of fettering you by an entail, trusts to your honour; and the heirs male of an estate so destined have in equity and in good faith, a *right* which it would be robbery in a moral sense, though not in a legal, to disappoint. Nairne was obstinate in his opinion, and his coldness upon my great principle of feudal honour disgusted me. I recollected Dr. Johnson's noble sentiments on the subject, and felt a superiority.

[1] His widow, Margaret Dundas, was a younger daughter of the Lord President. She was Scott's second wife. Lady Mary Hay, his first, ran away from him.

Mrs. Mitchelson and Mr. Stobie dined with us. I had something of a headache from last night's wine, though I had not drank to intoxication. Stobie had told me some days ago that my father did not seem inclined to pay my debt for Dalblair. This vexed me, after having pleased myself with the belief that he was to do it, as I have related on Saturday the 18 of November last. His going back was a sign to me of failure, and I was really perplexed. Stobie said that my father talked now of having an assignation to the debt to keep it up against me, as he thought I would call in question his settlement. I composed myself with thinking that I might, by gentle and prudent methods, get him to do as I could wish; and as an alteration of his settlements in my favour as his heir was in his power to the last hour of his life, I might perhaps in a *beau moment,* as the French say, persuade him to leave me at full liberty. Mrs. Mitchelson drank tea. I finished a long paper.

At supper my wife and I had a dispute about some trifle. She did not yield readily enough, and my passion rose to a pitch that I could not quite command. I started up and threw an egg in the fire and some beer after it. My inclination was to break and destroy everything. But I checked it. How curious is it that the thinking principle can speculate in the very instant of anger. My wife soon made up our difference. But I begged of her to be more attentive again.

SUNDAY 10 DECEMBER. (I am now writing on Wednesday the 13.) Was at New Church forenoon and afternoon, and at my father's between sermons. My wife and George Webster were there. I drank as much white wine as run in my head somewhat. Dr. Blair preached well in the afternoon on piety: "Cornelius, a devout man." [2] After church I walked with George Webster to the Abbey and King's Park. Drank tea comfortably at Sir George's, and got from him his father-in-law Ochiltree's grace after meat, which, being a very good one, I here preserve: "God of all glory, mercy, and peace, who created us, redeemed us, and at this time hath fed us; be blessed and bless us, both now and evermore. Amen." [3] I sat a little with Grange. Mr. Nairne supped with us and drank mulled port, according to a kind of Sunday's private party which he has had occasionally with us since ever we took up house. We were calmly social.

MONDAY 11 DECEMBER. My wife, after much entreaty, went with me to Donaldson's, and sat for a miniature picture for the first time. I did not do much in business today. In the evening I went with a number of my lodge to *The Recruiting Officer* with *Love à la Mode* played by desire

[2] Acts 10. 1–2. This was the sermon which caused Johnson to say, when he read it, "I wish Blair would come over to the Church of England" (*Life,* 8 May 1778).
[3] Sir George's father-in-law was William Cochrane of Ochiltree, Boswell's great-grandfather. See below, Appendix C, Chart V.

of the Free Masons.⁴ I went from the Theatre with Charles Hay to Princes Street Coffee-house to eat a bit of supper and drink a little brandy punch. George Webster joined us, and we drank pretty freely till my spirits rose and I proposed a rubber at whist. A Mr. Esdaile, a young Londoner, made a fourth hand. About one in the morning I sent a note to my wife by Joseph,⁵ who had found me out, told her I was sober, and hoped she would go to bed; and then I indulged my love of gaming, and insensibly resolved to make a night of it.

TUESDAY 12 DECEMBER. About seven in the morning my clerk, Mr. Lawrie, came and found us sitting like wizards. He told me that my wife had been up all night and was quite miserable. This shocked me. I thought, however, that it was in vain to go home now, but that I would play on till within a little of nine, when I was obliged to be in the Parliament House, having fifteen causes in the rolls, as Mr. Lawrie mentioned with much earnestness. He had the dismal look of a faithful servant who saw his master doing what was quite wrong. We retired from the coffee-room into a private room, and played on till near nine. I lost £2.7.6 upon the whole. If the Court had not been sitting, I believe we should have played on all day, for I was not at all saturated with gaming. I came home, washed, shifted, and put on my bar wig, and after being severely hurt by seeing my wife in sad uneasiness, I hastened to the House and struggled through my causes wonderfully. I could not help mentioning to several of my brethren the adventure of last night, but I mentioned it as a very extraordinary debauch for me *now*. I was very ill, and luckily had nothing absolutely necessary to be done this forenoon, so went home and went to bed immediately, Joseph bringing me onion soup. I lay till between seven and eight in the evening, and then got up and dictated a short paper. My wife, who had not been in bed since yesterday morning, was much indisposed, and very justly complained of my behaviour. I pacified her by sincere promises of future attention. Indeed she is wonderfully easy in forgetting my bad conduct. It is curious how differently bad conduct appears to a man when he himself is guilty of it from what it does in the abstract. What would I have thought had I been told of a counsellor-at-law and the father of a family doing what I did last night! I felt a kind of desponding impression that I was unfit for being a married man. I hope I shall be more firm in time coming. My good practice is never of sufficiently long continuance to have a stable consistency. It is shaken loose by occasional repetitions of licentiousness. The wounds of vice break out afresh.

⁴ The plays, respectively, were by George Farquhar and Charles Macklin.
⁵ Joseph Ritter, Boswell's Bohemian servant, had left his employ after the tour to the Hebrides, but had recently returned to him.

WEDNESDAY 13 DECEMBER. The election for the shire of Fife was a matter of some consequence to my cousin Balmuto, whose great friend Mr. Oswald was one of the candidates. I was quite well again this morning, and before nine called on Sir George Preston to sound him on the Fife politics; and when I came out of the Court I went out to Drumsheugh to Captain Archibald Erskine to sound him also, wishing to assist Oswald on Balmuto's account; but found that nothing could be done, Sir George having settled his estate on his son, and his son having passed no charter, and Captain Erskine being to go with Sir Robert Anstruther.[6]

I had been anxious from not having heard from my brother David for a good time. I was relieved today by a letter on the birth of my son. I had also a letter from Dr. Hall with accounts of my poor brother John, whose mind the Doctor described as in a twilight, but said he was insensible of his misfortune. He enclosed me an affidavit by him that he had no other place from Government than his lieutenancy on half pay. When I saw his subscription, and recollected his situation, it affected me so that I almost cried. Miss Dick called on us this forenoon, and I wrote a note to worthy Sir Alexander promising to dine with him on Saturday, wondering how I had been so long from Prestonfield, and telling him that I cherished a design of writing his life and hoped for his aid. Mr. Brown, writer in Kilmarnock, Mr. Blane of Blanefield,[6a] and young Mr. Robert Syme dined with us. I was perfectly moderate today. Mr. Syme drank tea. I dictated freely in the evening.

THURSDAY 14 DECEMBER. (I am now writing on Sunday the 17.) My late scenes of dissipation have hurt my mind. I have been quite a sensualist, quite a being for the immediate time, without thought of future existence. I am sensible that by habit a man may obliterate the traces of moral and religious duty. My thoughts at this period went only to gain and pleasure *de jour en journée,*[7] as the French say. I was abased in my own eyes when I turned them inwards for a moment. Lady Colville, Lady Anne Erskine, Captain Erskine, and Mr. Andrew drank tea with us. I played a rubber at sixpence whist.

FRIDAY 15 DECEMBER. This morning between nine and ten Lord Kennet, who had a long roll of causes, and was in a hurry to get through it, expressed himself to me (when I was pleading before him) in a manner that I thought rude. I checked my passion for a little, and spoke of his improper behaviour with some of my brethren, who seemed to think it

[6] His brother-in-law.
[6a] Gilbert Blane of Blanefield in the parish of Kirkoswald, Ayrshire, had been one of the pioneer "improvers" in Carrick. He was the father of Sir Gilbert Blane, F.R.S., the eminent physician, whose researches banished scurvy from the Royal Navy.
[7] "From day to day."

nothing extraordinary. I however did not like to put up with it; and therefore, after he was gone to the Inner House, I followed and got a word of him, and very calmly and seriously let him know that I thought he had used me ill. He declared he had no such intention, and that I had mistaken him. This was enough. I was put into a flutter with this incident. A judge is certainly obliged to treat counsel at the bar civilly, and if he is impertinent, may be called to account for it. But it is difficult and nice to determine *when* a judge has exceeded judicial propriety, as he no doubt has a right to proceed with due authority.

Mr. Donaldson, the painter, had been here either yesterday or the day before at another sitting for my wife's miniature. He was here again today. I was busy dictating a long paper. It refreshed me to go into the drawing-room now and then and see him painting. Between one and two I went to the burial of Colonel Gordon Graham's widow. It was a dismal misty day. Her son-in-law, Captain Donaldson of the Royal Highlanders, was chief mourner. I went principally out of compliment to him. I did not know him. But I could not think of being in any degree neglectful towards a brave Highland officer. In the evening I had Charles Hay, Mr. William Aytoun, and Mr. Samuel Mitchelson, Junior, at a whist party. The Hon. Mr. Alexander Gordon joined us later than the rest. Charles Hay went away to sup where he was engaged. We played till eleven, and upon the whole I lost just half a crown. We then supped. Mrs. Mitchelson was with us. I felt an itching to play more after supper. But luckily nobody proposed it. We drank moderately.

SATURDAY 16 DECEMBER. After the Court of Session rose, Mr. Donaldson, the painter, Dr. Boswell, and I walked out to Sir Alexander Dick's. This was reviving such a scene as I recollect sixteen years ago when [8] Donaldson was here and the Doctor was in high glee as a virtuoso. He was in brisk spirits today, and Donaldson and he disputed on many topics, especially on religion; Donaldson being a sort of infidel, and the Doctor a vigorous believer. We found Sir Alexander in the same gay, friendly temper as ever. He rejoiced with me on the birth of my Ascanius,[9] as he called my son. We walked a little before dinner, and in a summer-house which he has raised in a corner chosen by old Allan Ramsay, we saw upon the wall a sketch of that poet's head, very like, done by Sir Alexander from memory, in black lead.[1] Donaldson said it was a bold outline, and at my

---

[8] "From this page downwards till Sunday finished, written on Monday the 18": Boswell's note.

[9] The son of Aeneas.

[1] Ramsay, author of the pastoral drama, *The Gentle Shepherd,* was a close friend of Sir Alexander's. He had presented him with a set of his poems in 1755, inscribed with some dedicatory verses in his own hand.

suggestion agreed to copy it. I said that there might be good drawings made for our old Scotch songs: *The Auld Wife ayont the Fire, Muirland Willie,* etc. Donaldson thought so too. The Doctor told us he had prints of the scenes of *The Gentle Shepherd* done in England, but not good ones, as the artist did not understand the writing sufficiently. I spoke to Sir Alexander of writing his life. I had a pleasing card from him yesterday saying that it was only for private friends, and he today again modestly declined his being recorded. He said Proculeius was the only instance of a man celebrated merely for private virtue:

> Vivet extento Proculeius aevo,
> Notus in fratres animo paterno, etc.[2]

I however did not doubt that I should get from him the progressive circumstances of his life.

Esdaile, who sat up with me at Princes Street Coffee-house, dined here today. He put me in mind of a curious expression which I used when Mr. Lawrie wanted me to come home to my wife: "Tell her I'm doing harm neither to man nor beast." In the evening I called a little at home and then went to the Hon. A. Gordon's and played at whist and brag. A good many people were there. I was a gainer before supper, which was at twelve o'clock; but after it, when the rage of gaming came upon me, and I forgot or disregarded my resolution or promise never to play above half-crown whist and never to bet, I lost, besides my winning, £4. 14. We did not part till near three. I came home in great vexation of spirit. Luckily my wife was in a most gentle frame and soothed me, and I again resolved to be moderate, or give up play altogether. I considered that I might gradually become a deep gamester, and I shuddered at the thought.

SUNDAY 17 DECEMBER. Was at New Church forenoon and afternoon, and at my father's between sermons with Dr. Webster and George. Dr. Blair in the forenoon lectured excellently on St. Paul's voyage and shipwreck, and preached excellently on the same text as he did last Sunday: "Cornelius, a devout man." He had two observations which appeared new to me. He said we esteemed gratitude to benefactors when applied to men of high rank. We would do the same if an angel were the object of it. Strange that an amiable and respectable quality should not be as highly esteemed when applied to the Supreme Benefactor! And that, when it was objected that GOD is invisible, we should consider that the goodness, the generosity—in short, that which excites our gratitude towards our fellow creatures—is invisible to sense, being seated in the mind. In the afternoon Mr. Walker endeavoured to prove that the eternity of

---

[2] "Proculeius shall be known to distant ages for his fatherly affection towards his brothers": Horace, *Odes,* II. ii. 5–6, *animo paterno* for *animi paterni.*

punishment was nowise inconsistent with GOD's goodness. "For," said he, "in order to make us happy, which can only be by our living according to the Gospel, threatenings are necessary; and threatenings would not have the effect if we were not sure that they are to be executed. Therefore God, who cannot lie, hath threatened; and we cannot complain, as we have it in our choice to avoid the penalties." "But alas!" thought I, "What shall be said as to men of wavering faith and strong passions?" The afternoon's discourse darkened the fine tints of Blair in the forenoon. But I found that my mind had internal force enough to dissipate the mist. I steadily thought that eternity of punishment *could not be,* according to my notions of the Divinity.[3]

After church I called on David Hume and found him sitting after dinner with his sister and youngest nephew.[4] He had on a white nightcap and a hat above it. He called for a fresh bottle of port, which he and I drank, all but a single glass that his nephew took. I indeed took the largest share. Then we drank tea. Mr. Hume said that Armstrong's *Art of Preserving Health* was the most classical poem in the English language; that Thomson's *Seasons* had more luxuriance or splendour, but that it had no order and the transitions were rude. He said Armstrong was wonderfully ignorant, but affected to be still more so. That he had not met with the encouragement which he deserved as a man of genius, for Mr. Hume had known several men of letters who never had heard of him. That his *Almanac* was a sort of imitation of Rabelais, but that it had extravagance without being at all diverting.[5] Yet Armstrong thought better of it than of anything he had written. Mr. Hume said Armstrong said to him some of his friends told him it was the best thing he had written. "But," added Mr. Hume, "I found the friend who told him so was himself." He has said this to try if David would agree with his friends. Mr. Hume said that Armstrong set a very high value on poetry, for when he asked him one day if Wilkes was not a poet, "Poet!" said the Doctor, "he cannot write prose." "Ay, ay, Doctor," said David, "you do not consider that we prose

---

[3] With a return of orthodoxy, Boswell inked out this and the preceding sentence.

[4] Hume's only sister was named Catherine; the nephew was John, third son of John Home. David had changed the old-fashioned spelling of his family name. Long *o* in Scots had become the sound written ui (guid) and pronounced like French *u* or German *ü*.

[5] The Rabelaisian influence is apparent in the title-page, which reads in part as follows: "The Muncher's and Guzzler's Diary: the Wit's, the Critic's, the Conundrumist's, the Farmer's, the Petit-Maître's Pocket Companion . . . the Male, the Female, the Hermaphrodite Prognosticator: the Mole's, the Salamander's, the Butterfly's, the Flying-Fish's, the Whale's, the Alligator's, the Phoenix's, in a word, the Universal Almanac." It was printed in the first volume of Armstrong's *Miscellanies,* 1770.

writers think ourselves the strength of the army, the infantry, and you poets the horse, only for scouring the country."

Mr. Hume told me he went to France in the year 1734,[6] being ill, and stayed there three years. I told him that Dr. Maclaine at The Hague had shown me his first performance: a letter to the minister of Moffat (Dr. Wallace) on his sermon to prove that without revelation we had no reason to hope that the Deity would forgive offences. David said this was a mistake. The letter, which he commended as an acute, well-written piece, was by a minister who died young. He thought his name was Telfer;[7] and his own first publication was his *Treatise on Human Nature*. He said he had never written any verses. I had really a good chat with him this afternoon. I thought also of writing his life.

He told me that Herring, Archbishop of Canterbury, sent a message to him by Rouet that if ever he came to London he should have an apartment in his Palace at Lambeth. David was diverted with the thought of his being there among the chaplains. It was his *History* that pleased the Archbishop, and his Grace sent him a present of ten guineas. He never knew of it till after the Archbishop's death, when, on settling an account with Andrew Millar, he found stated, "ten guineas sent to you by the Archbishop of Canterbury."[8] He said he never was in London during the Bishop's life after the invitation. I said, "Perhaps the Archbishop did not know that you had written any bad book. You would have done very well at Lambeth; you would have given them good politics, and they would have given you good religion." It was curious to see David such a civil, sensible, comfortable looking man, and to recollect, "This is the Great Infidel." Belief or want of belief is not absolutely connected with practice. How many surly men are teachers of the gospel of peace! My wife and I went and sat a little at Sir George's in the evening.

MONDAY 18 DECEMBER. Dr. Black's lecture on gold really laid hold of my attention. My wife and I dined at Sir George's along with Surgeon Wood, and drank to Lady Betty Cochrane and Laird Heron, this being their marriage-day. The Hon. Mr. A. Gordon called on me a little in the forenoon. I read and dictated session business. We drank tea at Sir George's. Then I came home and dictated some, but had lived too full at dinner and was not easy. I was uneasy that I had not heard from Dr. Johnson for a long time. I feared that he was ill or had perhaps heard of

[6] Manuscript, "173 ." The *Treatise of Human Nature* was written during this period, chiefly at La Flèche.
[7] Probably the Reverend Charles Telfer, minister of Hawick from 1723 to 1731, in which year he died, aged thirty-eight.
[8] Millar was the publisher of Hume's *History of England*.

my defending the Americans, and was angry with me. I wrote to him this evening and to Mr. Thrale in case of his being ill.

TUESDAY 19 DECEMBER. The Court of Session by a great majority altered Lord Gardenstone's interlocutor in the cause, Scotlands against the Reverend Mr. Thomson, and were very severe on the latter.⁹ This was very unexpected to me, and I was a good deal hurt by it, having taken a fixed interest in the question, I suppose from its being connected with Colonel Campbell's success, and believing that Thomson thought himself right. I had today a letter from my brother David; thought him, at first reading, rather too anxious for his own interest, but checked the thought. I called a little on Sir George in the forenoon and on Grange in the afternoon. Was busy with law today. I need not mark particulars.

WEDNESDAY 20 DECEMBER. (I am now writing on Saturday the 23.) In the evening visited the military lodge of St. George's (from Edinburgh —No. 108), of the 31 Regiment, to whom I had given the use of our lodge-room for their occasional meetings. The Grand Master and several of his suite were there. Brother McCuming, their Deputy Master and Quartermaster to the Regiment, a worthy Scotsman raised by his merit from the ranks, told me that, of fifty of his lodge who left Edinburgh with the regiment in _____, he was the only one now in life.¹ This was a thought of awe and regret.

THURSDAY 21 DECEMBER. After dinner Mr. George Laing called on me to talk over a process in which he was agent and I was lawyer. He talked most sensibly, and as he has given me a good deal of business, and I never could perceive anything bad in his conduct, I felt a sort of humane warmth for him as one who has suffered from prejudice, his character in the Court being unfavourable, I know not for what. I called for wine and drank some glasses with him. Mr. Lawrie joined us after we had drank one or two. My constitution is now such, I suppose from habit, that I can hardly bear any wine at all. Though I drank but about a third of a bottle, my head was for a little disturbed. I however dictated some law and wrote a letter to Mr. Garrick, chiefly to recommend to him one Young, a Scotsman, who had gone upon the stage. I enclosed to him a letter to me from Lord Kames, asking me to recommend Young, who had been his clerk. I suggested to my Lord, when he spoke to me, to write such a letter as would be agreeable to Mr. Garrick. In writing to Garrick, I felt particles of vivacity rise by a sort of contagion of fancy.² At nine o'clock I went to the

---

⁹ He was fined £30 damages, and fifty guineas for expenses.
¹ The blank should be filled with 1762. The losses had mainly been owing to an epidemic of yellow fever at Pensacola in 1765.
² According to Lord Kames's letter to Boswell (19 December), Charles Young had been "more than a year with Mr. Digges; but being ambitious of figuring in the capital

Pantheon, of which I had been made an honorary member, and heard a debate whether or not lotteries are beneficial to Great Britain.

FRIDAY 22 DECEMBER. This being the day before the session rose for the Christmas recess, and as I was to dine at Lord Alemoor's and sup at Moncrieffe's, I wished to have nothing to do in the afternoon, and therefore finished the only paper necessary to be done directly, and so did not go to hear the last lecture of Dr. Black's course of chemistry. Indeed I have missed several of them. It is a certain fact that I have a mind incapable, or at least ill disposed, for science of any kind. I always remember Sir John Pringle's saying to me some years ago in London, "You know nothing." And now the remark is as just as then. There is an imperfection, a superficialness, in all my notions. I understand nothing clearly, nothing to the bottom. I pick up fragments, but never have in my memory a mass of any size. I wonder really if it be possible for me to acquire any one part of knowledge fully. I am a lawyer. I have no system of law. I write verses. I know nothing of the art of poetry. In short I could go through everything in the same way.

Mr. David Dalrymple, Mr. Nairne, Mr. John Davidson, and I went in a coach to Lord Alemoor's. Ilay Campbell, Lord Coalston, and John Mackenzie were there. We dined luxuriously, and my Lord kept us drinking claret till past nine, all but Lord Coalston. I have nothing worthy of registration at this meeting.[3] Ilay Campbell took John Davidson's place up to town. I went directly to Moncrieffe's. I was heated and elevated

---

scene of action, his heart is set upon going to London." Boswell's letter to Garrick was indeed written in a "contagion of fancy": "You theatrical sovereigns are, I believe, as much solicited for the places in your gift as any monarch in Europe. There is this difference, however, that I believe you never bestow them but according to merit real or imaginary. I am now to apply to Your Dramatic Majesty for the vacant place of my countryman Johnstone, not as Prime Minister, according to the popular cry of Scottish influence behind the curtain in Drury Lane as at St. James's, but as his successor in the parts which he played. . . . I shall never cease to renew my claim upon you for a visit to Scotland. Why will you not come and see a country where you have so many friends, and add a northern jewel to your diadem of fame? I could write a rhapsody upon this subject. I indeed wonder much at your neglect of us, and am a little angry or vexed. . . . I have had a son born to me since I saw you, so that I have now a wife and three children; and yet, I know not how, the cares of the world, of which I have read and heard a great deal, do not burthen me much. There is doubtless a knack of carrying our 'load of life' with more ease than common, without any remarkable strength of shoulders. It may be a kind of suppleness like the poles of English and Irish chairmen."

[3] "Only that my Lord held my hand cordially before parting—not again to meet in this life": marginal note by Boswell. Lord Alemoor died on 14 January.—The company was entirely legal. Coalston was a colleague of Alemoor's on the bench (see below, Appendix B), Davidson (Crown Agent) and Mackenzie were Writers to the Signet, and the other four were advocates. Ilay Campbell, whom Boswell in 1774 had called "the

pretty much; played at whist and lost a trifle, and then supped; but growing uneasy I came off soon after supper, and was ill after I came home, but not drunk. Strange are the manners of this country.

SATURDAY 23 DECEMBER. (I am now writing on Tuesday the 26.) The Session rose for the Christmas recess. I found business doing well this session, better even than last winter session. M. Dupont drank tea with us. This evening was the meeting of the examinators on civil and Scotch law, of whom I was one. We supped at Fortune's. Before supper I played a rubber at whist and won. Harry Dundas, Lord Advocate, our Dean, was with us, and he gave us so many parliamentary speeches, and talked so seriously on the decline of learning in Scotland, that I saw tonight what I never saw before: a company of advocates free from drunkenness, though we sat till past two in the morning. I was really pleased with Dundas tonight, and half resolved to be well with him, though his interference in the Ayrshire politics had exasperated me. I was in a good, rational, calm frame.

SUNDAY 24 DECEMBER. Slept too long for being in time for church in the forenoon. An account in the newspapers that St. John's Fort in Canada, commanded by my cousin, Major Charles Preston, was taken by the provincials agitated everybody.[4] I dined at my father's between sermons with Dr. Webster and George. My father was angry, supposing Preston had yielded the fort too easily. I said he was in want of provisions. "Then," said my father, "he might have eaten provincials." "Ha!" cried George Webster, "Cromwell could not have made a better speech." In the afternoon I heard Dr. Blair's third and concluding sermon on "Cornelius, a devout man"; but either I did not attend so well as before, or his sermon was not so good as the other two. I drank tea at young Donaldson's, talking of American news, and then sat awhile at Sir George's.

MONDAY 25 DECEMBER. (I am now writing on Thursday the 28.) Worthy Grange, who has never failed to dine with me on Christmas-day, was brought up in a chair,[5] and we were as comfortable as usual, and drank my brother David's health in rich Malaga. I went to the chapel in the afternoon, but the music was unpleasing, and my devotion was not aided. Grange drank tea with us. In the evening my wife and I took a fancy to play at brag, and my rage for gaming was such that we played till one in

---

first writing lawyer at our bar," became Lord President in 1789 and in 1808 was created a baronet.

[4] General Richard Montgomery, descending the Richelieu River from Lake Champlain, had laid siege to St. John's, which surrendered on 3 November. He then pressed on and took Montreal, some thirty miles away, and effected a junction with Benedict Arnold for the assault on Quebec, in which he was killed and Arnold severely wounded.

[5] He had hurt his leg. See above, 28 November.

the morning. I had sat awhile with Maclaurin in the forenoon. I sat a little
with Sir George at night.

TUESDAY 26 DECEMBER. My wife and I fell to brag again in the forenoon. I was sensible of my strange keenness for play, and resolved to guard
against it. Sir Walter had come to town last night on his way to London.
My wife was indisposed. I dined at Lady Colville's, and in the evening
played at whist.

WEDNESDAY 27 DECEMBER. In the forenoon sat with Robert Boswell a good while in the Advocates' Library consulting on a difficult cause.
Then went to my father's with a view of talking to him of paying my debt,
if I saw a proper opening. He came upon the subject himself, but was in
quite a different frame from what he was on Saturday the 18 November
as mentioned in this journal. He said he had made an entail and settled
that if I should even call it in question, I should forfeit all his own purchases; but that he saw this would not restrain me, and therefore he was
now determined to allow me no more than £100 a year, which he had
formally settled upon me, instead of £300, which he had hitherto allowed
me since my marriage; and instead of relieving me of my debt to Dalblair's creditors, he would get a trustee to pay it upon an assignation, and
then do diligence against me, and lay me in gaol.[6] He was in a shocking
humour today. I was quite calm; told him that I had pursued the very
plan of life which he was anxious I should follow, though it was disagreeable to me; that I was doing very well, and that I did not expect such
usage from him. That if he would entail the estate on heirs male without
stopping short and cutting off the descendants of Craigston, I would join
with him; but that as he told me that he went no farther than the heirs
male descending from my grandfather, and then went to heirs female, I
thought the entail unjust, and could not agree to it. I unluckily mentioned
something that Maclaurin had said. This made my father worse. He said,
"I see you have been consulting lawyers. I will guard against you." And
then he said, in a diabolical-like passion, "I shall put an end to it at once.
I shall sell it off and do with the money what I please." He also threw out

---

[6] See above, 17 November 1775 and below, 1 January and 10 February 1776. Lord
Auchinleck was surety (the Scots term is "cautioner") for the price of Dalblair, of
which Boswell still owed £1300. If Lord Auchinleck paid this in Boswell's place, he
would himself become legally an unpaid creditor of Boswell for the sum, and could
take against him all the measures that the law of debt allowed, including ultimately
that of imprisonment. Since it would have been considered outrageously harsh for
any father, however righteous his sternness, to lay his son and heir in gaol under
such circumstances, Lord Auchinleck is proposing the more decent course of getting
someone else (probably the trustee for Dalblair's creditors), with proper security, to
take his place as cautioner and pay the debt. "Then it will be out of my hands, and
he may do what he will with you."

some morose, contemptuous reflections: as if I thought myself a very wise man, and was the reverse, and how I went to London among the *geniuses,* who despised me. He abused Dr. Johnson, and when I mentioned keeping up a connexion with Lord Mountstuart, treated him with contempt. In short he was as bad as possible. I told him he no doubt had it in his power to do as he threatened; but I wished he would think seriously if he could do so with a good conscience, and that there was a Father in Heaven to whom both of us were answerable. He said that he himself would have settled the estate on my daughters, failing my sons, but that he had taken a race of heirs male to please me; that he believed I was the only man in Edinburgh who would insist to have his own children disinherited, but that I had not natural affection. I was a good deal agitated inwardly. He appeared truly odious as an unjust and tyrannical man. I recollected Dr. Johnson's saying that he would as soon hang himself as sell his estate, but yet I could not be sure what he might do. I however considered that I ought not to be accessory to injustice, to cutting off any of my brethren, and that if he should even sell the estate, I could reflect that I had been firm in what I thought honest and honourable. I pleased myself too with thinking that I might purchase the estate by the intervention of a friend, and so disappoint him totally. It was an abominable altercation.

Balbarton came to dine with him, and he asked me to stay, which I did. Lady Auchinleck was ill and did not dine with us. I appeared quite unconcerned, but was miserably vexed, and drank beer and porter in abundance and a good deal of white wine till I was somewhat intoxicated. I then went down to Peter Ramsay's, where Sir Walter was to take his chaise. He introduced me to his travelling companion, young Maxwell of Calderwood. The rattling conversation of the youths amused my mind and I drank freely of port and claret till they set out. I was very drunk and wandered in the streets about three hours, following girls but luckily retaining rationality enough to keep clear of them. I fell once or twice and came home all dirty and bruised and very ill of a cold immediately catched. My wife, to whom I told what had passed at my father's, which occasioned my drunkenness, was good enough not to upbraid me. I found a kind letter from Dr. Johnson, but was not able to read it perfectly, I was in such . . .'[7]

[SATURDAY 30 DECEMBER]. . . . . I put it to him if he would agree

[7] Four pages, containing the whole of the record for 28–29 December, have been removed from the journal at this point. We learn from the entry for 6 February 1776 that these pages probably contained, among other things, a "wild speech" against Lord Auchinleck which Boswell uttered at Grange's. They must also have recorded Boswell's realization that the bruises of his drunken nocturnal ramble included a severely sprained ankle. We recover the journal part way through the entry for 30 December, in the midst of another conversation concerning the entail, between Boswell and some older man.

to cut off so many heirs male, if he were in my place. He said he had not thought so much on the subject as I had done. I saw plainly that he approved of my firmness, but wished me to preserve a dutiful appearance towards a parent. I then went to Sir George's and, feeling myself in a most comfortable social humour, frankly offered to stay dinner if my wife would come. Miss Preston went immediately and secured her. We were made most heartily welcome, and so much kindness was shown that I observed tears in my wife's eyes. Sir George and Lady Preston have been really like parents to us for these several years, and I am happy to think that we have made an affectionate return. This day I was as warm-hearted with the worthy people and as much at my ease, relishing the comforts of life, as I could wish, and they were so much the same that I had no melancholy ideas of their being old. Sir George went to sleep between dinner and tea. I read some in Abercromby's *Lives of the Scots Writers.*[8] Sir James Wemyss and Miss Semple drank tea, and after they went Sir George and Miss Preston and my wife and I played at whist. While I sat here I received a letter from Mr. Garrick in answer to mine of the 21 current mentioned in this journal. He could not receive Young, but his letter was very polite. It was a pleasing dessert after my comfortable entertainment. In the evening at home, my wife was at great pains to soothe me, as she saw vexation on account of my father's treatment and my embarrassed circumstances distressing me.

SUNDAY 31 DECEMBER. (I am now writing on Tuesday 2 January 1776.) My cold and sprained ankle were worse. I lay in bed but did not enjoy that tranquillity which I have formerly done in that state of indolence. I read in *The Critical Review* an account of Priestley's edition of Hartley's *Observations on Man* with some essays of his own relative to the subject of that book. While I was carried into metaphysical abstraction, and felt that *perhaps* all our thinking of every kind was only a variety of modification upon matter, I was in a sort of amaze;[9] but I must observe that it did not affect me with "that secret dread and inward horror"[1] which it has occasioned at other times. There is no accounting for

---

[8] Boswell appears to have confused Patrick Abercromby's *Martial Achievements of the Scots Nation* and George Mackenzie's *Lives and Characters of the Most Eminent Writers of the Scots Nation.*

[9] Hartley, a physician and member of the empirical school, maintained that all our moral and religious ideas are complex aggregates, through association, of simple "ideas of sensation" (images), and explained thought by an ingenious mechanistic theory of minute vibrations in the nerves and brain. Though a sincere Christian, he denied free will in the philosophical sense. His book was published in 1749, but did not attract much attention until Priestley popularized it. His philosophy exerted a profound influence on Coleridge and Wordsworth.

[1] ". . . whence this secret dread, and inward horror, of falling into naught?" Addison's *Cato,* V. i. 4–5.

our feelings, but certain it is that what strikes us strongly at one time will have little influence at another. Speculation of this kind relieved me from the vexation of family differences, by changing objects and by making me consider, "If all thought and all volition and all that we denominate spirit be only properties of matter, why should I distress myself at present, while in full consciousness, about eventual successions of machines?" I however thought that philosophical theories were transient, whereas feudal principles remained for ages. In truth the mortality or immortality of the soul can make no difference on the enthusiasm for supporting a family, for, in either case, the matter must be of no moment to those who have departed this life. If they have ceased to exist, they know nothing of it. If they exist in another state, they perhaps even then know not what passes here, and, if they do, it is perhaps as trifling in their eyes as our childish concerns are in ours when we have arrived at manhood. How strange is it, then, that a man will toil all his life and deny himself satisfactions in order to aggrandize his posterity after he is dead. It is, I fancy, from a kind of delusion in the imagination, which makes us figure ourselves contemplating for ages our own magnificence in a succession of descendants. So strong is this delusion with me that I would suffer death rather than let the estate of Auchinleck be sold; and this must be from an enthusiasm for an *idea* for *the Family*.[2] The founder of it I never saw, so how can I be zealous for his race? and were I to be a martyr, I should only be reckoned a madman. But an *idea* will produce the highest enthusiasm. Witness the ardour which the individuals at the time have for the glory of their regiment, though they have no line of connexion with it, being picked out from all parts of the kingdom. The officers and soldiers of the Scots Greys boast that *"We* were never known to fly."—*"We* gained distinguished honour at such a battle." Yet the officers and soldiers under that *name* at former periods were as different from its officers and soldiers now as the Romans were. I don't mean that they were different in body or in mind, in any remarkable degree, but that there is not a trace of identity, unless that there is always a remain of a regiment to communicate the same discipline and gallantry of sentiment to those who come into it, so that *l'esprit du corps,* like the fire of Vesta, is kept incessantly burning, though the materials are different. I thought for a little that a man should place his pride and his happiness in his own individuality, and endeavour to be as rich and as renowned and as happy as he can. I considered that Dr. Johnson is as well as if he belonged to a *family*. Priestley's *material* sys-

---

[2] It seems likely that the second "for" is a slip of the pen, and that Boswell meant to write "for an *idea* of *the Family*." We do not venture to emend because it is possible to make sense of what he wrote, either with his own punctuation (which we follow) or with a comma after *idea:* "for an *idea,* for *the Family*."

tem affected me less that he declared his belief in Christianity, which teaches us that GOD bestows a future life. However, I thought myself strongly conscious of an immaterial something—of a soul. I read a pamphlet today, which I remember having looked at about twenty years ago: *The Trial of the Witnesses for the Resurrection of Jesus.*[8] I found it to be a piece of very good argument which confirmed me in my faith; but I was a little disgusted with its author's affecting a sort of easy smartness of dialogue in some places.

My wife went to church in the afternoon. I got up to tea, and afterwards I took from my drawers the account of our family drawn up by my grandfather, and read it with more attention than I had ever done; and I discovered that in fact my great-grandfather had got little better than a bankrupt estate from his uncle, and that it was so burthened with debt that it appeared to me a question if, at that period, when money was scarce in Scotland and interest high, it was prudent to take it. This at once, like a blaze of light, showed me that I had been in an error as to an obligation in *justice* to give the succession all along to heirs male, seeing that we had not received it as a sacred trust with that view; and if *principle* was removed, I could yield my *inclination* and agree with my father. I was apprehensive that this sudden light would not be steady, and was only struck out by my father's threatenings; at least that my mind was much biased by them. I therefore resolved to wait for some time and to consult Dr. Johnson. My wife, who was pleased not a little, cherished the discovery and suggested that if I had any scruple remaining, I might settle my estate of Dalblair on heirs male for ever. I was wonderfully relieved tonight. My feudal enthusiasm for the heirs male of our founder, Thomas Boswell, remained. But this I could yield or modify.

[8] Written by Thomas Sherlock, later Bishop of London, in 1729.

1776

MONDAY 1 JANUARY. (I am now writing on Wednesday the 3 January.) Nothing very remarkable filled my mind on this day, the beginning of a new year. Lord Hailes's *Annals of Scotland* came out and I read a little of them, wondering at his extreme assiduity.[1] Upon a review of my expense during the year, I found that, instead of £500 at which Sir William Forbes and I had calculated it on the 2 of January 1775, it amounted to upwards of £650. There were, however, a few extraordinary articles.[2] My wife and I resolved for this year to endeavour to spend less. I must indeed do her the justice to observe that, instead of exceeding what was allowed to her by the calculation, she was about £40 within it. I was in an indolent frame, with my legs resting on a stool to ease my sprained ankle. Young resolutions are sprightly. I pleased myself with hopes that I should be more economical in time coming. I made out a state of my debts and funds, and, abstracting from my debt to Dalblair's creditors, for which my father is bound, I had £100 clear. The Dalblair debt, principal and interest, came to £1,300, so that with the £100 retained of my last year's allowance, my father would have £1,200 to pay.

In the forenoon a curious incident happened to me in the course of my profession. ――――, a mason in Dundee, came and consulted me on a process which he had before the sheriff of Forfar.[3] After I had read several papers, heard him patiently, and written a note of my opinion, he asked me how much he should give me. I said whatever he pleased. Upon which he took out three shillings and said, "Will that do?" I smiled and bid him give it to "that young man" (Mr. Lawrie). The man appeared to me to have acted with honest simplicity. From his process I saw that he had by his business 1. 6 a day, and I suppose he thought two days' wages very good payment to me for less than two hours' work.

In the evening I wrote a long letter to my brother David, chiefly upon the unhappy differences between my father and me, and begging his advice what I should do as to the entail. I mentioned to him the discovery

[1] Only the first part, from the accession of Malcolm III to the accession of Robert I, had as yet appeared. The second part, which carried the history down to the accession of the House of Stuart, was published in 1779.
[2] Such as the thirty-guinea suit of laces, 13 April 1775.
[3] Patrick Chalmers of Auldbar.

which I had made on Sunday evening, and I sent him a second copy of my settlement on him, made out to his mind, he having objected to a clause in the original copy. I preserve the original copy with the alteration on it.

TUESDAY 2 JANUARY. During this recess I have indulged myself in lying long in bed. I had a consultation in the forenoon, but felt an unwillingness to the labour of the law. In the afternoon I wrote a long, serious, and earnest letter to Dr. Johnson upon the subject of the settlement of our estate, laid before him my discovery, and entreated a full opinion from him. He had formerly confirmed me in my resolution to be steadfast to heirs male for ever. But I stated to him that I had been in an error as to the *justice* of the case, seeing that my great-grandfather had got very little. My letter was too late for the post, so was to lie till Thursday. I made another discovery this night, which was that three sons of the family who went to Sweden to Gustavus Adolphus's wars were the next heirs after Balmuto, having come off a generation later than the Craigston branch, so that the dancing-master was placed at a much greater distance than we had been supposing, and gallant soldiers came forth.⁴ This other discovery showed me how very imperfectly either my father or I had studied the genealogy of our family. I this night made out a sort of tree or table of descent of our males to send to Dr. Johnson. I resolved to write a postscript still stronger than my letter to him, in favour of my liberty in point of *justice,* though my *inclination* for the male line of our founder was warm. There was an additional circumstance occurred to me tonight, which was that my great-great-grand-uncle did not give the estate to his brother James, but to his nephew David, which was a proof that he did not think of the strict male succession, and that he gave it to his nephew as a young man who might perhaps make something of it, when his brother could not. My wife suggested that the old laird was ashamed to let his indolence and extravagance be known, and was glad to get his nephew to undertake to pay his debts, instead of letting the estate be torn in pieces and his bad management exposed; and if his nephew could have a reversion, it was but factor fee or commission for his trouble and risk, for at that time it was difficult to get land sold. I wrote tonight to my friend Temple. There had been a cessation of above two months in our correspondence.

WEDNESDAY 3 JANUARY. A meeting was fixed for considering a submission between Mr. Craufurd of Auchenames and Adam Bell, formerly

---

⁴ These "gallant soldiers," William, George, and Matthew, were younger sons of James Boswell of Auchinleck (d. 1618), and brothers of David Boswell of Auchinleck (d. 1661). The Craigston branch was descended from John Boswell of Auchinleck (d. c. 1609). See below, Appendix C, Chart II.

his overseer, in which Mr. Ilay Campbell and I were arbiters, to be held this forenoon. Mr. Campbell obligingly came to my house, as my sprained ankle still required ease. I found my head clear enough, but indeed we had not much to consider at this time.

My wife and I were asked to dine this day at my father's. I was glad the invitation came, as it showed that notwithstanding our last disagreeable interview, we were not at war; but we sent our excuse on account of my lameness. Young Robert Syme drank tea with us. I was consulted today on a mercantile contract at Danzig. I have as yet little power of decision. I am uneasy when I have to give an opinion upon a case. I was at first view dubious as to this case, and rather against my client, but was to think of it more. My state of mind today was still affected by Hartley and Priestley's metaphysics, and was continually trying to perceive my faculties operating as machinery. My animal spirits were so light now that such sort of thinking did not distress me as it has done when I was more atrabilious. I felt an easy indifference as to what was my mental system. I liked present consciousness. Man's continuation of existence is a flux of ideas in the same body, like the flux of a river in the same channel. Even our bodies are perpetually changing. What then is the subject of praise or blame upon the whole? what of love or hatred when we are to contemplate a character? There *must* be *something*, which we understand by a *spirit* or a *soul,* which is permanent. And yet I must own that except the sense or perception of identity, I cannot say that there is any sameness in my soul now and my soul twenty years ago, or surely none thirty years ago. Though souls may be in a flux, each may have a distinct character as rivers have: one rapid, one smooth, etc. I read a little of Lord Hailes's *Annals.*

THURSDAY 4 JANUARY. Sir James Foulis of Colinton breakfasted with us. He threw out a number of conjectures and reveries on languages and antiquities and showed variety of knowledge; but there was a *mens agitat molem* [5] a-wanting, a sound understanding. He told me he was busy with an Erse dictionary.[6] I was dissatisfied to behold a representative of an ancient family, and a man who had been a soldier in Portugal and the East Indies as well as in the British Army, without either dignity or elegance. Sir Alexander Dick came in after breakfast, with Miss Dick. He always communicates to me vivacity and classical recollection. I read and considered to form an opinion on my Danzig case; thought differently from what I had done at first, but was still dubious.

[5] "Mind governing the mass": Virgil, *Aeneid*, vi. 727.
[6] It was never published. Sir James was, however, the first honorary member elected to the Society of Antiquaries of Scotland, and published several papers in the *Transactions* which show his knowledge of Gaelic.

In the afternoon I was quite charmed with Veronica. She could now sing a number of tunes: *Carrickfergus, O'er the Water to Charlie, Johnnie McGill, Wee Willy Gray, Nancy Dawson, Paddy Wake, Ploughman Laddie, Brose and Butter, O'er the Hills and Far Away.*[7] It was really extraordinary that a child not three years old should have such a musical memory, and she sung with a sweet voice and fine ear (if that expression be just). She could speak a great many words, but in an imperfect manner: "Etti me see u picture." (Let me see your picture.) She could not pronounce "f." "I hĕĕd." (I'm feared. English, I'm afraid.) She rubbed my sprained ankle this afternoon with rum, with care and tenderness. With eager affection I cried, "GOD bless you, my dearest little creature." She answered, "Od bess u, Papa." Yet she loved her mother more than me, I suppose because her behaviour to her was more uniform. Effie was a stout, cheerful child and very fond of me, but spoke almost none. She aimed at singing ———. I this afternoon felt so much tenderness for Veronica that after hearing my wife say that I might live to have a severe regret for disinheriting her, I for a little had a kind of inclination to let her perhaps be lady of the domains of Auchinleck, and I wrote a postscript to my letter to Dr. Johnson. I in a *copy* of it desired the author of *Rasselas,* as a man of tender feelings, to furnish me with philosophy in case Veronica should one day seem to upbraid me for disinheriting her. But I omitted it in the *principal,* having immediately resumed my feudal principle, and considered that a *family* must not be sunk for occasional fondness. That I could do much for Veronica without letting her have what males alone ought to get.[8]

Last night Mr. Adam Neill, the printer, called and sat awhile. I asked him many questions on the present operations of the press in Edinburgh, and the profits of publication in different ways; and he gave me such accounts as stimulated my appetite for money, and I wondered that I did not deal more in publication, as by that I might have a good additional income. He spoke of a new almanac and a new newspaper being proposed. He told me that Fleming sold in one year when he was with him nine thousand of the *Edinburgh Almanac.*[9] I found, however, that the clear profit came only to about ninety pounds. I have often thought of engaging in a new newspaper here. Mundell talked to me of a scheme of a daily

[7] Boswell left a line blank in order to enter more songs. "Brose" is made by pouring boiling water on to oatmeal or peasemeal.
[8] On 15 August 1773 Boswell had declared that Veronica "should have five hundred pounds of additional fortune" because of her fondness for Dr. Johnson. This promise was carried out, with express reference to "her infantine attention to my illustrious friend," in a grant of 3 March 1795 (manuscript at Malahide Castle).
[9] Robert Fleming was printer of *The Edinburgh Evening Courant* as well as publisher of the *Almanac.*

paper.[1] I am not sure which of us mentioned it first. But both had thought of it. I was at present thinking to write a pamphlet in favour of Lord Mountstuart's militia for Scotland; but I doubted of having enough to say, though I warmly wished it success. I still thought in a visionary way of engaging in a newspaper.

This afternoon Grange and young Donaldson drank tea with us. I had some papers to write, some to be printed by Thursday next (one of them a very long one), but I was very unwilling to begin. I put them off today. I was now in a calm frame by keeping the house. Read some of Lord Hailes's *Annals*. My letter and postscript to Dr. Johnson made three gilt sheets.[2] As I keep copies of all my letters to him, I copied one sheet, my wife another, and Mr. Lawrie another, that the letter might go by the post; yet it was too late tonight again. My wife very judiciously cautioned me against too much openness with Mr. Lawrie in letting him read and copy important letters, because though he was an honest, good lad, it was better not to be in his power, as it *might* happen that I would not like to keep him longer. I shall profit by this counsel to a certain degree. But really I have a kind of strange feeling as if I wished nothing to be secret that concerns myself. This is a weakness to be corrected. My wife wrote also to Dr. Johnson a very sensible, clear letter on the subject of my male succession, entreating his interest with me, that I might agree to my father's settlement; and she did not try to have heirs whatsoever brought in directly. I was much pleased with her letter.

FRIDAY 5 JANUARY. Sir James Foulis called in the forenoon and gave me an account of what had passed yesterday in the meeting of Midlothian freeholders on the Militia Bill. I had mentioned to him my design of writing a pamphlet on it. He was keen for my doing it. Afterwards Maclaurin, to whom I had sent a note, came and sat a little with me. He gave me some light on my Danzig case. I read papers by the late Arniston, Craigie, and James Graham, Junior, on a similar case, Carmichael and Stalker, 1735.[3] I mentioned to him Hartley and Priestley. He said he was *sure* he had a soul. He mentioned Whytt on the nerves and Porterfield on the eye as curious books, both ingenious on the hypothesis of an immaterial principle in man. Then Sir William Forbes, to whom I had sent as a merchant, came and assisted me likewise on my Danzig case. In the afternoon, after consulting books enough, I dictated an opinion on it. Dr. Young drank tea with us. Lord Hailes's *Annals* engaged me more and more.

---

[1] Robert Mundell, printer, was son of James Mundell, Boswell's schoolmaster.
[2] Professor Allen T. Hazen tells us that this means "three pieces (technically half-sheets) of folded letter paper, gilded on the edges by the stationer, probably of post size. Boswell's letter consequently filled twelve pages measuring about nine by seven inches."
[3] Lord Arniston was Robert Dundas, father of the Lord President.

SATURDAY 6 JANUARY. (I am now writing on Monday the 8.) Time now pressed me for session papers. I was obliged to begin to a perplexed one: answers, Sandeman and Company to the petition of Doig, a mercantile cause involved in circumstances which had perplexed me much before my father as Lord Ordinary, and even perplexed him. It was still difficult. Robert Boswell and I had met on it in the Advocates' Library.⁴ While Mr. Lawrie copied passages, I refreshed myself with Lord Hailes's *Annals.* Mr. William Wilson, Writer to the Signet, drank tea with us. His knowledge in business, and courteousness somewhat of the last age, pleased me. We talked of Sir Walter's ⁵ affairs, and he consulted me on two causes. I wrote some letters in the evening. I still possessed much tranquillity.

SUNDAY 7 JANUARY. There had been a fall of snow in the night. The whiteness and wintry appearance gave me a kind of lively sensation. It snowed all day. I read some of the Bible in English, and of the New Testament in French, which put me in mind of the French church at Utrecht. I read a great deal of Lord Hailes's *Annals.* My wife went to church in the afternoon. Young Donaldson, for whom I had sent, drank tea with us, gave me news, and showed me some strange pieces sent for his newspaper.

MONDAY 8 JANUARY. Got up early for the first time this winter and drudged at Sandeman and Company. Having my account with the Bank of Scotland up to the beginning of this year to settle, I took a chair in the forenoon and was carried thither. It still snowed, and after ten days' keeping the house, the appearance of the High Street struck me strongly. I have great satisfaction in seeing the steady application and regularity of business at the Bank. There is a good paper in *The Spectator* on the Bank of England.⁶ I have here an inferior species of the same contemplation. In the afternoon my old master for the violoncello, Mr. John Thomson, consulted me on a claim which he had. It was agreeable to me to have it in my power to help him. In the intervals of my drudgery I finished my reading of Lord Hailes's *Annals,* all but the dissertations. I wrote short remarks as I went along, to lay before him, for more information or to suggest doubts; and I put in marks at such passages as I wished to put into a commonplace-book as valuable fragments or quotations. I have taken a hint from Walton's life of Dr. Donne, to select all the passages which

⁴ One would guess that "Sandeman and Company" was the business of Robert Boswell's father-in-law, William Sandeman, linen manufacturer. The Glassite church, in which Robert Boswell was a teaching elder, is often called "Sandemanian." The name derives from William Sandeman's brother Robert, who married John Glas's daughter and founded churches of Glas's persuasion in England and America.
⁵ Sir Walter Montgomerie-Cuninghame.
⁶ *Spectator* No. 3.

strike me in every book that I read.[7] I have now a book of clean paper into which I am to transfer, not the passages at length, but references to them; for it is needless to take a copy when the book can be easily had to consult. If I meet with a rare book or manuscript, I shall transcribe the passages. Let me see of how many books I shall extract the *flores*. If any reflections of my own occur, I shall put them down with the references. I shall thus have a rich stock for composition.[8]

In the evening my wife had a letter from Dr. Cairnie informing her that her eldest sister[9] died at London on the 3rd current. She was a good deal moved. Though I could not regret that a woman who had disgraced herself by a low marriage, and was by that estranged from us, was removed, the recollection of former days made me be a little affected with some sort of tenderness on hearing she was no longer in life. But stern reason soon resumed its influence. When death is brought close to the mind by any particular event, a gloom must in general take place. I this night had something of the same kind of feeling as the night after seeing an execution. This page is worse expressed than usual. I wrote some letters.

TUESDAY 9 JANUARY. In the intervals while Mr. Lawrie copied passages, I read *The Monthly Review* on Priestley's edition of Hartley, and found his *material* system refuted with ability and spirit. I was much pleased, and wished to be acquainted with the writer of the article.[1] I could not but think what a strange life a man would lead who should fairly act according to metaphysical conviction or impression at the time. What inconsistency and extravagance should we find! Sometimes he would be rigidly virtuous, at other times abandoned to extreme licentiousness; and at both times acting from *principle*. I have thought of writing a kind of novel to show this: "Memoirs of a Practical Metaphysician." I remember I mentioned this to Dr. Reid, who writes on the mind ac-

---

[7] Donne "left the resultance of 1,400 authors, most of them abridged and analyzed with his own hand."

[8] This commonplace-book is now at Yale. It opens with notes on William Carstares's *State Papers and Letters* (1774), William Mason's *Life of Gray* (1775), and John Langhorne's edition of the *Poetical Works* of William Collins (1765); the notes on Hailes's *Annals* were never entered. It is useful as showing that Boswell's reading was more extensive and more thoughtful than one would infer from a hasty reading of the journal. The following will serve to illustrate his reflections: "Langhorne says, p. 133, 'We leave the *Oriental Eclogues* with the same kind of anxious pleasure we feel upon a temporary parting with a beloved friend.' I do not perceive the least propriety in this comparison. We are anxious when we part with a friend because we may never see him again, as his life is uncertain. But how can we have any such anxious feeling on closing a book, which is to last for ever, and which we may open when we please?"

[9] Mrs. Beaumont.

[1] He already was. The author was William Rose, of Chiswick.

cording to common sense.[2] He told me the same thought had occurred to him. Maclaurin observed very well, when he was last with me, that thinking metaphysically destroys the principles of morality; and indeed when a man analyses virtues and vices as a chemist does material substances, they lose their value as well as their odiousness. I was quite fatigued today with Sandeman and Company. Dr. Webster and Grange drank tea with us, which enlivened me somewhat. I sent for Grange. He does not visit me so often as he should. Dr. Grant sat awhile with me at night. Mr. Wood was with me before dinner, about my sprain.

WEDNESDAY 10 JANUARY. (I am now writing on Friday the 12.) Drudged on at Sandeman and Company, and got it finished to my satisfaction. Drew also a short paper to be in the boxes next day. Finished the dissertations at the end of Lord Hailes's *Annals.* In the evening Mr. Burnett, younger of Kemnay, who was secretary to Sir Andrew Mitchell, sat a little with me and revived somewhat my foreign ideas, as I had seen him at Berlin. After supper Robert Boswell came and we read over the proof-sheets of Sandeman and Company. It has been a harassing operation. We sat at it till near two in the morning.

THURSDAY 11 JANUARY. Read a view of the political writers in opposition in 1740, in a volume of pamphlets which I had bought at an auction;[3] was entertained with anecdotes, and struck to consider how much good writing was forgotten from being on temporary subjects; however, I thought that spiritual subjects, like material, serve their time and are transmuted and compounded in perpetual succession. Began to read Macquer's *Chemistry* while I was at stool, and thought that by getting a habit of reading it while at that operation, I would get through it by degrees, and each portion of it would be keenly seized.[4] Began also today to mark in my commonplace-book any passages which I had particularly observed in Carstares's *Letters,* a dull, uninteresting collection in general. Dictated a good part of another paper. Mrs. Grant, our neighbour, drank tea with us. Grange called in the evening and we prevailed with him to come back and sup. Maclaurin came and sat awhile. He was pleasanter than usual from having drank cheerfully. I was in good spirits though still lame.

I was full of metaphor. I said the Lords of Session were just sponges.

[2] Dr. Thomas Reid, Professor of Moral Philosophy at the University of Glasgow, was the author of *An Inquiry into the Human Mind on the Principles of Common Sense,* 1764. Boswell had been "refreshed and very happy" when he read the book in Berlin that year, because Reid had driven to pieces the "sceptical cobweb" of Hume.

[3] *An Historical View of the Principles . . . of the Political Writers in Great Britain,* London, 1740, by an anonymous supporter of Walpole's administration.

[4] Pierre Joseph Macquer, *Elements of the Theory and Practice of Chemistry:* Boswell's edition was probably that published at Edinburgh in 1768.

They absorbed matter from the papers which we give in to them, and pressed it out again. Some absorbed more; some less. I said the President squeezed them like lemons: "Come, Covington." Some were very juicy; others yielded very little. Alemoor was like a great melon. Alva, a little lime.

I had a letter tonight from Sir John Pringle, which should have come the night before, but the post was kept back by the deep snow. He argued against my quitting a certainty here and settling in London, and put his arguments so well together that I was really convinced. Indeed it is better for me to take London as a high enjoyment in the spring, unless I were sure of being settled there very advantageously. By being there only two months in the year, I feel myself welcomed by all my friends, and relish it more than if I lived always there. But is it not so extensive a place, such a world, that a man may always find novelty and vivid relish in it? And a man may as well think that it is better for him not to be in existence above two months in the year, that he may enjoy it more. My love for London is very strong. It is associated with a vast number of agreeable and grand ideas. My wife had today a beautiful letter from the Hon. Mrs. Stuart.

After I went to bed I had a curious fancy as to dreams. In sleep the doors of the mind are shut, and thoughts come jumping in at the windows. They tumble headlong, and therefore are so disorderly and strange. Sometimes they are stout and light on their feet, and then they are rational dreams.

FRIDAY 12 JANUARY. Wrote two papers for Campbell of Blythswood really as well as I would wish to write. I was sensible of having a knowledge of law as well as a faculty of expression. It was indeed but a limited knowledge, but it was quite sufficient for the present occasion. Maclaurin made an observation last night which pleased me. He said that speaking ill of people was a youthful thing and cured by age. I fancy he is right. As we grow old we either become convinced that mankind must not be tried by too strict a standard of virtue, or we grow prudent, or come to think with a sort of indifference. Miss Webster and Grange drank tea with us. The snow still continued.

SATURDAY 13 JANUARY. I had set apart this day for sorting a large parcel of my father's session papers, to select what were worth binding. I like such an operation wonderfully. The succession of different subjects and different lawyers passing quickly before me was amusing, and I had the pleasure of bringing order out of confusion as I arranged. Mr. Stobie called for a little in the forenoon. I said nothing to him on my father's difference with me, as I waited for Dr. Johnson's oracular response. I had now been a fortnight without tasting wine or having anybody to dine or sup. As Mr. Burnett was in town on his way to London, I had at supper him, Dr. and Mrs. Grant, Mr. George Wallace, Grange, and Lieutenant Martin, formerly of Montgomerie's Highlanders, who had brought me a letter from Dr. Donald Macqueen, and was an Isle of Skye man. I was in excellent spirits, was keen for a militia, and spoke with vivacity of Germany and of Lord Hailes's *Annals,* etc.; drank some Madeira, and sat till near one. Was a little disturbed by this small excess.

SUNDAY 14 JANUARY. Had taken physic the night before and was relieved by it today. It snowed a great deal today. My wife went to church both forenoon and afternoon. I had the children much with me. I read some of the Bible, and the story of Calas with Voltaire's verses upon it. A son of Calas had come to Edinburgh, I suppose to get contributions for the family as he had done in England, and I among others had a pamphlet sent to me by him containing what I have now mentioned. I was not very willing to contribute, at least till I should hear from some of my acquaintances that it really was charity; for the pamphlet had prefixed to it a list of great folks who had subscribed, which made me imagine he had no occasion for more.[5] I must own too that the story of Calas does not strike me as anything more than an instance of a man's having suffered death by an unjust sentence, if it really after all was so, which I have not had the means of judging; and his case is not the more piteous that the error by which he was condemned was owing to religious prejudice against a Huguenot. Had not Voltaire aggrandized the subject by his pen, Calas would have only added one to the number of those who have been executed on a charge of murder of which they were innocent. It will be curious if my opinion be found by Dr. Johnson to be just, after all Europe has been roused by the lyre of Voltaire.

I omitted to mention that on Thursday last I received from Sir John Pringle his last discourse before the Royal Society, and I read it that night. The subject being the attraction of mountains, and I being ignorant of the first principles of natural philosophy, I did not understand it. Miss Preston drank tea with us. I this day read over this volume of journal and was pleased upon the whole with my life. But it occurred to

[5] Jean Calas, a French Protestant merchant of Toulouse, was executed on the charge of having murdered his son Marc Antoine to prevent his becoming a Roman Catholic. Voltaire, always on the watch for instances of ecclesiastical oppression, made the Calas case famous throughout Europe, and finally procured an annulment of the proceedings and an official admission that Calas was innocent. The pamphlet sent to Boswell was *The History of the Misfortunes of John Calas . . . to which is added a Letter from M. Calas to his Wife and Children, Written by M. de Voltaire,* London, 1772 (another edition, Edinburgh, 1776). The verse letter, however, was not by Voltaire, but by Blin de Sainmore. The list of subscribers included the Queen, the Archbishop of Canterbury, and seventy-nine lords. The son seeking further subscribers was Louis, who had settled in London and practised as a surgeon.

me that if I keep in constant remembrance the thoughts of my heart and imaginations of my fancy, there will be a sameness produced, and my mind will not have free scope for alteration; so that I had better lay by my journal and read masses of it at distant intervals. However, I am persuaded that a man who mixes at all in society or has business to manage cannot have a sameness of mind. One new idea or former one revived will introduce a group. Nay, a monk of La Trappe, who never hears anything but prayers and *memento mori,* will, by the very change of seasons, of his health, and from memory, have his mind affected with alterations.

MONDAY 15 JANUARY. Mr. Lawrie came in the morning with accounts that Lord Alemoor had died yesterday. It gave me much satisfaction that I had dined with him cordially on Friday 22 December last, since we had lost him so soon. On the same day poor John Robertson, the writer, commonly called Black John or Rosebery John, had died. This struck me too, for I was preparing to write a memorial for him in a case where Lord Rosebery accused him of gross malversation. It was curious to think that he had escaped. I laid by a copy of the memorial against him with his notes on it, in which he said that while the house of Strowan remained, the sword should not depart from the Earl's house; so it seems he was of Strowan's family, though in low circumstances and of an unfavourable character.⁶ How vain did his retaliation now seem! Lord Alemoor's death, though he was a judge of distinguished abilities, did not strike me so much as Lord Strichen's, because there had not been such a period since a death, and because there was no Lockhart to be promoted. I finished today the only paper which I had upon my hands, except some that were chiefly to be done by Matthew Dickie. I was in good steady spirits.

TUESDAY 16 JANUARY. I was carried in a chair to the Court of Session and had a degree of pleasure in observing how many of my brethren inquired with seeming kindness how I was lame. Lord Alemoor's death was universally regretted. It still snowed some. Balmuto set me upon trying to get a voter on Henderson's side to stay away with my father, who was for Oswald; for he told me that the President and Advocate would set upon my father and prevent his going. He appeared to be very angry at them. This gave me great joy, for honest Balmuto's eyes were opened with regard to them. I tried Smith of Forret. But could not prevail. I grew very keen for Oswald, as the Dundases had joined Henderson by way of

---

⁶ Strowan in Perthshire was the estate of a line of Robertsons who had been forfeited in 1752 because of the participation of the Laird (Duncan Robertson) in the rising of 1745. It was restored to Duncan's son, Col. Alexander Robertson, in 1784. John Robertson the "writer" needed some kind of distinctive appellative, for the *Edinburgh Directory* for 1773–1774 lists three John Robertsons and a J. Robertson, writer. He had apparently been Lord Rosebery's agent.

making a show of carrying another election. Claud told me that the Advocate had said at a consultation, "Affleck[7] will not be at the election. He'll not get leave." This was very insolent, and Claud told my father of it. Though I disapprove of a judge's meddling in elections, I was desirous on *this* occasion that my father should go, as it galled me to think that he should be so much swayed by the Dundases. Donaldson, the painter, did something more today to my wife's picture. I kept him to dinner. I had received by the post this forenoon a most pleasant letter from Dempster and a friendly one from Dr. Johnson, but dated before my important one had reached him. I was put into high spirits, felt ambition in my breast, and thought that if properly supported, and indeed if not checked by my father, I would show the Dundases and the people in Scotland what I could do. I dictated well both law papers and a letter to *The London Chronicle.*[8]

WEDNESDAY 17 JANUARY. On Sunday evening I read some of *The Rambler* to my wife, and I wondered to think how long it was since I had read any of Dr. Johnson's works, though they are the food of my soul. I hope his excellent principles are firmly rooted in my mind. But to leave metaphor, as I am at a loss to carry it on longer, it is of great advantage to me to renew from time to time the impressions of *The Rambler*. Here I am still metaphorical, though in a more common style. This day was passed in the usual manner of a session day, without anything peculiar. After I went to bed, the absolute certainty of death and what either my wife or I *must* suffer by separation distressed me.

THURSDAY 18 JANUARY. (I am now writing on Sunday the 21.) My wife and I dined and drank tea at Sir George Preston's with the usual cordiality.

FRIDAY 19 JANUARY. Was at Moncrieffe's in the evening. Played at whist calmly without feeling the gaming rage. There were only eight of us at supper, so that I could not get away so soon as I hoped to do. It was past two in the morning before I rose. I left six sitting. I never choose to stay till the company breaks up, for then there is a kind of dreary feeling of *dissolution*. Whereas while the company is sitting, social jollity remains. I did not drink to great excess.

SATURDAY 20 JANUARY. The Dundases, finding that my father was *determined* to go to the Fifeshire election, had agreed that Smith of Forret

[7] This may imply that Boswell's father was usually called *Auch-in-leck.*
[8] A letter signed "Borax," lamenting the apathy of the Scots with regard to the American War. Boswell probably picked up the pseudonym (an uncommon word in 1776) from his daily reading in Macquer's *Chemistry.* He must have seen there the reference to borax as being "of great use in facilitating the fusion of metallic substances" (i. 36).

should stay away if he did so. I introduced Smith to him in the Parliament House, and they exchanged promises. My father had all this week been so indifferent about me that he had never once inquired how my sprain was. Today however he asked me; and I was a little with him and Lord Monboddo in the robing room, where we talked of Lord Hailes's *Annals,* and Scotch antiquities, and in favour of Skene.[9] Monboddo and I stayed awhile by ourselves. He had a curious thought that *attraction,* which philosophers cannot explain, may be *mind.* He pleases me by an enthusiasm for *spirit* against the *materialists.* Dr. Boswell and Mr. Donaldson, painter, were with me this forenoon. I dined at the anniversary meeting of Mundell's Scholars, and getting into more than common spirits, was exceedingly jovial and flashed a good deal. I do not recollect my sayings, which had an excellent effect at the time. I drank rather too much, and did not rise till near nine. When I came home I found a letter from Dr. Johnson in answer to my important one concerning the settlement of the estate. He said he was much impressed by my letter, but he could not yet form a satisfactory resolution. He suggested that Lord Hailes should be consulted, and he said, "I really think Lord Hailes could help us." I wondered that Dr. Johnson had not decided upon the full state of the case which I had laid before him.

SUNDAY 21 JANUARY. (I am now writing on Tuesday the 23.) Though I had not drank to intoxication last night and had left many of the Scholars sitting, I was somewhat uneasy with a headache. My lameness still continuing, I stayed at home and read some of the Bible and some of *Histoire philosophique et politique, etc.,*[1] which elevated me, but I was often interrupted by the children. In the evening I wrote a serious letter to Lord Hailes on the subject of my father's scheme of an entail and my difficulties. I had some doubt as to consulting him, as he was a Whig and a defender of female succession, and had not sentiments congenial with mine. But as Dr. Johnson had recommended applying to him as a Christian and a lawyer, I begged in confidence to have his lights, which I should transmit to Dr. Johnson.

MONDAY 22 JANUARY. (I am now writing on Wednesday the 24.) A number of papers to be written were now accumulated upon my table, none of them indeed very difficult or long, but it gave me uneasiness to perceive that I had so much to do. At one o'clock Captain Flint of the 26 [2] Regiment, an old Mundell's scholar whom I had seen for the first time on

[9] Presumably a reference to Sir John Skene's exposition of legal terms, *De verborum significatione,* 1597.
[1] By the Abbé Raynal—a history of European conquests in the East and West Indies; a powerful contribution to democratic propaganda. It had first appeared in 1770.
[2] An error for "25."

Saturday, called on me, as I had promised to give him my best advice in making good a privilege to recruit in the High Street of this city. I engaged to draw up for him a proper letter to the Lord Provost, wishing to have a license for the Edinburgh Regiment; but if that was refused, insisting on it as a *right*.[2a] I have a wonderful fondness for everything military, and I wrote the letter in the evening and sent it to Flint. Before dinner Mr. Glendonwyn of that ilk, Mr. McGeorge of Cocklick, and Mr. John Graeme, Writer to the Signet, and I met in my house as a quorum of the curators of Gordon of Crogo's daughters. They had chosen us, and we this day settled several points of their concerns. These three gentlemen, young Cowhill, Mr. Donaldson the painter, who had been this forenoon finishing my wife's picture, and Mr. Buchan, clerk to my old employer Mr. William Wilson, dined with me, and all but Buchan drank tea. At night the account of the execution of the two Perreaus affected me very much.[3] I could not fall asleep for a long time after going to bed; and the thoughts of my own death or that of my wife or of my children or of my father or brothers or friends made me very gloomy. My spirits were weak. I had this day dictated only a paper of three pages.

TUESDAY 23 JANUARY. I was somewhat better. The return of light and business removed gloom. I delivered into Lord Hailes's hands my letter to him on our family settlements. Balbarton dined with us today, which kept me idle till tea-time; but I could [not] think my time ill employed in entertaining a sensible kinsman aged seventy-five. I dictated none today at all, but studied a cause and made out a note of what the agent should do. Between seven and eight I and Adam Bell, writer, on one side, and David Armstrong, William Hay, Senior, and John Bushby at Dumfries on the other, met at Mrs. Dunbar's tavern and settled a cause, Barrow against Drew. It was a meeting not agreeable to me. But it helped a client. I was moderate in drinking and came home to supper.

WEDNESDAY 24 JANUARY. Lord Hailes returned me an excellent answer, which made the point of *justice* as to remote heirs male so clear against my former notion that I was enlivened to a high degree of cheerfulness, and felt myself quite at freedom. But I had still to get Dr. Johnson's full response, after he had seen what Lord Hailes wrote. I this day dictated a paper much to my satisfaction.

THURSDAY 25 JANUARY. Matthew Dickie dined with me and entertained me with his account of what a clever fellow Wedderburn was when at our bar, and how he was superior to others even in common law business. He said that he believed his last pleading before the Lords was in a

---

[2a] The Lord Provost was James Stoddart.

[3] The Perreaus and their fascinating accomplice, Mrs. Rudd, later to play an important part in Boswell's life, are dealt with in the Introduction, and below, pp. 344, 351, 352.

cause in which he was agent, Pillans against Clarke, a moving story of unjust imprisonment, and that he made the Lords weep.⁴ Perhaps Matthew exaggerated. But I felt a sort of comfortable acquiescence in Wedderburn's great superiority of parts, instead of that struggle which I have felt when ambitiously supposing it possible to vie with such a man. The news of Oswald's having carried his election had come this morning, and the Dundases were visibly chagrined. This pleased me. I consulted with Mr. Dickie after dinner on some causes, and at seven I was carried out in a chair to Macqueen's to a consultation. The soundness and vigour of his abilities humbled me. I had also consulted with Mr. Rae at John's Coffee-house⁵ in the forenoon, and been humbled by his quickness and knowledge of law business. I had a poor opinion of my own qualifications as an advocate, but reproached myself inwardly with want of application to the study of the law. Indeed I should recollect that I did not apply to it at any period as other students have done. I got eight guineas today. In the evening Annie Cuninghame arrived from London and lodged with us. We had Grange at supper and were comfortable.

FRIDAY 26 JANUARY. Annie Cuninghame went over to Fife on a visit.⁶ David Ross, who was to succeed Lord Alemoor, appeared today with a wig at the clerks' table. "We see," said I, "the gradual progress of making a judge. It is like seeing bees work in a glass hive." Said George Clerk: "The bees make the comb first and then fill it with honey; so Ross gets the wig first." The Solicitor⁷ said Ross was preparing to change his state; getting his wig was like getting wings with which he was to fly from the clerks' table to the bench. He alluded to an insect getting wings from being a worm. Such ready metaphorical vivacity is pleasant for the moment, and I like to recollect it. The Solicitor made a very prudent observation to me today when I was speaking strongly against the Dundases, and asking him if they were not bad people: "They never did me any harm. A bad man is one who is bad to me." Mr. Wemyss joined me heart-

----

⁴ Matthew Dickie should have known the facts, but his account is strangely at variance with that of Wedderburn's biographers. According to the usual story, Alexander Lockhart and Wedderburn were opposed in a cause in August 1757. Lockhart made an impassioned appeal to the judges, upon which Wedderburn remarked sarcastically, "Nay, my Lords, if tears could have moved your Lordships, tears, sure I am, would not have been wanting." The Lord President (Robert Craigie) rebuked him, and a quarrel ensued in the course of which Wedderburn was ordered by the whole Court to apologize. He refused, pulled off his gown and laid it on the bar, and left the Court never to return. He set out for London that night, was called to the English bar, and ultimately (1793) attained the Chancellorship. At this time he was Solicitor-General.

⁵ In Parliament Close, a favourite resort of men practising law.

⁶ Boswell inserted this sentence later, having forgotten that his entry for the day already contained the information.

⁷ Alexander Murray, the Solicitor-General.

ily against them, and told me that they made a kind of property of the Duke of Buccleuch, so that his relations, of whom Mr. Wemyss was one, were kept at a distance from him of late. Miss Cuninghame went to Fife today. Dr. Cairnie, who had come with her from London, drank tea with us. I laboured hardly any today. I was at Moncrieffe's at night, and though I loved to sit long, came away about one. Perhaps I check myself too much.

SATURDAY 27 JANUARY. (I am now writing on Monday the 29.) Nothing particular happened. Captain Martin of the Isle of Skye sat a little with me in the evening. I dictated freely.

SUNDAY 28 JANUARY. My lameness and the severe weather still continued. It was comfortable sitting by my dining-room fire. I read the history of Nebuchadnezzar in Daniel and was struck with its circumstances. My worthy uncle, the Doctor, dined with us between sermons. He said he believed Nebuchadnezzar was in heaven, and he thought him the greatest man that ever lived. I said that such a remarkable interposition of the Divinity to bring him to a proper frame of mind was an evidence of his greatness, of his superiority among human beings:

Nec deus intersit, nisi dignus vindice nodus.[8]

The Doctor was rather too flashy in his spirits, and showed symptoms of that unquiet temperament which is in our blood. But he and I were warmly affectionate. He said with sincerity that he would not change situations with my father. He would not give up the comfort which he had in his sons Robert and Bruce for four times my father's fortune. He and I joined in regretting my father's coldness, which deprived him of the great happiness of social intercourse and having his sons easy with him. We however agreed that he was at pains to make himself worse than he really was by checking every appearance of kindness of temper. The Doctor said my father had from his youth been set on wealth and on his own personal consequence. I observed that he had not liberal, extensive views of fame—to be known in other countries, to be respected by posterity—otherwise he would have published his researches into Scottish antiquities. He desired only the immediate and confined consequence of a Lord of Session.

I read today some of *Histoire philosophique, etc.,* but made slow progress. I was chiefly occupied in reading as an instructive and entertaining lesson the memorial for Ross of Pitcalnie by Mr. Francis Garden in 1761, giving an account of the weakness of the last Laird of Balnagowan and the imposition practised on him. As this cause was to be heard in the House of Lords in the spring, it was more interesting. I said to my wife that as one great circumstance to show Balnagowan's weakness was his being

[8] "God should not intervene unless the matter is worth it": Horace, *Ars Poetica,* l. 191.

under the influence of his lady, I was determined to guard against being so. I sent for young Donaldson to drink tea with me, which he did. My wife read some of the New Testament to me in the evening. I was quite comfortable. Annie Cuninghame returned tonight. Mr. Wood was with me in the forenoon, as I had sent for him. He said that there might be something of a rheumatism in my ankle and foot. He ordered me some camphorated spirits of wine.

MONDAY 29 JANUARY. As I wished to read with my own eyes in the records any charters of the estate of Auchinleck which I could find, before writing again to Dr. Johnson, I was carried in a chair to the Laigh Parliament House, and read Thomas Boswell's charters *heredibus,* which was clearly heirs general. But then I found my great-grandfather's charter to the heirs male of his own body, whom failing, *propinquioribus suis heredibus masculis.*[9] This for a moment made me return to heirs male *for ever;* but I considered that my grandfather's property was but a small share, and that it was enough to take in the heirs male descending from him. I had written some law with my own hand in the forenoon, and read some more of the Balnagowan cause. Grange dined with us. Annie was at my father's. Mrs. Mitchelson drank tea.

TUESDAY 30 JANUARY. (I am now writing on Thursday the 1 February.) Captain Flint called on me and gave me copies of letters which he had received from the Lord Provost and Sir Adolphus Oughton with regard to his requisition to beat up in the High Street.[1] The matter was settled in favour of the military; for the Lord Provost could not point out any privilege that the town had to restrain them, and therefore got the Commander-in-Chief to interpose. Balmuto called and was full of the Fife election. I spoke to him of the difference between my father and me as to the entail, and how my difficulties were much cleared up. He had not the least hesitation upon the subject and advised me to agree with my father, and to do it soon. He said he would freely resign his claim as heir male. I told him jocularly that he was a pagan and that I would take care of the right of his sons. My lameness still confined me, otherwise I should have gone to church, I mean the Episcopal meeting, to commemorate with regret the martyrdom of Charles I, since that fast is still kept. I remember Dr. Johnson seemed to think that it might cease after a certain term, I think he said a century.[2] I wrote to him today with Lord Hailes's opinion, which however I neglected to enclose, so that it could not go till Thursday. I was busy today with a long paper for the Earl of Eglinton. At eight at night I was at a consultation at Lord Advocate's on

[9] "To his nearest heirs male."
[1] That is, to solicit and enlist recruits. See above, 22 January 1776.
[2] He did, on 21 March 1772.

Ross against Mackenzie, which was to come on next day. George's Square looked very bleak to me. It was covered with snow and the frost was intense. I felt tonight again my own deficiencies as a lawyer, but was consoled with my superiority to Buchan of Kelloe, who was with us tonight as being the President's son-in-law.[3]

WEDNESDAY 31 JANUARY. (I am now writing on Friday the 2 February.) The cause, Ross against Mackenzie, came on, and as an instance of the instability of the Court of Session, Ross, who had formerly six of the Lords for him, and only four and the President against him, had today only one (Lord Covington) for him, and eleven against him. Lord Alemoor was dead and Lord Coalston was absent, by which he lost two votes, and perhaps many more, as Lord Alemoor had great weight and kept in awe the President, who was very keen for Mackenzie. It is very unpleasing when the inclination of a counsel is against his client. This was my situation today. My heart was touched with concern for the old family of Ross of Auchnacloich, which had for several generations struggled to recover its inheritance; and I felt a melancholy impression when the cause went against him, and hoped that the House of Lords would reverse the decree. I was conscious of having discharged my duty as *counsel* for Mackenzie, and I concealed my private thoughts as a *gentleman*. Perhaps it would be better for an advocate not to engage in a cause when his wishes are for the other side.

The Earl of Caithness, for whom I had been counsel and of whose family my ancestor Thomas Boswell's mother was a daughter, was now in town. My lameness was an apology for my not visiting him. He and his second son (a lieutenant in Fraser's Highlanders), Commissioner Lockhart and his lady, Miss MacLeod of Raasay, Dr. Boswell, Mr. and Mrs. Mitchelson, and Mr. Wood, the surgeon, supped with us.[4] Commissioner Lockhart had been very obliging to me in granting solicitations for offices in the Excise, yet by most unaccountable negligence I had never once waited on him. My wife had been lately introduced to Mrs. Lockhart, and we sent them a card to sup, after my wife had called and my lameness had been mentioned. It was very kind in them to come. I was in excellent spirits. Nothing disturbed me but the consideration of my knowing from undoubted authority that Mitchelson, whom I had asked because he was Lord Caithness's agent, disliked me much, I know not for what, and took every opportunity that he could to speak ill of me. His amiable wife being a great friend of my wife's, and as much prejudiced for me as her husband was against me, corrected his acidity, and he did very well tonight, as indeed he always does when we are together. I thought it not worth while

[3] George Buchan of Kelloe married Anne Dundas in 1773.
[4] The lieutenant was William Sinclair, who died in America on 30 October of this year.

to undeceive him, as he was a sordid fellow, and I was diverted with the contrast between *appearance* and *reality,* which I believe is too often to be found in the intercourse of men. Lord Caithness looked so jolly that after his son and Mr. Lockhart and the Doctor went away, I from a kind of benevolence joined him and Mitchelson and Wood in drinking strong rum punch, though I hate it and it disagrees with me. We sat till three. I was not drunk.

THURSDAY 1 FEBRUARY. I was very ill but was obliged to go to the Court of Session. I attended the determination of Hope against Wallace in the Inner House, and won it. The severe cold of the air pierced my frame. I had a violent headache, had been very sick before I went out, and was terrified that I should do as Antony did in the Senate House, which Cicero has so strongly arraigned.[5] The awe of disgrace had restrained my squeamishness while I was in the Court, but as soon as the cause was over, I was obliged to go to a corner of the Outer Hall. I got the Hon. Mr. Gordon to appear in my place for two small pieces of form which I had this forenoon, and went home, went to bed, and after some hours of severe uneasiness grew better, got up, and dictated some law. I sent off Lord Hailes's letter to me on the entail to Dr. Johnson.

FRIDAY 2 FEBRUARY. (I am now writing on Sunday the 4.) Matthew Dickie dined with me. I was very well today but for my lameness. I had attended a pleading in the Inner House all the forenoon by Dickson and Wight maintaining that the Act _____ is not to be applied to the wages of day labourers, because each day's wages cannot make a term, and there is none other fixed, as in the case of servants who are engaged yearly or half yearly; and by Armstrong and Maclaurin maintaining the contrary. It was well argued on both sides, but so little attention is paid to pleading in the Court of Session that I was the only lawyer who attended today from beginning to end; and for long intervals there was an absolute void in the benches. Ours is a court of *papers.* We are never seriously engaged but when we write. We may be compared to the Highlanders in 1745. Our pleading is like their firing their musketry, which did little execution. We do not fall heartily to work till we take to our pens, as they to their broadswords.

I began today a curious bargain which I made with the Hon. Henry Erskine in order to acquire correctness in writing. We were to give to each other a copy of every one of our printed papers, and each was to be censor on the other. For every ungrammatical expression and every Scotticism except technical phrases, a shilling was to be incurred; and for every error in punctuation which hurt the sense of a passage and every

[5] "You had drunk so much wine at Hippia's wedding that you had to vomit in the sight of the Roman people the next day": *Philippic* II. xxv. 63.

error of the press, sixpence was to be incurred. Each was to keep an account of debit and credit, and nothing was to be charged but what was acknowledged by the writer of the paper to be just. Erskine had many objections to a paper of mine today. Lord Hailes was once appealed to and gave it for me. Erskine was too nice; for it was not inelegance but incorrectness that was liable to a fine. The former was very arbitrary. The latter, Johnson and Lowth could determine.[6] He had three shillings against me today. I am persuaded that this will do me much good. In the afternoon I had before me ten papers to draw. So much work awaiting me appeared mountainous. One I did immediately and then went to Moncrieffe's, played moderately at whist and brag, heard Monboddo talk of savage nations, drank little, and came home before one. This day a fine thaw came on.

SATURDAY 3 FEBRUARY. At the consultation in the cause, Ross against Mackenzie, on Tuesday night last, a curious incident occurred which Lord Advocate and I recollected today. Macqueen asked if Ross had not made offer of a compromise. I said something that seemed to favour this as a prudent measure, as it was a deep stake to litigate for a man's whole estate. Mackenzie, a grave, stiff old gentleman like a lay moderator of the General Assembly of the Kirk of Scotland, all at once, with a slow, deliberate, north-country tone, answered, "Mr. Boswell, rather than agree to that compromise, I would put a pistol to my lug (ear)." Such an explosion from a man of so staid and decent an appearance made one start as if the pistol had gone off.

I had time after being in the Court today to dictate a paper. Then I went to dine at Lord Monboddo's. It seems he had asked a great many people of the law today, but not one was disengaged but Mr. David Rae and myself. I was at first disappointed, as I had come with my mind tuned for a large company and gay conversation; but I soon let it down to a good social key, and had a very agreeable meeting. My Lord's clerk dined with us, and his daughter came and sat a little after dinner; but the time was mostly spent in a *trio*.[7] My Lord said that he never asked company to his house but those for whom he had a regard, and he looked on this as the great privilege of his office as a judge. That a gentleman at the bar has not this in his power. Clients of any decent rank expect to be asked to dine. Rae observed that merchants entertain their customers. I said that an advocate is obliged to entertain many people whose company he does not like, both clients and agents. I wished to hear Lord Monboddo and

[6] Robert Lowth, who became Bishop of London in 1777, wrote *A Short Introduction to English Grammar,* first published in 1762; a very popular work.
[7] The daughter, Helen Burnett, later married the clerk, whose name was Kirkpatrick Williamson.

Rae on the propriety or expediency of entertaining agents, but the conversation took another turn. My Lord told me that Wedderburn was an excellent Greek and Latin scholar, that he had talked with him on Greek learning; that his parts were always remarkable, and his rising so high, though he was neither loved nor esteemed, was a proof certain both of his parts and education. We had various subjects started: Shakespeare, Pope, Dr. Johnson. My Lord's manliness of mind and store of knowledge humbled me. He and I drank each a bottle of claret slowly. Rae took wine and water. We all drank tea. In the evening I dictated another paper. Dr. Boswell called a little in the forenoon, and Miss Susie Dunlop in the evening.

SUNDAY 4 FEBRUARY. Was calm and quiet all day. Read Lord Monboddo (when Mr. Burnett) against Pitcalnie in the Balnagowan cause; altered my opinion a good deal. Read the Bible and some of *Histoire philosophique, etc.* Had young Donaldson at tea. Got from him Kenrick's review of Steele's scheme of recording the measure and melody of speech like music. It struck me a good deal. Also *The Edinburgh Review* of Lord Hailes's *Annals.*[8] Dr. Grant sat a little with us in the evening. My wife made a very ingenious remark on the advantage of getting the English language early to have the power of expressing our thoughts. She said that one bred in Scotland has a poverty of language, so that his ideas fade for want of expression as plants do in a poor soil. Mr. Wood had been with me in the forenoon and ordered me to pour cold water on my sprained ankle. My mind at present was in a sort of indifferent state. I was struck with a passage in Young's *Night Thoughts,* how man "resolves, resolves (to be better), and *dies the same.*"[9] It was very applicable to myself.

MONDAY 5 FEBRUARY. Was at home all day; finished one long paper and one of moderate size; had some consolation in seeing my mass of *work to be done* a little lessened. I was agreeably fatigued. I mean that the sensation which I felt at night after my labour was over was pleasing.

TUESDAY 6 FEBRUARY. (I am now writing on Thursday the 8.) I had dreamt in the night that my father was dead. All the natural affection and tenderness of my younger years was revived in sleep. I was much distressed and I awaked crying. My mind was much softened. I was anxious to make my father easy and to have nothing in my conduct towards him of later years to regret after he was gone. My instantaneous thought was to go to him and agree to his entail directly. But I waited to hear from Dr. Johnson. I recollected with some uneasiness my wild speech at Grange's on the

---

[8] Joshua Steele's *Essay towards Establishing the Melody and Measure of Speech* was reviewed in *The London Review* (edited by William Kenrick) for December 1775 and January 1776. *The Edinburgh Magazine and Review* (edited by William Smellie and Gilbert Stuart) carried a review of Hailes's *Annals* in the number for February 1776.
[9] Near the end of *Night the First:* "Resolves; and re-resolves; then dies the same."

29 of December last, of which he said I would repent. When I actually saw my father in the Court, his indifference froze my fine feelings. In the evening I was at a consultation at Mr. Macqueen's on Blythswood's cause, on which I had written so well; and being quite master of it, I did not feel a disagreeable inferiority at the consultation. It indeed vexed me a little that Macqueen as senior counsel was to draw the printed paper, as it deprived me of an opportunity of having a good paper of mine laid before all the judges. It is a common error that the senior counsel will always write best. Young Mr. Robert Syme drank tea with us. I advanced pretty well in my work.

WEDNESDAY 7 FEBRUARY. I intended to have gone this evening to *The Beggar's Opera,* which always inspires me with London sensations. But there was a consultation at Lord Advocate's on the great cause of Maclean against the Duke of Argyll.[1] We sat about two hours, and I had great pleasure in being instructed in law by Macqueen, Rae, and Lord Advocate. Formerly a young lawyer was educated by attending consultations.

There was tonight a ball in James's Court given by the inhabitants. I dislike such corporation meetings, and neither my wife nor I went to it. Worthy Grange came and supped with us, he being also a nonconformist. He said very well that if James's Court were in the middle of a wild moor, its inhabitants must from necessity associate together; but as we are in the middle of a large city, where we can choose our company, it is absurd to be like the inhabitants of a village. I believe we were ill thought of by the inhabitants who joined in this ball. But it was better to keep clear of a connexion which was not desirable.

I this night received an admirable letter from Dr. Johnson with a full opinion on our family settlements so far as *justice* was concerned. He had not received Lord Hailes's opinion on the subject when this was written, so that I got his own original thoughts, and he convinced me by masterly arguments that I was under no moral obligation to preserve strictly the male succession. I shall not attempt to abridge his letter.[2] My wife shed tears. I had now a kind of wavering if I should not agree to heirs whatso-

---

[1] Concerning the Maclean estate, which was in the possession of the Duke of Argyll. In the Hebrides Boswell had been strongly impressed in favour of Sir Allan Maclean, Chief of the Clan, and swore a covenant to him on what he thought was the black stone of Iona.

[2] The letter is printed in the *Life,* 3 February 1776. Johnson's conclusion is as follows: "Your ancestor for some reason disinherited his daughters, but it no more follows that he intended his act as a rule for posterity than the disinheriting of his brother. If, therefore, you ask by what right your father admits daughters to inheritance, ask yourself first by what right you require them to be excluded? It appears, upon reflection, that your father excludes nobody; he only admits nearer females to inherit before males more remote, and the exclusion is purely consequential."

ever, as *justice* did not interpose and *Veronica* was so engaging. But my brother David and feudal notions as to barons soon returned. I was struck with wonder at Dr. Johnson's abilities.

THURSDAY 8 FEBRUARY. I opened Sir Allan Maclean's cause before Lord Elliock. It was so full of Highland history and facts starting up on all hands that I was much interested. Mr. Rae supported me. Mr. Crosbie opened on the other side, but did not get his pleading finished; so we were to resume this cause at another time. I had to dine with us Mr. Daniel Wardrop, mason in Glasgow and lately one of the bailies of that town, a client of mine; Adam Bell, his agent; Balbarton, Matthew Dickie, and Mr. Donaldson, the painter, who had been today doing something more to my wife's miniature picture. I drank moderately. Balbarton and Matthew Dickie stayed to tea. Dr. Young came to tea. I dictated well in the evening.

FRIDAY 9 FEBRUARY. The day went on as usual during the session. In the evening I was at Moncrieffe's. My old circuit companion, David Kennedy, was there for the first time as Earl of Cassillis, and Crosbie took his seat for the first time. We were eighteen at table. I played rather too keenly at whist and brag, and lost a little. There was much noise. I sat till near three and drank too much, but did not expose myself by speaking.

SATURDAY 10 FEBRUARY. The wine which I had drank last night, though it had not intoxicated me exceedingly, had fevered me a good deal. I was however able to go to the Court and appear in several causes between nine and ten. I then grew very uneasy, went home, and was obliged to go to bed. My wife was exceedingly attentive to me. I got up to dinner. I received a letter from the factor for Dalblair's creditors proposing that the remainder of the price should be paid immediately. I was thrown into great uneasiness how to act. Sometimes I thought of going directly to my father and telling him that he might now make an entail such as he should think best, and I would agree to it, and so he and I might be on the best footing. But then I considered that he would be offended at my going to London in the spring, and I had better delay agreeing to the entail till that should be over. Then it hurt me to think of being absent from my wife and children, and yet I could not lose an opportunity of being with Dr. Johnson since he had been in France. My wife soothed me, for my mind was harassed. She advised me to write to Craigengillan, the trustee for the creditors, and beg of him either to pay the money himself on getting a right to my father's security or mine; or agree to assign the right to some person whom I should find, and this to be done privately without my father's knowledge; or to put off the payment for some time. I accordingly wrote in these terms. I got last night a letter from my friend

Temple, in great anxiety about a loan of £1,000 from Mrs. Compton as to which some obstacle had occurred. This added to my uneasiness, and my melancholy recurred. I was fretful and horridly passionate to my dear wife, and once *swore,* which is a sign of my mind being much disturbed. I have much reason for gratitude to GOD that my hypochondria comes upon me now so seldom. I prayed earnestly for a few minutes. It vexed me to think that my promise under the venerable yew at Mamhead, not to drink more than six glasses at a time, had been so ill observed.

I wrote a little law with my own hand, Mr. Lawrie having an acquaintance from Glasgow in town who took him out. It shocked me to think of a long paper which I had to write for the boxes of next Thursday. I was, in short, in a woeful state. My wife was a little jocular while I was on the rack, which occasioned my being passionate. I did however perceive inwardly, at the very time, that I had a kind of pride in being melancholy and fretful like my grandfather, and perhaps I exacted more attention than I had a right to expect. But she was in the wrong not to study my humour, for, though I might perhaps have governed it more than I did, I could not subdue it entirely. Sir Walter came tonight. He supped with us. I grew a little better.

SUNDAY 11 FEBRUARY. Was low-spirited beyond what I have been for a considerable time. Veronica was with me in the dining-room all the forenoon, and I read none, but just whiled away the time with the little sweet creature, who was a very pleasing companion to me. Between sermons Lord Cassillis sat awhile with me, as did Sir Walter. Annie Cuninghame dined at my father's. In the afternoon I hesitated whether to stay at home or go to the New Church or go to Bell's English Chapel.[3] I was weak and fretful, and it vexed me to find a return of that distemper of mind which formerly afflicted me so much. I should rather have been grateful to GOD for the wonderful good spirits which I have enjoyed of later years. Indeed upon reflection I was so. My wife comforted me by tracing my uneasiness from Friday's riot. I went to Bell's Chapel, as a quiet place of public worship, and was at prayers. I was somewhat pious, but there was a coldness and darkness in my mind. George Webster drank tea with us. His conversation on active life and his fancy amused me. I was also relieved by writing the journal of Saturday. We had George at supper too, and I drank a little claret and became tolerably social. But when the mind has been hurt by hypochondria, it is not soon quite easy again. I had resolved to go very early to bed and get up betimes next morn-

[3] After the New English Chapel had been built, Baron Smith's English Chapel in Blackfriars Wynd, where Johnson had attended service on 15 August 1773, was taken over as a proprietary "qualified" chapel by Dr. Robert Bell. It was styled either the "Old English Chapel" or, as here, "Bell's English Chapel."

ing, as I had a long paper to write; but I yielded to the present inclination and sat till near twelve.

MONDAY 12 FEBRUARY. I awaked relaxed and indolent, and though I recollected the task which I had to perform, I indulged myself in lying in bed till between eight and nine. After breakfast Sir Alexander Dick called and sat awhile with me. His amiable and classical manners pleased me; but my mind was still hurt, and I perceived his good qualities as a man who has a headache views the beauties of a fine prospect. He seemed more willing today than formerly that I should write his life. I had three different consultations this forenoon, one gratis. I was quite harassed with business, and thought of giving up practice. Captain Archibald Erskine then sat awhile with me. In short it was past one o'clock before I could get my long paper begun. Sir Walter and Miss Annie Boswell dined. I hurried away from table and drudged doggedly, as Dr. Johnson says,' so that at night I had about two-thirds of my task done. This gave me some relief. I received a letter from Dr. Johnson on our family settlements, after he had read Lord Hailes's opinion. It was excellently written, and my scruples as to excluding remote heirs male were quite removed. Dr. Johnson even showed the justice of the claims of females in the present state of manners. This however I could not yet receive. My mind was so clouded and shattered that I could not think even of Dr. Johnson as I used to do when in sound vigour of understanding. But I consoled myself with recollecting that even he has been afflicted with hypochondria. My wife was so kind and engaging tonight, by exerting herself to relieve me from the foul fiend, that I was all love and gratitude.

TUESDAY 13 FEBRUARY. I was somewhat better. I got home from the Court early and finished my long paper before dinner. My wife and I and Annie Cuninghame dined at Sir William Forbes's. Lord Cassillis and Colonel Seton and Mr. Hunter, Sir William's partner, and some more were there. I was not dismal, but dull and insipid. I drank very little. There was no conversation that pleased me, for I could have none with worthy Sir William alone. I went and drank tea comfortably with Grange, and then dictated well.

WEDNESDAY 14 FEBRUARY. (I am now writing on Friday the 16.) I walked to the Parliament House, but with difficulty, I believe chiefly from long disuse. Sir Walter dined with us. Mr. Donaldson, the painter, drank tea. I dictated tolerably. My spirits were better, but I felt much of the "stale, flat, and unprofitable."

THURSDAY 15 FEBRUARY. Mr. Donaldson finished the miniature picture of my wife. It pleased me to have her resemblance thus secured. He dined with us, as did Surgeon Wood. Either last night or the night before

' *Hebrides,* 16 August 1773.

I had again dreamt that my father was dead. It affected me not so tenderly as last time, but with gloom. This morning I had heard Crosbie, Ilay Campbell, and Solicitor Murray against Sir Allan Maclean, and Macqueen for him; then had called on Lord Eglinton and seen him for a few minutes, and on Lord Cassillis, who was not at home. I had also called at the Custom House for Commissioner Cochrane. He had been ill, and had an aged, failed appearance very different from what he appeared when I last saw him. This damped my spirits somewhat. After dinner I called on worthy Grange at his kind request, and drank a glass or two of sweet wine with him and Abercrombie and Currie. This, with the little which I had drank at dinner, made me restless and quite incapable of dictating, at least I fancied so; and though papers had come upon me as others were done—*labitur et labetur*[5]—I resigned myself to absolute indolence. Sir Walter and young Robert Syme drank tea with us.

FRIDAY 16 FEBRUARY. (I am now writing on Sunday the 18.) I was well entertained this forenoon with Maclaurin's pleading in favour of the freedom of Negroes in Britain in the case of Joseph Knight, one of that race.[6] An extensive subject enlarges the mind, as small subjects contract it. In a life of Nash said to be written by Goldsmith, it is said that his mind shrunk in proportion to the littleness of the objects about which he was occupied.[7] A great or small subject is to the mind like a great or small last, to stretch it or let it contract. I dictated pretty well today, but not with freedom and vigour. I drank tea at my father's, not having been under his roof since the 27th of last December. He was indifferent as usual. Robert Boswell and his father-in-law, Sandeman, were there. In the evening I was at Moncrieffe's, played whist ill, but won. I had ever since last Friday been in bad spirits. I this night felt a momentary sensation of gay pleasure while drinking a glass of white Cape wine. I came home between twelve and one, quite cool.

SATURDAY 17 FEBRUARY. My head was clearer than it had been for ten days before, and I made several little morning appearances at the bar with more ease than during that time. But still I was depressed with a general indifference and despondency. I went down awhile to the Advocates' Library to consult some English law books on a subject on which I had a petition to write. It was a case of much equity, whether a debtor has an action of damages against people who have maliciously combined to

---

[5] Boswell is comparing himself to Horace's rustic who waited for the river to run out, "yet it glides on, and will glide on for ever": *Epistles,* I. ii. 42–43.
[6] A famous case in which Boswell gave his services; in 1777 he persuaded Johnson to dictate an argument. Knight had been bought in Jamaica as a child by a Mr. Wedderburne, who afterwards took him to Scotland. He brought an action for his liberty on the ground that the laws of Scotland did not tolerate slavery, and finally won.
[7] Goldsmith's *Life of Richard Nash* was first published, anonymously, in 1762.

distress him by advancing money to his creditors to keep him in prison, and have accordingly gratified their resentment. Maclaurin put me upon what is called *maintaining*[8] in the law of England, and I found good argument under that title. A large library always comforts me somehow. I cannot at present tell distinctly how.

I then went and called on Mrs. Compton; found her inclined to assist Temple, but tedious and timorous. I used my best endeavours to persuade her to be friendly to him. I know not clearly how it happens, but I feel myself a man of more address when with English people than when with those of my own country. It pleased me today to be sensible that the faculty of address returned when I was with Mrs. Compton. I then went to the Exchange Coffee-house and was present at settling Sir Walter's purchase of a cornetcy in the Greys. I dined at Walker's as one of the *Parliament* of James's Court, as it is called, being a society of its inhabitants for police, which has subsisted since 1727. I was in bad spirits, but kept a decent social appearance; came home to tea. Then went to the Hon. A. Gordon's and played at brag and won. Worthy Grange had drank too much at the Parliament, and he would needs call for me and bring me home before supper. I complied. It was then twelve.

SUNDAY 18 FEBRUARY. My wife and I were at the New Church in the forenoon. A Mr. Burnside preached. I did not profit much. A curious thought came into my head on the great question of *soul*. I imagined that man is born with a *body* like a *hive,* and that the *soul* is the *honey* which is made in it. That by cultivation, particularly piety, *spirit* is increased. That the philosopher's window in his breast resembled a glass hive,[9] where the *working* of the bees is seen, and though in *Comus* we find

> Ye drones . . . in idle cell,[1]

yet really good monks are the best bees. This is a curious fancy. But what is the *bee*—the acting principle? I regretted my neglect of a religious course of life, and hoped to do better.

My wife went home between sermons to Annie Cuninghame, who was ill. Dr. Boswell dined with her. I dined at my father's with George Webster. In the afternoon heard Dr. Blair preach on "Enoch walked with

[8] Or *maintenance,* the action of wrongfully aiding and abetting litigation.
[9] Boswell perhaps forgot that he had found this comparison in *Tristram Shandy,* I. xxiii. It was Momus, god of censure, who wished that there had been a window in the breast of the man made by Hephaestus (Lucian, *Hermotimus,* § 20).
[1] From one of the songs inserted by John Dalton in the third act of his stage version of *Comus,* 1738:

> Preach not me your musty rules,
> Ye drones that mould in idle cell!

GOD."[2] My attention was not fixed. I drank tea at Sir George Preston's, and was consoled with anecdotes of the Dundonald and Kincardine families by my Lady. I say consoled, for good real ideas dispel the vapours of hypochondria. In the evening Miss Susie Dunlop sat a little at our house.

MONDAY 19 FEBRUARY. Dr. Boswell breakfasted with us. He and I had some vociferous talk of the nature of the soul of man. I called for a little at my father's. He talked of the extravagance of the age, and of the necessity of entailing; but, what was wonderful, he did not resume the subject of compelling my consent to his entail, so that I did not communicate to him my change of opinion. He talked of withholding my £300 a year in order to clear the debt for which he was bound with me. I said, "Then I cannot live." He spoke in an indifferent manner, as if he had never thought of the matter before. I just let things remain as they were till I should return from London. I was harassed today with dictating. In the evening I received another letter from Dr. Johnson with some parcels of Lord Hailes's *Annals,* in which he said something more of our entail. It hurt me to think that I was now indebted to this great man for no less than three letters. My indolence was quite shameful. Dr. Johnson wrote, "I long for a letter." This roused me. I was really vexed that I owed General Paoli two letters and Sir John Pringle one, and that I had not written to General Oglethorpe since I was last in London. *Non omnia possumus omnes.*[3] Law business consumes my time, and indolence wastes it. My mind was upon the whole quiet.

TUESDAY 20 FEBRUARY. Heard the Solicitor and Advocate plead against and for the Negro.[4] Dr. Boswell, who had attended the pleadings, dined with us, as did Sir Walter. I was pretty well but without any vivid sensations of felicity. I wrote to Dr. Johnson thanking him for his letters on the great question and entreating to be encouraged by him to come to London this spring. I could scarcely suppose that I should not, but I wished for a *viaticum,* as I was somewhat irresolute. I dictated tolerably. David Ross began his trials today to succeed Lord Alemoor. His promotion did not strike the mind as Lockhart's did.

WEDNESDAY 21 FEBRUARY. Was in gay happy spirits at breakfast; was quite charmed with Veronica, who was a pleasing child and wiser than is usual at her age. Effie was bustling and not so attentive or affectionate

[2] Genesis 5. 24.
[3] "We can't all do everything": Virgil, *Eclogues,* viii. 63.
[4] The Advocate's eloquence is here allowed to pass without comment. But when Boswell came to write the *Life,* and was seeking Dundas's favour, he remembered that this speech impressed him "with such feelings as were produced by some of the most eminent orations of antiquity" (*Life,* after 29 November 1777).

as her sister. It is impossible not to have a preference for one child over another. But a parent should not show it; and perhaps Effie may yet gain upon my heart.[5] The day was passed in the ordinary course during a session. My son was now a stout infant, and appeared to be of a sweet disposition.

THURSDAY 22 FEBRUARY. (I am now writing on Sunday the 25.) The perplexed cause of Sandeman and Company against Doig, which had tormented me, was this forenoon determined. The Lords seemed to know nothing of it, which hurt me though I won. I dined at Sir George's. Sir Walter supped with us after a consultation on his affairs.

FRIDAY 23 FEBRUARY. I was rather in better spirits than usual, or to speak more properly, was less uneasy. Hallglenmuir, Knockroon, and Matthew Dickie and Sir Walter dined with us. To find myself amongst Ayrshire people gave me a comfortable feeling. I drank tea at my father's, but there was still a cold distance between us. I had taken a resolute purpose of letter-writing today, and wrote to General Paoli, General Oglethorpe, Lord Pembroke, and Colonel Stopford. My mind was enlivened by such variety of connexions. I went at night to Moncrieffe's, it being the last meeting of his club for this session. Played at cards ill, and lost. Was overpowered at supper with Macqueen's noise. Came home quite cool before one.

SATURDAY 24 FEBRUARY. My papers to be written were grown numerous again. I finished one this forenoon; dined at the Hon. A. Gordon's. Monboddo was there and the claret had a fine flavour, so I drank too freely. I was then seized with the fever of gaming, and played at brag and whist till about three in the morning with different people who were there. Lost £3. 12; was vexed and ashamed of my disorderly conduct, and when I came home, was hurt to find my dear wife sitting up for me.

SUNDAY 25 FEBRUARY. (I am now writing on Tuesday the 27.) Got up with a headache, but went to the New Church. Dr. Blair preached on this text: "A wounded spirit—who can bear it?"[6] He said the spirit of man might be wounded by folly, by passion, or by guilt. He pointed out in a striking manner a man who has ruined himself in life by foolish conduct, and the pain which he must feel in looking up to those once his equals but now his superiors, and how miserable he must be to consider how he has degraded himself. I was in bad spirits today and applied this to myself. But I corrected the uneasy apprehension by considering, as Dr. Johnson once bid me do, how many had done worse than I had done, or

---

[5] She did. On 30 March 1777 Boswell wrote in his journal: "I shall regard her all my life for the strength of her affection. She will take the greatest care of me in my old age, though Veronica may be the most pleasing companion when I am well."
[6] Proverbs 18. 14.

rather to how many I was superior. It occurred to me that the true meaning of the text was the misery of melancholy or a distempered mind, and I felt it in some degree at the time. I felt a regret that I had not asked Dr. Blair to dine or sup with me nor been to see him since I came last from London, and I resolved to invite him soon.

My ankle was now surprisingly well. I walked out to George's Square between sermons, and sat a little with Commissioner Lockhart. I dined at my father's between sermons. Dr. Webster and George and Miss Farquhar of Gilmillscroft were there. My wife was at home with Annie Cuninghame. Veronica dined with us and was quite at home. After dinner George Webster and I walked down to see the Earl of Dundonald, whom I had not seen all this winter. He was much failed. He did not recollect that I was married. We drank a bottle of wine and then drank tea with Mrs. Cochrane, my Lady being ill. I was a little intoxicated and disapproved of my having paid a visit during divine service. I appointed to sup at Dr. Webster's, but first went home and wrote some journal. Sir Walter and Miss Dunlop were at our house a little. Dr. Webster did not sup at home; so I passed the evening with Annie, George, Lieutenant Wellwood, and Granty Seton.[7] I spoke little; I was drowsy and not in good humour.

MONDAY 26 FEBRUARY. Was at a consultation for a Justiciary trial of Gibson and others for an alleged attack of an excise officer, which was to come on next Monday. Felt my mind pretty able, but had no pleasant sensations of vigour or gaiety. Dictated pretty well in the afternoon; but from the trifling circumstance of not being able to find a passage which I had read in Hawkins's *Pleas of the Crown,* I was quite fretted. At last I perceived that I had the second volume before me instead of the first. I wrote to Sir John Pringle. Lady Wallace supped with us. I was in poor spirits and somewhat peevish. My favourite, Widow Grant, who came to town last night, called for a little before tea. I did not feel any lively agitation.

TUESDAY 27 FEBRUARY. For some time past my mind has been in a troubled, fretful state. I had a fit of gloomy passion this morning at breakfast, and threw a guinea note in the fire because my wife objected to my subscribing three shillings for a miscellany by a Miss Edwards.[8] I however rescued the note with the tongs before it was consumed, and, though a

---

[7] All Websters or Webster connexions. Annie and George were Dr. Webster's children, Lieutenant Wellwood was his wife's first cousin once removed, Grant Seton was his grand-nephew.

[8] *Miscellanies in Prose and Verse,* Edinburgh, 1776, which *The Critical Review* called "an excellent cargo for the use of pastry-cooks, and the other patrons of unfortunate publications."

good part of it was burnt, I got its value from the Royal Bank. This incident shocked me, because it made me dread that I might in some sudden rage do much worse. I attended to business tolerably in the forenoon, and dictated tolerably in the afternoon. Grange drank tea with us. At night I was in an inanimate, sullen frame, and sat poring over the fire in heavy uneasiness. My dear wife was at pains to console me, and relieved me somewhat; but I had a dismal apprehension of becoming as melancholy as my poor brother John, and the weakness of mind which is thought to occasion that distemper made me miserably vexed from the consideration of being despised. I wondered when I recollected how much of my life since my marriage had been free from hypochondria; and it galled me that at present I was so afflicted with it that I had no just ideas or sensations of any kind. I was anxious to be with Dr. Johnson; but the confused state of my affairs, and my tender concern at being absent from my wife and children, distressed me. I was exceedingly unhappy. I could fix my mind upon no object whatever that could engage it. Futurity was dark, and my soul had no vigour of piety. I know not if it be right thus to preserve my weakness and woe. Lord Monboddo said on Saturday that writing down hurts the memory. Could I extract the hypochondria from my mind, and deposit it in my journal, writing down would be very valuable. However, as Dr. Johnson said to me that it was right to keep a history of my mind,[9] I write exactly the state of it. Probably it will not be long till my present unhappiness will be recollected as a dream.

WEDNESDAY 28 FEBRUARY. (I am now writing on Saturday the 2 of March.) This day Hallglenmuir and Knockroon told me that they were to dine with Matthew Dickie. I bid them say nothing, and I would probably step in. I accordingly did so, and found them and old John Boswell and a Mr. John Young with him at dinner. I was still melancholy; but a society of this kind was a good variety to me. At five I went to Mr. Solicitor's and compared his notes with mine in the cause, Ross against Mackenzie. I drank tea with him socially. He made a very just observation on taking notes, that sometimes a man catches the expressions, but not the meaning. "Yes," said I, "as if one should grasp the clothes and let the body escape." He and I were well together, having been schoolfellows, and there having been a friendship between our fathers. I perceive I am writing this journal very ill; however, I shall persist. When the Solicitor talked of rising in life, I was in such a sickly frame of mind that I could not relish any scheme whatever. When I came home I found a letter from Dr. Johnson, being an answer in course of post to mine of the 20th current. He discouraged me from coming to London. This hurt me somewhat. I could not bear the thought of not seeing him this spring. I resolved to write to

[9] On 11 April 1773.

him more pressingly on the subject. My dear wife wished that I would not go; but, when she saw me desirous of going, indulged my inclination. It pained me to think of being absent from her. Yet I could not resolve to come to a final agreement with my father till I had heard Dr. Johnson upon particulars.

THURSDAY 29 FEBRUARY. Grange dined with us. Sir Walter came in from the hunting with a hare in his hand as we were finishing dinner, quite as if we had been in the country. His animal spirits shocked my nervous sensibility. Worthy Grange and I shook hands cordially, and talked of low spirits with which he has been afflicted, though not so severely as I have been. Talking with him, and hearing his calm reflections, did me good. I dictated pretty well, and wrote an earnest letter to Dr. Johnson; but was sensible that I might appear weak and troublesome to him. I trusted to his kindness for me, and his knowledge from experience of dejection of mind. I had read this week his *Marmor Norfolciense,* republished by some envious enemy with intention to hurt him.[1] I had pleasure in perusing it as a piece of composition; but, my *anti-Hanoverian* warmth being much abated, I had not so high a relish of it as I should have had formerly; and it appeared to me not to have so much force of genius as his later productions. My wife and I and Miss Cuninghame and Sir Walter supped at Lady Wallace's, where were her brother Dunlop, his son, who takes the title of Sir Thomas Wallace, Colonel Mure Campbell, and Mr. Wallace, our sheriff.[2] I was at first dull and awkward. Colonel Campbell pleased me, and the wine was generous, and by degrees I grew a little hearty, and sat till past one; drank rather too much.

FRIDAY 1 MARCH. (I am now writing on Sunday the 3.) This forenoon I was made acquainted with Mr. Addison, merchant at Borrowstounness, who took the principal charge of a cause at the instance of one

[1] "In this performance [Johnson], in a feigned inscription, supposed to have been found in Norfolk, the county of Sir Robert Walpole, then the obnoxious Prime Minister of this country, inveighs against the Brunswick succession and the measures of Government consequent upon it. To this supposed prophecy he added a commentary, making each expression apply to the times with warm anti-Hanoverian zeal" (*Life,* under April 1739, when *Marmor Norfolciense* was first published). In 1775 someone using the pseudonym "Tribunus" reprinted the pamphlet with an ironical dedication to Johnson. The intent, of course, was to discredit Johnson's political pamphlets by showing that he had ratted.

[2] Sir Thomas took the title unwarrantably. He was the son of John Dunlop of Dunlop. His mother (Burns's Mrs. Dunlop) was daughter of the late Sir Thomas Wallace of Craigie, and he claimed as heir of line. His son and grandson persisted in the assumption, which ceased only upon the death of the latter in 1892. "Sir Thomas's" wife was the beautiful and eccentric Eglantine Maxwell, sister of the Duchess of Gordon. Married in 1772, she divorced him in 1778, on the grounds of various adulteries committed in the year 1775.

Ritchie against the kirk session of that place, in which cause I was counsel. It is seldom that one is struck with the appearance of a stranger after one has lived as long in the world as I have done, there is such a sameness amongst mankind. But there was a stateliness about Addison, who was a large man with a wig like a London citizen, a scarlet cloak and a cane with a gold head of a form for which I have not a word: ⌐ , that really struck me. Grange dined with us today.

I drank tea at Maclaurin's along with Crosbie, consulting for the trial of Gibson and others. I was humbled by Crosbie's great knowledge of the British statutes, but played my part very well in argument. There was something in the west-country tone of the men that were to be tried that touched me with particular compassion, I believe from some association of it in my youth with distress, while I lived at Auchinleck, as that of a poor tenant unable to pay his rent, or of some one who had lost a father or brother. Their shabby clothes too made the scene piteous. I took no money from them; but Maclaurin and Crosbie did. Perhaps it is from my not having enough of knowledge of the real condition of men in their state of life that I am pained when I think of some guineas being taken from them. What a sum is a guinea to one of them! is my reflection when I see that all that he has on is hardly worth so much. But they were all smugglers that I saw tonight; and I remember Lord Hailes telling me that I should not think a man less able to give a fee because he had a bad coat; for he probably has the money which another lays out upon dress. My imagination melted down the fees into small money, and I thought how many bottles of small beer or such necessaries would two guineas buy, and I really was uneasy when I thought that the men were not guilty of the offence with which they were charged; yet could only be acquitted, and would not be indemnified of their costs. This is a severe circumstance in criminal law. I was a good deal better today. I dictated well in the evening.

We had at supper Mr. Solicitor and his lady, Dr. and Mrs. Young and Miss Plenderleith, Miss Jeanie Henderson, Miss Susie Dunlop and her brother *Sir Thomas*, Colonel Mure Campbell, Mr. George Wallace, Sir Walter, and Mr. Claud Boswell. We were fifteen at table. I was somewhat embarrassed at first; but by hob or nobbing got into lively spirits. There was no conversation to record; but time went on well, and I liked to keep up good connexions. Colonel Campbell, Sir Walter, and George Wallace sat about an hour longer than the rest. My heart warmed as I drank, but I did not go to excess. We parted at two. In the forenoon my wife and I had walked out to Lady Colville's; found only Captain Erskine, and sat awhile.

SATURDAY 2 MARCH. Melancholy had almost quite left me, it is impossible to explain how. The Solicitor had some friendly conversation with me in the House this morning upon my having good pretensions to something from Government on account of my father's merit. The Countess Dowager of Galloway had called for us two days before, and not finding us at home had left a message that she insisted on our dining with her this day at Lawson's tavern in Leith. I was curious to see what this entertainment would be; and luckily was now in such a state of mind that it would not be a burthen to me. My wife did not choose to go; but she convoyed me half way. It proved a very good party. My Lady was in coloured clothes,³ and more easy and cheerful than ever I saw her. She had for company Lord and Lady Aboyne, the Miss Mackenzies of Seaforth and their old governess, Mrs. Sinclair of Freswick, young Freswick, and a Mr. Bowdler, a student of physic.⁴ We had two courses and a dessert, and most luxurious Canary, of which I drank with relish, calling it nectar. I said it would be great happiness if one were so made as to be able to drink a long time of this, and neither be intoxicated nor sick. "Nay," said Miss Fanny Mackenzie, "if there were a pipe from whence it should drop continually into one's mouth." This was an exquisite fancy, quite epicurean paradise. I was good-humoured and pleasant; but I do not remember much that can bear being bottled. There is a form in our newspapers of putting in a death: "It is hoped his friends and relations will accept of this as a sufficient notification of his death." I said that the marriage of a beauty or of an heiress should be announced, "It is hoped her lovers will accept of this as a sufficient notification of her marriage." My ideas resumed their proper places in my mind. They had been jumbled in the dark gloom of melancholy.

I walked up with Bowdler; called at my father's, but found that a good many people who had dined with him were sitting in the drawing-room. So I did not go in. It gave me a momentary uneasiness to think that he had many entertainments, and did not ask me to them; so that I had not the advantage of being countenanced by him as a son should be; but I instantly checked any swelling on that account by considering that I did not endeavour to be intimate with him since his second marriage. I dictated some tonight very easily, and read a little of *The Spectator,* and had my mind furnished with pleasing ideas.

³ That is, no longer in mourning. Lord Galloway had died in 1773. Lady Galloway was of the Cochrane family and hence a distant relation of Boswell.
⁴ Mrs. Boswell had probably stayed away because she wished to avoid a tavern party. Her primness cost her a meeting with Thomas Bowdler, the future purifier of Shakespeare.

SUNDAY 3 MARCH. (I am now writing on Friday the 8th.) Was at the New Church forenoon and afternoon. Mr. Walker did not fix my attention in the forenoon, nor Dr. Blair so much as usual in the afternoon. I dined at my father's between sermons, as did Veronica. George Webster was there. He always sets my mind in motion somehow. I started this thought: that it is curious how the Lord President of the Session is an object of respect. For is he not a man paid by the community to undergo the drudgery of determining causes? If it is said he has great trust placed in him, may not the same thing be said of a coachman to whose skill and fidelity you trust your life? But the truth is that the qualities supposed to be possessed by a man who holds the office of Lord President, and his general authority, impress us with reverence. I drank tea at Sir George's.

MONDAY 4 MARCH. (I am now writing on Saturday the 9th.) This day came on the trial of Gibson and others. I had not appeared in the criminal court since John Reid's trial. I spoke a little on the relevancy, not much to my own satisfaction, knowing that it could have no effect. The trial was over and the panels acquitted by three. Crosbie, Maclaurin, and I, with Mr. James Hunter, chancellor of the jury, and David Steuart and Peter Kerr, agents for the panels, went to eat a beefsteak at Princes Street Coffee-house. We grew exceedingly merry; and who begun it, I cannot say. But we three advocates made a number of sketches of songs, by way of a *Criminal Opera*. As for instance, "We're not guilty yet," to the tune of, "We're gaily yet." [5] Such ludicrous extravagance diverted us extremely. We laughed and sung and drank claret till past eleven at night. Though I drank above two bottles I was not at all intoxicated, which was strange. During this scene I often looked back with wonder on my late melancholy. But I disapproved of such intemperance.

TUESDAY 5 MARCH. Craigengillan, Fairlie, Dunlop, his daughter Miss Susie, Dr. Blair, Knockroon, Matthew Dickie, and Sir Walter dined with us. I was in a sound cheerful frame. Dr. Blair sat by me, and we talked a little of Dr. Johnson and literary subjects. I told him that his sermons on "Cornelius, a devout man" had really done me good. He said his religion and mine were of the same kind. He had a good deal of enthusiasm; but I had much more. Dunlop, Fairlie, and Matthew Dickie sat a long time with me. I was in the humour of being social and cordial as an Ayrshire man, while surrounded by people of my own county. Yet I wished to

---

[5] This amusing skit was published, with considerable interpolations, by Sir Alexander Boswell in *Songs in the Justiciary Opera,* 1816. The Gibson cause is clearly the source: the prisoner, John Black, has been indicted for a supposed assault on Peter Brown, an exciseman. Black is unanimously acquitted by the jury, to the disgust of the bench. A manuscript copy of the skit exists at Yale. "Gaily" is a Scotticism: "in good health and spirits."

guard against having Auchinleck at a future period a house of riot. I was more intoxicated today, with one bottle and a little more, than yesterday with two. I dictated with vigour.

WEDNESDAY 6 MARCH. I was all forenoon, almost, attending the decision of the Lords upon Captain Dalrymple's vote in Fifeshire, upon which the election turned.[6] There was a most crowded audience, and all seemed to be much interested, as at any warm contest. It came at last to a casting-vote. My father was in the chair, and as he had expressed himself in a sort of dubious, figurative manner, calling the Captain's qualification "only a picture and a very ill-drawn picture," Lord Advocate and some other partisans of Henderson, the candidate against whom the Captain voted, sanguinely concluded that his opinion was to set aside the qualification. But when he gave his vote it was to support it. This made a prodigious hubbub. The Advocate was indecently extravagant in his gestures, and, when I came to the bar, he said to me under cover of great friendship for my father, "I would rather lose all the elections in Scotland than have to represent his conduct at the bar of the House of Commons as I must do. Speak one way, and vote another." I could only say to the Advocate that his Lordship was wrong. I was indeed confounded and uneasy. For I myself had apprehended that my father's opinion was for setting aside the vote. I was impatient to talk with my father of this strange affair. I went and called on him, and told him what Lord Advocate had said, not the whole, but that he had spoken one way and voted another. He said it was not true; that he had been much difficulted; but that as the Court had allowed qualifications as bad to pass, he could not set aside this. He was quite calm, and satisfied my mind that there was not any contradiction between his speech and his vote. Lady Auchinleck was very clear upon it. I told him that I had now freed myself of my scruple concerning remote heirs male. This seemed to please him. He asked me to stay and dine. Dr. Boswell dined, and we were pretty cordial, though my father would never let the Doctor enter upon conversation of what he had been reading, or rather would not let him expatiate, but broke the discourse into small talk. I dictated tolerably tonight. Grange supped with us very comfortably.

THURSDAY 7 MARCH. I was made uneasy by hearing murmurs and insinuations from people in the Court that there had not been a consistency between my father's speech and his vote. I avoided the subject, not being cool or firm enough upon it. After the House rose, I was easier. I had been at my father's before it sat down, and had a conversation with

[6] Two objections had been made to Captain Dalrymple's qualification to vote in the election of a representative to Parliament for the county of Fife after the death of General Scott. See below, p. 254, *n.* 9.

him, in presence of Mr. Stobie, upon a settlement of our affairs. He was in a placid, kind frame and put his entail into my hands. I read the clauses of it at home, and found them to be very rational. Mr. Matthew, clerk in the post-office, took his annual dinner with me. Sir Walter and Mr. Stobie also dined.

And now I am going to trace the origin and progress of a debauch of which I am ashamed. After dinner young Fairfield, who lived in the same stair, came and begged that I would come up to his house and play a rubber at whist.[7] I was a little heated with my share of two bottles, and agreed. I found with him Lieutenant Wellwood and Joseph Munro, a young *writer*. I drank some white wine, and, having won at whist, was in turbulent spirits. I made them all but Fairfield go with me to Canongate Kilwinning Lodge. The Brethren did not assemble, so there was no meeting. Wellwood and Munro insisted that as I had two hours to spare, I should go to Walker's Tavern, where Fairfield was to come when sent for. I yielded. We three played at lambskinet[8] (I for the first time), till Campbell came, and then whist went on till supper. Campbell went away, and I found myself engaged with two idle boys. We resolved to part at eleven; but the claret pleased me too much, and I drank freely till near one, I believe. I was then keen for whist. Wellwood was positive against playing at any game. I heard that Esdaile, with whom I had played at whist all night in Princes Street Coffee-house, was come into the next room. I went to it, and brought him and young Freswick to our company; and they joined Munro and me at whist.[9] Wellwood stayed awhile. We drank claret occasionally, and played on till about four in the morning. I had sent early in the evening to let my wife know where I was. It was truly distressing to me to find her ill and fretted when I came home. What a shameful loss of time do I now record!

FRIDAY 8 MARCH. (I am now writing on Sunday the 10th.) I was very ill in the morning, but went to the Court; came home about eleven and slept till two. Dined at Matthew Dickie's with Craigengillan and Fairlie. Drank very little. In the evening had a party at my house at cards and supper: young Fairfield and his wife, the Hon. A. Gordon, Mr. and Mrs. Mitchelson, and Mr. Buchan Hepburn. I had letters from Lord Pembroke and Sir John Pringle which revived me.

SATURDAY 9 MARCH. A petition in the Fife politics came in signed by Lord Advocate, who was set out for London. It contained a paragraph

---

[7] Young Fairfield was William Campbell.
[8] Or "lamb-skin-it": a corruption of *lansquenet,* a card-game of German origin.
[9] Young Freswick's name was William Sinclair; he was a cornet in the 2nd Dragoons. He died three years later in Guernsey, being then lieutenant in Lord Seaforth's newly formed Highland regiment.

which seemed to say that my father had *voted* in *opposition* to his *opinion*. I had been with Grange in the morning, who had told me that many impartial people had a notion that what he said was different from the import of his vote. He very properly advised me not to make a stir about the matter; but laugh it off with indifference. The petition however roused my spirit, and I meditated challenging the Advocate if he did not make an apology, or explain away the paragraph. This was the last day of the session; so the Court was all confusion. I was affected with a kind of confusion and uneasiness that there should be even a hint against the integrity of a man of so established a character as my father. I called on Claud, who was angry and anxious about it. I went to my father and found him quite calm. He said the Advocate could mean nothing against him. He was too much his friend. I wondered at his coolness, and blindness to these Dundases. In the afternoon Sir Walter, who dined and drank tea with us, and Mr. William Wilson, who also drank tea, had a conversation with me upon Sir Walter's affairs. I had a letter this evening from Dr. Johnson, very kind, and informing me that he was to set out for Italy next month. This put me in a flutter of spirits. I wrote to him begging that he might not be from London when I arrived. My mind was agitated about my father's character.

SUNDAY 10 MARCH. (I am now writing on Tuesday the 12 at Newcastle.) My wife was a little indisposed. I was at the New Church in the forenoon. Between sermons I went up to my father's. I had not resolution to tell him that I was to set out for London next day. I took Lady Auchinleck into another room, acquainted her of it, and asked her "friendly advice" how to proceed; told her that it distressed me to give any uneasiness to my father, but that I was convinced my going to London was for my interest. She said that my father looked on it as idle and expensive, and that I had formerly given him reason to think in that manner; but upon my giving her my reasons she seemed to be convinced that I was right, and she engaged to communicate the matter to him first, and then I might call on him in the evening. I was for the first time on a confidential footing with her, and I was sincere; but I saw she doubted my sincerity. I told her so. She owned it; but said that it never made any odds on her conduct. I assured her that she was wrong. That indeed I had once hated her; but that I now thought very differently, and she *must* have no longer any suspicion of me; that I had great faults, but was upon the whole one of the best men that ever lived; that it gave me uneasiness to be at enmity with anybody. She said, "You cannot be a better man than I wish you, on many accounts." She said that she had for some time been pressing my father to give up his Justiciary gown if something could be got for me; and that he was willing, but doubted of my prudence to negotiate the affair. It was a new and comfortable kind of feeling which I had now. I went and sat a little with Claud, and we talked together of an answer to a false account of my father's opinion which had appeared in last night's *Mercury*. Lady Auchinleck had yesterday and today also talked of the reflection against my father with such a serene contempt that I envied her strength of mind.

I dined at my father's along with Dr. Webster. I had called at home and found Dr. Boswell, who was to dine at our house. My mind was so much troubled about my father's character being even questioned that I could not bear the Doctor's flashiness. I called on Nairne. He was gone to Sir William Forbes's to dinner. I had said I would perhaps call on Sir William today, as he and my Lady were to set out for London next day. Dinner was over. I had drank a good deal of white wine at my father's. I drank more here. Instead of going to church, we three sat and drank till I declare I was intoxicated. It was a strange thought that I was drinking hard on Sunday, along with Sir W. Forbes and Nairne, two worthy, distinguished Christians. I mentioned its being wrong. They severally declared they did not think so, and they certainly did not at the time. I said I did; but could not resist. Our conversation was of religion, Dr. Johnson, and other good topics. I suppose neither of them was intoxicated, not having drank so much as I did before we met. But they had above a bottle of wine apiece after I joined them. I shall not forget this scene. I went home with Nairne to his house, and drank tea. I spoke of the insinuation against my father, and hinted that I would call Lord Advocate to account for it. Nairne said I would be wrong; for why cut a man's throat for a mistake into which he might naturally be led from what my father said, and his own warmth upon one side? Nairne declared that *before* my father gave his vote he imagined that he was of opinion against the qualification. But *after* the vote he saw nothing in what he had said inconsistent with it.

I was uneasy and restless. I went and took a ticket in the fly for Newcastle for next morning. Then called at Widow Grant's; found Miss Moncrieffe with her at tea. Drank tea again there; saw the widow with perfect indifference, and was ashamed of having been enamoured of her. Was too lively here from the wine which I had taken. Went home, and, instead of going to my father, wrote a letter telling him my reasons for going to London, and mentioning that I had had a return of melancholy and required relaxation. That I would be with him at Auchinleck this vacation, join in his entail, and do everything agreeable to him. I enclosed this in a short note to Lady Auchinleck, made an apology for not calling, and begged she would "soothe my worthy father." Indeed I was unfit to see him tonight.

I had called a little at Claud's as I came home. He seemed to think that my father was a little uneasy, though he did not say much. I was very ill with the wine after I came home, but grew better. It was very unlucky that I had fallen into a debauch the night before my journey. But how could I fear Sir William Forbes and Nairne? Grange was with me a little, and told me that Henderson's friends spoke strongly against my father, as if he had given his opinion with candour *against* the qualification when he thought it was lost; but, finding it come to his casting voice, had voted *for* it, as being for the side which he espoused. I was miserably vexed. I wrote to Sir John Pringle as my father's friend and my friend, stated the matter to him, and sent a sketch of a letter to Lord Advocate insisting that he should say if he meant to *impeach my father's integrity;* and, if he did not give it me under his hand that he did not, I told Sir John I would write to Lord Advocate that he was a *liar* and a *scoundrel.* That in my conscience and before GOD I should be justified in having a *duel;* that his nephew, Colonel Pringle, would perhaps be kind enough to be my second. That Sir John used to think I had bad nerves. It might be so; but that I hoped I was now determined. That I should be with him on Friday night or Saturday morning; but that this letter would come before me, to prepare him.

My excellent wife did not suspect what was in my mind. But comforted me as well as she could when she saw me vexed about my father. Said it would not hurt his established reputation to have such a reflection thrown out, as that he had been biased upon one political occasion, and that this was the worst that could be said; that it was unlucky that our judges talked jocularly and of private anecdotes like old women; and that if he had said nothing, but given his vote with firmness, nobody could have had anything to say as if he had been inconsistent; though no doubt, as he had declared for Mr. Oswald, the friends of Mr. Henderson would at any rate have called him partial. Her good sense and liveliness relieved me somewhat. But my heart was torn with anxiety. After we were in bed, I could not sleep for agitation, and I was in anguish to think that I was probably to expose my life in a few days and perhaps leave her and my children in a disconsolate situation. It was hard upon me that I could not communicate my distress to her. When I shut my eyes I saw a death's-head. I was quite gloomy and disturbed; but resolved to endure. At last I fell asleep, I think about four; but my rest was broken.

Journal

in London, Lichfield, Ashbourne, etc.

MONDAY 11 MARCH. I got up a little after five. My dear wife gave me tea. Mr. Lawrie was ready and serviceable, as was Joseph. But I was both gloomy and in pain. I took leave of my valuable spouse with an earnest embrace, and said, "GOD grant we may meet in a better world!" I had still a duel in view. I went in a chair to the fly. We were four passengers. I need not be particular in describing them. One was a Captain Bidlington, a sea captain, something like Sir John Douglas, and a man of English humour and pleasantry.[1] His manner was not violent, so did not offend me; but though I did not perceive it at the time, I dare say it insensibly did me good. I read some of Lord Monboddo's third volume on language.[2] I was perpetually thinking of my challenge to Lord Advocate. I dreaded that my nerves might fail me; yet I was conscious of being determined. I travelled like a criminal, or rather a condemned man not a criminal, in a coach to the place of execution. I was ever and anon figuring Lord Advocate and me upon the field. I hoped that Sir John Pringle and Dr. Johnson would invigorate my mind. I fancied that I might just think, think of a duel till I should overcome the fear of it by deadening my mind. That timorousness was a fault in my constitution; but that I had a noble principle of fortitude; and that I should have the advantage of Lord Advocate by being better prepared for it by the discipline of meditation. I slumbered a great deal in the coach. I read a little in the Bible which I got from Lord Mountstuart, and which I carry always with me. I got to bed before ten at Wooler. What misery does a man of sensibility suffer! I however fell asleep immediately.

TUESDAY 12 MARCH. (I am now writing on Monday the 18 at Messrs. Dillys' in the Poultry, London. I have fallen sadly behind.) "Sunshine broke in upon my mind" this day, as Dr. Johnson said it would.[3] I finished Lord Monboddo's third volume. His thoughts of the superiority of

---

[1] Sir John was Boswell's cousin, "a lively man but hurried away by fanciful projects."
[2] This volume of Monboddo's *Origin and Progress of Language* had just been published.
[3] In his letter of 5 March 1776.

mind in the ancient Greeks and Romans revived me, and a duel seemed quite easy to me. I had a warm affection for my wife and children. But magnanimity elevated me above it when honour called. Bidlington was perpetually rhyming in an odd manner. For instance, when one said the tea brought for breakfast was *Congo,* he cried, "Ah, I fear 'tis *wrongo.*"

We got to Newcastle to dinner. I sent for Dr. Hall, physician, and Mr. Leighton, surgeon. Hall came for a few minutes; told me that my poor brother John was not unhappy and that he thought it would be most desirable for the family that he should continue in his present state. Indeed it is better to be insensible than unhappy; better to have an obscurity of reason than as much light as to see one's self miserable. In passing, it occurs to me that much of human misery is for want of light enough. When there is a *lueur,* an imperfect light, we imagine we see hideous spectres. Full light shows us that there is nothing to fear; and fear is the great cause of our misery. How little is there of positive present evil. It is the imagination which torments us. This duel of mine, now, has alarmed and distressed me while in the dark. But, when I have an extensive view of it, I consider thus: If I am killed, the shock is momentary; and death comes as well at one time as another. My wife and children will be consoled in a short time. At any rate *I* shall not feel their uneasiness; but shall look on it as trifling, and expect them soon to join me in the world of spirits. If I am wounded, my spirits will be raised by a sense of honour and a sort of gallant vanity which a duel justly fought inspires. My greatest uneasiness was the fear of fear; an apprehension that my nerves, or whatever else it is, should yield to impressions of danger, though my *soul* was brave. I think there is a meaning here. I shall ask Dr. Johnson. I must after this leave a margin in my journal for after remarks, either by myself or others.[1]

I took a post-chaise and Wilson the landlord with me, and visited poor John. He looked better than when I saw him in May; but seemed to be quite in a stupor. I sat with him about ten minutes, I suppose, before he spoke a single word, though I said many different things to him, and shook him cordially by the hand. I thought of my duel at the time; and that it was well to have fought in a good cause before sinking into the state in which I saw my brother and which I feared might be my fate one day. I was going to leave him. He put forth his hand, seized mine and said, "Take me with you." I stopped awhile with him. I said, "Do you know me?" He said, "To be sure." He had accepted of some sweet oranges from me. He said, "Give me some money." I gave him two shillings. He said, "Give me some more." I gave him another. Dr. Hall had told me that it was not wrong to let him have a little to buy pepper-cake, a sort of ginger-

[1] He continued, however, to save paper and write to the edge of the page.

bread, or some such thing which pleased his taste. He said, "How is your wife?" and he said, "I am kept a prisoner here." I covered my face for a little, and shed tears. There was something very striking to me in this scene. It shook my mind somewhat. But it was comfortable to see that he was not in pain of body or anguish of mind.

When I returned to Newcastle I had Leighton the surgeon to drink coffee with me. His quiet, common-sense, practical talk pleased me. But I was still ruminating (if one may say so of the future) on my duel, and thought myself a being whose life was near its shallows. It is strange how an immediate prospect of death affects one. I sat up writing to my wife, and this journal, till near twelve. The coach was to set out at two. I could not sleep.

WEDNESDAY 13 MARCH. Our journey went on very well, and we had a lady from Northallerton, I believe an old kept mistress, now a bawd. Her voice was melodious. Her manners gentle. Her looks the remains of comeliness. She had cards with a text of Scripture on one side and verses in a Methodist strain on the other, some of them very pretty; and we drew cards as people do *jokes* put up in sugar at a dessert. The coach broke down a mile from Doncaster.[5] It was dragged along. I sat in it alone, read some of the Bible, and Collins's *Ode on the Poetical Character*. I was in good spirits, nay in high and fine flow of thought. My mind is a furnace. It melts and refines objects when there is a strong clear heat; but sometimes my furnace is smoky, and then the objects are blackened. We were to have lain at York; but the assizes being there, the inns (I am now writing on Tuesday the 19th at Oxford) were all full, so we took post-chaises, and went on to Tadcaster, where we had a comfortable supper and a good sleep. I was in the most perfect frame. I enjoyed the present, and was not afraid of death.

THURSDAY 14 MARCH. I was not quite so well; but was upon the whole manly. I was, however, like the thinking man in *The Rambler* who tried various ways of life, and served a campaign with *philosophical* courage.[6] We drove on all night.

---

[5] Since Doncaster is beyond Tadcaster, where Boswell slept Wednesday night, this incident must belong to the next entry. Or Doncaster has been substituted for some other place-name.

[6] Polyphilus, in No. 19. "Being much accustomed to think, he let the sense of danger sink into his mind, and felt at the approach of any action that terror which a sentence of death would have brought upon him. He saw that instead of conquering their fears, the endeavour of his gay friends was only to escape them; but his philosophy chained his mind to its object, and rather loaded him with shackles than furnished him with arms. He, however, suppressed his misery in silence, and passed through the campaign with honour, but found himself utterly unable to support another."

FRIDAY 15 MARCH. (I am now writing on Wednesday the 20th at Oxford.) The lady quitted the coach at Stilton. She was of that mixed character of licentiousness and enthusiasm [7] which we often find. I got upon the coach-box today from Stevenage to Hatfield. I was afraid I should fall; and I accustomed myself to overcome fear. The coachman was a stately fellow, as well dressed as a country squire, and quite a bishop in his line of life; for instead of driving one stage out and in, by which at an average two shillings a day may be got, he drove three, so that he got six shillings a day besides wages. There were two outside passengers, who sung and roared and swore as he did. My nerves were hurt at first; but considering it to have no offensive meaning whatever, and to be just the vocal expression of the beings, I was not fretted. They sang, *And A-Hunting We will Go,* and I joined the chorus. I then sung *Hearts of Oak, Gee Ho, Dobbin, The Roast Beef of Old England,* and they chorused. We made a prodigious jovial noise going through Welwyn and other villages. What a contrast to the solemnity of Young's *Night Thoughts* written at Welwyn. I kept my duel in view all the while, and felt, I suppose, quite as a soldier or sailor does before an action. I had, however, only *passive courage,* as I have heard my father observe Prince Charles had. I set myself to *endure* whatever might come. But then I was advancing into danger. Captain Bidlington was enough to dissipate gloom, he was so lively and comical and entertaining with anecdotes of what he had seen in the course of a great deal of sailing both in King's ships and merchantmen. He had a smattering too of many kinds of knowledge.

The coach had been robbed by footpads in the morning near London; and last night at six another coach had been robbed. It was past six when we were at Highgate. The fear which I felt till we got upon the stones was uneasy. The coachman bid us keep a look-out. Some fellows wanted him to stop under pretence of wanting to be up on the outside; but he drove quickly on, and some of us looked out on each side. When we got to the _____ in St. John Street, Smithfield, I was a little sorry to part with my fellow travellers; of so soft and warm a composition am I that I adhere a little to almost all with whom I come in contact, unless they have qualities which repel me.

I drove in a hackney-coach to Dilly's, was received by Ned with the briskest kindness; but as I was intent on seeing Sir John Pringle, and settling what I should do to vindicate my father, I was disturbed by his vivacity; and John Wilkes's contest for being Chamberlain, and Price's gold box, were so indifferent to me at the time that Dilly's keen, quick, and shrill talk of them was like letting off squibs close to my ears.[8] There

[7] Religious fanaticism.
[8] Dr. Richard Price, nonconformist minister, writer on morals, economics, and politics,

was a company in the house to cards and supper. Charles was entertaining them, so could not come to me.

After being shaved, and putting on a clean shirt, I hastened to Sir John Pringle's. He had received my letter, and, having gone out, had ordered John to come for him whenever I called. We met with ease and cordiality. I instantly started the subject of which I was so full. Sir John instantly made it vanish, by telling me that it would be quixotism to call a man out for abusing my father in a court of justice. That was no private affront to me; and I should let the matter take its course. "Everybody here," said he, "is abused in public and it is never thought there should be a duel on that account." He showed me from the reflection of his mind that I was confined and rash in my view. I was relieved as if he had cured me at once of some painful disorder. I eat some bread and drank some wine and water and was quite comfortable. He reproved me for not having waited on my father before I set out. I was stating to him the dispute whether the Court of Session did right in stating two votes when there were two objections to a qualification.⁹ He said, "Mr. Boswell, that appears of importance to you at Edinburgh. When you have been three days here, you will see it to be very uninteresting." I ceased therefore; but I thought him in the wrong from his dislike of our tedious law proceedings in general, and the custom of our advocates in introducing them into con-

---

had expressed strong opposition to the American War in a recently published pamphlet, *Observations on the Nature of Civil Liberty and the Justice and Policy of the War with America,* which had had very wide circulation. On the previous day the Court of Common Council of the City of London had tendered him official thanks and voted to present him the freedom of the city in a gold box worth £50. Price was an intimate friend of Benjamin Franklin, and his pamphlet is said to have encouraged the Colonies to declare their independence. In 1781 he was made LL.D. by Yale College, together with George Washington.—This was only the beginning of Wilkes's "contest for being Chamberlain." On 20 February of this year Sir Stephen Janssen had resigned the office, and both Wilkes and Benjamin Hopkins announced their candidacy for the post. Hopkins, having greater influence at Court, was elected and was re-elected each year thereafter until his death in November 1779. Wilkes, who had persisted in standing for the office, was then finally elected and held the chamberlainship for the rest of his life.

⁹ Captain Dalrymple's case had raised a nice and fundamental problem in procedure. Two objections had been made to his qualification. Eleven judges being present, it soon became evident that about half of them would uphold objection *a* and dismiss objection *b*, and the other half *vice versa*. Dalrymple's counsel thereupon moved to put the vote on the objections separately, whereupon both were thrown out, one by a vote of six to four and the other by a vote of six to five, Lord Auchinleck giving the casting-vote. This was a paradox, for if the question had been simply "Is Captain Dalrymple qualified?" the vote would (presumably) have been nine to one in the negative. Henry Dundas had appealed, his objection being principally to the mode of putting the vote.

versation in genteel company. For there *may* be a curious point discussed in our court, such a point as may entertain any sort of ingenious men; and it seemed to me that this was one. Sir John was very kind and agreeable when I did not offend him with what he did not like. I sat with him till near twelve.

I was desirous to see Dr. Johnson, and state the subject of my challenge to Lord Advocate to him also; but I was so much fatigued with my journey that I durst not enter his house at so late an hour, knowing that it might be much later before I could get away. London struck me less now than ever. It was more a home. I was better used to it. I slept at Dilly's. I found here tonight a letter from my dear wife.

SATURDAY 16 MARCH. Had resolved to walk out early to breakfast with Dr. Johnson, but time slips away fast in London while the mind is engaged with a variety of objects. I drank some tea with Messieurs Dilly, and got to the street about nine. I posted to Johnson's Court. But the great man had removed to Bolt Court, No. 7. I felt a foolish regret that he had left a court which bore his name; but it was better than foolish to be affected with some tenderness of regard for a place in which I had seen him a great deal, from whence I had often issued a better and a happier man than when I went in, and which had often appeared to my imagination, while I trod its pavement in the solemn darkness of the night, to be sacred to Wisdom and Piety. But he did not dwell long enough in it, nor was there such an association between him and it established, as to warrant a lasting value or veneration for it, as for "Marathon or Iona." [1] When I found his new house a much better one, I was cheered. He had good rooms and a pretty little spot of background. Frank, his Black, told me that he was at Mr. Thrale's, but that he would be home early in the forenoon. I said I should go to him directly. I saw Mr. Levett too, who assured me of his being very well. Even Levett and Frank raised my spirits as concomitants of the Great Man. I want a simile for this. I am sure many might be found. Such as that a fine lady is cheered even by seeing the case, the Great Mogul, of a pack of cards, or a drinker by hearing the sound of a cork drawn. [2] These are bad. My meaning is that objects, however unimportant in themselves, please us by reviving the impression of what was agreeable while they were present. Thus a happy lover talks fondly of the groves and streams which he saw at the same time with his mistress, though he would not care at all for them on their own account. Dr. Johnson's new house belonged to Mr. Allen the printer, who lived in

[1] "That man is little to be envied whose patriotism would not gain force upon the plain of *Marathon,* or whose piety would not grow warmer among the ruins of *Iona!*" (Johnson's *Journey to the Western Islands,* the landing at Iona).
[2] Fine playing-cards bore the device of the Great Mogul upon the box.

Bolt Court. I met him as I was coming out. "Well, Mr. Allen, you have now the Great Man" (or some such phrase) "for your *tacksman*." [3] We talked of his going to Italy. I said, "I wish him to see as much as possible that we may have the advantage by reflection. His mind is at once a magnifying glass and a prism. It enlarges and brightens, separates and colours objects."

I took a boat at Blackfriars Bridge, and sailed to Southwark. Knocked at Mr. Thrale's door. Just as the servant opened it, Baretti appeared. I coldly asked him how he did. Methought there was a shade of murderous blood upon his pale face. I soon made a transition from this disagreeable object to the parlour, where Mrs. Thrale and Dr. Johnson were at breakfast. My reception here was truly flattering. At once I had chocolade before me, and Dr. Johnson was in full glow of conversation. I was elevated as if brought into another state of being. Mrs. Thrale and I looked to each other while he talked (Baretti having soon left the room), and our looks expressed our congenial admiration of him. I said to her, "This is *Hermippus redivivus*.[4] I am quite restored by him, by transfusion of mind." Mr. Thrale joined us, and cordially welcomed me. Dr. Johnson said he had seen all the visibilities of Paris and around it; but that to have formed acquaintance with the people there would have required more time than he could stay. That he was just beginning to creep into acquaintance by means of Colonel Drumgold, a very high man, head of *L'École Militaire*, a most complete character, for he had been first a professor of rhetoric and then became a soldier.[5]

When I spoke with regret of the Laird of MacLeod's not acting as he should do to preserve the ancient family, and that it would be well if he were killed in America, Mrs. Thrale said she did not understand this preference of the estate to its owner; of the land to the man who walks upon that land. "Madam," said Dr. Johnson, "it is not a preference of the land to its owner. It is the preference of a family to an individual. Here is an establishment in a country which is of importance for ages, not only to the chief but to his people, which extends upwards and downwards; that this should be destroyed by one idle fellow is a sad thing."

He said entails were good, because it is good to preserve in a country serieses of men to whom the people are habituated to look up as to their

[3] Principal tenant. Johnson's *Journey* had recently brought the term to the attention of English readers.

[4] Boswell refers to Dr. John Campbell's version (published in 1743, a *jeu d'esprit*) of Cohausen's Latin work, *Hermippus redivivus*, 1742. The proposition of the book is that breathing "the breath of young women may probably contribute to the maintaining long life [perhaps to 115 years] and keeping off old age."

[5] Jean Drumgold was a member of an Irish Jacobite family that fled to Paris with James II.

heads. But he was for leaving a quantity of land in commerce, to excite industry and keep money in the country. "For," said he, "if no land were to be bought in a country, there would be no encouragement to get wealth, because a family could not be founded there. Or if it were got, it must be carried away to another country where land may be bought; and although the land in every country will remain the same, and produce as much when there is no money, yet all the happiness of civil life, which we know is produced by money being in a country, is lost." "Then," said I, "would it be for the advantage of a country that all its lands were sold at once?" "Sir," said he, "so far as money produces good, it *would* be an advantage; for then that country would have as much money circulating in it as it is worth. But to be sure this would be counterbalanced by disadvantages attending a total change of proprietors." (I believe this reflection occurred to me.)

I was for limiting the power of entailing thus: that there should be one-third, or perhaps one-half of the land of a country free for commerce. That the proportion allowed to be entailed should be parcelled out so as that no family could entail above a certain quantity. Let a family according to the abilities of its representatives be richer and poorer in different generations, or always rich if its heirs be always wise. But let its absolute permanency be moderate. In this way we should have a certainty of so many established roots; and as in the course of nature, there is in every age an extinction of so many families, there would be continual openings for men ambitious of perpetuity to plant a stock in the entailed ground. I would not have the very same land to be the entailed proportion, as probably it would not be so well improved. I mean that a man would have an opening in the allotted *quantity*. Indeed I would rather that an old family estate, when its proprietors fail, should go into the circle of commerce for a while, than be immediately transferred to a new family and again fixed. I would have the two races kept distinct. Dr. Johnson said that mankind could better regulate entails when the evil of too much land being fixed by them was felt than we could do at present when it was not felt.

I mentioned Adam Smith's book just come out,[6] and as Sir John Pringle had the night before given his opinion that Smith, who had never been in trade, could not be expected to write well on that subject, any more than I upon physic, I started this to Dr. Johnson. He thought that a man who had never traded himself might write well upon trade, and he said there was nothing that more required to be illustrated by philosophy. "As to mere riches," said he, "that is to say, money, it is plain that one nation or one individual cannot get more of it but by making

[6] *The Wealth of Nations.*

another poorer. But trade procures real riches: the reciprocation of the advantages of different countries. A merchant," said he, "seldom thinks but of his own particular trade. To have a good book upon it, we must have extensive views. It is not necessary to practice to write well upon a subject." I mentioned law. "Why, Sir," said he, "in England, where so much money is to be got by the practice of the law, most of our writers upon it have been in practice; though Blackstone had not been much in practice when he published his *Commentaries*. Upon the Continent, the great writers on law have not all been in practice. Grotius indeed was. But Pufendorf was not; Burlamaqui was not."

I stated to him with composed seriousness the affair of my father's opinion and vote by which I had been so much agitated. He said he saw no inconsistency. Here was a species of freehold right of which my father disapproved; but, as it had the sanction of the Court, he was obliged to give it effect; and here was a conveyance, unskilfully drawn indeed, but still sufficient to carry the right. He said I had no call whatever to challenge a lawyer for what he had said of my father in a court of law. It was before the Court; and it belonged to the judges from a high place to correct his insolence. "Pringle was right, Sir," said he. My mind was now quite clear. Dr. Johnson admitted, however, that if Lord Advocate were in my company to reflect upon my father, that would be a private impertinence to me which I might resent.

He told me that before going to Italy he was to take a jaunt to Oxford, Birmingham, Lichfield, his native town, and his old friend Dr. Taylor's at Ashbourne in Derbyshire, and he asked me to go with him. I said I should be very happy to go; but I must first see if Douglas would pay me the compliment of gratitude of having me one of the counsel in his appeal. Dr. Johnson said, "He will not ask you. I speak upon general knowledge of human nature. Mankind are too unmindful of favours, or too inattentive, or too unwilling to part with their money, to act as he should do upon such an occasion. I wish he may, not merely for the few guineas that you may get, but for the credit which a man gets by being employed in his profession."

I asked him if it was wrong in a lawyer to solicit employment. "No, Sir," said he. "It is wrong to stir up lawsuits; but when once lawsuits are to go on, there is nothing wrong in a lawyer's endeavouring that he shall have the benefit, rather than another." "You would not solicit employment, Sir," said I, "if you were a lawyer." "No, Sir," said he, "but not because I should think it wrong, but because I should disdain it." (I am now writing on Friday the 22nd at Henley in Warwickshire, while Dr. Johnson is getting up to be ready to set out at seven in the morning. Let me see what may be done in such a space of time.) This was a good distinction, and a good rule to a man of my family and just pride. He said, however, "Do not be wanting to yourself in using fair means. I would inject a little hint to him. Speak of his cause. Ask what hopes his lawyers give him, and let him have an opening."

We talked of regulating the succession of an estate, while Mrs. Thrale was by. He enlarged my view very much. "Where," said he, "a man gets the unlimited property of an estate, there is no obligation upon him in *justice* to leave it to one rather than to another. There is a motive of preference from *kindness,* and this kindness is generally entertained for the nearest relation. If I *owe* a particular man a sum of money, I am obliged to let that man have the next money I get, and cannot in justice let another have it. But if I owe money to no man, I may dispose of what I get as I please. There is not a *debitum justitiae* to my next heir. There is only a *debitum caritatis.* It is plain therefore that I have morally a choice according to my liking. If I have a brother in want, he has a claim from affection to my assistance. But I have also a friend in want, whom I like better. He has a preferable claim. The right of an heir-at-law is only this: that he is to have the succession in case no other person is appointed to it by the owner of an estate. He has only a preference to the King." Thus far at Henley. A page is thus gained from idleness. (I am *now* writing on the same day at Birmingham while Dr. Johnson is at the little house.) To have my mind enlarged from fetters of conscientious scrupulous justice was very cheering. At the same time my feudal *inclinations* for male succession remained warm.

We got into a boat, and while upon the Thames, we talked of a little volume advertised to come out under the title of *Johnsoniana.* (I am now writing on Saturday the 23 at Lichfield.) This was to be a collection of *bon mots* by Dr. Johnson and others. He said it was a mighty impudent thing. I asked if he could have no redress if he were to prosecute a publisher for bringing out under his name what he never said, and perhaps making him swear bloodily, as many of the *bon mots* related of him did."No, Sir," said he. "There will always be so much truth mixed, and how can it be ascertained how much is true and how much false? And what damages would a jury give me for my having been represented as swearing?" He is *above* such things. But there is many a man who would be much hurt by having bad things passed in his name, and I think it hard if there be no redress.

He said, "The value of every story depends on its being true. A story is a picture either of an individual or of human nature in general. If it be false, it is a picture of nothing. For instance, suppose a man should tell that Johnson, before setting out on his journey to Italy, as he had to cross the Alps, sat down to make himself wings. This many people would believe; but it would be a picture of nothing. Langton used to think a story a story till I showed him that truth was essential to it." "But," said I, "Foote entertains us with stories which are not true." I, however, corrected myself and added, "But it is not properly as stories that Foote's tales please us, but as collections of images." He said Foote was quite impartial, for he lied of everybody.

We landed at the Temple, and as we walked in that ill-inhabited seat of study, the external of which always composes my mind in a pleasing manner, we talked of the entail of Auchinleck. He owned that I was right to be resolute against excluding remote heirs male while I thought they had a claim *in justice,* but that I should now do as my father thought best; that is to say, I should not oppose any scheme of settlement by him at a great risk. I might choose what succession I liked best if I were at liberty. He said it was lucky that he advised me to apply to Lord Hailes. His being a strong partisan for the indiscriminate succession of males and females counterbalanced my prejudice for the male line.

He went home, and I marched away to the west end of the town. I called at Goodwin's in Gerrard Street, where I lodged last year. The first floor was taken, but I agreed with Goodwin that my lodgings should be at his house, all letters and cards be left for me there, and that I should on my return from Oxford, etc., have a bed in his second floor when I chose to come to it.

I called on David Cuninghame. Found him quite idle and unreasonable, despising £25, and unwilling to join his division of marines. I left him to come to himself. I called at the Duke of Queensberry's, but he was not at home. I met in the street Alves, the miniature painter, whom I had seen at Rome in 1765 and at Inverness in 1773. He told me he lodged in Bond Street opposite *Stewart's* Coffee-house. "At whose house?" said I. "At Mr. *King's,*" he answered. "Oh," said I, "I shall not forget it. There is such a connexion between *Stewart* and *King.*" I was now in that glow of good spirits which I enjoy on a fine day, walking the streets of London. I met Charles Fox, who was indifferently civil. I cannot expect that all men are to like me. Dr. Johnson had told me that our Club at the Turk's Head, upon being a member of which I had valued myself so highly, was now quite spoiled by the introduction of too many members, and that without attention to their being agreeable to all the rest.

I called on General Paoli; was received with the most benignant complacency and kindness. He reproved me for not coming to his house directly, showed me my room in readiness for me, told me I should come to it whenever it was convenient for me, that his house and servants and coach were all at my service. He said he would wait dinner today till half an hour past four, in case I could get back to him. I went to my amiable

Mrs. Stuart's, found her eating beefsteaks with her children and their governess at an early hour, which is her way when Mr. Stuart is not to dine at home. Here I was cordially received by a sweet creature whom I admire and who is my wife's intimate friend. Mr. Stuart came in to dress, and he was very friendly in his manner of talking to me. I then went to Lord Mountstuart's and was received, I thought, with a more earnest affection than ever. He was just going to dine at the London Tavern with his brother and some more friends. He asked me to dine with him next day. I told him I had refused to dine tête-à-tête with his sister-in-law next day, telling her that I durst not yet trust myself alone with her. I must first be a little longer in London and see some more fine faces. My Lord, in his sly humorous way, put this construction upon my words: "Why, that was just telling her, 'Madam, I am so lewd at present that I do not choose to be alone with you. I must first be at a bawdy-house.' "

I dined at General Paoli's. We had there Count Gentili, who has been with him for some years, a rough being; a cousin of his, also a Gentili, from Naples, who seemed to be still life; and the gallant Gentili who took Capraja, an amiable man whom I had seen at Sollacarò, though we did not remember one another; [7] and a Mr. Connolly, a forward, talking fellow.[7a] He disgusted me with an affected smartness and ignorant reflections upon Dr. Johnson's having a pension and being violent in his manner. I was happy in the society of the General and the gallant Gentili, between whom I sat, and I let Count Gentili and Connolly go on as the wind blows when one is in a good house. I drank wine very moderately today, being on my guard as I used to exceed here, and about seven I walked away and felt a calm and gay felicity much preferable to the fever and tumult which wine occasions; and I compared my present feelings going through Berkeley Square with those which I had frequently last year when going from General Paoli's after dinner. I had happiness without alloy.

I went to Ridley's, the bookseller, in St. James's Street, harangued a good while with wonderful fluency to him and a genteel man about town who was in the shop, and got him to promise to let me have two copies of *Johnsoniana* before publication, that Dr. Johnson and I might take them to the country with us. I then sauntered awhile in St. James's Park. Then drank tea with Spottiswoode, solicitor for Douglas in his appeal. I talked of it, and he said he was sending the case to the press. But there was

[7] Antonio Gentili had taken part in the struggle against the Genoese when only sixteen years old. Capraja, an island off the coast of Tuscany belonging to Genoa, was taken by the Corsicans under the leadership of Achilles Murati, 29 May 1767. Boswell had spent seven days on the island, 21–28 November 1765.

[7a] Boswell wrote "a forward, talking fellow of an   man," deleting the last three words. He probably intended to write "of an Irishman," but became uncertain as to the fact.

not the least hint of my being employed. I saw that Dr. Johnson was right. I met a girl in the Strand very like my favourite, Widow Grant, and still in a rural state. I took her to the Fountain and gave her a glass of wine to humour the fancy of similitude.

I then went to Dr. Johnson's, found him in Mrs. Williams's room, and Lady Knight, an Admiral's widow, and her daughter with them. When these ladies went away, I went up to Dr. Johnson's room and wrote to my dear wife, and then he and I came down again to Mrs. Williams, and he treated me with raw oysters and porter, in both of which Mrs. Williams joined. He eat oysters and drank water and then he had tea. The immediate transition from raw oysters to sweet tea was strange. Oysters and sugar are a composition which one is challenged to eat for a wager.

We talked of religious orders. He said it was as unreasonable for a man to go into a Carthusian convent for fear of being immoral as for a man to cut off his hands for fear he should steal. That there might be resolution in the very act of dismembering himself, but when that was once done, he had no longer any merit, for it was out of his power to steal; yet he might all his life be a thief in his heart. So when a man had once become Carthusian he was obliged to continue so whether he chose it or not. He said their silence was absurd. We read in the Gospel of being sent to preach, but not to hold one's tongue. He said all severity that did not tend to increase good or prevent evil was idle. I thought him rather laxer in his notions than in *The Rambler* and *Idler,* where he treats austerities with much solemnity. He told me he said to the abbess of a convent,[8] "Madam, you are here not for the love of virtue but the fear of sin." She said she should remember it as long as she lived.

He said he had no objection to a man's drinking wine if he could do it in moderation. That he had found himself apt to go to excess in it, and therefore, after having been for some time without it on account of illness, had thought it better not to return to it. He said every man was to judge for himself according to the effects which he experienced. One of the Fathers tells us he found that fasting made him so peevish that he did not practise it. I got home to Messieurs Dilly's not long after twelve.

SUNDAY 17 MARCH. Drank some tea at home first, then sallied forth to breakfast with Douglas. Had myself shaved at old Reid's, whose name I read upon his sign in the Strand. Found him to be an Atholl man, who had been about thirty years in London. I had ever since May last let my hair grow, thinking to wear it again to look younger to please my wife. But it was very troublesome, as I was obliged to wear a wig at the bar, and I thought my health and spirits a little hurt by the heat of my thick

[8] This is almost certainly "Mrs. Fermor, Abbess," whom Johnson met in Paris (*Life,* 16 October 1775).

hair. I therefore had it cut off today, and was sensibly lighter and easier. My wife had advised me to this. Such a small change has not a small influence upon my existence.

As I walked along the Strand, I observed a gentleman's servant in a one-horse chair. I thought I might get into it. If he damned me for asking, I should be no worse. If he agreed to my having a place in it, I should be amused with an adventure. So I stopped him and asked if he was going towards Pall Mall. He said yes. "I'll give you a pint of beer if you'll let me come up beside you." "Come up, Sir," said he. I accordingly mounted, was instantly quite frank and free, and in a few minutes had the reins and whip, and drove cheerfully along. The street was quiet, it being Sunday morning, so I got easily forward. The servant told me his master was Mr. Pritchard of Shelvock, ten miles beyond Shrewsbury, and that he had come up for a little while to London. In Cockspur Street I observed Mr. John Swinton. I hailed him and told him in French not to take notice, for that this good fellow did not know me. John seemed amazed. I liked this little adventure. I had a pleasant drive for almost nothing, for I gave the man only three halfpence, being all the copper in my pocket, and he was very well content. I dismounted in the Haymarket. Suppose anybody whom I knew had seen me, I was driving in a chair with a servant, and what then? If a man can but keep his own secret, he may do many amusing things in London.

I breakfasted with Douglas and Lady Lucy. It was a most insipid scene, and although I mentioned his appeal, he never once aimed at having me as one of his counsel. I thought meanly of him when I saw him void both of parts and of gratitude. I asked him if there was to be a blow ⁹ of British peers soon, and said I hoped he had his root in the ground. He has flattered himself with being created Earl of Douglas. I called next on the Duke of Queensberry and had a short audience of him, but found him cold and indifferent and unmeaning. I then called on Mr. Longlands, the solicitor, for a little. Then went to the Bavarian Minister's Chapel to mass, but was too late for the solemn music. It was St. Patrick's day, and seeing the Irish with the green cresses in their hats gave me sensations of spirit which I connect with Ireland. The elegance of the dress of some of the ladies whom I saw at mass refined my imagination. I was in the humour I was in when in Italy, pious and amorous. I hastened to visit a lady whom I had been in love with formerly. I suddenly was sensible of my influence. ———.¹ (I am now writing on Sunday the 24 March at Lich-

---

⁹ Blossoming.

¹ The dash is Boswell's own, and indicates that more happened than he chooses to record. See also 18, 21, 24, 29 March. He nowhere names the lady, but in his London journal of 1778, which appears to record a resumption of the intrigue, he styles her

field, catching a few minutes between eight and nine while Dr. Johnson gets up.)

Being absolutely wearied with walking, I took a coach in Oxford Street to have a shilling's worth of rest by being driven along. It was both ease and pleasure. I enjoyed London much. In Cavendish Square I saw Dr. Percy walking with a lady. I quitted my coach and joined him. The lady was his wife. He had invited me to dine with him today along with Dr. Johnson and Mrs. Williams. But I told him I was engaged at Lord Mount-stuart's. We had some lively literary talk. He told me he was writing the history of the wolf in Great Britain. I called on Colonel Archibald Campbell in Harley Street, but he was not at home.

Then I went to Langton's, who had a house in the same street. I had seen Beauclerk's name upon a door in Hertford Street yesterday, he having removed from the Adelphi. He was in bed, and I left a card for him. Lady Rothes came to the door of Langton's house just as I was going to knock, so she ushered me in to the parlour, where I found Langton quite domestic with books and children. He lamented The Club's being overwhelmed with unsuitable members. Dr. Johnson had said to me yesterday that Adam Smith was a most disagreeable fellow after he had drank some wine, which, he said, "bubbled in his mouth." He made a most excellent remark. "Drinking," said he, "does not improve conversation. It alters the mind so as that you are pleased with any conversation." He is certainly right. Wine debases the intellect and blunts the taste. May it not, however, be doubted if there are not some men whose dull constitutions require being agitated by fermentation? Langton delicately cautioned me against my usual fault of repeating to people what is said of them, and then told me that he could perceive Beauclerk had lost his relish for Adam Smith's conversation, about which we had disputed last year.[2] Beauclerk, it seems, was so ill that there was scarcely any hope of his recovery.[3] The tranquillity of Langton's parlour was a good shade

---

"No. 36" and reveals the fact that she lived with, or was familiarly visited by, a son. "Thirty-six" was probably the number of her house or lodging. By the law of parsimony one is led to Mrs. Love, the actress, a widow with a twenty-year-old son, who had been Boswell's mistress in 1761–1762. She was almost certainly in London, having played a small part at Drury Lane so recently as 7 March, and evidence is lacking that any other of Boswell's recorded mistresses was at hand. She was well past fifty, but the Contessa di San Gillio, whom Boswell had pursued ardently in Turin, was past fifty, and he describes himself as being in his Italian humour. The identification, however, must not be considered more than plausible. Boswell in all likelihood had more affairs with women of reputation than has been suspected, and in such affairs was capable of being very secretive.

[2] Probably on 2 April 1775.

[3] He lived until 1780.

in London. Talking of literary men, I said there were many of them whose books we may like, but with whom one would no more wish to be personally acquainted than with a musician or a painter, merely from admiring their works. He agreed with me, and gave a striking instance of the mistaken desire of the society of *men* whose *performances* are excellent. "When Johnson who rides three horses was at Oxford, Tom Warton did not go to see him ride. He did not care for that. But he sat an evening with him. He got nothing for his pains. The fellow never opened his mouth."

I then paid a visit to Mrs. Stuart. She was dressing, but I bid the servant ask if she would see me for a few minutes. I was shown up to her bedchamber, where her maid was assisting her at her toilet. Mr. Stuart came in. She said before him and her maid, "Lord help me, I have been reading Hume's essay on natural religion, and it has almost made me an infidel." [4] I said, "You shall not be an infidel as long as I live. Why do you read such books?" "Oh," said she, "let truth have a fair examination." I was sorry that she talked thus before her husband, who had not been taught religion or had forgot it, and her maid, who, I suppose, had it not firmly fixed. I resolved to have a serious conversation with her afterwards, and put good books into her hands. I had not arguments ready for her. I am not quite certain whether this incident happened on Sunday the 17 or Monday the 18. I then went to General Paoli's and dressed and had some most consolatory soup. I was quite at home there.

(I am now writing on the same day between one and two, to catch half an hour before dinner. I am fallen sadly behind in my journal. I should live no more than I can record, as one should not have more corn growing than one can get in. There is a waste of good if it be not preserved. And yet perhaps if it serve the purpose of immediate felicity, that is enough. The world would not hold pictures of all the pretty women who have lived in it and gladdened mankind; nor would it hold a register of all the agreeable conversations which have passed. But I mean only to record what is excellent; and let me rejoice when I can find abundance of that.)

Lord Mountstuart was to have had Dempster to dine with me, but he was engaged. It gave me pleasure to find that he now knew Dempster well and loved him much. Could I get all whom I really value to be well together and form one constellation (I am now writing on Monday the 25 March at Lichfield, while Dr. Johnson is dressing to be ready to go out to breakfast), it would be fine. That however is not to be expected in this state of being, where they will fight like meteors in the air, from contrary qualities. Lord Denbigh dined. He had been of the party at the London Tavern. They had drank hard and sat till four in the morning and were distressed after a riot. Lord Mountstuart said he was sober when

[4] The eleventh essay in *Philosophical Essays concerning Human Understanding*, 1748.

he came home, but when he got up in the morning, or rather *afternoon,* found himself drunk. It was a secret consolation to me that this elegant and noble-minded young peer could, like me, fall into intemperate drinking, and like me suffered for it. (I am now writing on Wednesday the 27 at Ashbourne.) My Lady was civil and obliging as I could wish. I was pleased with contemplating the plenty and elegance of the table of my *patron* (for I will call Lord Mountstuart so). Virgil says of his patron, "Namque erit ille mihi semper deus." [5] He indeed *had received* important favours. I have as yet received only marks of social affection and assurances of future solid support. But I have no doubt of Lord Mountstuart's determination to assist me. He told me today that when he spoke some time ago to the Duke of Queensberry of my getting Baron Maule's office of Clerk to the Register of Sasines, which I have had so long in view, the Duke hummed and ha'd and talked as if he had somebody else in his eye for it. Yet the Duke assured me that if the Baron would resign it he would do what he could for me. Lord Mountstuart confirmed me in my opinion that the Duke was a weak man. But if he is unfaithful to his word, that is a sad effect of weakness. It is a malignant fever from poverty of blood. It is wonderful and grieving to find how politicians are regardless of truth. Mr. Stuart told me yesterday that he had twenty promises of places under Lord North's hand, and yet they were given away to other people than those for whom he had the promises. My Lord asked me today if I knew his uncle, the Lord Privy Seal. [6] I told him no, but I wished much to have that honour. "Then," said he, "I'll introduce you." He said he was going to Bath for a little, that he would be back to the Duchess of Kingston's trial, and after that would not go away from London for a long while. [7] He said, "I promised to take you to see Luton, and I will do it." [7a] He was today quite as I could wish him to be. I said, "My Lord, you should do me all the good you can, for I am very grateful." "Well, I do," said he. We had the usual raillery upon my being suspected of popery and Jacobitism, of which my Lord often speaks with a complacency which I love, be-

[5] "Indeed for me that man will always be a god": *Eclogues,* i. 7. His patron was Octavian (the Emperor Augustus).

[6] James Stuart Mackenzie, brother of Lord Bute, had taken the name of Mackenzie on succeeding to an important property.

[7] Elizabeth Chudleigh (b. 1720), a woman of small fortune and great beauty, had secretly married the Hon. Augustus John Hervey (later Earl of Bristol), but she quarrelled with him and became the mistress of the Duke of Kingston. After a complicated suit in the Ecclesiastical Court (where she perjured herself), she married the Duke. Upon his death in 1773, she inherited his personal property and his real estate for life. Meantime the Duke's nephew had caused her to be indicted for bigamy. On 15 April (see below) she was brought to trial before the peers in Westminster Hall. Lord Mountstuart was one of her close friends and sureties.

[7a] Luton Hoo, in Bedfordshire, was the country residence of Lord Bute.

cause it shows that he thinks neither a scandal. He tells of my devotion in St. Peter's Church at Rome, which was true, and of my kissing the Old Stuart's hand, which was not true, but which he I really think believes, and which I never seriously contradict, as I have a pleasure in hearing him talk of it.

I told him I was making a collection of engraved heads of Scotsmen, as I could not attempt his extensive scheme of a British collection. I told him that Ridley, the bookseller, said he would have given £3,000 for the collection which his Lordship bought of Mr. Bull for £2,000. My Lord said he had not given _____, that he could not have afforded to give so much (which was a jest I thought). That he was not to tell how much he gave, for that Bull had two daughters, to make fortunes for whom his wife kept him from the use of money altogether; so he sold his prints to have a little purse for himself, the extent of which she should never know. My Lord said he had collected a great many prints himself before he bought Bull's. He said he hoped to get some preferment for Granger; that in the mean time he gave him his wine, and would give him money if he did not suppose it would affront him.[8] He said Granger was angry that I had not come to see him as I promised. I said I would make out[9] my visit.

We talked of the Scotch militia, for which my Lord was very zealous. He spoke quite in the style of a prince; said he fancied he had made some of the Scotch Members angry, for he had never consulted them. He had first shown them his bill. Then, when he had resolved on alterations, he sent for them to his house, and told them what these were to be, not submitting them at all to their consideration.

I should have mentioned yesterday that Dr. Johnson startled me somewhat upon this favourite ground. He said that as Scotland contributed so little land-tax towards the general support of the nation, it ought not to have a militia paid out of the general fund, unless it was thought for the general interest that Scotland should be protected from an invasion, which no man could think, because an enemy never would invade it. He was, I thought, wrong in this last proposition from an erroneous notion as to the poverty of Scotland; for he said he had been assured that, within these seven years, the Bank at Edinburgh could not pay three hundred pounds without previous notice being given, than which nothing almost can be more ridiculous, as it is certain that each of the banks there has a large sum of money always in readiness. Sir John Pringle afterwards wanted to know his authority for this strange fable. I asked Dr. Johnson,

[8] James Granger, the author of the *Biographical History of England,* which introduced a new word into the language. The book was published with blank leaves for the reception of engraved portraits or other illustrations; hence "to grangerize."
[9] "Succeed in making": a Scotticism.

but he had forgotten. The Doctor said that now that we had not the pay of English soldiers spent among us, as they were sent abroad, we were trying to get money another way, by having militia paid. That if we were afraid, and seriously desired to have an armed force to defend us, we should pay for it. That our scheme was to retain so much of our little land-tax, by way of paying and clothing a militia. I said he should not talk of *we* and *you*. That there was now an *Union*. He said there must be a distinction of interest while the proportions of land-tax were so unequal. He said, "If Yorkshire should say, 'Instead of paying our land-tax, we will keep so many more men as militia,' it would be unreasonable." Lord Mountstuart was of opinion that the French might probably land in Scotland, if left defenceless, and march from thence into England; and he observed that if the Scotch should be ill-treated upon this occasion, and have a militia refused them, they might naturally be as well inclined to France as to England, since the one would govern them at least as favourably as the other. I am not quite sure if this was his observation. I think it was.

He said he could not trust the Lord Advocate. I said I was glad he thought so, for he might depend upon it, the Lord Advocate was not in earnest in supporting the Scotch militia at this time, however loudly he might roar for it in the House of Commons. "I believe," said my Lord, "the Duke of Buccleuch is very sorry that he was not the proposer of it." "Well," said I, "there it is. The Duke of Buccleuch is a tool of the Advocate's, and the Advocate is sorry that so popular a bill has been proposed by your Lordship, whose interest is opposed to the Duke's. I know not whether he likes a militia at all. But I am sure he does not like this militia." Said my Lord with his princely air: "No. He does not like Lord Mountstuart's militia."

I felt a strong desire for Lord Mountstuart's interest prevailing in Scotland, as a noble Tory interest, and I was keen to give him any assistance in my power, and wished much to have power. Surely my parts might do something if properly directed. But the Scotch are so cold and selfish and cunning that I fear generous exertion would be lost upon them; and political interest is, since the death of Archibald, Duke of Argyll, so divided among different families hungry for advantages that I doubt if an extensive influence can again be established in one family. I have thoughts of writing "The Present Political State of Scotland." Lord Mountstuart bid me push Lord Mansfield this evening upon the subject of the Scotch militia. "If," said he, "he speaks against it, persevere in speaking for it, and hear what he has to say. If he smiles and says nothing, say, 'I am glad it has your Lordship's approbation'; and try to bring him out."

General Paoli's coach came for me. I had drank a bottle of old hock, and was just in good spirits. I called at my Chief, Mr. Bosville's in Great

Russell Street. Mrs. Bosville reprehended me for not answering Mr. Bosville's last letter, which I had received many months ago. I was ashamed of my neglect, and glad to get off so easily. Miss Bosville was as beautiful as ever. I was received here with attention and kindness as a valuable relation. Sir Alexander Macdonald, who had not been on speaking terms with me since Dr. Johnson and I saw him in the Isle of Skye, was here.[1] It was awkward to be at variance with the son-in-law of my Chief. I frankly said, "Sir Alexander and I have not been well together for some time. Let us have an end of it before this good company." Miss Bosville properly and pleasingly said, "*I* will make up the difference." But he was perverse, and said to her, "Don't be officious, Miss." So I turned off the subject quite easily, and chatted on twenty topics.

I then went to Lord Mansfield's. Found the same stiff formality without dignity. Somebody mentioned soldiers. I said it was a curiosity now to meet a soldier. There were so few to be seen in the country. Lord Coventry, who sat next me, said, "I hope they'll leave enough to defend us." *Then* was an opening for me. "I hope, my Lord," said I, "we shall soon be able to defend ourselves in Scotland by a militia." Lord Mansfield not seeming to take notice, I had assurance enough to address myself to him briskly. "I am saying, my Lord, I hope we shall have our Scotch militia." He looked constricted, and said, "I don't know," or some such unmeaning thing. Mr. Bacon, Member for Norwich, took up the subject a little, I could not tell on what side. Mr. Crosbie spoke for it. Lord Mansfield said, "From the divisions there have been upon it, I should think the bill will not pass"; and when some clauses of it were mentioned, he said, "I know nothing of it," which was most certainly not true. The Duke of Gordon, from feebleness or modesty, never opened his mouth. Lord Advocate said he hoped it would go through, but showed no warmth. I again with assurance sallied forth upon Lord Mansfield thus: "I don't like to see your Lordship shake your head so."

I went and took a place in the Oxford post-coach for Tuesday. I liked to see my name put down in the book directly under *Dr. Johnson.* I then went to Sir John Pringle's, found there Bruce, the traveller, Dr. Baker, Dr. Hunter, and many more, under some restraint, too. When Bruce and some of the circle were gone, I became lively and introduced a gaiety which I could perceive gladdened them all, though none of them had animal spirits to begin it and dissipate the cloud of gravity. Dr. Priestley

---

[1] See above, 22 March 1775. Sir Alexander's sulkiness did not last much longer. On his last day in London during this jaunt (16 May), Boswell took him to be introduced to Samuel Foote. A bitter controversy developed in 1785 when, in the *Tour to the Hebrides,* Boswell printed the reflections which he and Johnson had made in 1773 on his greed and penuriousness.

was there, with whom I renewed my acquaintance, though I disliked his opinions in religion and politics. I however erred tonight, for I owned that I was inclined to think the Americans in the right while they asserted their claim to the British Constitutional privilege of taxing themselves by their own representatives, as they should enjoy it as well as we, and it might be as well diffused over America under the same Sovereign with us as over Ireland. I say I erred for talking freely upon the question, which I had not enough studied, and saying that it was the only great point upon which I had got from under Dr. Johnson. This was imprudence, and I instantly perceived it with pain. Dr. Hunter fell to telling a long story of the bad behaviour of Dr. Harwood, to which Priestley listened with avidity.[2] Sir John Pringle nodded. I was patient for I suppose eight or ten minutes, but the story was so uninteresting, and Hunter spoke so tediously and so insipidly, that my mind was in such uneasiness as the lungs are when in want of air, when they are just teased with as much as keeps them in a wretched feeble motion. I could endure it no longer, and made my escape. Sir John Pringle, who was happy to have a respite, followed me into the passage. I mentioned to him my accompanying Dr. Johnson in his short tour, and he did not disapprove of it. But he was justly angry with me for having come away without seeing my father and asking his commands, which he said was strange in a man who talked of fighting for his father's honour. There is however no inconsistency here. I feel there is none. As a soldier, as *The Spectator* observes,[3] will mount a breach, though he trembles for fear of a ghost in the dark, so I may be depressed and made so uneasy by the habitual awe which comes upon me in my father's presence when he disapproves of my conduct, and yet I may have resolution enough to risk my life in his vindication. I told Sir John I should write to my father in proper terms. I got home to Messieurs Dilly's a little after twelve.

MONDAY 18 MARCH. This morning I resolved should be spent calmly, for I felt that dissipation was making me giddy notwithstanding my deliberate purpose of being quite cool and steady during this visit to London. There is no preventing giddiness but by having intervals of cessation, as boiling over is prevented by taking the liquor now and then off the

---

[2] William Hunter, the anatomist, was telling a story about a former friend of Priestley's. Edward Harwood, a very unpopular biblical critic because of his semi-Arian views, later (1785) defended Priestley when he denied the virgin birth of Christ. Priestley, whose Unitarian theology, mechanistic psychology (see above, 31 December 1775), and radical political theory Boswell found offensive, is now chiefly remembered as the discoverer of oxygen. Boswell had met him four years previously at a Whig club in London to which they both belonged.

[3] *Spectator* No. 12.

fire. Every time I have been in London, even last year, I have insensibly overheated my mind by the rapidity of amusement. I must grease the wheels with sober attention lest they flame and be consumed. I sent a note to General Paoli for his coach, and read some of a most elegant publication which my friends Messieurs Dilly were preparing, *Letters from Lord Chesterfield to his Friends,* and original letters from some of them to him. I was charmed with those which I read this morning to Madame de Boccage and Mr. Dayrolles. The publication was to contain all Lord Chesterfield's writings except his letters to his son, with his life by the editor, Dr. Maty, Secretary to the Royal Society. I was quite refreshed. After breakfast Mr. Mickle came and sat awhile with me.[4] I remember nothing that passed, except his acknowledgements of gratitude to me for interesting myself in his concerns. Then came David Cuninghame, who was become a little more rational, and willingly granted a receipt for £25 to account of what his brother owed him.

I had talked of him by description to Dr. Johnson on Saturday. He was against his brother's advancing money to him in his present idle, expensive state; "For," he said, "it might afterwards keep him alive when he had spent all he had." This led me to ask his opinion of the influence of education. He allowed the greatest effect to it. Did not deny but there was some original difference in minds, but that it was nothing in comparison of what is formed by education. That by negligence and want of use the powers of the human mind were lost. He instanced the science of *numbers* as what all minds were equally capable of attaining. That we found a prodigious difference in the powers of different men in that, when they were grown up, because their minds had been more or less exercised in it; and that he thought the same cause would explain the difference of excellence in other things, admitting always *some* difference in the first principles.[5] This is a difficult subject, but it is best to hope that diligence may do a very great deal. We are *sure* of what it can do in giving us mechanical force and dexterity.

Bruce Boswell was passing through the Poultry. We called him up. I took him and David Cuninghame with me in General Paoli's coach. I called for a little on Dr. Johnson, and took them with me. He was very courteous to them. Stockdale was there. He was now chaplain to a man-

[4] William Julius Mickle had, like Boswell, contributed to Donaldson's *Collection of Poems* in 1762. They had corresponded since 1768 and had occasionally met. In 1771 Mickle had published the first book of his most celebrated work, a translation of *The Lusiad* of Camoens, for which Boswell later solicited subscriptions. The complete translation had just been published.

[5] The *Life* shows that Johnson's remarks end here, the next two sentences being Boswell's commentary.

of-war lying at Portsmouth. (I am now writing on Saturday the 30 in London.) Dr. Johnson took occasion to expatiate on the wretchedness of a sea life, which I have heard him do more than once.[6] He said that a ship was worse than a gaol. That there is better air in a gaol, better company, more conveniency of every kind, and that a ship has the additional disadvantage of being in danger; and he said that when men came to like a sea life, they were not fit to live at land. "Then," said I, "it would be cruel to breed a son to the sea." "It would be cruel," said he, "in a father who thinks as I do." He said people went to sea before they knew the unhappiness of that way of life, and, when they knew it, they could not escape from it because it was then too late to choose another profession, as is the case with men in general when they have once engaged in a particular way of life.

I then carried the two young men to Sir Joshua Reynolds's and showed them my picture of Mary Queen of Scots being forced to resign her crown, painted by Hamilton.[7] I saw from Sir Joshua's manner of speaking before the picture was produced that he was not pleased with it. Indeed I was disappointed when I now saw it for the first time. All the figures were well but the Queen herself, who had neither beauty in a high degree nor grace in any degree. Sir Joshua was civil and obliging as usual, and asked me to dine with him today along with Dr. Johnson. I told him I was engaged at Mr. Montagu Stuart's.[8] It is agreeable when one can mention an engagement so creditable. Mrs. Cholmondeley was at Sir Joshua's.[9] She recollected having seen me at Mrs. Macaulay's, and we had a good deal of such chit-chat as passes in a picture room. I was quite easy and gay, but disliked her extreme effrontery. I was struck with an incident. While we looked at some drawings of the mode of burying the dead in Otaheite, or rather the mode of disposing of the dead, which is pleasing, or at least alleviating, as they are suspended among green boughs

[6] *Hebrides,* 31 August and 23 September 1773. Stockdale, a literary hack, had previously been an officer in the Army and chaplain to the Fleet Prison (*Boswell for the Defence,* 21 March 1772). Johnson's diatribes against a sea life involved Bruce Boswell as well as Stockdale, for Bruce Boswell was a sailor by profession (above, 11 October 1775), and had undoubtedly been presented to Johnson as such.

[7] While he was in Italy in 1765, Boswell, who then entertained very grand ideas, had commissioned this large picture from Gavin Hamilton.

[8] Lord Mountstuart's brother, Colonel James Archibald Stuart. He never actually took the name of Montagu, though he may have been called by it in order to identify him. His mother was the daughter of Edward and Lady Mary Wortley Montagu. Stuart, not his brother, was heir to the Wortley Montagu property, and later inherited that of his uncle Stuart Mackenzie. His grandfather, Lady Mary's husband, had originally been Wortley and added the name Montagu.

[9] Mary, younger sister of Peg Woffington, married the Hon. Robert Cholmondeley, son of the third Earl.

supported by two trees,[1] and the flesh is quickly consumed in the air without any bad smell, after which the skeletons are deposited in a mausoleum —while we looked at these mementoes of mortality, a kind of pleasantry was bandied between Mrs. Cholmondeley and Sir Joshua about "this sad thing death," and the Knight in particular was quite delicate and fine and smiling while he talked of it. I could not help steadfastly thinking, how strange is it that these two, who are themselves certainly to die, should even for a few moments treat the awful and tremendous destruction of this scene of existence with such levity. The thought grew full and solemn at once.—And then my mind made a transition to something else.

I dined very agreeably at Mr. Stuart's; nobody there but Sir William Cunynghame and Miss Monckton, daughter of the Earl of Galway, a little creature, all life and fashion. Stuart luckily was not in the humour for drinking today, so I only enlivened myself with wine. When Sir William was gone and the ladies had retired, Stuart talked to me, as to a friend whom he valued, of his gaming, and of the uneasiness it gave him, both on his own account and that of Mrs. Stuart, who had told me how much she suffered when he was at the gaming-table, as the evil that might happen was boundless, and that he had lost several thousands this winter. He said he wished to tie himself up, and he proposed that if I would give him ten guineas, which I might pay when he[2] pleased, he would grant me an obligation to pay me a thousand pounds in case of his ever playing or betting at hazard, or losing a hundred guineas at any game in one day, the fact to be proved by witnesses or by his word of honour, and he took my word of honour that I should exact the forfeit. I accordingly wrote out an obligation, which he signed, and when we went to drink coffee and tea with the ladies, I made Mrs. Stuart easy by showing the paper, and to add to its validity in a court of honour I made his own lady and Miss Monckton witness it.[3] I was rather too lively this afternoon, talked too much, and was too entertaining to impress any respect. It struck me when Stuart said, "Boswell, I dare say Miss Monckton thinks you mad." It is not easy to resist the immediate pleasure of perceiving a company entertained with one's vivacity, and yet one is sure to suffer for it in dignity of character. I shall here put down a remark of General Paoli's at breakfast, 30 March 1776.[4] Talking of Lord North and his chief excellence being pleasantry,

[1] Boswell is using this word in the obsolete sense of "poles" or "posts."

[2] *Sic,* but Boswell probably meant to write "I."

[3] The "obligation," in Boswell's hand, is among the papers at Yale. It was to last for five years from this date.

[4] *Sic.* Boswell was unusually far behind in posting his journal. See the beginning of the entry for 19 March.

he said, "Si fractus illabatur orbis, *indifferentem* ferient ruinae."[5] But he was not "impavidus." "Jamais des grands hommes ont étés des diseurs de jolis mots. Cicéron les a dits, mais jamais Caesar; jamais Auguste. Un homme qui nous fait rire se mette au dessous de nous."[6] I said an entertaining, merry man was the *jouet*[7] of a company. "Yet," I said, "Dr. Johnson makes us often laugh by his sayings." Poggi, the Italian painter, who was by, made a very just distinction. "Dr. Johnson," said he, "makes you laugh by his strong satire." I was struck with the distinction, and saw that the laughter excited by Dr. Johnson is at other people, not at himself or any circumstances inherent in himself; for all his jokes have a reference to the characters or opinions of somebody either present or absent.

I left Stuart's in a calm, cheerful frame, called at Ridley's, and got from his shopman two copies of *Johnsoniana*, which Ridley had procured for me before publication. Then called at the lady's with whom I was formerly in love, and again felt my influence with a masterly superiority. Got to Dilly's in good time. Wrote letters to my dear wife, my father, and Temple, and left a note for Dempster, as I had not had time to call on him at his lodgings. I should have marked, though, that I called for him today at the House of Commons and did not find him. I walked awhile in the Court of Requests with different people; was introduced to Mr. Oswald, on whom I had called with a letter of introduction from Claud; found him a plain, worthy fellow. Aberdeen talked of the *Scotch Ministry*, as they were called, or called themselves; that is to say, the Duke of Buccleuch, Lord Advocate, Sir Adam Fergusson, Andrew Stuart, etc. I treated them with indignant contempt, and said they should be watched. I said the Duke of Buccleuch was a tool to Dundas. That I feared he could only be a tool, but he was a tool of fine metal, and I wished he were in better hands. I walked a little with worthy John Swinton, who said that there was no wonder I was so universally liked, as I was so good-humoured. I perceived my gaiety cheering him at the time. But he was wrong in one thing, for he said there was nobody who disliked me. Whereas, as I told him, there are many people who think very unfavourably of me. I walked a little with Seton, the solicitor. I introduced the Fife election, and, with an air of despising indifference and a little resentment, mentioned the false charge against my father. "Poh!" says Seton (with a smile and a countenance perfectly expressive of confidence and contempt), "your

---

[5] "If the vault of heaven were to break and fall, the ruins, though they struck him, would not rouse him from indifference": paraphrased from Horace, *Odes*, III. iii. 7–8; *indifferentem* for *impavidum* (undismayed).

[6] "Great men have never been dispensers of fine phrases. Cicero was, but never Caesar, never Augustus. A man who makes us laugh puts himself below us."

[7] "Sport."

father's character is so well known that what they say is ridiculous." I was more relieved by Seton's view of the matter than by the more serious views of abler men. I catched his pure flippancy and walked with a brisk pace and a kind of lively triumph. The Advocate spoke to me, said he had not seen me but at Lord Mansfield's, and seemed to have the assurance to think that I should have waited on him. I was quite nonchalant. I went for a little into the House of Lords and heard Wedderburn pleading in an appeal between Sir John Eden and Lord Bute. I was disgusted with his priggish affectation, and vexed that such a fellow as I thought him should get so high. I called before dinner on my old friend Captain Hoggan, who had been in quest of me and was exceedingly glad to see me.[8] What a long history of one day!

TUESDAY 19 MARCH. (I am now writing in the Hon. Mrs. Stuart's dressing-room, London, Monday evening April 1.) Between eight and nine in the morning I was at the Somerset Coffee-house, and there I found Dr. Johnson waiting for the Oxford coach, and Mr. Gwynn, the architect, attending him. I breakfasted comfortably, and then we three got into the coach, which, when it is desired, calls at the Somerset. The fourth passenger was Mr. _____ of Merton College, a young gentleman of Gloucestershire. He very politely gave me his place that I might be drawn forward as Dr. Johnson was.

In my journal of yesterday I strangely omitted to mention that between ten and eleven at night I called on Mr. Garrick, found him sitting with Mrs. Garrick and Miss More, the poetess, and stayed with him till near twelve, drinking port and water and eating bread and a Hampton nonpareil.[9] He was quite easy and gay as usual. I said this morning in the coach that he would be relieved by his quitting the stage. Dr. Johnson seemed to doubt it. "Why," said I, "he will be Atlas with the burthen off his back." "But I know not," said Dr. Johnson, "if he will be so steady without his load." He was clear that he should never play any more, but be quite the gentleman, and not partly the player; and that he should not any longer subject himself to be hissed or to be insolently treated by the performers whom he used to rule with a high hand, and who would gladly retaliate. I said I thought he should play once a year for the benefit

[8] Captain James Hoggan had been, with Boswell, John Johnston, and William Johnson Temple, a member of Robert Hunter's Greek class at the University of Edinburgh in 1754–1755, and he and Boswell had travelled together in Ireland in 1769.

[9] Hannah More, best known now for her edifying books for children, was at this time paying the Garricks an extended visit. In a letter she described this meeting with Boswell as follows: "Mr. Boswell (Corsican Boswell) was here last night; he is a very agreeable and good-natured man; he perfectly adores Johnson" (*Letters of Hannah More*, ed. R. B. Johnson, London, 1925, p. 36).—A nonpareil was a kind of confectionery or an apple; Garrick's villa was at Hampton.

of decayed actors, as it was given out he was to do. "Sir," said Dr. Johnson, "he'll be a decayed actor himself."

(I am now writing at General Paoli's, London, Tuesday forenoon, April 2.) Dr. Johnson found fault with ornamental architecture, because it consumes labour disproportionate to its utility. For the same reason he satirized statuary. "Painting," said he, "consumes labour not disproportionate to its effect, but a fellow will hack half a year at a block of marble to make something in stone that resembles a man." This was a Gothic reflection, for certainly statuary is a noble art of imitation, and preserves the utmost expression of the human frame. Dr. Johnson said the value of statuary was owing to its difficulty; "For," said he, "you would not value the finest cut head upon a carrot." Here I take it he was not just; for although the difficulty may enter into the estimation of the value of a marble head, I take it the durability is the principal reason for a preference.

Gwynn was a rattling fellow,[1] but the Doctor kept him in pure subjection, calling him "Gwynnie." I could discover too that the Doctor was his good friend in recommending him to employment at Oxford.[2] It was a pleasant day. When we came to Oxford, we went immediately to University College to call on Mr. Scott, one of the fellows, who had accompanied the Doctor from Newcastle to Edinburgh. With him we should have lodged, but he was gone into the country for some days; so we put up at the Angel Inn, and had the very parlour where Dr. Johnson and Chambers and poor Frank Stewart supped with me in 1768.[3]

Either this night or the one after he spoke to me of the melancholy to which I am subject, said that I had a very ticklish mind, and that I must divert distressing thoughts, and not combat with them. "Remember always," said he, "_____."[4] I said I sometimes tried to *think them down.* He said I was wrong. He bid me have a lamp burning in my bedchamber, and take a book and read and so compose myself to rest. This I supposed was his own method. But I told him I seldom waked in the night. When I do at home, my excellent spouse consoles me with easy, sensible talk. He said to have the management of one's mind was a great art, and that it might be attained in a considerable degree by experience and ha-

[1] "and even swore a little": manuscript of the *Life,* deleted.
[2] Johnson had befriended John Gwynn as early as 1759, by publishing letters recommending his design for Blackfriars Bridge. Gwynn was visiting Oxford at this time to resume his supervision of the construction of Magdalen Bridge, which he had designed.
[3] Stewart was a cousin of the famous Sir James Macdonald and, like Macdonald, a nephew of Lord Eglinton. Like Sir James he was a most promising young man, and like Sir James he died young.
[4] Boswell left the greater part of a line blank, intending to write down Johnson's counsel when he recalled it. What he cannot remember is what Johnson tells him he must never forget!

bitual exercise. His sage counsel I treasured up. He commended Burton's *Anatomy of Melancholy* and said there was great spirit and great power in what Burton said when he wrote from his own mind. I fancied tonight that I was prepared by my revered friend for conducting myself through any future gloom.

We had a double-bedded room, and were as companionable as during our journey to the Hebrides, while I felt that kind of consolatory respectful frame which Oxford has ever produced in me.

WEDNESDAY 20 MARCH. After breakfasting, we went and waited on Dr. Wetherell, the Master of University College, with whom Dr. Johnson had some business in giving advice concerning the sale of the books printed for the University. I have observed that the Doctor loves business; that is, he loves to have his wisdom operate. Wetherell said that he would have given him a hundred guineas if he would have written a preface to his *Political Tracts,* which were now to be published in a volume—a preface by way of a discourse upon the British Constitution. I said that the Doctor, though in his writings a great friend to the Constitution both in Church and State, had never written *per expressum* in support of either, and that really there was a claim upon him for both. This is a serious truth. I am sure he could give a volume of no great bulk upon each, which would comprise the substance, and with his spirit would effectually maintain them. He should erect a fort on the confines of each. I could perceive that he was not pleased with our discourse. He said, "Why should *I* be always writing?" I hope he was conscious that the debt was just, and that he will discharge it, though he disliked being dunned. One evening at Aberdeen when he was in a heavenly frame, he, I think, undertook to write for Christianity.[5]

We then went to Pembroke College, the place of his education, and of which Dr. Adams of Shrewsbury, who had been his tutor, was now Master.[6] Gwynn, who is a Shrewsbury man, went with us. I had desired much to see Adams, and once thought of going to Shrewsbury to visit him, supposing that he could tell me a great deal of Dr. Johnson's university life. I got a little from him, which is marked in the little book of notes for Dr. Johnson's life.[7] We drank chocolade with Dr. Adams's lady and daughter, who was, as Gwynn told me, a very fine scholar. Adams was

---

[5] *Hebrides,* 22 August 1773.

[6] A mistake. In the *Life* Boswell wrote: "Dr. Adams, the worthy and respectable Master of Pembroke College, has generally had the reputation of being Johnson's tutor. The fact, however, is that in 1731 Mr. Jorden quitted the college, and his pupils were transferred to Dr. Adams; so that had Johnson returned, Dr. Adams *would have been his tutor*" (*Life,* under the year 1731).

[7] This small notebook, apparently the only one which Boswell devoted exclusively to Johnson, was published in 1925 by the late R. W. Chapman. It is now in the Hyde Collection.

a little fair [8] man, very civil and communicative. Though I had not read more than some extracts of his pamphlet against David Hume's treatise on miracles, I took the liberty to object to the politeness with which he treats the Infidel. He said he had met Hume in London at a dinner, who shook hands with him and said, "You have treated me much better than I deserve." That he had called on Hume and Hume had called on him; and I observed the quarto edition of Hume's *Essays* in Adams's library, bound in morocco. Of all this I disapproved. Where there is a controversy concerning a passage in a classic, or concerning a question in antiquities, or some such subject, one may treat an antagonist with politeness and respect. But where the controversy is concerning the government or religion of my country, it is of such vast importance to have the better, that the *person* of an opponent is not to be spared. If a man firmly believes that religion is a great treasure, he will consider a writer who endeavours to deprive mankind of it as a robber; he will look upon him as *odious* even though the infidel may think himself in the right. A robber who reasons as the gang do in *The Beggar's Opera,* who call themselves *practical* philosophers,[9] and may have as much *bona fides* as pernicious *speculative* philosophers, is not the less an object of just indignation. An abandoned profligate may have a notion that it is not wrong to debauch my wife; but shall I therefore not detest him, and if I catch him making an attempt, shall I treat him with politeness, nay with compliments upon his genteel address? No, I will kick him downstairs, or break his bones. That is, if I really love my wife, or have a true notion of honour. Hume, then, certainly should not be treated well by a Christian priest merely because he robs with ingenuity. Dr. Johnson joined me against Adams, and said that when a man voluntarily engages in an important controversy, he is to do all that he can to lessen his antagonist, because authority from personal respect has much weight and often more than the reasonings. "If," said he, "my antagonist writes bad language, though that may not be essential to the question, I will attack him for his bad language." Said Adams, in the common phrase: "You would not jostle a chimney-sweeper." "Yes, Sir," said Dr. Johnson, "if it were necessary to jostle him down."

Adams told us that in some of the colleges at Oxford the fellows had excluded the young men from social intercourse with them. Dr. Johnson said they were right; for there could be no real conversation, no fair exertion of mind, if the young men were by, as a man who has a character does not choose to stake it upon a debate in their presence. "But," said I, "may there not be conversation without a contest for superiority?" "No

[8] "Mrs. Thrale called Dr. Adams 'a parson in wax' ": Boswell's marginal note.
[9] Act II, scene i.

animated conversation," said Dr. Johnson; "for it cannot be but one or other must come off superior. I do not mean that he shall have the better in the argument, for he may take the weak side; but his superiority of parts and knowledge will necessarily appear, and he to whom he thus appears superior is lessened in the eyes of the young men. You know—— said, 'Mallem cum Scaligero errare quam cum Clavio recte sapere.'[1] In the same manner take Bentley's and Johnson's[2] comments upon Horace. You will admire Bentley more, though he be wrong and Johnson[2] right."

We then visited Dr. Bentham, Canon of Christ Church and Divinity Professor, a man of learning, abilities, and vivacity in conversation. Dr. Adams asked us to dine with him, and Dr. Bentham asked us to dine with the canons of Christ Church. But we were engaged to the Master of University. I was in a sound, cheerful state of mind today, and viewed Oxford with high relish. I told Dr. Johnson how I had been here in 1763, and though Sir James Macdonald carried me about with all advantage, I was so oppressed with a temporary melancholy that I was quite unhappy and that in a wretched degree, because I had no hope of relief upon earth when Oxford was a burthen to me. And, to be sure, that is the most dreadful state—when a man is miserable in a situation where he ought to be happy—because he cannot then flatter himself that he would be well in another place, as he can do when he is in a remote dull situation. It was St. Cuthbert's day, which is kept at University College, St. Cuthbert having been a saint of Durham, with which this college is much connected. We had an excellent dinner with the Master and fellows. An apothecary in the town and Dr. Johnson and I were the guests. At the foot of the table sat Mr. Coulson, I believe the Senior Fellow. Mrs. Thrale introduces him as an old friend of Dr. Johnson's into her translation of his Latin verses written in the opera-house.[3] But they have not been very long acquainted. I eat and drank too much, which clouded me somewhat; but I liked to be saturated with college luxury. There was not much conversation. Gwynn would needs enter the lists with Dr. Johnson, and he blun-

---

[1] "I had rather go wrong with Scaliger than be right with Clavius" (imitated from Cicero, *Tusculan Disputations,* I. xvii. 39). Christopher Clavius, a Jesuit mathematician and Cardinal, was commissioned by Gregory XIII to publish an explanation of the new calendar, with the calculations necessary for its verification, and thereby became involved in a bitter controversy with the great Protestant scholar Joseph Scaliger.

[2] Corrected in the *Life* to "Jason de Nores."

[3] Johnson's *In Theatro* was written 8 March 1771. Mrs. Thrale's imitation is given in her *Anecdotes of Johnson:*

> When threescore years have chilled thee quite,
> Still can theatric scenes delight?
> Ill suits this place with learned wight,
> May Bates or Coulson cry.

dered out an answer which the Doctor allowed to be a good one, in so much that he would have him rest his colloquial fame upon it, and cried, "Speak no more." The Doctor was angry that Gwynn was taking down a church which might have stood many years, only to have a direct road to a new bridge; and the expression he used was, "You are taking a church out of the way, that the people may go in a straight line to the bridge." "No, Sir," said Gwynn, "I am putting the church in the way, that the people may not go out of the way." [4]

The Doctor and I then went to Magdalen Hall, where he introduced me to Dr. Horne, the Master of it, who had once talked of publishing an edition of Izaak Walton's *Lives*, and had laid aside the design upon Dr. Johnson's telling him, from mistake, that Lord Hailes was to do it. I had above a year wished to be negotiator between Lord Hailes and Dr. Horne, that one or other of them should perform so good a work. Horne was a stout, complaisant scholar. He said he was publishing a *Commentary on the Psalms*, after which he would endeavour to find time for Walton. I told him Lord Hailes would give him a good deal of help. He did not seem very keen for the scheme. [5] It occurred to me that I might be the editor myself. Dr. Johnson said that it would be necessary to collect all the editions of Walton's *Lives;* that they had in a later edition left out a vision which he relates Dr. Donne had, by way of adapting the book to the present age, but that it should be restored; [6] and he said there should be a critical catalogue given of the works of the different persons whose lives were written by Walton; therefore their works should be read by the editor. We drank tea with Dr. Horne.

[4] This is a rare—perhaps a unique—instance of a failure by Boswell to "carry a *bon mot.*" Neither here nor in the *Life* is it possible to grasp the point of Gwynn's retort, for the reason that in the journal Boswell neglected to mention an essential circumstance, while in the *Life* he added one—that a new church was built at a different place—which completely falsifies the situation. The facts (for which we are indebted to Dr. L. F. Powell) seem to have been as follows: Gwynn was rebuilding Magdalen Bridge, Oxford. The approach on the London end was troublesome, as St. Clement's church and churchyard blocked the way. It was proposed to remove the church (which was in bad repair), but the scheme was not carried through. Instead a part of the churchyard was cut off, and the road brought flush up with the church, which then stood in the fork between two roads, being literally "in the way." It remained there till 1829, the present St. Clement's being then built in Marston Road. When Boswell posted the journal he perhaps understood Gwynn's reply, though he failed to record the essential fact that the demolition of the church was only proposed. When he came to write the *Life,* he had clearly lost the point himself.
[5] He never carried it out.
[6] Johnson seems to be referring to the *Life of Donne,* abridged from Walton, which was prefixed to Tonson's edition of Donne's poems, 1719. Many of the well-known anecdotes are omitted, amongst them Donne's vision of his wife. No other printing of the *Life of Donne* between 1675 and 1776 has been traced.

We then called on Dr. Wheeler, the Poetry Professor, but did not find him. Then we went to Mr. Thomas Warton of Trinity, whom I had long wished to see. We found him in a very elegant apartment ornamented with good prints, and with wax or spermaceti candles before him. All this surprised me, because I had heard that Tom kept low drunken company, and I expected to see a confused dusty room and a little, fat, laughing fellow. In place of which I found a good, sizable man, with most decent clothes and darkish periwig, one who might figure as a canon. He did not say much; but as Dr. Johnson had some time ago given him a memorandum from me to inquire about an ancient ballad for Lord Hailes, he very obligingly told me that he should send me it, and asked to have my address. There was no vivacity broke forth—no poetic flash. We talked of writing lives. Dr. Johnson said few people who lived with a man knew what to remark about him, and he instanced the chaplain of the late Pearce, Bishop of Rochester, whom he was to assist in writing some memoirs of that prelate, but who could tell almost nothing.

I said Dodsley's life should be written, as he had been so much connected with the wits of his time, and had risen from the state of a footman. Dr.[7] Warton said he had published a little volume under the title of *The Muse in Livery.* Dr. Johnson said Dodsley's brother would not thank a man who should write the life.[8] I mentioned the late Dr. John Campbell as we talked of biography. Dr. Johnson had said to me that he believed his disappointment on the bad success of his great work, the *Political Survey,* had killed him. He at Dr.[7] Warton's said that work was his death. Warton did not understand his meaning, and said, "I believe so too. The great attention which he employed upon it—" "Nay," said Dr. Johnson, "he died of want of attention if he died at all by that book."

I asked Warton to sup with us at our inn. He said he was particularly engaged. Dr. Johnson said to me afterwards that Warton did not like to be with us. He was not at his ease. He liked only company in which he could reign. "I am sure," said I, "I should have willingly let him reign." "Ay, but he would not have reigned before us," said he, "for all men who have that love of low company are also timid."

I was elevated in spirit while I walked in the cloisters of an Oxford college with Dr. Johnson in the stillness of moonlight. I said, "This is the road to a better world." He assented. I regretted that I had not been educated at Oxford, but said I would send my son thither, and should be

[7] Properly "Mr.," as given before in the journal, and as given at this place in the *Life.*
[8] The life of Robert Dodsley, the bookseller, dramatist, and poet, was not written until 1910, by Ralph Straus. *A Muse in Livery: or, The Footman's Miscellany* was printed for the author in 1732. Dodsley's brother James was also a bookseller, and was living when this anecdote was published in the *Life.*

happy in coming here to see him.[9] He said I should have him first educated at an English school; not at one of the great schools at a distance
from me, but at one in the north of England, where there were very good
ones. He said Durham would be a proper place to send him to if there
were a good school there, which there once was.

He went to sit with Miss Parker, sister to the booksellers[1] here of that
name, and I went and called on Dr. Smith, the Anatomy Professor, as an
Ayrshire man and one who had formerly been very civil to me. Having
been all day in agreeable English society, I was somewhat shocked to
find Smith and Mr. William Alexander, the merchant's son, a student,
drinking tea after a debauch in wine at a meeting of Scotchmen in Oxford. Smith, who indecently talks as an unbeliever, was full of the praises
of Gibbon's *Decline and Fall of the Roman Empire,* just published. I
said the style was beautiful, quite mellifluous, but that there was poison
conveyed in it, and it was a strange thing to meet with infidelity in a
history. That it was not fair to attack us thus unexpectedly, and that he
should have warned us of our danger, before we entered his garden of
flowers of eloquence, by an advertisement: "Springs and traps set here."[2]
Smith uttered the common cant about free inquiry, and truth standing
the test, and he seemed to applaud an attack upon the university establishments in Adam Smith's book on wealth.[3] I said it was ungrateful in Smith,
who owed his instruction to Oxford. Upon the whole this was a disagreeable interview.

I hastened to Parker's and sat a few minutes, and then my revered
friend and I went to our inn. I enjoyed his conversation much after
Smith's. We had excellent Oxford eel every night for supper, and I
thought him the better for having a social meal in the evening put in his
way. He seemed to relish it. He said tonight that if I saved good fortunes
for my daughters, they would have no right to call me unjust, though I
preferred an heir male to the succession of Auchinleck. He bid me make
no change in my way of life after getting possession of the estate until I
had first made my circumstances quite easy.

We were to set out for Birmingham and Lichfield next day. A *dili-*

[9] Alexander Boswell attended the University of Edinburgh, not Oxford. He also spent
some time at Leipzig, where Boswell had once (1764) promised to send a son. Boswell's younger son, James, graduated from Oxford, but his father did not live to see
him matriculate.

[1] Sackville Parker, who had a shop in Logic Lane, next to University College.
"Parker's," the present bookshop in Broad Street and the Turl, descends from a different establishment, which Sackville's grand-nephew Joseph joined in 1798.

[2] The reading of the *Life* is "spring-guns and man-traps."

[3] In Book V, chapter i: "Of the Expense of the Institutions for the Education of
Youth."

gence, that is, a post-chaise of the stage kind, was to pass through about three in the morning. I left orders to call us if there were two places. The name of this vehicle, I found, was corrupted into the "dilly." Dr. Johnson laughed at this, as he does at small sports often enough. Both these nights I have contrived that we should go to bed in good time. I have omitted to mention that this evening, when I talked to him of my forwardness in making myself known to people and getting information from them, and said, "I am afraid of lessening myself by this," "Sir," said he, "you are growing in reality greater as you increase your knowledge." This encouraged me.

THURSDAY 21 MARCH. (I am now writing in General Paoli's, London, Thursday 4 April.) The "dilly" did not disturb us, so we slept till between eight and nine. Dr. Wetherell had read in my presence part of a letter from Dr. Johnson, giving advice as to the sale of University books and explaining with his pointed perspicuity the trade of bookselling. I wished to have a copy of it, and Dr. Wetherell agreed to let me have it if Dr. Johnson consented. I obtained his consent last night, and this morning got the letter and copied it. I resolved to come to Oxford every time that I came to London. Dr. Johnson suggested this, and said I would establish such an acquaintance there that it would cost me no more than the expense of travelling. It pleased me to think that I might, at different periods of life, in some degree supply the want of an Oxford education.

I should have mentioned last night that at Mr. Thomas Warton's we talked of Gibbon's book, and I said that as he had changed his system several times—from the Church of England to popery, and then to infidelity—I did not despair of seeing him yet a Methodist preacher. Dr. Johnson said now that he had published his infidelity, he would probably persist in it. I mentioned Sir Richard Steele's publishing his *Christian Hero* in order to keep himself firm in religion, and yet his practice being very unsuitable. Dr. Johnson then said, "He practised the *lighter* vices." I catched at this saying as a kind of indulgence to licentiousness in women and wine. My two late visits to an amorous lady in London gave me an interest in desiring such an indulgence. I can declare that they did not affect my *mind* more than drinking a pot of porter when thirsty, but I was in some doubt whether this was owing to sensual thoughtlessness in me or to harmlessness in the acts. I was not quite easy, however, upon reflection, but I had recourse to patriarchal extensiveness.

Gwynn came to us a little this morning. About twelve o'clock we set out in a post-chaise. It was a delightful day. We drove through Blenheim Park, as I had never seen that celebrated place. Dr. Johnson had been through the house. I was satisfied with viewing the outside of the magnificent pile, and felt a grand impression when I thought that here was a grant by the British Parliament to a great general. When I looked at the bridge upon which an epigram was made,[4] I think in the following words,

> The arch the height of thy ambition shows,
> The stream, an emblem of thy bounty flows,

and saw that now there was abundance of water collected, I said, "They have drowned the epigram." I enjoyed very highly the present scene: beautiful weather—Blenheim—Dr. Johnson. I said, "You and I, Sir, have seen the extremes of what is to be seen: the rough, wild Mull, and now Blenheim Park."

At Chapel House, where we dined, Dr. Johnson said to me, as expressing his own sentiment, "You would not for a small sum give up the addition to your knowledge of human life which you got in our journey to the Hebrides?" "I would not give it up for £500," said I. "No, you would not," said he. After dinner, while we were driven rapidly in the post-chaise, which Dr. Johnson has always loved,[5] he said to me very seriously, "Life has not many things better than this." I agreed with him.

We stopped at Stratford upon Avon, and he ordered both coffee and tea. We were very comfortable here, and I mingled in the *cup of soul* some occasional relishes in my own mind of Shakespeare's birth-place, of the Jubilee at which I was in 1769, and of the fine sensations of love for my valuable spouse, who was then my bride.

He had spoken slightingly of Dyer's *Fleece,* and said the subject could not be made poetical. "How could one write poetically of serges and druggets?" And yet, he said, you would hear many people talk of "that excellent poem, *The Fleece.*" He[6] also spoke slightingly of Grainger's *Sugar Cane,* and said that Grainger did not consider how few could be interested by that subject. I mentioned the circumstance which Langton told me, of that poem, when produced in manuscript at Sir Joshua Reynolds's, making all the assembled wits laugh at a passage,

> Now, Muse, let's sing of rats,

which had *mice* originally written, rats being put in as more dignified.[7] Dr. Johnson said Percy was angry with him for laughing at the *Sugar*

---

[4] By Dr. Abel Evans.

[5] See above, 12 October 1774.

[6] The passage beginning with this word and extending down to "He said Grainger's *Tibullus,*" etc. was the occasion of one of the more important cancels in the *Life.* Boswell originally transferred it to his copy much as it stands here. But after the sheet was printed, he was persuaded by Percy to cancel a leaf and to rearrange and abridge the text so as to spare Percy and Grainger. In his second edition he restored a good deal of the omitted material.

[7] In the published version, Grainger did not introduce the rats so baldly, but alluded to them as "the whisker'd vermin race."

Cane, for he had a mind to make a great thing of Grainger's rats. He said he did not write the review of the *Sugar Cane* in *The London Chronicle* entirely, but only helped Percy, and was in jest. He said Grainger might have been made a very good poet, that he was an agreeable man, and a man who would have done one any good, but was quite void of principle. "I was told," said the Doctor, "by an officer who knew him well, that he did not think he had the moral sense." The Doctor said Grainger was very unlucky. He was for some years surgeon to a regiment. He then got a Scotch degree as physician, and set up in London. Not succeeding well there, he got an offer from Mr. _____,[8] a rich West Indian, to travel with him, or rather accompany him, for [four] years, for which he was to have £200 a year during his life. But Grainger fell in love with a wench who was in the ship, and, perhaps tired of Mr. _____, gave up his agreement, married the wench, and went to St. Christopher's and set up as a physician.[9] He wrote to Johnston, an apothecary in London, to send him out a man to compound his medicines. Johnston sent him one, with an apology for his dulness. This fellow set up as a rival to Grainger in the practice of physic, and got so much the better of him in the opinion of the people of St. Christopher's that he carried away all the business. Upon which Grainger returned to England, published his *Sugar Cane,* and soon died. He said Grainger's *Tibullus* was, he thought, very well. This was much from such a judge as Dr. Johnson. He said, "One might write *The Parsley Bed, a Poem,* or *The Cabbage Garden, a Poem,* as well as *The Fleece.*" I said, "You must then pickle your cabbage with the *sal Atticum.*" "You know," said he, "there is already *The Hop-Garden, a Poem.*[1] One could say a great deal about cabbage. The poem might begin with the advantages of civilized society over a rude state, exemplified by the Scotch, who had no cabbages till Oliver Cromwell's soldiers introduced them, and one might show how arts are introduced by conquest, as they were by the Roman arms." He seemed diverted with the fertility of his own mind.

In the chaise I had mentioned that Percy was writing of the wolf in Great Britain. Dr. Johnson ridiculed this. "Why does he not write of the bear, which we had formerly? Nay, it is said we had the beaver; or why does he not write of the grey rat?—the Hanover rat as it is called, because it is said to have come into this country about the time that the family of Hanover came. I should like to see *The History of the Grey Rat, by*

[8] Bourryau. By "West Indian" he means merely an Englishman who owned property in the West Indies.
[9] The "wench" was Daniel Mathew Burt, daughter of William Pym Burt, Chief Justice and Treasurer of St. Christopher.
[1] By Christopher Smart.

Thomas Percy, D.D., Chaplain in Ordinary to His Majesty." "I'm afraid," said I, "a court chaplain could not decently write of the grey rat." "He need not give it the name of the Hanover rat," said the Doctor.

We lay tonight at Henley, a Warwickshire village, a long range of very ordinary houses. The inn was good; we had each a bedroom.

FRIDAY 22 MARCH. After a sound sleep we got up well refreshed. Before we set out, Dr. Johnson resumed the subject of my melancholy, and was displeased with my notion of *thinking down* that malady. He said, "I have not been more shocked with anything that I have heard of a long time." "Sir," said I, "it was spirit and resolution." "Ay," said he, "but it was the spirit and resolution of a madman." I said I had been in a mistake, for I imagined that he approved of that method. While we were in the chaise driving to Birmingham to breakfast, he said, "When you have a place in the country, lay out twenty pounds a year upon a laboratory. It will be an amusement to you." I said I had last summer taken a course of chemistry. "Sir," said he, "take a course of chemistry, or a course of rope-dancing, or a course of anything to which you are inclined at the time. Contrive to have as many retreats for your mind as you can, as many things to which it can fly from itself." There was a liberal philosophy in this advice which pleased me much. I *thought* of a course of concubinage, but was afraid to mention it.

I had read yesterday in the chaise *Reflections on the Study of Divinity* by Dr. Bentham. Also a short Latin discourse on the same subject, and *De motibus Americanis*, both by the same professor.[2] I was well satisfied with them. I had bought a Minellius Horace at Oxford, and having heard Beauclerk mention Dr. Johnson's repeating "Truditur dies die,"[3] etc., one moonlight evening in London, soon after he got acquainted with him, holding by the rails, I got that ode in which the passage is by heart. By this time I had it not yet perfect. Amidst all this I had high happiness, and was warmly pious. Nothing disturbed me but a degree of unsettledness as to the consistency of concubinage, or rather occasional transient connexions with loose women, and Christian morals. I was sensible that there was a great weight of interpretation against such license. But as I did not see precisely a general doctrine for practice in that respect in the New Testament, and some Christians, even Luther, did not think it an indispensable duty to cohabit only with one woman, and my appetite that way was naturally strong and perhaps rendered stronger by encouragement,[4] I could not decide against it. I *must* venture to consult Dr. John-

---

[2] *De studiis theologicis*, 1764, and *De tumultibus* [not *De motibus*] *Americanis*, 1776. Edward Bentham died on 1 August of this year.

[3] "Day is driven on by day": *Odes*, II. xviii. 15.

[4] From his wife. See 8 March 1775.

son upon it. For he can, by his noble counsel, make my judgement clear and my resolution vigorous.

We put up at the Swan at Birmingham, breakfasted and dressed, and then walked out that I might see the town. We were first to call on Mr. Hector, the surgeon, the Doctor's old schoolfellow. He told me I should see at Mr. Hector's his sister, Mrs. Carless, a clergyman's widow, "the first woman," said he, "with whom I was in love." But he said his love for her dropped out of his head imperceptibly. He agreed with me that it was not true that a man never could be in love but once, and I think he also agreed with me that a man may be in love with several women at a time. He said Mrs. Carless and he should always have a kindness one for another. When we came to Hector's door, a very stupid maid answered. She told us her master was out, and Mrs. Carless too, and her master was in the country, but she could not tell when he was to return; in short she was a wretched receiver of his friends, and as Dr. Johnson said, "She would have behaved no better to people who might have wanted him hastily in the way of his profession." He said, "My name is Johnson; tell him I called. Will you remember the name?" She answered, "I don't hear you, Sir," or, "I don't understand you, Sir." "Blockhead," said he, "I'll write." I never heard *blockhead* applied to a woman before. However, he grew calm, and roared loud, "*Johnson*," and then she catched it.

We then called at Mr. Lloyd's, a Quaker.[5] His wife told us he was not in the house, but asked us to dine, and the Doctor accepted the invitation. He said to me, "After the uncertainty of all human things at Hector's, this invitation came very well." We walked and looked at the town, and saw ranges of good new buildings.

We talked of legitimation by subsequent marriage. Dr. Johnson thought it a bad thing, because the chastity of women being of the utmost importance, as all property depends upon it, they should not have any possibility of being restored to good character after losing it. I think he is right. Upon his principle there may at times [be] a hardship upon individuals, but the general good of society is better secured. And, after all, it is an unreasonable complaint of hardship for an individual to repine that he has not the advantage of a state different from his by social institution. A woman does not complain that her brother, who is younger than she, gets the father's estate. Why, then, should a natural son complain that a younger brother lawfully begotten gets it? The operation of law is similar in both cases. Besides, a natural child who has a brother by the same father and mother, who gets an estate, has no better claim to

---

[5] Sampson Lloyd the Third (1728–1807), with his father, Sampson the Second, one of the founders of Lloyds Bank. Their partners were John Taylor and his son John, button manufacturers.

it than if his brother and he had only the same father, from whom alone the estate descends.

Mr. Lloyd joined us in the street, and in a little we met *Friend Hector,* as he called him, who was a little man of easy, civil manners. I liked to see Dr. Johnson and him meet cordially. They went and sat at Mr. Lloyd's father's at the bank, while young Mr. Lloyd carried me to Mr. Taylor's manufactory, where I saw the best part of the process of making a gilt metal button, which I need not describe. We then went to the bank, a very neat one. Old Mr. Lloyd, a hale Quaker of seventy-seven, dined with us. Before dinner, while we called for a little at our inn, Dr. Johnson agreed with young Taylor that marriage was the best state for men in general, and that a man was a worse man in proportion as he was unfit for the married state. We had at table Mr. and Mrs. Lloyd, a sister of hers, and the old gentleman, and several most comely children of young Lloyd and his wife's. They had in all eleven.

Before dinner I had talked a little with young Lloyd of his religion, and having said that the essential part of religion was piety, a devout intercourse with the Divinity, I observed as to this that many a man was a Quaker without knowing it. Dr. Johnson had said to me as we walked that he liked individuals among the Quakers, but not the sect. I kept clear of introducing any question concerning their faith, but having asked to look at Baskerville's edition of Barclay's *Apology,* Dr. Johnson laid hold of it; and the chapter on baptism having turned up, he said, "He says there is neither precept nor practice for baptism in the Scriptures; that is false." Here he was the aggressor, and the good Quakers had the advantage, for he had read negligently and had not observed that Barclay speaks of *infant* baptism, which they calmly made him perceive. However, Lloyd was in as bad a mistake, for he argued that John the Baptist, speaking of Christ, said, *"My baptism* shall decrease, but *his* shall increase." Whereas the words are, *"I* shall decrease," * etc. Dr. Johnson afterwards insisted with me that the Quakers today wilfully misquoted Scripture, but I could not agree with him.

He answered them in a masterly manner, when they objected to the observance of days and months and years, by telling them that the Church did not superstitiously observe days merely as days, but as memorials of important facts, and that Christmas might be kept as well upon one day of the year as another. Only that there should be a stated day for commemorating the birth of our Saviour, as there is danger that what may be done upon any day will be neglected.

These Quakers were opulent people and kept a good table. They told me that in the manufacture of gilt buttons two hundred ounces of gold

* John 3. 30 ("He must increase, but I must decrease").

were consumed weekly. Mr. Hector and I went in a hackney-coach, which I remember was lined with red and white broad-striped check, which had a cleanly look, and saw Mr. Boulton's manufactory about two miles from the town.[7] Boulton seemed to be a clever, fine fellow. I regretted that I did not know mechanics well enough to comprehend the description of a machine lately invented by him, which he took great pains to show me. "I sell, Sir," said he, "what all the world desires to have—power." And indeed his machine seemed to have prodigious force in raising water. We drank tea with him and Mrs. Boulton. I was struck with the thought of a smith being a great man. Here I saw it. He had about seven hundred people at work. He was a sort of iron chieftain, and seemed to be fatherly to his tribe. A smith came to complain grievously of his landlord for seizing his goods. "Your landlord is in the right, Smith," said Boulton. "But I'll tell you what: find you a friend or neighbour who will lay down one-half of your rent, and I'll lay down the other half, and you shall have your goods again."

Mr. Hector told me several anecdotes of Dr. Johnson, which I have marked in a book of notes concerning the Doctor. I wished to be longer with him to get more, for Dr. Johnson said I might pretty well depend on what he related. I had a gloom or a weariness at Boulton's which I could not cure while I was obliged to attend to the present object.

Mr. Hector and I alighted at his house, where was Dr. Johnson with his first love, Mrs. Carless, who appeared to be an amiable woman, and had the remains of an agreeable countenance. Dr. Johnson lamented to Hector the state of their schoolfellow, the Reverend Mr. Charles Congreve, who now lived in London, quite as a valetudinarian, afraid to go into any house but his own, took a short airing every day in his post-chaise, had an old woman whom he called cousin who lived with him and jogged his elbow when his glass had stood too long empty, and encouraged him in drinking, in which he was very willing to be encouraged; not that he got drunk, for he was a very pious man, but was always muddy; that he confessed to one bottle of port every day and he probably drank more. That he was quite unsocial; his conversation was monosyllabical; and when Dr. Johnson asked what a clock[8] it was, this signal of his departure had so pleasing an effect on Congreve that he sprung up to look at his watch, like a greyhound bounding at a hare. When the Doctor took leave of Hector, he said, "Don't grow like Congreve, nor let me grow like him when you are near me."

When he again talked of Mrs. Carless tonight, he seemed to have had

[7] It was during this year that Matthew Boulton and James Watt had first begun to manufacture steam-engines commercially at "Soho," as the factory was called.
[8] A Scotticism.

his affection revived, for he said to this purpose: "If I had married her, it might have been as happy for me." "I suppose," said I, "there are fifty women with whom a man may be as happy as with any one in particular." "Ay, fifty thousand," said he. I doubted if he was right. I have a strong imagination that I could not have been so happy in marriage with any other woman as with my dear wife. I cannot tell why, so as to give any rational explanation to others. I only know or fancy that there are qualities and *compositions of qualities* (to talk in musical metaphor) which in the course of our lives appear to me in her that please me more than what I have perceived in any other woman, and which I cannot separate from her identity.

I wished to have stayed at Birmingham tonight, but Dr. Johnson would go forward to Lichfield. We set off I think about eight. The road was not very good, and the night not very clear, so this portion of our travelling was dull. We were long silent in the chaise. When we came within the focus of the Lichfield lamps, "Now," said he, "we are getting out of a state of death." His words were to that effect. We put up at the Three Crowns, none of the capital inns, but a good old-fashioned one kept by Mr. Wilkins in [Bread-market Street], the very next house to Dr. Johnson's, in which he was born and brought up. We had a little comfortable supper, I drank excellent Lichfield ale, which made me drowsy, and we had a tolerable two-bedded room.

SATURDAY 23 MARCH. (I am now writing Saturday 6 April.) After breakfast Dr. Johnson conducted me to Mrs. Lucy Porter's, his daughter-in-law, that is to say, Mrs. Johnson's daughter. She was a good maiden lady with much simplicity of manner. She had never been in London. She had a fortune of £10,000, and had laid out three in building a comfortable house and buying a piece of garden ground. We saw her brother, a merchant, who had lived some time at Leghorn.[9]

We then called on Mr. Peter Garrick, the elder brother of Roscius. His brother's letter announcing our coming to Lichfield had reached him this morning. He was engaged to dinner but asked us to tea in the afternoon, to take beds at his house, which the Doctor refused though I own I wished it, and to dine next day, which we accepted. The Doctor went to call on some friends. Mr. Garrick obligingly walked with me about the town. He said he doubted if his brother would be happy after quitting

[9] Lucy Porter (1715–1786), only daughter of Johnson's wife, Elizabeth Jervis, by her first husband, Harry Porter, had lived for many years with Johnson's mother (d. 1759). She died unmarried. Her fortune was inherited from her elder brother, Captain Jervis Henry Porter, R.N. The younger brother, Joseph, had settled in Leghorn by 1759 and died there in 1783, unmarried, leaving his fortune also to his sister.

the stage, for he had not little resources for amusement. He told me his brother and Quin were once at Chatsworth.[1] His brother said, "Mr. Quin, you must see the chapel." Quin grumbled, as having no mind to it, but went. Garrick took him into the gallery of the superb kitchen, from whence he could look down to cooks busy roasting and boiling and making grand preparations for dinner. "Ay, David," said Quin, "this *is* a chapel. The Lord be praised." He was literally one whose GOD was his belly. Mr. Garrick pleased me by his resemblance to his brother David, and at the same time by a calmness and tranquillity. He was David with a sourdine: the same instrument, but not so loud or sharp. I will not, however, hold him to be quite the same instrument, though Dr. Johnson seemed to think that we could not tell but if Peter had cultivated all the arts of gaiety as David has done, he might have been as brisk and lively. We walked in the garden of Mr. Docksey, who is married to a sister of the Garricks. I saw her, and she too had a strong family likeness.

At the inn Dr. Johnson and I dined and had with us Mr. [Harry] Jackson, an old schoolfellow of his, whom he treated with much kindness, though he seemed to be a low man, dull and untaught. He had coarse clothes, I think a greyish brown coat and black waistcoat, greasy leather breeches, a yellowish uncurled wig, and a countenance ruddy with drinking, as I supposed. It seems he had tried to be a cutler at Birmingham but had not succeeded, and now he lived poorly at home and was upon some scheme of dressing leather in a better way than usual, to his indistinct account of which Dr. Johnson listened with patient indulgence, that he might advise him.[2] He drank only ale. I never saw better than at Lichfield, brewed by our host, who had been a publican forty years. I drank here too for the first time oat ale, and saw oatcakes, soft like Yorkshire ones of wheat flour, at breakfast. It was pleasant to find *the food of horses* so much used in Dr. Johnson's own town.[3] He praised his town, said that they were the most sober, decent people of any town in England, the genteelest in proportion to their wealth, and spoke the purest English. I doubted a little as to this, for I thought they had provincial sounds, as *there* pronounced like *fear* or rather *feear*, instead of like *fair*. Also *once* pronounced *woonss*, instead of *wunss*; and I have heard Garrick imitate Dr. Johnson in pronouncing, "Who's for *poonch?*" (instead of punch).

There are no manufactures at Lichfield but two very strange ones

---

[1] The seat of the Dukes of Devonshire.

[2] At Ullinish Johnson had revealed his knowledge of tanning (*Hebrides,* 23 September 1773).

[3] An allusion to the famous definition of oats in Johnson's *Dictionary:* "A grain, which in England is generally given to horses, but in Scotland supports the people."

for so inland a place, sail-cloth and streamers for ships, and these very limited; and saddle-cloths, which is a more suitable manufacture for the situation. I observed a good deal of sheepskins dressing. I said to Dr. Johnson, "You're an idle set of people." "Sir," said he, "we are a city of philosophers. We work with our heads, not with our hands. We make the boobies of Birmingham work for us." I think that was his jocular expression.

There was here at present a company of players. Dr. Johnson said forty years ago he had been in love with an actress here, Mrs. Emmet, who acted Flora in *Hob in the Well*.[4] Mr. Stanton sent in his compliments and that he would be glad to wait on us.[5] I liked this. He was a plain, decent man and thanked Dr. Johnson for having got him moderate terms once at Ashbourne from Dr. Taylor. Garrick was soon introduced. "Garrick's conversation," said Dr. Johnson, "is gay and grotesque. It is a dish of all sorts, but all good things. There is no solid meat in it. There is a want of sentiment, not but that he has sentiment sometimes, and sentiment, too, very powerful and very pleasing; but it has not its full proportion in his conversation."

We drank coffee and tea at Mr. Peter Garrick's, where was a Miss Aston, an elderly maiden lady. I had seen in the forenoon with Mr. Garrick in the house of Mr. Newton, brother to the Bishop of Bristol, a fine portrait of Mr. David Garrick by Dance, and some East Indian curiosities; and this afternoon I saw with Dr. Johnson the museum of Mr. Greene, an apothecary, a wonderful collection to be made by a man like him in a country town. He had his curiosities neatly arranged, with their names printed at his own little press, and he had at the top of the first flat of his staircase a board with the contributors marked in gold letters. He had also a printed catalogue, which I bought at the bookseller's. He was a bustling, good-humoured little man. He said Dr. Johnson said he should as soon have thought of building a man of war as getting together such a museum. He drank a glass of wine with us at the inn in the evening.

I had yesterday talked of Dr. Boswell's museum, and Dr. Johnson asked why he quitted practice. I said because his whimsical change of religion had made people distrustful of him as a physician, which I thought unreasonable, as religion was unconnected with medical skill. Dr. Johnson said it was not unreasonable, for when people see a man absurd in what they understand, they may conclude the same of him in what they do not understand. If a physician were to take to eating of horseflesh, nobody would employ him, though one may eat horseflesh and be a very skilful physician. He admitted that if a man were educated in an absurd

---

[4] An adaptation of Colley Cibber's *Hob: or the Country Wake.*
[5] Samuel Stanton, manager of the company of travelling comedians.

religion, his continuing to profess it would not hurt him as a change to it would.

He this day, when we were at Peter Garrick's, as well as on the road to Oxford, attacked the French nation. Said that the great there lived very magnificently, but the rest miserably. That there was no happy middle station as in England. That the shops of Paris were mean, the meat in the markets such as would be sent to a gaol in England; and Mr. Thrale had justly observed that the French cookery was forced upon them by necessity, for they could not eat their meat unless they added some taste to it. He said they were an indelicate people, would spit in any place, that at Madame de Boccage's the footman lifted sugar with his fingers and put [it] into his coffee. He was going to have put it aside, but hearing it was made on purpose for him, he e'en tasted Tom's fingers. She would make tea *à l'anglaise*. The spout of the pot did not pour freely. She bid the footman blow into it. He said France was worse than Scotland in everything but climate. Nature had done more for them, but they had done less for themselves than the Scotch had done.

This evening, I think, I talked to him of Dr. Boswell's going to bawdy-houses and talking as if the Christian religion had not prescribed any fixed rule for intercourse between the sexes. He said, "Sir, there is no trusting to that crazy piety." I was humbled by this strong saying. After dinner I had visited his house.⁹ A beautiful, gentle, sweet maid showed it. In one of the garret rooms I kissed her, and she curtsied. I was charmed with her for the moment as with a rose or some pleasing object which makes a slight but very vivid impression.

SUNDAY 24 MARCH. We breakfasted with Mrs. Cobb, a widow lady, who lived in a sweet old sequestered place close by the town called the *Friary*, having been formerly a religious house. She had living with her Miss Adey, her niece. She was a sensible, well-bred woman, and Miss Adey was very well. They were great admirers of Dr. Johnson. They entertained us with the absurd forwardness of Twiss, the traveller, who had been some days at Lichfield. Miss Adey and I and Greene, the apothecary, who called there, went to the Cathedral. Dr. Johnson went to [St. Mary's Church] with Mrs. Cobb. I was much pleased with the Cathedral service here, having never heard the music so solemn and so accordant with the words. I

⁹ The manuscript of the *Life* adds the following: "I went and viewed the house in which my illustrious friend was born and which remained his own property as long as he lived. Mr. Hinckesman, the tenant of it, obligingly allowed me to go through it. It was a good large house; and an engraved view of it with the adjacent buildings is to be seen in *The Gentleman's Magazine* for [February 1785]." A deleted note in the margin reads: "Qu. Shall I get the plate and have it here?" He apparently did not get the plate, and for this or some other reason the paragraph was omitted from the *Life*. The plate is reproduced in this volume, following p. 134.

was quite elevated, but sensual connexions with women, particularly with the lady with whom I had been twice lately in London, came across me. I thought thus: "These are Asiatic satisfactions, quite consistent with devotion and with a fervent attachment to my valuable spouse." Mr. _____ preached on these words, "Be steadfast and immovable," [7] etc., and admirably represented the bad effects of relapsing into vice after a course of holy living. This struck me, "for," thought I, "what vice am I ever inclined to but sensual indulgence?" However, my former soothing sophistry returned. I walked with Miss Adey and Miss Docksey, the only child of the sister of the Garricks, in Mr. Docksey's garden. He joined us for a little, and told me he would be glad to see me at his house.

Dr. Johnson, Mr. Porter, and I dined at Mr. Peter Garrick's quite comfortably. The Doctor and I went to the Cathedral in the afternoon. It was grand to see him at worship in the Cathedral of his native city. Mr. Seward,[8] Canon-Residentiary, had asked me as a stranger to dine with him. He now asked Dr. Johnson and me, whom by this time he knew, to sup with him. I returned to Peter Garrick's to coffee and tea while Dr. Johnson went to visit Miss Aston. Mr. Porter was with us. Peter got into a livelier humour than usual, and told many little anecdotes of his brother's going on the stage, and of Dr. Johnson. He was quite a London *narrateur,* with that earnestness and mimicry which we often find in the wits of the metropolis. Here I wrote to my dear wife, and was quite at home.

Porter and I went to Mr. Seward's at the Bishop's Palace between eight and nine, and found that Dr. Johnson had drank tea and been all afternoon since church there, the weather, being a little cold and rainy, having kept him from going to Miss Aston's. Mr. Seward was a very becoming churchman, had travelled with Lord Charles Fitzroy, this Duke of Grafton's uncle, who died abroad, had Lady Burlington for his patroness, and had written verses in Dodsley's *Collection.* Mrs. Seward was a decent old woman, the daughter of Mr. Hunter, the schoolmaster who taught Dr. Johnson. Miss Seward was rather a pretty woman.[9] She had bright eyes but I thought a

[7] 1 Corinthians 15. 58.

[8] Boswell spelled the name Seyward, probably by analogy with Seymour. The regular English pronunciation of Seward is Seé-wuhd.

[9] This is Boswell's first meeting with Anna Seward, "the swan of Lichfield," an esteemed poetess and indefatigable writer of letters, which Walter Scott had to publish as the price of the flattery which he had gratefully received from her in the early days of his fame. Miss Seward furnished Boswell with anecdotes for the *Life,* but her constitutional inaccuracy and her hatred of Johnson vitiated nearly everything she ever wrote concerning him. When Boswell in the *Corrections and Additions* to his first edition pointed out some of her mistakes, an unseemly literary squabble ensued. What made his later severity worse is that, as we now know, he once made ardent advances to her.

bad mouth. I thought one might make an epigram in the old style of conceit, and compare her eyes and mouth to lights placed at the mouth of a coal-pit. Dr. Johnson had jocularly proposed to me to write a prologue to be spoken before the play on Monday, which we were to attend: "A Prologue by James Boswell, Esq., from the Hebrides." I really did think of writing one after he gave the hint. I was for "Prologue spoken before Dr. Johnson at Lichfield," like, "Prologue before the Duke of York" in Charles II's time. Much might be said of what Lichfield had done for Shakespeare by Johnson and Garrick. But I saw he was averse to it.

We were easy and cheerful at Seward's, but I do not recollect our conversation. He gave me an observation upon the strata of earth in volcanoes, which he himself had made, and which showed Brydone's anti-Mosaic flippancy to be quite erroneous.[1] Dr. Johnson had said before at dinner at Oxford that it would be strange if all the accumulated evidence of the history of the world should be overcome by an uncertain remark such as that of Brydone. I must get Mr. Seward to send me his observation in writing.

MONDAY 25 MARCH. This morning when I was pressing Dr. Johnson closely with some question concerning himself, he rebuked me smartly, and said that this questioning was not the conversation among gentlemen; that it was assuming a superiority; that a man might not wish to have parts of his former life brought under his view; that he was shocked yesterday and saw Peter Garrick was shocked when I asked if his brother was not bred to the wine trade.[2] That in their brother's state of splendour, they did not like to have his original state recalled; that nobody questioned people as I did. How should I like to have people ask me what estate my father had, and such questions? I acknowledged my fault, and that it was too much familiarity.

We breakfasted at Mrs. Porter's. We had sent an express to Dr. Taylor, who wrote in return that his chaise should come for us on Monday. While we were at breakfast, Dr. Johnson received a letter which seemed to agitate him much. When he had read it, he said, "One of the most dreadful things that has happened in my time." The phrase, *my time*, like the word *age*, is usually understood to apply to something public or general. I figured something like an assassination of the King, like a Gunpowder Plot car-

[1] Patrick Brydone had remarked in his *Tour through Sicily and Malta* that Mount Etna could not be so young as Moses makes the world. Seward had concluded from observation that it was impossible to ascertain the age of a volcano by studying its strata.

[2] Early in life David Garrick had been sent to Lisbon to learn the wine trade from his uncle David. He soon returned to England, where he continued in the trade until he was twenty-five, though with little interest in it.

ried into execution, or like another Fire of London. When asked, "What is it, Sir?" he answered, "Mr. Thrale has lost his only son." [3] This was to be sure a very great affliction to Mr. and Mrs. Thrale, and which their friends must consider as an event of sorrowful magnitude. But from the manner in which the intelligence of it was communicated, it appeared for the moment to be comparatively small. I was soon affected with sincere concern, and was curious to see how Dr. Johnson would feel. He said, "This is such a total _____ [4] to their family as if they were sold into captivity." I said Mr. Thrale had daughters to inherit his wealth. "Daughters!" said he, "he'll no more value his daughters than—" I was going to speak. "Sir," said he, "don't you know how you yourself think? Sir, he wishes to propagate his name." In short I saw masculine succession strong in the Doctor's mind. I said it was lucky he was not present. "It is lucky for me," said he. "People in distress never think that you feel enough." "And," said I, "they'll have the hope of seeing you, which will be a relief in the mean time, and when you get to them, the pain will be so far abated that they will be capable of being consoled by you, which in the first violence of it, I believe, would not be the case." "No, Sir," said he, "violent pain of mind, as of body, *must* be severely felt." I said I had not much *feeling* of another's distress, as some people have or pretend to have, but I have this: that I would do all I could to relieve them. He said it was affectation to pretend to feel another's affliction as much as they themselves, as if one should pretend to feel equal pain with a friend while his leg is cutting off; but I had expressed the true effect of concern. He said he would have gone to the extremity of the earth (I think these were his words) to have preserved this boy.

He was soon quite calm. The letter was from Mr. Thrale's clerk, and bore,[5] "I need not say how much they wish to see you in London." He said, "We shall hasten back from Taylor's."

Mrs. Porter told me a good deal about Dr. Johnson. Mrs. Adey, mother to Mrs. Cobb's niece, came on a visit, and while he was in the garden, we talked of him. It delighted me to find him *beloved* by those who knew him best in his native city. These two ladies were of opinion that he would have made an excellent physician and a still better counsellor; that his gestures would not have been so proper for the pulpit. I went and saw Greene's museum better.

Dr. Johnson went to Stowe Hill, just by the town, to dine with Mrs.

[3] Harry Thrale, nine years old, had died 23 March 1776.
[4] "Extinction": supplied from the *Life*.
[5] "Mentioned" is written as an alternative above the line. "Bore" in Boswell's sense is legal, and he probably suspected it of being a Scotticism.

Gastrell, sister to Miss Aston. From a strange want of facility or easy freedom among his friends, he did not ask me to go with him, but left me to
shift for myself. This was a double defect, first of ease as to his friends,
and then of attention to me. However, Mrs. Gastrell had asked after me,
for I received a card in the Doctor's handwriting to come and dine with
her, which I did. She and her sister were substantial old women. Each had
a good house and ground about it, Miss Aston having the property of
both. I was glad I did not know till afterwards that Mrs. Gastrell's husband was the clergyman at Stratford upon Avon who cut down Shakespeare's mulberry tree, and Dr. Johnson told me he did it to vex his
parishioners, who had differed with him.⁶ This was detestable. However,
Mrs. Gastrell appeared to me as a good, chatty, hospitable lady. She and
her sister spoke of Dr. Johnson's *goodness,* as Mrs. Adey and Miss Porter
had done, so that I could not help thinking, how different is the notion of
him here from that of many people. Their brother-in-law, Mr. Walmesley,
had been his great friend. Here he wrote to Mrs. Thrale. I would give a
good deal for the letter. We drank coffee and tea. He observed of Lord
Bute, "It was said of Augustus that it would have been better for Rome
that he had never been born, or had never died. So it would have been
better for this nation if Lord Bute had never been Minister, or had never
resigned."

We went to the theatre in the Town Hall, and saw *Theodosius* with
the *Jubilee.*⁷ It was curious to see him in the front of the pit. The scenes
and dresses were very, nay were wonderfully, good. A Mr. Penn was a better actor or as good as any in London but Garrick, and there was really
a good set of performers upon the whole. I fell in love with Mrs. Owen,
who played Athenais, a beauty very like Mrs. Stuart, but larger. I however transferred my fondness to Miss Stanton in the *Jubilee,* who sung
Sweet Willy O enchantingly. She was not a beauty, but had a genteel figure, a youthful, gay, and innocent face, and something of a cheerful light
in her eyes that enlivened one and made one love her so as to cry, "My
dear little creature." I know not if I have expressed my own sprightly sensation. There was a very good audience, and it was very pleasant to me
that not one person there knew me more than for a day or two, and very
few of those. I was quite easy, and well entertained.

Yesterday morning as we walked to Mrs. Cobb's, Dr. Johnson resumed
his conversation at Birmingham upon marriage. I have omitted the most

⁶ In a note to the *Life,* Boswell gave a reference to Malone's edition of Shakespeare,
where Gastrell is described as an ill-natured man, who had destroyed the mulberry
tree in order to save himself the trouble of showing it to visitors.
⁷ By, respectively, Nathaniel Lee and David Garrick.

of it in its place. I now recollect that he said a man stood much more in need of marriage than a woman, for he could do much less to supply himself with domestic comforts, and he often wondered at women marrying, when an unmarried woman has so much more freedom and so much more attention paid her than one who is married. He said yesterday morning, "I did not mention the strong reason, the mechanical reason." "Why," said I, "that is a strong one. But imagination makes it much more important than it is in reality. It is," said I, "a delusion in us as well as in women." "Yes, Sir," said he, "and a delusion that is always beginning again." This was admirably observed. I said I imagined there was more evil than good produced by that appetite. He said, "I don't think so." I must hear him more fully upon this.

Mr. Seward asked us to go home and sup with him. I said our inn was in his way, and he must not pass our door. He agreed to be our guest, and we had also Mr. Pearson, a curate here, a modest, well-behaved young man much esteemed by Mrs. Porter. They sat with us till it struck one. I remember none of our conversation, though it was agreeable enough at the time. I must however remark that Mr. Seward said to me, "Whenever you return to Lichfield, my doors shall be oiled to receive you, and I hope you'll take a bed at my house." "Sir," said Dr. Johnson, "there is no house which he enters into which they will not gladly receive him again." He is essentially good to me. Yet I offended him again tonight, for, having a copy of the *Johnsoniana* in my pocket, I took it out, and showed his head prefixed, very ill done indeed. He said I should never speak of a man in his own presence. No doubt it is indelicate. He and I sat till about two.

TUESDAY 26 MARCH. (I am now writing in London on Monday April 8.) We breakfasted at Mrs. Porter's, where was Mr. Pearson. I said that last night at the play, while I was gay and merry, I checked myself sometimes, and thought, "This is wrong when poor Mr. and Mrs. Thrale are in such distress." Dr. Johnson said I was wrong. "Twenty years hence," said he, "Mr. and Mrs. Thrale will not be severely pained from the death of their son. Distance of place as well as distance of time lessens distress. I would not have you gay in the presence of the distressed, as it would shock them, but you may be gay at a distance. Pain," said he, "for the loss of a friend or of a relation whom we love, is occasioned by the want which we feel. In time the vacuity is filled with something else, or sometimes the vacuity closes up of itself." He said Mrs. Thrale did not like Baretti, nor Baretti her. But he was the best teacher of Italian that she could have for her daughter, therefore she kept him in the house. Baretti was well entertained and well paid, therefore he stayed in the house. He lived there as at an inn. I suppose he meant, gave value for what he got, and did not mind whether the landlady liked him or no.

At Oxford I censured Baretti's dialogues between a cock and hens to Dr. Johnson.[8] He agreed with me, and said, "Nothing odd will do long. *Tristram Shandy* did not last." I at the same time expressed a desire to know Mrs. Rudd, as a woman of extraordinary address and insinuation. "Sir," said he, "never believe extraordinary characters which you hear of people. Depend upon it, they are exaggerated. You do not see one man shoot a great deal higher than another." I instanced Burke. He was going to controvert a little, but took himself and said, "Yes, Burke *is* an extraordinary man. His stream of mind is perpetual." I read at Mrs. Porter's verses to Dr. Johnson by a Mr. Maurice of University College, Oxford, in manuscript.[9] She was forbidden to give a copy of them. I may perhaps get them from the author.

We set out after breakfast in (I am now writing in London, Tuesday 9 April) goodly style, in Dr. Taylor's large post-chaise drawn by four stout plump horses, and driven by two jolly postilions. When I described this to our Solicitor-General Murray, he approved much of that fullness of Taylor's, and said that many people were narrow and scanty in their style. I said, "Let a man have such a plan of living as he can execute completely. Let him not draw an outline wider than he can fill up. We have in Scotland many skeletons of show and high living." We had an excellent drive to Ashbourne, and found Dr. Taylor quite at his ease in a house at the end of Ashbourne, to which he has built an octagon room, ten feet each lozenge or division, stuccoed and gilded. He has behind his house some pretty ground, a river, deer, horses, and cows. He has £1,000 a year in the church, and I understood more of land-rent. He is an excellent Justice of Peace, and has a considerable political interest, which he gives to the Devonshire family. He is like the father or sovereign of Ashbourne. He last winter gave away £200 among its inhabitants who were in want of assistance. He keeps a good deal of land in his own hand, breeds horses and remarkable large cattle and game fowls. He has no wit, but, as Dr. Johnson observed, a very strong understanding. His second wife was an unreasonable woman, and they have been parted many years. This was the only circumstance about him which was not agreeable to contemplate. He had an upper servant in a kind of purple dress and large white wig, like the butler of a bishop. Peters was his name. We dined well, and he and I drank a bottle of port.

[8] The dialogues, written in Italian and English, comprised a book entitled *Easy Phraseology for the Use of Young Ladies who Intend to Learn the Colloquial Part of the Italian Language,* 1775, and were designed to be light and fanciful.
[9] They were later printed in Thomas Maurice's *Poems and Miscellaneous Pieces,* 1779. In this same volume was published a translation of the *Oedipus Tyrannus* of Sophocles, with a Preface by Johnson.

Dr. Johnson told him of Congreve, as he had done Hector, and said, "There is nothing of which an old man should be more aware than putting himself to nurse." Taylor commended much Dr. Butter, physician at Derby, and said that he fought many battles for him, as many people in the country disliked him.[1] "But," said Dr. Johnson, "you should consider that by every one of your victories Butter is a loser, for every man of whom you get the better will be very angry, and will resolve not to employ him. Whereas if people get the better of you in argument about him, they'll think, 'We'll send for Butter nevertheless.' " This was a remark deep and sure in human nature.

Dr. Johnson went and paid a visit in the town. Dr. Taylor and I were very companionable. He is a prebendary of Westminster. I shall visit him there. I was pleased with his manly, plain English character. He said Dr. Johnson was a wonderful man. He said they were to talk together of some difficulties as to the title-deeds of an estate which he had bought. We had coffee and tea and supper, all suitable to the substantial style of the Doctor's living. He did not seem to be much of a literary man. He got into story-telling now and then. He went to bed early, and Dr. Johnson and I sat up till about twelve.

WEDNESDAY 27 MARCH. Mr. Flint, Dr. Taylor's clerk, whose wife (who had died a little before this time) was a relation of Dr. Johnson's, walked with me, and showed me Ashbourne, which like Lichfield is a place of hardly any manufacture. The church is one of the best in England belonging to a country town. Flint dined with us, and after dinner came in two farmers, Mr. ——— and Mr. ———. I had liked the country in the forenoon. But by some association of ideas which I cannot analyse, the appearance of these men brought on a fit of the *English malady* [2] upon me, and to live in the country seemed dismal. Taylor has many pictures which he believes are originals and were bought by him very cheap. I was wondering too implicitly, but Dr. Johnson, when we were alone, bid me not take all this for granted, for Sir Joshua Reynolds did not think that Taylor had such great bargains.

After dinner Dr. Johnson talked of some person who had attained to the state of the philosophical wise man, that is, to have no want of anything. "Then," said I, "the savage is a wise man." "Sir," said he, "I do not mean simply being without, but not having a want." I maintained it was

[1] William Butter, M.D., a Scotsman, was known for his treatises on hooping-cough and puerperal fevers.
[2] Probably an allusion to Dr. George Cheyne's book of this title, although melancholy had long been supposed, as Boswell wrote in *The Hypochondriack*, "almost universal" in England.

better to have fine clothes, for instance, than not to want them.[3] "No, Sir," said he, "fine clothes are only good as they supply the want of other means of having respect. Was Charles the 12, think you, less respected in his coarse blue coat and black neckcloth?[4] And you find the King of Prussia dresses plain because the dignity of his character is sufficient." Here I again brought myself into a scrape, for I heedlessly said, "Would not *you*, Sir, be the better of velvet and embroidery?" "Sir," said he, "you put an end to an argument when you introduce a man himself. Have you no better manners? That *you* want." I tried to apologize by saying, what was strictly true, that I mentioned him as an instance of one who wanted as little as anybody whom I knew. He went out of the room for a little. Taylor said I was wrong, and that he saw what was coming.

Dr. Johnson was in a hurry to see Mr. Thrale's family, so we set out in a post-chaise after tea. At Derby I called on Dr. and Mrs. Butter. The Doctor was in a violent passion that the Scotch Militia Bill was thrown out, and was for breaking the Union. "What Scotsman," said he, "has been made a peer since the Union?" This struck me somewhat. As to the militia, Dr. Johnson had reasoned strongly against it. "I am glad," said he, "that Parliament has had the spirit to throw it out. You wanted to take advantage of the timidity of our scoundrels" (meaning the Ministry).

We got at night to _____.[5] He had with him upon this jaunt a volume of *Il Palmerino d'Inghilterra*, a romance praised by Cervantes.[6] But Dr. Johnson did not like it much. He read it for the language, by way of preparation for Italy. He made a very solid defence of his choice of Cocker's *Arithmetic* on his journey to the Hebrides, "For," said he, "a book of science is inexhaustible, and therefore when a man carries but one book with him, it should be a book of science."[7]

THURSDAY 28 MARCH. We journeyed on very well. I talked of Sheridan's saying and persisting to say that Dr. Johnson had a black heart because Dr. Johnson had said, "If they have given him a pension, it is time for me to give up mine."[8] He said Macpherson had told this to Sheridan, for there were none present but he and Mr. and Mrs. Strahan, at whose house it was said. But that the half of what passed only was told, for he added, "I am glad he has got a pension, for he is a very good man." And he said now to me, "I'll tell Sheridan so when I see him. But supposing

[3] The *Life* reads, less ambiguously, "than not to feel the want of them."
[4] He was so dressed at his meeting with the King of Poland.
[5] Loughborough: supplied from the *Life*.
[6] This work, which is attributed to Francisco de Moraes, is praised in *Don Quixote*, I. vi.
[7] See above, 10 April 1775.
[8] See above, 7 April 1775.

I had not added this, how absurd is it in a man to load the saying with a black heart. It accused him of nothing. It was what everybody will at a time say of everybody in a fit of frowardness or bad humour." I said Sheridan complained of the ingratitude of General Fraser and Mr. Wedderburn. "Why, Sir," said Dr. Johnson, "a man is very apt to complain of the ingratitude of those who get far above him. A man when he gets into a higher sphere, into other habits of life, cannot keep up all his former connexions. Then, Sir, one who knew him formerly upon a level with himself may think that he ought still to be treated as on a level, which cannot be; and an acquaintance in a former situation may bring out things which it would be very disagreeable to have mentioned before higher company, even though perhaps everybody knows of them." He put this subject in a new light to me, and showed me that a man must not be condemned too hastily for being distant to former acquaintances, even though he may have been obliged to them. Yet a *proper* attention is to be shown, if they will be satisfied with it. But there is the difficulty. There are many people who have done me favours whom I should not wish to have at my table with Lord Mountstuart, or to accost me familiarly at an elegant rout in London, though I would do them a kindness if it were in my power.

I read upon this jaunt *Medicina Gymnastica* by Fuller, which pleased me exceedingly, and I resolved to follow his precepts.[9] We got at night to St. Albans. It was a cold inn, and we were ill served. The rattling of the chaise today prevented me from hearing Dr. Johnson talk. I told him so. "Then," said he, "you may go hang yourself." It is strange when such a sally bursts from him.

FRIDAY 29 MARCH. Yesterday, at Leicester I think, we saw Dr. James's death in the newspapers.[1] I thought the death of an old schoolfellow, and one with whom he had lived a good deal afterwards, would have affected Dr. Johnson much. However, he only said, "Ah, poor Jamie." Afterwards indeed in the chaise he said with more tenderness, "Since I set out on this jaunt I have lost an old friend and a young one: Dr. James and poor Harry" (meaning Mr. Thrale's son).

This morning we breakfasted at Barnet and were in excellent good humour. He said, "I have not brought my mind to any solid settling about apparitions. John Wesley put a story into my hands which he firmly believes happened, lately. I'll show you it."[2]

---

[9] Francis Fuller's book (1704; ninth edition, 1777) advocated exercise and chafing (massage) in the treatment of several diseases.
[1] Dr. Robert James had died on 23 March. He had been Johnson's schoolfellow at Lichfield Grammar School.
[2] At this point in the manuscript of the *Life* there are three sentences which have

I consulted with him about pushing my Lord Mountstuart to get something for me. He was of opinion that £200 a year would be of more advantage to me now than much more some years hence, and he said it was not difficult to get that if a man had interest. Garrick got it for his brother Peter, a sinecure in the Customs. I was inspirited with the hopes of making myself easy soon, and making my dear wife live as she deserves to do. I was somewhat abashed when Dr. Johnson talked to me today of my skill in Latin, as I could not say I knew much of it. He bid me read Buchanan's history in Latin. I had said to him at Lichfield that I was now quite easy with him, that I should have no difficulty to tell him of any folly that I committed. He was pleased with this, but cautioned me against too much openness. "A man," said he, "should never tell tales of himself. People may appear to laugh and be entertained, but they treasure them up, and bring them out against him."

I enjoyed the luxury of the approach to London in a post-chaise with Dr. Samuel Johnson. "Sir," said I, "you said one day at General Oglethorpe's that a man is never happy for the present but when he is drunk.[8] Will you not add, or when driving quick in a post-chaise?" "No, Sir," said he, "you are driving quick *from* something or *to* something."

He talked of the melancholy to which I am subject, and said that some men, and very thinking men too, had not these vexing thoughts, but that most men had, in the degree in which they were capable of having them. He said that if I was in the country, and felt myself so distressed, I should force myself to take a book, and every time I did this I would find it the easier. He said, "I should like to stay a summer at Auchinleck if it were yours." He bid me divert melancholy by every means but drinking. I thought then of women, but no doubt he no more thought of my indulging in licentious copulation than of my stealing.

We alighted at Dilly's. He took a coach and hastened to Thrale's. I found two letters from my dear wife, one from worthy Grange, one from Temple, and one from Dempster, who was set out for Scotland. I was thus feasted. Bruce Boswell called on me, and I undertook to solicit interest to assist him in getting a ship. Charles Dilly was gone to the country. I dined with Edward; and Smith, the miniature painter from Scotland, who was going to the East Indies, was there. I drank as much as intoxicated me somewhat, and I hastened to the lady's with whom I had once been amorously connected and had lately twice renewed the connexion. So wild was my mind now that I did not perceive the least doubt as to this

---

been deleted: "He afterwards gave me a letter of introduction to Mr. Wesley that I might talk of it. I waited on him at Edinburgh. But the evidence did not satisfy [alternative *convince*] me."

[8] See above, 10 April 1775.

casual intercourse, any more than any other gratification. She was not at home, which disappointed my desires. I called at my lodgings and to my agreeable surprise found the Douglas cases lying for me as one of the counsel. I was in a kind of brutal fever, went to the Park, and was relieved by dalliance. Suspicious that the cases might have been sent to me because it was known I was out of town, I called on Maconochie, and as he was not at home, left a note for him expressing what I had felt from an apprehension of neglect, all things considered, and my agreeable disappointment that I found myself one of the counsel. I supped at Mrs. Stuart's. Her husband did not come home. Oswald and Aberdeen were there. I madly drank a bottle of claret by myself, none of them drinking with me, and this, meeting what I had taken at dinner, made me brutally feverish. So I sallied to the Park again, and again dallied. But, what was worse, as I was coming home to General Paoli's, I was picked up by a strumpet at the head of St. James's Street, who went with me to the entry to the passage from Hay Hill by Lord Shelburne's, and in my drunken venturousness, I lay with her. Oh, what a sad apprehension then seized me! I got home between three and four, or a little earlier.

SATURDAY 30 MARCH. Awaked very ill with sickness and headache; wished to conceal my illness, or rather the cause of it. Got up at ten. The General discovered it, and genteelly reproved my drunkenness as a vice which hurts the character, and gives envious people an advantage over a man of parts. Poggi, an Italian painter, was taking a picture of him. We all breakfasted together this morning on tea. The General said no man was ever promoted to an office of trust, without merit or the appearance of merit. He said the Devonshire family had been hurt in this reign by the Court, which had occasioned much mischief. That the King would willingly cover the wound with a ribbon of any colour. I went and called on Spottiswoode, who told me that my being employed in the Douglas appeal was the suggestion of Douglas himself, who said it would be a shame if I were left out.[4] This pleased me very much.

Jenny Taylor, the girl with whom I had lain last night, told me that she lived in Peter Street, Westminster. I was much afraid of having catched the venereal disorder, and went this forenoon to find her and examine her. But I could get no intelligence of her. Probably she lied as to her name and residence. Returning through the Park about three o'clock, I observed a pretty, fresh-looking girl, as I thought, standing with another. She told me her name was Nanny Smith, that she lived as a servant-maid with Mr. Williams in New Bond Street, that she was out an[5] errand. She

[4] This is misdated: see the beginning of the next entry.
[5] A Scotticism.

agreed to go with me to the One Tun, Chelsea, a house of lewd entertainment in a garden, to which the other girl directed us, and there I enjoyed her. I dined at General Paoli's and drank coffee comfortably.

I should have mentioned that yesterday afternoon coming along from Mr. Dilly's, I called at Dr. Johnson's, at his desire, to tell Mrs. Williams of his safe return, when to my surprise I found him sitting with her at tea, and I thought not in very good humour; for it seems when he went to Mr. Thrale's, the coach was at the door to carry Mrs. Thrale and Miss and Baretti to Bath.[6] This was not the attention to *Imlac* which might have been expected; and they were gone. I was glad, however, to find that the Italian expedition was to hold, for Dr. Johnson had some doubts if it would, after the loss which had happened in Mr. Thrale's family. He said indeed that this was an additional reason for it, and if he were not to be of the party, he would drive them out. But he would not advise them unless his advice was asked, lest they might suspect that he spoke for what he wished on his own account. After all, though his intimacy in Thrale's family has done him much good, I could wish that he had been independent of it. He would have had more dignity. For undoubtedly he is at times under some restraint and submits to circumstances not quite agreeable, that he may not lose that intimacy. I sat this evening about two hours, from ten till near twelve, with Sir John Pringle. Our conversation was easy and agreeable.

SUNDAY 31 MARCH. I had called last night on Douglas, and he was not at home. I found him this morning, and my cousin, Willy Douglas of Kelhead, with him. It was not till after seeing him this morning that Spottiswoode told me of his grateful propriety towards me, so I said nothing at this time. I had General Paoli's coach this forenoon. I went and heard the conclusion of high mass in the Bavarian Chapel, in a snug closet in the lower storey of the house, with a window near to the altar. I found my way into it by that curiosity and forwardness which is in my character. Dr. Johnson, in rebuking me at Lichfield, told me, "They say you're not like a Scotsman, but like an Irishman. That is from your absurdity."

I must put down his sayings as I recollect them. He said at Dr. Taylor's that Andrew Stuart's letters could not give Lord Mansfield uneasiness, for either he acted honestly, or he meant to do injustice.[7] If he acted honestly, his own consciousness would protect him. If he meant to do injustice, he would be glad to see Stuart so much vexed. That his letters were the wail-

---

[6] Hester Maria, the Thrales's eldest child, was generally called "Queeney"; she was a great favourite of Johnson's.
[7] *Letters to Lord Mansfield,* 1773, subjected Mansfield's decision in the Douglas Cause to elegantly bitter review. Stuart was agent for the Duke of Hamilton.

ings of a dog that had been licked. I *think* these were Dr. Johnson's words, and I am confirmed in this by my recollecting that I objected, "But, Sir, a dog may bite."

I called at Dilly's for a few minutes. He had done with dinner. He made me drink a glass of wine, which run in my head, as a glass will do when the stomach is empty. I called on Dr. Johnson and showed him his translation of Lobo, which Sir John Pringle had lent me. He said, "Take no notice of it," or, "Don't talk of it," or used some such expression. He seemed to think it beneath him, though it was done at six-and-twenty. I said, "Sir, your style is much improved since you translated this." "I hope so," said he, with a sort of triumphant smile.

I dined at the Hon. James Stuart's. Nobody there but his sister, Lady Augusta, and Captain Corbet of the Horse Guards, her husband. A more fruitless afternoon of conversation (if *fruitless* may be used in this sense) I never passed. But we drank hard, and about ten o'clock I went away much in liquor. I went to Douglas's, thanked him for his attention, or rather, I believe, praised it as what was due to me. Lord and Lady Hope, Lady Louisa Hope, and a Mr. Randolph were there. I behaved pretty decently. But when I got into the street, the whoring rage came upon me. I thought I would devote a night to it. I was weary at the same time that I was tumultuous. I went to Charing Cross Bagnio with a wholesome-looking, bouncing wench, stripped, and went to bed with her. But after my desires were satiated by repeated indulgence, I could not rest; so I parted from her after she had honestly delivered to me my watch and ring and handkerchief, which I should not have missed I was so drunk. I took a hackney-coach and was set down in Berkeley Square, and went home cold and disturbed and dreary and vexed, with remorse rising like a black cloud without any distinct form; for in truth my moral principle as to chastity was absolutely eclipsed for a time. I was in the miserable state of those whom the Apostle represents as working all uncleanness with greediness.[8] I thought of my valuable spouse with the highest regard and warmest affection, but had a confused notion that my corporeal connexion with whores did not interfere with my love for her. Yet I considered that I might injure my health, which there could be no doubt was an injury to her. This is an exact state of my mind at the time. It shocks me to review it.

MONDAY 1 APRIL. Awaked very ill. Called on Captain James Erskine. Found him at his house in Pall Mall Court as last year. Sat awhile with him. "When shall we dine together?" said he. I answered, "I am engaged all this week." "This day sennight, then, at Le Telier's," said he. I am pretty firm in my resolution not to dine at a tavern in London unless with Dr. Johnson. But as Erskine is my relation, employed me last year as one

[8] Ephesians 4. 19.

of his counsel, and was at present I knew not in what circumstances, I could not refuse to meet him.

I went to Duck Lane, Westminster, and found my last night's harlot by the name of Nanny Cooms, and persuaded myself that she was not infected. But whom did I see in that blackguard lane but my pretended servant-maid, Nanny Smith, in a drummer's coat by way of a morning jacket! I was abashed and mortified at my simplicity. I asked Nanny Cooms and a girl who was with her about that jade Smith. They said she had lived in the house with them three months, and they could not answer for her, for the young man who lived with her, a corporal, was now in the hospital. This made me almost sick with fear. But Nanny Cooms had last night spoken to me of a pretty fair girl who was on call. I sent for her and enjoyed her, and ===== === a kind of license I never had ====. I thought this should be the last act of this fit of debauchery.[9]

I dined at General Paoli's, and drank coffee. Then called at Langton's. Found him so domestic in his parlour that it was so dull I could not bear it, especially as there was a young blear-eyed girl, some relation of his, who lived in the house, and whom he had taught to attend with a keen affectation to what was said, and to put *sensible questions*. I came off as soon as I decently could. Either this night or on Saturday last, I believe Saturday, I called and sat awhile with Tom Davies and his wife. Their strict conjugal union secretly reproached my licentiousness. We talked much of Dr. Johnson, and Tom put me in mind that I owed the Doctor to him. He certainly did introduce me, but I owe his friendship principally to my own perseverance. I went to Mrs. Stuart's and wrote part of my journal and to my wife and Temple, till she came in. Then I supped with her. Counsellor Macdonald was with us. His *smartness* displeased me. It made my nerves start like crackers going off.

TUESDAY 2 APRIL. Was at home all the forenoon writing journal. I should have mentioned that on Sunday morning the General communicated to me, in confidence, some important intelligence concerning Corsica and himself. My mind was roused by it, though it was as yet imperfect. It recalled his high dignity to my imagination. I had last year borrowed of him twenty-nine guineas. I this year borrowed six.[1] His kindness to me, and his perpetual good sense and good temper, made me admire him more and more. I lived in his house with as much ease or more than if it

---

[9] This whole passage, from "I went to Duck Lane" to "fit of debauchery" has been scored out in a recent ink, and two or three words which Boswell wrote in a cramped hand at the bottom of a page are so thoroughly obscured as still to defy decipherment. Everything here printed is certain except for "on call" and "license," and those words conform to the discernible traces. The word printed "on" is certainly either "on" or "in."

[1] At the beginning of 1777 Boswell owed Paoli £50.

had been my own. He was glad to see me at all times, for at all times I freely tried his civility. Yet he exacted no attention from me. My breakfast was brought into my bedchamber. I might have it carried into his. I might go out when I pleased. I might dine at home when I pleased. I might come home at any hour, and go quietly to bed. Giacomo Pietro, a Corsican, the General's own servant, shaved me and dressed my wig, and Jacob, a Swiss servant, went messages for me. Then I had the General's coach whenever I had occasion for it and he had it not out, which he seldom had. The General said to me that if he thought at all well he owed it to *The Spectator,* which he had read when very young at Naples, and to Nicole.[2] It pleased me much when he told me this of *The Spectator,* because my own mind was first touched with elegant thinking by it; and I wondered to hear him speak highly of Nicole, which I supposed to be a mere casuistical, or rather scrupulous, system of morals. I should have mentioned that yesterday I called on Lord Clifford at his house in Berkeley Square and was well received by his Lordship, who was very chatty and spoke with much regard of Temple. This forenoon my friend Hoggan came and sat with me awhile. I engaged him to dine at Le Telier's on Monday.

I dined today at Sir John Pringle's, where was the celebrated circumnavigator Captain Cook and his wife, General Graeme, his lady and brother, Sir George Hume, a navy captain who had been at Mundell's School with me, but whom I had not seen for five-and-twenty years, and Lady Erskine, Sir Harry's widow, with her son Sir James, and a daughter. Cook, as Sir John had told me before, was a plain, sensible man with an uncommon attention to veracity. My metaphor was that he had a balance in his mind for truth as nice as scales for weighing a guinea. Sir John gave me an instance. It was supposed that Cook had said he had seen a nation of men like monkeys, and Lord Monboddo had been very happy with this. Sir John happened to tell Cook of this. "No," said he, "I did not say they were like monkeys. I said their faces put me in mind of monkeys." There was a distinction very fine but sufficiently perceptible.

I talked a good deal with him today, as he was very obliging and communicative. He seemed to have no desire to make people stare, and being a man of good steady moral principles, as I thought, did not try to make theories out of what he had seen to confound virtue and vice. He said Hawkesworth made in his book a general conclusion from a particular fact, and would take as a fact what they had only heard.[3] He said it was

---

[2] Pierre Nicole (1625–1695), the French Jansenist. His best-known works were the *Essais de morale,* in fourteen volumes.

[3] Hawkesworth's *Account of the Voyages . . . in the Southern Hemisphere . . . Drawn up from the Journals which were Kept by the Several Commanders, and from the Papers of Joseph Banks, Esq.* was the first work to present the sexual mores of the

not true that Mr. Banks and he had revised all the book; and in what was revised Hawkesworth would make no alteration (I think he said this too). He said that a disregard of chastity in unmarried women was by no means general at Otaheite, and he said Hawkesworth's story of an *initiation* he had no reason to believe. "Why, Sir," said I, "Hawkesworth has used your narrative as a London tavern keeper does wine. He has *brewed* it." [4] It was curious to see Cook, a grave steady man, and his wife, a decent plump Englishwoman, and think that he was preparing to sail round the world.[5]

I went from Sir John's to the Queen's Arms in St. Paul's Churchyard, and supped at the monthly meeting of the partners of *The London Magazine*. I was quite the man of consequence, full of gaiety, and relished much the conversation of *the Trade*. Being apprehensive of venereal mischief, and desirous to hasten its appearance if it was lurking about me, I drank freely, but not to intoxication. Went home with Dilly comfortably to my room at his house.

WEDNESDAY 3 APRIL. After breakfast called on Mr. Forbes, banker in Aldermanbury, cousin german to Bruce Boswell, my cousin german, who lodged with him and to whom he was very friendly. Sat awhile with him and Bruce, and talked of trying every channel of interest for a ship. I relished Forbes's conversation upon the trade of a banker; what sums had been made by it, and how a young man might by degrees get a share in a capital house. I talked of my brother David. But found that it was very difficult to get into a good banking shop as a partner, unless by having been a clerk in it. I flattered myself with a possibility of getting him in with Coutts, and resolved to go and see Coutts, who is my relation and whom I ought not to neglect, as he was formerly very hospitable to me; and yet I have not called on him, I believe, for the two last times I have been in London.[6]

South Seas for the admiration of Britons. Hawkesworth had not been on any of the South Sea voyages. He was simply a clever man of letters, who, upon Garrick's recommendation, had been appointed by the Government to revise and publish the accounts of the voyages prepared by those who had made the expeditions. His book was generally condemned for impiety, inaccuracy, and indecency; indeed, the attacks made upon it are said to have hastened his end, which occurred in the year in which the book appeared (1773).

[4] That is, mixed other ingredients with it.

[5] Cook sailed from Plymouth on 12 July of this year, on what was to be his last voyage. He was killed by a mob of natives with whom he was having trouble over a stolen boat, on the beach of Kealakekua Bay, Hawaii, 14 February 1779.

[6] James Coutts and Boswell were third cousins in their maternal lines, both being great-great-grandsons of Sir John Cochrane of Ochiltree (died c. 1707). See Appendix C, Chart V. Sir John Cochrane was father of William Cochrane of Ochiltree. His daughter Grizel married John Ker of Morieston; Grizel's daughter Margaret married

I called on Dr. Johnson; found him putting his books in order. He had gloves on, and was all dusty. He was quite in the character which Dr. Boswell drew of him: "A robust genius! born to grapple with whole libraries!"[7] I gave him an account of Captain Cook, and told him I felt, while I was with the Captain, an inclination to make the voyage. "Why, so one does," said the Doctor, "till one considers how very little one learns." I said I was certain a great part of what we are told by the travellers to the South Sea Islands must be conjecture, because they cannot know language enough to understand so much as they tell. The Doctor was of that opinion. "But," said I, "one is carried away with the thing in general, a voyage round the world." "Yes," said he, "but one is to guard against taking a thing in general."

He agreed that we should dine today at the Mitre after my return from the House of Lords, this being the day when counsel were to be heard on Duke Hamilton's petition for putting off the cause between Lord Selkirk and Douglas till his Grace should also bring forward his claim. I went to the Temple and got a decent tie-wig from Mr. Tibbs, who let me have one last year.[8] The hire is half a crown a time. I called on Mr. Bigg, _____[9] of the Inner Temple, and got information when the commons were to begin for next term. I liked to think that I was of the society *Interioris Templi*.

I should have mentioned that Captain Cook told us that Omai, whom he was to carry home, begged to have two things for himself: port wine, which he loved the best of any liquor, and gunpowder; but the Captain said he would not let him have the power of fire-arms, which he supposed he wished to have from some ambitious design.[1] He said that for some time after Omai's return home he would be a man of great consequence, as having so many wonders to tell. That he would not foresee that when he had told all he had to tell, he would sink into his former state, and then,

---

Sir John Steuart of Allanbank; Margaret's daughter Jean married John Coutts, Lord Provost of Edinburgh and father of James and Thomas Coutts. Boswell seems not to have heard that James, the brother who had been so hospitable to him in 1762–1763, had been virtually insane for some years and had been bought out by Thomas in 1775.

[7] *Boswell in Search of a Wife*, 27 August 1769. Dr. Boswell said "Herculean" rather than "robust."

[8] Boswell mistook this name. David Tibson supplied wigs to the members of the Inner Temple for more than twenty years.

[9] "Butler," perhaps with a qualifying adjective. Joseph Bigg was at this time third butler; he was made chief butler in 1788.

[1] Omai was a young Society Islander who was brought to England by Captain Tobias Furneaux in the autumn of 1774. His intelligence and manners had delighted the English upper classes, who were determined to see in him the incarnation of the contemporary ideal of the noble savage.

the Captain supposed, he would wish to go to England again ("Britannia," the Otaheite people say, as they cannot pronounce "England"), but that the Captain would take care to leave the coast before Omai had time to be dissatisfied at home.[2]

In my way to the House of Lords, I called at Lord Lisburne's. He was abroad and was to go next day to Mamhead. I left a particular card for him, which I wrote upon his table, telling him that when he returned I should be happy to pay my grateful respects to him. He was very civil to me, and is very friendly to Temple. In Waghorne's Coffee-house, Douglas's counsel and agents met. Maconochie was very cordial towards me. He introduced me to Thurlow.[3] I must try to be acquainted with him. About three the counsel were called in. Hardinge spoke most distinctly in support of a delay. The Chancellor sent down a note to know if Douglas's counsel would agree to it, provided that Duke Hamilton should come forward expeditiously.[4] They agreed. This being known, Lord Mansfield rose and made a fine speech showing that in strict justice there was no reason for a delay, but lest the Duke should think that his cause might at all be hurt by the decision here, and as some of the points pleaded for him were pleaded for Lord Selkirk, and it would be better to avoid any danger of the House's determining the same points differently between different parties, he was for an adjournment if not opposed by Mr. Douglas; and the House would judge afterwards if there was any affected delay. I was quite in the humour of admiring Lord Mansfield today.

Mr. Solicitor Murray gladly accepted of a proposal which I made him that he should go and dine with Dr. Johnson and me at the Mitre. I observed to him that the Scotch who come up to London are like galley-slaves chained together. They only coast it, and never get into the main ocean. And what is very absurd, when a Scotsman asks you to dine with him here, instead of letting you see English company, he asks at the same time a number of the very people whom you see at home. He might as well give you broth and boiled beef. Swift said, "I am not satisfied with seeing your bill of fare. Let me see your bill of company."[5] We went first and called for a few minutes on his lady in Suffolk Street. (Writing Thursday 11.) Then I went with him to the Mitre, we ordered dinner, and I went for Dr. Johnson, who soon followed me.

I kept conversation a going very well. Mentioned Mr. Solicitor's rela-

[2] Omai died within three years of his return to the South Seas.

[3] Edward Thurlow, future Lord Chancellor, as counsel for Douglas in the appeal of 1769, had reflected so severely on Andrew Stuart that a duel had resulted. He was a man of considerable parts and extraordinarily impressive appearance. "No man," said Burke, "ever was so wise as Thurlow looks."

[4] The Chancellor was Lord Bathurst.

[5] In the *Journal to Stella,* 2 September 1711.

tion, Lord Charles Hay. Dr. Johnson said he wrote something for him, and he had nothing to fear from a court martial.[6] That he suffered a (I think a great) loss when Lord Charles died, that he was a mighty pleasing man in conversation, and a reading man. I then talked of the character of a soldier. Dr. Johnson said it was high. "Those," said he, "who stand forth the foremost in danger for the community," said he, "have the respect of mankind. An officer is much more respected than any other man who has as little money. In a commercial country money will always purchase respect. But you find an officer, who has properly speaking no money, is well received and treated with much attention. A soldier's character always stands him in stead." We objected that common soldiers were worse thought of than other men in the same rank of life, such as labourers. "Why," said he, "a common soldier is commonly a very gross man, and any quality which procures respect may be overwhelmed by grossness. A man of learning may be so ridiculous or so vicious that you cannot respect him. A common soldier, too, in the first place eats more than he can pay for. But when a common soldier is civil in his quarters, his red coat procures him a degree of respect." The military character being very high in France was mentioned. I said I should think that where military men are so numerous they would be less valued as not being rare. "Nay," said the Doctor, "wherever a particular character or profession is high in the estimation of a people, those who are of it will be valued above other men. We value an Englishman highly in this country, and yet Englishmen are not rare in it."

Mr. Solicitor praised the ancient philosophers for the candour with which philosophers of different sects disputed so as never to be in bad humour one with another. Said the Doctor, "They disputed with good humour because they were not in earnest as to religion. Had the ancients been serious in their belief, they would not have represented their gods in the manner we find them in the poets. The people would not have suffered it. They disputed with good humour upon their fanciful theories because they were not interested in their truth. When a man has nothing to lose, he may be in good humour with his opponent. Accordingly you see in Lucian, the Epicurean, who argues only negatively, keeps his temper. The Stoic, who has something positive to preserve, grows angry. Being angry with one who controverts an opinion which you value is a necessary

---

[6] In censuring Lord Loudoun's dilatory tactics against the French at Halifax, Hay was said to have observed that "the General was keeping the courage of His Majesty's troops at bay, and expending the nation's wealth in making sham sieges and planting cabbages when he ought to have been fighting." For this remark he was sent back to England and court-martialed, but died in prison (1 May 1760) before the decision of the court had been made public.

consequence of the uneasiness which you feel. Every man who attacks my belief diminishes in some degree my confidence in it, and therefore makes me uneasy; and I am angry with him who makes me uneasy. Only those who believed in revelation have been very angry at having their faith called in question, because they only had something upon which they could (writing Friday 12 April) rest as matter of fact." "But," said the Solicitor, "truth will always bear an examination." "Yes," said Dr. Johnson, "but it is uneasy to be forced to defend [it]. Consider, how should you like, though conscious of your innocence, to be tried before a jury for a capital crime once a week?"

The Solicitor talked of education at great schools. Dr. Johnson said what I have marked in my journal at Aberdeen.[7] But I must here add a remark which he made at Ashbourne, that no man whatever is so grossly unfaithful as the master of a great school. He professes to teach all the boys who come to him equally, yet he does nothing but for a very few who are forward to learn; and he does not inform the relations of the rest that they are unfit for being made scholars.

I introduced today the topic which is often ignorantly urged, that the universities of England are too rich; so that learning does not flourish as it would do if those who teach had smaller salaries and depended on their assiduity for a great part of their income. Dr. Johnson said the very reverse was the case in the English universities. "For," said he, "they are not rich enough. Our fellowships are only sufficient to support a man during his studies to fit him for the world, and accordingly in general they are kept no longer than till an opportunity offers of getting away. Now and then, perhaps, there is a fellow who grows old in his college, but this is against his will, unless he be a man very indolent indeed. A hundred a year is reckoned a good fellowship, and that is no more than is necessary to keep a man decently as a scholar. We do not allow our fellows to marry, because we consider that state only as a nursery for the world. It is by being a tutor and having pupils that anything more than a livelihood is to be had. To be sure, a man who has enough without teaching will not probably teach, for we would all be idle if we could. In the same manner, a man who is to get nothing by teaching will let it alone. There was Gresham College intended as a place of instruction for London; as the professors were to read lectures gratis, they contrived to have no scholars; whereas, if they had been to be paid but sixpence a lecture,[8] they would have been emulous to have a number of 'em. Everybody will agree that it should be the interest of those who teach to have scholars; and this is

[7] *Hebrides,* 22 August 1773.
[8] This page of the journal was used directly as copy for the *Life.* In revising, Boswell added "by each scholar" at this point.

the case in our universities. That they are too rich is certainly not true, for they have nothing good enough to keep a man of eminent learning for his life. In the foreign universities, a professorship is a high thing. It is as much almost as a man can make of his learning; and therefore we find the most learned men in the universities abroad. It is not so with us. Our universities are impoverished of learning by the poverty of their provisions." He said this to me during our last jaunt, and added that he wished there were "half a dozen places of a thousand a year at Oxford to keep first-rate men of learning from quitting the University." To be sure, literature then would have a dignity and splendour at Oxford, and there would be grander living sources of instruction.

I started Maclaurin's uneasiness on account of the ridicule thrown on his father in Goldsmith's *Animated Nature,* and I regretted that there was no legal reparation to be had, when a man's deceased relation was traduced in a publication.[9] The Solicitor maintained there *should* be reparation, unless the author could justify himself by proving the fact. "No, Sir," said Dr. Johnson, "it is of so much more consequence that truth should be told than that individuals should not be made uneasy, that it is much better that the law does not restrain writing freely concerning the characters of the dead. Damages will be given to a man who is traduced in his lifetime, because he may be hurt in his worldly interest, or at least hurt in his mind. But the law does not regard that uneasiness which a man feels on having his ancestor traduced. That is too nice. Let him deny what is said, and let the matter have a fair chance by discussion. But if a man could say nothing against a character but what he can prove, history could not be written; for a great deal is known of men of which proof cannot be brought. A minister may be notoriously known to take bribes, and yet you may not be able to prove it." The Solicitor stood to it a little that the author should be obliged to show some sort of evidence, though he would not require a strict legal proof; but the Doctor firmly and resolutely opposed any legal investigation as dangerous to free discussion of the characters of mankind.

I should have mentioned that when the Doctor said one was angry at a man for controverting an opinion which one believes and values, the Solicitor said, "One rather pities him." "No, Sir," said Johnson. "To be sure when you wish a man to have that belief which you consider as an

---

[9] Goldsmith had written that the father, Colin Maclaurin (a distinguished mathematician and a professor at Edinburgh University), was likely to dislocate his jaw if he yawned, and was likely to yawn if he saw anyone else doing it—a situation full of possibilities for a man teaching undergraduates. When he threw his jaw out, he had to stand "speechless, with his mouth wide open, till his servant, from the next room, was called in to set his jaw again."

advantage, you wish well to him; but your primary consideration is your own quiet. If a madman were to come into this room with a stick in his hand, no doubt we should pity the state of his mind; but our primary consideration would be to take care of ourselves. We should knock him down first, and pity him afterwards." He said too, "A man will dispute with great good humour upon a subject in which he is not interested. I will dispute very calmly upon the probability of another man's son being hanged; but if a man pushes a dispute with me upon the probability that my own son shall be hanged, I shall certainly not be in good humour with him." I added this illustration: "If a man endeavours to convince me that my wife, whom I love very much, and in whom I have great confidence, is a disagreeable woman, and is even unfaithful to me, I shall be very angry; for he is putting me in fear of being unhappy."

The Solicitor made a very tolerable figure, was very complaisant, and repeated a pretty long passage from Cicero and justly remarked that the seeming infidelity in it as to a future state was somewhat strange considering his other writings. This was a very good meeting. The Solicitor set me down at Beauclerk's, where I found him better than last year. He had with him Sir Charles and Lady Bingham and Mr. Gibbon, and in a little, Adam Smith came. He and Gibbon went away, and the rest of us had a sort of irregular repast. Beauclerk was keenly engaged in collecting plays, both English and French, and he spoke with much relish of the pleasure of making collections.[1] He asked me to come to him on Friday evening.

THURSDAY 4 APRIL. In the forenoon I called at Mrs. Stuart's. Lord Cassillis came there. I then called on Dr. Johnson. I said it was a pity that truth was not so firm as to bid defiance to all attacks, to be shot at as much as people chose to attempt, and yet be not hurt. "Then," said he, "it would not be shot at. Nobody attempts to dispute that two and two make four. But with moral truth, passions are mixed." I dined at General Paoli's and drank tea and wrote journal all the evening. I had noted since yesterday morning a few signs of the venereal disorder, though moderate ones.[2]

FRIDAY 5 APRIL. This being Good Friday, I intended as usual to breakfast with Dr. Johnson, but in my way called on Sir John Pringle, found him in his drawing-room, and the sun beaming upon it. He talked of having visited officially last year some madhouses, and that when he

[1] The sale of his library of thirty thousand volumes in 1781, the year after his death, lasted fifty days, five of which were devoted to the collections of plays.
[2] Boswell, who was using this leaf of his journal directly as copy for the *Life*, has inked this sentence over with unusual thoroughness. "I had . . . of the venereal disorder, though . . . ones" is certain; the other words are reconcilable with the discernible traces of the original pen strokes.

asked the keepers if they gave the lunatics any medicine to try to do them good, they answered, "You know, Sir, nothing will do them good." "It is true," said he; "and I wonder that this has not been used as an argument for the reality of demoniacs, for if madness were a bodily distemper, something might be done for it by medicine." He said he had read Farmer on demoniacs but was not satisfied by him. Sir John seemed not to be quite clear in his belief upon this subject, but talked of it with a delicate gravity. He said there was no more occasion to believe the Evangelists to be inspired to have a belief in Christianity than to believe the Roman historians inspired to have a belief that Caesar reigned, and did what is recorded of him, and was killed in the way we read. He seemed to think Mahomet had a divine commission, for he converted a vast proportion of people to the belief of one GOD. I agreed with him, and said I believed both Mahomet and Confucius to be messengers of revelation. He was in an easy, communicative frame. My mind was unquiet with the thoughts of having acted immorally. Yet I was not quite clear. A man is not steady in his conviction of the truth of a principle which his warm passions are ever melting and the transgression of which gives him pain. I said to Sir John I did not see any positive precept as to the connexion between the sexes. He insisted that the rule was explicit enough, but rather avoided an argument upon it.

As I was hastening up the Strand to breakfast at the Somerset Coffee-house, before going to St. Clement's Church where Dr. Johnson goes, I met Bruce Boswell, and took him to the Somerset with me, where over chocolade we talked a little of his affairs. I then went to St. Clement's, and was so late that I would not go into the seat with Dr. Johnson, but after service was over joined him at the door of the church, and walked home to his house with him. When we had sat some time, Mr. Thrale called.

We had talked of the Romish Church. Dr. Johnson said that in the barbarous ages priests and people were equally deceived, but afterwards there were gross corruptions by the clergy, such as indulgences to priests to have concubines, and the worship of images, though not inculcated yet knowingly permitted. I mentioned the licensed stews at Rome. That he strongly censured. "Then, Sir," said I, "you would allow no fornication at all." "To be sure, Sir," said he. "I would punish it much more than is done, and so restrain it. In all countries there has been fornication, as in all countries theft; but there may be more or less of the one as well as of the other by the force of law. All men will naturally commit fornication, as all men will naturally steal." I urged the common topic that whores were necessary to prevent the violent effects of lewdness, and prevent our wives and daughters from being ravished. But he was of opinion that severe laws, regularly enforced, would be sufficient, and would pro-mote marriage. (By writing my journal so long after hearing him, my recollection of his conversation is very imperfect.)

While we sat, a packet was brought to him by a boy as from the post-office, said to have come from Lisbon, and was charged £7. 10. This was a strange thing. I advised him not to pay for it, as it could not be worth the money. He accordingly made the boy take it away, and after he was gone it was plain it was a trick (writing on Saturday 13 April), for the direction was "To Dr. Johnson in Bolt Court," and it could not possibly be known at Lisbon when this packet was sent that he was to remove from Johnson's Court. He regretted he had not stopped the boy.

Thrale bore the loss of his son with so manly a composure that it was not painful to be with him, which is much in a case of so great affliction. I introduced the intended tour of Italy which Mr. and Mrs. and Miss Thrale and Dr. Johnson were to make, and on which they were to set out early in April. At Beauclerk's on Wednesday evening it was men-tioned, and Beauclerk said that Baretti, who was to go with them, would keep them so long in the little towns of his own country that they would not have time to see Rome. I repeated this today to put them on their guard. Dr. Johnson was angry. Said he: "We do not thank Mr. Beauclerk for supposing that we are to be directed by Mr. Baretti"; and he desired Thrale to go to Jackson (the "all-knowing") and get from him a plan for seeing the most in the time that they had to travel.[3] "We must, to be sure," said he, "see Rome, Naples, Florence, and Venice, and as much more as we can." Thrale appeared to me to have some difficulty about going, and I feared that he might lay aside the design if he was not hur-ried away. I therefore pressed their setting out speedily, for I was very desirous that Dr. Johnson should see Italy and give us his grand remarks.

He said (I am not sure what day) that he did not see that he could make a book upon Italy, as so much had been said of it; but he added, "I should be glad to get £200 or £500," which was a proof that he sup-posed he *might* compose a valuable journal. Beauclerk said on Wednesday that Baretti could not go to several of the towns in Italy, as he should be hanged. "Ay," said I, "the gallows is a roadpost for his direction at several places: *Turn from this.*" But I added what Dr. Johnson told me: that it was not for crimes such as murder or robbery that he would be hanged, but for some political daring writings. Beauclerk and I had a dispute as to his killing a man in London. I said I thought it murder. Beauclerk said

[3] Richard Jackson, politician, bencher of the Inner Temple, because of his remarkable store of general information was usually styled "Omniscient Jackson." Johnson, according to Boswell's note in the *Life,* substituted "all-knowing" because "omniscient" was a *"verbum solenne,* appropriated to the Supreme Being."

he was not in the least to blame. That what he did was in self-defence, and what any of us might do. Adam Smith having just come in while we disputed, we asked his opinion. He said he thought it manslaughter, but a very brutal manslaughter.[4]

Dr. Johnson told us today that he had received a letter from a Mr. Fowke in the East Indies, whom he formerly knew very well; that he came home with a genteel fortune, was a scholar and an agreeable man, and lived very prettily in London while his wife lived.[5] That after her death he took to dissipation and gaming, and lost all he had. "One evening he lost a thousand pounds to a gentleman whose name I am sorry I have forgotten. Next morning he sent him £500, telling him it was all he had in the world. The gentleman sent it back to him, told him he would not have it, and, if Mr. Fowke had occasion for other £500, he would lend it him. Fowke resolved to go out again to the East Indies and make his fortune anew. He was appointed _____. I thought of going out with him, and had I thought then as I do now, I should have gone, but I had objections then to quitting England." BOSWELL. "I am glad you did not go. We should not have had the *Dictionary*." JOHNSON. "Yes, you would. This was about the year 1746." (I am wrong. The *Dictionary* did not come out till 1754.[6] I must get more from him about this oriental scheme.)

Beauclerk had told me of a society called the New Club where people played to a desperate extent. JOHNSON. "Depend upon it, Sir, this is mere talk. *Who* is ruined by gaming? You will not find six instances in

[4] See above, 28 March 1775, note 9. A woman of the town accosted Baretti, and he struck her. Thereupon three men attacked him, or at least threatened to do so, and he gave one of them a wound with a pocket-knife which proved mortal. In his defence he testified that the woman struck him in the genitals, causing him exquisite pain, and that only then did he strike her over the hand; that he was shoved about and repeatedly struck; that it was dark and he was near-sighted and terrified; and that after drawing his weapon (a small knife he habitually carried to pare fruit and cut his meat) he warned his assailants to keep off. Even if one discounts some of this, it is hard to see how by the most unfavourable construction his act could have been rated worse than manslaughter. The jury acquitted him after a deliberation of only a few minutes (*Gentleman's Magazine,* Oct. 1769, xxxix. 508).

[5] It was, as events later proved, Joseph Fowke who had sent the packet which Johnson had just refused. It had come from India on a ship which had called at Lisbon.

[6] Still wrong; it was 1755. But it does not appear to be possible to set up for the story as Boswell tells it a chronology that can be reconciled with the known facts. Fowke went out to India in 1736 and came home in 1752, after having been member of Council at Madras. It was not till 1770 that he returned to India, this time as a free merchant to Calcutta. The scheme in which he was to be associated with Johnson can hardly have been under active consideration so late as 1770. Probably Johnson failed to make clear that Fowke also abandoned that scheme, or was greatly delayed in realizing it.

an age. There is a strange rout made about this, whereas you have many more people ruined by adventurous trade, and yet we do not hear such an outcry about it." THRALE. "There may be few absolutely ruined, but very many are hurt in their circumstances." JOHNSON. "Yes, Sir, and so are there by other kinds of expense." (I have heard him before upon the same subject. At Oxford he said he wished he had learnt to play at cards.)

We sat till it was too late for the afternoon service. Thrale asked me if he dined. I told him no; he kept the fast strictly, and I kept it with him. So we were to go to prayers at seven, Thrale having said he came to go to church with us. Dr. Johnson ordered coffee. I slipped away to Dilly's, where I was not a little disappointed in finding no letters from my dear wife. Mindful of the Father of whom Dr. Johnson told me, who was peevish if he fasted and therefore did not fast, I had taken some soup at the King's Arms Coffee-house opposite the Exchange; and there I was accosted by Mr. _____ Wilson, son of Mr. Wilson, merchant in Kilmarnock. I own that the sudden appearance of a Kilmarnock man, while I was quite wrapped up in the London humour, was disagreeable, and I got rid of him as soon as I civilly could. My prejudice at what is Scotch is perhaps unreasonably strong. At Dilly's I met my acquaintance, John Scott the Quaker, and found a copy of *Amwell*, a descriptive poem of his place in the country, which he had put up for me with a card in a parcel.

I returned to Dr. Johnson's, and drank some coffee. He and I and Mr. Thrale went to St. Clement's at seven, and heard prayers read by a fellow of high-keyed affectation. I was quite disgusted, and *could* not be devout. I should have gone away in the midst of the service had it not been for the awe of Dr. Johnson. He told me afterwards that the man's manner was so disagreeable to him that if the man was to be the constant reader, he would drive him from that church. I walked away quietly, called at Churchill's, apothecary, and got some [7] . . . and this was some relief to me.

I omitted to mention that I stated to Dr. Johnson today this case: "If I have a daughter who is debauched by a man, but nobody knows of it, should I keep her in my house?" He said I should. BOSWELL. "But, Sir, am not I accessory to an imposition upon the world? And perhaps a worthy man may come and marry this strumpet unless I tell him her worthlessness." JOHNSON. "Sir, you are accessory to no imposition. Your daughter is in your house, and if a man courts her, he takes his chance. If indeed a friend, or indeed any other man, asks your advice if he should marry her, you should advise him against it without telling why, because

---

[7] At this point two pages have been cut away. The last four words before the gap, and the first seven after it, as here printed, have been inked over, apparently by Boswell.

your real opinion is then required. Or if you have other daughters who know of her wickedness, you ought not to keep her in your house. You are to consider this is the state of life. We are to judge of other people's characters as well as we can, and a man is not bound in honesty or honour to tell us the faults of his daughter or of himself. A man who has debauched his friend's daughter is not obliged to tell everybody, 'Take care of me. Don't let me into your houses without suspicion. I once debauched a friend's daughter. I may debauch yours.' "

After I had written to my wife, I went and paid a visit to a lady, who argued with me that marriage was certainly no more but a political institution, as we see it has subsisted in so many different forms in different parts of the world.[8] "Therefore," said she, "it is merely a mutual contract which if one party breaks, the other is free. Now," said she, "my husband I know has been unfaithful to me a thousand times. I should therefore have no scruple of conscience, I do declare, to have an intrigue, and I am restrained only by my pride, because I would not do what is thought dishonourable in this country, and would not put myself in the power of a gallant." I argued that the chastity of women was of much more consequence than that of men, as the property and rights of families depend upon it. "Surely," said she, "that is easily answered, for the objection is removed if a woman does not intrigue but when she is with child." I really could not answer her. Yet I thought she was wrong, and I was uneasy, partly from my own weakness as a reasoner, partly from the pain which one feels on perceiving established principles sapped.

SATURDAY 6 APRIL. All the conversation with a lady which is marked as of last night was on the evening of this day. Claxton (I am now writing in London, Wednesday 24 April) had asked me to come and breakfast with him and talk of some affairs of Temple's. I begged he would come to me any time in the forenoon. He obligingly came. I had taken pretty smart physic. I wrote journal, and at five dined at Beauclerk's, where was Langton, and there was also Miss Floyd, whom I saw at Wilton. I was now certainly ill with a morbus.[9]

SUNDAY 7 APRIL. This being Easter day, I went through my usual forms. I breakfasted at the Chapter Coffee-house, then went to St. Paul's, heard an excellent discourse by Mr. Winstanley, and was solemnly devout. Mr. Thrale sat by me. I received the Holy Sacrament, being a sin-

[8] Boswell nowhere lifts the veil of anonymity, and in this case it seems better not to guess, since the only plausible guesses would involve ladies of hitherto unblemished reputation.

[9] The last two words are very uncertain. Boswell, apparently, has inked over the whole sentence.

cere Christian in faith, and hoping to be better in practice. Mrs. and Miss Thrale were also here. I had written a few lines of condolence to Mrs. Thrale on her son's death, when I arrived in town with Dr. Johnson. She seemed in tender grief today, and said to me, "What we have been now about is the true comfort." I went to Dr. Johnson's to my annual dinner. Mr. Macbean, author of *Ancient Geography,* and who had been several years librarian to Archibald, Duke of Argyll, was there.[1] He said he had been forty years from Scotland. "Ay," said Johnson, smiling, "Boswell, what would you give to be forty years from Scotland?" I said I should not like to be so long absent from the seat of my ancestors. This gentleman, Mrs. Williams, and Mr. Levett dined with us.

I repeated to [Johnson] the argument of a lady of my acquaintance, who maintained that her husband's having been guilty of numberless infidelities released her from her conjugal obligations, because they were reciprocal. JOHNSON. "This is sad stuff, Sir. To the contract of marriage, besides the man and wife, there is a third party—society; and, if it be considered as a vow—GOD; and therefore it cannot be dissolved by their own consent alone. Laws are not made for particular cases, but for mankind in general. A woman may be unhappy with her husband, but she cannot be freed from him without the approbation of the civil and ecclesiastical power. A man may be unhappy because he is not so rich as another, but he is not to seize upon another's property at his own hand."[2]

Dr. Johnson made a remark which both [Macbean] and I thought new, which was that the law against usury is for the protection of creditors as well as of debtors; for if there were no such check, people would be apt, from the temptation of great interest, to lend to desperate persons, by whom they would lose their money. Accordingly there were instances of

[1] Alexander Macbean had also been one of the six amanuenses whom Johnson had employed on the *Dictionary*. Later Johnson had written a preface to Macbean's *Dictionary of Ancient Geography.*—Ten pages of the manuscript of the journal, involving the Johnsonian conversation for 7 April, the whole of the record for 8 and 9 April, and part of that for 10 April, have been torn out at this point. Boswell's first draft of the *Life,* with slight rearrangement, serves as the text for the rest of 7 April. This part of the manuscript of the *Life* is in the collection of Mr. Arthur A. Houghton, Jr., New York City.

[2] Apparently when he came to revise his draft, Boswell extended the conversation as follows: "BOSWELL. 'But, Sir, this lady does not want that the contract should be dissolved; she only argues that she may indulge herself in gallantries with equal freedom as her husband does, provided she takes care not to introduce spurious issue into his family. You know, Sir, what Suetonius has told us of Faustina.' JOHNSON. 'This lady of yours, Sir, I think, is very fit for a brothel.'" In the proof or the revise, "Suetonius" and "Faustina" were changed to "Macrobius" and "Julia." Macrobius reported in a metaphor what the lady had said plainly; see above, 5 April 1776.

ladies being ruined by having injudiciously sunk their fortunes upon high annuities, which have paid but for a few years.

Mrs. Williams was very peevish; and I wondered at Johnson's patience now, as I had often done on similar occasions. After coffee we went to afternoon service in St. Clement's church. As we observed beggars in the street, I said to him I supposed there was no civilized country whatever, where misery in the low people was prevented. JOHNSON. "I believe there is not; but it is better that some should be unhappy than that none should be happy, which would be the case in a general state of equality."

I went home with him, and we sat quietly by ourselves. He recommended Dr. Cheyne's books. I said I thought Cheyne had been reckoned whimsical. "So he was," said he, "in some things; but there is no end of objections."

Upon the question whether a man who had been guilty of vicious irregularity would do well to force himself into solitude and [3] sadness: JOHNSON. "No, Sir, unless it prevent him from being vicious again. Sometimes gloomy penitence is only madness turned upside down. A man may be gloomy, till, in order to be relieved from gloom, he has recourse again to vice."

MONDAY 8, TUESDAY 9 APRIL. [The record for these days is missing.]

[WEDNESDAY 10 APRIL.] [4] . . . with me thinking him a more rigid moralist. I began again to imagine that irregularity of commerce between the sexes was a trivial offence. We talked of Johnson, and if he ever went to women. I said I durst not ask him. Said Sir John: "I would not live with a man whom I durst not ask that." "Why," said I, "I durst not ask you, Sir John." I paused to try if he would tell me of his own accord, but he said nothing. He said he would teach Latin very easily by having the Arabian tales translated into it, so as to engage children; for what entertainment could they have in the books which are read at schools? No matter whether the Latin taught them at first was elegant or not. He would teach the language, and improvements would be made gradually. He would have a grammar quite simple, without any irregular verbs. Let the scholars find them out in the course of their reading. He would not begin with grammar, but teach boys Latin as they are taught their mother tongue. I am always afraid of new schemes of education.

I drove to Dilly's and found there a most agreeable letter from my dear wife, which cheered me pleasingly. I then walked over London Bridge to Mr. Thrale's. I had called at Dr. Johnson's with a letter to de-

---

[3] "into solitude and": apparently added later.
[4] Here the text is resumed from the manuscript of the journal. Boswell has screwed up his courage to consult Sir John Pringle concerning his illness, and is surprised to find him so tolerant.

fend myself against his severity.[5] He was gone. I found him at Mr. Thrale's, where we were to dine. I had an awful timidity lest he should be so much offended with me as to treat me with distant coldness. He accosted [me,] "How d'ye do, Sir?" in his usual tone, and Mrs. Thrale and he and I and Baretti sat some time together. I found it was resolved they were not to go this year to Italy. This disappointed me much. Baretti left the room. I said I thought an Italian journey would do Mr. and Mrs. Thrale good. "No, Sir," said Dr. Johnson, "while grief is fresh, every attempt to [6] [divert only irritates. You must wait till grief be *digested,* and then amusement will dissipate the remains of it." I perceived that he had so warmly cherished the hope of enjoying classical scenes that he could not easily part with the scheme; for he said, "I shall probably contrive to get to Italy some other way. But I won't mention it to Mr. and Mrs. Thrale, as it might vex them.—I am disappointed, to be sure; but it is not a great] disappointment." I wondered to see him have such a manly calmness in a situation in which *I* should have been very peevish, or at least discontented. I said to him, "All evils lose their force in your presence," and I really had that impression.

Murphy entertained us a good deal with the history of Joe Simpson, a schoolfellow of Dr. Johnson's, a barrister-at-law, of very good parts, but who ruined himself by drinking, married a strumpet, and lived upon charity, but still with a dignity of deportment.[7] He wrote "Leonidas, a Tragedy." Sir Joseph Yates, when it was read in a company of lawyers, criticized it in the law phraseology, as, "I demur to that"; and so many corrections were suggested that Joe wrote his tragedy over again; so then he had two tragedies called "Leonidas." Dr. Johnson said he had one of

[5] On one of the days for which the record is missing (7–10 April) it would seem that Boswell had done or said something that offended Johnson to an unusual degree, though there is no hint in the *Life* of any such disturbance. In the last paragraph for Easter we find that Boswell raised "the question whether a man who had been guilty of vicious irregularity would do well to force himself into solitude and sadness." The reference is, of course, to himself. During the whole of this London jaunt he had been trying to get Johnson to talk about concubinage and fornication, hoping thereby to receive an indulgence for his own wayward actions. On both Good Friday and Easter he had steered the conversation into that channel. Perhaps he finally reached the stage of a confession and was severely scolded. Or possibly Johnson simply got tired of the tone which the conversation, under Boswell's leading, seemed always to be acquiring, and told him that he had had enough of it.
[6] Here two pages have been torn out. Since only a small part of the conversation as reported in the *Life* is unaccounted for, it is probable that the missing portion contained an account of Boswell's reconciliation with Johnson. We have filled the gap with a few sentences from the *Life*, rearranged so as to make a proper transition.
[7] Simpson was not a schoolfellow of Johnson's, except in the sense that they both attended the same school.

them still.[8] Murphy said his life would be very instructive. He was an excellent bankrupt lawyer, got £800 a year at the bar[9] for some time, and was in the high road to be of considerable eminence when vanity and intemperance destroyed him. He said to Murphy that Dr. Johnson told him, "A man is not so much in danger from great creditors. They have a liberality of mind. It is small creditors that distress a man. Few are killed in a battle by cannon. It is small shot that does the execution. Therefore try to get all your debts concentrated in a few hands." So poor Joe's plan was to borrow more money of his great creditors to pay his small ones, as if they would lend it to him for that purpose. The Doctor seemed willing to write Joe's life, and wished to have materials collected. Murphy is very good company when Dr. Johnson is present to keep him in good order and to prevent him from growing tedious. He abounds with anecdotes, but he is not to be trusted for exact veracity, as indeed few people are. Today he and Mr. and Mrs. Thrale all maintained that it was at their table that Dr. Johnson and I had the dispute about drinking. They have heard it related; but it actually happened at the Crown and Anchor in 1771, when I supped there with him and Langton and Lord Binning.[1]

This was my first day of water-drinking.[2] It was really uneasy to me, especially as Thrale produced some champagne which he had brought with him from Paris. When we went to coffee and tea, I felt by habit a sensation of being somewhat intoxicated, as one feels a rolling motion at land after having been tossed at sea, but had a comfortable consciousness of being in reality quite sober. When I talked to Mrs. Thrale of my drinking water, Dr. Johnson was angry a little. "Who cares whether you drink water or not?" As the French critic quoted in *The Spectator* says of Montaigne's mentioning that he liked white wine better than red, "Who the devil cares? *Qui diable?*"[3] I however thought with Pope:

[8] The manuscript was printed in 1785, with a title which was intended to make the public think that Johnson was the author: *The Patriot, a Tragedy. From a Manuscript of the Late Dr. Samuel Johnson, Corrected by Himself.*

[9] "Dr. Johnson since told me he was informed by Joe himself <he> never got more than £400": Boswell's note in the margin.

[1] Boswell recalls the occasion, the scene, and the company precisely as he had recorded them at the time in his journal, but his date is wrong: not 1771 but 1772 (15 April). This is characteristic. His memory for concrete circumstance was remarkably full and accurate, but he had no greater power to fix a date than other people have.

[2] Boswell had given his word to Paoli to drink no more, and kept this resolution until 11 May, when he weakened, having been plagued by Garrick and others about his water-drinking, and having received a "dispensation" from the General.

[3] Though Boswell closes his quotation of Johnson's remark with the previous sentence, it is possible (since his use of quotation marks is notably erratic) that Johnson said everything down to this point. For proof that Johnson occasionally allowed himself

I love to pour out all myself as plain
As downright Shippen, or as old Montaigne.[4]

Murphy mentioned a design that Dr. Johnson had to publish an edition of Cowley. The Doctor said he did not know but he should. He was very angry at Hurd's mutilated edition. Murphy said it was a very bad precedent. Any author might be used in the same manner. One loved to see the varieties of an author's composition. I mentioned Flatman's *Poems* which I had picked up on a stall, the fourth edition. I was abashed to find that he was a poet of eminence, and that Pope had borrowed his *Dying Christian* from him, as Mrs. Thrale mentioned. Dr. Johnson repeated Rochester's lines upon Flatman. I put down all the passages that I hear him repeat. He stamps a value on them.

We talked of the *Lives of the Poets* by Cibber. Dr. Johnson said the book was all done by Shiels, a Scotsman. The. Cibber, who was in prison, got ten guineas for leave to put *Mr. Cibber* as the author. And a double lie was intended. In the first place, that it was the work of a Cibber at all, and, in the second place, that it was the work of old Cibber.[5] The Doctor said most of the lives were taken from books, and that it was a collection one would wish to have, as being the only one of the kind. To hear him and Murphy talk of literature gave me an unusual relish for it; and I perceived there was hardly any book which in a critical mouth might not be made to appear of some worth, as in the chemist's laboratory all substances whatever have a certain degree of value. Murphy said Gray's life set him much higher in his estimation than his poems did, for you see a man eternally at work in literature. Dr. Johnson and he agreed that Akenside was superior to Gray or Mason.

We talked of the reviews. Dr. Johnson said he thought them very impartial. He did not know an instance of partiality. "The King," said he, "did me the honour to ask me about the *Monthly* and *Critical Reviews*. I said the *Monthly* was done with more care, the *Critical* upon better principles." He expatiated a little more on them this evening, said that the *Monthly* reviewers were not deists, but Christians with as little Christianity as might be, and were for pulling down all establishments; whereas the *Critical* were for supporting Church and State. He said the latter, he

---

such expressions as "How the devil," see *Hebrides*, 12 October 1773 (in 1962 edition, pp. 292 *n.* 3, 433). The *Spectator* referred to is No. 562; the critic was Joseph Scaliger.
[4] "First Satire of the Second Book of Horace," ll. 51–52.
[5] An article by Ralph Griffiths modifying this passage, in *The Monthly Review* for May 1792, was reprinted by Boswell as a note in later editions of the *Life*. The whole matter has been studied by Professor Nichol Smith, who concluded that Shiels (who was one of Johnson's amanuenses) wrote the entire work, except for the lives of Hill, Budgell, and Mrs. Chandler. Theophilus Cibber, not his father Colley, revised it.

believed, often reviewed without reading the books, but laid hold of an idea and wrote from their own minds. The *Monthly* were duller men, and were glad to read the books.

He talked of Lord Lyttelton's anxiety as an author; how he took about thirty years to write, and how he employed _____ ° to point, his *History*— as if another man could point his sense better than himself; and said he had seen a letter from him thanking the *Monthly* reviewers for their candid account of his *History*. Murphy said he understood his *History* was kept back several years for fear of Smollett. Said Dr. Johnson: "All this seems wonderful to Murphy and me, who never felt that anxiety, but sent what we wrote to the press, and let it take its chance." "The time has been," said Mrs. Thrale, "when you felt it." "Why really, Madam," said the Doctor, "I do not recollect when that was the case."

He mentioned Dr. Barry's system of physic. "A man," said he, "who had acquired a high reputation in Dublin, came over to England and brought his reputation with him, but had not great success. His notion was that pulsation occasions death by attrition, and therefore the way to preserve life is to retard pulsation. But we know that pulsation is strongest in infants, and that we increase though ⁷ it operates in its regular course; so it cannot be the cause of destruction. Somebody told Barry that I laughed at his book." The Doctor said something complaisantly to Mrs. Thrale, wishing her long life. I said, "If Barry's system be true, you have now shortened Mrs. Thrale's life perhaps some minutes by accelerating her pulsation." She thought this very well.

Murphy and I went together in a hackney-coach. He wearied me with a long story which ended in Tom Davies's writing against him in the newspapers; so that he was now at variance with poor Tom. Got home in good time.

THURSDAY 11 APRIL. Went early in the morning to Douglas's in Pall Mall. Told him my case, with expressions of concern that drunkenness should have made a married man get into such a scrape. Said he: "It is thought very little of in this town," and immediately he prescribed to me; said I was doing very well, but he would give me an electuary better than the lenitive, and he dictated the receipt for it in case I should at any other time have occasion for it. He said there was now an injection which produced a speedy cure with great safety; that he had altered his opinion as to injections, and that Sir John Pringle approved of this, but it was a secret known only to a few. I found him the same quiet, obliging man as

° Andrew Reid: supplied from Johnson's *Life of Lyttelton*. The *History* was of Henry II.

⁷ "This, and I am not sure how much before it, written on Thursday the 25": Boswell's note in the margin.

ever, and I was entertained with talking of the cure, and hearing him mention old Sainthill as a master in that branch. Sir John Pringle desired me to give him two guineas at the beginning, and two when I was well. I gave him two this morning.[8]

I called on Sir William Forbes, who had often tried to find me. He was abroad. I left a note to engage him to sup with Dr. Johnson at the Crown and Anchor on Saturday; then called on Nairne, and engaged him also. Then came home to breakfast, and drank tea plentifully, and then was introduced to Count Nény, a Flemish nobleman of £ 5,000 a year, one of the Council of Six in the Low Countries, and a great favourite at the Imperial Court. He had visited Corsica the year after I was there, and had procured for General Paoli the kindness and esteem of the Emperor and Great Duke of Tuscany.[9] He was a very polite man, and had read a great deal; he had made English a particular study, admired Dr. Johnson, and was well acquainted even with the *Journey to the Hebrides.* He was very desirous to see Mr. Garrick play Abel Drugger this evening, but could not get a place to take at the theatre.[1] He imagined that by calling on Garrick with a card as *un étranger,* he might obtain a place. I told him that was not enough. His rank must be made known. And I would give him a note to Garrick. I accordingly did so. Sir William Forbes called and sat a little with the General and me.

I then called on Garrick, having gone out in the General's coach. I found him in his study with a little table *à un couvert,* as he dines lightly alone the days on which he acts. He had not as yet received my note. I told him of it. He affected to be angry. He could not possibly find a place. Did I make him a box-keeper? "By no means," said I. "But a foreigner, a man of such high rank, should have particular attention paid to him." I gave him some hasty anecdotes of Dr. Johnson's late jaunt in which I ac-

---

[8] Up to this point in the entry, enough words have been inked out, presumably by Boswell, to prevent a casual reader from grasping the sense. His intention seems to have been to leave cues enough so that he himself could recover the deleted portions without too much labour. Andrew Douglas, surgeon, had already treated Boswell twice: in 1760, on the occasion of his first infection, and again in 1763 when the Louisa affair provided a surprise ending. Boswell had then considered him so much a friend that on his arrival in London at the end of 1762 he had lived for a week in Douglas's house while he was looking for lodgings. He had dined at Douglas's on 24 July 1763, shortly before his departure to the Continent, and apparently had never called on him since. In 1763 he had paid (or at least had expected to pay) Douglas five guineas for his cure, but on that occasion he was under Douglas's sole care. This time he is in the hands of Sir John Pringle, who has called in Douglas for consultation.

[9] The Emperor Joseph II, and his brother Leopold I, who became Emperor in 1790.

[1] Garrick had publicly declared that this was to be his last appearance as Abel Drugger (in Jonson's *Alchemist*).

companied him. The little theatrical sovereign was not pleased when I told him how well Dr. Johnson and I thought of the players at Lichfield. He said Johnson had not any idea of good acting. "But don't tell him so." "Oh," said I, "I'm cured of repeating to people anything said of them which they would dislike." "I am glad of it," said he. "You had once like to have made sad mischief by that. I will not tell you between whom, as I have it in confidence." Garrick some years ago spoke to me very seriously on this subject, and I think with good effect.

While we were talking, Count Nény came to the door in his coach, and sent in my note. Garrick fluttered, and would say he was not at home. I said, "You had better receive him, and make an apology yourself." He agreed. In came the Count. And Garrick was at once taken with his appearance. He at first told him, "C'est impossible"; and though before he would not be thought a box-keeper, yet now he showed a whole heap of cards soliciting places. I said the Count might press into the pit amongst the mob. "No, no," said Garrick, "that would distress him," or some such word. "I would willingly be distressed" (or some such word), said the Count, "to have the pleasure of seeing you." Garrick, with the pause and start of reflection and expedient, found out that *peut-être* he might find a place, and desired the Count to send his servant to the theatre early.

He talked of Abel Drugger as a very small part, and told the Count with pleasant vanity how a Frenchman had seen him in one of the inferior characters and exclaimed, "Comment! Je ne le crois pas. Ce n'est pas Monsieur Garrick, ce grand homme!" [2] He said, "If I were to begin life again, I think I should not play those low characters." "Sir," said I, "you would be in the wrong, for your great excellence is your variety of playing —the very different characters which you represent."

Dr. Johnson said at dinner today that Garrick was not in earnest in what he said, for to be sure his peculiar excellence was his variety, and perhaps there was not any one character which had not been acted as well by somebody as he could do it. "Why, then," said I, "did he talk so?" "Why, Sir, to make you answer as you did." "I don't know," said I; "he seemed to dip deep into his mind for the reflection." JOHNSON. "He had not far to dip, Sir. He had said the same thing probably twenty times before." Count Nény was very thankful to me for my assistance in this matter, of importance in its own way; and I was a little vain to find myself undoubtedly proved to this Flemish nobleman to have the intimacy of the celebrated arbiter of the drama in London.

I went to Dr. Johnson's and brought him in the General's chariot to dinner. As we drove along Berkeley Square, I mentioned Lord Shelburne. Dr. Johnson said his parts were pretty well for a lord, but would not be

[2] "What! I don't believe it. *That* isn't the great Garrick!"

distinguished in a man who had nothing else but his parts. This is the meaning, but it was much more pointedly expressed. After dinner Dr. Johnson said, "Mr. Boswell is a sprightly ³ man, and has no need of wine."

He said, "A man who has not been in Italy is always conscious of an inferiority, of not having seen what it is expected a man should see." "But," said I, "where is this travelling to end?" "Why, Sir," said he, "the grand object of travelling is to see the shores of the Mediterranean. On these shores were the four great empires of the world: the Assyrian, the Persian, the Grecian, and the Roman. All our religion, almost all our law, almost all our arts, almost all that sets us above savages, has come to us from the shores of the Mediterranean." The General said a thought then came into his mind that the Mediterranean would be a noble subject of a poem.

We talked of translation. I said I could not define it, nor make a similitude to illustrate what it is. I said the translation of poetry must be only imitation. Dr. Johnson said, "You may translate books of science exactly. You may also translate history, in so far as it is not embellished with oratory, which is poetical. Poetry, indeed, cannot be translated, and therefore it is the poets that preserve languages; for we would not be at the trouble to learn a language when we can have all that is written in it just as well in a translation. But as we cannot have the beauties of poetry but in its original language, we learn it."

The General maintained that the art of printing had hurt real learning by disseminating idle writings. Dr. Johnson said if it had not been for the art of printing, we should have now no learning at all, for books would have perished faster than they could have been transcribed. I did not well understand this, considering for how many ages books were preserved by writing alone. I must ask him.

The General maintained that a diffusion of knowledge among a people was a disadvantage, for it made the vulgar rise above their humble sphere. The Doctor opposed this and said that while knowledge was a distinction, those who were possessed of it would naturally rise above those who were not. That to read and write was a distinction at first, but we see when reading and writing have become general, the common people keep their own stations. In the same proportion will it be with respect to other kinds of knowledge.

He and I took a hackney-coach and drove to Hoole's, Shire Lane. But here let me glean a little of past days. When I said at Barnet that I had at times an anxious apprehension that my wife or children might be dead while I was absent, and that reason certainly could not cure this, he said, "Consider how unreasonable you would think it in them to be anxiously

³ *"Lively,* I think": a later interlinear addition.

apprehensive that you may be dead." He said, "Goldsmith referred everything to vanity; his virtues and his vices too were from that motive. He
was not a social man. He never exchanged mind with you."

Last day when I dined at Beauclerk's, Langton said to me, "Shall we
petition to have the young gentleman brought in?" (I am now writing
on Saturday the 27 at Bath.) He meant Beauclerk's son, a child about two
year old. Thinking this affectation in Langton, willing to check him and
to indulge the spirit of contradiction, especially as I had heard Beauclerk
satirize Langton's affectation of this sort and his plaguing people with his
own children, I answered, "I'll petition for no such thing. I don't like
other people's children. I think it is pretty well if a man can bear his
own." Here I affected more roughness than I always possess, though in
general it is certainly true that I do not like to have young children
brought in, as I am disgusted with them, and dislike being in a manner
forced to pay foolish compliments to their parents. Dr. Johnson said last
night at Thrale's that I was right. He maintained too that there were
many people who had no concern about their children, who, from being
engaged in business, or from their course of life in whatever way, seldom
saw their children. "*I*," said he, "should not have had much fondness for
a child of my own." "Nay," said Mrs. Thrale. "At least," said he, "I never
wished to have a child."

He spoke last night of *The Spectator;* said that it was wonderful that
there was such a proportion of bad papers in the half of the work which
was not written by Addison. "For," said he, "there was all the world to
write that half; yet not a half of that half is good." He praised very highly,
as one of the finest pieces in English, the paper on novelty.[4] "Yet," said
he, "one does not hear it talked of." He said it was written by Grove, a
dissenting *teacher.* He would not, I observed to myself, call him a *clergyman;* but he was candid enough to allow very great merit to his composition. Murphy said he remembered when there were several people alive
in London who enjoyed a respectable reputation merely upon having written a paper in *The Spectator.* He remembered particularly Mr. Ince, who
used to come to Tom's Coffee-house. "But," said the Doctor, "you must
consider how highly Steele speaks of Mr. Ince." Murphy said he did not
know till lately that Lord Hardwicke had written the paper "Philip
Homebred."[5] Dr. Johnson said it had no merit, it was quite vulgar, had
nothing luminous.

On the road from Ashburnham[6] he said that it was commonly a weak
man who married for love, and that it was a mistake to think that a woman
(writing Sunday 28 April at Bath) who brings no fortune will be a better

---

[4] *Spectator* No. 626.
[5] *Spectator* No. 364.
[6] Boswell must have meant "Ashbourne," which he has hitherto spelled "Ashburn."

economist than one who does. "No, Sir," said he, "such women are not used to the handling of money. It is new to them, and they take great delight in spending."

He said that in France they had not the tavern life which is so agreeable in this country, where people meet all upon a footing, without any care or anxiety; for there is always some uneasy restraint when there is an entertainer and people entertained. The entertainer is anxious lest his guests should not be pleased; the guests are obliged to pay particular attention to *him*. There is a rivalship, too, in entertaining, which produces care. I have not his exact words, but his meaning.

I said at Lichfield that it was strange how well Scotsmen were known to one another, though born in very distant counties; that you do not find the gentlemen of two or three neighbouring counties in England known to one another. Dr. Johnson at once explained this. "Why," said he (I am now writing Tuesday 30 April at Bath), "You have Edinburgh, where the people from all your counties meet, and which is not so large but that they are all known. There is no such common place of collection in England except London, where from its great size and diffusion but a few can be known to each other."

At Hoole's we drank tea. There was a Mr. Dun, his lady, and daughter, a pretty young creature whom Dr. Johnson fondled, for he really loves the fair sex. Mickle also was there. Dr. Johnson said that Thomson had a true poetical genius, the power of viewing everything in a poetical light. That his fault was such a cloud of words sometimes that the sense could hardly peep through. He said Shiels, who compiled Cibber's *Lives of the Poets,* was one day with him. He took down Thomson and read a good portion to Shiels, and then asked if this was not very fine. Shiels was high in admiration. "Well," said Dr. Johnson, "I have missed every other line." I related the dispute between Goldsmith and Dodsley at Tom Davies's, ———— 1763,[7] whether there was any poetry in this age; when Goldsmith said there was none, and Dodsley quoted his own *Collection,* I mean appealed to it, and said that perhaps you could not find a palace like Dryden's *Ode,*[8] but you had villages of very pretty houses. "I think," said Dr. Johnson, "Dodsley gave up the question. He and Goldsmith said the same thing, only that he said it in a softer manner than Goldsmith did; for he acknowledged that there was no poetry, nothing that towered above the common mark. You may find wit and humour in verse, and yet it is not poetry. *Hudibras* has a profusion of these, yet it is not to be reckoned a poem." I said Dodsley mentioned *The Spleen*[9] in his *Collection.* Dr. Johnson said that was not poetry. I said, "Did not Gray's poetry tower above

[7] According to *Boswell's London Journal,* the dispute was on Christmas-day, 1762.
[8] *Alexander's Feast,* the second title of which is *An Ode in Honour of St. Cecilia's Day.*
[9] By Matthew Green.

the common mark?" "Yes," said he, "but we must attend to the difference between doing what men in general cannot do if they would, and what every man may do if he would. Sixteen-string Jack towered above the common mark." [1] I asked, "Then, Sir, what is poetry?" "Why," said he, "it is much easier to tell what it is not. We all know what light is, but it is not easy to tell what it is." I wished to get from him a definition of poetry, but could not at this time.

At supper I talked of words peculiar to the Scottish dialect. Dr. Johnson, as he has formerly done, encouraged me in collecting them. I unknowingly brought out one tonight which had a ludicrous effect. I was talking of the Methodists' using common song tunes in their chapels, and I said that one day when I was at Whitefield's Chapel, to my no small surprise they *banged* up the tune of "GOD *save the King.*" Mickle got hold of this, as I had detected him in a Scotticism a little before. I was so used to the word *bang* that I could hardly believe it was not English; but the expression in English is *struck up.* When Dr. Johnson asked, as not having heard distinctly, "They *banged* up what?" there was much laughter.

I could not help wondering tonight to think that Hoole had written tragedies, when I perceived so little fire in his conversation, and indeed so little imagery or genius of any kind. But there is a species of tragedy which may be drawn up like an attorney's narrative, or woven like damask; and genius is not to be expected in the author any more than in the attorney or in the weaver. The versification may be correct and even elegant, as the narrative may be distinct and well expressed, or the damask prettily executed; but superiority of mind is not there.

I took a hackney-coach home. Mickle went with me as far as Bond Street, where I set him down to find his way near to Portland Chapel. He again disgusted me with his dwarfish talk.

FRIDAY 12 APRIL. (I am now writing Thursday 2 May in London.) Called at Douglas's, the surgeon, in the morning. Breakfasted with Lord, or rather Lady, Eglinton.[2] Was received so well that I agreed to breakfast there every morning. (I am now writing Saturday 4 May in London.) I came home and wrote some journal.

SATURDAY 13 APRIL. Walked through Covent Garden between two and three in my way to dinner at Tom Davies's. Saw a very fine woman, elegantly dressed, moving along by herself. I passed her, but as everybody looked at her with the appearance of admiration, I could not resist stop-

---

[1] John Rann, a notorious highwayman, had been executed at Tyburn, 30 November 1774. He had been known for foppishness in his dress, particularly for wearing breeches with eight strings at each knee: hence his appellation.

[2] Lady Jean Lindsay, eldest daughter of Mrs. Boswell's friend the Countess of Crawford, had married Lord Eglinton early in her sixteenth year, and was not yet twenty.

ping till she came up, and at once begged to know where she lived. She told me in Greek Street, Soho, and her name was upon the door—*Mrs. Price.* I walked in the Piazza with her, and was easy and gay and complimentative, and fancied I was agreeable. I trusted that nobody knew me, but Dr. Johnson has counselled me not to trust too much to that.[3]

At Tom Davies's were Dr. Johnson, Mr. Cradock (a Leicestershire gentleman of good fortune, author of *Zobeide,* a tragedy, a pleasing man, who told me he would furnish me some good anecdotes of Dr. Johnson, and asked me to his house, which was very little out of my way to Scotland; I was sorry to find that his tragedy, which I bought and read after this, was not excellent); and there was the Reverend Dr. Harwood, who has translated the New Testament in modern phraseology, a ridiculous work, and Mrs. Williams.[4] I introduced Aristotle's doctrine of the κάθαρσις τῶν παθημάτων [5] by tragedy. "But how by terror and pity?" said I, with an air of ignorance. "Why, Sir," said Johnson, "you are to consider what is the meaning of purging in the original sense. It is to expel impurities from the human body. The passions are the great movers of human action, but they are mixed with such impurities that it is necessary they should be purged or refined by means of terror and pity. For instance, ambition is a noble passion; but by seeing upon the stage that a man who is so excessively ambitious as to raise himself by injustice is punished, we are terrified at the effects of such a passion. In the same manner a certain degree of resentment is necessary; but if we see that a man carries it too far, we pity the object of it, and are taught to moderate that passion." I am recording this very ill. Dr. Johnson was grandly eloquent. Mr. Cradock said to me, "Oh! that his words were written in a book." [6]

I said that the great defect of *Othello* was that it had not a moral, for that no man could resist the circumstances of suspicion which were artfully suggested to Othello's mind. The Doctor said, "In the first place, we learn from *Othello* this very useful moral: not to make an unequal match. In the second place, we learn not to yield too readily to suspicion.

---

[3] *Hebrides,* 23 September 1773.
[4] Croker gives the following (possibly apocryphal) anecdote of Johnson, which he had from Mr. Wickins of Lichfield: "The first book he laid his hands upon was Harwood's *Liberal Translation of the New Testament.* The passage which first caught his eye was from that sublime apostrophe in St. John, upon the raising of Lazarus, 'Jesus wept'; which Harwood had conceitedly rendered, 'and Jesus, the Saviour of the world, burst into a flood of tears.' He contemptuously threw the book aside, exclaiming, 'Puppy!'" (*Johnsonian Miscellanies,* ii. 429). Harwood's rendition of John 11. 35 is actually "Jesus burst into a flood of tears."
[5] "The purging of the passions": Boswell's translation in the *Life.*
[6] "Oh that my words were now written! oh that they were printed in a book!": Job 19. 23.

The handkerchief is merely a trick, though a very pretty trick; but there are no other circumstances of reasonable suspicion, but that of Cassio talking in his sleep, which too was not sufficient. No. I think *Othello* has more moral than almost any play."

He said Sir Alexander Macdonald was narrow, not so much from avarice as from an impotence to lay out money. He could not find in his heart to pour out a bottle of wine, but he would not much care though it should sour.

He said he wished to see Dennis's critical works collected. Tom Davies said they would not sell. The ⟨Doctor⟩ seemed to think otherwise.

Tom said that Murphy lived upon potted stories, and that he made his way as Hannibal did—by vinegar,[7] having begun with attacking people (he mentioned, I think, the players).[8] He told Dr. Johnson today that he was present when Murphy paid him the highest compliment that could be paid to a layman—asked his pardon, because in telling a story he had to introduce some oaths.

I mentioned Lord Bathurst's having told at his table in 1763, before Dr. Hugh Blair, who repeated it to me, that he had seen Pope's *Essay on Man* in Lord Bolingbroke's handwriting. Dr. Johnson doubted the fact in its full extent, and put this striking question. "Did Blair ask Lord Bathurst if he had read it? I dare say, Sir, he did not read it."[9] He is the best detector of inaccurate stories that I ever knew. He would have made a capital judge.

We drank tea. Harwood was a clumsy fellow. I had fixed a meeting with Dr. Johnson this evening at the Crown and Anchor. He went home with Mrs. Williams. I stayed and wrote a letter to my wife, and then went to the Crown and Anchor; found Nairne and in a little came Sir Joshua Reynolds, whom I had visited in the forenoon, and engaged to be with

[7] Hannibal, according to Livy, made a road for his elephants through the Alps by heating the rock with great fires and then pouring vinegar on it.

[8] In the *Life* Boswell wrote: "particularly the players." Murphy's name was there suppressed.

[9] When Johnson was engaged in writing his *Life of Pope*, Boswell received a letter from Hugh Blair (written 21 September 1779) which elucidated this story. Lord Bathurst had said that the *Essay on Man* "was originally composed by Lord Bolingbroke in prose, and that Mr. Pope did no more than put it into verse; that he had read Lord Bolingbroke's manuscript in his own handwriting, and remembered well that he was at a loss whether most to admire the elegance of Lord Bolingbroke's prose, or the beauty of Mr. Pope's verse" (*Life*, 10 October 1779). Blair's conversation with Bathurst took place on 22 April 1763. A few days afterwards, meeting Boswell, Blair repeated the conversation; but Boswell did not record it in his *London Journal*. Bolingbroke's manuscript is lost; it is unlikely, however, that he contributed more than some outlines for the argument of Pope's poem.

us. He gave me the genuine story of Johnson and Mudge. Mudge was a young lad about sixteen, grandson to the Mudge of whom Johnson has given a high character; he was waiting at Sir Joshua's before breakfast, eager to meet Dr. Johnson, and he observed that he thought the Doctor had drawn his own character in _____ in *The Rambler*. When Dr. Johnson came, Sir Joshua, who thought this a very pretty observation for a young man, repeated it to Dr. Johnson, who answered, "Does Mudge say so? Then Mudge lies." [1] I observed it could not possibly be a *lie*. Sir Joshua agreed that was clear; he besides was of opinion that the character was really Johnson's own. He said Johnson was like his macaw: very good humoured at times, but all at once without any reason that you can see, would grow angry and _____ [2] you.

He said that he was once with him in Devonshire.[3] The company, and Sir Joshua among the rest, had been out a-hunting; so at dinner Dr. Johnson was left out of the conversation. Sir Joshua with a polite desire to bring him into it said, just by way of saying what occurred first, "Well, Sir, I have been galloping over fields and jumping hedges and ditches to-day, and that is one thing I can do better than you." Johnson angrily answered, "Sir, when I have as mean a mind as you, I shall be vain of such things." Sir Joshua said, "It was a humbling thing that Johnson might say such things without people taking notice of them."

Sir William Forbes and Langton came, and Dr. Johnson arrived at last. There was an admirable dispute whether drinking improved conversation and benevolence. Sir Joshua maintained it did. "No, Sir," said Dr. Johnson. "Before dinner men meet with great inequality of understanding, and those who are conscious of their inferiority have the modesty not to talk. When they have drank wine, every man feels himself happy and loses that modesty, and grows impudent and vociferous. But he is not improved. He is only not sensible of his defects." Sir Joshua said that the Doctor was talking of the effects of excess in wine, but that a moderate glass enlivened

[1] It is not clear which this was among the twenty children of the thrice-married Dr. John Mudge. Johnson's godson, William Mudge, would have been only thirteen at the time of this entry in the journal, and Boswell does not write as though the encounter were recent. Johnson's character of the grandfather, the Reverend Zachariah Mudge, which Boswell quoted in full in the *Life* (March 1781), first appeared in *The London Chronicle* for 2 May 1769. Johnson told Mrs. Thrale he had drawn himself in *The Idler* as Sober (No. 31) and Gelaleddin (No. 75) but admitted no self-portrait in *The Rambler*. None of the named characters in *The Rambler* seems to have more than a touch or two suggestive of Johnson.
[2] Blank in manuscript. Boswell later added above the line: "(I suppose peck at)."
[3] 16 August–26 September 1762. One wonders whether Johnson was especially prone to irascibility when Mudges were at hand. On the occasion of the rude remark about to be reported, he and Reynolds were guests of Dr. Mudge, young Mudge's father.

the mind by giving a proper circulation to the blood. "I am," said he, "in very good spirits when I get up in the morning. By dinner-time I am exhausted. Wine puts me in the same state as when I got up, and I am sure that moderate drinking makes people talk better." "No, Sir," said Johnson, "wine gives not light, gay, ideal hilarity, but tumultuous, noisy, clamorous merriment. I have heard none of those drunken—nay, drunken is a coarse word—none of those *vinous* flights." Sir Joshua said, "Because you have sat by quite sober, and felt an envy of the happiness of those who were drinking." "Perhaps," said Johnson, "a contempt. And it is not necessary to be drunk one's self to relish the wit of drunkenness. Do we not judge of the drunken wit of Iago and Cassio, the most excellent in its kind, when we are quite sober? Wit is wit, by whatever means it is produced; and if good, will appear so at all times." He admitted that the spirits are raised by drinking by the common participation of pleasure, but that cock-fighting or bear-baiting will raise the spirits of a company as drinking does, though surely they will not improve conversation. He also admitted that there were some sluggish men who were improved by drinking, as there are fruits which are not good till they are rotten. "There are such men," said he, "but they are medlars." But he candidly allowed that there might be a very few improved by drinking; but he maintained that he was right as to drinking in general and he observed that there is nothing which is not true of some man. Sir William Forbes said, "Might not a man be like a bottle of beer which is improved by being set before the fire?" "Nay," said Johnson contemptuously, "I cannot answer that. That is too much for me." Worthy Sir William luckily did not mind this. Langton acquiesced in Dr. Johnson's doctrine. Nairne either durst not speak or had nothing to say.

I said I knew wine did me harm; it inflamed me; did not improve my mind, but confused and irritated it; but that the experience of mankind had declared in favour of moderate drinking. Johnson said, "I do not say it is wrong to produce this self-complacency by drinking. I only deny that it improves the mind. I scorned to take wine when I had company. I have drank many a bottle by myself; in the first place, because I had need of it to raise my spirits; in the second place, because I would have nobody to witness its effects upon me."

He said almost all his *Ramblers* were written just as they were wanted for the press; that he sent so much of a paper, and wrote the rest as they were printing. He said he waited till the last, as he was then sure he should do it. I wondered at this. But he has a rich store in his mind, and only requires a little external force to make it play like a fountain.

He said that for general improvement a man should read just what his immediate inclination prompted; though, to be sure, if a man has a science to learn, he must regularly and resolutely advance. He said, "What we read with inclination makes a much better impression. If we read without inclination, half the mind is employed in fixing the attention, so there is but one half to be employed on what we read." He said he read *Amelia* through, standing with a chair in his hand *thus* (and he stood holding a chair with its back turned to his side). He said, "If a man begins to read in the middle of a book and feels an inclination to go on, let him not quit it to go to the beginning. He may perhaps not feel again the inclination."

Sir Joshua mentioned Cumberland's *Odes,* which were just published. Dr. Johnson said they would have been thought as good as odes commonly are if Cumberland had not put his name to them; but that a name immediately draws censure, unless it be a name that bears down everything before it. "Nay," said he, "Cumberland has made his *Odes* introduce a man into the world. They might have run well enough by themselves, but he has loaded them with a name; nay, he has made them carry double." [4]

We talked of the reviews, and Dr. Johnson spoke of them as he did at Thrale's.[5] Sir Joshua said, what I have often thought, that he many a time wondered to find so much good writing employed in them. "Nay," said Dr. Johnson, "those who write in them write well in order to be paid well." Johnson said Adam Smith was as dull a dog as he had ever met with. I said it was strange to me to find my old professor in London, a professed infidel with a bag-wig. This was a very good meeting. Langton set me down at the General's.

SUNDAY 14 APRIL. I had been engaged to dine today at Mr. Stuart's with Lord Cassillis, but being informed that Lord Eglinton, Lord Kellie, and other Caledonian drinkers were to be there, I begged to be off. Mrs. Stuart said I had better come and dine at Lady Eglinton's, where she was to be. I breakfasted with Lady Eglinton, she asked me to dine, and I readily agreed. She was preparing for being introduced to the King, and was not the least in a flutter. I heard high mass in the chapel of the Neapolitan Ambassador. I asked at his house when mass began, and a servant very obligingly showed me into a seat entering from the house, a genteel closet with glass windows just looking out close to the altar. I was pious and elegantly happy. The Ambassador was il Conte Pignatelli, whom I had seen at Turin in 1765. I sent in my name and he received me with

[4] They were dedicated to Romney, the painter, who was by no means unknown in 1776. But Reynolds disliked Romney, and this is a Reynolds faction.
[5] On 10 April 1776.

engaging affability, said he remembered me very well, and hoped to see me often, and called me "Un ancien ami qui je respecterai toujours."[6] I was delighted to find myself thus regarded by a foreign minister, and thought I would make the Laird of Auchinleck distinguished in Europe. It is hard that the difference between my father and me checks my aspiring and extending spirit.

I came home and dressed in a full suit of black clothes of the Abate Cigli, a Florentine castrato, not having a full suit made yet for myself. I said, "I shall dine with Lady Eglinton and Mrs. Stuart in an eunuch's dress, so they will be very safe." This was nonsense. I went to Court in a chair, and was pleased to find myself treated by the pretty young Countess with perfect civility and good humour. But I should not wonder so much at being well treated, for although educated very narrowly, and still depressed by my father from mistake, I ought to remember that my character as a man of parts and extensive acquaintance makes people fond of my attention. I talked a good deal with an officer who stood next to me. I learnt it was General Haldimand. Lord Eglinton introduced me to him. We had talked in French, and with much *franchise*.[7] It pleased me to see our young Ayrshire Countess [8] make so fine a figure at Court. Lord Pembroke was in waiting. He came and spoke to me very obligingly, and told me that if the King should recollect me, he would speak to me; if not, I might be presented the first levee day.[9] I came home, put off the full suit, and went in my frock dress to Lady Eglinton's and dined with her Ladyship, Mrs. Stuart, and Miss Gregory. Mrs. Stuart said I was the Grand Turk. I was at first dissatisfied that I was not very entertaining; but I was patient, and Mrs. Stuart was very lively, so that no blank appeared. We drank coffee and tea in the evening. My Lady said she had no notion of being unhappy. I called a little at Lord Mountstuart's, who was just come from Bath, and then supped with Mrs. Stuart, quite in an intimate style.

MONDAY 15 APRIL. I did not apply for a ticket to the Duchess of Kingston's trial, thinking it exceedingly difficult to get one, but Lady Eglinton offered me one, which I accepted and was flattered with receiving.[1] I relished as much as I could wish the grandeur of the peers of Great Britain in their robes, and of all the other apparatus of a noble trial, and

[6] "An old friend whom I shall always respect." Boswell should have written "que."
[7] "Frankness." They talked in French because Lieutenant-General Sir Frederick Haldimand was a Swiss, and never learned to speak English well.
[8] Lady Eglinton.
[9] Boswell had been presented to the King on 18 February 1766, but had not been at Court since.
[1] The trial began on this day, and was continued on 16, 19, 20, and 22 April, on which day the peers unanimously pronounced her guilty of bigamy. Her rank enabled her to escape the usual sentence: imprisonment and burning on the hand with a hot iron.

I was quite enchanted with the beautiful exhibition of ladies. I did not think there had been so many fine women in the universe; and I thought the mode of dressing, with a deal of hair and feathers and flowers of various colours, more beautiful than what I had ever seen before. I could hear very little. I came away about two o'clock. I called on Sir John Pringle and sat a little, as also with Surgeon Douglas. I had engaged to dine with Langton. I had no great mind to it, but I valued him for his learning and worth, and thought I should get some anecdotes of Johnson from him. As I walked to his house, I called at Egan's, wigmaker, now hair-merchant, just by Oxford Chapel, and saw the room in which I lodged when I first came to London in spring 1760. He was a plain, worthy Roman Catholic. I found I could have his second floor for sixteen shillings, and I thought I would have it next time that I came to London. It pleased me to find him alive and in the same house. He did not recollect me. Indeed I never was much acquainted with him. It was rather dull at Langton's with him and his lady and a Mrs. Tadwell, and no elegance of living. He seemed to be quite dull and recluse and gloomy from too strict notions of religious duty. I got him to talk of Johnson, and he told me some particulars which are to be found in the little book which I keep solely for Dr. Johnson's life. I hope I shall have many of them filled.[2] I drank tea with him, and supped with Lord Mountstuart very cordially. He bid me come to him tomorrow morning and he would take me into a good place at the trial where I should hear well.

TUESDAY 16 APRIL. Breakfasted with Lord Mountstuart, and went with him in his carriage to Westminster Hall. He got from Mr. Laroche, who attended the Duchess, a ticket which admitted me close to the bar.[3] I heard for the first time Dunning speak, and was pleased with his shrewdness and vivacity.[4] I also heard Dr. Harris, a civilian, whom I liked very well. When the peers adjourned, I went to the House of Lords for a little; and when they were to return, Lord Mountstuart said to me, "Come, Boswell, I'll carry you in as a peer's eldest son. Stand you by that beefeater till I come out after we are marshalled, and I'll take you under the arm, and you shall walk in the procession along with me." Accordingly amongst "Peers' eldest sons, two and two,"[5] did I strut, and got to the throne,

[2] There is no evidence that Boswell had more than this one notebook of Johnsonian materials separate from the journal when he began writing the *Life*.

[3] James Laroche, M.P. for Bodmin, was created a baronet in September.

[4] Hannah More, whose vivid account of the trial has often been quoted, wrote, "Dunning's manner is insufferably bad, coughing and spitting at every three words; but his sense and his expression pointed to the last degree; he made her Grace shed bitter tears" (*Letters of Hannah More*, ed. Johnson, p. 42). John Dunning, later first Baron Ashburton, was one of the counsel for the prosecution.

[5] Boswell is quoting from the printed order for the procession.

where I was excellently placed; but the House adjourned till Friday. My Lord would have had me to dine with him, but I begged leave to go and see Garrick play Benedict. I got no dinner, and the only place I could find was in the shilling gallery, so that I saw imperfectly, though I heard pretty well. I supped at Lord Mountstuart's. My mind for these several days was placid and gay.

WEDNESDAY 17 APRIL. (Writing early on Tuesday 7 May.) Breakfasted Lord Eglinton's. He put an Erse grammar in manuscript into my hands to give an opinion how it was done.[9] I afterwards read all I could of it, and thought it distinct enough; only his ignorance of English pronunciation made his rules as to sounds erroneous. I visited Beauclerk in the forenoon, while he was in bed. He kept his spirits wonderfully. I promised to come to him in the evening.

Dined at Lord Mountstuart's; Sir William Cunynghame was there, and after dinner he and my Lord talked only scandal and bawdy. Their judgements as to many ladies were, I dare say, mistaken. Dr. Johnson maintained to me the day we came last to London that the women of this age are more faithful to their husbands than formerly, for their understandings are better cultivated. I wish he may be right as to the effect of the cultivation. Forrester, the English lawyer, came in. I had long wished to be acquainted with him. He took to me at once, said he had a great respect for my father, and would be glad to see me. I told him how lucky I thought myself in thus meeting with him. I had a satisfaction in seeing him a *man*—a character, I think, become rare, there is such light juvenility. I had a tolerable simile. I said speaking to a thin audience was like swimming in shallow water; whereas a crowded audience bears one up like deep waves. My Lord and Forrester were quite social. It gave me some uneasiness that I could not drink wine today, Forrester looked so hearty, and it seemed to me so benevolent to encourage him in taking a social cup; but I checked my regret by considering the consequences.

My Lord and I were some time by ourselves. He made me write a letter to the nephew of Granger, the curious man for engraved portraits, who was just dead. He dictated it, though it was to be from me, my Lord being so much hurried with the trial. He did not wish to get into correspondence with a man whom he did not know. I doubted whether one word in the epistle was English. "No matter," said my Lord jocularily,[6a] "English or not, you are to sign it." I think, however, I did not put down

---

[9] By William Shaw. Boswell later turned the manuscript over to Johnson, who approved of its publication and wrote "Proposals" for it. It was published in 1778, with the title *An Analysis of the Galic Language.*

[6a] A lapse of Boswell's own into non-English, doubly amusing in the context.

the word, or altered it. I went to Beauclerk's and sat with him and Lady Di. I recollect nothing.

THURSDAY 18 APRIL. Breakfasted Lord Eglinton's. General Paoli and I dined at the Mitre with Sir John Pringle and some more members of the Royal Society. I placed myself next to Captain Cook, and had a great deal of conversation with him; but I need not mark it, as his book will tell it all. Only I must observe that he candidly confessed to me that he and his companions who visited the South Sea Islands could not be certain of any information they got, or supposed they got, except as to objects falling under the observation of the senses; their knowledge of the language was so imperfect they required the aid of their senses, and anything which they learnt about religion, government, or traditions might be quite erroneous. He gave me a distinct account of a New Zealander eating human flesh in his presence and in that of many more aboard, so that the fact of cannibals is now certainly known. We talked of having some men of inquiry left for three years at each of the islands of Otaheite, New Zealand, and Nova Caledonia, so as to learn the language and (I am now writing on Wednesday the 22 of May at Edinburgh) bring home a full account of all that can be known of people in a state so different from ours. I felt a stirring in my mind to go upon such an undertaking, if encouraged by Government by having a handsome pension for life. We drank coffee at Brown's Coffee-house, and I felt myself as much at home and in as much tranquillity in London as I could wish to be.

I then went to the Royal Society and heard two pieces read. After Sir John Pringle had come down from the chair, I mentioned to him my inclination to go with Captain Cook. "Take care," said he, "your old spirit" (or some such word) "is reviving." I should have mentioned that at the Mitre, as the company was rising from table, and Sir John making an apology for our not having had a very good dinner, I made a tolerable pun. "I have had a feast," said I (pointing to the Captain); "I have had a good dinner, for I have had a good *Cook*." I had some conversation with Dr. Solander at dinner, and with Mr. Banks at the Society. The General, who I found was now a Fellow of the Royal Society, carried me in his coach, first home, where I wrote to my wife, and then he and I and Signor Gentili went to a rout at Mrs. Bosville's, where I was completely easy. We stayed a very short while, and then went to a Subscription City Ball at Haberdashers' Hall, to which the General had tickets for himself and his two friends. There was a goodly company of city ladies and gentlemen, who seemed to be very courteous and cheerful. (I am now writing May 25 at Edinburgh.)

I met here with the Chief of the Mohawks, Theandénaigen, grandson of him who visited England in Queen Anne's reign.[7] (I am now writing on Thursday 30 May at Auchinleck, where I am calmly refreshing myself in the country, and where it is curious to recall the variety of ideas during my late travels by recording them.) I was told that an officer whom I saw here had conducted the Chief to England. I began a conversation with him, and found him very affable. He told me his name was Tice. And he did what should always be done when a name is mentioned for the first time: he spelt it—T i c e. The ear never almost catches a new name exactly, so it should be assisted by spelling. He was of English extraction, but had never been in Britain before. He had served in the last war, and during the present troubles in America had been at Fort St. John with my cousin, Major Charles Preston, having with him this Mohawk Chief and a good many Indians. But he had left it in September. He spoke with high esteem of Preston, and I am not sure whether it was before or after knowing my connexion with him that, upon my proposing to pay him a visit, he said he would be glad to see me any morning to drink tea with the Chief and him at the Swan with Two Necks in Lad Lane.[8] They had put up at that inn on their arrival in London, and the Chief thought the people so civil that he would not leave the house to go into lodgings. I talked a little with the Chief tonight. He spoke English quite well. But I shall not put down any particulars concerning him here, as I am to draw up some account of him for *The London Magazine*.[9] Came home with General Paoli in good time.

FRIDAY 19 APRIL. Was late of going abroad. Called at Lord Mountstuart's. Somebody was with him on business (I am now writing after supper, 31 May, at Auchinleck) for a little. I had some breakfast in the parlour by myself. My Lord's brother Frederick[1] called, and was with me a little.

[7] The Indian's name is usually spelled Thayendanegea, but Boswell's article (mentioned later) shows that he made an effort to get the right pronunciation. Better known as Joseph Brant, Thayendanegea was a young Mohawk chief who had risen to a position of prominence in Indian affairs through the influence of his sister, Molly Brant, Sir William Johnson's common-law wife. He had been educated at Moor's Charity School, Lebanon, Connecticut, was a convert to the Church of England, and (as he later told Boswell) was engaged in a translation of the New Testament into his own tongue. He had been brought to England by the Government, who hoped to induce him to lead his people against the Colonists. In this they succeeded. Brant returned to America early in May and spread the Indian terror throughout the Mohawk Valley, directing the Cherry Valley massacre and others.

[8] For more than a century this inn was the booking-office for coaches to the North.

[9] Boswell's account was printed as the leading article in *The London Magazine* for July 1776. It was accompanied by an engraved portrait of Brant in what purported to be "the dress of his nation." The engraving (see following page 134) was "from an original drawing in the possession of James Boswell, Esqr." The drawing has disappeared.

[1] The Hon. Frederick Stuart, M.P. for the Ayr burghs.

He said, in answer to a question from me, that he did not think his brother would ever be a man of business, for that he could not persist. We were soon introduced to my Lord's study, and I was cheered with that princely benevolence which uniformly appears in him.

I called on Lord Eglinton and walked out to Hyde Park with him and Captain Hoggan, but soon tired and left them. Coming along Piccadilly, I was overtaken by Foote, and he asked me into his chariot. (I am now writing at Auchinleck, Sunday 2 June, after breakfast, before setting out for church.) I accepted of the invitation. He said he had seen Dr. Johnson at Paris, and I might figure what an appearance he would have to the French, in the same brown clothes and the same wig which he wears in England, and a plain shirt. He spoke of Lord Mansfield's strange behaviour in the case of the Duchess of Kingston. I said it was shocking to see a Lord Chief Justice so partial.[2] That we saw the[3] oracle a prostitute even on the tripod.

[EDITORIAL NOTE: Boswell's rough notes, some of the most obscure in the entire collection, constitute the daily record for the remainder of his visit to London.[4] The whirl continued; usually each mealtime was spent with different people, in different parts of London. He was out for breakfast and chocolate, tea, dinner, tea again, supper, and sometimes late in the evening he might call at a coffee-house. Almost always there were other visits for "gallant compliments" or for good talk or to arrange for good talk in the future. Lord Mountstuart practised his speech on the Scotch Militia Bill before him, and a few days later Boswell stayed up all night to copy it. By the time he had finished, the coaches from a masquerade were rolling past in the early morning sunshine, while thoughts of his "elegant connexion softened [the] dire labour." This friendship was confirmed in Lord Mountstuart's gift of his portrait by William Hoare, and that with young Lady Eglinton by a kiss and a relic (a lock of Boswell's hair). He flirted openly and self-consciously with Mrs. Stuart, but slyly and meanly with "la bella Contessa" Eglinton, appeasing his conscience with the excuse that he was fortifying her against the wiles of Lord Pembroke. Nevertheless Boswell was "vastly gay" when he was with her, with Mrs. Stuart he was elated, and he was calm and happy a great part of the time.

[2] Mansfield seems to have given the general impression of being the Duchess's partisan on the first day of the trial, but he soon swung into line, "his cowardice" (to quote an unfriendly critic, Horace Walpole) "always supplanting his knavery" (letter to Mason, 21 April 1776).

[3] The journal breaks off here at the foot of a page, and is not resumed until 12 June. The sentence is completed from the notes.

[4] In this section in the quotations from Boswell's notes all abbreviated words are expanded by the editors; interpolated words are placed within brackets.

The familiar names appear frequently in these notes. We read of conversations with Paoli, Reynolds, Burke, Garrick, Percy, Wilkes, Colman, Oglethorpe, Lord Pembroke. There are also records concerning one or two acquaintances who have just entered his journal: Joseph Brant, the Mohawk Chief, and Captain Cook, whom Boswell saw at Mile End, where they had tea in the garden. A blackbird sang; it was "quite pleasant. Was in *perfect* London spirits." Boswell found a similar rapport with his world when he was in Bath. He was "quite in Bath spirits, not a grain of melancholy or of timidity." Johnson had gone there for a brief visit with the Thrales, and Boswell followed him on 26 April. Boswell, who had never been to Bath, saw everything expected of an eager tourist. He felt giddy at the first glimpse of the assembly rooms. He heard a "curious" discourse at the Countess of Huntingdon's fashionable Methodist chapel; he went out to the late Ralph Allen's famous mansion, Prior Park, and from the sweeping portico and the arcades he could view the city. On the 29th he and Johnson made an excursion to Bristol to look into the authenticity of the Rowley poems: Johnson was shown the very chest out of which Chatterton's manuscripts were said to have come, but remained skeptical, though he thought it "wonderful (or some such word) how this whelp had written such things."

In London again, Boswell saw much of Burke, who was in high elation because of Howe's retreat from Boston. He engaged in a competition with Garrick in imitating Johnson, and again slept under Johnson's roof. Johnson had assured him that a bedroom was always at his disposal ("Mrs. Williams must tell you [that] nobody will come to it more welcome than you"), but "would give no hint" when Boswell next night had a mind to occupy it. He hinted himself, Johnson was delighted, held him with both hands, and said, "Glad to have you here." Boswell then jotted in his notes: "Curious! [to sleep] under [the] roof of [the] Rambler." And with childlike simplicity added, "But [it was] not right to think of [the] Contessa."

The most remarkable event of April and May 1776 is Boswell's interview with Mrs. Rudd. As Boswell indicated in his notes (and since we have printed it at the end of this volume), the reader will find the "history of this apart." The extraordinary first scene of the drama with that adventuress was on the night of 22 April. Boswell called again at her lodgings on 13 May, but she was not at home. The following night, between eight and nine, he visited her, and afterwards he tried unsuccessfully to write some verses in her honour. He then met Wilkes. "Wilkes . . . carried me into Parliament Street to see a curious procession pass: the funeral of a lamplighter attended by some hundreds of his fraternity with torches. Wilkes, who either is, or affects to be, an infidel, was rattling

away, 'I think there's an end of that fellow. I think he won't rise again.'
I very calmly said to him, 'You bring into my mind the strongest argument that ever I heard against a future state'; and then told him David
Hume's objection that Wilkes and his Mob must be immortal. It seemed
to make a proper impression, for he grinned abashment, as a Negro grows
whiter when he blushes." [4a]

The next day, 15 May, was the great dinner at Dilly's at which he
brought Wilkes and Johnson together, justly the most celebrated portion
of the *Life*, and one which loses none of its glory when we discover that
it was written from rough notes at a distance of nearly fifteen years. Before the dinner (presumably about four o'clock), Boswell had managed to
make the calls of a typical morning in London: chocolate with Paoli, tea
with Lord Mountstuart, returned home accompanied by Hoggan, then to
Sir John Pringle's to leave a note, home again to get a greatcoat, a farewell to Hoggan in the Haymarket, to Goodwin's (where all letters for
Boswell were left), to Lord Pembroke's to leave a message, somewhere to
receive a call from Dr. Patrick Russell, who had been physician to the
English factory at Aleppo and who wished to meet him, and finally to
Dr. Johnson's. The record of the rest of the day follows below, taken from
the manuscript of the *Life*.[5]]

Upon the much-expected Wednesday, I called on him about half an
hour before dinner, as I often did when we were to dine out together, to
see that he was ready in time and to accompany him. I found him battling
with his books, as upon a former occasion, covered with dust and making
no preparation for going abroad. "How is this, Sir?" said I. "Don't you
recollect that you are to dine at Mr. Dilly's?" JOHNSON. "Sir, I did not
think of going to Dilly's. It went out of my head. I have ordered dinner
at home." BOSWELL. "But my dear Sir, you know you were engaged to
Mr. Dilly, and I told him so. He will expect you and will be much dis-

---

[4a] Quoted not from the journal for 14 May 1776, which gives no details, but from a
later recollection in the account of his last interview with Hume, 7 July 1776, "partly
enlarged from my memory, 3 March 1777."

[5] We have attempted, so far as we can determine it, to give the first draft. This part
of the manuscript of the *Life* is in the collection of Mr. Arthur A. Houghton, Jr.,
New York City. The leaves show signs of having been separated from the rest of the
manuscript and folded, with the following docket and note on the outside: "First
Conversation between Dr. Johnson and Mr. Wilkes, 1776. It is prefaced in the book
with a full account of the *Negotiation* by which I led Johnson to affirm that meeting
Mr. Wilkes would be nothing to him (affecting perfect ease of manners), so that when
I brought them together, he was *obliged* not to find f<ault>." Clearly Boswell submitted this portion of the manuscript of the *Life* to various of his friends—perhaps
even to Wilkes—before sending it to the printer.

appointed if you don't come." JOHNSON. "You must talk to Mrs. Williams."

Here was a sad dilemma. I feared that what I was so confident I had secured would yet be frustrated. He stood in some degree of awe of Mrs. Williams and if she should be obstinate he would not stir. I ran downstairs to the blind lady's room and told her I was in great uneasiness, for Dr. Johnson had engaged to me to dine this day at Mr. Dilly's, but that he told me he had forgotten his engagement and had ordered dinner at home. "Yes, Sir," said she pretty peevishly, "Dr. Johnson is to dine at home." "Madam," said I, "his respect for you is such that I know he will not leave you unless you absolutely desire it. But as you have his company so often, I hope you will be good enough to forego it for a day, as Mr. Dilly is a very worthy man, has often had agreeable parties at his house for Dr. Johnson, and will be vexed if the Doctor neglects him today. And then, Madam, be pleased to consider my situation. I carried the message, and I assured Mr. Dilly that Dr. Johnson was to come; and, to be sure, he has made a dinner and invited a company and boasted of the honour he was assured he was to have. I shall be quite affronted if he does not go."

She gradually softened to my entreaties, which were certainly as earnest as most entreaties to ladies upon any occasion, and was graciously pleased to empower me to tell Dr. Johnson that, "All things considered, she thought he should certainly go." I flew back to him, still in dust and careless of what should be the event, indifferent in his choice—Dilly's or home—and the moment I had announced to him Mrs. Williams's consent, he roared: "Frank, a clean shirt," and was very quickly dressed. When I had him fairly in the hackney-coach with me, I exulted as much as a fortune hunter who has an heiress in the post-chaise with him.

When we entered Mr. Dilly's dining-room, he found himself in the midst of a company whom he did not know. I kept myself snug and silent, watching how he would conduct himself. I observed him whispering to Mr. Dilly, "Who is that gentleman, Sir?" "Mr. Arthur Lee."⁹ "Tut, tut, tut" (which was one of his habitual mutterings). Mr. Arthur Lee was not only a Patriot, but an American and afterwards Minister from the United States at the Court of Madrid. "And who is the gentleman in lace?" "Mr. Wilkes, Sir." This information confounded him still more. He had some

⁹ Arthur Lee, born in Virginia, was educated at Eton and then at Edinburgh (M.D., 1764), where he had been one of Boswell's light-hearted companions in the Soaping Club. He was admitted to the English bar in 1775. During the American War he performed various missions abroad for the Continental Congress, and then embarked on a diplomatic career which was marred by quarrels and unjust attacks upon his colleagues, one of whom was Benjamin Franklin.

difficulty to restrain himself, and, taking up a book, sat down at a window and read, or at least kept his eyes upon it intensely for some time till he composed himself. His situation, I dare say, was awkward enough. But he no doubt recollected his having rated me for supposing that he could be at all disconcerted by any company, and he therefore tuned himself up to appear quite as an easy man of the world, who can adapt himself at once to the manners of those whom he may chance to meet.

The cheering sound of dinner being upon the table dissolved his reverie, and we all sat down in good humour. There were present besides Mr. Wilkes and Mr. Arthur Lee, who was an old companion of mine when he studied at Edinburgh, Mr. (now Sir John) Miller, Dr. Lettsom, the Quaker physician, and Mr. Slater, the druggist. Mr. Wilkes placed himself next to Dr. Johnson, and behaved to him with so much attention and politeness that he gained upon him insensibly. No man eat more heartily than Johnson, or loved better what was nice and tasty. Mr. Wilkes was at great pains in helping him with some fine veal. "Pray give me leave, Sir—It is better here—A little of the brown—Some fat, Sir—A bit of the stuffing—Some gravy—Let me have the pleasure of giving you some butter—Allow me to recommend a squeeze of an orange—or the lemon perhaps may have more zest." "Sir, Sir, I am obliged to you, Sir," cried Johnson, bowing and turning his head to him with a look for some time of "surly virtue,"[r] but in a short time of complacency.

Foote being mentioned, Johnson said, "He is not a good mimic." One of the company added, "A merry andrew, a buffoon." JOHNSON. "Why yes, but he has wit too, and is not deficient in ideas or in fertility and variety of imagery, and not empty of reading; he has knowledge enough to fill up his part. One species of wit he has in an eminent degree: that of escape. You drive him into a corner with both hands; but he's gone, Sir, when you think you have got him—like an animal that jumps over your head. Then he has a great range for his wit. He never lets truth stand between him and a jest. And he is sometimes mighty coarse. The first time I was in company with Foote was at Fitzherbert's. Having no good opinion of the fellow, I was resolved against being entertained by him, and went on eating my dinner pretty sullenly, affecting not to mind him. But the dog was so very diverting that I was obliged to lay down my knife and fork, throw myself back upon my chair, and fairly laugh it out. No, Sir, he was irresistible. He upon one occasion had an extraordinary proof of the power of his talents. Amongst the many and various ways which he tried of getting money, he became a partner with a small-beer

---

[r] A reference to Johnson's *London*, l. 145:

> How, when competitors like these contend,
> Can surly virtue hope to fix a friend?

brewer,[7a] and he was to have a share of the profits for procuring customers amongst his numerous acquaintance. Fitzherbert was one who took his small beer; but it was so bad that the servants resolved not to drink it. They were at some loss how to notify their resolution, being afraid of offending their master, who they knew liked Foote much as a companion. At last they pitched upon a little black boy, who was rather a favourite, to be their deputy and deliver their remonstrance, and, having invested him with the whole authority of the kitchen, he was to speak to Fitzherbert in all their names upon a certain day that they would drink Foote's small beer no longer. On that day Foote happened to dine at Fitzherbert's, and this boy served at table. He was so delighted with Foote's stories and merriment and grimace that when he went downstairs, he told them, 'This is the finest man I have ever seen. I will not deliver your message. I will drink his small beer.' "

Somebody observed that Garrick could not have done this. WILKES. "Garrick would have made the small beer still smaller. He is now leaving the stage, but he will play *Scrub*[8] all his life." I knew that Johnson would let nobody attack Garrick but himself, as Garrick once said to me, and I had heard him praise his liberality, so to bring out his commendation of his celebrated pupil, I said loud: "I have heard Garrick is liberal." JOHNSON. "Yes, Sir. I know that Garrick has given away more money than any man in England I know, and that not from ostentatious views. Garrick was very poor when he began life; so when he came to have money, he probably was very unskilful in giving away, and saved when he should not. But Garrick began to be liberal as soon as he could, and I am of opinion the reputation of avarice, which he has had, has been very lucky for him and prevented his having many enemies. You despise a man for avarice, but you don't hate him. Garrick might have been much better attacked for living with more splendour than is suitable to a player. If they had had the wit to have attacked him in that quarter they might have galled him more. But they have kept clamouring about his avarice, which has rescued him from much obloquy and much envy.

"When I was a young fellow I wanted to write the life of Dryden, and in order to get materials I applied to the only two persons then alive who had seen him. These were old Swinny[9] and old Cibber. Swinny's information was no more than this, that at Will's Coffee-house Dryden had a particular chair for himself which was set by the fire in winter, and was then

[7a] Charles Price, a notorious swindler, who hanged himself in 1786 on being apprehended for counterfeiting bank-notes.

[8] The tapster, server, and man of all work to Lady Bountiful's household in Farquhar's *Beaux' Stratagem*. The part was one of Garrick's most famous comic impersonations.

[9] Owen MacSwinny, the playwright.

called his winter chair, and that it was carried out for him to the balcony in summer, and was then called his summer chair. Cibber could tell no more but that he remembered him a decent old man, arbiter of critical disputes at Will's. You are to consider that Cibber was then at a great distance from Dryden, had perhaps one leg only in the room and durst not draw in the other." BOSWELL. "Yet Cibber was a man of observation." JOHNSON. "I think not." BOSWELL. "You will allow his *Apology* to be well done." JOHNSON. "Very well done, to be sure, Sir. That book is a striking proof of the justice of Pope's remark,

> Each might his several province well command
> Would all but stoop to what they understand."

BOSWELL. "And his plays are good." JOHNSON. "Yes. But that was his trade, *l'esprit du corps.* He had lived always among players and play writers. I wondered that he had so little to say in conversation, for he had kept the best company and learnt all that can be got by the ear. He abused Pindar to me, and then showed me an ode of his own with this couplet,

> Perched on the eagle's soaring wing
> The lowly linnet loves to sing.[1]

I told him that when the ancients made a simile, they always made it like something real."

Mr. Arthur Lee mentioned some Scotch who had taken possession of a barren part of America, and wondered why they should choose this. JOHNSON. "Why, Sir, all barrenness is comparative. The *Scotch* would not know it to be barren." BOSWELL. "Come, come. He is pleasing the English. You have now been in Scotland, Sir, and [1a] say if you did not see meat and drink enough there." JOHNSON. "Why, meat and drink enough to give the inhabitants strength sufficient to run away from home." All these quick and lively sallies were said quite sportively, quite in jest, and with a smile which showed that he meant only wit. Upon this topic he and Mr. Wilkes could perfectly assimilate. Here was a bond of union between them, and I was conscious that as both had visited Caledonia, both were fully satisfied of the strange narrow ignorance of those who imagine that it is a land of famine. But they amused themselves with persevering in the old jokes. When I claimed a superiority in Scotland over England in one respect, that no man can be arrested there for a debt merely because

---

[1] As Johnson told Boswell on 21 September 1777, Cibber "had heard of the wren perching on the eagle's wing, and had mistaken it for the linnet."

[1a] A reproduction of the page of the copy that begins with this word will be found among the illustrations following p. 134. "N89" in the left-hand margin is the proof-reader's notation that signature N, p. 89 of the second volume of Boswell's book began in the proofs at that point.

another swears it against him; but there must first be the judgement of a court of law ascertaining its justice; and that summary arrestment of the person can take place only if his creditor should swear that he is about to fly from the country, or, as it is technically expressed, is *in meditatione fugae:*[2] WILKES. "That, I should think, may be safely sworn ⟨of⟩ all the Scotch nation." JOHNSON (to Mr. Wilkes). "You must ⟨know, Sir,⟩ I lately took my friend Boswell to see genuine civilized life in an English provincial town. I turned him loose at Lichfield, my native city, that he might for once see real civility. For you know he lives among savages at home, and among rakes in London." WILKES. "Except when he is with grave, sober, decent people like you and me." JOHNSON. "And we ashamed of him." WILKES. "Boswell, you have kept a great deal of bad company."

After dinner and at tea we had an accession of Mrs. Knowles, the amiable accomplished Quaker,[3] and of Mr. Alderman Lee.[4] Amidst some patriotic groans, somebody (I think the Alderman) said, "Poor old England is lost." JOHNSON. "It is not so much to be lamented that old England is lost, as that the Scotch have found it."

Mr. Wilkes held a candle to show a fine print of a beautiful female figure which hung in the room, and pointed out the elegant contour of the bosom with the hand of a master. He afterwards waggishly insis⟨ted⟩ with me that all the time Johnson showed visible signs of a fervent admiration of the corresponding charms of the fair Quaker.

This imperfect record will serve to give a notion of this very curious interview, which was not only pleasing at the time, but had the agreeable and benignant effect of reconciling any differences and sweetening any acidity, which, in the various bustle of political contest, had been produced in the minds of two men, who, though widely different, had so many things in common—classical learning, political knowledge, modern literature, wit and humour and ready repartee—that it would have been much to be regretted if they had been forever at a distance from each other.

I attended Dr. Johnson home, and had the satisfaction to hear him tell Mrs. Williams how much he had been pleased with Mr. Wilkes's company, and what an agreeable day he had passed.

[EDITORIAL NOTE: From the history of the past two years of Boswell's life, the reader may suspect that all the notes relating to the English visit will not be pleasant and convivial. And they are not completely so. On 1 May, for example, when he left Bath to return to London, he wrote

---

[2] "Contemplation of flight."

[3] A beautiful woman and a clever conversationalist, she was best known for her needlework portraits.

[4] William Lee, a brother of Arthur Lee, was like him a native of Virginia.

that he was "low a very little," though he "recovered on arrival." He suffered from a venereal disease; in addition he was plagued because he could drink only water. His pledge of total abstinence for a year was kept about the usual length of time: that is to say, one month, whereupon he got a dispensation from Paoli to drink three glasses of wine at a time. After hearing that Boswell had told Thrale that he had been drunk twelve times since he came to London (perhaps after learning from Boswell himself the unhappy consequences of his drinking), Johnson had lectured him sharply and earnestly. Boswell had also been warned that he asked too many questions about Johnson. "You have but two topics," Johnson said, "yourself and me, and I'm sick of both." On Boswell's last day in London, Johnson wrote to Mrs. Boswell: "You will now have Mr. Boswell home; it is well that you have him; he has led a wild life." The notes, as well as his journal in London, show that this was no playful exaggeration.

The last day was 16 May. Boswell saw Mrs. Rudd ("charming") and was "lively" and a "man of fashion." He sang his song on her, *The Snake.* And at the end of his note for the day, he made a brief report of the interview. An interlinear addition above the heading ("Mrs. R. 16 May") reads, "Like water corrupted and grown fresh again, her art is become purest simplicity." Thereafter follows the record—the last we shall read of Mrs. Rudd until 9 August 1785, when Boswell received a card from her begging him to pay a visit.]

[SHE. "I will] show you [a] miniature [of myself] if you'll return it upon honour. This [was] taken when I was in confinement, in case of any accident." [J.] "What, Madam, do you talk with so much ease? Do you mean losing [your] life?" [SHE.] "Yes." [J.] "What, being hanged?" [SHE.] "No, I assure you [I] should never have been hanged. [I] had taken care of that." [J.] "What! had you resolution [to destroy yourself?" SHE.] "I promise you [I am] not afraid of death. [This is] no affectation. [I am] above it. As I said to a gentleman, 'I have too [much] virtue to be a prude, and too much sense to be a coquette.' " [J.] "The latter [is] very true. As for virtue, one cannot answer for another's. One can hardly answer for one's own. But why too much virtue to be [a] prude? I've seen a virtuous prude." SHE. "No, they have only the affectation of it." [She] pushed me to stay.[5] [J.] "You could make me commit murder. [But] you would be sorry afterwards to have made so ungenerous a use of your power. You have no occasion to be convinced of your power over the human heart. You know it. I dare say you could make me do anything—make me commit murder." [6] For [the] first [time] delirium [seized me. J. "Is a] pretty

[5] Reading uncertain; perhaps "to tell."
[6] The repetition is probably inadvertent, this part of the conversation (from "you would be sorry") being on a new leaf, which was no doubt written later.

ankle one of your perfections?" [SHE.] "Yes." [I. "Your] eyes—" [SHE.] "Poets and painters have told me enough of them." [When I took a] kiss, [she said, "I have] heard I had [a] fine mouth." [Snatched] several, [with] passion. Twice [I said] "Adieu"; at last, "God bless you."

[EDITORIAL NOTE: The last hours of this day were spent at Johnson's house, and the first few hours of the next morning, the 17th, when, after three hours of half-sleep, Boswell was on his way to Edinburgh. Before going to bed, he was bidden another farewell, this time stern yet gentle. Johnson accompanied him to his bedroom, while Boswell complained that nothing had been said that day.]

[JOHNSON.] "Why, Sir, [there] seldom [is." BOSWELL.] "Why then meet?" [JOHNSON.] "To eat and drink and promote kindness. And, Sir, 'tis better so than by solid conversation, for *then* people differ. And for this Sir Robert Walpole said he talked bawdy at his table, as all could join. Lord Hailes's *Annals* has not that painted form which people like nowadays. But 'twill be a book [that] will always sell, [it has] such a stability of dates, certainty of facts, and punctuality of citation. I never before read Scotch history with certainty. Take care of yourself. Don't drink. ['Tis] as important [for you] as 'To be or not [to] be': To be in one's wits or not. You may [when drunk] do what you deserve to be hanged for next day. Every man is to take existence on the terms on which it is given to him. Yours is given to you on condition of your not using liberties which other people may. Don't talk of yourself or of me. ([You may] talk of me to Mrs. Boswell and Veronica and your son.) Don't make yourself and me a proverb. Have no one topic, that people can say, 'We'll hear him upon it.' " Asked how [I should] read [the] Bible—with [a] commentary? [JOHNSON. "Read] Lowth and Patrick [on the] Old Testament, Hammond [on the] New." He was not very fluent. [I said,] "Thank you for all your kindness." [JOHNSON. "You are] very welcome. Nobody repays it with more."

Boswell's Interview with the Celebrated Margaret Caroline Rudd, London, 22 April 1776

[EDITORIAL NOTE: The notorious Margaret Caroline Rudd, for some months the most talked-of woman in Great Britain, has no article in *The Dictionary of National Biography,* nor is it easy for the uninitiated to find much concerning her elsewhere. In his books, *Some Distinguished Victims of the Scaffold* and *Trial of Henry Fauntleroy and other famous Trials for Forgery,* Mr. Horace Bleackley has given two excellent sketches of her career, based upon extensive research in eighteenth-century periodicals; but these studies have too frequently escaped attention because of their inclusion under titles which do not contain Mrs. Rudd's name. We therefore venture to prefix to Boswell's account of his first meeting with Mrs. Rudd a few notes on the remarkable woman he describes. For these notes we are largely indebted to Mr. Bleackley.

Margaret Caroline Rudd was born in the north of Ireland about 1745. Her father, Patrick Youngson (or, as she herself insisted, Patrick Young), was a surgeon and apothecary. Her mother, Marjorie Stewart, was the natural daughter of "Major W. Stewart of the Dragoons." This Major Stewart appears to have been of the family of Stewart of Ballymoran in Ireland, the Stewarts of Ballymoran being cadets of the Stewarts of Garlies (after 1623 Earls of Galloway) in Scotland. A more intriguing line of descent which Boswell seems never to have mentioned and perhaps was unaware of links Mrs. Rudd with Boswell himself. If her grandfather was a Stewart of Ballymoran, then, like Boswell, she was descended from Lady Marie Stuart, Countess of Mar and daughter of the Duke of Lennox, and could claim cousinship with her Sovereign.[1] She married at the age of seventeen a Lieutenant Valentine Rudd, but soon left him and embarked on the career of a woman of pleasure. In her early and more humble days she seems to have posed as a foreign lady of mysterious but noble origin, using a position as French teacher or governess to lead her to profitable connexions with wealthy men whom she afterwards blackmailed. We pick her up in these years under the varied names of Miss de la Rochette, Miss Malfaisans, Mrs. Potter, and Miss de Grosberg. She appears to have taught for a time in a young ladies' school at Exeter, and to have served briefly as governess in the family of Governor Floyer. At the end of 1764 she secured an appointment as governess to the daughters of the Earl of Lauderdale and was unmasked, apparently with little effect on her fortunes. In 1767 she seems still to have been calling herself Countess de Grosberg; later she dropped the Countess and became Mrs. Gore. The rich Jewish money-lender Salvadore was said to have been generous to her, and scandal (perhaps without much truth) numbered John Wilkes and the young Duke of Cumberland among her admirers.

In 1770 she accepted the protection of a certain Daniel Perreau, who introduced her as his wife, and to whom she bore three children. Perreau was a man of expensive tastes but no certain occupation, who, after having been three times a bankrupt, was now playing the dangerous game of

[1] See below, Appendix C, Charts IV and I. Mrs. Rudd, at least at a later time, was well aware of her Graham (which implied the Lennox) descent, for in 1789 she published a pamphlet which not only asserted it but hinted that she had a presumptive claim to the dormant (Graham) earldom of Menteith. The seven generations on her side as compared with only four on Boswell's are explained by the fact that he descended through late marriages—one a second, the other a third—of two men advanced in years.

speculation in Exchange Alley. He had a twin brother, Robert, an apothecary (that is, general medical practitioner), who had always borne the reputation of being as honest and hard-working as Daniel was frivolous. The trio soon became involved in criminal transactions on a large scale. Certain evidence is lacking, and will always be lacking, but it is probable that the desperate expedient of forgery was first employed to cover some of Daniel's speculations, and that, as generally happens in such cases, further forgeries became necessary to conceal the first. At any rate we know that Mrs. Rudd, who was an adept at feigned handwriting, forged bonds or promissory notes in the name of a rich Army agent, William Adair, and that Daniel and Robert Perreau borrowed money against these notes. As each came due, a larger note was forged to cover it. It was no doubt hoped that a lucky *coup* of Daniel's would bring in money enough to enable them to pay off their forgeries and retire from the game. But Daniel continued to be unlucky, and the inevitable crash followed.

When, in March 1775, Robert was challenged in passing one of the bonds, both brothers tried to save their own necks by professing themselves to be the innocent dupes of Daniel's supposed wife, who, they said, had told them that she was the natural daughter of Mr. Adair's kinsman, James Adair, and that the bonds were the free gift of a doting relative.[a] That Mrs. Rudd furnished the brains of the association is evident, but that the Perreaus were not also guilty seems hardly credible. As men of the world, they could hardly have believed that a man of Mr. Adair's wealth would choose to advance money only by notes of hand, or that he would steadily refuse to meet those for whom he professed so high a regard. Mrs. Rudd, who had shown the most admirable loyalty on the occasion of Robert's detection, now met the treachery of her accomplices by offering herself as evidence for the Crown against them. The Perreaus were found guilty and sentenced to be hanged. And Mrs. Rudd found herself in some danger of sharing their fate. Lord Mansfield thought her claim to immunity unsatisfactory. She had confessed to signing William Adair's name to one bond, but maintained that Daniel had compelled her to do so by holding a knife to her throat. Consequently, said his Lordship, she was not an accomplice, and as claiming innocence, should have no objection to being tried! Furthermore, though there were known to be several of the forged bonds, she admitted knowledge of only one: therefore she had forfeited immunity by not telling *all* the truth. The question of trying a person who had been admitted to evidence was so important that the opinion of twelve judges was finally taken, the resulting decision being that she must stand trial.

[a] The fact seems to have been that she was (with Daniel's connivance) mistress of James Adair, who was one of the sources of the personal "fortune" to which she frequently referred.

After having been kept in gaol for six months, she appeared on 7 December 1775 before the Court in the Old Bailey. Gaetano Bartolozzi's print of her in the prisoner's box (following page 134) will give some indication of the histrionic gifts she displayed there. The public generally considered her the victim of injustice. She therefore carefully avoided all appearance of the grand lady and dressed in a quiet suit of "second mourning," every article of her costume and every detail of her posture being intended to emphasize her smallness, her fragility, and her helplessness.

The case for the prosecution proved really to be weak. The only persons besides Mrs. Rudd who knew the facts were the unfortunate brothers, who were not called. Their animus against her was evident, and their story had failed to convince a jury on the occasion of their own trials. A frank confession of guilt from them would probably have hanged her, but they still had hopes of a pardon.

She conducted her own defence with remarkable skill, handing her lawyer more than fifty notes during the progress of the trial. At the end she spoke briefly to the jury, concluding her plea with these words: "I have no reliance but on you. You are honest men, and I am safe in your hands." When the jury, after a deliberation of only thirty minutes, returned a verdict of "Not Guilty," "there were," says a contemporary account, "the loudest applauses almost ever known in a court of justice." The Perreaus had meantime been kept in prison waiting the outcome of her trial. Her acquittal sealed their fate, and though extraordinary exertions were made to secure a pardon for them, the King was adamant, and they were hanged at Tyburn on 17 January 1776, still protesting their innocence. It was only a little more than three months after this that Boswell first met Mrs. Rudd.

That Boswell wrote the account here presented has been known since the publication of his letters to Temple. On 28 April 1776 he wrote to his friend, "You know my curiosity and love of adventure. I have got acquainted with the celebrated Mrs. Rudd. I was sending an account of this to my wife; but as it appeared to me highly entertaining, I thought you should have a reading of it. I therefore send it. Pray take the greatest care of it, and return it to me by the first or second post." If there were any doubt that this is the identical document, it would be removed by Boswell's endorsement: "To my wife—but not sent."]

London, between 12 and 1 in
the morning of 23 April 1776

My dearest life,

Before I go to bed, and while the impressions of the extraordinary scene which I am going to mention are fresh and lively, I sit down to write to you. Many a time you heard me rave with a strange force of imagination about the celebrated Mrs. Rudd—Margaret Caroline Rudd—and how I should certainly see her while I was in London. My curiosity did not go off, and I resolved to gratify it. I heard where she had taken lodgings in Westminster, and this forenoon I went and knocked at the door. A woman came. "Does Mrs. Rudd lodge here?" "Yes, Sir." "Is she at home?" "I'll call her maid." The maid came and said she was not at home but would be at home in the evening, or I might find her any morning. Would I please leave my name? I said it was unnecessary to leave my name, but she would be so good as tell her mistress that a friend of Mr. Macqueen's from Scotland had called and would call again.[3] A quarter after nine in the evening I called again at her lodgings, No. 10 Queen Street. The maid said, "She is just gone out, Sir, but will be home in half an hour. You will oblige me if you will walk up stairs. I told her that you called." My answer was that I would call again in half an hour. I sauntered calmly to Westminster Bridge, and did not return till about ten. Still she was not come home, but I agreed to walk up stairs. I had a sort of palpitation at my heart when I knocked at the door. I was shown into a dining-room, decent enough, but how poor in comparison of her former magnificence! A couple of tallow candles gave me light. My fancy began to form fearful suppositions in this solitary situation. I thought the ghosts of the Perreaus might appear. I thought that there might be murderers or bullies in the house. But then the street was too public for that. Her books were a Court Calendar, Duncan's *Logic*, Watts' *Logic*, *Johnsoniana*, two copies of her *Genuine Letter to Lord Weymouth* and a defence of her around it, a letter to her from Mrs. Christian Hart,[4] Pope's *Essay on Man* and his *Essay on Criticism* bound together, and *The Small Talker,* a very good novel against the practice of some men in gaining the affections of young ladies only for conquest, as they soon neglect them. I sat half an hour reading in the two last books.

[3] Probably Robert Macqueen, later Lord Braxfield. Mrs. Rudd, according to her own story, had visited relatives in Scotland in December 1772, and while there had "acquired many friends, persons of the first sense and consequence."

[4] A selection from the spate of pamphlets produced by the trials. Lord Weymouth, as Secretary of State for the Southern Department, would have had the responsibility of bringing to the King a recommendation for a pardon. On 15 January 1776, two days before the date set for the execution of the Perreaus and while extraordinary pressure was being brought on the executive to pardon Robert, Mrs. Rudd addressed this letter to Lord Weymouth, asserting Robert's guilt in the strongest manner. Christian Hart, formerly her servant, one of the witnesses against her at her trial, testified that Mrs. Rudd had attempted to bribe her to commit perjury. She was to swear that she had seen Mrs. Robert Perreau forge the bond for which Mrs. Rudd was being tried, and that Mrs. Perreau and Sir Thomas Frankland (see below) were in a conspiracy to secure Mrs. Rudd's conviction and execution.

Then I heard her coming up stairs. I was all impatience and trepidation, when there entered rather a little woman, delicately made, not at all a beauty, but with a very pleasing appearance and much younger than I imagined. In short, the first view of her surprised me somewhat, as it was not by any means such as to strike me with the awe either of dignity or of high elegance. She was dressed in black clothes, with a white cloak and hat. I begged pardon for intruding upon her, but I was a friend of Mr. Macqueen's, and though I had no direct instructions from that family, she might believe that they would be glad to have accounts of her. She said she was much obliged to me for my civility. We sat down opposite to one another at a little distance, and I asked her how she was now. She said, "As well as could be expected," and immediately entered upon her unhappy story, which she told (I went to bed when I had written to the foot of the last page; I now continue my narrative, 24[5] April, between nine and ten in the morning) with wonderful ease and delicacy and an air of innocence quite amazing when one thought of what had been proved. She said the *Per*reau[6] family (as she called it) was a little commonwealth, it was so numerous and so spread over England and Ireland, and that all the connexions endeavoured to throw the guilt upon *her*. I said it was shocking that the Perreaus had died denying as they did. "Yes," said she, "it must shock everybody who has any tenderness of conscience. They should have died in silence." She said she was to carry on a suit against Sir Thomas Frankland by which, if she got the full value of what he carried off belonging to her, she would recover £5,000 besides high damages.[7]

She spoke with much earnestness of her anxiety to know whether her husband, Mr. Rudd, was alive or not, and said she would go to Ireland to see if a man whom some would have to be he, and others an impostor, was he or not, though she thought that his long neglect of her set her free from him.[8] But she would not think of marrying again after having

[5] Probably a mistake for 23. The notes seem to indicate that he saw Mrs. Rudd late on the evening of the 22nd, began the account after midnight that same night, and completed it the next morning.

[6] That is, she stressed the first syllable, not the last.

[7] It was on Admiral Sir Thomas Frankland's charge that Mrs. Rudd was committed, and he was the nominal prosecutor at her trial. A client and friend of Robert Perreau, he had lent him £4,000 on the security of a bond for £10,600 signed William Adair and payable to Robert Perreau. It was for forging and publishing this bond that Mrs. Rudd was being tried. When the Perreaus were apprehended, Daniel attempted to secure Sir Thomas's silence by giving him a bill of sale of his house, whereupon Sir Thomas carried off Mrs. Rudd's jewels and clothes. Mrs. Rudd sued for their return on the amusing but apparently inexpugnable ground that she was neither a criminal nor the wife of Daniel Perreau.

[8] He outlived her, and did not die until 1809.

been twice so unlucky; and indeed, unless it was a man of rank and fortune that could bear her up notwithstanding what had happened to her, she should not think of marriage. She said she loved reading, and that if she had not had resources in her own mind, she must have been very unhappy. She said her confinement was very severe upon her. She had formerly been consumptive two years. She was almost blind when she came out again to the light, and her eyes, I saw, were still weak. When I looked at her narrowly she seemed to have some flushy heat on her cheeks, her nose contracted as she breathed, and she spoke through her teeth. Yet there was upon the whole—"Celia altogether" [9]—something so pleasing and insinuating that I could believe her power to be what we have read. I said she was reckoned quite a sorceress, possessed of enchantment. She smiled and did not contradict me as to the past, but said she could enchant nobody. I begged her pardon and, with exquisite flattery, said, "My dear Mrs. Rudd, don't talk so. Everything you have said to me till now has been truth and candour"; and I told her I was convinced she could enchant, but I begged she would not enchant me too much, not change me into any other creature, but allow me to continue to be a man with some degree of reason. I was as cautious as if I had been opposite to that snake which fascinates with its eyes. Her language was choice and fluent and her voice melodious. The peculiar characteristic of her enchantment seemed to be its delicate imperceptible power. She perfectly concealed her design to charm. There was no meretricious air, no direct attempt upon the heart. It was like hearing the music of the spheres which poets feign, and which produces its effect without the intervention of any instrument, so that the very soul of harmony immediately affects our souls. She said she had formerly deluded herself with hopes of enjoying happiness. She now was satisfied with insensibility, not however in the extreme, but comparatively speaking. "You must not be insensible," said I, and rose and seized her silken hand, and afterwards, upon the argument being renewed a little, kissed it. This was all experiment, and she showed neither prudery nor effrontery, but the complaisance, or compliance if you please, of a woman of fashion.

She asked if Miss Macqueen [1] was married; said she promised to be a

[9] "There is a very good song in one of the collections of smaller pieces of poetry, in which a lover *analyses his mistress,* if that phrase may be used, and after examining her title to different perfections one by one, and still being obliged to acknowledge her deficiency, he accounts for his preference by saying, in short ' 'Tis Celia all together.' " (*Hypochondriack* No. 11, August 1778. The song in William Whitehead's *The Je ne sais quoi,* which Boswell no doubt found in Dodsley's *Collection.*)

[1] If "Mr. Macqueen" was Braxfield, this was his eldest daughter, Mary, who next year married William Honyman, advocate, later a baronet and Lord of Session with the title Lord Armadale.

fine woman; said she liked Scotland and would perhaps visit it again, and would go to the house of Mr. Stewart of Physgill,[2] to which she had many invitations. She spoke of our New Town with commendation. She said she had seen Mr. Macqueen only once at his own house. She seemed much displeased with Lord Galloway; said he was the most insincere man that could be, but very successful in making his way at a court. I said he was good-humoured and lively. She said that was partly natural, but a good deal mechanical. This was a very just remark and showed her knowledge of human nature. We talked then on forming a character by habit, and she said we might be anything we pleased. This is Dr. Johnson's opinion. She said Lady Gower[3] was a worthy, friendly woman and very sincere, which was not a little remarkable, as she had been so long a Court lady and excelled so much in that way; "which," says she, "is every morning having a plan—a part to play—for the day. Lady Gower," said she, "is a good relation in every respect: a good wife, a good mother, and behaves exceedingly well to all Lord Gower's connexions." She praised Keith Stewart[4] too, as sincere and friendly. I said nothing. She talked of Lady Galloway's building a house on her jointure lands, and never was at a loss for chit-chat.

I sometimes kept silence on purpose to observe how she would renew the conversation. She never let the pause be long, but with admirable politeness, when she found that I did not begin again to speak and might perhaps be embarrassed, said something quite easily, so as not to have the appearance of abruptness, to make me feel that I had stopped short, but rather of a continuation of our discourse, as if what she then said had grown out of what we had talked of before. Another thing which I remarked was that she did not aim at being witty. She did not dazzle with brilliance, but cheered one with a mild light. And what I thought also an uncommon excellence, she did not whine about her distress or affect to be plaintive, for she was sensible that the representation of unhappiness gives a certain degree of pain, and though pity is said to be akin to love, gaiety is a much more engaging relation. Seeing her eyes weak, I set the candles upon a table at some distance from her, but as she was then in such obscurity that I could hardly discern the pretty turns of her countenance as she talked, I soon brought back one of them to a table near her,

[2] John Hathorn (Stewart), d. 1780. The real owner of Physgill was his wife, Agnes Stewart, d. 1786. The Stewarts of Physgill, like the Stewarts of Ballymoran, were cadets of the Stewarts of Garlies, ancestors of the Earls of Galloway. John Stewart, brother of the founder of the family of Physgill, Alexander Stewart, purchased Ballymoran, County Down, Ireland, early in the seventeenth century. It is probably from him that Mrs. Rudd was descended.

[3] Lord Galloway's sister.

[4] Lord Galloway's brother.

saying that I must not deny myself altogether the pleasure of seeing her.

She said that during her confinement she was quite alone all the night. She would not have a maid in the same room with her, "because," said she, "there were hours when I did not wish to be at all disturbed, as I employed them in thought; and I hope I shall be the better for it. I hope I am wiser." When she talked of insensibility, I said she might as well be a nun. She said if it were not for her children she would retire to a convent. She liked France, but she would not be a nun. She would not shut herself up for life. She said people made many stories concerning her. It was said she lived with Lord Lyttelton. "But," said she, "though one who has been a good deal at public places knows most people of distinction by sight, I really do not know Lord Lyttelton by sight, and he has contradicted the report. Besides, Lord Lyttelton is not a person with whom one would form a connexion, as he is quite a profligate." "Nay, Madam," said I, "I heard today that you and Lord Loudoun were very well acquainted." "To be sure," said she, "if Lord Loudoun were to come into this room, I should know him; but as to any intimacy—" "It is amazing," said I, "with what confidence people will tell lies, but there is a vanity in being thought to know particularly about a lady so celebrated as you." Said she: "People are apt to form an idea of one whom they have never seen. A gentleman told me he had imagined that I was old and ugly." "Why," said I, "that was very extraordinary, though indeed it may have been owing to the reputation of your enchantment, as witches were said to be old and ugly. You are, however, much *younger* than I supposed." "But," said she, "I am not a young woman. I am nine-and-twenty, and I do not think that young."

She mentioned Cummyng, the herald-painter and Keeper of the Lyon Records, and said he and Sir John Dalrymple went to Scotland a month ago, but had business to transact for Government somewhere upon the road. Such absurd airs of consequence had been assumed, and I was silent upon that head. I spoke of her pedigree. She said, "They would not allow me to be a gentlewoman and said my pedigree was forged—as if one would forge a pedigree when certainly one cannot raise money upon it." The easy, unconcerned pleasantry with which she talked of forgery was wonderful.

While she again said something about her confinement and trial, she showed a pretty little foot, and I got up in a kind of lively sudden surprise and said, "I cannot believe that you have gone through all this. Are you really Mrs. Rudd?" She smiled and said, "I *am* Mrs. Rudd." I said she must forget all the ill that had passed and be happy for the future, and I thought love would be the best remedy for her. She said very gently she did not think so. I run out in the commonplace style upon the happiness of love, but said she must now be very cautious in her choice. I said I hoped she would forgive the liberty I had taken in waiting upon her. I thought I might avail myself of being a friend of Mr. Macqueen's, while I had a desire very natural to see a lady so distinguished for enchantment, and I should be much obliged to her if she would give me leave to call on her sometimes. She made me very welcome and said she was always at home. I returned her a thousand thanks.

During all this interview I was quite calm and possessed myself fully, snuffed the candles and stirred the fire as one does who is at home, sat easy upon my chair, and felt no confusion when her eyes and mine met. Indeed her eyes did not flash defiance but attracted with sweetness, and *there* was the reason of the difference of effect between her eyes and those of more insolent or less experienced charmers. She was not a robber but a thief. I wished her good night with a kiss which she received without affectation of any kind. I was *then* a little confused. Churchill satirizes Lord Lyttelton for being *curious in grief* in his *Monody* on the death of his first lady. I was here actually *curious in kissing.*[5] I thought of Mrs. Rudd's fame for enchantment and all her history. I concluded from every *circumstance* that she was now upon the town, though her conversation was so superior to that of common women. But I might be mistaken, for I never hinted at an intrigue. I wondered what she thought of me. I imagined I was very agreeable, and it pleased me much that she never asked my name or anything at all about me, which showed perfect good breeding. I would not for a good deal have missed this scene. We crowd to see those who excel in any art, and surely the highest excellence of art is the art of pleasing, the art of attracting admiration and fondness.

[5] The manuscript has the alternative "taking a kiss."

APPENDIX A

[Draft of a letter in Boswell's hand, bearing the following heading: "This is a letter which I wrote for David Boswell at Leith, to my father. He copied it over, signed it, and sent it. But it had no effect."]

[Edinburgh, late 1775]

My Lord:—It gives me great uneasiness to be under the necessity of intruding upon your Lordship, but your general character and the kindness with which you was pleased to treat me in my younger days make me hope that you will forgive me for applying to you while in absolute want, for to whom can I look up but to Lord Auchinleck, whom I have all my life been accustomed to reverence as a patron? My father had the honour of being your Lordship's companion, and from the manner in which I have heard you speak of Craigston I am persuaded your Lordship will not hear that his grandson is starving without doing something to help him.

Your Lordship may remember that I was bred a weaver and succeeded Mr. Bruce Campbell at Riccarton. But that business turned out as ill with me as it did with him, so that I was reduced to a very poor situation so as to be glad to do anything in an honest way to make a livelihood. I therefore set up in the way of teaching to dance, by which I have been able hitherto to support myself and a wife and several children without being a burthen to my relations. I have contracted no new debt since I set up in that way, but am owing about £40, which was what I owed by former losses; and I have kept it just as it was by changing creditors, being always in hopes that things would do better with me. But by the late failures in credit I find myself much worse. My school which I keep at Leith is so diminished that I have but five scholars; and in short I am in a very miserable state.

I always flatter myself that my uncle in Jamaica will do for me. Your son, Mr. James Boswell, has been so kind as to write to him strongly in my favour. But as he has done nothing yet, I hope your Lordship will not refuse me your assistance.

May I also entreat that your Lordship will get me put into any place that will be bread to me? I would humbly suggest that as my wife's grandfather Mr. Fergusson was a relation of Lord Kilkerran's,[1] I may be recom-

---

[1] "Sir Adam Fergusson's" (deleted). Sir James Fergusson, Lord Kilkerran, was Sir Adam Fergusson's father. Lord Auchinleck had been his colleague on the bench from 1754

mended by your Lordship to Sir Adam Fergusson, the present Member of Parliament for Ayrshire, especially as I understand that he owes his seat in a great measure to your Lordship,[2] and Sir Adam might get me some employment in the Customs. Or your Lordship's great interest with the Lord President might perhaps procure me the post of macer, which your Lordship procured for Monkland. Or by speaking to the Reverend Dr. Webster your Lordship might get me some small office about the City of Edinburgh.[3]

In the mean time I must earnestly implore your Lordship's humane interposition, as indeed my family is at present as great an object of charity as you can find. I am with the greatest respect, my Lord, your Lordship's most devoted humble servant.

APPENDIX B

The Scottish Courts and Legal System 1774–1776 [1]

On 26 July 1766, James Boswell "passed advocate," that is, was admitted to the Faculty of Advocates, and three days later he began to practise in the Scottish courts. For the next twenty years, with complete regularity and a fair degree of assiduity, he followed his professional career in Scotland, not abandoning it until early in 1786, when, in fulfilment of a long-cherished dream, he was admitted to the English bar and took up residence in London. Since so much of his daily life from 1766 onwards was spent in and about courts, especially the Court of Session in Edinburgh, the reader may find himself helped by an extended note on the principal features of the Scottish judicial system.

Both in its law and in its court procedure, the Scottish system differed

---

to 1759. For the connexions between the Craigston and the Knockroon Boswells, see Chart II in Appendix C.

[2] Lord Auchinleck probably had little difficulty in assigning this sentence to its true author.

[3] "I am willing to follow any way of life" (deleted).

[1] This sketch is repeated, with proper revision, from *Boswell for the Defence, 1769–1774.*

widely from the usage of England.[2] The basis of Scots law was the Roman Civil Law as expounded by the Dutch commentators, which explains why so many Scots advocates, including Boswell, his father, and his grandfather, studied for a time in Dutch universities. In one respect, though following a different nomenclature, the Scots professional arrangements agreed with those of England as opposed to those of the United States. In America, the vast majority of lawyers today are members of the bar and hence are qualified to plead in court, as well as to advise clients, to draw documents, and to manage cases (*causes* is the correct Scots terminology). In England there is a sharp division between *solicitors,* who prepare and manage cases, and *barristers,* who plead them; and the same distinction obtained in Scotland, though the terminology there was *writers* and *advocates.* (A Writer to the Signet was a writer whose membership in an ancient legal society entitled him to certain privileges.) Boswell was an advocate, which means that he was commonly engaged and briefed by a writer who was managing the cause. Advocates and Writers to the Signet were as a rule members of the same social class—upper middle, though many were of the aristocracy—but the profession of advocate was considered rather more "liberal" than that of writer, and might lead to promotion to the bench.

The principal courts in which Boswell appeared during the period of his Scottish practice were the Court of Session and the General Assembly of the Church of Scotland, which sat in Edinburgh, the High Court of Justiciary, which sat in Edinburgh and at circuit towns in the country, and the House of Lords, which sat in London.

The Court of Session was the supreme court for civil causes in Scotland. It sat in its own rooms in the Parliament House in Edinburgh on all week-days except Monday from 12 June to 11 August (Summer Session) and from 12 November to 11 March (Winter Session), with a short recess at Christmas. The bench consisted of fifteen judges, known as Senators of the College of Justice or Lords of Council and Session: fourteen Ordinary Lords and a fifteenth or presiding judge who was styled the Lord

---

[2] Since the purpose of this appendix is merely to elucidate Boswell's text, we have used the past tense throughout, though a good deal of the information here given would be as true for the present century as for the eighteenth. Our main sources are Hugo Arnot, *The History of Edinburgh,* 1788; Robert Bell, *A Dictionary of the Law of Scotland,* 2 vols., 1807; George Brunton and David Haig, *An Historical Account of the Senators of the College of Justice,* 1832; Henry Cockburn, *Memorials of His Time,* 1856; Sir Francis J. Grant, *The Faculty of Advocates in Scotland, 1532–1943,* Scottish Record Society, 1944; C. A. Malcolm, "The Parliament House and its Antecedents," in Stair Society *Publications,* xx. 449–458; and various English and Scottish annual calendars for the years 1774–1776.

President. Each judge bore the style of Lord, his further designation being usually that of his country estate. (Thus Alexander Boswell was styled Lord Auchinleck; James Burnett, Lord Monboddo. All judges, however, signed their Christian and family names, even to official acts.) By custom only advocates of considerable experience in the Court of Session were appointed judges, and such eventual promotion was the aim of most advocates. In 1776 the stated salary of the Lord President was £1,300 a year and that of the Ordinary Lords £700.[a]

The business of the Court was transacted in two divisions known as the Outer House and the Inner House. The court-room of the Outer House was the Parliament Hall, the stately apartment in which the Scots Parliament had sat from 1639 until the Union of 1707. Each week, in turn, one of the Ordinary Lords sat as a single judge in what had been the Sovereign's throne, and summarily decided the simpler legal actions. When his verdict was not acceptable to one of the parties, appeal was made to the Inner House, where the Court of Session, headed by the Lord President, sat to review the judgements of the Ordinaries. The proceedings in the Court of Session were carried on very largely in writing, advocates having to present their causes and arguments by way of minutes, representations, informations, memorials, replies, etc.—often in printed form—for the judges to consider. Only rarely, in causes of special importance, did the Court order a hearing in presence, that is, permit the opposing advocates to argue the cause viva voce. All causes in this Court were tried without juries. Appeal could be taken to the House of Lords from its final judgement. The Lords of Session wore gowns of purple cloth with cape and facings of crimson velvet. On the cape and facings were knots of cloth which had formerly been bows for tying the halves of the gown together in front. Eighteenth-century portraits indicate that full-bottomed wigs and long white cravats were normal accessories.

Six of the Lords of Session held dual appointments, and constituted the High Court of Justiciary, the supreme court of Scotland for criminal causes. This Court was in theory headed by the Lord Justice-General, a peer of exalted rank (the Duke of Queensberry held the office during the period covered by this volume). But if the Lord Justice-General did not hold the office as a pure sinecure, he no longer took part in trials and may for our purposes be ignored. The actual head of the Court was the Lord Justice-Clerk, one of the fifteen, who received an addition of £500 to his salary as Lord of Session. The other five Lords or Commissioners of Justiciary received an addition of £200 each. They met in their own room in

[a] Arnot says (p. 479) that, though the stated salary remained unchanged, Lord President Dundas was given an addition for his lifetime of £300 annually, beginning in 1769.

the Council House adjoining the Parliament Hall at its north-west end (the site now occupied by the lobby of the Signet Library) during the terms of the Court of Session, Mondays being entirely reserved for Justiciary business. Prosecutions for the Crown were conducted by His Majesty's Advocate for Scotland (commonly styled the Lord Advocate) and the Solicitor-General, generally assisted by other advocates. Criminal causes were tried before juries of fifteen citizens, a majority of votes being sufficient for a verdict. Scots law permitted not two but three verdicts: Guilty, Not Guilty, and Not Proven, the last being no less a full acquittal from the pains of the law than Not Guilty. The Lords of Justiciary wore scarlet gowns with cape and facings of white. Generally speaking, an appointment as Ordinary Lord of Session was terminated only by death or total incapacity to act, but a Justiciary Lord commonly relinquished his office on finding that age or infirmity was reducing his capacity for work.

Some time in the spring after the rising of the Court of Session and again in September, the Lords of Justiciary went on circuit: that is, presided at criminal courts at various stated towns in three areas into which Scotland was divided. The Western Circuit sat at Stirling, Glasgow, and Inveraray; the Northern at Perth, Aberdeen, and Inverness; the Southern at Jedburgh, Dumfries, and Ayr. Two judges were appointed for each circuit, but the duty was often actually performed by one. Each judge was allowed from £300 to £360 a year for circuit expenses, which included fairly lavish hospitality in circuit towns. Young lawyers acquired practice by "going the circuits"; older and better-established lawyers were less likely to take the trouble.

No appeal lay from the sentence of the High Court of Justiciary, and a prisoner capitally convicted in that Court could hope for reversal or mitigation of sentence only by exercise of the royal mercy. To allow time for appeal to the Crown, no capital sentence could be carried into execution to the south of the Forth within less than thirty days, or to the north of the Forth within less than forty.

There were several changes in the bench during the period covered by the present volume. Alexander Fraser, Lord Strichen, died on 15 February 1775, and Andrew Pringle, Lord Alemoor, on 14 January 1776. Their places were taken respectively by Alexander Lockhart, Lord Covington, and David Ross, Lord Ankerville. Lords Coalston and Pitfour resigned as Lords of Justiciary and were succeeded (30 April 1776) by Lords Gardenstone and Hailes. The following table gives the complete roster of the College of Justice from 12 February 1767 to 6 November 1776. Lords of Justiciary are indicated by asterisks.

Judicial Title	Family Name	Born / Died	Appointed Judge
Lord President	Robert Dundas	1713–1787	1760
*Lord Justice-Clerk	Thomas Miller	1717–1789	1766
Lord Alemoor	Andrew Pringle	d. 1776	1759
Lord Alva	James Erskine	c. 1723–1796	1761
Lord Ankerville	David Ross	c. 1727–1805	1776
*Lord Auchinleck	Alexander Boswell	1707–1782	1754
*Lord Coalston	George Brown	d. 1776	1756
Lord Covington	Alexander Lockhart	c. 1700–1782	1775
Lord Elliock	James Veitch	1712–1793	1761
*Lord Gardenstone	Francis Garden	1721–1793	1764
*Lord Hailes	Sir David Dalrymple	1726–1792	1766
*Lord Kames	Henry Home	1696–1782	1752
*Lord Kennet	Robert Bruce	1718–1785	1764
Lord Monboddo	James Burnett	1714–1799	1767
*Lord Pitfour	James Ferguson	c. 1700–1777	1764
Lord Stonefield	John Campbell	d. 1801	1763
Lord Strichen	Alexander Fraser	c. 1699–1775	1730

The Lord Advocate from 1766 to May 1775 was James Montgomery (1721–1803), who was then appointed Chief Baron of the Exchequer. The Solicitor-General, Henry Dundas (1742–1811), thereupon became Lord Advocate, and Alexander Murray (1736–1795) was made Solicitor-General.

The judges of another Scottish court receive frequent mention in Boswell's journal, but he himself did little or no business there. The Court of Exchequer tried causes relating to customs, excise, and other matters concerning Crown revenue. It consisted of a Lord Chief Baron and four other Barons. This Court followed the forms of English law, and English barristers as well as Scots advocates were eligible for appointment to its bench. The salaries of three of the Barons were the same as those of the Ordinary Lords of Session, but Baron Winn received £1,200 and the Lord Chief Baron received £2,000 annually. This court was almost completely reconstituted during the period covered by the present volume. Baron Mure died, and Barons Ord and Winn resigned. The full roster, 1774–1776, was as follows:

Lord Chief Baron	Robert Ord (resigned 1775; d. 1778)
Lord Chief Baron	James Montgomery (appointed 27 May 1775)
Baron	Sir John Dalrymple (1726–1810; appointed 11 May 1776)
Baron	John Grant (d. November 1776)
Baron	John Maule (1706–1781)
Baron	William Mure (1718–25 March 1776)
Baron	Fletcher Norton (1740–1820; appointed 27 February 1776)
Baron	George Winn (1725–1798; resigned early 1776)

Boswell went every day during term to the Parliament House, arriving at nine o'clock. If he had no cause to plead, he joined the other advocates in the Parliament Hall, where they paced back and forth in the Outer House, which was promenade and waiting-room as well as courtroom. (An area at the north end, fenced off by a slight wooden partition running half-way to the ceiling, was occupied by the stalls of stationers and booksellers, later of jewellers and cutlers.) Scots advocates did not have offices or chambers distinct from their dwellings. Boswell dictated his papers at home and made appointments with clients in a tavern. As will be seen from the dates given above, the sessions of the courts covered only six months of the year. During the long vacations, the professional demands on an advocate were few. If he were ambitious and prudent, he studied law then, for the Scots bar was crowded and a commanding practice had to be fought for. Boswell was restive under this discipline, and oftener than not rushed off to London as soon as the Court rose in the spring. In 1775 and 1776 he could plead the excuse of business—in 1775, indeed, he got forty-two guineas in fees—but he really needed no excuse except his own strong inclination. Term-time, however, was sacred. Not once in seventeen years (from 1766 to 1782) did he absent himself from Scotland when the Court of Session was sitting.

The fact that it cut into vacation may have been one of the reasons why he came to entertain such hearty dislike for the business of the General Assembly of the Church of Scotland. This, the supreme ecclesiastical court of the kingdom, sat each May in an apartment appropriated to its use in St. Giles's church. It was made up of ministers and elders elected annually from each presbytery, was presided over by a Moderator chosen at each Assembly from its own members, and was attended by a Lord High Commissioner representing the King. The best-known of Boswell's causes in this Court concerned a clergyman who was refused induction and ordination because of previous immoral behaviour. Most of his causes appear to have dealt with the then very lively issue of patronage: whether the chief landholder of a parish could present ministers, or whether they should come at the direct call of the parish.

The House of Lords of the Parliament of Great Britain, besides being a house of the legislature, was also the final court of appeal from most of the courts in Great Britain though not (as has already been mentioned) from the criminal courts of Scotland.[4] It sat as a court on stated days of the week throughout the legal year, even during prorogation or dissolution of Parliament. Any member of the House (all the peers of England

[4] The sources for this part of the sketch are mainly Michael Macdonagh, *The Book of Parliament*, 1897, and Sir Frank MacKinnon, "The Law and the Lawyers," in *Johnson's England*, ed. A. S. Turberville, 2 vols., 1933.

and of Great Britain, sixteen representative Scots peers, and twenty-six bishops) could attend and could vote on an appeal, and members sometimes exercised this privilege, but the decisions were usually left to the "law lords," that is, to the Lord Chancellor and the judges of the supreme courts of England who held the rank of peers. In 1775 and 1776 there were only two law lords: Lord Apsley (Bathurst after 16 September 1775), the Chancellor, and Lord Mansfield, Lord Chief Justice of the King's Bench. Apsley was present on all the various occasions in April and May 1775 when Boswell's case of Alexander *et al.* v. Paterson *et al.* came up; Mansfield was present on all but one. The case was finally put off to the autumn and was decided when Boswell was in Scotland. Both Apsley (by that time Bathurst) and Mansfield were present when the decision was made to postpone the Earl of Selkirk v. Douglas (above, 3 April 1776). Cases in the House of Lords were managed by solicitors and pleaded by advocates or barristers. The respective cases of the appellant and the respondent, forming the subject-matter of the appeal, were printed and bound in a considerable number of copies at the expense of the appellant and lodged with the House in advance of the trial; some of these were bound in purple cloth for the use of the law lords. Only two counsel could be heard on each side.

Contested elections of Scots Members of Parliament were tried by Select Committees of the House of Commons. The elaborate procedure of balloting by which the Committees, which consisted of fifteen members, were constituted, is described above, p. 121, *n.* 2. The balloting took place in the House, and the Committee sat in such court-room or committee room as was vacant. Boswell first served as counsel before a Select Committee in 1775. The Committee on that occasion met in the Court of Chancery.

Glossary of Legal Terms

ADVOCATION. The act of a superior court in calling before itself an action lying in an inferior court, on the motion of one of the parties to the action.

ARRESTMENT JUDICIO SISTI. Apprehension by judicial warrant of a defender who is believed to be meditating flight, until he finds caution to stand judgement within the jurisdiction.

BOX. To lodge a printed copy of a petition or answers to the Court of Session in the box of each judge.

CESSIO BONORUM. A total surrender by a debtor of his whole property, on oath, in favour of his creditors, so that he may escape perpetual imprisonment.

DEFENDER. The defendant or respondent.

DUPLY. A second reply; a defender's rejoinder to a pursuer's reply.

HERITABLE SECURITY. Security in land, or whatever is connected with land, for the interest and principal of a loan.

INFEFTMENT. Investiture in heritable property.

INFORMATION. A written pleading ordered by the Lord Ordinary when he takes a cause to report to the Inner House.

INTERLOCUTOR. The judgement of the court, or of the Lord Ordinary, which, unless reclaimed or appealed, has the effect of deciding the cause.

IRRITANCY. A clause in a deed by which any infringement of the conditions by one party entitles the other to treat the deed as null and void.

MEMORIAL. A statement of facts drawn up to be submitted for counsel's opinion. Also, an advocate's brief.

MINUTE. A notice of intention presented to the court by a party to a suit.

PANEL. The defendant (accused) in a criminal action.

PRECOGNITION. A preliminary examination of witnesses by the Lord Ordinary or by justices of the peace, in a criminal cause; also, the evidence uncovered in this examination.

PURGATION, OATH OF. The affirmation on oath of his innocence by the accused in a spiritual court, confirmed by the oaths of several of his peers. The General Assembly had enacted in 1707 that the oath was to be administered only in cases where there was strong presumption of guilt.

PURSUER. The plaintiff or prosecutor.

REPRESENTATION. A written pleading presented to the Lord Ordinary when his judgement is brought under review.

SUBMISSION, DEED OF. A contract by which the parties in a dispute agree to submit the disputed matters to arbitration.

SUSPENSION AND LIBERATION. A petition to the court asking for the sentence of imprisonment to be set aside and the debtor liberated. Since the failure to pay a debt after a judicial order for payment was considered an offence against the King, a debtor besides paying his debt had to present a bill of suspension and liberation and pay a fee before he could obtain his release.

TRUST OATH. A long and detailed oath which could be put to a freeholder presenting himself to vote at an election for a Member of Parliament for a county, stating that his title to his estate was "not nominal or fictitious, created . . . in order to enable me to vote for a member to serve in Parliament, but that the same is a true and real estate in me, for my own use and benefit, and for the use of no other person whatsoever."

APPENDIX C

Genealogical Tables

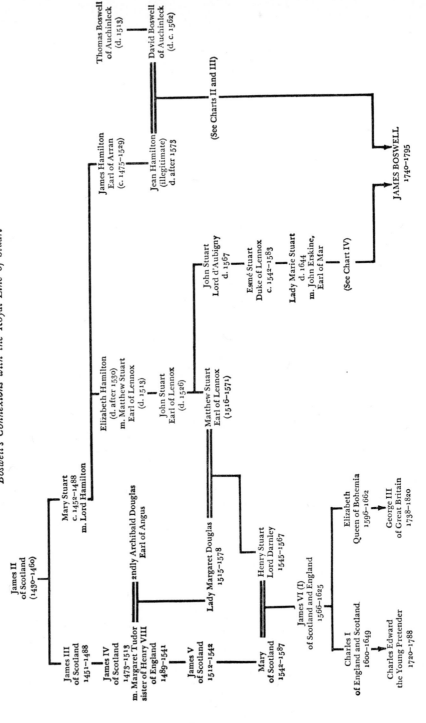

Chart I

Boswell's Connexions with the Royal Line of Stuart

James II
of Scotland
(1430–1460)

James III
of Scotland
1451–1488

James IV
of Scotland
1473–1513
m. Margaret Tudor
sister of Henry VIII
of England
1489–1541

2ndly Archibald Douglas
Earl of Angus

James V
of Scotland
1512–1542

Lady Margaret Douglas
1515–1578

Mary
of Scotland
1542–1587

Henry Stuart
Lord Darnley
1545–1567

James VI (I)
of Scotland and England
1566–1625

Charles I
of England and Scotland
1600–1649

Charles Edward
the Young Pretender
1720–1788

Elizabeth
Queen of Bohemia
1596–1662

George III
of Great Britain
1738–1820

Mary Stuart
c. 1452–1488
m. Lord Hamilton

Elizabeth Hamilton
(d. after 1530)
m. Matthew Stuart
Earl of Lennox
(d. 1513)

John Stuart
Earl of Lennox
(d. 1526)

Matthew Stuart
Earl of Lennox
(1516–1571)

James Hamilton
Earl of Arran
(c. 1475–1529)

Jean Hamilton
(illegitimate)
(d. after 1573)

John Stuart
Lord d'Aubigny
d. 1567

Esmé Stuart
Duke of Lennox
c. 1542–1583

Lady Marie Stuart
d. 1644
m. John Erskine,
Earl of Mar

(See Chart IV)

Thomas Boswell
of Auchinleck
(d. 1513)

David Boswell
of Auchinleck
(d. c. 1562)

(See Charts II and III)

JAMES BOSWELL
1740–1795

374

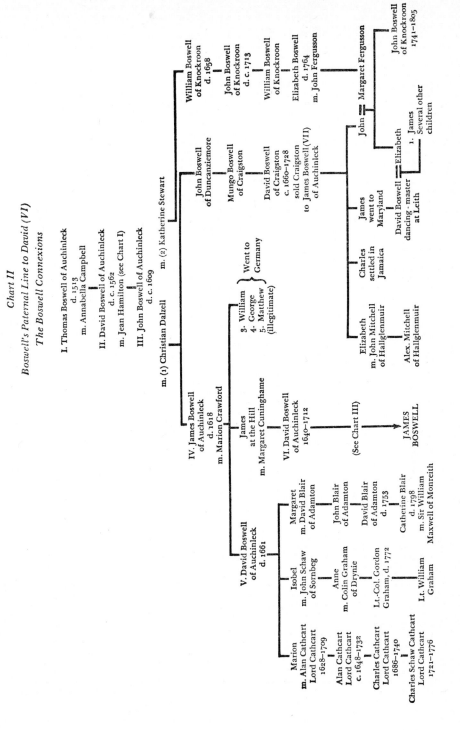

Chart II
Boswell's Paternal Line to David (VI)
The Boswell Connexions

I. Thomas Boswell of Auchinleck
d. 1513
m. Annabella Campbell

II. David Boswell of Auchinleck
d. c. 1562
m. Jean Hamilton (see Chart I)

III. John Boswell of Auchinleck
d. c. 1609

m. (1) Christian Dalzell   m. (2) Katherine Stewart

William Boswell
of Knockroon
d. 1658

John Boswell
of Knockroon
d. c. 1713

William Boswell
of Knockroon

Elizabeth Boswell
d. 1764
m. John Fergusson

John Boswell
of Knockroon
1741–1805

John ═ Margaret Fergusson

Elizabeth

1. James   Several other
              children

John Boswell
of Duncanziemore

Mungo Boswell
of Craigston

David Boswell
of Craigston
c. 1660–1728
sold Craigston
to James Boswell (VII)
of Auchinleck

James
went to
Maryland

David Boswell
dancing- master
at Leith

Charles
settled in
Jamaica

Elizabeth
m. John Mitchell
of Hallglenmuir

Alex. Mitchell
of Hallglenmuir

3. William ⎫
4. George   ⎬ Went to
5. Matthew ⎭ Germany
(illegitimate)

IV. James Boswell
of Auchinleck
d. 1618
m. Marion Crawford

James
at the Hill
m. Margaret Cuninghame

VI. David Boswell of Auchinleck
1640–1712

(See Chart III)

JAMES
BOSWELL

V. David Boswell
of Auchinleck
d. 1661

Margaret
m. David Blair
of Adamton

John Blair
of Adamton

David Blair
of Adamton
d. 1753

Catherine Blair
d. 1798
m. Sir William
Maxwell of Monreith

Isobel
m. John Schaw
of Sornbeg

Anne
m. Colin Graham
of Drynie

Lt.-Col. Gordon
Graham, d. 1772

Lt. William
Graham

Marion
m. Alan Cathcart
Lord Cathcart
1628–1709

Alan Cathcart
Lord Cathcart
c. 1648–1732

Charles Cathcart
Lord Cathcart
1686–1740

Charles Schaw Cathcart
Lord Cathcart
1721–1776

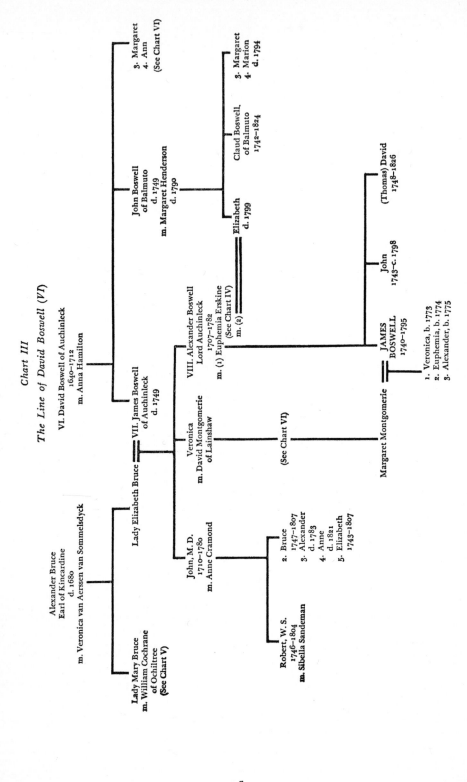

Chart III

The Line of *David Boswell (VI)*

Alexander Bruce
Earl of Kincardine
d. 1680
m. Veronica van Aerssen van Sommelsdyck

David Boswell of Auchinleck
1640–1712
m. Anna Hamilton

Lady Elizabeth Bruce

VII. James Boswell
of Auchinleck
d. 1749

John Boswell of Balmuto
d. 1749
m. Margaret Henderson
d. 1790

3. Margaret
4. Ann
(See Chart VI)

Claud Boswell
of Balmuto
1742–1824

3. Margaret
4. Marion
d. 1794

Elizabeth
d. 1799

VIII. Alexander Boswell
Lord Auchinleck
1707–1782
m. (1) Euphemia Erskine
(See Chart IV)
m. (2)

John
1743–c. 1798

(Thomas) David
1748–1826

Lady Mary Bruce
m. William Cochrane
of Ochiltree
(See Chart V)

Veronica
m. David Montgomerie
of Lainshaw

(See Chart VI)

JAMES
BOSWELL
1740–1795

Margaret Montgomerie

1. Veronica, b. 1773
2. Euphemia, b. 1774
3. Alexander, b. 1775

John, M. D.
1710–1780
m. Anne Cramond

Robert, W. S.
1746–1804
m. Sibella Sandeman

2. Bruce
1747–1807
3. Alexander
d. 1783
4. Anne
d. 1821
5. Elizabeth
1743–1807

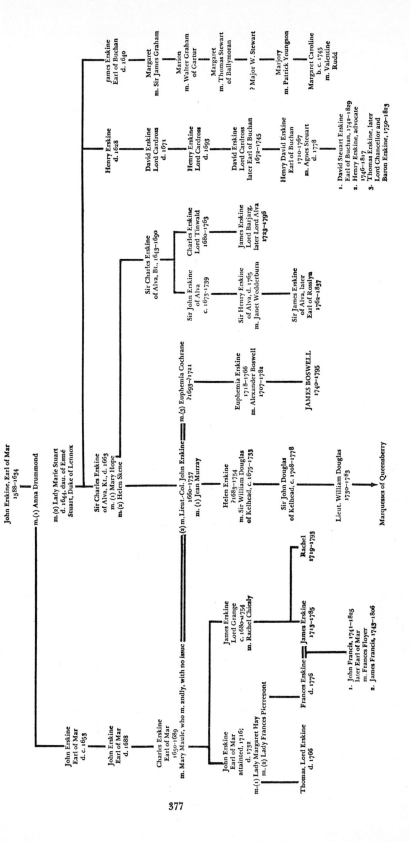

Chart IV
Boswell's Maternal Line
The Erskine and Douglas Connexions

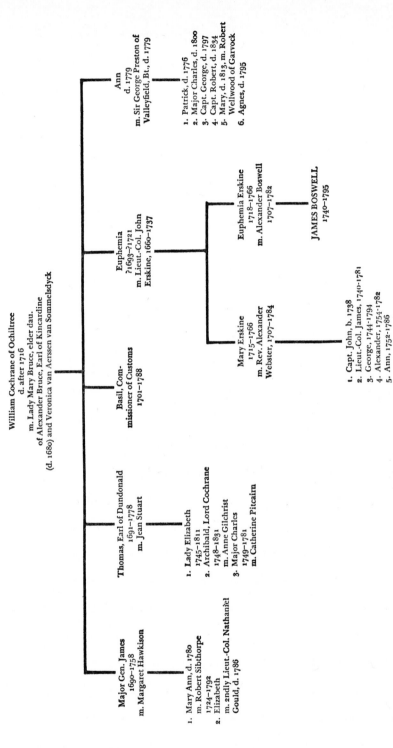

Chart V

The Cochrane, Preston, and Webster Connexions

William Cochrane of Ochiltree
d. after 1716
m. Lady Mary Bruce, elder dau.
of Alexander Bruce, Earl of Kincardine
(d. 1680) and Veronica van Aerssen van Sommelsdyck

Ann
d. 1779
m. Sir George Preston of
Valleyfield, Bt., d. 1779

1. Patrick, d. 1776
2. Major Charles, d. 1800
3. Capt. George, d. 1797
4. Capt. Robert, d. 1834
5. Mary, d. 1813, m. Robert
   Wellwood of Garvock
6. Agnes, d. 1795

Euphemia
?1693–?1721
m. Lieut.-Col. John
Erskine, 1660–1737

Basil, Com-
missioner of Customs
1701–1788

Euphemia Erskine
1718–1766
m. Alexander Boswell
1707–1782

Mary Erskine
1715–1766
m. Rev. Alexander
Webster, 1707–1784

JAMES BOSWELL
1740–1795

1. Capt. John, b. 1738
2. Lieut.-Col. James, 1740–1781
3. George, 1744–1794
4. Alexander, 1754–1782
5. Ann, 1752–1786

Thomas, Earl of Dundonald
1691–1778
m. Jean Stuart

1. Lady Elizabeth
   1745–1811
2. Archibald, Lord Cochrane
   1748–1831
   m. Anne Gilchrist
3. Major Charles
   1749–1781
   m. Catherine Pitcairn

Major Gen. James
1690–1758
m. Margaret Hawkison

1. Mary Ann, d. 1780
   m. Robert Sibthorpe
   1724–1792
2. Elizabeth
   m. 2ndly Lieut.-Col. Nathaniel
   Gould, d. 1786

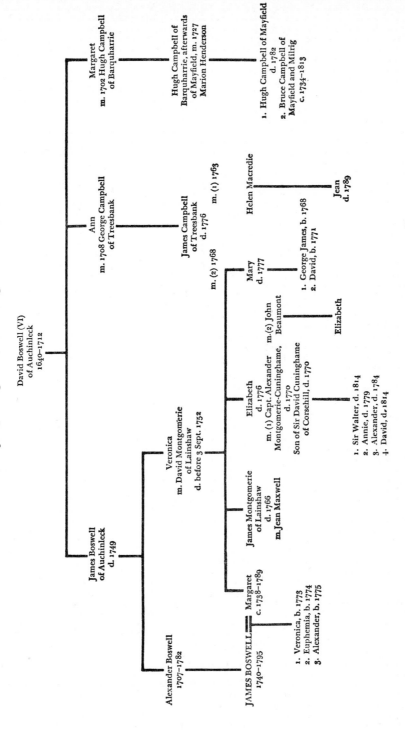

Chart VI

The Campbell, Montgomerie, and Cuninghame Connexions

David Boswell (VI)
of Auchinleck
1640–1712

Margaret
m. 1702 Hugh Campbell
of Barquharrie

Ann
m. 1708 George Campbell
of Treesbank

James Boswell
of Auchinleck
d. 1749

Hugh Campbell of
Barquharrie, afterwards
of Mayfield, m. 1727
Marion Henderson

James Campbell
of Treesbank
d. 1776

m. (2) 1768   m. (1) 1763

1. Hugh Campbell of Mayfield
   d. 1782
2. Bruce Campbell of
   Mayfield and Milrig
   c. 1734–1813

Helen Macredie

Alexander Boswell
1707–1782

Veronica
m. David Montgomerie
of Lainshaw
d. before 3 Sept. 1752

Elizabeth
d. 1776
m. (1) Capt. Alexander
Montgomerie-Cuninghame,
d. 1770
Son of Sir David Cuninghame
of Corsehill, d. 1770

m. (2) John
Beaumont

Mary
d. 1777

1. George James, b. 1768
2. David, b. 1771

Jean
d. 1789

James Montgomerie
of Lainshaw
d. 1766
m. Jean Maxwell

Elizabeth

JAMES BOSWELL
1740–1795

Margaret
c. 1738–1789

1. Sir Walter, d. 1814
2. Annie, d. 1779
3. Alexander, d. 1784
4. David, d. 1814

1. Veronica, b. 1773
2. Euphemia, b. 1774
3. Alexander, b. 1775

379

INDEX

This is in general an index of proper names with analysis of actions, opinions, and personal relationships under the important names. Buildings, streets, and other locations in Edinburgh and London are listed under those headings. Observations on a person are ordinarily listed under that person; for example, opinions of various men on Adam Smith are indexed under Adam Smith and not under other names. An exception is made in the case of Samuel Johnson, whose opinions on various people are listed in Part III of the article under his name although they may be mentioned under the names of the persons in question. Details of Boswell's personal relationship with Johnson are indexed in Part II of the article under Johnson. Sovereigns appear under their Christian names; noblemen and Lords of Session under their titles. The titles are usually those proper to the period 1774–1776. Maiden names of married women are given in parentheses. Titles of books are listed under the name of the author. Abbreviations used are D. (Duke), M. (Marquess), E. (Earl), V. (Viscount), B. (Baron), Bt. (Baronet), Kt. (Knight), W.S. (Writer to the Signet), JB (James Boswell), SJ (Samuel Johnson).